江苏统计年鉴

STATISTICAL YEARBOOK OF JIANGSU

1999

(总第16期)

江苏省统计局 编

中国统计出版社

（京）新登字 041 号

图书在版编目(CIP)数据

江苏统计年鉴　1999/江苏省统计局编.－北京：中国统计出版社，1999

ISBN 7-5037-2981-3

Ⅰ.江…
Ⅱ.江…
Ⅲ.统计资料－江苏－1999－年鉴
Ⅳ.C832.53-54

中国版本图书馆 **CIP** 数据核字(1999)第 17663 号

中国统计出版社出版
（北京西城三里河月坛南街 75 号 100826）
南京人民印刷厂印刷
*
889×1194 毫米　16 开本　35 印张　26 彩页　130 万字
1999 年 7 月第 1 版　　1999 年 7 月第 1 次印刷
印数：1－3000 册
*
定价：160.00 元

江泽民总书记在江苏

江泽民总书记视察无锡小天鹅股份有限公司

朱镕基总理在夫子庙小商品市场与个体业主亲切交谈

1999年2月1日至2月7日江苏省第九届人民代表大会第二次会议在南京隆重召开

省委书记、省人大主任陈焕友投下庄严的一票

省长季允石作政府工作报告

陈焕友同志参加苏州代表团讨论

季允石同志在代表中

代表们郑重行使选举权

代表们纷纷举手表决

大会场景

服务“两会”再现风采

服务于江苏省第九届人民代表大会第二次会议的统计信息查询系统，以准确、丰富的资料，直观、形象的图象，又一次吸引了到会党政领导和代表们关注的目光，赢得了一片异

省长季允石亲临操作统计信息查询系统

副省长王荣炳凝神注视富于变化的屏幕

副省长张连珍前来畅谈“新感觉”

副省长金忠青兴趣盎然现场“点评”

江苏省统计局 统计信息查询系统 剪影

口同声的称赞。省委副书记、省长季允石，省委副书记顾浩，副省长王荣炳、张连珍、金忠青，省长助理、秘书长张长胜以及老同志储江、凌启鸿等先后到查询系统前，仔细询问系统功能，并亲自操作，查询所需资料。

采用先进的“多媒体”微机系统为人大会议服务开始于1997年。在总结前两年成功经验基础上，省统计局在“软件”和“硬件”两方面又作了进一步的改进和完善，使这一独特的服务受到越来越广泛的认可和欢迎。据不完全统计，会议期间共接待前来咨询的代表500多人次，打印各种资料600多份。江苏卫视台在“江苏新闻联播”节目中作了现场采访报道，“扬子晚报”以彩色照片形式作了介绍宣传。

江苏水利

省领导视察泰州引江河工程建设。省委书记陈焕友对工程建设质量表示非常满意。

1998年，全省广大水利干部职工高举旗帜，深化改革，加快发展，创建产业，圆满完成了省委、省政府交办的各项任务。

面对长江流域性大洪水，水利系统认真贯彻省委、省政府“三防五保”方针，

望虞河常熟水利枢纽

水利部部长汪恕诚在江苏视察江堤建设，在听取省水利厅厅长翟浩辉汇报后，汪部长赞誉江苏水利为全国提供了很多借鉴经验。

顽强拼搏，严防死守，及时消除险情180处，夺取了抗洪斗争的全面胜利，全省水利工程无一失事，减免灾效益250亿元。汛后，水利建设者全面落实省委、省政府关于进一步加快防洪保安基础设施建设的决定，水利建设规模空前。淮河入海水道、新沂河堤防加固等一批重点工程开工建设，治太望虞河、太浦河全面建成，泰州引江河实现初通，江海堤防达标整体推进，新沂河海口控制、黄墩湖滞洪闸、蔷薇河送清水等工程陆续建成；农田水利基本建设坚持不懈，全省改造中低产田325万亩，发展旱改水67万亩，治理水土流失256平方公里。1998年水利建设共完成总投资57亿元，全省防洪保安和水资源供给能力得到较大提高。精神文明建设、队伍建设、科教兴水、水政执法、行业管理等不断得到加强，一个崭新的水利产业正在崛起。

黄墩湖滞洪闸工程建成投运

在98年长江特大洪水面前，江苏堤外滚滚洪流、堤内安然无恙。

在创业中不断改革　在发展中创造辉煌

——江苏省国税局

江苏省国税局于1994年7月由原江苏省税务局分设成立以来，江苏国税系统在国家税务总局和江苏省委、省政府的领导下，坚持以组织收入为中心、以征管改革为突破口，高起点、快速度、规范化地推进改革，国税各项工作得到了全面发展，取得了显著成绩。

一是大力组织税收收入，连年超额完成各项税收收入任务。连续四年位列全国第三。

二是新的征管模式已经形成，税收管理发生了深刻变化，征管质量进一步提高。全面推行了上门申报纳税制度。全省基本普及计算机应用，手工征管逐步向计算机征管转变。

三是强化税务稽查工作，依法治税进程大大推进。维护了正常的经济与税收秩序，为国家挽回了大量经济损失。

四是精神文明建设取得丰硕成果。广泛开展“三爱一树两争创”活动，全系统先后涌现全国劳模1名、全国“五一”劳动奖章获得者2名；全国税务先进个人3名，先进集体7个，示范窗口（青年文明号）6个；省劳模和“勤政廉政好干部”10名，省级文明单位（青年文明号）17个，省级文明窗口13个；连续4年有72%以上的市县局被当地党委政府评为先进单位或文明单位，有39个在当地党政行风测评中名列前茅。65个县级局中已有34个被当地党政评为县级“文明行业”，淮阴市国税系统被评为市级“文明行业”，在社会上树立了“公正、廉洁、文明、高效”的国税新形象。

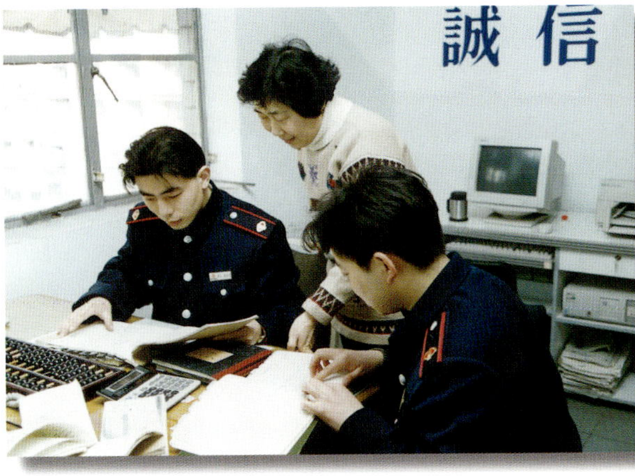

江 苏 地 税

地税部门负责征收和管理的税包括：营业税、资源税、企业所得税、个人所得税、土地增值税、城镇土地使用税、城市维护建设税、固定资产投资方向调节税、房产税、车船使用税、印花税、屠宰税等，同时承担各项基金（费）的征集任务。

江苏地税成立以来，坚持依法治税，实施征管改革，加强队伍建设，大力组织收入，取得了累累硕果。全省地方工商税收从1995年的73.73亿元上升到1998年的149.02亿元，累计完成455.71亿元，年平均增收23.58亿元，增长28.5%，实现三年翻一番。

在迈向新世纪的征途中，江苏地税将进一步深化征管改革，充分发挥税收的职能作用，为推动江苏经济持续、快速、健康发展作出新的贡献。

修桥铺路　造福江苏

江苏省委书记陈焕友、省长季允石在公司董事长、总经理张伯端陪同下视察新长铁路。

新大桥施工一景

江苏省铁路有限责任公司是直属省政府领导的具有投资性质的国有合资公司，负责全省铁路建设的投资、筹资还贷、工程建设和经营管理，负责铁路投资所形成的国有资产、保值、增值。公司以加快我省铁路建设为已任，努力追求"一个企业与多条铁路"这一丰碑般的成就。

1998年，该省与铁道部、浙江省联合投资建设的新长铁路已正式开工建设，全年共完成投资12亿。根据江苏省铁路网规划，我省境内还将新建一批重要的干线铁路和区域性铁路及支线、专用线，建设总里程达1820公里。

公司贯彻"一业为主，多元开发"的经营方针。坚持以铁路建设为中心，围绕铁路建设积极开展多种经营，不断壮大公司实力，增强筹措铁路建设资金的能力，最终将公司建设成为铁路投资、建设、管理为主体的集团公司。

1998年9月16日，新长铁路开工典礼在淮安隆重举行。图为江苏省委书记陈焕友、省长季允石、铁道部党组副书记、副部长孙永福等领导为新长铁路奠基。

机声隆隆，挖掘机、载重车开赴铁路施工一线

江苏常熟发电有限公司

江苏常熟发电有限公司（常熟发电厂）位于江南名城常熟市东北郊24公里的扬子江畔，东临上海、南接苏州、西连无锡、北依长江，与南通隔江相望，水陆交通十分便利。4台3000MW装机系中国电力投资公司 、江苏省国际信托投资公司、江苏省电力公司和苏州市信托投资公司合资建设。该发电公司始建于1990年9月2日，1994年11月7日全部建成投产，1995年11月15日通过国家验收，为国家特大型企业。1997年10月，企业改制为江苏常熟发电有限公司。

公司现有职工1848人，其中各类专业技术人员439人。投产以来，全体职工弘扬“爱厂爱岗、尽心尽职、团结奋进、争创一流”的企业精神，致力于企业内部机制的转换，不断强化基础建设，狠抓设备的完善和整治，提高基础管理和专业管理水平，取得了显著的经济效益。到1998年末，4台机组共发电282.72亿千瓦时，实现利税116762.36万元。

1993年以来，公司（常熟发电厂）先后多次荣获“江苏省先进集体”、江苏省电力系统和苏州市“双文明单位”等各项荣誉，1996年被电力部命名为“安全文明生产双达标”企业，1998年顺利实现“无泄漏发电厂”目标。

江苏经济管理干部学院

江苏经济管理干部学院是独立设置的成人高等学校，江苏省人民政府的直属单位，由江苏省计划与经济委员会代管并具体领导。

建院十几年来，该院坚持以岗位培训为重点，学历教育为基础，走教学、科研、信息、咨询服务多功能办学的路子，为江苏经济建设服务。

学院现有教职工200多人，100多名专任教师中，具有研究生学历的占23%，大学本科毕业的占77%；26%的教师具有高级职称，具有中级职称的占52%。学院还聘请了一批专家、学者担任兼职教师。

学院教学、生活设施齐全，可容纳1200余名学生开课。电教设备较齐全，两个语音室共100余座，高档次微机150余台。新建的图书馆、网络实验室进一步改善了教学条件。正在筹建的有多媒体教室和多个专用实验室。

学院现设5系2部，即管理系、经济贸易系、财会金融系、法律系、计算机系和培训部、函授部。经江苏省教育委员会批准，开设成人高等教育大专层次专业15个、本科（专科起点升本科）专业3个，高等职业教育专业4个。目前本、专科在校学生1500余人，以工商管理培训为主的各类培训年规模达1500人次。

地址：南京市花园路5号

邮编：210042　电话：(025)5412912

传真：5412819

常务副校长：王宽亚

江苏省中华会计函授学校

全省在职会计继续教育培训基地

十年来，江苏省中华会计函授学校为全省培养了六万多名具有中专以上学历的财会人员；全省有近半数的在职会计人员，在这所学校里接受过各种短期专业培训。

该校是根据财政部的要求和我省经济建设的需要建立起来的。建校以来，在全省十三个省辖市建立了分校，在八十个县(市)区建立了函授站，形成了统一领导、分级管理覆盖全省的三级教育培训网络。全省各级函校部建立了教学基地，累计投资达一亿多元，教学建筑面积五万多平方米，配备了电视机、录象机、微机、传真机等教学设备2600多台(套)。学校还配备了专职管理人员，专兼职教师1300多人，为完成大规模的会计继续教育和培训提供了良好的环境和条件。

办学十年来，学校贯彻“从严治学，质量第一”的办学方针，坚持以质量求生存，以改革促发展，以特色创信誉，严格按照“自学、电教、面授”三位一体的教学组织形式，开展多媒体的业余教育。在实践中不断改革创新，探索和总结出适合远距离成人教育规律和特点的新经验和新方法，取得了显著成果。创造了“三段作业”教学法，得到了国家教委的肯定，被财政部总校在全国函授系统推广应用。为此，王宽亚副校长受国家教委委派，出席了在新西兰召开的太平洋国际远距离教育研讨会，并介绍了这一科研成果，受到了与会专家和学者的首肯。

校长：施学道　（兼）　常务副校长：王宽亚
校址：南京新模范马路92号　邮编：210003　电话：3401482　传真：3431106

总经理蔡正兴

江蘇利錫拉鏈股份有限公司

JIANGSU RIXI ZIPPER CO,LTD.

江苏利锡拉链股份有限公司是一家专业生产拉链企业，采用最先进的德国、台湾拉链生产技术。从模具制作至成品拉头、拉链原材料至拉链成品均自行生产，为较好的质量控制、成本控制、时间控制奠定了基础。

公司现有员工 850 人，建筑面积 37200m^2、距上海仅 1.5 小时车程。

本公司实施 ISO9002 运作管理方式，以“诚信”为经营宗旨生产的 TH 牌树脂、尼龙、金属拉链安全可靠、外观精致，并深受国内外用户欢迎，产品直销欧、美、亚地区。我们致力于开发其它市场，使我们的产品进一步全球化，竭诚欢迎国内外用户惠顾。

地址：江苏省锡山市扬市镇星火东大街 27 号
电话：(0510)3551646
传真：3551355
邮编：214154

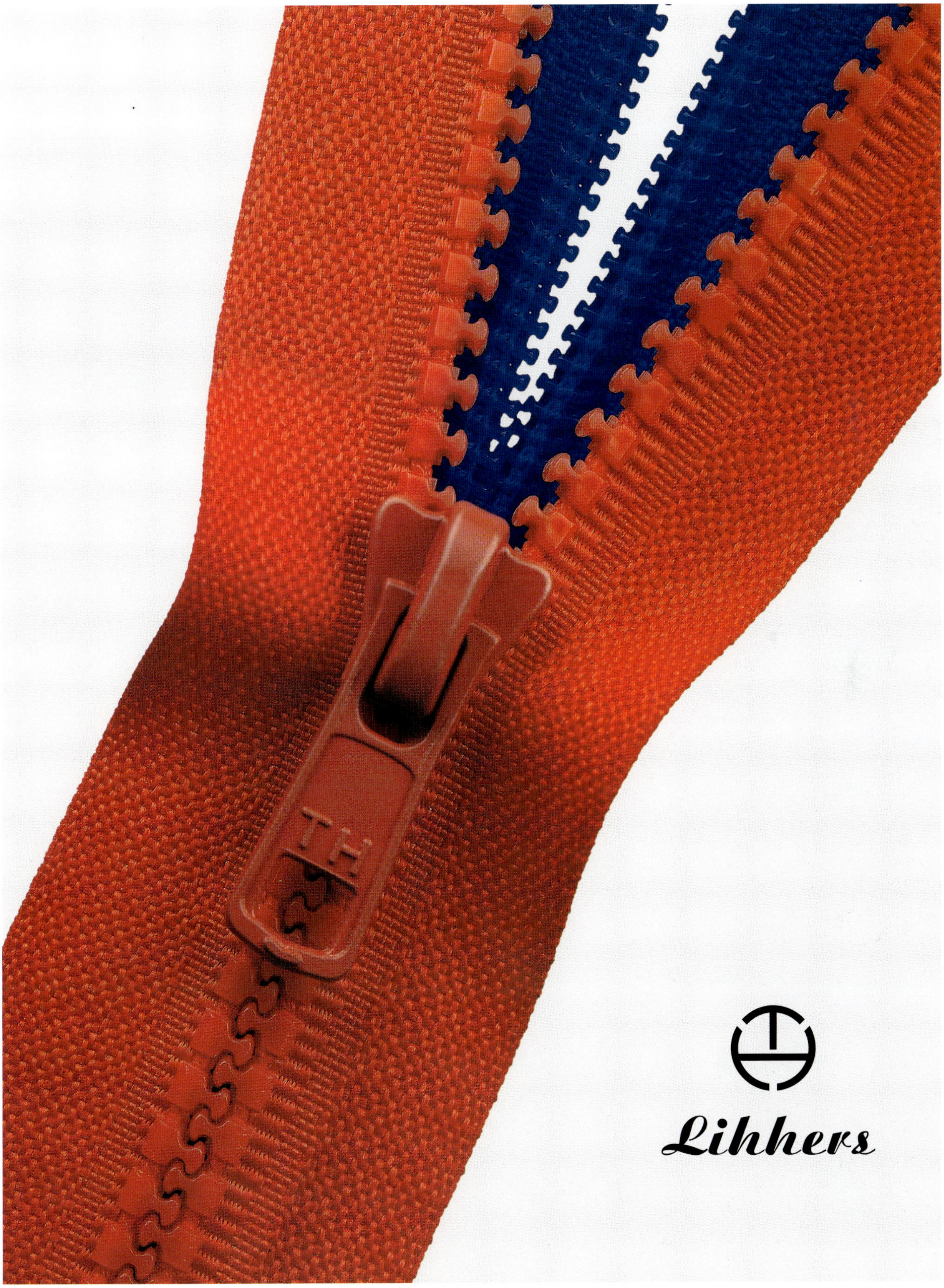
TH

江苏碘盐技术培训中心

无锡市盐务管理局

江苏省盐业公司无锡分公司

无锡市盐务管理局暨江苏省盐业公司无锡分公司，下辖无锡盐业批发部和江阴、宜兴两个支公司，负责无锡一城三市的工、食盐供应和盐业市场的管理。

公司积极开拓经济发展新路，在原有盐产品的基础上，又推出了海盐系列品种盐－低钠盐、加钙盐、加硒盐、加锌盐等等，主业创利在省盐业系统名列前茅。集会议、办公、餐饮、客房、娱乐等于一体的盐务大厦即将投入运行，江阴华夏包装机械公司、宜兴金海包装公司等综合经营为公司走向市场奠定了基础。公司切实加强精神文明建设，被誉为省公司“明星企业”，并授予市级“文明单位”。

法人代表：孙永有

地址：无锡市工艺路40号

邮编：214005

电话：(0510)2302127，2303184

传真：(0510)2303102

电子邮件：WXYWJ@126.com

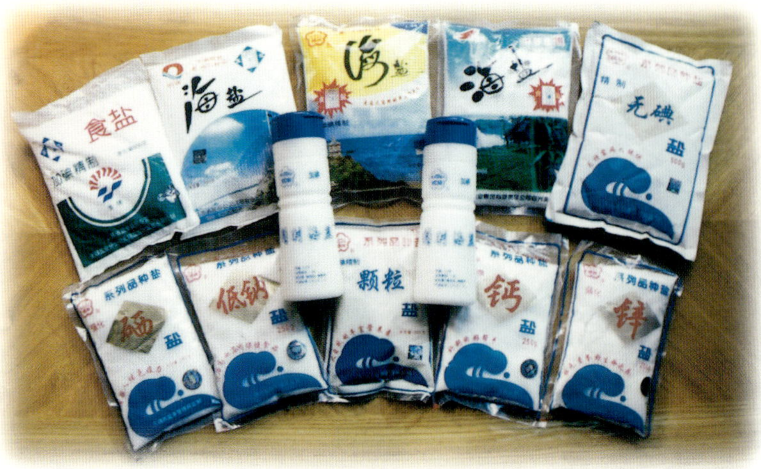

镇江
钛白粉有限公司

公司董事长兼总经理：法浩然

镇江钛白粉股份有限公司是国家大型企业。现有职工1110人，其中各类专业技术人员279人，固定资产8000多万元。企业先后被部、省、市命名为“清洁文明工厂”、“省先进企业”、“重合同守信用企业”、“双文明先进企业”。

公司现有“环球”、“太白”、“号角”三个注册商标。主产品“环球”牌钛白粉曾在全国同行业质量评比中获第一名，并获得江苏省名牌产品称号；高粘树脂切片、聚合硫酸铁在省高科技产品评比中，分别获金、银质奖。环球牌钛白粉不但畅销国内而且远销日本、巴西、美国、法国、韩国、西班牙、印度、台湾、香港等国家和地区。

企业不断上规模、上水平，追求高新技术。现已步入“中国500家最大化学工业企业”和“中国技工贸收入超亿元企业”的行列，并被省科委命名为“高新技术企业”。

地址：镇江市长江路27号
邮编：212001
电话：(0511)5273715　5271181
传真：(0511)5273715　5278129

南京宏图建筑安装集团有限公司

戴品文总经理在公司开业典礼大会上讲话

公司领导在浇钢跨天车梁改造工程竣工庆祝大会上

南京宏图建筑安装集团有限公司是南京宏图建安集团核心层企业，企业法人营业执照注册资本一千五百万元人民币，企业类型为有限责任公司，企业资质等级二级。承包工程范围：工业与民用，建筑安装可承担25层以下、30米跨度以下的房屋建筑安装，高度100米以下的构筑物建筑等。以工业与民用建筑安装工程、地基基础工程、设备安装工程、建筑装饰工程和装饰工程设计为主，并经销建材等业务。

该集团公司一贯重合同、守信誉，坚持质量第一、安全第一的服务宗旨，承包建设的工程均经建设单位一次性验收，达到优良工程，得到建设单位好评，被誉为善打硬仗、信得过企业，并先后被南京市政府和有关部门评为［重合同、守信用企业］、［AAA级信用企业］、和［南京市明星企业］等。

南钢炼钢厂房技术改造现场

董事长兼总经理：戴品文
地址：南京市大厂区宁钢路88号
邮编：210035

南京市秦淮区城镇建设综合开发总公司

公司总经理法定代表人：唐玉华

南京市秦淮区城镇建设综合开发总公司是国家房地产开发一级企业。自1984年成立以来先后开发建设秦虹、弓箭坊、白鹭、琵琶等七个片区，累计竣工面积200万平方米，拓宽改造中山南路(一期)、中华路、城东干道（秦淮段)、秦虹大道等17条城市道路，完成各类公建配套设施逾30万平方米。

公司目前在建和可供合作的项目主要有毗邻夫子庙繁华地区和白鹭洲公园，总建筑面积5.6万平方米的夫子庙花园城；有位于中华路三山街商业中心，总建筑面积5万平方米的中华广场；有地处中山南路，总建筑面积2.6万平方米的弓箭坊商住综合楼以及弓箭坊小区高层公寓等。

公司连续多年被省、市政府评为全省房地产“五十强”、南京市房地产内资“十强”；连续四年被省市建行、工商行评为“AAA”特级资信企业；98年被国家统计局评为“全国房地产领先企业”。

体现明清建筑风格的夫子庙美食街

地址：南京市中华路465号
邮编：210006
电话：(025) 6629698　6629094
传真：(025) 2306018

弓箭坊小区高层住宅群

鸟瞰秦虹小区

董事长、总经理：杨柏勋

中美合资 **启东威勋杰时装有限公司**

本公司创建于1987年，专业生产内销中高档时装，全厂占地面积10亩，建筑面积2500平方米。技术力量雄厚，专用设备齐全，年产服装50多万件，质量上档次，获得中外客户一致好评。“威勋杰”牌系列服装，1997年获得“中国名牌”称号。

产品畅销全国各大城市。企业管理严格，效益显著，连续多年被评为市重合同守信用企业和“双文明”单位。

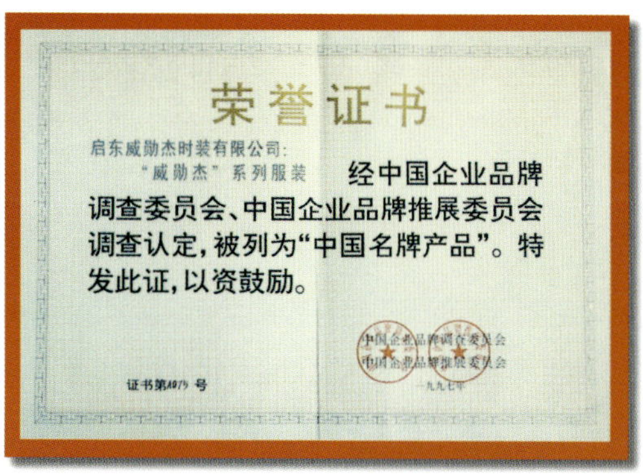

荣誉证书

启东威勋杰时装有限公司：

“威勋杰”系列服装 经中国企业品牌调查委员会、中国企业品牌推展委员会调查认定，被列为“中国名牌产品”。特发此证，以资鼓励。

厂址：江苏省启东市寅阳镇　　邮编：226259

电话：0513-3497352　3497781　传真：0513-3773017

南京市

祖堂山 精神病院

风景秀丽的院区

南京市祖堂山精神病院属市民政局领导下的社会福利事业单位。该院创建于1952年10月，地处南京市南郊区松竹苍翠的祖堂山南麓，古“幽栖寺”遗址，距南京市中心23公里，占地面积50496m²，建筑面积8217m²。全院现有职工121名，机构设置有：党政办公室、医务科、总务科、护理部、门诊部、4个护理病区(3个男病区、1个女病区)，医护专技人员47名，固定资产620万元。

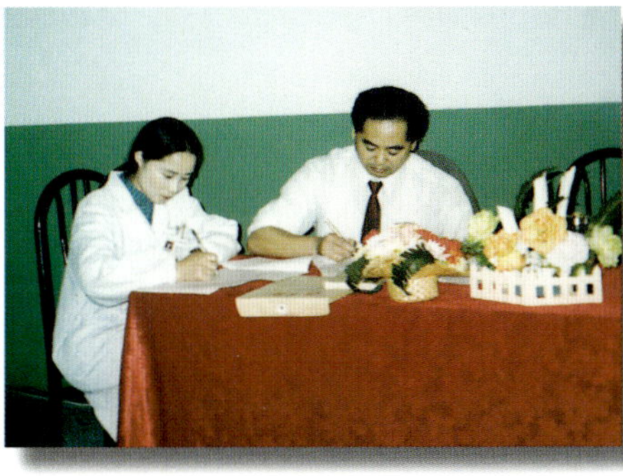

98年叶安义院长与部门签定综合目标管理责任书

四十六年来，共收治慢性精神病患者12972人次，年均282人次。1985年2月，南京市政府定该院为二级医疗单位。

近年来，该院增加更新医疗设备的资金投入，先后添置了B超机、心电路机、心理监护仪、200毫安X光机、16支笔脑电图机、血糖测定仪、自动生化仪、血细胞分析仪、自动尿液分析仪、抢救仪疗仪器设备等，使医疗设备基本配套。

1999年将投入400万元，新建门诊大楼2500m²。

四十六年的发展变化，特别是改革开放为病院建设带来新的机遇和挑战，该院全体干部职工正以奋发向上的精神，决心经过三至五年的努力，使该院的整体管理水平和医疗质量达到民政二级和卫生二级甲等水平，为维护社会稳定，为南京市国民经济和社会发展，为全市第二个三年面貌大变做出应有的贡献。

丰富多彩的娱乐生活(第三届休养员与医护人员文艺会演)

杨正清书记与三区共度中秋佳节

地址：南京祖堂山精神病院 电话：025-2740129 2740140 传真：025-2740129 邮编：211154

金　陵　重　镇

燕子矶镇

素有“金陵重镇”之称的燕子矶镇，位于南京市城北市郊，土地面积18.5平方公里，总人口5.7万，是南京市“十强乡镇”。燕子矶镇参与联合开发的“南京市经济技术开发区”已有包括荷兰飞利浦、日本夏普、德国赫司特等国际著名企业在内的400多家中外企业在此共图发展大业。

镇内基础设施齐全，水陆交通发达，区位优势明显。南京第二热电厂和在建的50万吨城北水厂座落在镇境内，水、电、汽资源丰富；南京长江二桥引线与绕城公路、沪宁高速公路相连，可直达禄口机场，纬一路、太新路等四条高等级公路和四条铁路专用线贯穿全镇，我国内河最大的江海换装港－新生圩港辐射世界。

燕子矶镇环境优美、风景秀丽、人文氛围浓郁，镇内有十多家国有大中型企业、五所院校和多所科研机构。

该镇坚持两个文明一起抓，先后被评为省、市“文明单位”、“省先进集体”、“省科技先进乡镇”，并荣获“全国群众性体育先进乡镇”和“全国双拥先进乡镇”等光荣称号。

兴化市第一镇——戴南

迎宾楼

镇党委书记：刘元太

戴南镇是一座历史悠久的水乡古镇，位于兴化市的东南端。境内水网交织，河道纵横，省宁盐一级公路穿镇而过，水陆交通十分便利。

镇域总面积47.9平方公里，可耕地面积3.6万亩，辖31个行政村，4个居委会，总人口4.8万人，是区、镇两级

居民小区

政府所在地和经济文化中心。1998年全镇实现社会总产值14.02亿元，比上年增长20.9%，其中工业产值9.89亿元，比上年增长22.9%。该镇小城镇建设初具规模。镇区宽阔的水泥街道与宁盐公路相连，路灯、路牙、绿岛相互配套，一批批办公楼、营业楼、教学楼、住宅楼和农民别墅给戴南增添了现代化气息；全镇自发电装机容量达到2.4万千瓦，程控电话扩容到8000门，有线电视实现了全省联网入户率达到90%以上，兴建了第二农贸市场、戴南大厦、星地超市、保龄球馆、明珠广场等一批标志性工程，在苏北第一家开通了乡镇公交车。文化、教育、卫生、体育等社会事业得到较快的发展，人民生活水平逐年提高。先后获得了省百家名镇、科技、体育先进乡镇、苏中百强乡镇新型示范小城镇等先进称号，并被列为全国500家现代化小城镇建设试点镇之一。

人民路

兴化市委常委、戴南镇党委书记：刘元太　戴南镇人民政府镇长：高学军

党委书记：莫鹏程

镇长：姚连岳

姜堰市—娄庄镇

苏北明珠娄庄镇总面积32平方公里，辖23个行政村、1个居委会、200个村民小组、2.8万人口。

该镇经济实力不断增强，1998年全镇实现利税2000万元。先后被江苏省命名为教育、科技、体育、群众文化先进镇、安全文明镇、电话小康镇等，被泰州市命名为红旗党组织、文明镇、经济十强镇。

以个体私营企业为主体的乡镇工业如今已成为全镇经济的支柱产业，现有镇办、村办中外合资及个体企业156家，职工近5000人。主要有机械、建筑、建材、电子、食品、纺织等行业，产品有5大类100多个品种，畅销全国29个省市自治区，部分产品出口海外。

目前，邮电、广电、金融、文化及宾馆、饭店等公益设施配套齐全，道路宽敞整洁、小城镇建设初具规模，社会文明安定，投资环境良好。

镇机关大楼

欣欣向荣的集镇新貌

乡党委书记：王 景

乡长：陈锦富

兴化市—刘陆乡

刘陆乡位于兴化城区南侧，兴泰公路穿乡而过。总人口34673人，户数9623户，面积57.6平方公里，现有耕地50402亩，辖26个行政村，有202个村民小组。1998年全乡实现三业总产值38260万元，全年财政收入840万元，农民人均纯收入3074元。近年来，全乡加大了结构调整的力度，效益农业成为主导产业；以特种水产养殖为重点的多种经营生产是本乡主要特色；工业有玩具、纺织、建材、机械、纸品、农副产品加工等六大门类，应运而生的私营企业发展旺盛。

刘陆舒乐玩具公司与外地厂家商家联手，生产的长毛绒、布绒等动物玩具系列几十个品种，远销韩国、日本、欧美等十几个国家和地区。在里下河地区被誉为“玩具之乡”。

刘陆乡集镇总体规划业经兴化市人民政府批准。新规划的集镇由原辖刘陆村，改辖刘陆、大王、水产三村，确定了“三纵三横”以及新区发展格局。全乡开通程控电话3072门，完成和基本完成了扶贫通电及电器化，基本实现了村村通公路，全乡全面完成了改水任务。

刘陆农修厂生产的TGJ6型船用挂浆机，是通过省农机研究所鉴定的优质产品。

江都市——曹王林园场

江都市曹王林园场书记、场长：杜信祥

江都市曹王林园场是以培花育苗为主，林、副、工综合经营的省重点国有场圃，省绿化先进单位和省育苗达标单位。全场占地3.63Km²，境内佳木葱茏，鸟语花香，是闻名遐迩的花木之乡。

日臻繁荣的曹王花木市场

该场拥有固定资产4000余万元，下辖18个育苗单位，千余户花农和4个场办工厂，花木生产面积3000亩，年产苗木1000余万株，盆花，盆景百万盆，花木品种达千余种，尤以五宝杜鹃、广陵芍药、扬州琼花、扬派盆景为特色，产品远销全国二十二个省、市、自治区，并与日本、澳大利亚、意大利、荷兰、香港等国家和地区发生业务往来。

全国人大农委主任高德占（右三）在江都市委副书记仲祖云（左一）陪同下视察曹王。

德国朋友参观曹王林园场花木市场

江都市曹王林园场是一个外向型的综合经济实体，融千余年花木生产之技艺，汇千余种花木品种于一体，集新、奇、特产品于一市，致力于花木产业化发展，开发园林绿化设计、施工等，为绿化大地，保护地球，造福人类多做贡献。

编者说明

一、《江苏统计年鉴——1999》(以下简称《年鉴》)是一部全面、系统反映江苏省1998年及历史重要年份国民经济和社会发展情况的资料性年刊。本书收录了江苏省及各市、县大量的社会、经济、科技统计信息。

二、全书内容分为二十个部分,即:1.行政区划和自然资源;2.综合;3.人口、劳动力;4.人民生活;5.固定资产投资;6.物价;7.农业;8.工业、能源;9.建筑及地质勘查业;10.交通运输、邮电业;11.国内贸易;12.对外经济贸易和旅游业;13.财政、金融、保险;14.科技、教育;15.文化、体育、卫生、环保;16.档案、司法、社会福利、其他;17.城市经济建设;18.区域经济;19.市县社会经济;20.县(市)社会经济序列。书末还附有部分省市社会经济主要指标;我国经济与主要国家比较;主要统计指标解释;企事业单位选介等。

三、资料中所使用的度量衡单位均采用国际统一标准计量单位。

四、《年鉴》表中"…"表示数据不足本表最小单位数;"空格"表示该项统计指标数据不详或无该项数据;"#"表示其中项。

五、感谢国内外广大读者多年来对《年鉴》编辑出版工作的支持和帮助,欢迎继续提出宝贵意见,使《年鉴》的形式和内容更趋完善。

COMPLIER'S NOTE

Ⅰ. Jiangsu Statistical Yearbook 1999 (abbreviated as Yearbook hereafter) is an annual publication which provides comprehensive and systematic data about the national economy and social development in Jiangsu Province in 1998 and some important years in history. It includes much statistical information on social, economic, scientific and technological development in the province and in various cities and counties.

Ⅱ. The Yearbook is composed of altogether twenty parts: 1. Division of Administrative Districts and Natural Resources; 2. General Survey; 3. Population and Employment; 4. People's Livelihood; 5. Fixed Assets Investment; 6. Commodity Price; 7. Agriculture; 8. Industry, Energy; 9. Construction and Geological Prospecting; 10. Transportation, Post and Telecommunication; 11. Domestic Trade; 12. Foreign Economy, Trade and Tourism; 13. Finance, Banking and Insurance; 14. Science, Technology and Education; 15. Culture, Sports, Health Care and Environmental Protection; 16. Archives, Judgement, Social Welfare and Other; 17. Urban Economy and Construction; 18. Regional Economy; 19. City (County) Social Economy; 20. County (City) Social Economic Alignment. Appended at the end of the book there are Major Social and Economic Indicators of Some Provinces and Municipalities; Comparison of Economy between China and other Major Countries; Explanatory Notes to Major Statistical Indicators; Business Enterprises Selected Introductions of The Units.

Ⅲ. The units of weights and measures used in the Yearbook are all internationally standard measurement units.

Ⅳ. In the Yearbook, "…" indicates that the data are not large enough to be rounded into the minimal unit; "space" indicates that little is not avaiable; "#" indicates major component items.

Ⅴ. We express thanks to the general readers of domestic and abroad for surpporting and helping to the work of compilation and publication of the Yearbook; welcome continued valuable suggestions from the general readers, so that the form and content of the Yearbook can be further improved.

目　录

CONTENTS

5 固定资产投资 FIXED ASSETS INVESTMENT

7　农业
AGRICULTURE

8 工业、能源
INDUSTRY, ENERGY

9 建筑业及地质勘查业
CONSTRUCTION AND GEOLOGICAL PROSPECTING

10 交通运输、邮电业
TRANSPORTATION, POSTAL AND TELECOMMUNICATION SERVICES

17 城市经济与建设
URBAN ECONOMY AND CONSTRUCTION

18 区域经济
REGIONAL ECONOMY

19 市县社会经济
CITY（COUNTY）SOCIAL ECONOMY

20 县(市)社会经济序列
COUNTY (CITY) SOCIAL ECONOMIC ALIGNMENT

附录一 部分省市经济主要指标
APPENDIX Ⅰ MAJOR ECONOMIC INDICATORS OF SOME PROVICES AND MUNICIPALITIES

附录二 我国经济与主要国家比较

APPENDIX Ⅱ COMPARISION OF ECONOMY BETWEEN CHINA AND OTHER MAJOR COUNTRIES OF THE WORLD

江苏省统计局关于1998年国民经济和社会发展的统计公报

1998年是极不平凡的一年,是经历了国内外形势的严峻考验并取得重大胜利的一年。在党中央、国务院以及省委、省政府的领导下,全省上下同心同德、顽强拼搏,努力克服经济生活中出现的各种困难,特别是亚洲金融危机的冲击和特大洪涝灾害的影响,经济保持稳定增长格局,各项改革继续深化,社会事业取得新进步,基本完成了全年经济和社会发展预期调控目标。

一、综　　合

全省经济保持较快增长,经济整体素质进一步提高。初步统计,全年完成国内生产总值7199.95亿元,比上年增长11.0%,增幅高于全国平均水平3.2个百分点。其中,第一产业增加值1016.27亿元,增长2.1%;第二产业增加值3640.1亿元,增长12.0%;第三产业增加值2543.58亿元,增长12.9%。全省人均国内生产总值10021元,比上年提高10.4%。经济结构和所有制结构得到调整。第一、第二、第三产业增加值在国内生产总值中的构成比例,由上年的15.1∶51.1∶33.8调整为14.1∶50.6∶35.3。公有制经济在改革开放中稳定发展,混合所有制经济和个体、私营经济发展迅速。财政收支情况良好,金融形势基本平稳,市场价格保持低位走势。

扩大内需政策的效果逐步显现,经济增长的拉动力增强。积极启动投资需求,特别是水利、交通等基础设施建设投资力度明显加大,重点项目建设进度加快,成为拉动经济回升的主要因素。努力扩大消费需求,重视市场开拓和名牌产品销售。产品市场占有率有所提高。出口需求在极其困难的情况下保持了一定增长。抗洪斗争取得伟大胜利。全省人民团结奋斗,严防死守,英勇抗御长江特大洪水的袭击,境内堤防无一决口,水利工程无一失事,也没有因洪水死亡一人,有效地保证了经济建设的正常进行和人民生命财产安全。

劳动就业和社会保障工作进一步加强。年末全省城镇在岗职工752.8万人,其中国有单位471.5万人,城镇集体单位161.9万人,其他类型单位119.4万人;农村个体从业人员281.7万人,农村私营企业从业人员133.7万人。国有企业下岗职工基本生活保障和再就业工作取得显著成效。有下岗职工的国有企业全部建立了再就业服务中心或类似机构,年末24.5万名国有企业下岗职工进入再就业服务中心,下岗职工的基本生活得到了保障。企业离退休人员养老金基本上做到了按时足额发放。全年29.2万名国企下岗职工通过多种途径实现再就业,再就业比例达54.3%。年末全省城镇登记失业率为2.6%。

经济社会发展中存在的主要困难和问题是:结构性矛盾仍较突出;最终消费需求不旺,城乡集体和个体投资增长乏力,出口需求增幅减小;部分企业生产经营困难,经济效益较差;农业结构调整步伐不够快,农业服务体系尚待进一步加强;就业与再就业压力较大;居民收入增长减缓,部分低收入居民生活比较困难。

二、农林牧渔业

农业生产平稳发展。夏季粮油因灾大幅度减产,但由于以秋补夏措施得力和秋季气候条件良好,秋粮亩产、总产双超历史,其中水稻亩产连续五年过千斤。全年粮食总产量3415.1万吨,比上年减少148.7万吨,下降4.2%,总产仍属历史较高年份。棉花总产量46.2万吨,比上年下降9.0%;油料总产量115.6万吨,其中油菜籽64.3万吨,分别下降18.5%和36.1%;蚕茧总产量8.5万吨,下降1.5%;水果总产量144.4万吨,增长2.8%。

林业、牧业、渔业生产持续增长。全年完成造林面积15.1千公顷,比上年下降20.4%。主要畜产品中,肉类总产量295.3万吨,比上年增长10.8%;禽蛋总产量157.1万吨,增长3.9%;牛奶总产量12.1万吨,增长9.5%。全年水产品产量282.0万吨,比上年增长6.1%;其中淡水产品产量193.8万吨,海水产品产量88.2万吨,分别增长7.3%和3.7%。

农业综合开发得到加强,农业生产条件进一步改善。全年围垦滩涂7.7千公顷,改造中低产田216.7千公顷,建设高产稳产农田138.7千公顷,新增节水灌溉面积293.3千公顷。水利建设取得新进展,一批水利建设工程如期完成,农田有效灌溉面积达3855.4千公顷,比上年增加16.1千公顷,农业物质装备水平有新的提高,年末全省农业机械总动力2594.8万千瓦,比上年末增长3.8%。

农村改革进一步深化,农村产业结构调整取得新成绩。稳定和完善土地承包关系,组织实施并基本完成延长全省农村土地承包期三十年不变的二轮承包工作。稳步推进粮食流通体制改革,认真执行"按保护价敞开收购余粮,收储企业实行粮食顺价销售,收购资金实行封闭运行"三项政策,深化国有粮食企业改革,粮食收购工作进展顺利。农业结构有所调整.农业产业化经营进一步推进,优质高产作物面积扩大,江南、淮南、淮北高效畜牧业和园艺业十大基地建设初见成效,全省形成年销售收入亿元以上的龙头企业84家。农村非农产业继续较快发展,全省农村工业、建筑业、运输业和批发、零售贸易业、餐饮业产值比上年增长12.1%,占农村社会总产值比重由上年的83.7%提高到84.4%。

三、工业和建筑业

工业生产保持较快增长。全年完成工业增加值3157.7亿元,比上年增长10.8%。

全年全部国有及年销售收入500万元以上的非国有工业企业完成总产值8053.02亿元,比上年增长12.5%。国有和集体工业稳定发展,其他经济类型工业增长较快。国有控股工业企业产值2653.00亿元,比上年增长4.5%,集体工业企业产值3056.04亿元,增长4.5%;股份制工业企业产值1097.95亿元,增长26.8%;外商港澳台投资工业企业产值1829.37亿元,增长28.6%;联营、私营等其他经济类型工业企业产值449.38亿元,增长46.7%。大中型工业企业完成产值3810.99亿元,增长2.4%。受增加投资的拉动,重工业增速有所加快。全年轻工业完成产值3709.65亿元,增长14.3%;重工业完成产值4343.38亿元,增长10.8%。

稳步推进各项企业改革。国有大中型企业建立现代企业制度的步伐加快,至年底有40%的国有大中型企业初步建立了现代企业制度。采取引进外资、股份合作制、股份制、承包、租赁、出售等多种形式,进一步搞活国有小企业。乡镇企业改制面由上年的60%上升到85%。

积极开展'98工业结构调整促进年活动,工业结构调整取得新进展。组建发展了一批企业集团,到年底全省已有各类企业集团2000多家。优化资本结构工作取得一定进展,全年资产重组超过200亿元。全省完成81万锭的压锭任务。产品结构有所调整,技术含量高、市场需求较旺的产品增长较快,一些生产能力严重过剩的加工工业产品、市场滞销产品呈现负增长。在列入统计考核的83种主要工业产品产量户,保持增长的有41种,下降的有42种。其中,与上年相比,纱下降1.0%、机制纸及纸板增长3.2%、原盐下降10.8%、家用洗衣机增长4.5%、彩色电视机增长41.5%、原煤增长4.9%、发电量增长0.4%、原油加工量增长1.4%、成品钢材增长12.4%、水泥增长1.8%、金属切削机床增长2.8%、平板玻璃增长25.6%、纯碱增长28.7%、微型电子计算机增长107.0%、汽车下降9.2%、组合音响增长191.7%、程控交换机增长24.3%、化肥下降1.2%、房间空调器下降16.7%、化学纤维增长6.0%。产品质量和档次稳步提高,名牌产品的市场竞争力得到增强。

工业企业产销衔接状况有所改善,但经济效益尚未明显好转。全省工业产品销售率为96.0%,比上年提高0.3个百分点。库存积压增幅减缓,年末工业产成品库存增长2.72%,增幅比年初回落13.7个百分点。企业扭亏增盈力度加大,亏损额升幅缩小,效益下滑之势得到一定程度遏止。但企业总体效益仍不理想。全省国有及年销售收入500万元以上非国有独立核算工业企业实现利润总额151.51亿元,比上年下降7.9%.其中国有企业下降15.4%,大中型企业下降12.2%;亏损企业亏损额114.33亿元,上升22.8%,其中国有企业上升14.0%;企业亏损面24.3%,上升1.8个百分点。全年工业经济效益综合指数为99.3%,比上年下降2.1个百分点。企业资本保值增值率为108.2%,下降5.8个百分点;资产负债率为62.6%,下降0.21个百分点。

建筑业发展加快。全年完成建筑业增加值482.4亿元,比上年增长22.2%。全省建筑施工企业共承接65841个施工项目,实行招投标的工程个数29293个,招投标面为44.5%,比上年增加11.5个百分点。工程质量管理得到加强,工程质量优良品率为33.0%,比上年提高2.7个百分点。全年建筑企业施工的房屋建筑面积17803.33万平方米,比上年增长10.0%;房屋竣工面积9958.90万平方米,增长13.3%;实现利税总额42.71亿元,增长13.5%。

四、固定资产投资

固定资产投资增长较快。全年全社会完成固定资产投资2535.5亿元,比上年增长15.1%,计算物价因素,实际工作量增长16.5%。其中,国有经济投资1031.8亿元.增长24.8%;集体经济投资475.4亿元,增长6.1%;城乡居民个人投资319.2亿元,下降7.8%;其他各种经济类型投资709.0亿元,增长21.8%。按投资管理渠道划分,基本建设投资747.2亿元,增长27.1%;更新改造投资296.0亿元,增长10.1%;房地产开发投资300.2亿元,增长24.3%;其他投资311.3亿元,增长33.4%。

投资结构调整取得明显进展。资金投入向基础产业和基础设施倾斜,全省第一产业完成投资102.6亿元,比上年增长33.2%,比全部投资增幅高出18.1个百分点;第二产业完成投资1091.8亿元,增长8.6%;第三产业完成投资1341.1亿元,增长19.7%。在基本建设和更新改造中,用于能源工业投资153.7亿元,增长12.8%;原材料工业投资78.9亿元,下降17.4%;机电工业投资50.5亿元,下降39.7%;轻纺工业投资126.5亿元,增长104.6%;交通运输邮电业投资274.1亿元,增长37.3%;文教卫科投资72.0亿元,增长34.6%。

水利、交通、能源等一批重点项目建设得到加强。全省大中型基本建设项目和限上技改项目共完成投资278.5亿元,比上年增长19.8%。治淮治太、江海堤防达标等省重点水利工程取得新进展,沂沭泗洪水东调南下工程正在实施,泰州引江河工程建设实现初通水和通航,淮河入海水道工程开工建设,通榆河工程加快进行。南京至马鞍山、南京至高淳(一期)高速公路建成通车,江阴长江公路大桥、南京长江第二大桥和广靖、锡澄、淮江、连徐高速公路等建设步伐加快。新长铁路、华东江苏50万伏输变电工程等开工建设。

固定资产投资成果显著。全年基本建设和更新改造建成投产项目7820个,项目建成投产率为71.0%;新增固定资产795.7亿元,新增固定资产交付使用率为76.3%。全省基本建设新增的主要生产能力有:天然原油开采30万吨/年;火力发电机组容量155.1万千瓦,输电线路长度536公里,变电设备能力301万千伏安;新建公路799公里,其中高速公路63公里;新扩建港口码头泊位12个,年吞吐量296万吨;水泥70万吨/年;城市自来水供水能力18.5万吨/日。

五、交通和邮电业

交通运输生产继续增长。全年完成增加值322.9亿元,比上年增长6.3%。铁路、公路、水运、民航基础设施不断改善,综合运输能力得到加强。全省各种运输方式完成的货物周转量1482.6亿吨公里,比上年增长2.0%。其中,铁路343.4亿吨公里,下降3.5%;公路337.5亿吨公里,增长3.2%;水运769.8亿吨公里,增长3.9%;管道31.7亿吨公里,增长5.5%。各种运输方式完成的旅客周转量717.4亿人公里,比上年增长2.3%。其中,铁路141.2亿人公里,下降2.4%;公路564.8亿人公里,增长3.2%;水运1.3亿人公里,下降38.7%;航空10.1亿人公里,增长34.0%。主要港口货物吞吐量12115万吨,比上年增长1.9%;其中外贸货物吞吐量2721万吨,增长2.9%。

邮电通信业快速发展。全年完成增加值112.9亿元,比上年增长44.1%。完成邮电业务总量167.8亿元,比上年增长26.6%;业务收入173亿元,增长41.5%。公用通信能力进一步提高,邮政新型业务发展迅速。年末局用交换机总容量达1292.2万门,净增236.7万门。其中市内电话已装容量772.3万门,净增52.7万门;农话已装容量519.9万门,净增184.0万门。城乡住宅电话用户达637万户,新增139万户。全省电话普及率达每百人18.7部,比上年提高4.4部。农村电话在上年行政村村村通电话的基础上继续加快发展。年末移动电话新增用户52万户,达到140万户,比上年末增长59.1%;计算机互联网络用户达到7.4万户,增长3.1倍。

六、国内贸易和市场物价

国内消费品销售在买方市场格局下保持稳定增长。全年社会消费品零售总额2238.0亿元,比上年增长5.7%,计算物价因素,实际增长7.6%。其中,城市(包括县城)实现1509.6亿元,比上年增长6.3%;农村实现728.4亿元,增长4.3%。分经济类型看,国有经济零售额475.9亿元,比上年下降4.7%;集体经济616.6亿元,下降2.8%;私营经济137.0亿元,增长49.7%;个体经济557.2亿元,增长17.9%。分行业看,批发零售贸易业零售额1540.5亿元,比上年增长6.5%;餐饮业175.6亿元,增长13.6%;各种其他行业522.0亿元,上升0.9%。流通体制改革继续深化,现代流通业态发展较快。市场建设迈出新步伐,全省商品交易市场达6018个,其中年成交额超亿元的市场338个,超10亿元的市场42个。各类要素市场达300多家。

全省百家重点批发零售贸易企业全年销售收入净额154.0亿元,比上年下降13.1%;经营费用率为5.4%,上升0.4个百分点。经济效益状况仍未明显改观。全年利润总额2.2亿元,比上年下降27.1%;销售利润率为1.4%,下降0.3个百分点。

全省居民消费价格比上年下降0.6%,其中城乡居民消费价格分别与上年持平和下降1.0%。分项目看,食品价格下降2.7%,其中粮食上涨3.9%、油脂上涨2.3%、肉禽及其制品下降10.2%、蛋类上涨5.4%、水产品下降4.9%、鲜菜上涨2%.衣着类下降0.7%,家庭设备及用品类下降1.3%,医疗保健上涨2.7%,交通和通讯工具下降3.9%,娱乐教育文化用品下降1.5%,居住类上涨0.7%,服务项目上涨8.6%。全省农业生产资料价格下降7.5%,工业企业原材料、燃料、动力购进价格下降8.6%,工业品出厂价格下降5.5%。全省商品零售价格比上年下降1.8%,其中城乡商品零售价格分别下降1.8%和1.9%。

七、对外经济

面对亚洲金融危机的冲击。全省对外贸易仍取得较好成绩。据海关统计,全年进出口总额264.3亿美元,比上年增长11.9%。其中:进口107.8亿美元,增长13.0%;出口156.5亿美元,增长11.1%。出口市场多元化战略取得明显成效,商品销往193个国家和地区,欧盟、美国等传统市场得到巩固和发展,出口分别增长33.6%和26.3%;对非洲、拉美、大洋洲等新兴市场的出口,分别增长20.9%、20.6%和14.6%。外商投资企业成为全省外贸发展的主要力量,全年出口80.6亿美元,增长20.1%,占全省出口总额的51.5%,比上年提高3.9个百分点。出口商品结构进一步改善,初级产品出口额的比重由上年的5.7%下降为4.5%，工业制成品出口比重比上年提高1.2个百分点，其中高技术含量、高附加值的机电产品出口额达62.0亿美元，增长31.2%，比全省平均增幅高出20.2个百分点。

利用外资稳步增长。全省实际利用外资总额达69.6亿美元，其中外商直接投资66.5亿美元，比上年增长14.8%；全省新批外商投资企业1818家，合同外资75.7亿美元，分别比上年下降12.9%和18.4%，降幅比年初有所减小。其中新批总投资在1000万美元以上的项目达189个，超亿美元的项目4个，有近60个国家(地区)的客商和21个世界著名跨国公司踊跃来苏投资。外商独资企业保持强劲增长势头，新批外商独资企业合同外资增长15.0%，占全省的比重由上年的41.4%上升到58.3%。外商投资结构逐步改善，全年新批增资项目由上年的331个上升到519个，基础设施、基础产业项目也有所增加。

各类开发区已成为全省对外开放的重要窗口。79家国家级、省级开发区外商实际出资和外贸出口分别占全省总数的67.9%和30.5%。

对外经济技术合作业务继续拓展。全年国际公司新签对外承包劳务合同额6.3亿美元，比上年增长31.3%；完成营业额5.2亿美元，增长35.6%。

国际旅游业继续发展。全年共接待旅游、参观、访问及从事各项活动的海外游客115.4万人次、395.9万人天，旅游外汇收入5.3亿美元，分别比上年增长7.5%、33.7%和24.8%。

八、财政、金融和保险业

财政收支状况良好。全年财政总收入579.9亿元，比上年增长13.1%；其中地方财政收入308.2亿元，增长12.8%。全年财政支出434.2亿元，比上年增长14.4%。全省财政收支平衡，已全部消化了历史性财政赤字。认真执行中央制定的积极的财政政策，扩大对重点水利工程和交通等基础设施的投资，促进了经济稳步发展。

金融形势基本平稳。年末全社会各项存款余额6578.8亿元，贷款余额5063.6亿元，分别比年初增加898.7亿元和609.9亿元，存贷差比去年增加288.8亿元。在存款中，企业存款余额2484.3亿元，城乡居民储蓄存款余额3656.5亿元，分别比年初增加273.8亿元和553.3亿元。在贷款中，短期贷款余额4094.2亿元，中长期贷款余额651.5亿元，分别比年初增加486.2亿元和47.8亿元。年末现金(M0)增长20.8%，狭义货币(M1)增长14.3%，广义货币(M2)增长17.2%。

保险事业继续发展。全年承保总额16351.9亿元，比上年增长36.3%；保费收入99.0亿元，增长19.1%；赔付总额18.7亿元，增长4.2%。

九、科学技术和教育

科技队伍继续扩大。年末全省各类专业技术人员202.2万人，比上年增长4.5%。科技机构2166个，其中，政府部门属独立研究与开发机构394个，高等院校属科研机构369个，大中型工业企业办科研机构1403个；从事科技活动人员49.1万人，其中科学家和工程师23.5万人。全省拥有中国科学院院士46人，中国工程院院士25人。

科学研究成果累累。全省获国家级科技成果奖47项，其中国家发明奖2项，国家科技进步奖45项；获省科技进步奖299项，其中特等奖1项，一等奖14项，二等奖60项，三等奖244项。

技术市场日趋活跃。全年共签订各类技术合同4.4万项；技术贸易成交额33.1亿元，比上年增长14.7%。专利事业发展较快。全年申请专利5828件，授权专利3787件，分别比上年增长11.4%和42.7%。

高新技术产业化进程加快。建成43个国家和省级工程技术研究中心、53个国家和省级企业技术中心及15个高新技术创新服务中心与园区。国家级和省级高新技术产业开发区实现技工贸总收入890亿元，比上年增长36.5%。全省高新技术企业812家，当年认定省级高技术产品450项，省级新产品642项。与中国科学院合作，成功举办了高新技术及其产业化合作交易洽谈会。

继续实施教育现代化和教育促小康工程，深化教育教学改革，素质教育得到广泛重视，各级各类教育事业全面发展。改造和更新薄弱学校1334所。全省招收研究生5640人，在学研究生1.52万人。普通高校招收本专科生8.49万人，在校学生27.32万人，分别比上年增加0.66万人和3.42万人。各类中等专业学校在校学生48.11万人，比上年增加2.23万人。全省普通中学在校学生324.24万人，小学在校学生751.82万人，分别比上年增加3.55万人和19.76万人。职业中学在校学生22.91万人，比上年减少2.16万人。技工学校在校学生11.16万人，比上年减少0.29万人。小学学龄儿童入学率达99.8%，初中入学率达95.1%。普及九年义务教育及扫除青壮年文盲的成果得到巩固。成人教育进一步发展。全年成人高等学校招收本专科生7.05万人，在校学生20.02万人，分别比上年增加0.13万人和1.4万人。成人中专在校学生17.39万人，比上年减少0.44万人。教师队伍建设得到加强，办学条件有所改善。教师住房建设速度加快，新建教师住房面积229万平方米。

十、文 化 和 体 育

文化大省建设步伐加快。"五个一工程"建设取得新成绩，一批优秀剧目和作品在全国获奖。文化基础设施改善，文化市场健康活跃。年末全省共有文化馆 108 个，公共图书馆 99 个，博物馆 79 个，档案馆 163 个，向社会开放档案 115 万卷，省辖市以上广播电台 14 座，中短波广播发射台和转播台 21 座，电视台 14 座，广播人口覆盖率和电视人口覆盖率分别达 97.7% 和 97.8%。共有艺术表演团体 132 个，各类电影放映单位 2772 个。全年报纸出版 18.6 亿份，各类杂志出版 9240 万册，图书出版 4.68 亿册。

体育事业蓬勃发展。在国际国内重大比赛中，全省共有 169 人次获奖牌。其中，在世界最高水平比赛中获金牌 10 枚、银牌 14 枚、铜牌 9 枚；亚洲最高水平比赛中获金牌 36 枚、银牌 15 枚、铜牌 8 枚。在全国性重大比赛中获金牌 30 枚、银牌 27 枚、铜牌 20 枚。在第十三届亚运会上全省有 36 人次夺取金牌，居全国第一，荣获国家体育总局颁发的 1998 年全国体育工作五项大奖，其中突出贡献奖和亚运会贡献奖双双名列全国各省市之首。

十一、卫生和环境保护

卫生工作得到加强。全省以县(市、区)为单位全面达到初级卫生保健合格标准，解决了淮北高氟和污染严重地区 450 万人口卫生饮水问题。年末共有各类卫生机构 14572 个。其中医院、卫生院 2610 个，卫生防疫和防治机构 264 个，妇幼卫生保健机构 114 个。各类卫生机构拥有病床 17.0 万张，其中医院、卫生院病床 15.9 万张。共有卫生技术人员 25.7 万人，其中医生 11.6 万人；拥有中西医师 7.8 万人，护师和护士 7.1 万人；拥有卫生防疫和防治人员 1.2 万人，妇幼卫生人员 0.3 万人。

环保执法力度加大，环保工作取得新成绩。年末全省共有各级环境监测站 95 个，设立自然保护区 18 个。全年共完成环境污染治理项目 1510 项，完成总投资 17.4 亿元；建成烟尘控制区 121 个，面积达 1302.9 平方公里；建成环境噪声达标区 126 个，面积为 829.5 平方公里；工业粉尘排放量、回收量分别为 55 万吨和 145 万吨，全省新增废水天处理能力 114.6 万吨。太湖、淮河和长江等重点流域水污染治理取得阶段性成果。

十二、人口和人民生活

计划生育工作成效显著，人口保持低速增长。全年人口出生率 10.97‰，下降 0.46 个千分点；死亡率 6.84‰；人口自然增长率为 4.13‰，下降 0.46 个千分点。年末全省常住人口 7182.5 万人，比上年末增加 34.6 万人。

城乡居民生活质量继续提高。全年城镇居民人均可支配收入 6018 元，比上年增长 4.4%；人均消费性支出 4889 元，增长 7.8%。全年职工工资总额 652.9 亿元，比上年增长 2.7%；职工平均工资 7516 元，增长 5.7%。全年农民人均纯收入 3377 元，比上年增长 3.3%；人均生活消费支出 2337 元，下降 6.1%。全省继续实施扶贫攻坚计划，脱贫成果得到巩固。

城乡居民居住条件进一步改善。全年城镇新建住宅 2198 万平方米，农村新建住宅 7381 万平方米。城镇居民人均居住面积为 11.1 平方米，农村居民人均住房面积为 32.0 平方米，分别比上年增加 0.5 平方米和 1.3 平方米。

STATISTICAL COMMUNIQUE OF JIANGSU PROVINCE STATISTICAL BUREAU ON 1998 NATIONAL ECONOMIC AND SOCIAL DEVELOPMENT

The year 1998 was extremely unusual, having gone through the severe test in domestic and foreign situations and won important victories. Under the Leadership of the Central Party Committee, the State Council, and the Provincial Party Committee and the Government, the people all over the province from top to bottom, with one heart and one mind, had carried on an indomitable struggle and made great efforts to overcome all kinds of difficulties occurred in the economic life, among them the impact of the Asian financial crises and the disaster caused by the monstrous floods. Consequently, the economy maintained a stable growth, various reforms continued to deepen, social undertakings gained new progress, so the adjusting and controlling targets set for the whole year in economic and social development had been basically fulfilled.

Ⅰ. General Survey

The economy of the province remained a faster growth, with a further heightened economic quality. According to preliminary statistics, the GDP of the year reached 719.995 billion yuan, an increase of 11% than the previous year, 3.2% higher than national average in terms of range of rise, of which, the added value of the primary industry reached 101.627 billion yuan, 2.1% increase of the previous year; the added value of secondary industry was 364.01 billion yuan, 12.0% increase; and the added value of the tertiary industry was 254.358 billion yuan, 12.9% increase. The per capita GDP was 10,021 yuan, 10.4% higher than the previous year. The structure of the economy and the ownership had been adjusted. For the respective component proportion to the GDP of the added value of the primary, secondary and tertiary industries, there was the change from the previous year's 15.1:51.1:33.8 to this year's 14.1:50.6:35.3. The public owned economy assumed a stable development in the course of reform and opening, while the mixed owned economy and the private economy had a rapid growth. Financial revenue and expenditure were in good conditions. Basic stability was remained in monetary situation. The market price kept low rank performance.

The effects of the policy of enlarging the domestic demands gradually became visible. The motive power of economic growth was strengthened. The investment demands were started positively, especially referred the dynamic for the investment of infrastructure construction, such as the water conservancy, transportation, were obviously strengthened. The rate of progress of the key projects construction was quickened. All of these had become the main elements in rejuvenating the economic growth. The rate of the market occupation was heightened, as the consumptive demand was enlarged with great effort, and more attention was paid for the sales of the famous products and market development. In spite of the most troublesome situation, export demands remained increasing to some extent. Great victories had been won in fighting the flood. People all over the province, united, guarded steadily, resisted bravely to protect the hitting of the flood. There was no gap on dykes, no accident in water conservancy projects, and nobody died from the flood calamity. An effective guarantee was given for the normal order of the economic construction and the safety of the people's life and property.

Employment and social insurance were further emphasized. By the end of the year, there were 7528 thousand employees on the post in city and town, of which, 4715 thousand were in state-owned units 1619 thousand were in urban collective-owned units, 1194 were in other tpye units. In rural area, the number of the people engaged in individual business was 2817 thousand, in private enterprises was 1,337 thousand. Remarkable effect was made in basic life insurance and reemployment task of the workers who were laid off in state-owned enterprises. Centers of re-employment service and the like were established in all of the state-owned enterprises provided with laid off workers. By the end of the year, 245 thousand laid off workers had entered the centers of reemployment service, basic guarantee was given to their life, old-aged pension was fully provided for the retirees of the enterprises on time. 292 thousand laid off workers were reemployed through numerous channels, with 54.3 % as the reemployment rate. By the end of the year, the rate of registered unemployments reached 2.6 % in city and town.

The existing main problems in the course of economic and social development were: The structural contradiction was still outstanding, the final demand was not prosperous, the growth strength of the investment by city and town collective units and individual was weak, the export demand showed a smaller increase than before, part of enterprises were having a difficult time in production and management. The economic result was worse. The adjustment step of rural structure was not quick enough. Parts of the rural service systems were further to be strengthened. There were more pressures in employment and reemployment. The income of the residents increased slowly. There was difficulty in the life of part low-income residents.

Ⅱ. Farming, Forestry, Animal Husbandry and Fishery

There was stable development in agricultural production. Owing to the natural calamities, the production of summer grain and oil crop were decreased by a big margin. However, thanks to the strong measure of "Taking the autumn to Compensate the Summer" and the fine weather, the production of the autumn grain broke past records in both total output and per mu area output, of which, per mu output of paddy had surpassed thousand jins for five years running. The annual total output of grain was 34,151 thousand tons, a minus of 1.487 million tons than the previous year, 4.2 % less than in 1997, but still was a higher harvest year. The total output of cotton was 462 thousand tons, 9 % decrease of the previous year. The total output of oil-bearing crops was 1.156 million tons, of which, the rapeseeds was 643 thousand tons, a drop of 18.5 % and 36.1 % respectively. The total output of silkworm cocoon was 85 thousand tons, 1.5 % decrease. The total output of fruits was 1.444 million tons, 2.8 % increase over the previous year.

Continual growth was seen in production of forestry, animal husbandry and fishery. The year's afforestation area was 15.1 thousand hectares, a decrease of 20.4 % than the previous year. Among the major animal products, the total output of meat was 2.953 million tons, up 10.8.1 % of the previous year. The total output of poultry and eggs was 1.571 million tons, 3.9 % increase than 1997. The total output of milk was 122 thousand tons, up 9.5 % of the previous year. The total output of aquatic products was 2.82 million tons, 6.1 % increase over 1997, with the output of fresh water products being 1.938 million tons, and that of the marine products being 882 thousand tons, up by 7.3 % and 3.7 % over the previous year respectively.

The agricultural synthetical development was strengthened. The conditions of agricultural production were further ameliorated. In this year, 7.7 thousand hectares of beaches were surrounded and cultivated. 216.7 thousand hectares of medium and low production farmland were reformed, 138.7 thousand of farmland with high and stable production were built, and 293.3 thousand hectares of irrigated farmland area were newly increased. New progress was made in the construction of water conservancy. A number of water conservancy projects were completed as scheduled, the effective irrigated area of farmland reached 3855.4 thousand hectares, 16.1 thousand hectares increase of the previous year. Material equipment for agriculture was newly improved. By the end of the year, the total power of agricultural machinery was 25.948 million kilowatts, 3.8 % increase of the previous year's end.

The reform in countryside was further deepened; new records were also made in the adjustment of rural structure. The relation of land contracting was stable and improved. The task of the second turn of the rural land contracting, which would be unchanged for 30 years, had been organized and carried out, and basically prolonged in whole province. The reform for the system of grain circulation was pushed on. As three policies of "Purchasing the Surplus Grain According to the Protective Price and Selling the Grain with Positive Price by Purchasing and Storage Enterprises, and Revolving the Purchasing Funds in Closed Manner" were carried out with conscientious effort, the reform of the grain enterprises was deepened, and the work for the grain purchasing was developed smoothly. Progress was also somewhat made in the adjustment of agricultural structure, and the management of agriculture industrialization was further pushed on. The crop areas with good quality and high production were enlarged. The construction for the ten bases of high effective animal husbandry and gardening industries in the areas to the south of the Yantze River, and to the south as well as to the north of the Huaihe River had been shown the initial effect. 84 dragon-head-leading-enterprises with 100 million yuan per year revenue of product sales had already formed throughout the province. Non-agricultural industries in rural area continued to have a quicker development. The output value of industry, construction, transportation, wholesale and retail sale trade was 12.1 % more than in 1997, and that of the proportion in the gross rural social output value had risen from previous year's 83.7 % to 84.4 %.

Ⅲ. Industry and Construction

There was a sustained rapid growth in industrial production. The whole year's industrial added value was 315.77 billion yuan, 10.8 % increase over 1997.

805.302 billion yuan of the output value were completed by all of the state-owned enterprises, and non-state-owned enterprises with 5 million yuan above of annual revenue of product sales, an increase of 12.5 % than previous year. There was a steady development in state-owned and collective-owned industry, other types of industry also had a faster growth. The output value of the state-owned shareholding industry was 265.30 billion yuan, 4.5 % increase over 1997; among them, the output value of state-owned industry was 221.06 billion yuan, 6 % increase, and that of the collective-owned industry was 368.12 billion yuan, 4.5 % increase; shareholding industry was 109.795 billion yuan, 26.8 % increase; the output value by foreign, Hongkong, Macao and Taiwan funds invested enterprises was 182.937 billion yuan, 28.6 % more than 1997; the output value of joint-venture, private and other type industry was 44.938 billion yuan, 46.7 % increase. The output value of large and medium-sized industrial enterprises was 381.099 billion yuan, up 2.4 % over the previous year. Thanks to the motive power of investment, the growth of the heavy industry was quicker to some extent. The annual output value of light industry was 370.965 billion yuan, 14.3 % increase over the previous year; the output value of the heavy industry was 434.338 billion yuan, 10.8 % increase.

Various reforms of the enterprises were steadily going on. The step of the establishment of the enterprise-modernized system was quickened in state-owned large and medium industrial enterprises. By the end of the year, 40 % of the state-owned large and medium-sized enterprises had tentatively built such system. The state-owned small enterprises were further activited by taking numerous type of measures such as foreign funds introducing, cooperative stocking system, stocking system, contracting, rent and sale etc. The proportion of enterprises reformed in township had risen to 85 % from previous year's 60 %.

After the compaign of '98 adjustment and advancement of the industrial structure, new progress was made in structure adjustment. A number of the enterprises groups were established and developed. By the end of the year, there were more than 2000 various kinds of enterprise groups. There were certain progresses in the work of the capital funds structure optimization. More than 20 billion of capital assets were reorganized. The task of cutting down 810 thousand of spindles was completed throughout the province. The structure of the products was adjusted. The products with high technical contents and meeting the prosperous marketing demands showed a faster growth, while the industrial processing products, with surplus production capacity and market unsalable goods assumed a negative growth. Among the output of 83 kinds of major industrial products (placed on statistics), 41 kinds of the output of major products were increased, and that of 42 kinds of major products dropped. Compare with 1997, the output of cotton yarn, 1.0 % decrease; machine-made paper and paper-board, 3.2 % increase; salt, 10.8 % decrease; household washing machines, 4.5 % increase; color TV Sets, 41.5 % increase; coal, 4.9 % increase; electricity, 0.4 % increase; crude oil processing, 1.4 % increase; rolled-steel and final products, 12.4 % increase; cement, 1.8 % increase; metal-cutting machines, 2.8 % increase; plate glass, 25.6 % increase; soda ash, 28.7 % increase; microelectronic computer, 107 % increase; motor vehicle, 9.2 % decrease; hi-fi systems, 191.7 % increase; distance controlling switchboards, 24.3 % increase; chemical fertilizers, 1.2 % decrease; air conditioners, 16.7 % decrease, chemical fiber, 6.0 % increase. The quality and grade of the products were steadily heightened, and the marketing competitive capacity of the famous brand products was reinforced.

The condition of the connection between production and sale of the industrial enterprises was somewhat improved, however, the economic result had not yet become favorable. The rate between sale and production was 96.0 %, 0.3 percentage point higher than the previous year. The overstock was decreased slowly, by the end of the year, the stock of the industrial finished products was 2.72 % increase of the previous year, but with the redropped growth rang of 13.7 percentage point than the beginning of the year. More efforts were given to eliminate deficits and to raise profits. The growth range of deficits was shrinked. The decline in industrial economic benefit was checked to some extent. However, as a whole, the economic result of the enterprises was not yet ideal. The total amount of the profit of state-owned and non-state-owned independent accounting industrial enterprises, each with 5000 thousand or more of revenue of products sales per year, was 15.151 billion yuan, 7.9 % decrease of the previous year, of which, state-owned enterprises was 15.4 % decrease, large and medium-sized enterprises was 12.2 % decrease. The deficit in loss making enterprises was 11.433 billion yuan, an increase of 22.8 % than 1997, of which the state-owned was 14.0 % increase. The deficit scale was 24.3 %, an increase of 1.8 percentage point. The year's aggregative index of the industrial economic result was 99.3 %, 2.1 percentage point lower than 1997. The rate of capital remained and value added of the enterprises was 108.2 %, a decrease of 5.8 percentage point than the previous year. The rate of capital liabilities was 62.6 %, a decrease of 0.21 percentage point.

There was a faster development in construction industry. The year's added value accomplished by construction industry was 48.24 billion yuan, 22.2 % increase over 1997. There were 65,841 construction projects for the construction enterprises in the province, and 29,293 of them were opened for bidding, the scale of those was 44.5 %, went up by 11.5 percentage point than 1997. The management for the quality of projects was strengthened, with 33.0 % as the good quality rate, an increase of 2.7 percentage point than the previous year. The year's floor space of housing built by the construction enterprises was 178,033 thousand square meters, topping 1997 by 10.0 %, and the floor space of the housing completed was 99,589 thousand square meters, an increase of 13.3 %. The total pre-tax profit reached 4.271 billion yuan, an increase of 13.5 % over 1997.

Ⅳ. Fixed Assets Investment

There was a quicker growth in fixed assets investment. Of all the social fixed assets investment completed in 1998 was 253.55 billion yuan, up by 15.1 % of the previous year. The actual amount of work (price factor deducted) was 16.5 % increase of the previous year, of which, invested by state-owned economy was 103.18 billion yuan (24.8 % increase); collective-owned economy 47.54 billion yuan (6.1 % increase); individual residents in city and county 31.92 billion (7.8 % decrease); and other types of economy 70.90 billion yuan (21.8 % increase). Grouped by channel of investment, in capital construction was 74.72 billion yuan (27.1 % increase of the previous year), in technical updating and transformation 29.60 billion yuan (10.1 % increase), real estate development 30.02 billion yuan (24.3 % increase), other investment was 31.15 billion yuan (33.4 % increase).

Obvious progress had been made in the adjustment of investment structure. Funds furnished was inclined to the basic industry and infrastructure. Of the whole province, investment for the primary industry was 10.26 billion yuan (33.2 % increase of the previous year), the growth range was 18.1 percentage point higher than the overall investment; and for the secondary industry was 109.18 billion yuan, 8.6 % increase; and for the tertiary industry was 134.11 billion yuan, 19.7 % increase. Among the investment in capital construction and technical updating and transformation, 15.37 billion was used for energy industry, 12.8 % increase; 7.89 billion yuan for raw material industry, 17.4 % decrease; 5.05 billion yuan for machinery and electronic industry, 39.7 % decrease; 12.65 billion yuan for light and textile industry, 104.6 % increase; 27.41 billion yuan for transportation, post and telecommunication, 37.3 % increase; 7.20 billion yuan for culture, education, health, science and technology,. 34.6 % increase.

A number of key construction projects were emphasized, regarding water conservancy, transportation and energy etc.. Of the whole province, 27.85 billion yuan of investment was used for the capital construction of large and medium-sized and above-norm technical updating and transformation projects, 19.8 % increase than previous year. New progress had been made in the provincial focus water conservancy projects, regarding Huaihe River and Taihu Lake harnessing, and river and sea dykes standardization. The projects of introducing the water to the east and south from Yihe River, Suohe River, Sihonghe River were carrying out. The construction project of introducing the water from river to Taizhou was put into navigation and circulation initially. The waterway project of introducing the Huihe River onto the sea was started. Tongyuhe River project was quickly going on. The express highway from Nanjing to Ma'anshan and Nanjing to Gaochun (first-phase) were completed and put into operation. The construction step of Jiangyin Yantze River highway bridge and Nanjing No.2 Yangtze River highway bridge, and Guangling-Jinjiang, Wuxi-Jiangyin, Huaiying-Jiangduo, Lianyungang-Xuzhou express highway was quickened. The construction of railway from Xinyi to Changxing and Jiangsu eastern China 500 thousand volt-amperes of substation capacity projects etc. were also starting.

Significant result was made in investment for the capital construction. 7,820 projects of capital construction and technical updating and transformation had been put into operation. The rate of completion and putting into operation was 71.0 %; 79.57 billion yuan were newly added to fixed assets, and its commissioning and utilization rate for these fixed assets was 65.2 %. The major production capacity newly added to capital construction were: 300 thousand tons per year of the natural curd oil extraction; 1.551 million kilowatts of power generation, 536 kilometers of transmission line, 3010 thousand volt-amperes of substation capacity. There were 799 kilometers of newly-built highway (including 63 kilometers of expressway), 12 units of newly enlarged berth for dock at ports, with 2,960 thousand of cargo handled per year; 700 thousand tons of cement per year, 185 thousand tons of tap water per day in city.

Ⅴ. Transportation, Post and Telecommunication

The production of transportation and communication were continually increasing. The added value completed in the year amounted to 32.29 billion yuan, 6.3 % increase of the previous year, with the improving of the infrastructure of railway, highway, waterway and civil aviation. The aggregative transportation ability was strengthened. The freight turnover by various means of transportation was 148.26 billion ton kilometers, 2.0 % increase of the previous year, of which, 34.34 billion by railway (3.5 % decrease); 33.75 billion by highway (3.2 % increase); 76.98 billion by waterway (3.9 % increase); and 3.17 billion by pipeline (5.5 % increase). The turnover volume of passenger traffic by various means of transportation was 71.74 billion person kilometers, 2.3 % increase of the previous year, of which, 14.12 billion by railway (2.4 % decrease); 56.48 billion by highway (3.2 % increase); 0.13 billion by waterway (38.7 % decrease); 1.01 billion by civil aviation (34.0 % increase). The volume of the freight handled in major ports was 121.15 million tons, 1.9 % increase of the previous year, of which, the cargo handled of foreign trade was 27.21 million tons, 2.9 % increase.

The industry of posts and telecommunication developed rapidly. The added value achieved over the year was 11.29 billion yuan, 44.1 % increase of the previous year. The total volume of post and telecommunication services was 16.78 billion yuan, 26.6 % increase; business revenue was 17.3 billion yuan, 41.5 % increase. Public communication capacity was further improved. New type of post business was quickly developed. By the end of the year, the total switchboard capacity reached 12.922 million sets, with a net increase of 2.367 million, of which, urban telephone capacity was 7.723 million sets, a net increase of 527 thousand; rural telephone capacity was 5.199 million sets, with a net increase of 1.84 million. In city and countryside, there were 6.37 million residence telephone users, with 1.39 million as new users. On the average, there were 18.7 telephones per 100 persons, 4.4 telephones higher than the previous year. Rural telephone continued to develop rapidly, following the last year, with the telephone had already provided for all of the administrative villages in Jiangsu as the base. By the end of the year, there were 1.40 million mobile telephone users, with 520 thousand as new users, 59.1 % increase over the last year end. The users of the computer exchange network reached 74 thousand, three times increase than 1997.

Ⅵ. Domestic Trade and Market Price

Under the pattern of buying party market, the sale of domestic consumer goods remained a stable growth. For the year, the total value of retail sales of consumer goods was 223.80 billion yuan, 5.7 % increase of the previous year, there was an actual 7.6 % increase (price factor deducted). Among the total value of retail sales of consumer goods, 150.96 billion was from the city (including county town), 6.3 % increase; 72.84 billion was from the countryside, 4.3 % increase. Grouped by the type of ownership, 47.59 billion was from state-owned economy, 4.7 % decrease; 61.66 billion yuan was from collective economy, 2.8 % decrease; 13.70 billion yuan was from private economy, 49.7 % increase; and 55.72 billion was from individual economy, 17.9 % increase. Grouped by the branches of trade, 154.05 billion yuan was from wholesale and retail sale trade, 6.5 % increase of the previous year; 17.56 billion yuan was from catering trade, 13.6 % increase; 52.20 billion from other branches, 0.9 % increase. With the deepening of reform in circulation system, there was a quicker development in modern circulation industry, a new step was starting in construction of market. There were 6,018 commodity transaction markets over the year, of which, 338 markets each with surpassing 100 million yuan of transaction value per year, and 42 markets each with surpassing 1000 million yuan of transaction value per year. There were more than 300 factor markets of various kinds and levels.

Of the whole province, the sales revenue of 100 focus wholesale and retail sale trade enterprises was 15.40 billion yuan (net value) yearly, 13.1 % decrease than the previous year, the rate of management cost was 5.4 %, 0.4 percentage point higher than in 1997, there was still no obvious change in economic result. The total after-tax profits amounted 220 million yuan, 27.1 % decrease than 1997. The rate between the pre-tax profits and sales was 1.4 %, 0.3 percentage point decrease than the previous year.

Of the whole province, the residents consumer price was a 0.6 % decrease than the previous year, of which, the urban and rural residents consumer price were unbaised and 1.0 % decrease than the previous year respectively. Seen from the articles, food price fell by 2.7 %, of which, 3.9 % increase in grain; 2.3 % increase in oil; 10.2 % decrease in meat and poultry and their finished products, 5.4 % increase in eggs and their products; 4.9 % decrease in aquatic; 2 % increase in flesh vegetable; 0.7 % decrease was in clothes, 1.3 % decrease was in home appliances and articles; 2.7 % increase in medical treatment and health protection; 3.9 % decrease in means of transportation and telecommunication; 1.5 % decrease in articles for recreational, educational and cultural purpose; 0.7 % increase in residence and the like; 8.6 % increase in service items. The price for means of agricultural production had a 7.5 % decrease. Purchasing price for raw material, fuel and power in industrial enterprises had a 8.6 % decrease. Producer's price of manufactured products had a 5.5 % decrease. Retail price had a 1.8 % decrease than the previous year, of which, retail price for urban and rural residents had a 1.8 % and 1.9 % decrease respectively.

Ⅶ. Foreign Economy

Facing the lashing by Asian financial crisis, there was still a better achievement in foreign trade of the province. According to the statistics of the customs, the year's gross value of import and export reached 26.43 billion US dollars, 11.9 % increase of the previous year, of which, 10.78 billion US dollars was for import, 13.0 % increase; 15.65 billion US dollars was for export, 11.1 % increase. Obvious result was made in the strategy of the export pluralization, commodities were sold to 193 countries and districts. The traditional markets in European Union and USA were consolidated and developed, with 33.6 % and 26.3 % increase in export respectively. Export for the newly arising markets in Africa, Latin America, and Oceania were 20.9 %, 20.6 % and 14.6 % increase respectively. Foreign invested enterprises had become the major force of the provincial foreign trade, with 8.06 billion US dollars of export, an increase of 20.1 % than 1997, and occupied 51.5 % of the gross export value of the whole prinvince, 3.9 percentage point higher than the previous year. Improvements were made in export structure, the proportion of export value for primary products fell to 4.5 % from previous year's 5.7 %, and that of the manufactured products rose 1.2 percentage point than in 1997, of which, the export value of machinery and electronic products with high technical content and high added value was 6.20 billion US dollars, up by 31.2 % than the previous year, and 20.2 percentage point higher than average growth range of the province.

The utilization of foreign capital saw a steadily increasing. 6.96 billion US dollars of foreign capital was actually utilized in whole province, of which, the direct investment from foreign businessmen was 6.65 billion US dollars, 14.8 % increase than 1997. There were 1,818 newly permitted foreign-invested enterprises, with 7.57 billion US dollars of contractural foreign capital, 12.9 % and 18.4 % decrease respectively, the decreasing range was less than the beginning of the year to some extent, of which, there were 189 projects with newly permitted investment value exceeding 10 million US dollars, and 4 projects exceeding 100 million US dollars. There were travelling traders from nearly 60 countries and districts and 21 famous transnational corporations invested to Jiangsu eagerly. Solely foreign invested enterprises kept a momentum of strong growth. There was an increase of 15 % of contractual foreign funds by newly permitted solely foreign invested enterprises, and that of the proportion in the province had risen to 58.3 % from 41.4 % of the previous year. The structure of foreign investment was improved gradually. Newly permitted funds added projects had risen to 519 from 331 of the previous year. There was some increase in the projects of infrastructure and base industry.

Various kinds of developing zones had become the important windows of the opening Jiangsu province. The proportion of the actual foreign investment and foreign trade export by 79 national level and provincial developing zones had occupied 67.9 % and 30.5 % of the whole province respectively.

Foreign economic and technical cooperative business continued to develop. The value of newly signed foreign contracts on labor service by international company reached 630 million US dollars, 31.3 % increase of the previous year, 520 million US dollars of sales turnover were completed, an increase of 35.6 %.

There was a sustained increase in international trurism. In 1998, the number of overseas tourists engaged in travelling, looking around, visiting and other activities reached 1.154 million person times, 3.959 million person days, and foreign exchange income from tourism amounted to 530 million US dollars, 7.5 %. 33.7 % and 24.8 % increase over the previous year respectively.

Ⅷ. Finance, Banking and Insurance

Financial revenue and expenditure were in good conditions. The year's total financial revenue was 57.99 billion yuan, 13.1 % increase over the previous year, of which, the local financial revenue was 30.82 billion yuan, 12.8 % increase. The financial expenditure was 43.42 billion yuan, an increase of 14.4 % than 1997. Balance was made in financial revenue and expenditure. The historical financial deficit had been wiped out thoroughly. The economic development was being promoted steadily, as the positive financial policy formed by the central government was carried out conscientiously, and the infrastructure investments for the key water conservancy project and transportation were enlarged.

Basic stability was maintained in monetary situation. By the end of the year, balance held on various deposits of the whole society was 657.88 billion yuan, and that on loans was 506.36 billion yuan, 89.87 billion and 60.99 billion increase over the beginning of the year respectively, 28.88 billion yuan of the surplus in deposits was increased than the same period of 1997. Among the deposits, 248.43 billion yuan was from the enterprises, 365.65 billion yuan was from the savings of urban and rural residents, 27.38 billion and 55.33 billion increase respectively over the beginning of the year. Among the loans, 409.42 billion yuan was for short-term loans, 65.15 billion yuan was for long and medium-term loans, 48.62 billion and 4.78 billion increase over the beginning of the year. By the end of the year, the cash (M0) was an increase of 20.8 %; the currency in narrow sense (M1) was an increase of 14.3 %; and the currency in broad sense (M2) was an increase of 17.2 %.

Insurance business continued to expand. The total underwriting amount was 1635.19 billion yuan, 36.3 % increase than the previous year. Premium income was 9.9 billion yuan, 19.1 % increase. As many as 1.87 billion cases of indemnity were handled, 4.2 % increase.

Ⅸ. Science, Technology and Education

The scientific and technical ranks were growing steadly in size continually. By the end of the year, there were 2.022 million specialized technical personnels of various kinds, 4.5 % increase of the previous year. There were 2,166 scientific and technological institutions, of which, 394 scientific institutions were independent under government department; 369 were under colleges and universities, 1,403 were run by large and medium-sized enterprises. A total of 491 thousand people were engaged in scientific and technological activities, of which, 235 thousand were scientists and engineers. The province held 46 academicians of the Chinese Academy of Science, and 25 academicians of the Chinese Academy of Engineering.

Remarkable accomplishments had been made in scientific research. There were 47 national awards won for scientific and technological achievements, of which, 2 were national awards for invention, 45 were national awards for scientific and technological progress, 299 were provincial awards for scientific and technological progress, among which, 1 was top grade a ward, 14 first class, 60 second class and 244 third class awards.

Technology market was more and more enlivened. The number of the various technological contracts signed in the year was 44 thousand. The turnover of technology trade reached 3.31 billion yuan, 14.7 % increase of the previous year. A quicker development was made in patent business. 5,828 patents were applied for, 3787 were authorized, 11.4 % and 42.7 % increase respectively over the previous year.

The process of industrialization for high and new-technology was quickened, 43 national and provincial engineering and technological research centers, 53 national and provincial enterprises technological centers, 15 high and new technological creative service centers and gardening districts were established. The total income from technology, industry, and trade amounted to 89 billion yuan, for the national and provincial developing zones with high and new technology, 36.5 % increase of the previous year. There were 812 enterprises with high and new technology, 450 provincial level products with high technology, and 642 provincial new products got affirmed in this year. A meeting of high and new technology and its industrialization was held successfully in cooperating with the China Academy of Science.

The process of education modernization and the project of promoting comfortable living by education were continually carried on. With the deepening of reform in education and teaching, more attention was paid to the quality education extensively, various levels and kinds of educational cause were developing in an all round way. 1,334 weak schools were reformed and renewed. 5,640 graduate students were newly admitted to institutions of higher learning, thus making the total number of graduate students 15,200. 84,900undergraduate and two-years college students were admitted to regular high learning institutions, making the total number of students 273.2 thousand, a respective increase of 6600 and 34.2 thousand people over the previous year. In the province, the number of students in various specialized technical schools was 481.1 thousand, with an increase of 22,300 people than 1997. There were 3.2424 million students in general high school, and 7.5812 million students in primary schools, with a respective increase of 35.5 thousand and 197.6 thousand people. There were 229.1 thousand students in vocational schools, a decrease of 21.6 thousand people over the previous year, 111.6 thousand students in technical schools, with a decrease of 2900 people than the previous year. The enrollment rate of school-age pupils was 99.8 %, and the enrollment rate of the student in junior middle schools was 95.1 %. The achievement of nine-year compulsory education and the task of eliminating illiteracy of the young people were consolidated. The adult education was further developed. In the year, 70,500 people were enrolled by universities and colleges for adult, there were 200,200 students in these schools, 1,300 and 14,000 more than 1997 respectively. There were 173,900 students in secondary technical schools for adults, 4,400 less than the previous year. The construction of the ranks of the teacher was strengthened. The conditions were improved in running a school. The speed of residence construction for teachers was quickened, the floor space of newly built teachers' residence reached 2.29 million square meters.

Ⅹ. Culture and Sports

The pace of constructing a "Great Province in Cultural" was quickened. New records were made in the construction of " Project Five Ones". A number of excellent programs and works had won national awards. The cultural infrastructure was improved. The cultural market was healthy and brisk. By the end of the year, there were 108 cultural centers, 99 public libraries, 79 museums, 163 archives; 1.15 million volumes of files opened to public, 14 radio stations in cities under the jurisdiction of the provincial government and above, 21 medium and short wave broadcast and relay stations, 14 TV stations. The population coverage rate of the broadcast and TV reached 97.7 % and 97.8 % respectively. There were 132 artistic performance groups, 2,772 various kinds of film projects units. 1.86 billion copies of newspapers, 92.40 million copies of magazines, and 468 million copies of books were published and issued.

Sports cause was enjoying great vitality. In major international competitions, 169 person-times of medals were won by Jiangsu province, of which, 10 gold, 14 silver, 9 bronze medals were won in the highest level competitions of the world; and 36gold, 15 silver, 8 bronze medals were won in Asian highest level competitions; 30 gold, 27 silver, 20 bronze medals were won in national major competitions; 36 person-times gold medals were won in 13th Asian athletic meeting, and obtained the national first place, and had the honor to get 5 items of large medals of the national sport work issued by the State General Bureau of Sports, of which the outstanding contribution award and the Asian athletic meeting contribution award were obtained the national (of all provinces and municipalities) first place in pairs.

Ⅺ. Health and Environmental Protection

Sanitary work was strengthened. The elementary sanitary and health care had overall standardized taking the counties

(Cities and districts) as the units. The problem of 4.5 million people's drinking water had solved in northern Huaihe River Area, a district of high fluorine and severely polluted. By the end of the year, there were 14,572 various sanitary organizations, of which, 2,610 were hospitals and commune hospitals; 264 were sanitation and epidemic prevention organizations, sanitation and disease control organizations; 114 were maternal and child sanitation and health care organizations. There were altogether 170 thousand hospital beds in various kinds of sanitary organizations, of which, 159 thousand beds were belonging to hospitals and commune hospitals. There were 257 thousand professional medical workers, among them, 116 thousand were doctors. The number of Chinese and western medicine doctors was 78 thousand, senior nurses and nurses was 71 thousand. There were 12,000 epidemic prevention and disease control personnels, 3,000 maternal and child health care personnels.

The dynamic of the enforcement of the law for environmental protection was strengthened. New achievements were made in environmental work. By the end of the year, there were 95 environmental monitoring stations on various levels over the province, 18 natural reserves were established, 1,510 projects were completed for the treatment and improvement of environmental pollution with a total investment of 1.74 billion yuan. 121 smoke and dust control zones were set up, with 1,302.9 square kilometers of area; 126 noise standardized zones were completed with 829.5 kilometer of the area. The total emission and reclamation volume of industrial dust were 550 thousand tons and 1.45 million tons, respectively. The day capacity of sewage handling equipment newly built was 1.146 million tons. Gigantic achievements were made for the sewage pollution treatment of major river basins as Taihu Lake, Huaihe River and Yangtze River etc.

XII. Population and People's Livelihood

Remarkable achievements were made in family planning, a slow growth was remained in population. In the year, the birth rate of whole province was 10.97 ‰, 0.46 per thousand point decrease of the previous year; the death rate was 6.84 ‰. The natural growth rate was 4.13 ‰, 0.46 per thousand point decrease than 1997. By the end of the year, the resident population was 71.825 million, an increase of 346 thousand over the previous year.

The life quality of urban and rural residents was further improved. For the city and town residents, the per capita allocatable income of the year was 6,018 yuan, 4.4 % increase over the previous year. The per capita consumptive expenditure of city and town residents was 4,889 yuan, 7.8 % increase than 1997. The year's total wage bill of the staff and workers was 65.29 billion yuan, 2.7 % increase; the average wage was 7,516 yuan, 5.7 % increase. The year's per capita net income of farmers was 3,377 yuan, 3.3 % increase, and that of the per capita consumptive expenditure was 2,337 yuan, 6.1 % decrease. The plan of "Assisting the Poor" was continually carried out with great effort. The fruit of eliminating the poverty was consolidated.

Housing conditions for urban and rural residents were further improved. This year newly built residence for city and town residents reached 21.98 million square meters, and 73.81 million square meters were for rural residents; 11.1 square meters of per capita floor space were for city and town residents, and 32.0 square meters of per capita floor space were for rural residents, 0.5 and 1.3 square meters increase than 1997 respectively.

1. 行政区划和自然资源

DIVISIONS OF ADMINISTRATIVE AREAS AND NATURAL RESOURCES

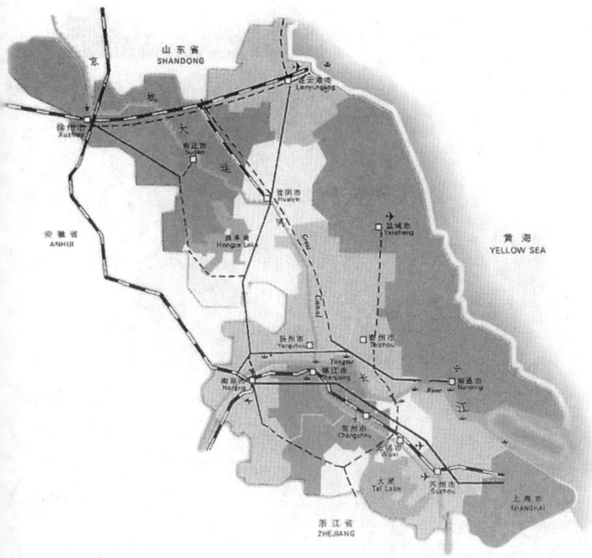

1 行政区划和自然资源
DIVISIONS OF ADMINISTRATIVE AREAS AND NATURAL RESOURCES

自 然 概 况

位 置

江苏简称苏，位于我国大陆东部沿海中心，介于东经116°18′－121°57′，北纬30°45′－35°20′之间。东濒黄海，西连安徽，北接山东，东南与浙江和上海毗邻。

江苏地处美丽富饶的长江三角洲，平原辽阔，主要有苏南平原、江淮平原、黄淮平原组成，自然条件优越，经济基础较好。

面 积

全省面积10.26万平方公里，占全国总面积的1.06%。其中平原面积7.06万平方公里，水面面积1.73万平方公里，海岸线长954公里，耕地面积500.79万公顷。

河 流

全省境内河川交错，水网密布，长江横穿东西400多公里；大运河纵贯南北690公里，西南部有秦淮河，北部有苏北灌溉总渠、沂沭河、通扬运河等。有属全国"五大淡水湖"之列的太湖和洪泽湖，还有阳澄湖、高邮湖等。

资 源

江苏以地形地势低平，河湖众多为特点，平原、水面所占比例之大，在全国居首位，成为江苏一大地理优势；水产资源丰富，有广阔的海涂、浅海，东部沿海渔场面积达15.4万平方公里，其中包括著名的吕泗渔场和海州湾渔场，盛产黄鱼、带鱼、昌鱼、虾类、蟹类及贝藻类等。我省也是全国鳗鱼苗的主要产地。内陆水面2600多万亩，有淡水鱼类140余种，已利用的有40多种。矿产资源分布广泛，品种较多，已发现的有112种，粘土类矿产、建材类矿产、化工原料矿产、冶金辅助原料矿产和特种用途矿产，是江苏矿产资源的优势。

气 候

全省气候具有明显的季风特征，处于亚热带向暖温带过渡地带，大致以淮河——灌溉总渠一线为界，以南属亚热带湿润季风气候，以北属暖温带湿润季风气候。全省气候温和，雨量适中，四季分明。

DIVISIONS OF ADMINISTRATIVE AREAS AND NATURAL RESOURCES NATURAL SITUATIONS

LOCATION

Jiangsu (Short for Su) lies in the east of the country. It is situated in the center of the costal area, between 116°18′ – 121° 57′E and 30°45′ – 35°20′N, with Yellowsea on the east, Anhui province on the west, Shandong on north, and Zhejiang and Shanghai as its neighbours in the southeast.

Jiangsu seats on the beautiful and abundent Yangtze River Delta. Composed of vast plains, mianly South – Su, Jianghui and Huanghui plain, the province provides favorable natural conditions and good economic bases.

AREA

The area of Jiangsu is 102600 square kilometres, occupied 1.06 % of the total national area, among which 70600 square kilometres are plain areas, 17300 square kilometres are water surface. The coastline of the province is as long as 954 kilmetres, and the 44354400 hectares of cultivated land.

RIVERS AND LAKES

In Jiangsu, there are rivers crisscrossing throughout the province, and distributes the network of waterways. The Yangtze River travels whole area of Jiangsu, from west to east, for more than 400 kilometres. The Grand Canal flows sourh to north for 690 kilometres.

There are Qinhui River in the southeast of Jiangsu, Subei general irrigation canal, Qishu River and Tongyang canal etc. in the north part. The Taihu Lake and Hongzehu Lake are both listed among the national "Five Large Fresh Water Lakes". Besides there are Yangchenghu Lake and Gaoyouhu Lake, etc.

RESOURCES

The province is characteristic of topographical features in low and flat terrains, with numerous rivers and lakes. The proportion of plain and watersurface area is so large that it ranks the first in China and become a geographical superiority proportion. There are plentiful aquatic resources, vast shallow sea beaches and epeiric seas. There are 154000 square kilometres of fishing grounds on the eastern coastal area, composed of famous Lushi and Haizhouwan fishing grounds, abound in yellow croaker, hairtail, butterfish, shrimp and crab, and shellfish and algae. Jiangsu is also a main production area of young eel in the country. There are more than 26000 thousand mu of interior water surface, with more than 140 kinds of flesh water fishes, more than 40 kinds of them are utilized. Numerous varieties of mineral resources are widely dispersed, 112 kinds of them have been discovered. The minerals as clay, construction materials, sand, chemical raw materials, metallurgical assistance raw materials, and special purpose minerals become a mineral superiority of Jiangsu.

CLIMATE

Located in a transition area from subtripical zone to temperature zone, Jiangsu shows a distinct characteristic of monsoon. Taking the Huai river to general irrigation canal as an approximate line of demarcation, the climate to the south of the line belongs to monsoon of tropical moist zone, while the climate to the north of the line belongs to monsoon of warm moist zone. Jiangsu has a warm climate, with moderate rainfall and distinct seasons.

1-1 主要城市月平均气温(1998)
MONTHLY AVERAGE TEMPERATURE IN MAJOR CITIES

单位:摄氏度 (℃)

市名 City	1月 Jan.	2月 Feb.	3月 Mar.	4月 Apr.	5月 May	6月 June	7月 July	8月 Aug.	9月 Sept.	10月 Oct.	11月 Nov.	12月 Dec.
南京市 Nanjing	2.3	6.6	9.1	17.9	20.5	24.2	29.5	28.6	23.6	18.9	13.2	6.0
无锡市 Wuxi	3.3	6.9	9.0	17.6	20.5	24.1	29.5	29.1	23.4	19.2	14.3	7.3
徐州市 Xuzhou	-0.1	5.0	8.4	16.6	18.8	24.5	28.6	26.1	23.9	18.1	10.9	3.8
常州市 Changzhou	3.3	6.9	9.2	18.0	20.9	24.4	29.9	29.7	24.0	19.7	14.9	7.6
苏州市 Suzhou	3.9	7.4	9.4	17.9	20.8	24.1	29.6	29.5	23.8	19.9	15.1	8.3
南通市 Nantong	3.4	6.7	8.8	16.6	19.8	23.1	28.6	28.7	23.4	19.0	14.2	7.2
连云港市 Lianyungang	0.3	4.8	8.3	15.1	18.6	22.6	28.4	26.5	24.2	18.8	11.9	4.5
淮阴市 Huiyin	0.8	5.3	8.5	16.4	19.1	22.8	28.5	26.9	23.8	18.5	12.6	5.2
盐城市 Yancheng	1.6	5.5	8.1	15.6	18.7	22.0	28.2	27.6	23.6	18.6	12.9	6.0
扬州市 Yangzhou	2.3	6.3	9.1	17.7	20.3	24.1	29.3	28.6	24.1	19.1	13.9	6.3
镇江市 Zhenjiang	2.4	6.3	8.7	17.3	20.2	23.9	28.8	28.3	23.5	19.1	13.5	6.5
泰州市 Taizhou	2.3	6.0	8.6	16.9	19.7	23.2	28.7	28.3	23.4	18.7	13.3	6.4
宿迁市 Suqian		5.0	8.4	16.2	18.9	23.4	28.1	26.0	23.3	18.2	11.4	3.9

1-2 主要城市月降水量(1998)
MONTHLY PRECIPITATION IN MAJOR CITIES

单位:毫米 (mm)

市名 City	1月 Jan.	2月 Feb.	3月 Mar.	4月 Apr.	5月 May	6月 June	7月 July	8月 Aug.	9月 Sept.	10月 Oct.	11月 Nov.	12月 Dec.
南京市 Nanjing	112.8	32.1	134.6	130.5	112.5	222.0	285.5	109.4	23.9	41.7	10.4	23.6
无锡市 Wuxi	153.0	59.7	160.6	78.5	51.1	213.5	166.0	97.4	109.6	32.6	17.6	49.6
徐州市 Xuzhou	41.9	36.2	115.5	103.3	133.8	69.7	267.3	317.2	0.6	34.7	0.0	8.7
常州市 Changzhou	149.4	54.5	159.7	183.3	62.3	172.6	248.3	84.2	112.5	40.6	9.8	50.6
苏州市 Suzhou	181.3	55.0	138.8	65.1	54.3	187.5	255.1	42.3	291.5	36.4	15.5	51.7
南通市 Nantong	139.2	48.8	165.2	67.9	48.1	234.5	209.2	36.4	161.5	30.2	12.8	32.1
连云港市 Lianyungang	28.1	33.7	81.9	104.2	103.8	100.4	104.9	310.6	0.0	34.8	0.0	15.8
淮阴市 Huiyin	68.9	28.2	72.0	118.8	120.2	326.2	196.9	248.8	6.8	17.6	8.3	16.8
盐城市 Yancheng	105.1	34.7	99.4	81.3	200.7	197.8	243.1	148.9	83.4	33.6	9.9	23.8
扬州市 Yangzhou	128.4	39.7	178.8	131.5	181.9	198.4	160.2	100.1	24.3	49.6	5.0	40.1
镇江市 Zhenjiang	147.2	40.3	153.8	127.7	135.8	215.9	401.8	877.9	34.5	53.0	11.8	48.1
泰州市 Taizhou	142.6	33.2	164.7	107.8	132.5	216.6	196.5	156.7	33.9	57.6	6.0	32.9
宿迁市 Suqian	62.2	30.7	95.8	76.9	173.7	152.3	165.8	586.3	0.0	13.7	0.2	11.2

1-3 行 政 区 划 (1998)
ADMINISTRATIVE DIVISIONS

单位:个 (number)

市 名 City		县级单位数 Number of Counties	#县级市 Cities	各级市单位数 Number of Cities	市辖区数 Districts Under City Administration
合 计	**Total**	**64**	**31**	**44**	**44**
南京市	Nanjing	5		1	10
无锡市	Wuxi	3	3	4	5
徐州市	Xuzhou	6	2	3	5
常州市	Changzhou	3	3	4	4
苏州市	Suzhou	6	6	7	4
南通市	Nantong	6	4	5	2
连云港市	Lianyungang	4		1	4
淮阴市	Huaiyin	6	1	2	2
盐城市	Yancheng	8	2	3	1
扬州市	Yangzhou	5	3	4	2
镇江市	Zhenjiang	4	3	4	2
泰州市	Taizhou	4	4	5	2
宿迁市	Xuqian	4		1	1

续表 Continued

单位:个 (number)

市 名 City		镇 Town	乡 Township	街道办事处 Subdistrict Office	居民委员会 Neighbourhood Committee	村民委员会 Villagers' Committee
合 计	**Total**	**1015**	**959**	**206**	**6119**	**35031**
南京市	Nanjing	67	52	51	1115	1597
无锡市	Wuxi	95	22	27	689	2083
徐州市	Xuzhou	71	114	35	465	3501
常州市	Changzhou	81	55	19	459	1903
苏州市	Suzhou	154	4	22	1101	3135
南通市	Nantong	104	152	9	379	4358
连云港市	Lianyungang	47	72	8	256	2041
淮阴市	Huaiyin	47	116	8	156	2600
盐城市	Yancheng	103	93	5	425	4321
扬州市	Yangzhou	81	74	4	398	2201
镇江市	Zhenjiang	63	26	10	305	1408
泰州市	Taizhou	72	83	8	296	3602
宿迁市	Xuqian	30	96		75	2281

2. 综合

GENERAL SURVEY

2 综　　合
GENERAL SURVEY

从统计看1998年的江苏
JIANGSU IN STATISTICS'98

江 苏 的 地 位
POSITION OF JIANGSU IN THE COUNTRY

国内生产总值	Gross Domestic Products	占全国	9.1%	Percentage in the country
#第三产业	Tertiary Industry	占全国	9.7%	Percentage in the country
全社会固定资产投资总额	Gross Value of Total Investment by Fixed Assets	占全国	8.9%	Percentage in the country
社会消费品零售总额	Total Retail Sales of Consumer Goods	占全国	7.7%	Percentage in the country
外贸进出口总额	Total Value of Imports and Exports	占全国	8.2%	Percentage in the country
#出口总额	Total Value of Exports	占全国	8.5%	Percentage in the country
粮食产量	Output of Grain	占全国	7.0%	Percentage in the country
棉花产量	Output of Cotton	占全国	10.3%	Percentage in the country
油料产量	Output of Oil-Bearing Crops	占全国	5.0%	Percentage in the country
大学在校学生数	Students Enrollment in Institution of Higher Education	占全国	8.0%	Percentage in the country

江 苏 的 人 口
POPULATION OF JIANGSU

年末人口	Population (year-end)	7182.46	万人	(10000 persons)
从业人员	Employment	3687.85	万人	(10000 persons)
#职工人数	Staff and Workers	870.01	万人	(10000 persons)
出生人数	Births	78.60	万人	(10000 persons)
死亡人数	Deaths	49.01	万人	(10000 persons)
结婚人数	Marriages	52.27	万对	(10000 pairs)
离婚人数	Divorces	7.08	万对	(10000 pairs)
人口密度	Density of Population	700	人/平方公里	(person/sq·km)
人口平均期望寿命(1995年)	Life Expectancy (1995)	72.66	岁	(year)

江 苏 经 济 的 发 展
ECONOMIC DEVELOPMENT OF JIANGSU

		1952－1998 年 平均增长 1952－1998 Average Annual Growth Rate	1978－1998 年 平均增长 1978－1998 Average Annual Growth Rate
国内生产总值	Gross Domestic Products	8.3	12.6
#第三产业	Tertiary Industry	8.8	15.4
工农业总产值	Gross Output Value of Agriculture	13.1	18.8
农业产值	Gross Output Value of Agriculture	4.8	6.9
工业产值	Gross Output Value of Industry	15.1	19.9
货物运输量	Freight Traffic	9.0	8.9
全社会固定资产投资	Total Investment in Fixed Assets	18.0	26.9
社会消费品零售总额	Total Retail Sales of Consumer Goods	11.1	17.8
外贸出口总额	Total Value of Exports by Foreign Trade		19.9
财政收入	Financial Revenue	10.1	11.9

江 苏 的 一 天
ONE DAY IN JIANGSU

国内生产总值	Gross Domestic Products	19.73	亿元	(10^8 yuan)
#第三产业	Tertiary Industry	6.97	亿元	(10^8 yuan)
工农业总产值	Gross Output Value of Industry and Agriculture	41.19	亿元	(10^8 yuan)
#工业总产值	Gross Output Value of Industry	36.13	亿元	(10^8 yuan)
货物运输量	Freight Traffic	220.35	万吨	(10000 ton)
全社会住宅竣工面积	Total Floor Space of Residence Completed	25.89	万平方米	(10000 sq·m)
社会消费品零售总额	Total Retail Sales of Consumer Goods	6.13	亿元	(10^8 yuan)
财政收入	Financial Revenue	15888	万元	(10000 yuan)
出版报纸	Newspapers Published	510	万份	(10000)
邮寄函件	Letters Delivered	141	万件	(10000)

国内生产总值(亿元)

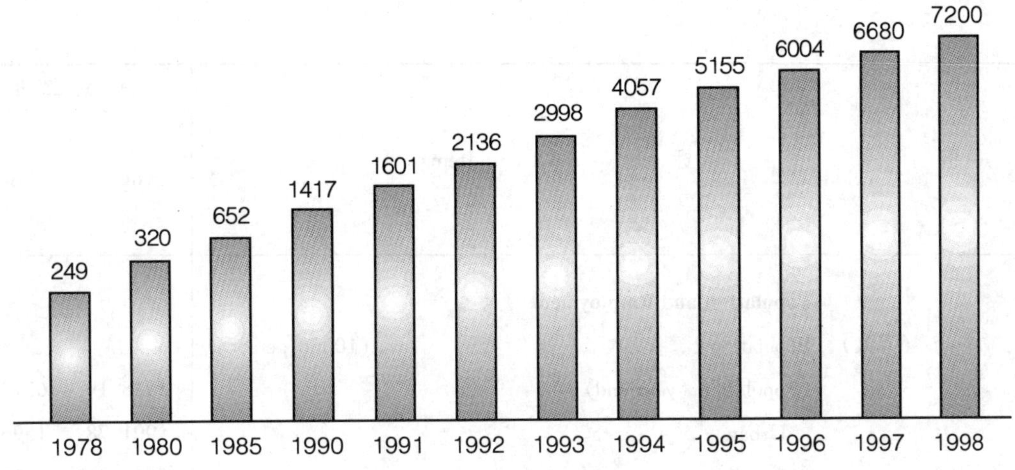

国内生产总值构成(%)

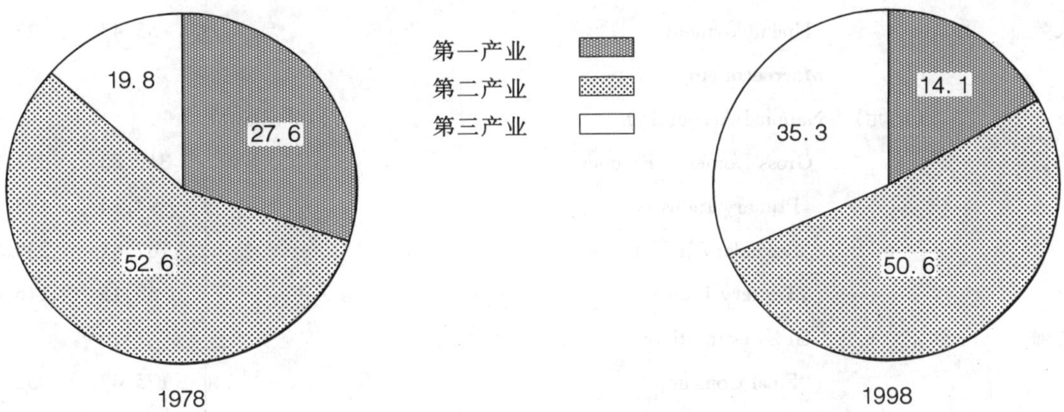

国内生产总值指数(1978=100)

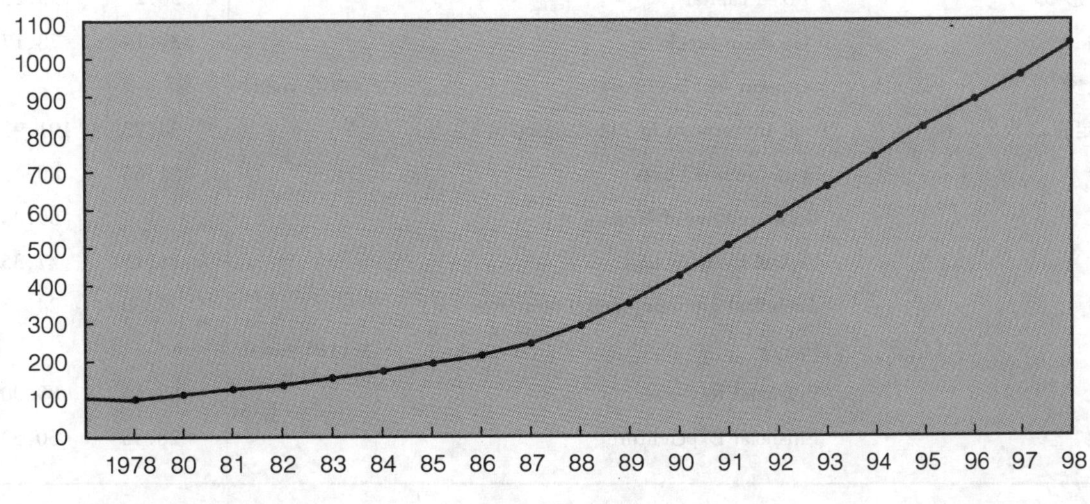

2－1 国民经济和社会发展总量与速度指标

指标		Items		总量指标 1980	1985
人口与就业		**Population and Employment**			
人　　口	（万人）	Population	(10000 persons)		
年末人口		Population (year-end)		5938.19	6213.48
市镇人口		Urban		901.78	1596.15
乡村人口		Rural		5036.41	4617.33
就　　业	（万人）	Employment	(10000 persons)		
从业人数		Employment		2821.03	3262.97
#职工人数		Staff and Workers		644.15	782.44
#国有经济		State Owned Units		401.98	468.80
城镇失业人数		Unemployment		55.47	23.63
宏观经济		**Macroeconomy**			
国民核算	（亿元）	National Accounting	(10^8 yuan)		
国内生产总值		Gross Domestic Products		319.80	651.82
第一产业		Primary Industry		94.24	195.66
第二产业		Secondary Industry		167.41	339.56
第三产业		Tertiary Industry		58.15	116.60
国内支出总额		Gross Domestic Expenditures			
#最终消费		Final Consumption		175.47	353.72
居民消费		Resident Consumption		154.72	300.86
政府消费		Govemment Consumption		20.75	52.86
资本形成总额		Total Capital		97.44	271.42
固定资本形成		Fixed capital		58.25	193.25
存货增加		Goods in Stock		39.19	78.17
固定资产投资	（亿元）	Investment in Fixed Assets	(10^8 yuan)		
全社会固定资产投资总额		Total Investment in Fixed Assets		34.73	191.93
#国有单位		State Owned Units		31.65	80.43
集体单位		Colletive Owned Units			59.06
#基本建设		Capital Construction		26.15	47.35
更新改造		Technical Updating and Transformation		5.50	24.73
财　　政	（亿元）	Finance	(10^8 yuan)		
财政收入		Financial Revenue		62.45	89.00
财政支出		Financial Expenditure		28.95	50.53

INDICES OF TOTAL NUMBER AND SPEED OF NATIONAL ECONOMY AND SOCIAL DEVELOPMENT

Number				速 度 指 标 Speed					
				指 数 （1998年为下列各年%） 1998 As The Percentage Of Following Years				平均增长% Average Annual Growth Rate	
1990	1995	1997	1998	1985	1990	1995	1997	1981－1990	1981－1998
6766.90	7066.02	7147.86	7182.46	115.6	106.1	101.6	100.5	1.3	1.1
1458.94	1929.09	2133.64	2262.47	141.7	155.1	117.3	106.0	4.9	5.2
5307.96	5136.93	5014.22	4919.99	106.6	92.7	95.8	98.1	0.5	－0.1
3569.13	3649.69	3658.05	3687.85	113.0	103.3	101.0	100.8	2.4	1.5
879.85	915.98	893.74	870.01	111.2	98.9	95.0	97.3	3.2	1.7
536.88	576.24	577.54	552.47	117.8	102.9	95.9	95.7	2.9	1.8
52.72	42.32	46.38	46.81	198.1	88.8	110.6	101.0	－0.5	－0.9
1416.50	5155.25	6680.34	7199.95	492.5	305.6	139.5	111.0	11.6	13.1
355.17	848.35	1008.41	1016.27	163.1	150.5	115.5	102.1	5.5	5.4
692.59	2715.26	3411.86	3640.10	575.6	356.5	141.6	112.0	12.3	14.5
368.74	1591.64	2260.07	2543.58	821.2	354.1	147.3	112.9	16.6	16.8
717.36	2250.66	3020.94	3161.88	301.9	233.8	133.1	106.4	8.5	9.7
608.29	1806.43	2417.77	2513.52	268.3	214.0	131.1	105.6	7.8	8.8
109.07	444.23	603.17	648.36	516.6	345.7	141.3	109.5	13.1	14.7
588.44	2479.30	2925.28	3321.44	622.3	342.2	138.3	116.3	17.1	16.9
374.12	1756.88	2295.97	2642.29	664.6	389.4	150.7	116.5	18.4	18.5
214.32	722.42	629.31	679.15	534.3	255.0	112.0	115.9	14.9	13.8
356.30	1680.17	2203.09	2535.50	1321.1	711.6	150.9	115.1	26.2	26.9
134.86	602.70	826.60	1031.95	1283.0	765.2	171.2	124.8	15.6	21.4
74.87	491.08	447.94	475.36	804.9	634.9	96.8	106.1		
74.32	362.15	588.05	747.18	1578.0	1005.4	206.3	127.1	11.0	20.5
41.53	218.78	268.77	296.01	1197.0	712.8	135.3	110.1	22.4	24.8
136.20	350.08	512.90	579.90	651.6	425.8	165.6	113.1	8.0	13.1
100.97	253.49	379.50	434.17	859.2	430.0	171.3	114.4	13.3	16.2

续 表 1

指 标	Items		总量指标 1980	1985
物 价 （上年=100）	Price	(preceeding year=100)		
商品零售价格总指数	Overall Retail Price Index		105.8	109.5
城市居民消费价格总指数	Overall Urban Residents Cost of Living Index		105.7	109.6
农副产品收购价格总指数	Overall Farm and Sideline Products Purchasing Price Index		104.3	106.9
利用外资 （亿美元）	Utilization of Foreign Capital	(10^8 USD)		
签订利用外资协议额	Value of Foreign Capital Through Signed Contracts		0.05	1.96
实际利用外资额	Value of Foreign Capital Actually Used			0.93
产 业	**Industry**			
农 业	Agriculture Production			
农林牧渔业劳动力 （万人）	Farming, Forestry, Animal Husbandry and Fishery Labor Force	(10000 persons)	1810	1703.20
农林牧渔业总产值 （亿元）	Gross Output Value of FFAF	(10^8 yuan)	138.45	288.55
主要农产品产量 （万吨）	Output of Major Farm Products	(10000 tons)		
粮 食	Grain		2417.95	3126.52
棉 花	Cotton		41.81	47.91
油 料	Oil-Bearing Crops		38.64	108.78
糖 料	Sugar Crops		5.15	26.34
蚕 茧	Silkworm Cocoons		3.82	7.31
猪牛羊肉	Pork, Beef and Mutton		107.24	138.9
水 产 品	Aquatic Products		42.71	67.54
工 业	Industry			
工业总产值 （亿元）	Gross Output Value of Industry	(10^8 yuan)	467.82	1036.67
轻 工 业	Light Industry		267.97	552.23
重 工 业	Heavy Industry		199.85	484.44
主要工业产品产量 （万吨）	Output of Major Products	(10000 tons)		
钢	Steel		68.17	98.97
成品钢材	Rolled-Steel		104.87	145.18
发 电 量 （亿千瓦小时）	Electricity	(10^8 kwh)	156.32	234.48
原 煤	Coal		1690.00	2193.85
农用化肥(折 100%)	Chemical Furtilizers		111.61	121.71
化学农药	Chemical Pesticide		5.75	4.27
水 泥	Cement		629.19	1116.90
化学纤维	Chemical Fiber		3.26	12.52
机制纸及纸板	Machine-Made Paper and Paperboard		28.76	50.00

Continued 1

Number				速　度　指　标　Speed					
				指　数（1998年为下列各年%） 1998 As The Percentage Of Following Years				平均增长% Average Annual Growth Rate	
1990	1995	1997	1998	1985	1990	1995	1997	1981－1990	1981－1998
102.3	114.3	99.3	98.2	321.3	187.9	104.1	98.2	7.0	7.5
103.4	116.2	101.3	100.0	392.9	227.3	112.3	100.0	7.5	8.9
98.7	114.3	94.8	94.6	309.3	182.5	91.5	94.6	7.3	7.5
3.62	130.23	98.13	76.86	3921.4	2123.2	59.0	78.3	53.5	50.3
4.39	52.87	67.85	69.57	7480.6	1584.7	131.6	102.5		
1714.49	1541.33	1532.52	1531.46	89.9	89.3	99.4	99.9	-0.5	-0.9
580.53	1686.78	1816.37	1849.20	228.8	190.4	120.2	103.9	6.6	7.4
3264.15	3286.30	3563.79	3415.12	109.2	104.6	103.9	95.8	3.0	1.9
46.42	56.16	50.75	46.19	96.4	99.5	82.2	91.0	1.1	0.6
112.39	159.46	141.93	115.63	106.3	102.9	72.5	81.5	11.3	6.3
22.26	23.37	23.34	19.64	74.6	88.2	84.0	84.1	15.8	7.7
12.00	18.62	8.64	8.51	116.4	70.9	45.7	98.5	12.1	4.6
158.38	217.79	186.42	209.31	150.7	132.2	96.1	112.3	4.0	3.9
118.25	219.47	265.72	282.03	417.6	238.5	128.5	106.1	10.7	11.1
2764.10	9807.19	12542.40	13185.70	1249.8	597.7	151.9	113.2	16.4	20.2
1510.57	4785.42	6382.96	6843.38	1230.1	588.7	156.9	115.3	16.4	20.1
1253.53	5021.77	6159.44	6342.40	1231.1	588.2	141.2	110.0	16.4	20.1
190.18	360.40	475.01	523.78	529.2	275.4	145.3	110.3	10.8	12.0
203.01	787.89	856.79	933.63	643.1	459.9	118.5	109.0	6.8	12.9
404.47	700.41	777.00	763.49	325.6	188.8	109.0	98.3	10.0	9.2
2407.79	2650.72	2506.01	2378.53	108.4	98.8	89.7	94.9	3.6	1.9
145.90	191.85	187.98	170.12	139.8	116.6	88.7	90.5	2.7	2.4
4.51	12.18	9.27	8.59	201.2	190.5	70.5	92.7	2.4	2.3
1532.89	3966.42	4031.73	3856.30	345.3	251.6	97.2	95.6	9.3	10.6
40.76	102.20	139.11	140.94	1125.7	345.8	137.9	101.3	28.7	23.3
74.82	167.55	186.31	126.81	253.6	169.5	75.7	68.1	10.0	8.6

续 表 2

指 标 Items			总量指标 1980	1985
建筑业	Construction			
建筑业企业人数 (万人)	Enployment	(10000 persons)	68.18	124.09
建筑业总产值 (亿元)	Gross Output Value	(10^8 yuan)	27.33	82.63
施工房屋面积 (万平方米)	Floor Space of Building Under Construstion	(10000 sq·m)	3189.80	5570.32
竣工房屋面积 (万平方米)	Floor Space of Building Completed	(10000 sq·m)	2296.09	3527.20
交通运输	Transportation			
货运量 (万吨)	Freight Traffic	(10000 tons)	16527	46842
#铁路	Railways		3420	4037
公路	Highways		4427	23255
水运	Waterways		6482	18117
客运量 (万人)	Passenger Traffic	(10000 persons)	34002	53935
#铁路	Railways		3364	4819
公路	Highways		26463	45751
水运	Waterways		4175	3365
港口货物吞吐量 (万吨)	Cargo Handled at Seaports	(10000 tons)	12053	16022
邮电通信业	Postal and Telecommunication Services			
邮电业务总量 (亿元)	Business Revenue of PTS	(10^8 yuan)	1.12	1.97
函件 (亿件)	Letters Delivered	(10^8 pieces)	2.00	2.78
订销报刊累计份数 (亿份)	Newspapers and Magazines Distributed Accumulately		9.63	17.06
电话机 (万部)	Telephone	(10000)		43.27
城市	Urban			28.37
农村	Rural			14.90
国内商业	Domestic Trade			
社会消费品零售总额 (亿元)	Total Retail Sales of Consumer Goods	(10^8 yuan)	122.56	262.57
对外经济贸易和旅游	Foreign Trade and Tourism			
进出口总额 (亿美元)	Total Value of Imports and Exports	(10^8 USD)	9.46	19.87
进口	Imports		0.92	4.01
出口	Exports		8.54	15.86
旅游人数 (人)	Number of Tourists	(10000 persons)	26.28	50.71
金融保险 (亿元)	Banking and Insurance	(10^8 yuan)		
金融机构存款	Deposits of Banking Organization		95.54	247.12
金融机构贷款	Loans of Banking Organization		159.11	387.06
国内保险承保额(中保)	Domestic Insurance Value			962.95

Continued 2

Number				速　度　指　标 Speed					
				指　数（1998年为下列各年%）1998 As The Percentage Of Following Years				平均增长% Average Annual Growth Rate	
1990	1995	1997	1998	1985	1990	1995	1997	1981－1990	1981－1998
124.31	232.94	215.69	232.32	187.2	186.9	99.7	107.7	6.2	7.0
147.23	998.11	1102.12	1224.42	1481.8	831.6	122.7	111.1	18.3	23.5
5240.98	16646.14	16191.85	17803.33	319.6	339.7	107.0	109.9	5.1	10.0
3307.93	8739.38	8787.36	9958.90	282.3	301.1	114.0	113.3	3.7	8.5
49399	81830	82290	80429	171.7	162.8	98.3	97.7	11.6	9.2
4235	4143	4131	3793	94.0	89.6	91.6	91.8	2.2	0.6
27904	49578	52441	54328	233.6	194.7	109.6	103.6	20.2	14.9
15908	27161	24826	21363	117.9	134.3	78.7	86.1	9.4	6.9
48339	84803	93684	97033	179.9	200.7	114.4	103.6	3.6	6.0
4788	5185	4433	4451	92.4	93.0	85.8	100.4	3.6	1.6
41850	78947	88826	92215	201.6	220.3	116.8	103.8	4.7	7.2
1701	623	341	273	8.1	16.0	43.8	80.0	-8.6	-14.1
17002	20177	32795	32885	205.2	193.4	163.0	100.3	3.5	18.0
4.95	72.24	132.52	167.81	8518.3	3390.1	232.3	126.6	16.0	32.1
3.30	5.31	5.26	5.16	185.6	155.9	97.2	98.1	5.1	5.4
10.99	18.16	19.14	19.77	115.9	179.9	108.9	103.3	0.3	4.1
89.94	491.98	900.64	1160.42	2681.8	1290.2	235.9	128.8		
63.30	333.90	516.27	601.22	2119.2	949.8	180.1	116.5		
26.64	158.08	384.37	559.20	3753.0	2099.1	353.7	145.5		
515.43	1650.00	2118.12	2238.01	852.3	434.2	135.6	105.7	15.4	17.5
41.39	162.78	236.21	264.26	1329.9	638.5	162.3	111.9	15.9	20.3
11.95	64.96	95.32	107.75	2687.0	901.7	165.9	113.0	29.2	30.3
29.44	97.82	140.89	156.51	986.8	531.6	160.0	111.1	13.2	17.6
72.48	76.77	101.71	115.40	227.6	159.2	150.3	113.5	10.7	8.6
860.33	3500.49	5623.68	6578.80	2662.1	764.7	187.9	117.0	24.6	26.5
1013.45	2875.39	4454.56	5063.57	1308.2	499.6	176.1	113.7	20.3	21.2
2667.04	5472.66	8432.94	12106.28	1257.2	453.9	221.2	143.6		

续 表 3

指 标	Items	总量指标 1980	总量指标 1985
教育、科技、文化	**Education, Science and Technology and Culture**		
教 育	Education		
高等学校在校学生 (万人)	Students Enrollment in Institutions of Higher Education (10000 persons)	8.41	11.96
中等专业学校在校学生 (万人)	Students Enrollment in Specialized Secondary Schools (10000 persons)	6.11	9.25
普通中学在校学生 (万人)	Students Enrollment in Regular Secondary Schools (10000 persons)	320.49	284.73
小学在校学生 (万人)	Students Enrollment in Primary Schools (10000 persons)	836.90	677.92
科 技	Science and Technology		
县以上科研机构数 (个)	Number of Scientific & Technological Research Institutions of County Level and Above		274
各类专业技术人员 (万人)	Scientific and Technical Personnel (10000 persons)	43.87	83.41
文 化	Culture		
图书出版量 (亿册)	Books Published (10^8)	2.12	2.67
杂志出版量 (万册)	Magazines Issued (10000)	2373	5091
报纸出版量 (亿份)	Newspapers Issued (10^8)	2.68	9.33
家庭、生活、环境	**Family, People's Livelihood and Environment**		
家 庭	Family		
家庭总户数 (万户)	Total Households (10000 households)	1471.76	1633.62
城镇居民平均每户家庭人口 (人)	Average Persons Per Household in Urban Area (persons)	4.20	3.64
农村居民平均每户家庭人口 (人)	Average Persons Per Household in Rural Area (persons)	4.90	4.38
居 住	Housing		
城市居民人均居住面积 (平方米)	Urban Residents Per Capita Living Space (sq·m)	6.40	7.20
农村居民人均生活用房面积 (平方米)	Rural Residents Per Capita Living Space (sq·m)	12.48	16.37

Continued 3

Number				速　度　指　标　Speed					
				指　　数（1998年为下列各年%） 1998 As The Percentage Of Following Years				平均增长% Average Annual Growth Rate	
1990	1995	1997	1998	1985	1990	1995	1997	1981－1990	1981－1998
14.69	20.86	23.90	27.32	228.4	186.0	131.0	114.3	5.7	6.8
13.99	31.87	45.88	48.11	520.1	343.9	151.0	104.9	8.6	12.1
281.97	316.75	320.69	324.24	113.9	115.0	102.4	101.1	－1.3	0.1
612.29	644.77	732.35	751.82	110.9	122.8	116.6	102.7	－3.1	－0.6
326	337	328	321	117.2	98.5	95.3	97.9		
158.86	184.97	193.46	202.15	242.4	127.3	109.3	104.5	13.7	8.9
3.44	4.05	4.63	4.68	175.3	136.5	115.6	101.1	5.0	4.5
4107	7005	7748	9240	181.5	225.0	131.9	119.3	5.6	7.8
8.27	15.95	18.81	18.60	199.4	224.9	116.6	98.9	11.9	11.4
1806.78	2066.09	2133.69	2087.92	127.8	115.6	101.1	97.9	2.1	2.0
3.34	3.19	3.14	3.10	85.2	92.8	97.2	98.7	－2.3	－1.7
4.1	4.0	3.9	3.8	86.8	92.7	95.0	97.4	－1.8	－1.4
9.06	10.59	10.86	11.08	153.9	122.3	104.6	102.0	3.5	3.1
22.33	25.71	30.80	32.00	195.5	143.3	124.5	103.9	6.0	5.4

续 表 4

指 标		Items		总量指标 1980	总量指标 1985
生 活		People's Livelihood			
城镇居民人均可支配收入	(元)	Urban Household Per Capita Allocatable Income	(yuan)	433	766
农村居民人均纯收入	(元)	Rural Household Per Capita Net Income	(yuan)	218	493
城乡居民储蓄存款余额	(亿元)	Deposits Balance in Urban and Rural Areas	(10^8 yuan)	23.72	99.35
工资和福利	(亿元)	Wage and Welfare	(10^8 yuan)		
工资总额		Total Wage		41.63	86.17
职工平均工资	(元)	Average Wage for Staff	(yuan)	667	1135
职工保险福利费		Labor Insurance and Welfare Funds		4.12	11.02
离退休、退职职工保险福利费		Labor Insurance and Welfare for Retiree		2.94	9.16
卫 生		Health Care			
卫生机构数	(个)	Number of Health Care Organizations	(unit)	9943	11515
#医 院		Hospital		2457	2460
床位数	(万张)	Number of Hospital Beds	(10000)	12.75	14.29
#医 院		Hospital		11.62	12.65
卫生技术人员数	(万人)	Number of Medical Technical Personnels	(10000 persons)	15.04	18.28
#医 生		Doctors		6.10	7.65
市政建设		Urban Civil Construction			
自来水供应量	(亿吨)	Volume of Tap Water Supply	(10^8 tons)	4.52	7.66
排水管道长度	(公里)	Length of Sewer Pipelines	(km)	1650	2277
年末实有道路长度	(公里)	Year-end Length of Paved Road	(km)	1881	2437
环 境		Environment			
治理污染资金使用额	(亿元)	Funds Used for Pollution Treatment	(10^8 yuan)	0.91	1.65
安排治理项目	(个)	Treatment Projects Arranged	(unit)	1412	1615
工业废水处理量	(亿吨)	Volume of Industrial Waste Water Treatment	(10^8 tons)	1.53	5.00
工业粉尘回收量	(万吨)	Volume of Industrial Dust Retrieved	(10000 tons)		71

Continued 4

Number				速度指标 Speed					
				指数（1998年为下列各年%） 1998 As The Percentage Of Following Years				平均增长% Average Annual Growth Rate	
1990	1995	1997	1998	1985	1990	1995	1997	1981－1990	1981－1998
1464	4634	5765	6018	785.6	411.1	129.9	104.4	13.0	15.7
884	2457	3270	3377	685.0	382.0	137.4	103.3	15.0	16.4
470.86	1922.33	3101.89	3656.46	3680.4	776.5	190.2	117.9	34.8	32.3
184.60	541.62	635.44	654.56	749.2	349.7	119.2	101.6	16.1	16.5
2129	5943	7108	7516	662.2	353.0	126.5	105.7	12.3	14.4
31.56	63.87	80.04	78.53	712.6	248.8	123.0	98.1	22.6	17.8
29.37	103.75	145.75	156.40	1707.4	532.5	150.7	107.3	25.9	24.7
12366	12039	13386	14572	126.5	117.8	121.0	108.9	2.2	2.1
2491	2534	2620	2610	106.1	104.8	103.0	99.6	0.1	0.3
16.45	17.46	17.03	17.01	119.0	103.4	97.4	99.9	2.6	1.6
14.54	15.48	15.90	15.91	125.8	109.4	102.8	100.1	2.3	1.8
21.35	24.55	25.48	25.67	140.4	120.2	104.6	100.7	3.6	3.0
9.94	11.22	11.58	11.61	151.8	116.8	103.5	100.3	5.0	3.6
25.67	38.23	34.31	35.90	468.7	139.9	93.9	104.6	19.0	12.2
4099	8262	8812	9574	420.5	233.6	115.9	108.6	9.5	10.3
5812	8163	9440	9618	394.7	165.5	117.8	101.9	11.9	9.5
2.48	5.42	8.06	23.33	1413.9	940.7	430.4	289.5	10.5	19.7
1382	919	738	2524	156.3	182.6	274.6	342.0	－0.2	3.3
5.92	11.28	16.55	16.92	338.4	285.8	150.0	102.2	14.5	14.3
81	112	163	145	204.2	179.0	129.5	89.0		

2-2 国民经济和社会发展结构指标
STRUCTURAL INDICATORS OF NATIONAL ECONOMY AND SOCIAL DEVELOPMENT

单位:% (percent)

指标	Items	1990	1995	1997	1998
人口与就业	**Population and Employment**				
人　口	Population				
城乡结构	Urban and Rural Composition				
城　镇	Urban	21.5	27.3	29.9	31.5
乡　村	Rural	78.5	72.7	70.1	68.5
性别结构	Sex				
男	Male	50.9	50.8	50.8	50.7
女	Female	49.1	49.2	49.2	49.3
就　业	Employment				
产业结构	Industrial Structures				
第一产业	Primary Industry	48.9	42.9	42.5	42.1
第二产业	Secondary Industry	33.8	34.8	33.3	32.2
第三产业	Tertiary Industry	17.3	22.3	24.2	25.7
经济类型结构	Structures by Ownership				
国有单位	State-owned	15.0	15.8	15.8	15.0
城镇集体单位	Collective-owned	9.1	7.5	6.6	6.0
其他经济类型单位	Others	0.5	1.8	2.1	2.7
城镇私营企业和个体劳动者	Urban Private Enterprises and Individual Laborers	0.7	1.8	2.5	3.5
乡村劳动者	Village Laborers	74.7	72.8	72.8	72.4
宏观经济	**Macro Economy**				
国民核算	National Accounting				
国内生产总值产业结构	GDP Structures				
第一产业	Primary Industry	25.1	16.4	15.1	14.1
第二产业	Secondary Industry	48.9	52.7	51.1	50.6
第三产业	Tertiary Industry	26.0	30.9	33.8	35.3
国内支出结构	Domestic Expenditures				
总消费	Total Consumption	50.6	43.7	45.2	43.9
居民消费	Final Consumption	42.9	35.1	36.2	34.9
农村居民	Agricultural Resident	28.5	20.0	20.8	19.0
城镇居民	Urban Resident	14.5	15.1	15.4	15.9
政府消费	Government Consumption	7.7	8.6	9.0	9.0
资本形成总额	Total Capital	41.5	48.1	43.8	46.1
固定资本形成	Fixed Assets	26.4	34.1	34.4	36.7
存货增加	Goods in Stock	15.1	14.0	9.4	9.4
净出口	Net Export	7.8	8.2	11.0	10.0

续表1 Continued 1

单位：%　　(percent)

指　标	Items	1990	1995	1997	1998
投　资	Investment				
经济类型结构	Structures by Ownership				
国有单位	State-owned	37.9	35.9	37.5	40.7
集体单位	Collective-owned	21.0	29.2	20.4	18.7
其他经济单位	Others		22.2	26.4	28.0
个　体	Individual	41.1	12.7	15.7	12.6
#农　村	Rural	40.1	11.9	15.0	11.8
资金来源结构	Structures of Finance Sources				
国家预算资金	State Appropriation	4.2	1.5	1.4	2.0
国内贷款	Domestic Loans	12.8	16.1	13.3	13.1
利用外资	Foreign Investment	4.5	13.6	17.7	16.3
自筹资金	Fundraising	29.9	52.4	54.4	55.4
其他投资	Others	48.7	16.4	13.2	13.2
财　政	Public Finance				
财政支出结构	Structure of Financial Expendicture				
#农业支出	Agriculture	9.1	5.9	7.9	7.2
基本建设	Capital Construction	5.6	7.4	6.8	7.1
教　育	Education	18.1	20.9	19.9	20.7
利用外资	Utilization of Foreign Capital				
实际利用外资结构	Structures of Value of Foreign Capital Actually Used				
对外借款	Loans from Abroad	63.1	7.9	6.5	2.7
外商直接投资	Direct Investment by Foreigners	32.2	90.4	85.4	95.6
外商其他投资	Other Investment by Foreigners	4.7	1.7	8.1	1.7
产业经济	**Industrial Economy**				
农　业	Agriculture				
农林牧渔业产值结构	Structures of Gross Output Value of FFAF				
农　业	Farming	62.4	58.4	59.8	59.3
林　业	Forestry	1.4	1.3	1.2	1.3
牧　业	Animal Husbandry	27.7	28.2	23.7	23.6
渔　业	Fishery	8.5	12.1	15.3	15.8
工　业	Industry				
按经济类型分	Grouped by Ownership				
#国有工业	State-owned	34.3	21.4	17.7	14.9
集体工业	Colletive-owned	39.6	36.3	29.8	23.2
按轻重分	Grouped by Light and Heavy Industry				
轻工业	Light Industry	54.6	47.7	50.9	51.9
重工业	Heavy Industry	45.4	52.3	49.1	48.1

续表2 Continued 2

单位：% (percent)

指 标	Items	1990	1995	1997	1998
建筑业	Construction				
建筑企业总产值结构	Structures of Gross Output Value of Construction Enterprises				
国有经济	State-owned	21.7	25.8	32.0	27.4
地方	Local-owned	14.6	20.8	26.7	22.3
部属	Central-owned	7.1	5.0	5.3	5.1
城镇集体经济	Colletive-owned	20.2	26.0	28.0	31.6
乡镇企业及其它经济	Rural and Township Industry and Others	58.1	48.2	40.0	41.0
运输业	Transportation				
货运量结构	Structures of Freight Traffic Volume				
按运输方式分	By Type				
铁路	Railways	8.6	5.1	5.0	4.7
公路	Highways	56.5	60.6	63.7	67.5
水运	Waterways	32.2	33.2	30.2	26.6
国内商业	Domestic Trade				
社会消费品零售总额结构	Total Retail Sales of Consumer Goods				
国有经济	State-owned	34.5	30.1	23.6	21.3
集体经济	Collective-owned	40.2	32.2	29.9	27.5
个体和私营经济	Indivial	15.8	20.4	26.6	31.0
其他经济单位	Others	9.5	17.3	19.9	20.2
对外经济贸易和国际旅游	Foreign Trade and International Tourism				
出口商品结构	Structures of Export Commodities				
#亚洲地区	Asia		62.4	56.3	49.8
欧洲地区	Europe		16.3	18.6	22.5
北美洲	North America		16.3	19.0	21.3
来华旅游人数结构	Structures of Tourists				
外国人	Foreigners	30.2	63.4	63.2	60.3
华侨	Overseas Chinese	2.3	2.1	1.8	2.6
港澳台同胞	Hongkong, Macao and Taiwan Chinese	67.5	34.5	35.0	37.1
教育、科技、文化	**Education, Science and Culture**				
教育	Education				
在校学生结构	Structures of Student Enrollment				
大学生	College and University Students	1.6	2.0	2.1	2.3
中学生	Secondary School Students	33.2	36.0	34.1	33.7
小学生	Primary School Students	65.2	62.0	63.8	64.0
专任教师结构	Full-time Teachers by Type				
大学	College and University	5.6	5.2	5.1	5.2
中学	Secondary School	39.8	42.4	42.8	43.2
小学	Primary School	54.6	52.4	52.1	51.6
科技	Science and Technology				
各类专业技术人员结构	Structures of Scientific & Technical Personnel				

续 表 3　Continued 3

单位：%　　(percent)

指　　标　Items		1990	1995	1997	1998
工程技术人员	Engineering	20.0	15.3	23.0	23.5
农业技术人员	Agriculture	1.5	1.4	2.0	2.2
科学研究人员	Scientific Research	1.2	0.3	1.0	0.9
卫生技术人员	Health Care	8.7	8.4	11.4	11.2
教学人员	Teaching	28.0	27.4	32.3	31.6
家庭、生活、环境	**Family, People's Livelihood and Environment**				
家　庭	Family				
家庭户结构	Structures of Members of Household				
一人户	Single	7.4	6.5	6.9	6.1
二人户	Two People	12.4	17.2	18.7	17.8
三人及以上户	Three People and Above	80.2	76.3	74.4	76.1
生　活	People's Livelihood				
城镇居民消费结构	Structures of Urban Household Consumption				
食品类	Food	55.5	51.9	47.7	45.1
衣着类	Clothing	13.2	12.8	11.4	9.2
用品及其他	Daily Use Article and Others	24.9	28.0	32.4	35.9
居　住	Residence	6.4	7.3	8.5	9.8
农村居民消费结构	Structures of Rural Household Consumption				
食品类	Food	52.3	54.8	48.9	47.8
衣着类	Clothing	7.4	6.5	6.5	5.8
用品及其他	Daily Use Article and Others	15.8	20.9	27.4	29.3
居　住	Residence	24.5	17.8	17.2	17.1
福　利	Social Welfare				
职工保险福利费结构	Structures of Staff Insurance and Welfare				
国有单位	State-owned	72.3	70.1	73.5	72.6
城镇集体单位	Urban Colletive-owned	25.0	22.1	17.5	14.8
其他单位	Others	2.7	7.8	9.0	12.6
离退休人员结构	Structures of Retired Staff and workers				
国有单位	State-owned	64.9	70.8	72.4	71.8
城镇集体单位	Urban Colletive-owned	33.3	25.4	23.3	21.3
其他单位	Others	1.8	3.8	4.3	6.9
卫　生	Health Care				
医生结构	Doctors by Type				
中　医	Doctors of Traditional Chinese Medicine	15.1	13.5	12.8	12.7
西医师	Doctors of Western Medicine	63.3	65.2	66.7	67.9
西医士	Junior Doctors of Western Medicine	21.6	21.3	20.5	19.5
医院床位结构	Hospital Beds by Structures				
县以上医院	Hospitals at County Level and Above	57.2	59.1	58.6	57.8
环境、灾害	Environment, Disaster				
治理污染资金使用结构	Uses of Funds in Pollution Treatment				
治理废水	Waste Water Treatment	57.7	61.6	76.3	77.2
治理废气	Waste Gas Treatment	25.7	24.8	17.6	13.4
治理固体废物	Waste Residue Treatment	9.6	8.4	2.2	5.9
治理噪声	Noise Abatement	2.1	3.6	1.2	0.3
其　他	Others	4.9	1.6	2.7	3.2

2-3 江苏的一天
ONE DAY IN JIANGSU

指标	Items	1990	1995	1997	1998
全省每天创造的财富	**Daily Production**				
国内生产总值 （亿元）	Gross Domestic Products (10^8 yuan)	3.88	14.12	18.30	19.73
工农业总产值 （亿元）	Gross Output Value of Industry and Agriculture (10^8 yuan)	9.16	31.49	39.34	41.19
农业总产值	Gross Output Value of Agriculture	1.59	4.62	4.98	5.07
工业总产值	Gross Output Value of Industry	7.57	26.87	34.36	36.13
财政收入 （万元）	Financial Revenue (10000 yuan)	3732	9591	14052	15888
钢 （万吨）	Steel (10000 tons)	0.52	0.99	1.30	1.44
成品钢材 （万吨）	Rolled Steel (10000 tons)	0.56	2.16	2.35	2.56
发电量 （亿千瓦小时）	Electricity (10^8 kwh)	1.11	1.92	2.13	2.09
原煤 （万吨）	Coal (10000 tons)	6.60	7.26	6.87	6.52
水泥 （万吨）	Cement (10000 tons)	4.20	10.87	11.05	10.57
布 （万米）	Cloth (10000 m)	792	1340	1108	869
机制纸及纸板 （吨）	Machine-Made Paper and Paperboards (tonss)	2050	4590	5104	3474
全省每天消费量	**Daily Consumption**				
城乡居民消费额 （亿元）	Consumption of Urban and Rural Residents (10^8 yuan)	1.67	4.95	6.62	6.89
平均每人消费额 （元）	Per Capita Consumption (yuan)	2.48	7.03	9.29	9.62
城镇居民每人生活费支出 （元）	Per Capita Living Expenditure of Urban Residents (yuan)	3.67	10.34	12.42	13.40
#食品消费	Food Consumption	2.04	5.36	5.92	6.04
农民每人生活消费支出 （元）	Per Capita Living Expenditure of Rural Residents (yuan)	2.16	5.31	6.82	6.40
#食品消费	Food Consumption	1.13	2.91	3.33	3.06
社会消费品零售总额 （亿元）	Total Retail Sales of Consumption Goods (10^8 yuan)	1.41	4.52	5.80	6.13
每天其他经济活动	**Other Daily Economic Activities**				
货物运输量 （万吨）	Freight Traffic (10000 tons)	135.34	224.19	225.45	220.35
旅客运输量 （万人）	Passenger Traffic (10000 persons)	132.44	232.34	256.67	265.84
房屋建筑竣工面积 （万平方米）	Floor Space Completed of Buildings (10000 sq·m)	32.14	34.12	38.49	36.37
#住宅竣工面积	Floor Space Completed of Residential Housing	27.97	24.76	28.61	25.89
出版报纸 （万份）	Newspaper Published (10000 copies)	227	437	515	510
邮寄函件 （万件）	Letters Delivered (10000 pieces)	90	145	144	141
每天人口变动和婚姻	**Daily Population Changes and Marriages**				
出生人数 （人）	Births (persons)	3780	2377	2232	2153
死亡人数 （人）	Deaths (persons)	1202	1266	1336	1343
结婚对数 （对）	Marriages (couples)	1432	1576	1447	1432
离婚对数 （对）	Divorces (couples)	78	120	143	194

注：国内生产总值、工业、农业总产值均按当年价格计算(下同)。

Note: Gross domestic produst, gross output value of industry and agriculture were counted by current price (so did the following).

2－4 江苏国民经济占全国的比重（1998）
PERCENTAGE OF JIANGSU'S NATIONAL ECONOMY IN THE COUNTRY

指标	Items	全国 Country	江苏 Jiangsu	江苏占全国的比重（%） Percentage in the Country of Jiangsu
年末总人口（万人）	Year-end Total Population (10000 persons)	124810	7182.46	5.8
国内生产总值（亿元）	Domestic Gross Products (10^8 yuan)	79553	7199.95	9.1
第一产业	Primary Industry	14299	1016.27	7.1
第二产业	Secondary Industry	39150	3640.10	9.3
第三产业	Tertiary Industry	26104	2543.58	9.7
全社会固定资产投资（亿元）	Total Investment in Fixed Assets (10^8 yuan)	28457.50	2535.50	8.9
#基本建设	Capital Construction	11904.3	747.18	6.3
更新改造	Technical Updating and Transformation	4467.2	296.01	6.6
财政收入（亿元）	Finacial Revenue (10^8 yuan)	9853	579.90	5.9
财政支出（亿元）	Finacial Expenditure (10^8 yuan)	10771	434.17	3.9
社会消费品零售总额（亿元）	Total Retail Sales of Consumer Goods (10^8 yuan)	29152.5	2238.01	7.7
对外贸易进出口总额（亿美元）	Total Value of Imports and Exports (10^8 USD)	3239.3	264.26	8.2
#出口总额	Exports	1837.6	156.51	8.5
实际利用外资（亿美元）	Value of Foreign Capital Actually Used (10^8 USD)	585.6	69.57	11.9
普通高等学校在校学生数（万人）	Students Enrollment in Institutions of High Education (10000 persons)	340.9	27.32	8.0
医院病床数（万张）	Hospital Beds (10000)	291.4	15.91	5.5
卫生技术人员（万人）	Medical Technical Personnel (10000 persons)	442.4	25.67	5.8
#医生	Doctors	200.0	11.61	5.8
在岗职工平均工资（元）	Average Wage of Staff and Workers Employed (yuan)	7479	8252	
农民人均纯收入（元）	Per Capita Net Income of Rural Residents (yuan)	2162	3377	
城镇居民年平均可支配收入（元）	Annual Per Capita Allocatable Income of Urban Residents (yuan)	5425	6018	
城乡居民储蓄存款余额（亿元）	Savings Deposit Balance of Urban and Rural Residents (10^8 yuan)	53408	3656	6.8
工农业主要产品产量（万吨）	Output of Major Industrial Products and Agricultural Products (10000 tons)			
粮食	Grain	49000	3415.12	7.0
棉花	Cotton	450.1	46.19	10.3
油料	Oil-Bearing Crops	2313.9	115.63	5.0
钢	Steel	11559	523.78	4.5
成品钢材	Rolled-steel	10518	933.63	8.9
原煤	Coal	125000	2378.53	1.9
发电量（亿千瓦小时）	Electricity (10^8 kwh)	11670	763.49	6.5
水泥	Cement	53600	3856.30	7.2
农用化肥（折100%）	Chemical Fertilizers (convert into 100 %)	3010.0	170.12	5.7
化学纤维	Chemical Fibers	510	140.94	27.6
布（亿米）	Cloth (10^8 m)	241.0	31.72	13.2
机制纸及纸板	Machine-Made Paper and Paperboard	2126	126.81	6.0
家用电冰箱（万台）	Household Refrigerators (10000)	1060	68.71	6.5
彩色电视机（万台）	Television Sets (10000)	3497	394.14	11.3

2-5 全省人均国民经济主要指标
MAJOR PER CAPITA INDICATORS OF JIANGSU NATIONAL ECONOMY

指　　标	Items	1990	1995	1997	1998
国内生产总值（元）	Gross Domestic Products (yuan)	2103	7299	9344	10021
工农业总产值（元）	Gross Output Value of Industry and Agriculture (yuan)	4980	16319	20141	20983
农业产值	Output Value of Agriculture	864	2395	2548	2581
工业产值	Output Value of Industry	4115	13924	17593	18403
财政收入（元）	Financial Revenue (yuan)	203	497	719	809
财政支出（元）	Financial Expenditures (yuan)	150	360	532	606
全社会固定资产投资额（元）	Total Value of Investment in Fixed Assets (yuan)	530	2385	3090	3539
#基本建设	Capital Construction	111	514	825	1043
更新改造	Technical Updating and Tranformation	62	311	377	413
城镇集体	Rural Collective	31	127	104	106
农民人均纯收入（元）	Per Capita Net Income of Rural Residents (yuan)	884	2457	3270	3377
城镇居民年均可支配收入（元）	Annual Per Capita Allocatable Income of Urban Residents (yuan)	1464	4634	5765	6018
年末城乡居民储蓄存款（元）	Year-end Savings Deposit of Urban and Rural Residents (yuan)	696	2721	4340	5091
社会消费品零售额（元）	Total Retail Sales of Consumer Goods (yuan)	767	2343	2971	3123
外贸自营出口总额（美元）	Total Value of Exports of Foreign Trade by Self-management (USD)	44	139	198	218
高等学校在校学生数（人/万人）	Student Enrollment in Institution of Higher Education (person/10000 persons)	22	30	33	38
年末医院病床数（张/万人）	Year-end Hospital Beds (bed/10000 persons)	21	22	22	22
年末卫生技术人员数（人/万人）	Year-end Medical Technical Personnel (person/10000 persons)	32	35	36	36
#医　　生	Doctors	15	16	16	16
主要工农业产品产量（千克）	Output of Major Industrial and Agricultural Products (kg)				
粮　　食	Grain	486	467	500	477
棉　　花	Cotton	7	8	7	6
油　　料	Oil-Bearing Crops	17	23	20	16
钢	Steel	28	51	67	73
原　　煤	Coal	358	376	352	332
发 电 量（千瓦小时）	Electricity (kwh)	602	994	1090	1066

2-6 历　年　总　产　出
TOTAL OUTPUT OVER THE YEARS

本表按当年价格计算　　　　(At current prices)

年　份 Year	总产出（亿元） Total Output (10^8 yuan)	第一产业 Primary Industry	第二产业 Secondary Industry	#工　业 Industry	第三产业 Tertiary Industry	#商　业 Commerce
1952	81.54	31.87	27.19	25.53	22.48	11.12
1955	100.53	36.22	35.77	32.82	28.54	12.94
1957	114.15	36.81	44.63	41.01	32.71	15.08
1962	133.12	40.15	56.38	53.36	36.59	12.90
1965	192.52	57.27	97.49	88.08	37.76	14.60
1970	273.85	71.33	149.65	135.47	52.87	18.23
1975	412.28	91.66	260.23	235.28	60.39	21.03
1976	438.59	100.71	271.19	247.59	66.69	21.21
1977	487.98	89.16	326.37	297.12	72.45	22.33
1978	566.85	105.87	378.99	337.65	81.99	22.39
1979	661.26	145.25	427.36	386.05	88.65	29.12
1980	750.12	138.45	515.71	467.82	95.96	32.37
1981	816.27	153.62	557.41	504.94	105.24	34.47
1982	897.85	188.11	593.52	534.87	116.22	35.47
1983	1014.55	206.86	679.67	600.70	128.02	43.11
1984	1239.44	253.82	836.02	745.36	149.60	52.99
1985	1642.70	288.55	1157.52	1036.67	196.63	62.44
1986	1960.44	332.66	1380.16	1235.38	247.62	75.83
1987	2472.22	380.25	1771.85	1590.31	320.12	113.59
1988	3409.56	497.95	2370.81	2152.93	540.80	220.49
1989	3839.67	522.25	2713.50	2507.42	603.92	218.49
1990	4208.23	580.53	2978.51	2764.10	649.19	219.68
1991	4820.22	580.93	3416.59	3161.60	822.70	300.50
1992	6862.87	673.82	5089.59	4673.57	1099.46	415.46
1993	10245.27	875.37	7757.28	7096.46	1612.62	634.18
1994	14163.89	1335.23	10601.01	9826.50	2227.65	816.07
1995	17699.96	1686.78	13053.11	11995.30	2960.07	1104.21
1996	20304.53	1907.54	14764.02	13425.15	3632.97	1331.32
1997	22314.78	2045.68	16342.27	14703.65	3926.83	1462.21
1998	23433.26	2071.28	16967.90	15163.56	4394.08	1549.66

2-7 历年总产出指数
INDICES OF TOTAL OUTPUT OVER THE YEARS

按可比价格计算，1952＝100　　(At comparable price 1952＝100)

年份 Year	总产出 Total Output	第一产业 Primary Industry	第二产业 Secondary Industry	#工业 Industry	第三产业 Tertiary Industry	#商业 Commerce
1952	100.0	100.0	100.0	100.0	100.0	100.0
1955	120.1	113.0	134.3	129.7	123.6	113.3
1957	127.0	109.1	169.4	165.9	132.1	123.1
1962	121.8	93.4	200.8	208.5	121.4	86.5
1965	181.6	139.7	372.6	365.0	129.2	101.0
1970	263.7	166.3	653.9	651.2	179.4	129.6
1975	390.0	204.4	1164.8	1165.2	207.2	145.9
1976	420.8	212.3	1267.0	1285.1	232.1	149.2
1977	463.9	191.0	1524.5	1543.0	249.8	157.0
1978	544.0	232.1	1776.6	1755.8	285.4	157.6
1979	598.9	257.4	1983.5	2000.3	291.2	193.4
1980	671.6	243.2	2380.5	2417.9	304.9	213.6
1981	732.4	262.4	2589.9	2618.8	342.2	229.5
1982	802.5	301.5	2796.8	2820.2	376.6	234.2
1983	908.5	319.4	3242.2	3211.5	415.6	284.8
1984	1090.8	371.9	3955.8	3959.1	477.5	342.1
1985	1379.6	383.5	5250.3	5280.7	599.0	384.3
1986	1595.5	407.5	6115.4	6161.6	731.7	446.8
1987	1912.0	420.2	7474.4	7631.1	906.9	650.5
1988	2399.8	448.1	9385.3	9590.3	1288.2	1153.4
1989	2492.6	449.6	9671.7	10036.5	1422.0	1039.8
1990	2697.8	460.9	10591.2	11042.5	1502.8	1033.3
1991	3052.3	455.7	12113.2	12642.6	1807.1	1356.6
1992	4303.5	515.0	18047.4	18865.3	2272.1	1786.3
1993	5829.5	573.2	25275.4	26796.3	2888.1	2362.6
1994	7479.3	642.4	33358.5	35832.0	3354.2	2502.0
1995	8885.4	730.4	39896.8	42819.2	3904.3	2962.4
1996	10211.3	803.0	46066.3	49214.0	4471.7	3325.8
1997	11538.8	856.0	52377.4	55710.2	5035.1	3648.4
1998	12692.7	885.1	57667.5	61114.1	5674.6	3918.4

2-8 历年国内生产总值
GROSS DOMESTIC PRODUCTS OVER THE YEARS

本表按当年价格计算 (At current prices)

年份 Year	国内生产总值(亿元) Gross Domestic Products (10^8 yuan)	第一产业 Primary Industry	第二产业 Secondary Industry	#工业 Industry	第三产业 Tertiary Industry	#商业 Commerce	人均国内生产总值(元) Per Capita GDP (yuan)
1952	48.41	25.49	8.53	7.63	14.39	7.14	131
1955	58.96	29.69	11.29	10.06	17.98	8.61	150
1957	65.11	29.94	14.40	12.51	20.77	9.72	157
1962	69.20	29.10	17.34	15.69	22.76	9.65	161
1965	95.10	41.20	30.26	26.87	23.64	9.29	208
1970	129.23	51.03	46.16	42.33	32.04	12.88	249
1975	184.16	67.59	79.61	72.70	36.96	14.15	329
1976	187.97	62.38	85.04	78.48	40.55	15.48	332
1977	202.40	53.22	105.35	97.15	43.83	16.00	353
1978	249.24	68.71	131.09	117.10	49.44	13.63	430
1979	298.55	104.04	141.14	126.25	53.37	17.64	509
1980	319.80	94.24	167.41	151.22	58.15	18.04	541
1981	350.02	109.39	178.01	161.11	62.62	19.24	586
1982	390.17	135.15	185.52	168.09	69.50	20.84	645
1983	437.65	150.41	210.81	191.52	76.43	23.86	716
1984	518.85	179.00	250.39	228.58	89.46	29.66	843
1985	651.82	195.66	339.56	307.89	116.60	32.98	1053
1986	744.94	224.26	376.32	337.77	144.36	40.09	1193
1987	922.33	246.86	493.69	443.23	181.78	61.60	1462
1988	1208.85	319.18	586.82	526.92	302.85	103.63	1891
1989	1321.85	324.18	657.06	599.91	340.61	102.69	2038
1990	1416.50	355.17	692.59	634.13	368.74	103.25	2103
1991	1601.38	345.14	793.92	725.83	462.32	140.27	2347
1992	2136.02	393.82	1119.26	1017.94	622.94	201.91	3097
1993	2998.16	490.59	1598.05	1451.97	909.52	308.21	4308
1994	4057.39	671.94	2186.77	2002.22	1198.68	389.41	5785
1995	5155.25	848.35	2715.26	2467.63	1591.64	516.89	7299
1996	6004.21	965.29	3074.12	2754.80	1964.80	621.01	8447
1997	6680.34	1008.41	3411.86	3016.44	2260.07	683.86	9344
1998	7199.95	1016.27	3640.10	3157.69	2543.58	724.85	10021

2-9 历年国内生产总值指数
INDICES OF GROSS DOMESTIC PRODUCTS OVER THE YEARS

按可比价格计算，1952＝100 （At comparable price 1952＝100）

年份 Year	国内生产总值 Gross Domestic Products	第一产业 Primary Industry	第二产业 Secondary Industry	#工业 Industry	第三产业 Tertiary Industry	#商业 Commerce	人均国内生产总值 Per Capita GDP
1952	100.0	100.0	100.0	100.0	100.0	100.0	100.0
1955	118.9	115.9	133.5	132.0	121.6	117.4	111.3
1957	121.9	111.0	174.3	166.0	131.0	123.6	108.8
1962	103.8	84.6	202.6	212.1	118.0	100.9	89.2
1965	147.6	125.6	375.0	371.4	126.4	100.1	119.1
1970	200.9	148.7	663.6	671.7	176.0	142.6	143.1
1975	277.5	188.4	1179.3	1216.2	198.1	152.9	182.8
1976	280.3	164.4	1320.2	1382.9	220.4	169.8	182.3
1977	297.9	142.6	1636.2	1711.7	236.0	173.8	191.7
1978	371.4	188.3	2038.8	2110.7	268.8	149.5	236.3
1979	415.9	231.3	2183.9	2279.2	284.1	189.5	261.8
1980	436.0	207.0	2580.8	2729.0	288.6	180.6	272.1
1981	483.3	233.6	2767.9	2928.1	340.3	210.8	298.5
1982	530.9	270.9	2928.6	3107.3	375.8	227.2	324.0
1983	596.1	290.3	3376.3	3596.3	426.7	268.7	359.8
1984	689.8	327.9	3890.4	4121.0	489.1	302.2	413.7
1985	809.2	325.1	5097.1	5418.5	577.6	329.5	482.4
1986	893.1	342.5	5587.5	5894.1	689.3	386.1	527.9
1987	1013.2	344.1	6598.9	6914.9	804.3	549.8	592.7
1988	1211.6	359.1	7772.8	8173.8	1126.7	777.6	699.5
1989	1241.7	348.9	7807.8	8344.1	1252.4	761.7	706.4
1990	1303.9	352.5	8228.5	8838.6	1339.1	756.9	714.2
1991	1412.2	338.6	8964.1	9617.3	1592.9	958.6	763.4
1992	1773.5	374.7	11823.6	12584.2	2010.0	1325.6	948.4
1993	2124.5	384.2	14583.3	15501.2	2515.3	1762.7	1126.4
1994	2475.5	404.3	17841.2	19044.8	2801.8	1860.5	1302.4
1995	2856.7	459.3	20713.6	21977.7	3219.3	2143.3	1492.6
1996	3205.3	494.9	23261.9	24389.2	3681.1	2397.1	1664.2
1997	3589.9	519.6	26192.9	27145.2	4200.1	2653.6	1852.4
1998	3984.8	530.5	29336.0	30076.9	4741.9	2876.5	2045.4

2-10 历年国内生产总值构成
COMPOSITION OF GROSS DOMESTIC PRODUCTS OVER THE YEARS

本表按当年价格计算 (At current prices)

年份 Year	国内生产总值 (%) Gross Domestic Products	第一产业 Primary Industry	第二产业 Secondary Industry	#工业 Industry	第三产业 Tertiary Industry	#商业 Commerce
1952	100.0	52.7	17.6	15.8	29.7	14.7
1955	100.0	50.4	19.1	17.1	30.5	14.6
1957	100.0	46.0	22.1	19.2	31.9	14.9
1962	100.0	42.1	25.0	22.7	32.9	13.9
1965	100.0	43.3	31.8	28.3	24.9	9.8
1970	100.0	39.5	35.7	32.8	24.8	10.0
1975	100.0	36.7	43.2	39.5	20.1	7.7
1976	100.0	33.2	45.2	41.8	21.6	8.2
1977	100.0	26.3	52.0	48.0	21.7	7.9
1978	100.0	27.6	52.6	47.0	19.8	5.5
1979	100.0	34.8	47.3	42.3	17.9	5.9
1980	100.0	29.5	52.3	47.3	18.2	5.6
1981	100.0	31.3	50.8	46.0	17.9	5.5
1982	100.0	34.6	47.6	43.1	17.8	5.3
1983	100.0	34.4	48.2	43.8	17.4	5.5
1984	100.0	34.5	48.3	44.1	17.2	5.7
1985	100.0	30.0	52.1	47.2	17.9	5.1
1986	100.0	30.1	50.5	45.3	19.4	5.4
1987	100.0	26.8	53.5	48.1	19.7	6.7
1988	100.0	26.4	48.5	43.6	25.1	8.6
1989	100.0	24.5	49.7	45.4	25.8	7.8
1990	100.0	25.1	48.9	44.8	26.0	7.3
1991	100.0	21.5	49.6	45.3	28.9	8.8
1992	100.0	18.4	52.4	47.7	29.2	9.5
1993	100.0	16.4	53.3	48.4	30.3	10.3
1994	100.0	16.6	53.9	49.3	29.5	9.6
1995	100.0	16.4	52.7	47.9	30.9	10.0
1996	100.0	16.1	51.2	45.9	32.7	10.3
1997	100.0	15.1	51.1	45.2	33.8	10.2
1998	100.0	14.1	50.6	43.9	35.3	10.1

2-11 分行业国内生产总值
GROSS DOMESTIC PRODUCTS BY SECTOR

本表按当年价格计算　　　　(At current prices)

年 份 Year	国内生产总值(亿元) Gross Domestic Products (10^8 yuan)	第一产业 Primary Industry	第二产业 Secondary Industry	工 业 Industry	建筑业 Construction	第三产业 Tertiary Industry	运输邮电业 Transportation Postal and Telecommunication Services	商 业 Commerce
1978	249.24	68.71	131.09	117.10	13.99	49.44	6.85	13.63
1980	319.80	94.24	167.41	151.22	16.19	58.15	8.10	18.04
1981	350.02	109.39	178.01	161.11	16.90	62.62	9.14	19.24
1982	390.17	135.15	185.52	168.09	17.43	69.50	10.48	20.84
1983	437.65	150.41	210.81	191.52	19.29	76.43	12.36	23.86
1984	518.85	179.00	250.39	228.58	21.81	89.46	16.67	29.66
1985	651.82	195.66	339.56	307.89	31.67	116.60	26.07	32.98
1986	744.94	224.26	376.32	337.77	38.55	144.36	33.67	40.09
1987	922.33	246.86	493.69	443.23	50.46	181.78	43.25	61.60
1988	1208.85	319.18	586.82	526.92	59.90	302.85	59.62	103.63
1989	1321.85	324.18	657.06	599.91	57.15	340.61	62.66	102.69
1990	1416.50	355.17	692.59	634.13	58.46	368.74	63.64	103.25
1991	1601.38	345.14	793.92	725.83	68.09	462.32	80.27	140.27
1992	2136.02	393.82	1119.26	1017.94	101.32	622.94	100.55	201.91
1993	2998.16	490.59	1598.05	1451.97	146.08	909.52	144.11	308.21
1994	4057.39	671.94	2186.77	2002.22	184.55	1198.68	187.19	389.41
1995	5155.25	848.35	2715.26	2467.63	247.63	1591.64	253.52	516.89
1996	6004.21	965.29	3074.12	2754.80	319.32	1964.80	314.91	621.01
1997	6680.34	1008.41	3411.86	3016.44	395.42	2260.07	369.54	683.86
1998	7199.95	1016.27	3640.10	3157.69	482.41	2543.58	435.77	724.85

续表　Continue

年 份 Year	金融保险业 Banking and Insurance	房地产业 Real Estate Management	社会服务业 Social Services	卫生体育社会福利业 Health Care, Sports and Social Welfare	教育文艺广播电影电视业 Education, Culture, Art, Radio Film and Television	科学研究综合技术服务业 Scientific Research and Polytechnical Services	国家政党机关社会团体 Government Agencies, Party and Social Orgnizations	其 他 Others
1978	10.43	5.50	2.89	1.44	4.65	1.45	2.60	
1980	11.52	6.08	3.20	1.60	5.13	1.60	2.88	
1981	12.32	6.50	3.42	1.71	5.51	1.70	3.08	
1982	13.74	7.25	3.81	1.91	6.14	1.90	3.43	
1983	14.47	7.64	4.02	2.01	6.45	2.00	3.62	
1984	15.52	8.19	4.30	2.15	6.94	2.15	3.88	
1985	18.91	11.93	5.47	2.92	9.73	2.69	5.90	
1986	25.56	13.50	6.73	3.69	11.44	3.30	6.29	
1987	25.14	14.59	7.79	3.98	14.06	5.10	6.27	
1988	47.44	21.25	16.91	8.42	19.17	7.81	18.60	
1989	65.45	24.72	16.69	10.00	21.92	8.97	27.51	
1990	72.53	27.02	19.88	11.66	24.79	11.09	34.88	
1991	77.81	33.51	25.96	13.92	28.89	14.06	40.90	6.73
1992	109.27	43.89	35.79	17.74	35.49	17.92	51.05	9.33
1993	144.81	74.56	59.79	25.43	45.68	24.75	70.26	11.92
1994	200.34	99.26	82.36	33.53	65.37	34.42	97.79	9.01
1995	270.50	143.61	102.98	44.16	88.37	47.50	112.12	11.99
1996	333.51	194.24	131.81	54.99	106.92	58.53	134.25	14.63
1997	376.04	234.28	166.12	61.67	124.67	66.02	160.94	16.93
1998	381.81	286.66	210.39	71.82	150.64	73.71	188.28	19.65

2－12 分行业国内生产总值指数

INDICES OF GROSS DOMESTIC PRODUCTS BY SECTOR

按可比价格计算，1978＝100　　(At comparable price 1978＝100)

年 份 Year	国内生产总值 Gross Domestic Products	第一产业 Primary Industry	第二产业 Secondary Industry	工 业 Industry	建筑业 Construction	第三产业 Tertiary Industry	运输邮电业 Transportation Postal and Telecommunication Services	商 业 Commerce
1978	100.0	100.0	100.0	100.0	100.0	100.0	100.0	100.0
1980	117.4	109.9	126.6	129.3	105.6	107.3	108.0	120.8
1981	130.2	124.1	135.8	138.7	112.8	126.6	133.5	141.0
1982	143.0	143.9	143.6	147.2	116.0	139.8	152.3	151.9
1983	160.5	154.2	165.6	170.4	128.6	158.7	185.5	179.7
1984	185.8	174.1	195.2	195.3	195.1	181.9	226.3	202.1
1985	217.9	172.7	250.0	256.7	198.0	214.8	346.9	220.3
1986	240.5	181.9	274.1	279.3	233.9	256.4	433.1	258.2
1987	272.8	182.8	323.7	327.6	293.1	299.2	514.1	367.6
1988	326.3	190.7	381.2	387.3	334.6	419.1	595.9	520.0
1989	334.4	185.3	383.0	395.3	287.2	465.9	619.2	509.3
1990	351.1	187.2	403.6	418.8	286.2	498.1	619.9	506.1
1991	380.3	179.8	439.7	455.6	316.1	592.5	725.1	641.0
1992	477.6	199.0	579.9	596.2	453.4	747.7	850.6	886.4
1993	572.1	204.1	715.3	734.4	566.5	935.6	1099.5	1178.6
1994	666.6	214.7	875.1	902.3	661.0	1042.2	1355.5	1244.0
1995	769.3	243.9	1016.0	1041.3	826.9	1197.5	1562.9	1433.1
1996	863.2	262.8	1141.0	1155.6	1044.5	1369.3	1855.8	1602.8
1997	966.8	275.9	1284.8	1286.2	1293.1	1562.4	2136.0	1774.3
1998	1073.1	281.7	1439.0	1425.1	1580.2	1763.9	2469.2	1923.3

续表　Continue

年 份 Year	金融保险业 Banking and Insurance	房地产业 Real Estate Management	社会服务业 Social Services	卫生体育社会福利业 Health Care, Sports and Social Welfare	教育文艺广播电影电视业 Education, Culture, Art, Radio Film and Television	科学研究综合技术服务业 Scientific Research and Polytechnical Services	国家政党机关社会团体 Government Agencies, Party and Social Orgnizations
1978	100.0	100.0	100.0	100.0	100.0	100.0	100.0
1980	100.8	101.0	101.0	101.3	100.8	100.6	101.0
1981	118.0	118.3	118.3	118.3	118.5	117.0	118.3
1982	131.0	131.2	130.9	131.7	131.4	130.2	131.2
1983	142.4	142.7	142.6	143.0	142.6	141.5	142.8
1984	163.3	163.6	163.1	163.3	161.1	159.8	154.4
1985	165.1	197.8	172.2	184.8	190.8	168.6	206.7
1986	215.1	215.8	204.4	224.7	216.3	199.4	212.3
1987	196.1	216.1	218.9	224.7	246.2	286.2	196.1
1988	311.0	264.6	400.0	399.4	282.3	367.9	490.5
1989	424.3	304.1	389.9	468.4	319.1	417.6	714.7
1990	464.7	328.7	459.3	540.5	356.8	511.3	891.9
1991	487.2	388.7	575.3	619.3	399.5	622.0	1020.3
1992	648.5	458.2	644.4	744.0	462.0	747.4	1185.8
1993	734.9	686.3	735.4	891.9	515.4	863.1	1359.4
1994	822.6	741.7	850.0	986.4	597.1	996.7	1587.2
1995	971.5	927.1	874.7	1121.5	705.8	1155.2	1592.0
1996	1121.5	1147.3	997.0	1277.7	760.5	1286.1	1714.7
1997	1272.9	1394.0	1082.7	1442.5	892.8	1437.4	2069.6
1998	1322.5	1725.8	1274.3	1710.8	1098.1	1638.6	2464.9

2-13 国内生产总值构成项目(1998)
STRUCTURE OF GROSS DOMESTIC PRODUCTS

本表按当年价格计算 (At current prices)

行业	Items	增加值(亿元) Added Value (10^8 yuan)	劳动者报酬 Payment for Laborer	固定资产折旧 Depreciation of Fixed Assets	生产税净额 Net Amount of Production Tax	营业盈余 Business Surplus
国内生产总值	**Gross Domestic Products**	**7199.95**	**3664.08**	**1034.88**	**866.25**	**1634.74**
第一产业	Primary Industry	1016.27	889.99	47.55	24.48	54.25
第二产业	Secondary Industry	3640.10	1633.64	473.29	602.08	931.09
工　业	Industry	3157.69	1343.88	441.17	555.50	817.14
建筑业	Construction	482.41	289.76	32.12	46.58	113.95
第三产业	Tertiary Industry	2543.58	1140.45	514.04	239.69	649.40
农林牧渔服务业	Farming, Forestry, Animal Husbandry and Fishery Services	30.89	20.49	3.52	1.45	5.43
地质勘探业、水利管理业	Geological Prospecting and Water Conservancy	19.08	11.34	4.68	0.99	2.07
交通运输、仓储、邮电通讯业	Transportation, Storage, Postal and Telecommunications Services	435.77	219.22	110.96	40.75	64.84
批发和零售贸易、餐饮业	Wholesale, Retail Trade and Food Services	724.85	364.96	69.31	108.80	181.78
金融保险业	Banking and Insurance	381.81	45.33	11.48	36.72	288.28
房地产业	Real Estate Management	286.66	21.27	224.20	14.57	26.62
社会服务业	Social Services	210.39	110.20	22.68	26.54	50.97
卫生体育社会福利事业	Health Care, Sports and Social Welfare	71.82	52.21	10.28	1.74	7.59
教育文艺广播电影电视业	Education, Culture, Art, Radio, Film and Television	150.64	115.79	19.86	2.74	12.25
科学研究和综合技术服务业	Scientific Research and Polytechnical Services	23.74	13.84	3.11	2.16	4.63
国家政党机关、社会团体	Government Agencies, Party Agencies and Social Organizations	188.28	153.19	31.21	2.61	1.27
其　他	Others	19.65	12.61	2.75	0.62	3.67

2-14 按支出法计算的国内生产总值
GROSS DOMESTIC PRODUCTS BY EXPENDITURES

本表按当年价格计算 (At current prices)

年份 Year	国内生产总值(亿元) Gross Domestic Products (10^8 yuan)	最终消费 Final Consumption	居民消费 Resident Consumption	政府消费 Government Consumption	资本形成总额 Total Capital	固定资本形成 Fixed Capital	存货增加 Goods in Stock	货物和服务净出口 Net Export
1978	249.24	130.55	115.15	15.40	77.98	40.40	37.58	40.71
1980	319.80	175.47	154.72	20.75	97.44	58.25	39.19	46.89
1981	350.02	198.64	174.30	24.34	97.03	56.83	40.20	54.35
1982	390.17	232.12	203.38	28.74	133.09	95.71	37.38	24.96
1983	437.65	251.98	215.96	36.02	142.21	105.49	36.72	43.46
1984	518.85	297.65	257.86	39.79	198.62	131.39	67.23	22.58
1985	651.82	353.72	300.86	52.86	271.42	193.25	78.17	26.68
1986	744.94	393.05	339.37	53.68	341.74	240.37	101.37	10.15
1987	922.33	478.89	406.84	72.05	411.70	303.45	108.25	31.74
1988	1208.85	594.76	501.62	93.14	528.45	390.46	137.99	85.64
1989	1321.85	662.01	557.60	104.41	528.44	336.24	192.20	131.40
1990	1416.50	717.36	608.29	109.07	588.44	374.12	214.32	110.70
1991	1601.38	835.07	656.99	178.08	694.80	461.98	232.82	71.51
1992	2136.02	960.21	735.62	224.59	1069.20	747.29	321.91	106.61
1993	2998.16	1251.08	984.44	266.64	1589.93	1201.41	388.52	157.15
1994	4057.39	1721.45	1350.89	370.56	2018.95	1434.95	584.00	316.99
1995	5155.25	2250.66	1806.43	444.23	2479.30	1756.88	722.42	425.29
1996	6004.21	2721.84	2218.68	503.16	2798.62	2062.17	736.45	483.75
1997	6680.34	3020.94	2417.77	603.17	2925.28	2295.97	629.31	734.12
1998	7199.95	3161.88	2513.52	648.36	3321.44	2642.29	679.15	716.63

2-15 按支出法计算的国内生产总值指数
INDICES OF GROSS DOMESTIC PRODUCTS BY EXPENDITURES

按可比价格计算 1952=100 (At comparable price 1952=100)

年份 Year	最终消费 Final Consumption	居民消费 Resident Consumption	政府消费 Government Consumption	资本形成总额 Total Capital	固定资本形成 Fixed Capital	存货增加 Goods in Stock
1952	100.00	100.00	100.00	100.00	100.00	100.00
1978	367.65	352.29	545.30	695.68	593.18	847.12
1980	468.42	448.72	696.31	809.30	811.28	806.38
1981	528.62	503.92	814.43	849.00	843.18	857.61
1982	611.53	582.11	952.01	1187.54	1456.27	790.53
1983	665.48	619.66	1195.64	1296.10	1647.21	777.37
1984	769.46	724.13	1293.96	1722.43	1947.21	1390.33
1985	824.00	757.37	1594.97	2156.64	2572.98	1541.56
1986	880.49	816.62	1619.46	2755.48	3325.63	1913.17
1987	989.62	904.00	1980.20	3063.62	3803.90	1969.96
1988	1003.10	901.68	2176.51	3574.92	4429.39	2312.55
1989	1000.32	885.30	2331.21	3610.71	3998.61	3037.65
1990	1063.67	949.62	2383.22	3922.26	4390.95	3229.84
1991	1191.31	987.60	3734.51	4538.10	5330.60	3410.70
1992	1341.42	1090.32	4500.08	6389.60	7745.40	4491.90
1993	1523.85	1250.59	4945.59	7693.10	9542.30	5125.30
1994	1709.80	1403.20	5558.80	8470.10	9952.60	6355.40
1995	1868.80	1550.50	5831.20	9706.70	11346.00	7353.20
1996	2113.61	1775.32	6291.86	10755.02	13093.28	7434.09
1997	2337.65	1924.45	7525.06	11540.14	14677.57	7106.99
1998	2487.26	2032.22	8239.94	13421.18	17099.37	8237.00

2－16 最终消费及其构成

FINAL CONSUMPTION AND COMPOSITION

本表按当年价格计算 (At current prices)

年份 Year	最终消费（亿元） Final Consumption (10^8 yuan)	居民消费 Resident Consumption	农村居民 Village Resident	自给性 Self-Sufficient	商品性 Commodity Consumption	文化生活服务性 Cultural Life Services	住房及水电 Housing, Water and Electricity	住房 Housing
1978	130.55	115.15	76.11	28.31	37.48	4.43	5.89	5.54
1980	175.47	154.72	105.13	35.06	54.39	5.68	10.00	9.59
1981	198.64	174.30	121.83	44.83	59.96	6.13	10.91	10.91
1982	232.12	203.38	147.65	54.04	74.67	7.94	11.00	11.00
1983	251.98	215.96	158.02	58.20	77.66	9.97	12.19	9.70
1984	297.65	257.86	188.60	70.81	95.15	11.75	10.89	10.07
1985	353.72	300.86	219.98	77.57	117.73	12.20	12.48	11.55
1986	393.05	339.37	241.01	84.65	123.71	19.28	13.37	12.11
1987	478.89	406.84	282.48	91.99	143.66	28.90	17.93	13.53
1988	594.76	501.62	352.23	118.16	180.18	31.07	22.82	14.90
1989	662.01	557.60	386.40	136.33	193.07	33.54	23.46	19.36
1990	717.36	608.29	403.29	144.96	197.79	38.62	21.92	19.34
1991	835.07	656.99	423.60	149.83	208.63	40.72	24.42	21.12
1992	960.21	735.62	459.99	159.07	228.28	43.56	29.08	24.20
1993	1251.08	984.44	569.94	159.47	300.24	45.43	64.80	48.30
1994	1721.45	1350.89	782.19	265.06	344.82	76.75	95.56	75.56
1995	2250.66	1806.43	1029.92	327.11	406.11	125.84	170.86	133.59
1996	2721.84	2218.68	1314.01	327.98	553.94	192.43	239.66	186.79
1997	3020.94	2417.77	1390.51	310.10	643.41	195.27	241.73	224.27
1998	3161.88	2513.52	1370.53	285.68	616.77	221.36	246.72	229.04

续表 Continued

年份 Year	城镇居民 Urban Residents	商品性 Commodity Consumption	文化生活服务性 Cultural Life Services	住房及水电 Housing, Water and Electricity	住房 Housing	政府消费 Government Consumption
1978	39.04	33.18	5.11	0.75	0.50	15.40
1980	49.59	42.20	6.43	0.96	0.56	20.75
1981	52.47	45.00	6.44	1.03	0.59	24.34
1982	55.73	48.26	6.39	1.08	0.60	28.74
1983	57.94	50.15	6.41	1.38	0.76	36.02
1984	69.26	58.99	8.69	1.58	0.88	39.79
1985	80.88	69.58	9.63	1.67	0.94	52.86
1986	98.36	83.75	11.65	2.96	1.52	53.68
1987	124.36	103.76	17.21	3.39	1.67	72.05
1988	149.39	125.55	19.71	4.13	1.87	93.14
1989	171.20	142.79	23.48	4.93	2.16	104.41
1990	205.00	163.47	36.09	5.44	2.61	109.07
1991	233.39	188.14	38.41	6.84	3.00	178.08
1992	275.63	225.50	40.42	9.71	4.23	224.59
1993	414.50	305.25	87.15	22.10	6.79	266.64
1994	568.70	403.39	130.72	34.59	11.50	370.56
1995	776.51	534.89	183.64	57.98	30.66	444.23
1996	904.67	588.76	241.14	74.77	39.85	503.16
1997	1027.26	689.15	251.57	86.54	43.03	603.17
1998	1142.99	769.96	277.06	95.97	49.01	648.36

2-17 按产业分资本形成总额
TOTAL CAPITAL BY TYPE OF INDUSTRY

本表按当年价格计算 (At current prices)

年 份 Year	资本形成总额 (亿元) Total Capital (10^8 yuan)	固定资本形成 Fixed Capital	存货增加 Goods in Stock	第一产业 Primary Industry 资本形成总额 Total Capital	固定资本形成 Fixed Capital	存货增加 Goods in Stock
1978	77.98	40.40	37.58	6.36	2.23	4.13
1980	97.44	58.25	39.19	6.95	2.44	4.51
1981	97.03	56.83	40.20	7.84	3.22	4.62
1982	133.09	95.71	37.38	8.17	3.76	4.41
1983	142.21	105.49	36.72	8.29	3.85	4.44
1984	198.62	131.39	67.23	11.60	3.51	8.09
1985	271.42	193.25	78.17	12.86	4.50	8.36
1986	341.74	240.37	101.37	12.54	6.29	6.25
1987	411.70	303.45	108.25	16.30	8.50	7.80
1988	528.45	390.46	137.99	21.74	12.49	9.25
1989	528.44	336.24	192.20	19.60	10.76	8.84
1990	588.44	374.12	214.32	26.32	11.97	14.35
1991	694.80	461.98	232.82	27.37	12.94	14.43
1992	1069.20	747.29	321.91	36.29	15.69	20.60
1993	1589.93	1201.41	388.52	45.58	21.87	23.71
1994	2018.95	1434.95	584.00	86.38	48.26	38.12
1995	2479.30	1756.88	722.42	113.74	41.94	71.80
1996	2798.62	2062.17	736.45	149.17	45.41	103.76
1997	2925.28	2295.97	629.31	184.87	59.73	125.14
1998	3321.44	2642.29	679.15	201.22	68.37	132.85

续表 Continued

年 份 Year	第二产业 Scondary Industry 资本形成总额 Total Capital	固定资本形成 Fixed Capital	存货增加 Goods in Stock	第三产业 Tertiary Industry 资本形成总额 Total Capital	固定资本形成 Fixed Capital	存货增加 Goods in Stock
1978	53.94	27.26	26.68	17.68	10.91	6.77
1980	67.72	39.70	28.02	22.77	16.11	6.66
1981	64.95	36.21	28.74	24.24	17.40	6.84
1982	79.99	53.64	26.35	44.93	38.31	6.62
1983	80.46	54.46	26.00	53.46	47.18	6.28
1984	108.91	61.18	47.73	78.11	66.70	11.41
1985	145.25	89.82	55.43	113.31	98.93	14.38
1986	192.05	114.86	77.19	137.15	119.22	17.93
1987	215.64	141.10	74.54	179.76	153.85	25.91
1988	225.51	146.03	79.48	281.20	231.94	49.26
1989	256.83	125.75	131.08	252.01	199.73	52.28
1990	286.30	139.92	146.38	275.82	222.23	53.59
1991	336.72	196.80	139.92	330.71	252.24	78.47
1992	593.59	399.80	193.79	439.32	331.80	107.52
1993	923.38	669.43	253.95	620.97	510.11	110.86
1994	1073.66	736.45	337.21	858.91	650.24	208.67
1995	1262.85	829.54	433.31	1102.71	885.40	217.31
1996	1356.02	931.49	424.53	1293.43	1085.27	208.16
1997	1370.20	1037.52	332.68	1370.21	1198.72	171.49
1998	1495.48	1133.67	361.81	1624.74	1440.25	184.49

2-18 历年工农业总产值
GROSS OUTPUT VALUE OF INDUSTRY AND AGRICULTURE OVER THE YEARS

本表按当年价格计算 (At current prices)

年份 Year	工农业总产值（亿元） Gross Output Value of Industry and Agriculture (10^8 yuan)	农业 Agriculture	工业 Industry	轻工业 Light Industry	重工业 Heavy Industry
1949	38.48	22.59	15.89	15.01	0.88
1950	43.27	24.27	19.00	17.94	1.06
1952	57.40	31.87	25.53	23.97	1.56
1955	69.04	36.22	32.82	29.57	3.25
1957	77.82	36.81	41.01	34.78	6.23
1962	93.51	40.15	53.36	42.95	10.41
1965	145.35	57.27	88.08	66.28	21.80
1970	206.80	71.33	135.47	83.14	52.33
1975	326.94	91.66	235.28	130.28	105.00
1976	348.30	100.71	247.59	134.12	112.62
1977	386.28	89.16	297.12	158.12	139.00
1978	443.52	105.87	337.65	176.94	160.71
1979	531.30	145.25	386.05	208.11	177.94
1980	606.27	138.45	467.82	267.97	199.85
1981	658.56	153.62	504.94	307.98	196.96
1982	722.98	188.11	534.87	317.54	217.33
1983	807.56	206.86	600.70	348.56	252.14
1984	999.18	253.82	745.36	433.00	312.36
1985	1325.22	288.55	1036.67	552.23	484.44
1986	1568.04	332.66	1235.38	671.24	564.14
1987	1970.56	380.25	1590.31	859.40	730.91
1988	2650.88	497.95	2152.93	1151.00	1001.93
1989	3029.67	522.25	2507.42	1338.53	1168.89
1990	3344.63	580.53	2764.10	1510.57	1253.53
1991	3742.53	580.93	3161.60	1682.76	1478.84
1992	5347.39	673.82	4673.57	2379.00	2294.57
1993	7971.83	875.37	7096.46	3439.50	3656.96
1994	11161.73	1335.23	9826.50	5014.54	4811.96
1995	11493.97	1686.78	9807.19	4785.42	5021.77
1996	13379.79	1824.19	11555.60	5676.47	5879.13
1997	14358.77	1816.37	12542.40	6382.96	6159.44
1998	15034.90	1849.20	13185.70	6843.38	6342.40

注：从1995年开始，工业总产值按新规定统计。

Note: Total output value of industry were counted by new regulation since 1995.

2-19 历年工农业总产值指数
INDICES OF GROSS OUTPUT VALUE OF INDUSTRY AND AGRICULTURE OVER THE YEARS

按可比价格计算 1949=100 (At comparable price 1949=100)

年份 Year	工农业总产值 Gross Output Value of Industry and Agriculture	农业 Agriculture	工业 Industry	轻工业 Light Industry	重工业 Heavy Industry
1949	100.0	100.0	100.0	100.0	100.0
1950	113.5	109.1	119.5	119.2	123.1
1952	149.7	144.2	160.6	159.1	178.6
1955	181.0	163.0	208.3	194.9	368.4
1957	202.3	157.4	266.6	230.2	700.9
1962	218.6	134.7	334.8	270.6	1102.6
1965	355.9	201.4	577.0	448.2	2117.1
1970	573.9	239.7	1040.8	599.4	6318.8
1975	950.8	294.7	1861.2	944.4	12870.8
1976	1038.0	306.2	2050.5	1021.0	14475.3
1977	1194.7	275.4	2461.8	1189.7	17929.2
1978	1370.9	334.6	2797.8	1330.2	20707.9
1979	1555.3	371.1	3186.6	1561.8	22875.3
1980	1822.3	350.7	3847.3	2021.4	25552.8
1981	1974.4	378.4	4171.8	2360.5	25144.9
1982	2141.0	434.8	4490.8	2474.5	28080.5
1983	2419.4	460.6	5113.9	2790.0	32420.7
1984	2965.2	536.3	6304.5	3378.2	40947.6
1985	3866.0	553.1	8408.9	4425.1	55903.7
1986	4479.3	587.7	9811.6	5264.6	63611.0
1987	5480.6	605.9	12151.6	6336.4	81715.9
1988	6824.3	646.1	15271.4	7975.7	102496.3
1989	7126.5	648.3	15981.9	8303.0	107964.6
1990	7811.7	664.6	17583.9	9246.4	117011.0
1991	8889.1	657.1	20131.3	10304.4	138466.3
1992	13133.5	742.5	30039.9	14934.2	213695.0
1993	18177.3	826.4	42668.4	20680.9	312033.2
1994	23933.2	926.3	57057.8	28386.0	405576.0
1995	28840.2	1052.7	69176.9	34693.4	487583.5
1996	33776.9	1130.6	81725.4	40979.5	576131.6
1997	38201.7	1217.7	92840.0	47208.4	625678.9
1998	42938.7	1265.6	105094.9	54431.3	688246.1

2-20 个体工商业基本情况(1998)
SELF-EMPLOYMENT BUSINESS

单位:万元 (10000 yuan)

行业 Sector		户数(户) Households	从业人数(人) Personal (person)	注册资金 Registered Capital	总产值 Total Output Value	销售总额 Total Sales Value
总计	**Total**	**1556637**	**2817208**	**1513266**	**2775207**	**10828809**
按行业分	Grouped by Sector					
#农林牧渔业	Farming, Forestry, Animal Housbandry and Fishery	42944	105802	28844	187545	2614
制造业	Manufacturing	198900	462986	259336	2426521	
建筑业	Construction	4852	13556	12059	143482	
交通运输业	Transportation	155513	258568	253023		1261154
批发零售	Wholesale, Retail Sales	950944	1634199	792304		8631926
贸易业、餐饮业	Catering Trade					
#餐饮业	Catering Trade	126240	280898	123611		883526
社会服务业	Services	197621	331843	162254		898536
#日用品修理业	Repairing Business of Daily Use Goods	66967	98164	36558		215761

2-21 私营企业情况(1998)
PRIVATE ENTERPRISES

单位:万元 (10000 yuan)

行业 Sector		户数(户) Households	雇工人数(人) Employees (person)	投资者人数(人) Owners (person)	注册资金 Registered Capital	总产值 Total Output Value	销售总额 Total Sales Value
总计	**Total**	**107714**	**1135484**	**201512**	**4919547**	**5029588**	**4805968**
按行业分	Grouped by Sector						
#农林牧渔业	Farming, Forestry, Animal Housbandry and Fishery	909	8453	1577	51951	127987	18880
制造业	Manufacturing	56981	682992	93394	2214489	4545943	
建筑业	Construction	2219	27880	5402	239843	349580	
交通运输业	Transportation	701	7196	1553	43438		154214
批发零售	Wholesale, Retail Sales	38105	333653	80314	1941983		4134260
贸易业、餐饮业	Catering Trade						
#餐饮业	Catering Trade	1206	10451	1854	45417		125169
社会服务业	Services	6594	55113	14234	241465		380684
#日用品修理业	Repairing Business of Daily Use Goods	195	1675	300	4715		10740

3. 人口、劳动力

POPULATION & EMPLOYMENT

3 人口、劳动力
POPULATION & EMPLOYMENT

1 9 9 8

年末总人口	Population (Year-end)	7182.46	万人	10000 persons
#男性	Male	3643.21	万人	10000 persons
#农业人口	Agricultural Population	5251.81	万人	10000 persons
年末总户数	Total Households (Year-end)	2087.92	万户	10000 household
人口密度	Density of Population	700	人/平方公里	person/sq·k
人口自然增长率	Population Natural Growth Rate	4.13	‰	‰
从业人员	Employment	3687.85	万人	10000 persons
第一产业	Primary Industry	1551.87	万人	10000 persons
第二产业	Secondary Industry	1189.22	万人	10000 persons
第三产业	Tertiary Industry	946.76	万人	10000 persons
职工人数	Staff and Workers	870.01	万人	10000 persons
年末离休、退休、退职人员数	Number of VCSR and RRSW by Year-end	227.95	万人	10000 persons
城镇失业率	Unemployment Rate	2.6	%	percent

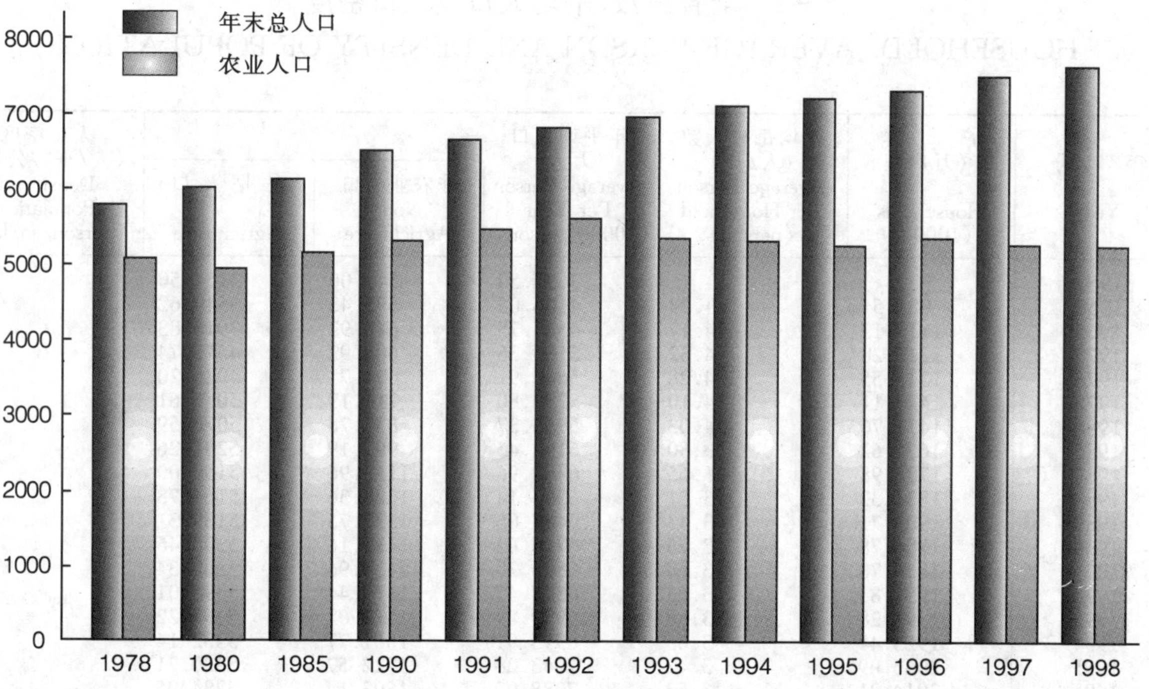

3-1 全省人口数及构成

POPULATION AND COMPOSITION

单位:万人 (10000 persons)

年 份 Year	总人口 Total	按性别分 Grouped by Sex				按农业人口、非农业人口分 Grouped by Agriculture and Non-Agriculture			
		男 Male		女 Female		农业人口 Agriculture		非农业人口 Non-Agriculture	
		人口数 Population	比重(%) Proportion	人口数 Population	比重(%) Proportion	人口数 Population	比重(%) Proportion	人口数 Population	比重(%) Proportion
1949	*3512.00	1778.80	50.6	1733.20	49.4	2991.00	85.2	*521.00	14.8
1952	*3739.00	1891.60	50.6	1847.40	49.4	3188.00	85.3	*551.00	14.7
1957	4182.71	2087.06	49.9	2095.65	50.1	3562.05	85.2	620.66	14.8
1965	4623.74	2319.92	50.2	2303.82	49.8	3968.56	85.8	655.18	14.2
1970	5252.09	2635.02	50.2	2617.07	49.8	4651.52	88.6	600.57	11.4
1975	5636.12	2842.86	50.4	2793.26	49.6	4958.86	88.0	677.26	12.0
1978	5834.33	2950.45	50.6	2883.88	49.4	5106.22	87.5	728.11	12.5
1980	5938.19	3003.75	50.6	2934.44	49.4	5085.67	85.6	852.52	14.4
1985	6213.48	3168.25	51.0	3045.23	49.0	5199.87	83.7	1013.61	16.3
1987	6348.00	3241.71	51.1	3106.29	48.9	5172.72	81.5	1175.28	18.5
1988	6438.27	3289.49	51.1	3148.78	48.9	5156.84	80.1	1281.43	19.9
1989	6535.85	3339.10	51.1	3196.75	48.9	5161.79	79.0	1374.06	21.0
1990	6766.90	3443.68	50.9	3323.22	49.1	5345.85	79.0	1421.05	21.0
1991	6843.70	3451.96	50.4	3391.74	49.6	5392.84	78.8	1450.86	21.2
1992	6911.20	3483.24	50.4	3427.96	49.6	5403.18	78.2	1508.02	21.8
1993	6967.27	3513.59	50.4	3453.68	49.6	5331.25	76.5	1636.02	23.5
1994	7020.54	3534.09	50.3	3486.45	49.7	5333.03	76.0	1687.51	24.0
1995	7066.02	3589.56	50.8	3476.46	49.2	5308.39	75.1	1757.63	24.9
1996	7110.16	3610.72	50.8	3499.44	49.2	5261.52	74.0	1848.64	26.0
1997	7147.86	3628.08	50.8	3519.78	49.2	5257.13	73.5	1890.73	26.5
1998	7182.46	3643.21	50.7	3539.26	49.3	5251.81	73.1	1930.65	26.9

注:1998年全省常住人口为7182.46万人,户籍人口为6983.09万人。

Note: Resident population was 7182.46 ten thousand people, and household population was 6983.09 ten thousand people in 1998.

3-2 全省户数、平均人口及人口密度

HOUSEHOLD, AVERAGE PERSON AND DENSITY OF POPULATION

年 份 Year	户 数(万户) Households (10000)	平均每户人数(人/户) Average Person Per Household (person)	年平均人口(万人) Average Person Per Year (10000 persons)			人口密度(人/平方公里) Density of Population (person/sq·km)
				非农业人口 Non-Agriculture	农业人口 Agriculture	
1952			3697.50	543.00	3154.50	364
1957	985.51	4.24	4136.05	595.43	3540.62	408
1965	1110.13	4.17	4567.75	648.92	3918.83	451
1970	1215.28	4.32	5185.36	609.92	4575.74	512
1975	1315.55	4.28	5600.91	674.71	4926.20	549
1978	1423.11	4.10	5799.80	713.19	5086.61	569
1980	1471.76	4.03	5915.37	838.78	5076.59	579
1985	1633.62	3.80	6192.45	991.19	5201.26	606
1987	1736.98	3.65	6308.96	1158.96	5150.00	619
1988	1834.32	3.51	6393.14	1228.36	5164.78	628
1989	1903.71	3.43	6487.06	1327.75	5159.31	637
1990	1806.78	3.75	6716.62	1411.16	5305.46	660
1991	1859.70	3.68	6805.30	1435.96	5369.34	667
1992	1957.85	3.53	6877.45	1479.44	5398.01	674
1993	1893.28	3.68	6939.24	1572.02	5367.22	679
1994	1923.44	3.65	6993.91	1661.77	5332.14	684
1995	2066.09	3.42	7043.28	1722.57	5320.71	689
1996	2014.21	3.53	7088.09	1803.14	5284.95	693
1997	2133.69	3.35	7129.01	1869.69	5259.32	697
1998	2087.92	3.44	7165.16	1910.69	5254.47	700

3-3 全省人口自然变动
POPULATION NATURAL CHANGE

单位:万人 (10000 persons)

年份 Year	出生 Birth 人数 Population	出生 Birth ‰	死亡 Death 人数 Population	死亡 Death ‰	自然增长 Natural Growth 人数 Population	自然增长 Natural Growth ‰
1949	*121.94	34.72	*57.77	16.45	*64.17	18.27
1952	*131.93	35.68	*57.98	15.68	*73.95	20.00
1957	142.19	34.38	42.45	10.26	99.74	24.12
1965	168.59	36.91	43.30	9.48	125.29	27.43
1970	159.06	30.68	35.51	6.85	123.55	23.83
1975	100.01	17.86	36.18	6.46	63.83	11.40
1978	90.62	15.63	35.32	6.09	55.30	9.54
1980	86.90	14.69	38.87	6.57	48.03	8.12
1985	67.11	10.84	36.35	5.87	30.76	4.97
1987	97.27	15.42	36.50	5.79	60.77	9.63
1988	102.46	16.03	37.65	5.89	64.81	10.14
1989	111.27	17.15	36.31	5.60	74.96	11.55
1990	137.96	20.54	43.86	6.53	94.10	14.01
1991	116.03	17.05	44.23	6.50	71.80	10.55
1992	108.04	15.71	46.49	6.76	61.55	8.95
1993	96.94	13.97	45.87	6.61	51.07	7.36
1994	96.38	13.78	47.98	6.86	48.40	6.92
1995	86.77	12.32	46.20	6.56	40.57	5.76
1996	85.84	12.11	46.64	6.58	39.20	5.53
1997	81.47	11.43	48.76	6.84	32.71	4.59
1998	78.60	10.97	49.01	6.84	29.59	4.13

3-4 全省市、镇、县人口数及其构成
CITY, COUNTY POPULATION AND COMPOSITION

单位:万人 (10000 persons)

年份 Year	总人口数 Total Population	市 City 人口数 Population	市 City 占总人口% Proportion	镇 City 人口数 Population	镇 City 占总人口% Proportion	县 County 人口数 Population	县 County 占总人口% Proportion
1957	4182.71	471.18	11.3				
1965	4623.74	496.91	10.8	191.23	4.1	3935.60	85.1
1970	5252.09	476.33	9.1	179.91	3.4	4595.85	87.5
1975	5636.12	530.38	9.4	211.09	3.8	4894.65	86.8
1978	5834.32	570.14	9.8	230.63	3.9	5033.55	86.3
1980	5938.19	636.41	10.7	265.37	4.5	5036.41	84.8
1985	6213.48	966.64	15.6	629.51	10.1	4617.33	74.3
1987	6348.00	1803.65	28.4	1077.63	17.0	3466.72	54.6
1988	6438.27	1947.01	30.2	1265.62	19.7	3225.64	50.1
1989	6535.85	2148.50	32.9	1344.96	20.6	3042.39	46.5
1990	6766.90	1043.45	15.4	415.49	6.1	5307.96	78.5
1991	6843.70	1163.43	17.0	424.31	6.2	5255.96	76.8
1992	6911.20	1182.59	17.1	461.13	6.7	5267.48	76.2
1993	6967.27	1199.26	17.2	474.32	6.8	5293.69	76.0
1994	7020.54	1255.58	17.9	477.43	6.8	5287.53	75.3
1995	7066.02	1331.30	18.8	597.79	8.5	5136.93	72.7
1996	7110.16	1328.18	18.7	614.32	8.6	5167.66	72.7
1997	7147.86	1465.31	20.5	668.33	9.4	5014.22	70.1
1998	7182.46	1537.05	21.4	725.42	10.1	4919.99	68.5

3-5 全省人口年龄构成情况
POPULATION AGE COMPOSITION

1998年人口变动情况抽样调查资料　　Sampling Survey in 1998

年龄（岁）Age (Year)	人口数（人）Population			占总计的% Proportion		
	合计 Total	男 Male	女 Female	合计 Total	男 Male	女 Female
总计 Total	**39788**	**19723**	**20065**	**100.00**	**49.57**	**50.43**
0-4	1988	1100	888	5.00	2.76	2.24
5-9	3289	1782	1507	8.27	4.48	3.79
10-14	3273	1672	1601	8.23	4.20	4.03
15-19	2443	1285	1158	6.14	3.23	2.91
20-24	2497	1116	1381	6.28	2.80	3.48
25-29	3542	1686	1856	8.90	4.24	4.66
30-34	3981	1870	2111	10.01	4.70	5.31
35-39	3016	1466	1550	7.58	3.68	3.90
40-44	3456	1771	1685	8.69	4.45	4.24
45-49	2985	1514	1471	7.50	3.81	3.69
50-54	2349	1190	1159	5.90	2.99	2.91
55-59	1687	831	856	4.24	2.09	2.15
60-64	1617	806	811	4.06	2.03	2.03
65-69	1376	676	700	3.46	1.70	1.76
70-74	1071	484	587	2.69	1.22	1.47
75-79	704	301	403	1.77	0.76	1.01
80-84	338	127	211	0.85	0.32	0.53
85-89	129	41	88	0.32	0.10	0.22
90及以上 90 and over	47	5	42	0.12	0.01	0.11

3-6 全省15岁及以上人口的婚姻状况
BASIC STATISTICS ON AGE 15 AND ABOVE POPULATION MARRIAGE

1998年人口变动情况抽样调查资料　　Sampling Survey in 1998

婚姻状况 Indication	人口数（人）Population (Person)	占15岁及以上人口的% Proportion of 15 Age and above Population			
		1990	1995	1997	1998
总计 Total	**31238**	**100.00**	**100.00**	**100.00**	**100.00**
未婚 Unmarried	4640	21.65	17.60	14.63	14.85
初婚有配偶 First Marriage	23834	71.48	73.91	76.20	76.30
再婚有配偶 Remarriage	421		1.58	1.48	1.35
离婚 Divorce	208	0.41	0.55	0.79	0.67
丧偶 Widowed	2135	6.46	6.36	6.90	6.83

3-7 全省家庭户规模
HOUSEHOLD SCALE

1998年人口变动情况抽样调查资料　　Sampling Survey in 1998

规模 Scale		户数（户） Households			占总计的% Proportion	
	1990	1995	1998	1990	1995	1998
总　计　Total	**17815925**	**157122**	**11567**	**100.00**	**100.00**	**100.00**
一　人　户　Single	1313477	10241	701	7.37	6.52	6.06
二　人　户　Two People	2213696	26939	2056	12.43	17.15	17.77
三　人　户　Three People	5282876	54650	3964	29.65	34.78	34.27
四　人　户　Four People	4527948	34694	2486	25.42	22.08	21.49
五　人　户　Five People	2662200	19352	1528	14.94	12.32	13.21
六　人　户　Six People	1067291	7645	567	5.99	4.86	4.90
七　人　户　Seven People	436168	2348	180	2.45	1.49	1.56
八人及以上户　Eight People and Above	312269	1253	85	1.75	0.80	0.73

3-8 全省分年龄育龄妇女生育孩次状况
LIVE BIRTH AND LIVING CHILDREN FOR WOMEN

1998年人口变动情况抽样调查资料　　Sampling Survey in 1998

年龄（岁） Age (Year)	出生人数（人） Birth Persons	孩次状况 Children			生育率（‰） Birth Rate
		一孩（%） One Child Proportion	二孩（%） Two Children Proportion	三孩及以上（%） Three and above Children Proportion	
总计　Total	**432**	**91.44**	**7.64**	**0.92**	**38.48**
15－19	1	100.00			0.87
20－24	204	98.04	1.96		143.86
25－29	194	90.21	8.76	1.03	100.18
30－34	25	68.00	28.00	4.00	11.84
35－39	6	16.67	83.33		4.03
40－44	2	50.00		50.00	1.20

3-9 从 业 人 数
EMPLOYMENT

单位:万人 (10000 persons)

年 份 Year	从业人数 Total Employment	职工人数 Staff and Workers	国有经济单位 State-Owned Units	城镇集体经济单位 Collective-Owned Units	其他经济类型单位 Other-Ownership Units	城镇私营企业从业人员和个体劳动者 Urban Self-Employment	乡村劳动者 Rural Collective Labors	其他从业人员 Others
1978	2777.72	581.50	366.37	215.13		1.62	2194.60	
1980	2821.03	644.15	401.98	242.17		2.75	2174.13	
1985	3262.97	782.44	468.80	305.39	8.25	11.86	2468.67	
1986	3350.02	816.00	487.91	318.73	9.36	11.69	2522.33	
1987	3429.69	845.26	506.68	326.72	11.86	14.53	2569.90	
1988	3502.65	873.00	527.52	331.40	14.08	16.13	2613.52	
1989	3519.83	867.55	525.24	324.73	17.58	19.09	2633.19	
1990	3569.13	879.85	536.88	323.34	19.63	23.57	2665.71	
1991	3600.27	899.27	551.52	324.91	22.84	21.92	2679.08	
1992	3613.90	904.09	562.69	313.81	27.59	23.63	2686.18	
1993	3639.04	914.73	574.02	293.57	47.14	37.11	2674.39	12.81
1994	3639.90	909.83	571.39	277.77	60.67	52.99	2666.04	11.04
1995	3649.69	915.98	576.24	273.96	65.78	65.89	2657.32	10.50
1996	3647.09	905.52	575.48	256.91	73.13	72.80	2657.98	10.79
1997	3658.05	893.74	577.54	239.61	76.59	90.12	2662.90	11.29
1998	3687.85	870.01	552.47	219.73	97.81	129.89	2671.54	16.41

3-10 分三次产业的从业人数
THREE INDUSTRY EMPLOYMENT

单位:万人 (10000 persons)

年 份 Year	从业人数 Employment	第一产业 Primary Industry		第二产业 Secondary Industry		第三产业 Tertiary Industry	
		人数 Population	比重 (%) Proportion	人数 Population	比重 (%) Proportion	人数 Population	比重 (%) Proportion
1978	2777.72	1937.06	69.7	544.57	19.6	296.09	10.7
1980	2821.03	1987.28	70.4	546.48	19.4	287.27	10.2
1985	3262.97	1738.09	53.2	1065.75	32.7	459.13	14.1
1986	3350.02	1678.71	50.1	1140.36	34.0	530.95	15.9
1987	3429.69	1652.89	48.2	1213.67	35.4	563.13	16.4
1988	3502.65	1654.31	47.2	1251.03	35.7	597.31	17.1
1989	3519.83	1714.69	48.7	1215.40	34.5	589.74	16.8
1990	3569.13	1745.12	48.9	1208.00	33.8	616.01	17.3
1991	3600.27	1770.76	49.2	1200.37	33.3	629.14	17.5
1992	3613.90	1722.00	47.6	1220.76	33.8	671.14	18.6
1993	3639.04	1652.07	45.4	1258.31	34.6	728.66	20.0
1994	3639.90	1616.51	44.4	1250.49	34.4	772.90	21.2
1995	3649.69	1564.70	42.9	1271.74	34.8	813.25	22.3
1996	3647.09	1551.79	42.5	1246.84	34.2	848.46	23.3
1997	3658.05	1554.22	42.5	1219.15	33.3	884.68	24.2
1998	3687.85	1551.87	42.1	1189.22	32.2	946.76	25.7

3-11 分行业从业人数（1998）
CATEGORY EMPLOYMENT

单位：万人　　　　(10000 persons)

行业	Items	从业人数 Employment	国有单位职工 State-Owned Units	城镇集体单位职工 Collective-Owned Units	其他单位职工 Other
总计	**Total**	**3570.6**	**471.52**	**161.85**	**119.39**
农、林、牧、渔业	Farming, Forestry, Animal Husbandry and Fishery	1555.73	22.42	0.69	0.09
采掘业	Excavation	22.20	17.48	1.08	3.35
制造业	Manufacturing	787.28	124.30	75.24	92.83
电力、煤气及水的生产和供应业	Power, Gas and Water Production and Supply	13.05	10.71	0.70	1.54
建筑业	Construction	282.14	18.13	12.65	2.15
地质勘查业、水利管理业	Geological Prospecting and Water Conservancy	6.03	5.74	0.23	
交通运输、仓储及邮电通信业	Transportation, Storge, Postal and Telecommunication Service	144.39	34.17	10.17	3.36
批发和零售贸易、餐饮业	Wholesale, Retail Sales and Catering Trade	272.85	47.34	38.93	11.15
金融、保险业	Banking and Insurance	18.55	10.89	3.35	1.46
房地产业	Real Estate	5.89	4.13	0.83	0.69
社会服务业	Social Service	60.63	18.07	4.81	2.31
卫生、体育和社会福利业	Health Care, Sports and Social Welfare	39.64	19.62	8.97	0.02
教育、文化艺术和广播电影电视业	Education, Culture, Art, Radio, Film and Television	100.28	82.24	2.42	0.07
科学研究和综合技术服务业	Scientific Research and Polytechnical Service	10.51	7.82	0.14	0.10
国家机关、政党机关和社会团体	Goverment Agencies, Party Agencies and Social Organizations	62.10	43.19	0.67	
其他行业	Others	189.33	5.27	0.97	0.09

续表 Continued

单位：万人　　　　(10000 persons)

行业	Items	城镇私营企业从业人员和个体劳动者 Urban Self-Employment	乡村劳动者 Rural Labors	其他从业人员 Others
总计	**Total**	**129.89**	**2671.54**	**16.41**
农、林、牧、渔业	Farming, Forestry, Animal Husbandry and Fishery	0.22	1531.46	0.85
采掘业	Excavation	0.06		0.05
制造业	Manufacturing	27.02	462.51	5.38
电力、煤气及水的生产和供应业	Power, Gas and Water Production and Supply			0.10
建筑业	Construction	2.14	245.70	1.37
地质勘查业、水利管理业	Geological Prospecting and Water Conservancy			0.06
交通运输、仓储及邮电通信业	Transportation, Storge, Postal and Telecommunication Service	4.33	91.17	1.19
批发和零售贸易、餐饮业	Wholesale, Retail Sales and Catering Trade	78.20	95.12	2.11
金融、保险业	Banking and Insurance		2.17	0.68
房地产业	Real Estate			0.24
社会服务业	Social Service	15.69	18.75	1.00
卫生、体育和社会福利业	Health Care, Sports and Social Welfare		10.25	0.78
教育、文化艺术和广播电影电视业	Education, Culture, Art, Radio, Film and Television		13.92	1.63
科学研究和综合技术服务业	Scientific Research and Polytechnical Service		2.20	0.25
国家机关、政党机关和社会团体	Goverment Agencies, Party Agencies and Social Organizations		17.58	0.66
其他行业	Others	2.23	180.71	0.06

注：本表从业人数不包括下岗职工。
Note: Laid off staff and workers were excluded in employment.

3-12 城镇单位(不含私营、个体)从业人员(1998)
URBAN UNITS EMPLOYMENT
(Excluded Privates and Individuals)

单位:万人 (10000 persons)

项目	Items	从业人员年末人数 Year end Employment	在岗职工 Employed	其他从业人员 Other	离开本单位仍保留劳动关系的职工 Workers Left-self Units but Still Remained Labor Relation
总计	**Total**	**769.17**	**752.76**	**16.41**	**117.25**
按登记注册类型分	**Grouped by Type of Registeration**				
国有单位	State-owned Units	480.57	471.52	9.05	62.07
城镇集体单位	Urban Collective-owned Units	165.40	161.85	3.55	40.68
其他单位	Other Units	123.20	119.39	3.81	14.50
#内资经济	Inner Funded	76.65	74.82	1.83	11.89
外商投资经济	Foreign Funded	26.41	25.41	1.00	1.38
港、澳、台投资经济	Hong Kong Macao and Taiwan Funded	20.14	19.16	0.98	1.23
按企业、事业、机关分	**Grouped by Character of the Units**				
企业	Enterprises	562.40	550.06	12.34	115.42
事业	Institutions	163.29	159.78	3.51	1.59
机关	Government Agencies	43.48	42.92	0.56	0.24
按国民经济行业分	**Grouped by Sector**				
农、林、牧、渔业	Farming, Forestry, Animal Husbandry and Fishery	24.05	23.20	0.85	1.75
采掘业	Excavation	22.14	22.09	0.05	4.00
制造业	Manafacturing	297.75	292.37	5.38	76.48
电力、煤气及水的生产和供应业	Electric Power, Gas and Water Production and Supply	13.05	12.95	0.10	0.27
建筑业	Construction	34.30	32.93	1.37	3.80
地质勘查业、水利管理业	Geological Prospecting and Water Conservency	6.30	5.97	0.06	0.29
交通运输、仓储及邮电通信业	Transportation, Storage, Postal and Telecommunication Services	48.89	47.70	1.19	5.89
批发和零售贸易、餐饮业	Wholesale, Retail Trade and Food Services	99.53	97.42	2.11	21.82
金融、保险业	Banking and Insurance	16.38	15.70	0.68	0.02
房地产业	Real Estate Management	5.89	5.65	0.24	0.26
社会服务业	Social Services	26.19	25.19	1.00	1.56
卫生、体育和社会福利业	Health Care, Sports and Social Welfare	29.39	28.61	0.78	0.12
教育、文化艺术和广播电影电视业	Education, Cultrue and Arts, Radio, Film and Television	89.36	84.73	1.63	0.26
科学研究和综合技术服务业	Scientific Research and Polytechnical Services	8.31	8.06	0.25	0.20
国家机关、政党机关和社会团体	Government Agencies, Party Agencies and Social Organizations	44.52	43.86	0.66	0.15
其他行业	Other Sectors	6.39	6.33	0.06	0.38

3-13 城镇单位(不含私营、个体)在岗职工人数(1998)
NUMBER OF STAFF AND WORKERS EMPLOYED (ON POST)
(Excluding Privates and Individuals)

单位:万人 (10000 persons)

项目	Items	在岗职工年末人数 Number of Staff and Workers Employed (year end)	国有单位 State-Owned Units	城镇集体单位 City and Town Collective Units	其他单位 Other Units
总计	**Total**	**752.76**	**471.52**	**161.85**	**119.39**
按企业、事业、机关分	**Grouped by Character of the Units**				
企业	Enterprises	550.06	283.95	146.77	119.34
事业	Institutions	159.78	144.09	14.74	0.05
机关	Government Agencies	42.92	42.58	0.34	
按国民经济行业分	**Grouped by Sector**				
农、林、牧、渔业	Farming, Forestry, Animal Husbandry and Fishery	23.20	22.42	0.69	0.09
采掘业	Excavation	22.09	17.48	1.08	3.53
制造业	Manafacturing	292.37	124.30	75.24	92.83
电力、煤气及水的生产和供应业	Electric Power, Gas and Water Production and Supply	12.95	10.71	0.70	1.54
建筑业	Construction	32.93	18.13	12.65	2.15
地质勘查业、水利管理业	Geological Prospecting and Water Conservency	5.97	5.74	0.23	
交通运输、仓储及邮电通信业	Transportation, Storage, Postal and Telecommunication Services	47.70	34.17	10.17	3.36
批发和零售贸易、餐饮业	Wholesale, Retail Trade and Food Services	97.42	47.34	38.93	11.15
金融、保险业	Banking and Insurance	15.70	10.89	3.35	1.46
房地产业	Real Estate Management	5.65	4.13	0.83	0.69
社会服务业	Social Services	25.19	18.07	4.81	2.31
卫生、体育和社会福利业	Health Care, Sports and Social Welfare	28.61	19.62	8.97	0.02
教育、文化艺术和广播电影电视业	Education, Cultrue and Arts, Radio, Film and Television	84.73	82.24	2.42	0.07
科学研究和综合技术服务业	Scientific Research and Polytechnical Services	8.06	7.82	0.14	0.10
国家机关、政党机关和社会团体	Government Agencies, Party Agencies and Social Organizations	43.86	43.19	0.67	
其他行业	Other Sectors	6.33	5.27	0.97	0.09

3－14 制造业在岗职工人数（1998）
NUMBER OF STAFF AND WORKERS EMPLOYED（ON POST）IN MANUFACTURING INDUSTRY

单位：万人 (persons)

项目	Items	在岗职工年末人数 Number of Staff and Workers Employed (year end)	国有单位 State-Owned Units	城镇集体单位 City and Town Collective Units	其他单位 Other Units
制造业总计	**Manufacturing Total**	**292.37**	**124.30**	**75.24**	**92.83**
食品加工业	Food Processing	9.90	6.62	1.20	2.08
食品制造业	Food Producting	6.47	3.05	0.78	2.64
饮料制造业	Beverage Producting	5.53	3.09	0.35	2.09
烟草加工业	Tobacco Processing	0.55	0.55		
纺织业	Textile Industry	50.04	22.78	15.24	12.02
服装及其他纤维制品制造业	Garments and Other Fiber Products	12.60	1.45	5.71	5.44
皮革、毛皮、羽绒及其制品业	Leather, Furs, Down and Related Products	2.60	0.69	0.92	0.99
木材加工及竹、藤、棕、草制品业	Timber Processing and Bamboo, Rattan, Palm and Straw Works	0.88	0.18	0.26	0.44
家具制造业	Furniture Manufacturing	0.84	0.13	0.61	0.10
造纸及纸制品业	Papermaking and Paper Products	3.94	1.40	1.35	1.19
印刷业、记录媒介的复制	Printing and Record Processing	3.71	1.87	1.03	0.81
文教体育用品制造业	Stationery, Education and Sports Goods	2.93	0.25	1.80	0.88
石油加工及炼焦业	Petroleum Processing and Coking Products	3.16	2.31	0.49	0.36
化学原料及化学制品制造业	Raw Chemical Material and Chemical Products	27.32	13.91	4.00	9.41
医药制造业	Medical and Pharmaceutical Products	6.66	3.31	0.87	2.48
化学纤维制造业	Chemical Fibers	4.48	1.31	0.25	2.92
橡胶制品业	Rubber Products	3.23	0.82	0.92	1.49
塑料制品业	Plastic Products	5.29	0.59	2.47	2.23
非金属矿物制品业	Nonmetal Mineral Products	16.20	7.96	3.89	4.35
黑色金属冶炼及压延加工业	Smelting and Processing of Ferrous Metals	8.83	4.58	1.12	3.13
有色金属冶炼及压延加工业	Smelting and Processing of Nonferrous Metals	1.72	0.84	0.38	0.50
金属制品业	Metal Products	8.70	1.44	3.07	4.19
普通机械制造业	Ordinarty Machinery Manufacturing	28.13	12.88	6.61	8.64
专用设备制造业	Special Purpose Equipment Manufacturing	17.56	9.04	5.12	3.40
交通运输设备制造业	Transportation Equipment Manufacturing	18.03	9.08	5.12	3.83
电气机械及器材制造业	Electric Equipment and Machinery	15.75	5.27	4.61	5.87
电子及通信设备制造业	Electronic and Telecommunication	14.97	5.65	2.27	7.05
仪器仪表及文化、办公用机械制造业	Instruments, Meters, Cultural and Official Machinery	5.22	2.01	1.16	2.05
其他制造业	Other Manufacturing	6.82	0.99	3.64	2.19

3-15 分经济类型女职工人数与比重
FEMALE STAFF AND WORKERS BY OWNERSHIP AND PROPORTION

年份 Year	年末女职工人数(万人) Female Staff and Workers (Year-end) (10000 person)				占全部职工人数的比重(%) Proportion in Total (percent)			
	合计 Total	国有单位 State-Owned Units	城镇集体单位 Urban Collective-Owned Units	其他单位 Other Units	合计 Total	国有单位 State-Owned Units	城镇集体单位 Urban Collective-Owned Units	其他单位 Other Units
1978	198.19	105.64	92.55		34.1	28.8	43.0	
1980	237.52	128.00	109.52		36.9	31.8	45.2	
1985	295.21	157.13	133.97	4.11	37.7	33.5	43.9	49.8
1986	310.84	165.56	140.65	4.63	38.1	33.9	44.1	49.5
1987	324.33	172.83	145.55	5.95	38.4	34.1	44.5	50.2
1988	337.34	182.03	148.31	7.00	38.6	34.5	44.8	49.7
1989	338.45	182.00	147.66	8.79	39.0	34.7	45.5	50.0
1990	346.63	188.95	147.98	9.70	39.4	35.2	45.8	49.4
1991	355.28	194.27	149.74	11.27	39.5	35.2	46.1	49.3
1992	358.94	200.95	144.38	13.61	39.7	35.7	46.0	49.3
1993	364.71	207.50	134.34	22.87	39.9	36.1	45.8	48.5
1994	362.29	204.80	128.00	29.49	39.8	35.8	46.1	48.6
1995	370.57	211.04	127.47	32.06	40.5	36.6	46.5	48.7
1996	367.41	210.95	120.77	35.69	40.6	36.7	47.0	48.8
1997	362.32	212.57	112.67	37.08	40.5	36.8	47.0	48.4
1998	346.11	201.40	99.04	45.67	39.8	36.5	45.1	46.7

3-16 离休、退休、退职人数
NUMBERS OF VCSR, RETIRED AND RESIGNED

单位:万人 (10000 persons)

年份 Year	年末人数 Population (Year-end)	国有单位 State-Owned Units	城镇集体单位 Urban Collective-Owned Units	其他单位 Other Units	离退休人员与退职职工比例 VCSR, Retired Quited Staff and Workers as percentage of Staff and Workers	(以职工为100) Formal Staff and Workers=100		
						国有单位 State-Owned Units	城镇集体单位 Urban Collective-Owned Units	其他单位 Other Units
1978	21.77	14.19	7.58		3.7	3.9	3.5	
1980	61.52	35.37	26.15		9.6	8.8	10.8	
1985	111.17	61.83	48.35	0.99	14.2	13.2	15.8	12.0
1986	114.50	64.34	48.96	1.20	14.0	13.2	15.4	12.8
1987	125.35	70.07	53.87	1.41	14.8	13.8	16.5	11.9
1988	130.90	74.92	54.15	1.83	15.0	14.2	16.3	13.0
1989	140.42	81.16	57.00	2.26	16.2	15.5	17.6	12.9
1990	153.59	90.68	60.32	2.59	17.5	16.9	18.7	13.2
1991	158.37	93.91	61.50	2.96	17.6	17.0	18.9	13.0
1992	164.68	100.01	61.15	3.52	18.2	17.8	19.5	12.8
1993	173.15	106.09	61.49	5.57	18.9	18.5	20.9	11.8
1994	190.40	110.70	72.43	7.27	20.9	19.4	26.1	12.0
1995	200.39	121.11	71.29	7.99	21.9	21.0	26.0	12.1
1996	205.02	130.85	64.66	9.51	22.6	22.7	25.2	13.0
1997	216.55	139.25	67.01	10.29	24.23	24.11	28.0	13.4
1998	227.95	147.42	70.52	10.01	26.20	26.70	32.10	10.20

3－17 城镇失业人数及失业率
UNEMPLOYED POPULATION AND UNEMPLOYED RATE IN URBAN

单位:万人 (10000 persons)

年份 Year	本年失业人数 Total Unemployees	本年失业人员就业人数 Unemployed-Reemployees	年末尚有失业人数 Unemploy-ment	#失业青年 Unemployment Younger	#女失业青年 Unemployment Female Younger	城镇失业率(%) Unemploy-ment Rate
1979	89.00	54.70	34.30			5.4
1980	55.47	32.78	20.29			3.1
1985	23.63	15.25	7.15	5.09	3.17	0.9
1986	26.12	16.23	8.36	6.68	3.95	1.0
1987	27.32	16.93	9.35	7.81	4.39	1.1
1988	31.92	18.94	12.02	9.40	5.20	1.3
1989	51.45	22.03	27.76	18.53	10.93	3.0
1990	52.72	28.06	22.52	17.23	9.21	2.4
1991	43.90	23.33	18.68	13.42	7.81	2.0
1992	42.15	21.43	18.81	14.61	8.44	2.0
1993	41.84	20.64	19.43	15.08	8.36	2.0
1994	43.01	22.19	19.58	14.71	8.20	2.0
1995	42.32	21.49	20.13	14.68	8.02	2.0
1996	45.19	20.78	22.34	13.74	7.37	2.2
1997	46.38	21.40	23.80	14.39	7.67	2.4
1998	46.81	21.61	24.26	13.14	7.17	2.6

3－18 单位从业人员变动情况(1998)
NUMBER OF EMPLOYEES CHANGES

单位:万人 (10000 persons)

指标	Items	职工变动人数 Number of Staff and Workers Changes	国有单位 State-Owned Units	城镇集体单位 Urban Collective-Owned Units	其他单位 Other Units
增加人数	**Number of Persons Increment**	**42.57**	**23.25**	**7.01**	**12.31**
从农村招收	Recruited from Rural	4.36	1.38	1.23	1.75
从城镇招收	Recruited from Urban	5.38	1.88	0.97	2.53
录用的复员转业军人	Demobilized Soldiers	1.43	1.05	0.20	0.18
录用的大、中专、技工学校毕业生	Graduates from University, College, Secondary School and Technical School	10.80	7.46	1.17	2.17
调入人数	Number of the Transferred into	12.49	7.47	1.95	3.07
#省外调入	From Outside City	0.65	0.59	0.02	0.04
其他	Others	8.11	4.01	1.49	2.61
减少人数	**Number of Persons Reduction**	**114.15**	**61.71**	**34.37**	**18.07**
离休、退休、退职	VCSR Retire and Resigned	17.79	11.95	3.87	1.97
开除、除名、辞退	Expel, Name Removed, Discharge	4.04	1.68	1.35	1.01
终止、解除合同	Stop and Terminate the Contract	13.82	5.93	3.98	3.91
调出人数	Number of the Transferred Out	12.27	7.53	2.35	2.39
#调往省外	To Outside City	0.28	0.24	0.02	0.02
其他	Others	66.23	34.62	22.82	8.79

4. 人民生活

PEOPLE'S LIVELIHOOD

4 人 民 生 活
PEOPLE'S LIVELIHOOD

1 9 9 8

职工工资总额	Total Wage Bill of Staff and Workers	654.56	亿元	(10^8 yuan)
#国有经济	State-Owned Units	455.05	亿元	(10^8 yuan)
职工平均工资	Average Wage Bill of Staff and Workers	7516	元	(yuan)
#国有经济	State-Owned Units	8232	元	(yuan)
保险福利费用总额	Total Value of Insurance and Welfare Funds	234.93	亿元	(10^8 yuan)
#职工保险福利费	Insurance and Welfare Funds of Staff and Workers	78.53	亿元	(10^8 yuan)
城镇居民人均可支配收入	Per Capita Allocatable Income Urban Residents	6018	元	(yuan)
城镇居民人均消费性支出	Per Capita Consumptive Expenditures of Urban Residents	4889	元	(yuan)
农民人均纯收入	Per Capita Net Income of Rural Residents	3377	元	(yuan)
农民人均生活消费支出	Per Catia Living Expenditures of Rural Residents	2337	亿元	(10^8 yuan)

职工平均工资（元）

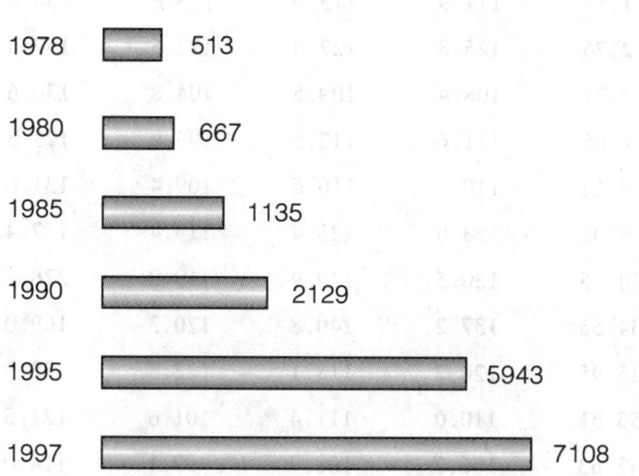

城乡居民生活消费支出构成(%)
1998

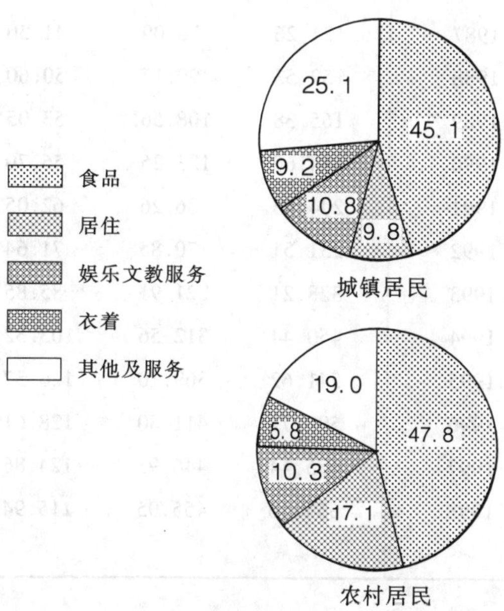

4-1 职工工资总额及指数
TOTAL WAGE BILL AND INDEX OF FORMAL EMPLOYEES

年份 Year	绝对数（亿元） Value (10^8 yuan)				指数（以上年为100） Index(previous year=100)			
	全部职工 Total	国有经济单位 State-Owned Units	城镇集体经济单位 Collective-Owned Units	其他经济类型单位 Other-Ownership Units	全部职工 Total	国有经济单位 State-Owned Units	城镇集体经济单位 Collective-Owned Units	其他经济类型单位 Other-Ownership Units
1971	16.38	11.82	4.56					
1972	18.51	13.04	5.47		113.0	110.3	120.0	
1973	19.38	13.49	5.89		104.7	103.5	107.7	
1974	20.22	13.76	6.46		104.3	102.0	109.7	
1975	21.20	14.03	7.17		104.8	102.0	111.0	
1976	22.50	14.59	7.91		106.1	104.0	110.3	
1977	26.24	17.91	8.33		116.6	122.8	105.3	
1978	29.05	19.84	9.21		110.7	110.8	110.6	
1979	33.10	22.46	10.64		113.9	113.2	115.5	
1980	41.63	27.99	13.64		125.8	124.6	128.2	
1981	44.13	29.60	14.53		106.0	105.8	106.5	
1982	48.14	32.35	15.79		109.1	109.3	108.7	
1983	50.78	34.41	16.37		105.5	106.4	103.7	
1984	67.28	43.34	23.25	0.69	132.5	126.0	142.0	
1985	86.17	55.10	30.09	0.98	128.1	127.1	129.4	142.0
1986	105.56	67.93	36.28	1.35	122.5	123.3	120.6	137.8
1987	121.26	78.09	41.30	1.87	114.9	115.0	113.8	138.5
1988	152.53	99.17	50.60	2.76	125.8	127.0	122.5	147.6
1989	165.38	108.56	53.05	3.77	108.4	109.5	104.8	136.6
1990	184.60	123.25	56.70	4.65	111.6	113.5	106.9	123.3
1991	204.43	136.26	62.05	6.12	110.7	110.6	109.4	131.6
1992	251.51	170.85	71.64	9.02	123.0	125.4	115.4	147.4
1993	328.21	221.91	85.85	20.45	130.5	129.9	119.8	226.7
1994	450.44	312.56	103.32	34.56	137.2	140.8	120.3	169.0
1995	541.62	369.10	126.57	45.95	120.2	118.1	122.5	132.9
1996	595.72	411.30	128.61	55.81	110.0	111.4	101.6	121.5
1997	635.44	446.95	124.86	63.63	106.7	108.7	97.1	114.0
1998	654.56	455.05	115.94	83.57	103.0	101.8	92.9	131.3

注：本表包括下岗职工。

Note: The figure included laid off staff and workers.

4-2 城镇单位(不含私营、个体)从业人员劳动报酬(1998)
LABOUR REWARD OF URBAN UNITS EMPLOYMENT (Excluding Privates and Individuals)

单位:亿元 (10⁸ yuan)

项目	Items	从业人员全年劳动报酬 Annual Labour Reward of Employment	在岗职工工资总额 Total Wage Value of Staff and Workers (on Post)	其他从业人员劳动报酬 Labour Reward of Other Employment	离开本单位仍保留劳动关系职工生活费 Living Income of Workers Left-self Unit Still Remian Labour Relation
总计	**Total**	**642.02**	**628.49**	**13.53**	**26.07**
按登记注册类型分	**Grouped by Type of Registeration**				
国有单位	State-owned Units	427.79	422.34	5.45	15.30
城镇集体单位	Urban Collective-owned Units	101.18	99.49	1.69	6.80
其他单位	Other Units	113.05	106.66	6.39	3.97
#内资经济	Inner Funded	66.04	64.48	1.56	3.27
外商投资经济	Foreign Funded	29.03	25.57	3.46	0.42
港、澳、台投资经济	Hong Kong Macao and Taiwan Funded	17.98	16.61	1.37	0.28
按企业、事业、机关分	**Grouped by Character of the Units**				
企业	Enterprises	444.30	432.88	11.42	25.42
事业	Institutions	151.35	149.57	1.78	0.57
机关	Government Agencies	46.37	46.04	0.33	0.08
按国民经济行业分	**Grouped by Sector**				
农、林、牧、渔业	Farming, Forestry, Animal Husbandry and Fishery	13.73	13.42	0.31	0.23
采掘业	Excavation	18.46	18.43	0.03	1.32
制造业	Manafacturing	227.93	221.43	6.50	17.11
电力、煤气及水的生产和供应业	Electric Power, Gas and Water Production and Supply	17.00	16.91	0.09	0.10
建筑业	Construction	28.50	27.68	0.82	1.04
地质勘查业、水利管理业	Geological Prospecting and Water Conservency	5.00	4.98	0.02	0.09
交通运输、仓储及邮电通信业	Transportation, Storage, Postal and Telecommunication Services	46.99	46.09	0.90	1.44
批发和零售贸易、餐饮业	Wholesale, Retail Trade and Food Services	64.08	62.76	1.32	3.73
金融、保险业	Banking and Insurance	18.55	17.94	0.61	0.01
房地产业	Real Estate Management	6.41	6.15	0.26	0.08
社会服务业	Social Services	24.09	23.21	0.88	0.48
卫生、体育和社会福利业	Health Care, Sports and Social Welfare	28.81	28.36	0.45	0.04
教育、文化艺术和广播电影电视业	Education, Cultrue and Arts, Radio, Film and Television	79.65	78.89	0.76	0.08
科学研究和综合技术服务业	Scientific Research and Polytechnical Services	9.94	9.76	0.18	0.09
国家机关、政党机关和社会团体	Government Agencies, Party Agencies and Social Organigations	47.37	47.01	0.36	0.06
其他行业	Other Sectors	5.51	5.47	0.04	0.17

4－3 城镇单位(不含私营、个体)在岗职工工资总额(1998)
TOTAL WAGE BILL OF STAFF AND WORKERS (ON POST) IN CITY AND TOWN UNITS
(Excluded Privates and Individuals)

单位:亿元 (10^8 yuan)

项目	Items	在岗职工全年工资总额 Annual Total Wage	国有单位 State-Owned Uints	城镇集体单位 Collective-Owned Uints	其他单位 Other Uints
总计	**Total**	**628.49**	**422.34**	**99.49**	**106.66**
按企业、事业、机关分	**Grouped by Character of the Units**				
企业	Enterprises	432.88	239.48	86.81	106.59
事业	Institutions	149.57	137.14	12.36	0.07
机关	Government Agencies	46.04	45.72	0.32	
按国民经济行业分	**Grouped by Sector**				
农、林、牧、渔业	Farming, Forestry, Animal Husbandry and Fishery	13.42	12.94	0.42	0.06
采掘业	Excavation	18.43	15.71	0.52	2.20
制造业	Manafacturing	221.43	96.39	44.22	80.82
电力、煤气及水的生产和供应业	Electric Power, Gas and Water Production and Supply	16.91	14.13	0.72	2.06
建筑业	Construction	27.68	17.06	8.61	2.01
地质勘查业、水利管理业	Geological Prospecting and Water Conservency	4.98	4.81	0.17	
交通运输、仓储及邮电通信业	Transportation, Storage, Postal and Telecommunication Services	46.09	36.56	5.78	3.75
批发和零售贸易、餐饮业	Wholesale, Retail Trade and Food Services	62.76	32.46	20.37	9.93
金融、保险业	Banking and Insurance	17.94	12.64	3.05	2.25
房地产业	Real Estate Management	6.15	4.42	0.82	0.91
社会服务业	Social Services	23.21	17.16	3.77	2.28
卫生、体育和社会福利业	Health Care, Sports and Social Welfare	28.36	20.35	7.99	0.02
教育、文化艺术和广播电影电视业	Education, Cultrue and Arts, Radio, Film and Television	78.89	77.25	1.55	0.09
科学研究和综合技术服务业	Scientific Research and Polytechnical Services	9.76	9.49	0.13	0.14
国家机关、政党机关和社会团体	Government Agencies, Party Agencies and Social Organigations	47.01	46.40	0.61	
其他行业	Other Sectors	5.47	4.57	0.76	0.14

4－4 制造业在岗职工工资总额（1998）
TOTAL WAGE BILL OF STAFF AND WORKERS (ON POST) OF MANUFACTURING INDUSTRY

单位：亿元 (10^8 yuan)

项　　目	Items	全年工资总额 Annual Total Wage Bill	国有单位 State-Owned Units	城镇集体单位 Urban Collective-Owned Units	其他单位 Other Units
制造业总计	**Manufacturing Total**	**221.43**	**96.39**	**44.22**	**80.82**
食品加工业	Food Processing	5.79	3.85	0.63	1.31
食品制造业	Food Producting	4.46	1.77	0.41	2.28
饮料制造业	Beverage Producting	3.44	1.80	0.11	1.53
烟草加工业	Tobacco Processing	0.97	0.97		
纺织业	Textile Industry	31.86	15.10	8.19	8.57
服装及其他纤维制品制造业	Garments and Other Fiber Products	7.66	0.99	2.90	3.77
皮革、毛皮、羽绒及其制品业	Leather, Furs, Down and Related Products	1.50	0.42	0.42	0.66
木材加工及竹、藤、棕、草制品业	Timber Processing and Bamboo, Rattan, Palm and Straw Works	0.55	0.10	0.12	0.33
家具制造业	Furniture Manufacturing	0.46	0.09	0.31	0.06
造纸及纸制品业	Papermaking and Paper Products	2.46	0.79	0.72	0.95
印刷业、记录媒介的复制	Printing and Record Processing	2.45	1.25	0.61	0.59
文教体育用品制造业	Stationery, Education and Sports Goods	1.92	0.11	1.22	0.59
石油加工及炼焦业	Petroleum Processing and Coking Products	4.07	3.06	0.61	0.40
化学原料及化学制品制造业	Raw Chemical Material and Chemical Products	22.82	10.70	2.62	9.50
医药制造业	Medical and Pharmaceutical Products	5.52	2.44	0.61	2.47
化学纤维制造业	Chemical Fibers	4.32	0.94	0.19	3.19
橡胶制品业	Rubber Products	2.54	0.73	0.53	1.28
塑料制品业	Plastic Products	4.08	0.50	1.68	1.90
非金属矿物制品业	Nonmetal Mineral Products	10.56	5.41	2.04	3.11
黑色金属冶炼及压延加工业	Smelting and Processing of Ferrous Metals	8.94	3.89	0.76	4.29
有色金属冶炼及压延加工业	Smelting and Processing of Nonferrous Metals	1.39	0.70	0.25	0.44
金属制品业	Metal Products	6.76	1.45	1.71	3.60
普通机械制造业	Ordinarty Machinery Manufacturing	22.30	10.95	4.05	7.30
专用设备制造业	Special Purpose Equipment Manufacturing	13.16	7.21	3.03	2.92
交通运输设备制造业	Transportation Equipment Manufacturing	16.21	9.14	3.24	3.83
电气机械及器材制造业	Electric Equipment and Machinery	12.46	4.48	2.84	5.14
电子及通信设备制造业	Electronic and Telecommunication	13.97	5.26	1.47	7.24
仪器仪表及文化、办公用机械制造业	Instruments, Meters, Cultural and Official Machinery	4.24	1.59	0.73	1.92
其他制造业	Other Manufacturing	4.39	0.56	2.22	1.61

4－5 职工年平均货币工资及指数

ANNUAL AVERAGE MONEY WAGE AND INDEX OF STAFF

年 份 year	绝 对 数(元) Value (yuan)				指 数(以上年为 100) Index(preceding year＝100)			
	全部职工 Total	国有经济单位 State-Owned Units	城镇集体经济单位 Collective-Owned Units	其他经济类型单位 Other-Ownership Units	全部职工 Total	国有经济单位 State-Owned Units	城镇集体经济单位 Collective-Owned Units	其他经济类型单位 Other-Ownership Units
1971	467	502	396					
1972	481	515	415		103.0	102.6	104.8	
1973	476	523	396		99.0	101.6	95.4	
1974	495	543	416		104.0	103.8	105.1	
1975	491	534	423		99.2	98.3	101.7	
1976	483	531	414		98.4	99.4	97.9	
1977	474	517	402		98.1	97.4	97.1	
1978	513	563	432		108.2	108.9	107.5	
1979	565	618	478		110.3	109.8	110.9	
1980	667	721	578		117.8	116.7	120.7	
1981	672	718	594		100.7	99.6	102.8	
1982	703	748	626		104.6	104.2	105.4	
1983	723	768	643		102.8	102.7	102.7	
1984	931	1003	820	1012	128.8	130.6	127.5	
1985	1135	1211	1015	1237	121.9	120.7	123.8	122.2
1986	1327	1430	1166	1468	116.9	118.1	114.9	118.7
1987	1471	1581	1295	1639	110.9	110.6	111.1	111.6
1988	1796	1936	1564	2059	122.1	122.5	120.8	125.6
1989	1918	2082	1639	2185	106.8	107.5	104.8	106.1
1990	2129	2331	1776	2444	111.0	111.9	108.4	111.9
1991	2302	2501	1932	2773	108.1	107.3	108.8	113.5
1992	2800	3057	2292	3370	121.6	122.2	118.6	121.5
1993	3615	3896	2937	4434	129.1	127.4	128.1	131.6
1994	4974	5491	3728	5827	137.6	140.9	126.9	131.4
1995	5943	6441	4621	7137	119.5	117.3	124.0	122.5
1996	6603	7186	4990	7740	111.1	111.6	108.0	108.4
1997	7108	7745	5183	8376	107.6	107.8	103.9	108.2
1998	7516	8232	5250	8588	105.7	106.3	101.3	102.5

注：本表包括下岗职工。

Note：The figures included laid off staff and workers.

4-6 城镇单位(不含私营、个体)从业人员年平均劳动报酬 (1998)
URBAN UNITS EMPLOYMENT ANNUAL AVERAGE LABOUR REWARD (Excluding Privates and Individuals)

单位:元 (yuan)

项目	Items	从业人员年平均劳动报酬 Annual Average Labour Reward of Employment	在岗职工年平均工资 Annual Average Wage of Staff and Workers on Post	其他从业人员年平均劳动报酬 Annual Average Labour Reward of Other Employment	离开本单位仍保留劳动关系的职工年平均生活费 Annual Average Living Income of Workers Left-self Unit Still Remian Labour Relation
总计	**Total**	**8252**	**8256**	**8051**	**2377**
按登记注册类型分	**Grouped by Type of Registeration**				
国有单位	State-owned Units	8816	8872	5928	2654
城镇集体单位	Urban Collective-owned Units	6000	6033	4524	1764
其他单位	Other Units	9104	8867	16399	2946
#内资经济	Inner Funded	8479	8481	8383	2947
外商投资经济	Foreign Funded	11174	10246	33775	3353
港、澳、台投资经济	Hong Kong Macao and Taiwan Funded	8853	8607	13548	2485
按企业、事业、机关分	**Grouped by Character of the Units**				
企业	Enterprises	7760	7731	9018	2356
事业	Institutions	9324	9422	4988	3656
机关	Government Agencies	10750	10816	5754	3388
按国民经济行业分	**Grouped by Sector**				
农、林、牧、渔业	Farming, Forestry, Animal Husbandry and Fishery	5672	5747	3610	1377
采掘业	Excavation	8312	8320	5278	3995
制造业	Manafacturing	7474	7398	11421	2388
电力、煤气及水的生产和供应业	Electric Power, Gas and Water Production and Supply	12884	12929	7529	4889
建筑业	Construction	8250	8298	6890	2933
地质勘查业、水利管理业	Geological Prospecting and Water Conservency	8214	8252	4307	3307
交通运输、仓储及邮电通信业	Transportation, Storage, Postal and Telecommunication Services	9524	9582	7279	2604
批发和零售贸易、餐饮业	Wholesale, Retail Trade and Food Services	6319	6328	5942	1807
金融、保险业	Banking and Insurance	11322	11393	9563	5435
房地产业	Real Estate Management	10877	10899	10352	3770
社会服务业	Social Services	9216	9263	8126	3313
卫生、体育和社会福利业	Health Care, Sports and Social Welfare	9909	10034	5556	3491
教育、文化艺术和广播电影电视业	Education, Cultrue and Arts, Radio, Film and Television	9301	9391	4649	2098
科学研究和综合技术服务业	Scientific Research and Polytechnical Services	11858	11986	7563	4872
国家机关、政党机关和社会团体	Government Agencies, Party Agencies and Social Organigations	10734	10812	5508	4255
其他行业	Other Sectors	8590	8637	5175	4398

4－7 在岗职工平均货币工资（1998）
AVERAGE MONEY WAGE OF STAFF (ON POST)

单位:元 (yuan)

项目	Items	在岗职工年平均工资 Annual Average Wage of Staff (on post)	国有单位 State-Owned Uints	城镇集体单位 Collective-Owned Uints	其他单位 Other Uints
总计	**Total**	**8256**	**8872**	**6033**	**8867**
按企业、事业、机关分	**Grouped by Character of the Units**				
企业	Enterprises	7731	8262	5794	8866
事业	Institutions	9422	9528	8375	13354
机关	Government Agencies	10816	10824	9814	
按国民经济行业分	**Grouped by Sector**				
农、林、牧、渔业	Farming, Forestry, Animal Husbandry and Fishery	5747	5738	5981	6060
采掘业	Excavation	8320	8869	4778	6565
制造业	Manafacturing	7398	7522	5708	8627
电力、煤气及水的生产和供应业	Electric Power, Gas and Water Production and Supply	12929	13020	10509	13359
建筑业	Construction	8298	9148	6888	9102
地质勘查业、水利管理业	Geological Prospecting and Water Conservency	8252	8282	7530	5857
交通运输、仓储及邮电通信业	Transportation, Storage, Postal and Telecommunication Services	9582	10669	5520	11155
批发和零售贸易、餐饮业	Wholesale, Retail Trade and Food Services	6328	6745	5131	8742
金融、保险业	Banking and Insurance	11393	11559	9089	15434
房地产业	Real Estate Management	10899	10715	9976	13086
社会服务业	Social Services	9263	9497	7951	10154
卫生、体育和社会福利业	Health Care, Sports and Social Welfare	10034	10496	9021	9945
教育、文化艺术和广播电视业	Education, Cultrue and Arts, Radio, Film and Television	9391	9488	6179	11186
科学研究和信息技术服务业	Scientific Research and Polytechnical Services	11986	11997	9125	15321
国家机关、政党机关和社会团体	Government Agencies, Party Agencies and Social Organigations	10812	10839	9094	
其他行业	Other Sectors	8637	8662	7860	15588

4－8 制造业在岗职工年平均工资（1998）
ANNUAL AVERAGE WAGE OF STAFF AND WORKERS (ON POST) OF MANUFACTURING INDUSTRY

单位：元 (yuan)

项目	Items	制造业在岗职工年平均工资 Annual Average Wage	国有单位 State-Owned Units	城镇集体单位 Urban Collective-Owned Units	其他单位 Other Units
制造业总计	**Total**	**7398**	**7522**	**5708**	**8627**
食品加工业	Food Processing	5797	5708	5312	6367
食品制造业	Food Producting	6689	5619	5153	8375
饮料制造业	Beverage Producting	6210	5742	3346	7390
烟草加工业	Tobacco Processing	17434	17434		
纺织业	Textile Industry	6057	6159	5226	6901
服装及其他纤维制品制造业	Garments and Other Fiber Products	6054	6725	5011	6995
皮革、毛皮、羽绒及其制品业	Leather, Furs, Down and Related Products	5544	6086	4376	6252
木材加工及竹、藤、棕、草制品业	Timber Processing and Bamboo, Rattan, Palm and Straw Works	5837	5064	4345	6998
家具制造业	Furniture Manufacturing	5343	7151	4810	6474
造纸及纸制品业	Papermaking and Paper Products	6139	5415	5063	8475
印刷业、记录媒介的复制	Printing and Record Processing	6512	6627	5730	7288
文教体育用品制造业	Stationery, Education and Sports Goods	6626	4455	7028	6466
石油加工及炼焦业	Petroleum Processing and Coking Products	12760	13037	12376	11439
化学原料及化学制品制造业	Raw Chemical Material and Chemical Products	8218	7513	6463	10031
医药制造业	Medical and Pharmaceutical Products	8213	7235	7023	9960
化学纤维制造业	Chemical Fibers	9400	6629	7311	10931
橡胶制品业	Rubber Products	7757	8717	5658	8537
塑料制品业	Plastic Products	7488	8024	6544	8409
非金属矿物制品业	Nonmetal Mineral Products	6355	6558	5144	7070
黑色金属冶炼及压延加工业	Smelting and Processing of Ferrous Metals	9758	8275	6399	13105
有色金属冶炼及压延加工业	Smelting and Processing of Nonferrous Metals	7880	8232	6327	8460
金属制品业	Metal Products	7389	9500	5141	8377
普通机械制造业	Ordinarty Machinery Manufacturing	7839	8373	6001	8469
专用设备制造业	Special Purpose Equipment Manufacturing	7352	7921	5745	8292
交通运输设备制造业	Transportation Equipment Manufacturing	8830	10027	6063	9824
电气机械及器材制造业	Electric Equipment and Machinery	7692	8126	5986	8651
电子及通信设备制造业	Electronic and Telecommunication	9281	9205	6142	10431
仪器仪表及文化、办公用机械制造业	Instruments, Meters, Cultural and Official Machinery	7908	7560	5952	9444
其他制造业	Other Manufacturing	6469	6197	5838	7741

4-9 职工平均工资指数
AVERAGE WAGE INDEX OF STAFF AND WORKERS

(1978=100)

年份 Year	全部职工 Total		国有经济单位 State-Owned Units		城镇集体经济单位 Collective-Owned Units		其他经济类型单位 Other Ownership Units	
	平均货币工资指数 Index of Average Money Wages	平均实际工资指数 Index of Average Real Wages	平均货币工资指数 Index of Average Money Wages	平均实际工资指数 Index of Average Real Wages	平均货币工资指数 Index of Average Money Wages	平均实际工资指数 Index of Average Real Wages	平均货币工资指数 Index of Average Money Wages	平均实际工资指数 Index of Average Real Wages
1978	100.0	100.0	100.0	100.0	100.0	100.0		
1980	130.0	121.7	128.1	119.9	133.8	125.3		
1985	221.2	174.9	215.1	170.0	235.0	185.8	122.2	111.5
1986	258.7	192.2	254.0	188.7	269.9	200.5	145.1	124.4
1987	286.7	192.8	280.8	188.8	299.8	201.6	162.0	125.7
1988	350.1	192.0	343.9	188.6	362.0	198.6	203.5	128.8
1989	373.9	176.8	369.8	174.8	379.4	179.4	215.9	117.8
1990	415.0	189.8	414.0	189.3	411.1	188.0	241.5	127.4
1991	448.7	190.5	444.2	188.6	447.2	189.9	274.0	134.2
1992	545.8	213.2	543.0	212.1	530.6	207.3	333.0	149.9
1993	704.7	231.9	692.0	227.7	679.9	223.7	438.1	166.1
1994	969.6	254.6	975.3	256.1	863.0	226.6	575.8	174.2
1995	1158.5	261.7	1144.0	258.5	1069.7	241.7	705.2	183.6
1996	1287.1	262.5	1276.4	260.3	1155.1	235.5	764.8	179.7
1997	1385.6	278.9	1375.7	276.9	1199.8	241.5	827.7	192.0
1998	1465.1	295.0	1462.2	294.4	1215.3	244.7	848.6	196.6

4-10 保险福利费用总额及指数
TOTAL VALUE AND INDEX OF INSURANCE AND WELFARE FUNDS

年份 Year	绝对数(亿元) Value (10^8 yuan)				指数(以上年为100) Index(previous year=100)			
	保险福利费总额 Total Value of Insurance and Welfare Funds	国有经济单位 State-Owned Units	城镇集体经济单位 Collective-Owned Uints	其他经济类型单位 Other-Ownership Uints	保险福利费总额 Total Value of Insurance and Welfare Funds	国有经济单位 State-Owned Units	城镇集体经济单位 Collective-Owned Units	其他经济类型单位 Other-Ownership Units
1978		2.82						
1980	7.06	5.07	1.99		122.5			
1985	20.17	13.57	6.33	0.27	126.5	126.5	125.1	180.0
1986	26.95	18.20	8.40	0.35	133.6	134.1	132.7	129.6
1987	31.86	21.41	9.95	0.50	118.2	117.6	118.5	142.9
1988	42.01	28.39	12.85	0.77	131.9	132.6	129.1	154.0
1989	49.16	33.28	14.82	1.06	117.0	117.2	115.3	137.7
1990	60.94	41.90	17.65	1.39	124.0	125.9	119.1	131.1
1991	68.97	47.87	19.29	1.81	113.2	114.2	109.3	130.2
1992	85.41	60.20	22.83	2.38	123.8	125.8	118.4	131.5
1993	112.04	77.99	29.31	4.74	131.2	129.6	128.4	199.2
1994	136.65	95.74	33.99	6.92	122.0	122.8	116.0	146.0
1995	167.62	118.25	40.44	8.93	122.7	123.5	119.0	129.0
1996	201.26	143.57	45.24	12.45	120.1	121.4	111.9	139.4
1997	225.79	164.30	48.05	13.44	112.2	114.4	106.2	108.0
1998	234.93	173.14	48.81	12.98	104.0	105.4	101.6	96.6

4－11 职工保险福利费用构成情况（1998）
COMPOSITION OF INSURANCE AND WELFARE FUNDS FOR STAFF AND WORKERS

单位:亿元 （10^8 yuan）

指标	Items	合计 Total	国有单位 State-Owned Units	城镇集体单位 Collective-Owned Uints	其他类型单位 Other-Ownership Uints
总计	**Total**	**78.53**	**57.05**	**11.61**	**9.87**
集体福利事业补贴费及集体福利设施费	Subsidy Funds for Collective Welfare Services and Facilities	21.95	16.35	2.75	2.85
文体宣传费	Expenses for Culture Activities, Sports and Publicity	4.12	3.02	0.69	0.41
医疗卫生费	Expenses for Medical Care	38.96	27.78	6.37	4.81
其他	Others	13.50	9.90	1.80	1.80

4－12 离休、退休、退职人员的保险福利费用构成（1998）
COMPOSITION OF INSURANCE AND WELFARE FUNDS FOR RETIRED AND QUITED PERSONNEL

单位:亿元 （10^8 yuan）

指标	Items	合计 Total	国有单位 State-Owned Units	城镇集体单位 Collective-Owned Uints	其他类型单位 Other-Ownership Uints
保险福利费用总计	**Total Funds for Insurance and Welfare**	**156.40**	**112.34**	**33.27**	**10.79**
离休金	Pension for VCSR	11.53	10.28	0.88	0.37
退休金	Pension for Retirement	116.83	80.83	27.40	8.60
退职生活费	Living Expenses for Resignation	2.08	1.15	0.80	0.13
医疗卫生费	Expenses for Medical Care	19.20	14.64	3.28	1.28
其他	Others	6.76	5.44	0.91	0.41

4－13 城镇居民家庭基本情况
BASIC INDICATORS OF URBAN HOUSEHOLD INCOME AND EXPENDITURES

指 标	Items	1990	1995	1997	1998
调查户数 (户)	Household Surveyed (household)	2220	2020	2120	2120
平均每户家庭人口 (人)	Average Person Per Household (person)	3.34	3.19	3.14	3.10
平均每户就业人口 (人)	Average Employment Per Household (person)	2.00	1.85	1.80	1.74
平均每一就业人口负担人数 (人)	Persons Supported By Each Employee (person)	1.67	1.72	1.74	1.78
平均每户就业面 (%)	Percentage of Employees Per Household (%)	59.9	58.0	57.3	56.1
平均每人居住面积 (平方米)	Average Living Floor Space Per Capita (sq·m)	9.06	10.59	10.86	11.08
平均每人辅助面积 (平方米)	Average Subsidiary Floor Space Per Capita (sq·m)	3.94	5.72	6.31	6.28
平均每人全年可支配收入 (元)	Annual Average Allocatable Income Per Capita (yuan)	1463.79	4634.42	5765.20	6017.85
现金收入 (元)	Cash Income Per Capita (yuan)	1852.45	5454.33	6995.72	7723.39
实际收入	Actual Income	1613.05	4647.33	5807.35	6064.45
借贷收入	Debit and Credit Income	239.40	807.00	1188.37	1658.94
#提取储蓄存款	Per Capita Draw Money from Bank	182.39	584.82	912.36	1125.53
兑售有价证券	Exchange and Sell Valuable Negotiale Securities	2.41	12.34	22.68	44.60
在实际收入中 (元)	Among Actual Income (yuan)				
国有(集体)职工工资性收入	Wages of Staff in State and Collective Units	1053.01	3156.78	3541.26	3534.27
国有(集体)职工非工资性收入	Other Nonwage Income of Staff	146.93	208.24	268.59	265.79
个体经营劳动者(含被雇)收入	Income of Individual Laborers	10.12	41.27	80.72	98.69
离退休再就业人员收入	Reemployment Income of Retirees	17.64	58.18	68.33	59.64
其他就业者收入	Income of Other Employees	2.70	2.21	4.49	3.63
其他劳动收入	Part-Time Income	13.77	56.52	136.24	172.38
财产性收入	Property Income	22.59	65.35	145.92	150.55
转移性收入	Pensions, Subside, Donations and Other	276.48	989.41	1386.23	1609.05
平均每人全年现金支出 (元)	Annual Cash Expenditures Per Capita (yuan)	1816.04	5372.69	6670.95	7583.06
实际支出	Annual Expenditures	1470.88	4343.08	5424.99	6047.70
#消费性支出	Living Expenditures	1338.66	3772.28	4533.57	4889.43
借贷支出	Debit and Credit Expenditures	345.16	1029.61	1245.96	1535.36
#存入储蓄款	Deposit Money in Bank	278.48	810.72	905.57	1147.13
购买有价证券	Buy Valuable Nogotiable Securities	6.50	38.72	57.02	75.71

注：1990 年的人均可支配收入为生活费收入数。

Note: The figure of income, in 1990 was indicated with income avialabe for living.

4－14 城镇居民家庭年人均现金收入和可支配收入
URBAN HOUSEHOLD ANNUAL PER CAPITA CASH INCOME AND ALLOCATABLE INCOME

单位:元 (yuan)

分　组	Grouped	1990	1991	1992	1993	1994
人均现金收入	**Cash Income Per Capita**	**1852.45**	**2101.16**	**2541.31**	**3337.90**	**4630.54**
最低收入户	Lowest Income	1068.15	1201.39	1521.15	1816.94	2314.76
低收入户	Low Income	1318.24	1490.39	1676.98	2090.30	3052.39
中等偏下户	Medium-Low Income	1533.10	1771.37	2035.41	2571.58	3339.26
中等收入户	Medium Income	1785.93	2023.75	2447.28	3077.59	4338.93
中等偏上户	Medium-High Income	2093.00	2390.08	2848.71	3879.69	5330.16
高收入户	High Income	2531.07	2808.41	3372.60	4712.31	6863.42
最高收入户	Highest Income	3219.55	3681.83	4859.25	6617.17	9408.40
人均可支配收入	**Per Capita Allocatable**	**1463.79**	**1622.93**	**2138.34**	**2773.77**	**3778.87**
最低收入户	Lowest Income	857.36	938.98	1237.24	1541.77	1728.32
低收入户	Low Income	1064.04	1182.13	1474.30	1850.57	2418.39
中等偏下户	Medium-Low Income	1229.19	1359.89	1767.59	2209.65	2940.38
中等收入户	Medium Income	1430.24	1596.83	2055.08	2640.04	3541.25
中等偏上户	Medium-High Income	1661.72	1856.58	2450.00	3218.38	4407.06
高收入户	High Income	1947.48	2138.21	2865.44	3814.04	5491.23
最高收入户	Highest Income	2448.00	2739.33	3790.74	5071.50	7181.04

续表 Continued

单位:元 (yuan)

分　组	Grouped	1995	1996	1997	1998
人均现金收入	**Cash Income Per Capita**	**5454.33**	**6293.40**	**6995.72**	**7723.39**
最低收入户	Lowest Income	2997.31	3259.67	3168.65	3425.85
低收入户	Low Income	3704.65	3746.43	4079.83	4206.15
中等偏下户	Medium-Low Income	4096.05	4689.78	4904.93	5374.23
中等收入户	Medium Income	5267.97	5612.64	6353.01	6758.68
中等偏上户	Medium-High Income	6166.18	7596.71	8297.20	8881.33
高收入户	High Income	7383.49	8960.23	10421.05	11559.50
最高收入户	Highest Income	10524.32	12615.85	15544.83	18947.82
人均可支配收入	**Per Capita Allocatable**	**4634.42**	**5185.79**	**5765.20**	**6017.85**
最低收入户	Lowest Income	2495.82	2763.02	2848.76	2803.84
低收入户	Low Income	3001.30	3392.76	3592.34	3676.10
中等偏下户	Medium-Low Income	3684.44	4054.41	4396.98	4533.94
中等收入户	Medium Income	4498.76	4902.08	5368.70	5577.79
中等偏上户	Medium-High Income	5307.41	5996.52	6828.38	7152.31
高收入户	High Income	6394.87	7366.83	8355.77	8881.42
最高收入户	Highest Income	8388.31	9471.69	11304.96	12165.92

注：1991 年以前(含 1991 年)为生活费收入指标,其余年份为可支配收入指标。

Note: The figure of income before 1991 (including 1991) was indicated with aviablable for living, other years was indicated with allocatable income.

4－15 城镇居民家庭年人均收入支出情况（1998）

单位:元

指　　标	Items	全省调查户平均水平 Total Average	最低收入户占10% Lowest Income Make up 10%	#更低收入户占5% Lower Income Make up 5%
可支配收入	**Annual Allocatable Income Per Capita**	**6017.85**	**2803.84**	**2464.40**
现金收入	**Cash Income**	**7723.39**	**3425.85**	**3267.16**
实际收入	**Actual Income**	**6064.45**	**2839.23**	**2498.19**
全民所有制职工收入	Income of Staff in State-Owned Units	3081.54	1272.59	924.33
集体所有制职工收入	Income of Staff in Collective-Owned Units	718.51	687.61	723.14
其它所有制职工收入	Total Income of Staff in Other Owned Units	167.90	28.62	28.56
个体经营者的净收益	Net Income of Individual Laborers	78.84	16.32	28.53
个体被雇者收入	Income of Employed Individual Laborers	19.85	16.31	12.89
离退休再就业人员收入	Replacement Income of Retirees	59.64	24.46	8.74
其他就业者收入	Other Employee's Income	3.63	7.76	4.34
其他劳动收入	Part-Time Income	172.38	130.58	119.54
财产性收入	Property Income	150.55	24.58	21.34
#利息	Interest	77.70	9.82	11.96
转移性收入	Transfer Income	1609.05	630.41	626.78
#离退休金	Pensions for Retirees	1268.98	515.88	499.55
家庭副业生产收入	Household Sideline Production Income	2.56		
借贷收入	Debit and Credit Income	1658.94	586.62	768.97
#提取储蓄存款	Draw Money from Bank	1125.53	488.09	702.23
兑售有价证券	Exchange and Sell Valuable Negotiable Securities	44.60	3.10	2.82
现金支出	**Cash Expenditures**	**7583.06**	**3293.53**	**3175.24**
实际支出	**Actual Expenditures**	**6047.70**	**3067.87**	**3022.78**
消费性支出	Living Expenditures	4889.43	2631.26	2556.00
非消费性支出	Nonliving Expenditures	1155.92	436.51	466.58
家庭副业生产支出	Household Sideline Production Expenditures	2.35	0.11	0.20
借贷支出	Debit and Credit Expenditures	1535.36	225.66	152.46
#存入储蓄存款	Deposit Money in Bank	1147.13	166.09	103.14
购买有价证券	Buy Valuable Negotiable Securities	75.71	5.95	7.09
食品	Food	2205.40	1458.19	1360.49
#粮食	Grain	214.98	196.32	200.02
淀粉及薯类	Starches and Tubers	20.38	17.11	17.60
干豆类及制品	Beans and Bean Products	49.47	39.92	38.90

URBAN HOUSHOLD ANNUAL PER CAPITA INCOME AND EXPENDITURE

(yuan)

按收入水平分组 Grouped by Level of Income					
低收入户 占 10 % Low Income Make up 10%	中等偏下户 占 20 % Medium-Low Income Make up 20%	中等收入户 占 20 % Medium Income Make up 20%	中等偏上户 占 20 % Medium-High Income Make up 20%	高收入户 占 10 % High Income Make up 10%	最高收入户 占 10 % Highest Income Make up 10%
3676.10	**4533.94**	**5577.79**	**7152.31**	**8881.42**	**12165.92**
4206.15	**5374.23**	**6758.68**	**8881.33**	**11559.50**	**18947.82**
3713.69	**4582.14**	**5621.25**	**7200.64**	**8935.02**	**12230.77**
1650.79	2167.83	2969.40	3670.81	4756.26	6595.09
828.40	750.45	741.08	750.41	542.35	597.36
57.54	132.76	158.18	291.79	177.39	303.31
111.88	70.61	33.30	78.52	25.71	296.30
12.48	19.87	27.38	25.90	22.39	0
24.33	30.36	25.46	70.02	144.56	189.74
1.87	1.05	1.39	9.79	0	1.86
205.05	164.67	167.33	160.04	194.83	219.77
45.46	76.35	118.89	205.57	253.38	465.42
11.08	23.74	51.05	109.29	157.36	286.82
775.90	1155.76	1378.83	1937.81	2818.15	3561.93
662.31	936.78	1097.72	1567.42	2285.97	2490.07
	12.42				
492.46	792.09	1137.44	1680.68	2624.48	6717.05
349.86	562.63	876.95	1325.71	2180.08	3312.77
6.29	35.57	18.16	10.40	107.52	241.06
4071.43	**5233.34**	**6585.81**	**8632.42**	**11544.13**	**18984.01**
3662.05	**4445.33**	**5538.50**	**6900.19**	**8747.98**	**13178.62**
3292.24	3815.85	4614.62	5557.44	6683.49	9642.48
367.03	621.10	923.04	1342.14	2064.48	3535.93
2.78	8.38	0.84	0.61	0.02	0.20
409.38	788.01	1047.30	1732.23	2796.15	5805.39
260.24	564.71	752.40	1331.67	2184.44	4347.07
23.75	21.40	55.55	80.86	90.72	377.05
1771.65	2010.76	2158.81	2413.73	2796.71	3209.84
194.34	218.70	213.80	225.18	226.08	224.65
17.60	19.82	19.62	21.41	26.46	22.80
41.00	48.33	47.57	53.51	58.28	61.57

续 表

单位:元

指标	Items	全省调查户平均水平 Total Average	最低收入户占 10 % Lowest Income Make up 10 %	#更低收入户占 5 % Lower Income Make up 5 %
油脂类	Oil and Fats	78.05	70.32	69.61
肉禽及制品	Meat, Poultry and Related Products	512.57	351.69	332.04
蛋类	Eggs	78.18	62.38	59.34
水产品类	Aquatic Products	238.27	151.74	134.37
菜类	Vegetables	210.21	161.68	153.66
调味品	Flavorings	32.66	26.15	27.10
糖类	Sugar	24.75	15.32	15.79
烟草类	Tobacco	108.00	59.79	51.47
酒和饮料	Liquor	95.97	52.17	47.82
干鲜瓜果类	Dried and Fresh Melons and Fruits	108.09	68.77	56.49
坚果及果仁	Muts and Grains	26.75	17.93	15.48
糕点类	Cake	44.17	28.49	20.13
奶及奶制品	Milk and Dairy Products	50.48	24.28	20.58
其它食品	Other Foods	43.86	18.74	17.26
衣着支出	Clothing	449.21	195.24	175.27
#服装	Garments	284.58	108.67	93.96
衣着材料	Clothing Materials	39.60	19.96	19.03
鞋袜帽及其它	Shoes, Hats, Socks and Other Clothing	107.49	57.89	53.12
设备用品及服务	Facilities, Artical and Service	579.34	138.38	111.61
耐用消费品	Durable Consumer Goods	361.24	64.90	47.06
室内装饰品	Interior Decorations	28.00	2.59	1.18
床上用品	Bed Articals	17.67	7.80	6.68
家庭日用杂品	Daily Use Articals	101.39	55.44	49.42
家具材料	furniture Materials	7.39	0.10	0.07
家庭服务	Household Services	63.64	7.54	7.20
医疗保健	Medicine and Medical Services	164.15	80.87	86.24
交通和通讯	Transportation and Communications	255.65	95.97	92.53
#交通费	Transportation	44.85	20.18	18.50
电讯费	Communications	114.10	57.29	54.30
娱乐文教服务	Recreation, Education and Cultural Services	530.38	223.81	227.17
#耐用消费品	Durable Consumer Goods	130.99	16.88	15.90
教育	Education	284.36	160.57	172.35
文化娱乐	Cultural Recreation	115.02	46.36	38.92
居住	Residence	478.54	340.67	418.19
#房租	Rent	62.02	36.33	34.62
水	Water	27.57	18.95	17.92
电	Electricity	122.85	75.26	79.48
杂项商品和服务	Miscellaneous Commodities and Services	226.77	98.13	84.51
#旅游	Tour	41.95	6.94	7.27

Continued

(yuan)

按 收 入 水 平 分 组 Grouped by Level of Income					
低收入户 占 10 % Low Income Make up 10%	中等偏下户 占 20 % Medium-Low Income Make up 20%	中等收入户 占 20 % Medium Income Make up 20%	中等偏上户 占 20 % Medium-High Income Make up 20%	高收入户 占 10 % High Income Make up 10%	最高收入户 占 10 % Highest Income Make up 10%
75.48	78.12	77.30	77.10	92.97	79.92
436.94	483.97	523.80	567.90	610.30	631.87
72.76	73.71	74.16	82.38	92.12	101.70
174.12	206.74	241.11	270.40	313.85	348.97
179.12	203.09	206.86	228.53	249.79	255.16
31.07	30.64	32.61	34.90	37.07	38.38
18.57	22.61	24.98	26.38	35.00	35.09
92.80	107.65	119.21	111.80	125.64	136.51
69.05	87.61	96.82	105.77	117.62	159.40
77.82	96.03	102.23	127.92	137.68	164.36
17.24	24.20	25.80	30.23	35.63	41.42
31.26	37.29	42.85	48.89	63.22	70.02
31.21	43.55	49.72	56.46	82.49	80.75
32.25	39.97	41.74	49.75	74.56	60.78
275.13	328.46	469.34	576.04	636.70	757.30
167.26	197.90	301.02	371.84	410.60	500.31
24.43	31.61	37.23	49.66	58.21	66.98
74.89	85.01	113.71	131.88	145.62	157.27
188.05	272.68	413.09	635.57	781.60	2408.16
86.20	140.58	243.28	365.26	522.44	1703.69
2.38	3.83	20.95	63.44	22.52	92.41
9.35	12.92	18.84	22.09	25.94	30.97
70.19	78.38	99.07	109.15	141.92	200.44
0.24	2.50	6.31	13.36	13.23	20.53
19.68	34.47	24.64	62.27	55.54	360.12
169.87	123.51	160.90	190.07	204.78	268.00
150.20	198.16	246.84	309.10	403.59	479.65
18.46	32.79	42.51	54.49	83.59	83.00
70.16	96.45	117.86	131.41	171.31	178.31
302.02	391.46	491.43	677.31	814.74	1013.08
32.62	48.25	110.50	176.07	279.68	393.00
202.30	261.17	278.91	359.08	339.44	390.50
67.11	82.03	102.01	142.16	195.61	229.59
310.72	350.38	471.51	486.18	647.73	994.37
53.26	57.19	49.20	78.67	74.15	97.96
21.59	27.93	26.58	30.26	32.03	36.99
97.66	101.93	124.28	140.46	158.65	185.80
124.60	140.43	202.71	269.44	397.64	512.07
10.60	12.11	35.11	40.05	125.22	133.02

4－16 城镇居民家庭平均每人全年购买主要商品数量
URBAN HOUSEHOLD ANNUAL PER CAPITA PURCHASES OF MAJOR COMMODITIES

单位：公斤 (kg)

项目	Items	1980	1985	1990	1995	1997	1998
粮食（贸易粮）	Grain (Processed)	162.60	128.60	119.00	96.31	86.17	86.97
植物油	Edible Vegetable Oil	4.20	7.30	6.98	7.31	7.46	8.25
鲜菜	Fresh Vegetables	181.20	122.00	117.73	112.30	109.65	109.13
猪肉	Pork	18.00	16.40	18.49	19.86	18.10	19.50
牛羊肉	Beef and Mutton	2.40	1.10	2.38	1.40	1.95	1.64
家禽	Poultry	2.40	6.00	4.35	7.11	8.88	8.38
鲜蛋	Fresh Eggs	4.20	8.50	7.54	10.89	12.98	12.12
鱼虾	Fish and Shrimp	9.00	9.90	10.76	14.31	15.75	17.15
食糖	Sugar	3.00	2.80	2.83	2.04	2.18	2.41
卷烟（盒）	Cigarettes (pack)	30.00	48.70	33.62	26.10	22.03	23.20
白酒	Liquor		2.30	2.78	2.71	2.47	2.48
茶叶	Tea	0.18	0.20	0.18	0.13	0.14	0.15
鲜瓜果	Fresh Mealon and Fruits	15.00	38.00	45.32	48.87	52.50	56.71
糖果	Candy	1.20	1.00	0.62	0.66	0.57	0.50
糕点	Cake	3.00	4.40	3.94	3.11	3.00	2.97
鲜奶	Fresh Dairy	3.60	5.50	3.72	3.84	4.72	5.89
服装（件）	Clothing (peice)				4.82	5.12	5.29
棉布（米）	Cotton Cloth (m)	4.48	2.59	1.23	0.47	0.40	0.35
化纤布（米）	Chemical Fiber Cloth (m)	2.24	2.21	1.52	1.33	1.10	0.99
呢绒（米）	Woolen Fabric (m)	0.31	0.51	0.30	0.23	0.12	0.08
绸缎（米）	Silk and Stins (m)	0.44	0.80	0.41	0.22	0.10	0.07
布鞋（双）	Cloth Shoes (pairs)	0.65	0.30	0.28	0.15	0.14	0.12
皮鞋（双）	Leather Shoes (pairs))	0.58	0.63	0.52	0.64	0.63	0.61
肥皂（块）	Soap (pcs)	9.14	5.80	3.12	1.75	1.82	1.95
洗衣粉	Detergent	0.41	0.80	0.73	0.85	0.86	1.01

注：家禽、鲜蛋、鱼虾、鲜瓜果，1995年以后（含1995年）均包括其他禽及制品、其他蛋及制品、其他鱼及制品、其他鲜瓜果及制品。

Note: Poultry, fresh eggs, fish and shrimp, fresh mealon and fruits include other poultry, eggs, fish, fresh mealon and fruits, and their relative products, since 1995 (including 1995).

4-17 城镇居民家庭居住情况
HOUSING CONDITIONS OF URBAN HOUSEHOLD

单位:户 (household)

指 标	Items	1990	1995	1997	1998
总 计	**Total**	**2220**	**2020**	**2120**	**2120**
按居住面积分	Grouped by Residential Space				
无房户	No Housing				
4平方米以下	Lower 4 sq·m	40	27	12	12
4-6平方米	4-6 sq·m	287	212	152	136
6-8平方米	6-8 sq·m	496	437	380	369
8-10平方米	8-10 sq·m	1307	452	414	395
10-12平方米	10-12 sq·m		272	399	394
12-14平方米	12-14 sq·m		229	278	277
14平方米以上	Over 14 sq·m		391	485	538
按卫生设备拥有分	Grouped by Possession of Sanitary Equipment				
无卫生设备	No Sanitary Equipment	1204	775	578	578
有浴室厕所	Provided with Bathroom and Toilet	296	865	1011	1027
有厕所无浴室	Provided with Toilet but No Bathroom	547	306	413	411
公用卫生设备	Public Sanitary Equipment	173	74	118	105
按厨房使用分	Grouped by Usage of Kitchen				
无厨房	No Kitchen	217	89	104	99
独用厨房	Sole Kitchen	1891	1870	1964	1984
公用厨房	Public Kitchen	112	62	52	37
按房屋产权分	Grouped by Ownership of Housing				
公房	Residence of Public Property	1664	1173	852	704
租赁私房	Rent Private Owned Residence	23	13	29	13
自有房	One's Own Residence	532	834	923	1001
部分产权的自有房	One's Own Residence Provided with part estate Right			315	403
其他	Others	1		1	
按燃料使用分	Grouped by Usage of Fuel				
管道煤气	Piping Gas	174	313	401	407
液化石油气	Liquified Petroleum Gas (LPG)	629	1089	1326	1372
煤	Coal	1416	606	392	339
其他	Others	1	11	1	2
按住宅建筑式样分	Grouped by Type of Construction				
家庭单栋配套楼房	Single Household Flat Storied Building		21	44	43
单元式配套住宅	Multi-Entrances Flat Residence		1036	1200	1241
一居室	One Room		130	63	70
二居室	Two Rooms		573	760	785
三居室	Three Rooms		313	358	362
四居室及以上	Four Rooms Over		19	19	24
普通楼房	Ordinary Storied Building		287	192	176
其它住宅	Others		676	684	661

4－18 城镇居民家庭平均每百户年末耐用品拥有量

URBAN HOUSEHOLD YEAR-END POSSESION OF DURABLE CONSUMER GOODS PER 100 HOUSEHOLDS

项目		Items	1985	1990	1995	1997	1998
毛皮大衣	(件)	Fur Coats	16.00	23.90	31.31	37.42	41.35
呢大衣	(件)	Woolen Coats	148.00	206.90	257.18	249.42	254.66
毛毯	(条)	Woolen Blankets	76.00	112.83	130.54	137.38	137.96
地毯	(平方米)	Carpets (m^2)			138.29	108.40	104.47
大衣柜	(个)	Wardrobes	97.00	105.92	93.60	91.05	90.91
沙发	(个)	Sofas	116.00	149.20	152.55	139.23	144.75
写字台	(张)	Writting Desks	83.00	97.87	99.34	97.34	97.93
组合家具	(套)	Combined Furniture	2.00	9.41	29.68	35.91	38.45
沙发床	(个)	Sofa Beds	2.00	10.73	20.97	29.73	30.36
自行车	(辆)	Bicycles	166.00	217.04	237.46	225.32	228.34
缝纫机	(架)	Sewing Machines	73.10	71.79	69.48	65.89	65.44
电风扇	(台)	Electric Fans	102.00	220.16	259.07	254.62	259.88
洗衣机	(台)	Washing Machines	48.00	85.81	95.35	94.98	96.14
电冰箱	(台)	Refrigerators	6.00	48.09	69.42	77.68	78.61
冰柜	(台)	Freezers			1.93	2.05	1.78
摩托车	(辆)	Motorcycles	1.00	1.90	6.77	15.57	17.08
影碟机	(台)	VCD				5.98	12.28
彩色电视机	(台)	Color TV Sets	9.00	51.46	85.22	101.11	105.23
收录机	(台)	Recorders	41.00	70.71	74.73	55.54	56.35
录放像机	(台)	Videorecorders		2.45	20.57	24.84	24.19
照相机	(架)	Cameras	7.00	17.11	28.57	32.83	34.42
中高档乐器	(件)	Medium and High-Grade Musical Instruments	3.00	7.45	5.37	3.20	2.44
钢琴	(架)	Pianoes			0.52	0.63	0.66
空调器	(台)	Air Conditioners		0.07	10.53	22.89	25.82
电炊具	(个)	Electric Cooking Tools	3.00	45.83	111.05	129.20	133.86
组合音响	(套)	Hi-Fi Systems		0.62	10.09	13.11	13.94
家用电脑	(台)	Computers				2.22	3.46
淋浴热水器	(台)	Showers			30.80	43.79	46.12
脱排油烟机	(台)	Range Hoods			34.26	48.73	51.48
吸尘器	(台)	Vacuum Cleaners			13.37	12.82	12.82
摄像机	(台)	TV Cameras				0.41	0.50
微波炉	(台)	Microwave Strove				7.59	12.57
健身器材	(件)	Health Care Instruments				2.15	2.95
移动电话	(台)	Mobile Telephones				1.79	2.50

4-19 农民家庭基本情况
BASIC INDICATORS OF RURAL HOUSEHOLDS

指　　标	Items	1990	1995	1997	1998
调查户数　（户）	**Households Surveyed　(household)**	**3400**	**3400**	**3400**	**3400**
调查户人口　（人）	**Residents Surveyed　(person)**				
常住人口	Permanent Residents	14071	13644	13229	13018
平均每户常住人口	Average Permanent Residents Per Household	4.1	4.0	3.9	3.8
平均每户整、半劳动力	Average Full-Time and Part-Time Laborers Per Household	2.78	2.79	2.65	2.61
平均每个劳动力负担人口（包括劳动力本人）	Average Persons Suported by Each Laborer (including the laborer-self)	1.5	1.4	1.5	1.5
平均每人全年收入　（元）	**Average Per Capita Annual Income　(yuan)**				
总收入	Total Revenue	1182.0	3290.9	4193.4	4258.2
纯收入	Net Income	883.8	2456.9	3269.9	3376.8
现金收入	Cash Income	1119.1	2696.4	3926.9	4014.2
按人均纯收入水平分组的户数占调查总户数的比重（%）	**Percentage of Households by Per Capita Annual Net Income　(%)**				
300元以下	Below 300 yuan	6.0	0.4	0.4	0.1
300－500元	300－500 yuan	16.5	0.6	0.1	0.2
500－800元	500－800 yuan	28.8	2.8	0.5	0.8
800－1500元	800－1500 yuan	35.0	20.2	8.8	7.2
1500－2000元	1500－2000 yuan	8.2	18.4	13.2	12.2
2000元以上	2000 yuan and Over	5.5	57.6	77.0	79.5
平均每人全年支出　（元）	**Average Per Capita Annual Expenditures　(yuan)**				
总支出	Total Expenditures	1095.0	2861.6	3456.3	3261.8
#家庭经营性支出	Household Business Expenditures	234.5	675.2	729.1	691.8
生活消费支出	Living Expenditures	787.0	1938.0	2487.7	2336.8
其他非借贷性支出	Other Non-Credit Expenditures	17.6	79.1	63.1	74.3
现金支出	Cash Expenditures	1049.7	2466.1	3535.1	3562.7
#生产性费用	Productive Costs	208.5	579.9	686.4	654.3
缴纳税金、上交集体承包费、集体提留和摊派	Taxes and Payments to Collective	42.8	83.9	98.0	102.6
生活消费支出	Consumptive Expenditures	569.7	1285.8	1898.1	1831.3
储蓄借贷支出	Savings and Credit Expenditures	153.8	357.8	599.3	725.0

4－20 农民家庭平均每人总收入和纯收入
ANNUAL PER CAPITA REVENUE AND NET INCOME OF RURAL HOUSEHOLDS

单位:元　　(yuan)

指标	Items	1990	1995	1997	1998
总收入	**Total Revenue**	**1182.0**	**3290.9**	**4193.4**	**4258.1**
基本收入	Basic Income	1148.9	3189.9	4044.2	4079.6
劳动者的报酬收入	Reward of Labourers	300.6	821.9	1235.1	1464.1
#在集体组织中劳动的报酬收入	Collective Organizes	30.0	81.8	150.0	231.8
在企业劳动得到的报酬收入	Enterprises	270.6	715.4	1001.3	899.3
家庭经营收入	House Business Revenue	848.3	2368.0	2809.1	2615.5
#种植业收入	Faming	458.3	1452.5	1486.9	1331.3
林业收入	Forestry	8.7	12.7	17.7	28.3
牧业收入	Animal Husbandry	233.6	483.0	632.9	540.8
渔业收入	Fishery	18.7	44.6	45.8	70.0
手工业收入	Handicraft	19.4	62.7	87.7	75.0
采集捕猎收入	Gathering and Hunting	1.9	2.8	2.6	3.7
工业收入	Industry	14.3	31.6	76.9	94.1
建筑业收入	Construction	26.8	99.9	170.1	119.6
运输业收入	Transportation	21.5	60.3	114.0	117.6
商业收入	Commerce	14.8	54.4	76.8	95.5
饮食业收入	Food Services	2.7	7.3	10.7	23.8
服务业收入	Services Trade	12.4	26.4	47.2	60.5
转移性收入	Transfer Income	33.1	75.5	114.6	136.3
财产性收入	Property Income		25.5	34.6	42.2
纯收入	**Net Income**	**883.8**	**2456.9**	**3269.9**	**3376.8**
劳动者的报酬收入	Reward of Labourers	300.6	821.9	1235.1	1464.1
家庭经营收入	Household Business	557.5	1544.4	1901.0	1754.1
转移性收入	Transfer Income	25.7	65.0	99.1	116.0
财产性收入	Property Income		25.6	34.7	42.3

4-21 农民家庭平均每人生活消费支出
PER CAPITA RURAL HOUSEHOLD LIVING EXPENDITURES

单位:元 (yuan)

指标	Items	1990	1995	1997	1998
生活消费支出	**Total Living Expenditures**	**787.0**	**1938.0**	**2487.7**	**2336.8**
食品	Food	411.6	1061.4	1216.5	1117.0
主食	Grain	81.0	412.3	353.3	328.4
副食	Non-Staple Food	231.4	456.0	570.2	491.1
其他	Others	99.2	193.1	293.0	297.5
衣着	Clothing	57.9	126.8	161.5	135.1
居住	Residence	193.2	344.6	427.2	399.0
住房和电费	Housing and Electricity	168.5	294.3	351.0	315.4
燃料	Fuel	24.7	33.0	42.7	41.4
其他	Others		17.3	33.5	42.2
家庭设备、用品及服务	Household Facilities, Articales and Services	53.3	133.0	188.5	153.8
医疗保健	Medicine and Medical Services	22.7	49.1	80.9	99.6
交通和通讯	Traffic and Communications	10.0	52.3	126.3	132.4
文化教育娱乐用品及服务	Cultural, Education and Recreation Artical and Services	34.7	139.2	225.4	240.0
其他商品和服务	Other Commodity and Services	3.6	31.6	61.4	59.5

4-22 农民家庭房屋情况
RURAL HOUSEHOLD HOUSING CONDITIONS

指标	Items	1990	1995	1997	1998
平均每人年末生活用房面积 (平方米)	Living Floor Space Per Capita of Houses by the End of Year (sq.m)	22.3	25.7	30.8	32.0
#砖木结构	Brick and Wood Structures	16.5	19.5	18.9	19.8
钢筋混凝土结构	Reinforced Concrete Structures	3.1	4.8	11.0	11.5
平均每户本年新建房屋	Rooms Newly Built Per Household Within the year				
新建房屋间数占使用间数比重 (%)	The Proportion of Rooms Newly Built in the Rooms Used (%)	5.8	4.5	5.4	4.0
新建房屋每间价值 (元)	Value of Per Room Newly Built (yuan)	3479.0	7750.0	9417.3	7310.9
每平方米价值 (元)	Value of Per Square Metre (yuan)	145.8	308.5	370.1	308.3
平均每人年内新建房屋面积 (平方米)	Per Capita Space of the Rooms Newly Built Within the Year (sq.m)	1.7	1.3	1.7	1.3
#砖木结构	Brick and Wood Structures	1.3	0.8	0.6	0.5
钢筋混凝土结构	Reinforced Concrete Structures	0.4	0.5	1.0	0.7
生活用房	Living Houses	1.6	1.2	1.5	1.1
楼房	Multi-Floor Houses	0.9	0.6	0.9	0.5

4-23 农民家庭平均每人全年主要消费品消费量
RURAL HOUSEHOLD PER CAPITA CONSUMPTION ON MAJOR CONSUMER GOODS

指 标		Items		1990	1995	1997	1998
粮　食(原粮)	(公斤)	Grain (Unprocessed Grains)	(kg)	275.9	264.0	273.0	262.4
#稻　谷	(公斤)	Paddy	(kg)	163.8	184.4	190.3	183.4
蔬　菜	(公斤)	Fresh Vegetables	(kg)	129.2	120.2	120.6	110.3
植 物 油	(公斤)	Edible Vegetable Oil	(kg)	6.6	7.6	8.5	7.6
动 物 油	(公斤)	Edible Animal Oil	(kg)	0.4	0.6	0.7	0.7
肉　类	(公斤)	Meat	(kg)	9.5	10.5	14.5	12.1
#猪　肉	(公斤)	Pork	(kg)	9.0	10.0	12.5	10.3
家　禽	(公斤)	Poultry	(kg)	1.5	3.2	5.3	4.6
蛋　类	(公斤)	Eggs	(kg)	6.0	7.6	9.8	6.7
鱼　虾	(公斤)	Fish and Shrimp	(kg)	4.9	6.8	9.1	7.5
食　糖	(公斤)	Sugar	(kg)	1.9	1.7	1.8	2.1
卷　烟	(盒)	Cigarettes	(packs)	36.4	27.8	30.3	27.9
酒	(公斤)	Liquor	(kg)	7.1	8.3	9.8	10.2
棉　布	(米)	Cotton Cloth	(m)	0.9	0.4	0.4	0.3
化 纤 布	(米)	Chemical Fiber	(m)	2.1	2.1	2.0	1.8
呢　绒	(米)	Woolen Fabric	(m)	0.09	0.09	0.12	0.11
绸　缎	(米)	Silk and Satin	(m)	0.05	0.02	0.01	0.01
毛线及毛线织品	(公斤)	Knitting Wool and Knitwear	(kg)	0.08	0.16	0.18	0.13
肥　皂	(块)	Soaps	(pcs)	0.7	0.2	0.2	0.2

4-24 农民家庭年末平均每百户耐用消费品拥有量
RURAL HOUSEHOLD YEAR-END POSSESSION OF DURABLE CONSUMER GOODS PER 100 HOUSEHOLDS

指 标		Items	1990	1995	1997	1998
自 行 车	(辆)	Bicycles	159.1	183.4	184.7	182.9
缝 纫 机	(架)	Sewing Machines	49.8	63.0	65.3	66.2
收 音 机	(台)	Radio Sets	52.2	42.3	34.1	33.1
钟　表	(只)	Clocks and Watches	259.0	293.0	272.6	274.3
#手　表	(只)	Wristwatches	197.6	202.6	175.6	171.5
电 视 机	(台)	TV Sets	54.4	96.6	112.0	114.8
#彩色电视机	(台)	Color TV Sets	6.2	21.9	34.4	38.1
收 录 机	(台)	Recorders	19.1	32.7	36.3	35.7
洗 衣 机	(台)	Washing Machines	15.0	29.8	41.5	42.3
电 风 扇	(台)	Electric Fans	86.2	167.6	195.3	202.5
电 冰 箱	(台)	Refrigerators	1.5	9.1	15.9	17.1
摩 托 车	(辆)	Motorcycles	1.5	8.6	18.5	21.1
照 相 机	(架)	Cameras	1.1	2.3	4.4	4.4
大型家具 (每件价值 50 元以上的)	(件)	Large Size Furnitures (Each Cost 50 Yuan Over)	411.5	745.1	796.6	778.8
#沙　发	(件)	Sofas	49.2	86.3	104.7	104.4
大 衣 柜	(个)	Wardrobes	93.9	109.1	98.0	97.6
写 字 台	(张)	Writing Desks	81.4	96.6	101.2	98.7

5. 固定资产投资

FIXED ASSETS INVESTMENT

5 固定资产投资
FIXED ASSETS INVESTMENT

1 9 9 8

全社会固定资产投资完成总额	Total Investment in Fixed Assets	2535.50	亿元	(10^8 yuan)
#国有经济	State-Owned	1031.95	亿元	(10^8 yuan)
集体经济	Collective-Owned	475.36	亿元	(10^8 yuan)
#基本建设	Capital Construction	747.18	亿元	(10^8 yuan)
更新改造	Technical Updating and Transformation	296.01	亿元	(10^8 yuan)
房地产开发	Real Estate Development	300.24	亿元	(10^8 yuan)
房屋施工面积	Floor Space of Building Under Construction	17059.16	万平方米	(10000 sq·m)
房屋竣工面积	Floor Space of Building Completed	13273.75	万平方米	(10000 sq·m)

全社会固定资产投资完成额(亿元)

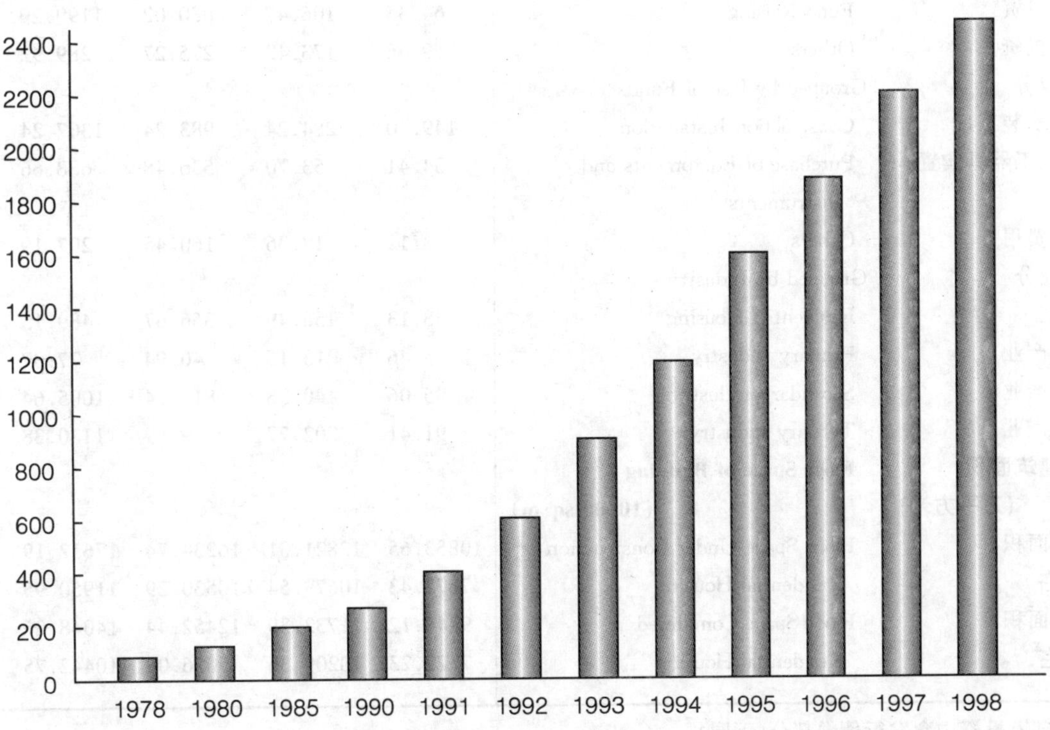

5-1 全社会固定资产投资
TOTAL INVESTMENT IN FIXED ASSETS

指 标	Items	1985	1990	1995	1997	1998
投资总额（亿元）	**Total Value of Investment (10^8 yuan)**	**191.93**	**356.30**	**1680.17**	**2203.09**	**2535.50**
按种类分	Grouped by Type of Construction					
基本建设	Capital Construction	47.35	74.32	362.15	588.05	747.18
更新改造	Technical Updating and Transformation	24.73	41.53	218.78	268.77	296.01
房地产开发	Real Estate Development		11.71	240.85	241.55	300.24
城镇集体	City and town Collective Units	19.60	20.79	89.30	74.01	75.81
农村集体	Rural Collective Units	39.46	54.08	451.52	451.06	485.82
城镇个人	City and Town Individuals	1.55	3.83	14.42	16.42	20.01
农村个人	Rural Individuals	50.89	142.74	199.80	329.88	299.17
其他投资	Others	8.35	7.30	103.35	233.35	311.26
按经济类型分	Grouped by Ownership					
国有经济	State Owned Units	80.43	134.86	602.70	826.60	1031.95
集体经济	Collective Owned Units	59.06	74.87	491.08	447.94	475.36
其他经济	Others	52.44	146.57	586.39	928.55	1028.19
按资金来源分	Grouped by Sources of Finance					
国家预算内投资	State Appropriation	17.25	15.02	25.83	29.63	49.46
国内贷款	Domestic Loans	36.79	45.47	270.16	293.66	331.83
利用外资	Foreign Investment	3.98	15.92	228.89	390.59	413.66
自筹投资	Fund Raising	64.45	106.47	880.02	1199.29	1406.39
其他投资	Others	69.46	173.42	275.27	289.92	334.16
按构成分	Grouped by Use of Funds					
建筑安装工程	Construction Installation	149.40	284.24	983.24	1307.24	1503.62
设备、工器具购置	Purchase of Equipments and Instruments	34.41	53.70	536.48	688.66	755.02
其他费用	Others	8.12	18.36	160.45	207.19	276.86
按产业分	Grouped by Industry					
# 住宅	Residential Housing	58.13	156.49	366.67	489.15	529.70
第一产业	Primary Industry	5.46	13.15	40.94	77.07	102.64
第二产业	Secondary Industry	95.06	140.38	819.54	1005.64	1091.81
第三产业	Tertiary Industry	91.41	202.77	819.69	1120.38	1341.05
房屋建筑面积（万平方米）	**Floor Space of Building (10000 sq·m)**					
施工面积	Floor Space Under Construction	10853.65	12821.31	16234.74	17612.19	17059.16
#住宅	Residential Housing	7673.43	10679.54	10530.29	11950.95	11251.03
竣工面积	Floor Space Completed	9246.12	11732.39	12452.44	14048.26	13273.75
#住宅	Residential Housing	7122.23	10209.36	9036.00	10442.75	9451.28

注：自筹投资中含发行债券部分(下同)。

Note: Fund raising included bond publishing (so did follows).

5－2 按经济类型分的全社会固定资产投资（1998）

TOTAL INVESTMENT IN FIXED ASSETS GROUPED BY OWNERSHIP

单位：亿元 　　　　　　　　　　　　　　　　　　　　(10^8 yuan)

指标	Items	总计 Total	#基本建设 Capital Construction	#更新改造 Technical Updating and Transformation	#房地产开发 Real Estate Development	#城镇集体 City and Town Collective	#农村集体 Rural Collective	#城乡个人 Urban and Rural Individual
投资总额	**Total**	**2535.50**	**747.18**	**296.01**	**300.24**	**75.81**	**485.82**	**319.18**
按登记注册类型分	Grouped by Type of Registeration							
内资	Domestic Funds	2021.27	624.74	256.70	239.90	75.81	419.21	319.18
#国有	State-owned	1031.95	569.51	237.19	158.73			
股份有限公司	Share Holding Co. Ltd.	92.33	39.42	15.00	14.84		18.76	
港澳台商投资	Hongkong, Macao and Taiwan Funds	127.32	9.04	11.36	44.41		32.71	
#合资经营	Cooperative Operation Funds	72.50	8.31	9.72	34.98		12.13	
外商投资	Foreign Funds	386.91	113.40	27.95	15.93		33.90	
#合资经营	Cooperative Operation Funds	205.32	103.09	24.25	9.27		18.81	
按资金来源分	Grouped by Sources of Finance							
国家预算内投资	State Appropriation	49.46	47.09	2.00	0.32	0.05		
国内贷款	Domestic Loans	331.83	134.11	45.35	69.05	10.26	35.97	6.42
利用外资	Foreign Investment	413.66	114.37	23.96	9.87	2.59	50.53	
自筹投资	Fund Raising	1406.39	381.16	210.98	87.01	53.42	342.32	270.13
其他投资	Others	334.16	70.45	13.72	133.99	9.49	57.00	42.63
按构成分								
建筑安装工程	Construction Installation	1503.62	492.54	98.67	214.86	41.73	223.88	301.65
设备、工器具购置	Purchase of Equipment and Instruments	755.02	145.08	174.98	5.09	28.86	225.74	17.53
其他费用	Others	276.86	109.56	22.36	80.29	5.22	36.20	
按产业分	Grouped by Industry							
#住宅	Residential Housing	529.70	48.23	1.72	196.15	4.40	17.00	258.92
第一产业	Primary Industry	102.64	41.55	1.85		1.30	25.78	30.39
第二产业	Secondary Industry	1091.81	283.47	164.71		45.42	341.24	5.25
第三产业	Tertiary Industry	1341.05	422.16	129.45	300.24	29.09	118.80	283.54
房屋建筑面积（万平方米）	**Floor Space of Building (10000 sq·m)**							
施工面积	Floor Space Under Constrution	17059.16	2479.82	255.91	3809.78	330.53	1966.76	7874.62
#住宅	Residential Housing	11251.03	796.89	23.69	2879.63	75.04	310.73	7150.48
竣工面积	Floor Space Completed	13273.75	1350.53	168.69	1824.62	259.83	1773.90	7700.62
#住宅	Residential Housing	9451.28	497.83	18.85	1471.62	66.34	274.19	7109.48

5-3 固定资产投资完成额

FULFILMENT VALUE OF FIXED ASSETS INVESTMENT

单位:亿元 (10⁸ yuan)

行业	Sector	1990	1995	1997	1998
总计	**Total**	**155.65**	**1014.43**	**1371.73**	**1678.50**
农、林、牧、渔业	Farming, Forestry, Animal Husbandry and Fishery	2.04	2.13	4.24	8.54
采掘业	Excavation	7.71	14.07	20.82	15.86
制造业	Manufacturing	66.69	340.32	454.84	529.61
电力、煤气及水的生产和供应业	Electric Power, Gas and Water Producation and Supply	17.90	77.87	137.39	162.98
建筑业	Construction	0.07	8.82	9.72	9.76
地质勘查业、水利管理业	Geological Prospect and Water Conservancy	1.85	8.41	21.26	36.39
交通运输、仓储及邮电通讯业	Transportation, Storage, Postal and Telecommunication Services	19.02	141.77	231.05	311.80
批发和零售贸易、餐饮业	Whole Sale, Retail Trade and Catering Trade	5.44	39.19	39.40	37.77
金融、保险业	Banking, Insurance	1.15	6.50	9.10	12.70
房地产业	Real Estate	17.56	244.90	246.98	306.50
社会服务业	Social Services	1.64	39.36	67.77	82.41
卫生、体育和社会福利业	Health Care, Sports and Social Welfare	1.85	8.62	10.64	15.59
教育、文化艺术及广播电影电视业	Education, Culture and Arts, Radio, Film and Television	7.25	26.16	46.12	56.88
科学研究和综合技术服务业	Scientific Research and Polytechnical Services	0.85	2.63	3.45	3.55
国家机关、政党机关和社会团体	Government Agencies, Party Agencies and Social Organizations	2.75	40.01	49.04	58.79
其他行业	Other Sectors	1.88	13.67	19.91	29.37

注：本表不含农村集体及城乡个体投资完成额。
Note: Rural collective units, urban and rural individual investment were not included in this table.

5-4 固定资产投资新增的固定资产

NEWLY INCREASED FIXED ASSETS THROUGH INVESTMENT

单位:亿元 (10⁸ yuan)

行业	Sector	1990	1995	1997	1998
总计	**Total**	**167.91**	**768.65**	**1071.00**	**1297.71**
农、林、牧、渔业	Farming, Forestry, Animal Husbandry and Fishery	1.80	2.10	3.60	3.84
采掘业	Excavation	3.61	10.87	10.61	11.76
制造业	Manufacturing	89.07	292.16	315.41	418.66
电力、煤气及水的生产和供应业	Electric Power, Gas and Water Producation and Supply	16.48	59.02	65.21	140.81
建筑业	Construction	0.49	8.27	6.71	9.77
地质勘查业、水利管理业	Geological Prospect and Water Conservancy	1.68	5.81	11.40	24.55
交通运输、仓储及邮电通讯业	Transportation, Storage, Postal and Telecommunication Services	17.44	97.64	217.84	189.32
批发和零售贸易、餐饮业	Whole Sale, Retail Trade and Catering Trade	5.92	34.15	41.51	31.85
金融、保险业	Banking, Insurance	0.91	5.48	7.63	10.97
房地产业	Real Estate	15.24	147.79	207.34	234.10
社会服务业	Social Services	1.41	30.03	66.55	82.64
卫生、体育和社会福利业	Health Care, Sports and Social Welfare	1.66	7.46	7.84	13.48
教育、文化艺术及广播电影电视业	Education, Culture and Arts, Radio, Film and Television	7.16	22.56	39.72	46.02
科学研究和综合技术服务业	Scientific Research and Polytechnical Services	1.22	2.66	1.89	2.37
国家机关、政党机关和社会团体	Government Agencies, Party Agencies and Social Organizations	2.49	33.46	51.36	53.53
其他行业	Other Sectors	1.33	9.19	16.38	24.04

注：本表不含农村集体及城乡个体投资新增的固定资产。
Note: Rural collective units, urban and rural individual investment of newly increased fixed assets were not included in this table.

5-5 国有单位固定资产投资(1998)

FIXED ASSETS INVESTMENT BY STATE OWNED UNITS

单位:亿元 (10[8] yuan)

指标	Items	合计 Total	基本建设 Capital Construction	更新改造 Updating and Transformation	其他投资 Others	房地产开发 Real Estate Development
建设项目个数 (个)	Number of Construction Projects (units)					
施工项目	Projects Under Construction	7252	4224	3028		
#大中型项目或限上技改项目	Large and Medium Projects or Over-Norm Items	76	37	39		
全部建成投产项目	Total Projects Completed Put Into Operation	5176	2836	2340		
#大中型项目或限上技改项目	Large and Medium Projects or Over-Norm Items	14	5	9		
建成项目投产率 (%)	Rate of Projects Completed Put Into Operation (%)	71.4	67.1	77.3		
建设周期 (年)(按项目个数计算)	Construction Cycle (Year, By Number of Projects)	1.40	1.49	1.29		
财务拨款、贷款合计	Total Financial Allocation and Loans	1045.52	583.87	244.20	22.26	195.19
国家预算内投资	State Appropriation	37.90	35.71	1.99		0.20
国内贷款	Domestic Loans	190.36	108.36	36.63	5.36	40.01
利用外资	Foreign Investment	24.70	16.37	7.66		0.67
自筹投资	Fund Raising	569.05	323.08	178.89	16.83	50.25
其他投资	Others	147.17	57.85	13.05	0.07	76.20
投资总额	Total Value of Investment	991.95	569.51	237.19	26.52	158.73
按构成分	Grouped by Use of Funds					
#建筑工程	Construction Projects	587.97	404.38	50.48	25.75	107.36
安装工程	Installation Projects	63.42	26.78	33.12	0.07	3.45
设备、工具、器具购置	Purchase of Equipment, Tools and Instruments	191.74	54.02	135.92	0.17	1.63
按产业分	Grouped by Industry					
第一产业	Primary Industry	43.22	41.42	1.80		
第二产业	Secondary Industry	266.81	153.29	110.10	3.42	
第三产业	Tertiary Industry	681.92	374.80	125.29	23.10	158.73
#运输邮电通讯业	Transportation, Postal and Telecommunication	261.25	140.31	97.84	23.10	
住宅	Residential Housing	160.34	46.12	1.38		112.84
按建设性质分	Grouped by Type of Construction					
#新建	New Construction	250.98	239.39	11.59		
扩建	Expension	516.29	221.64	135.92		158.73
改建	Replacement	212.69	103.46	82.71	26.52	
房屋建筑面积 (万平方米)	Floor Space of Building (10000 sq·m)					
施工面积	Floor Space Under Construction	4561.59	2289.24	176.69	0.07	2095.59
#住宅	Residential Housing	2483.58	775.59	20.28		1687.71
竣工面积	Floor Space Completed	2410.51	1289.93	120.14	0.07	1000.37
#住宅	Residential Housing	1325.78	485.41	16.04		824.33

注:本表不包括5~50万元零星固定资产投资。

Note: Odd pieces of fixed assets (50-500 thousand yuan) were excluded in this table.

5-6 基本建设、更新改造和房地产开发投资（1998）

INVESTMENT IN CAPITAL CONSTRUCTION, UPDATING AND TRANSFORMATION, AND REAL ESTATE DEVELOPMENT

指标	Items	合计 Total	基本建设 Capital Construction	更新改造 Updating and Transformation	房地产开发 Real Estate Development
投资总额（亿元）	**Total Value of Investment (10^8 yuan)**	**1343.43**	**747.18**	**296.01**	**300.24**
按资金来源分	Grouped by Sources of Finance				
国家预算内投资	State Appropriation	49.41	47.09	2.00	0.32
国内贷款	Domestic Loans	248.51	134.11	45.35	69.05
利用外资	Foreign Investment	148.20	114.37	23.96	9.87
自筹投资	Fund Raising	679.15	381.16	210.98	87.01
其他投资	Others	218.16	70.45	13.72	133.99
按隶属关系分	Grouped by Administrative Relationship				
中央项目	Central Government Projects	308.94	204.41	103.04	1.49
地方项目	Local Projects	1034.49	542.77	192.97	298.75
按构成分	Grouped by Use of Funds				
建筑安装工程	Construction and Installation	806.07	492.54	98.67	214.86
设备、工器具购置	Purchase of Equipment and Instruments	325.15	145.08	174.98	5.09
其他费用	Others	212.21	109.56	22.36	80.29
按建设性质分	Grouped by Type of Construction				
#新建	New Construction	394.19	376.19	18.00	
扩建	Expension	731.05	259.95	170.86	300.24
改建	Replacement	197.56	105.72	91.84	
按用途分	Grouped by Industry				
#住宅	Residential Housing	246.10	48.23	1.72	196.15
第一产业	Primary Industry	43.40	41.55	1.85	
第二产业	Secondary Industry	448.18	283.47	164.71	
第三产业	Tertiary Industry	851.85	422.16	129.45	300.24
新增固定资产（亿元）	**Newly Incraesed Fixed Assets (10^8 yuan)**	**1024.77**	**531.25**	**264.41**	**229.11**
建设项目个数（个）	**Construction Projects**				
施工项目	Projects Under Construction	7820	4405	3415	
#大中型项目或限上技改项目	Large and Medium Projects or Over-Norm Item	112	46	66	
全部建成投产项目	Total Projects Completed Put Into Use	5549	2940	2609	
#大中型项目或限上技改项目	Large and Medium Projects or Over-Norm Item	26	9	17	
房屋建筑面积（万平方米）	**Floor Space of Building (10000 sq·m)**				
施工面积	Floor Space Under Construction	6545.51	2479.82	255.91	3809.78
#住宅	Residential Housing	3700.21	796.89	23.69	2879.63
竣工面积	Floor Space Completed	3343.84	1350.53	168.69	1824.62
#住宅	Residential Housing	1988.30	497.83	18.85	1471.62

5－7 基本建设、更新改造投资完成额(按农轻重分)
FULFILMENT VALUE OF CAPITAL CONSTRUCTION, UPDATING AND TRANSFORMATION INVESTMENT
(Grouped by Agriculture, Light Industry, Heavy Industry)

单位:亿元 (10^8 yuan)

年份 Year	农业 Agriculture	轻工业 Light Industry	重工业 Heavey Industry	#能源工业 Sources of Energy	运输邮电通信业 Transportation, Postal and Telecommunication
1980	1.91	6.00	13.63	6.28	1.92
1985	1.16	13.29	30.47	11.44	7.40
1986	1.01	18.27	15.43	14.67	9.44
1987	1.78	23.50	58.45	22.65	12.51
1988	1.94	29.87	70.94	24.07	11.16
1989	1.64	21.40	54.34	18.61	12.48
1990	2.58	19.31	54.55	22.52	15.92
1991	3.49	26.63	72.63	30.52	20.14
1992	4.40	43.78	103.45	40.22	37.48
1993	6.77	63.89	126.10	45.15	55.31
1994	8.35	83.56	146.34	47.66	82.24
1995	9.94	86.57	205.97	79.22	125.87
1996	13.30	69.14	263.58	112.60	168.55
1997	24.22	91.27	314.42	136.26	199.65
1998	43.40	161.29	278.92	153.68	274.08

5－8 基本建设、更新改造投资完成额(按建设性质分)
FULFILMENT VALUE OF CAPITAL CONSTRUCTION, UPDATING AND TRANSFORMATION INVESTMENT
(Grouped by Type of Construction)

单位:亿元 (10^8 yuan)

年份 Year	基本建设 Capital Construction				更新改造 Updating and Transformation			
	投资额 Investment Value	#新建 New Construction	#扩建 Expension	#改建 Replacement	投资额 Investment Value	#新建 New Construction	#扩建 Expension	#改建 Replacement
1980	26.15	7.63	11.07	7.38	5.50	0.29	2.30	2.75
1985	47.35	19.01	22.76	4.87	24.73	0.48	9.83	11.84
1986	60.42	26.62	26.46	6.46	34.04	1.57	17.24	13.92
1987	78.89	40.15	29.27	7.30	43.04	1.66	21.98	8.10
1988	90.85	45.40	33.67	9.12	54.15	3.44	30.02	19.22
1989	75.12	34.34	29.83	8.49	41.12	2.04	22.54	15.12
1990	74.32	31.80	43.12	10.18	41.53	1.44	22.75	16.07
1991	92.09	38.61	40.35	12.02	58.92	1.98	32.31	22.70
1992	155.84	81.09	57.10	15.45	93.72	4.24	49.73	38.08
1993	212.11	106.53	76.18	26.55	145.13	8.94	78.60	55.40
1994	274.79	124.75	113.06	33.31	170.53	12.42	91.62	62.49
1995	362.15	159.88	148.14	47.76	218.78	32.91	108.02	72.19
1996	481.07	206.92	198.51	68.25	238.23	18.71	138.24	74.85
1997	588.05	262.43	248.13	70.32	268.77	15.11	157.14	80.71
1998	747.18	376.19	259.95	105.72	296.01	18.00	170.86	91.84

5-9 基本建设施工项目计划总投资及完成情况
FULFILMENT OF GENERAL INVESTMENT PLAN BY CAPITAL CONSTRUCTION PROJECTS UNDER CONSTRUCTION

单位:亿元 (10^8 yuan)

指标	Items	1990	1995	1997	1998
施工项目 (个)	Projects Under Construction	3171	3878	3785	4405
全部建成投产项目 (个)	Projects Fully Completed Put Into Operation	1739	2523	2473	2940
计划总投资	Plan of General Investments	449.42	1138.60	1946.97	2607.96
自开始建设至本年底累计完成投资	Total Investment value Completed Since the Beginning of Construction to the End of This Year	305.81	725.44	1161.60	1357.45
本年完成投资	Investments Completed in This Year	74.32	362.15	588.05	747.18
累计新增固定资产	Newly Increased Fixed Assets Accumulatively	209.68	423.06	658.11	675.57
未完工程累计完成投资	Accumulation of Investment of Projects Incompleted	88.14	299.07	493.56	565.00
全部建成尚需投资	Investment Needed For the Completion of Projects	143.61	413.16	785.37	1250.51
项目建成投产率 (%)	Rate of Investment of Projects Completed (%)	54.8	65.1	65.3	66.7
未完工程占用率 (%)	Occupied Rate of Projects Incompleted (%)	118.6	82.6	83.9	75.6
建设周期 (年)	Construction Cycle (year)	6.05	3.14	3.31	3.49

5-10 基本建设施工大中型项目计划总投资及完成情况
FULFILMENT OF GENERAL INVESTMENT PLAN BY LARGE AND MEDIUM CAPITAL CONSTRUCTION PROJECTS UNDER CONSTRUCTION

单位:亿元 (10^8 yuan)

指标	Items	1990	1995	1997	1998
施工项目 (个)	Projects Under Construction	50	49	50	46
全部建成投产项目 (个)	Projects Fully Completed Put Into Operation	7	7	10	9
计划总投资	Plan of General Investments	316.64	602.07	1000.61	1232.77
自开始建设至本年底累计完成投资	Total Investment value Completed Since the Beginning of Construction to the End of This Year	221.78	332.22	512.78	557.95
本年完成投资	Investments Completed in This Year	38.70	115.62	186.41	240.32
累计新增固定资产	Newly Increased Fixed Assets Accumulatively	157.62	190.76	271.21	217.26
未完工程累计完成投资	Accumulation of Investment of Projects Incompleted	54.79	139.50	240.87	232.72
全部建成尚需投资	Investment Needed For the Completion of Projects	94.86	269.85	487.83	674.82
项目建成投产率 (%)	Rate of Investment of Projects Completed (%)	14.0	14.3	20.0	19.6
未完工程占用率 (%)	Occupied Rate of Projects Incompleted (%)	141.6	120.7	129.2	96.8
建设周期 (年)	Construction Cycle (year)	8.18	5.21	5.37	5.13

5-11 基本建设投资完成额

FULFILMENT VALUE OF CAPITAL CONSTRUCTION INVESTMENT

单位:亿元 (10[8] yuan)

年份 Year	农业 Agriculture	轻工业 Light Industry	重工业 Heavey Industry	#能源工业 Sources of Energy	运输邮电通信业 Transportation, Postal and Telecommunication
1980	1.83	4.23	10.59	4.91	1.67
1981	0.49	2.11	7.55	2.93	1.05
1982	0.44	3.92	6.67	2.57	2.04
1983	0.80	4.77	8.22	3.19	3.15
1984	0.86	3.60	13.29	6.05	4.40
1985	0.88	3.46	19.23	7.15	6.30
1986	0.76	5.62	25.05	10.66	8.47
1987	1.11	7.08	39.11	18.24	10.33
1988	0.29	9.51	46.24	18.76	9.23
1989	0.17	7.21	35.55	14.99	9.79
1990	1.92	6.70	34.79	17.64	12.19
1991	2.77	7.38	44.33	23.94	13.93
1992	3.49	12.46	57.14	34.24	30.27
1993	5.48	17.50	58.86	35.71	36.39
1994	7.34	34.94	65.48	37.58	52.94
1995	8.65	28.73	94.94	59.22	88.08
1996	11.90	22.48	148.53	90.20	104.52
1997	22.60	46.74	187.39	110.61	119.12
1998	41.55	116.98	159.58	119.45	172.27

5-12 基本建设投资施工和竣工的房屋建筑面积

CAPITAL CONSTRUCTION INVESTMENT UNDER CONSTRUCTION AND FLOOR SPACE COMPLETED OF BUILDING

单位:万平方米 (10000 sq·m)

年份 Year	施工的房屋建筑面积 Floor Space of Building Under Construction	#住宅 Residential Housing	竣工的房屋建筑面积 Floor Space of Building Completed	#住宅 Residential Housing	房屋建筑面积竣工率(%) Rate of Floor Space of Building Completed
1978	880.00	359.91	466.00	213.67	53.0
1980	1631.61	854.76	834.19	461.86	51.1
1985	1753.88	855.80	821.30	451.61	46.8
1986	1737.06	830.80	949.44	520.87	54.7
1987	1526.00	561.40	808.23	380.89	53.0
1988	1518.05	595.00	766.81	345.94	50.5
1989	1272.83	504.40	689.11	295.63	54.1
1990	1112.59	400.68	567.96	218.37	51.0
1991	1190.25	433.99	586.45	225.52	49.3
1992	1602.51	568.41	779.75	322.07	48.7
1993	1645.87	449.19	858.13	277.20	52.1
1994	1731.45	517.24	921.61	334.04	53.2
1995	1895.78	541.01	1031.75	353.06	54.4
1996	2027.22	574.07	1097.57	372.03	54.1
1997	2179.48	608.77	1198.14	410.46	55.0
1998	2479.82	796.89	1350.53	497.83	54.5

5－13 国民经济各行业按建设性质分的基本建设投资（1998）
CAPITAL CONSTRUCTION INVESTMENT OF STATE-OWNED UNITS BY TYPE OF CONSTRUCTION AND SECTOR

单位：亿元 （10^8 yuan）

行业	Sector	投资额 Investment	#新建 New Construction	#扩建 Expension	#改建 Replacement
全省总计	**Provincial**	**747.18**	**376.19**	**259.95**	**105.72**
农、林、牧、渔业	**Farming, Forestry, Animal Husbandry and Fishery**	**6.63**	**0.49**	**1.56**	**4.58**
农业	Farming	4.66	0.32	1.06	3.28
林业	Forestry	0.04		0.01	0.03
畜牧业	Animal Husbandry	0.16	0.09	0.07	
渔业	Fishery	0.07		0.05	0.02
农林牧渔服务业	FFAF Services	1.70	0.08	0.37	1.25
采掘业	**Excavation**	**7.62**	**0.72**	**6.63**	**0.27**
煤炭采选业	Coal Mining and Processing	3.60	0.70	2.86	0.04
石油和天然气开采业	Petroleum and Natural Gas Extraction	3.30		3.30	
黑色金属矿采选业	Ferrous Metals Mining and Processing				
有色金属矿采选业	Nonferrous Metals Mining and Processing				
非金属矿采选业	Nonmetal Minerals Mining and Processing	0.72	0.02	0.47	0.23
其他矿采选业	Other Minerals Mining and Processing				
木材及竹材采运业	Logging and Transport of Timber and Bamboo				
制造业	**Manufacturing**	**144.73**	**95.70**	**43.56**	**4.99**
食品加工业	Food Processing	0.33	0.17	0.07	0.09
食品制造业	Food Production	0.43	0.23	0.10	0.08
饮料制造业	Beverage Production	0.10	0.03	0.02	0.05
烟草加工业	Tobacco Processing	0.03			0.03
纺织业	Textile Industry	0.55	0.19	0.05	0.31
服装及纤维制品制造业	Garments and Other Fiber Products	0.73	0.08	0.13	0.52
皮革毛皮羽绒及制品业	Leather, Furs, Down and Related Products				
木材加工及竹藤棕草制品业	Timber Processing, Bamboo, Cane, Palm Fiber and Straw Products				
家具制造业	Furniture Manufacturing	0.12		0.11	0.01
造纸及纸制品业	Papermaking and Paper Products	78.85	78.73	0.06	0.06
印刷业记录媒介的复制	Printing and Record Pressing	0.07		0.06	0.01
文教体育用品制造业	Stationery, Education and Sports Goods				
石油加工及炼焦业	Petroleum Processing and Coking Products	2.46	0.02	2.39	0.05
化学原料及制品制造业	Raw Chemical Materials and Chemical Products	19.75	5.19	13.68	0.54
医药制造业	Medical and Pharmaceutical Products	2.47	0.26	2.20	0.01
化学纤维制造业	Chemical Fibers	15.66	3.28	12.37	
橡胶制品业	Rubber Products				
塑料制品业	Plastic Products	0.14		0.06	0.08
非金属矿物制品业	Nonmetal Mineral Products	3.62	1.03	2.48	0.10
黑色金属冶炼及压延加工业	Smelting and Pressing of Ferrous Metals	0.41	0.27		0.14

续表 1 Continued 1

单位:亿元 (10⁸ yuan)

行业	Sector	投资额 Investment	#新建 New Construction	#扩建 Expension	#改建 Replacement
有色金属冶炼及压延加工业	Smelting and Pressing of Nonferrous Metals	0.01			0.01
金属制品业	Metal Products	4.28	3.46	0.39	0.43
普通机械制造业	Ordinary Machinery Manufacturing	0.96	0.33	0.28	0.35
专用设备制造业	Special Purposes Equipment Manufacturing	5.36	0.02	5.01	0.26
交通运输设备制造业	Transportation Equipment Manufacturing	2.99	0.81	0.77	1.38
电气机械及器材制造业	Electric Equipment and Machinery	1.66	0.99	0.46	0.21
电子及通信设备制造业	Electronic and Telecommunications	3.18	0.40	2.68	0.10
仪器仪表及文化办公用机械制造业	Instruments, Meters, Cultural and Official Machinery	0.19		0.02	0.17
其他制造业	Other Manufacturing	0.38	0.21	0.17	
电力、煤气及水的生产和供应业	**Electric Power, Gas and Water Production and Supply**	**124.21**	**69.48**	**47.56**	**7.17**
电力、蒸气、热水生产和供应业	Electric Power, Steam and Hot Water Production and Supply	107.25	57.88	43.23	6.14
煤气的生产和供应业	Gas Production and Supply	2.85	0.24	2.47	0.14
自来水的生产和供应业	Tap Water Production and Supply	14.11	11.36	1.86	0.89
建筑业	**Construction**	**6.91**	**2.87**	**1.01**	**3.03**
土木工程建筑业	Civil Engineering Construction	6.42	2.50	1.01	2.91
线路、管道和设备安装业	Circuit, Pipelines and Equipment Installation	0.47	0.37		0.10
建筑物的装修装饰业	Building Fitting up and Decorations	0.02			0.02
地质勘查、水利管理业	**Geological Prospecting and Water Conservancy**	**35.07**	**3.90**	**15.91**	**15.25**
地质勘查业	Geological Prospecting	0.15		0.07	0.08
水利管理业	Water Conservancy	34.92	3.90	15.84	15.17
交通运输、仓储及邮电通信业	**Transportation, Storage, Postal and Telecommunications Services**	**175.90**	**117.73**	**27.86**	**30.00**
铁路运输业	Railways	19.93	12.36	0.25	7.31
公路运输业	Highways	56.04	41.25	6.93	7.60
管道运输业	Pipelines				
水上运输业	Waterways	0.94	0.02	0.04	0.88
航空运输业	Airways	1.53	0.99	0.54	
交通运输辅助业	Subsidiary Transportation	56.28	39.08	5.13	12.04
其他交通运输业	Other Transportation	12.95	12.95		
仓储业	Storage	3.63	3.07	0.54	0.02
邮电通信业	Postal and Telecommunications Services	24.60	8.01	14.43	2.15
批发和零售贸易餐饮业	**Wholesale, Retail Trade and Food Services**	**21.66**	**8.24**	**11.02**	**2.40**
食品饮料烟草和家庭用品批发业	Wholesale Food, Drink, Tobacco and Household Articles	9.94	1.83	6.70	1.40
能源材料和机械电子设备批发业	Wholesale Energy, Material and Electronic Equipment	2.00	1.26	0.50	0.23

续 表 2 Continued 2

单位:亿元 (10^8 yuan)

行业	Sector	投资额 Investment	#新建 New Construction	#扩建 Expension	#改建 Replacement
其他批发业	Other Wholesale	1.07	0.19	0.84	0.04
零售业	Retail	6.82	3.83	2.68	0.31
商业经纪与代理业	Commercial Management and Agencies	0.60	0.44		0.16
餐饮业	Food Services	1.23	0.69	0.30	0.24
金融、保险业	**Banking and Insurance**	**10.72**	**2.66**	**7.05**	**1.01**
金融业	Banking	9.81	2.21	6.65	0.94
保险业	Insurance	0.91	0.45	0.40	0.07
房地产业	**Real Estate**	**4.67**	**1.47**	**2.81**	**0.39**
房地产开发与经营业	Real Estate Development and Management	0.52	0.49	0.02	0.01
房地产管理业	Real Estate Management	4.07	0.98	2.79	0.30
房地产代理与经纪业	Real Estate Management and Agencies	0.08			0.08
社会服务业	**Social Services**	**68.58**	**26.70**	**24.66**	**16.54**
公共设施服务业	Public Facilities Services	57.72	19.86	21.49	16.11
居民服务业	Residential Services	0.92	0.18	0.44	0.03
旅馆业	Hotels	6.68	4.58	1.87	0.17
租赁服务业	Rentals				
旅游业	Touism	1.28	0.53	0.75	
娱乐服务业	Recreational Services	1.28	1.10	0.04	0.07
信息、咨询服务业	Information and Consultancy Services	0.01			
计算机应用服务业	Computer Supply Services	0.33	0.32		
其他社会服务业	Other Social Services	0.36	0.13	0.07	0.16
卫生体育和社会福利业	**Health Care, Sports and Social Welfare**	**13.48**	**2.67**	**8.73**	**1.73**
卫生	Health Care	11.98	1.81	8.22	1.59
体育	Sports	1.30	0.78	0.38	0.14
社会福利保障业	Social Welfare	0.20	0.08	0.13	
教育、文化艺术和广播电影电视业	**Education, Culture and Arts, Radio, Film and Television**	**52.88**	**8.82**	**35.68**	**6.84**
教育	Education	46.11	6.25	32.55	6.08
文化艺术业	Culture and Arts	2.77	1.38	0.99	0.27
广播、电影、电视业	Radio, Film and Television	4.00	1.19	2.14	0.49
科学研究和综合技术服务业	**Scientific Research and Polytechnical Services**	**3.12**	**0.43**	**0.95**	**1.73**
科学研究业	Scientific Research	2.25	0.21	0.73	1.30
综合技术服务业	Polytechnical Services	0.87	0.22	0.22	0.43
国家机关、政党机关和社会团体	**Government Agencies, Party Agencies and Social Organizations**	**56.13**	**23.94**	**20.62**	**9.63**
#国家机关	Government Agencies and Party	53.12	22.00	16.69	9.53
政党机关	Agencies	1.76	1.70	0.03	0.02
其他行业	**Other Sectors**	**14.87**	**10.37**	**4.34**	**0.16**

5－14 国民经济各行业基本建设施工、投产项目个数（1998）
CAPITAL CONSTRUCTION PROJECTS UNDER CONSTRUCTION AND PUT INTO USE BY SECTOR

行业	Sector	施工项目（个）Project under Construction (units)	#新开工 Starting This Year	全部建成投产项目（个）Fully Completed Project Turn Over for Production (unit)	项目建成投产率（%）Rate of Projests Completed & Put into Use (%)
全省总计	**Provincial**	**4405**	**3053**	**2940**	**66.7**
农、林、牧、渔业	**Farming, Forestry, Animal Husbandry and Fishery**	**59**	**45**	**35**	**59.3**
农业	Farming	17	14	8	47.1
林业	Forestry	2	2	1	50.0
畜牧业	Animal Husbandry	7	5	4	57.1
渔业	Fishery	3	3	2	66.7
农林牧渔服务业	FFAF Services	30	21	20	66.7
采掘业	**Excavation**	**13**	**5**	**4**	**30.8**
煤炭采选业	Coal Mining and Processing	6	1	1	16.7
石油和天然气开采业	Petroleum and Natural Gas Extraction	1			
黑色金属矿采选业	Ferrous Metals Mining and Processing				
有色金属矿采选业	Nonferrous Metals Mining and Processing				
非金属矿采选业	Nonmetal Minerals Mining and Processing	6	4	3	50.0
其他矿采选业	Other Minerals Mining and Processing				
木材及竹材采运业	Logging and Transport of Timber and Bamboo				
制造业	**Manufacturing**	**296**	**180**	**189**	**63.9**
食品加工业	Food Processing	21	16	18	85.7
食品制造业	Food Production	13	10	8	61.5
饮料制造业	Beverage Production	6	4	5	83.3
烟草加工业	Tobacco Processing	1		1	100.0
纺织业	Textile Industry	26	17	21	80.8
服装及纤维制品制造业	Garments and Other Fiber Products	3	2	3	100.0
皮革毛皮羽绒及制品业	Leather, Furs, Down and Related Products				
木材加工及竹藤棕草制品业	Timber Processing, Bamboo, Cane, Palm Fiber and Straw Products				
家具制造业	Furniture Manufacturing	2	1	2	100.0
造纸及纸制品业	Papermaking and Paper Products	6	4	3	50.0
印刷业记录媒介的复制	Printing and Record Pressing	5	3	4	80.0
文教体育用品制造业	Stationery, Education and Sports Goods				
石油加工及炼焦业	Petroleum Processing and Coking Products	3		2	66.7
化学原料及制品制造业	Raw Chemical Materials and Chemical Products	35	18	21	60.0
医药制造业	Medical and Pharmaceutical Products	8	4	5	62.5
化学纤维制造业	Chemical Fibers	5	2	2	40.0
橡胶制品业	Rubber Products				
塑料制品业	Plastic Products	4	2	4	100.0
非金属矿物制品业	Nonmetal Mineral Products	20	14	12	60.0
黑色金属冶炼及压延加工业	Smelting and Pressing of Ferrous Metals	4	4	2	50.0

续表1 Continued 1

行业	Sector	施工项目（个） Project under Construction (units)	#新开工 Starting This Year	全部建成投产项目（个） Fully Completed Projest Turn Over for Production (unit)	项目建成投产率（%） Rate of Projests Completed & Put into Use (%)
有色金属冶炼及压延加工业	Smelting and Pressing of Nonferrous Metals	2	1	1	50.0
金属制品业	Metal Products	10	7	8	80.0
普通机械制造业	Ordinary Machinery Manufacturing	26	17	14	53.8
专用设备制造业	Special Purposes Equipment Manufacturing	17	10	13	76.5
交通运输设备制造业	Transportation Equipment Manufacturing	33	18	13	39.4
电气机械及器材制造业	Electric Equipment and Machinery	19	14	12	63.2
电子及通信设备制造业	Electronic and Telecommunications	16	5	9	56.3
仪器仪表及文化办公用机械制造业	Instruments, Meters, Cultural and Official Machinery	7	4	2	28.6
其他制造业	Other Manufacturing	4	3	4	100.0
电力、煤气及水的生产和供应业	**Electric Power, Gas and Water Production and Supply**	**182**	**104**	**88**	**48.4**
电力、蒸气、热水生产和供应业	Electric Power, Steam and Hot Water Production and Supply	120	70	62	51.7
煤气的生产和供应业	Gas Production and Supply	13	7	3	23.1
自来水的生产和供应业	Tap Water Production and Supply	49	27	23	46.9
建筑业	**Construction**	**86**	**67**	**68**	**79.1**
土木工程建筑业	Civil Engineering Construction	79	62	62	78.5
线路、管道和设备安装业	Circuit, Pipelines and Equipment Installation	6	4	5	83.3
建筑物的装修装饰业	Building Fitting up and Decorations	1	1	1	100.0
地质勘查、水利管理业	**Geological Prospecting and Water Conservancy**	**109**	**82**	**64**	**58.7**
地质勘查业	Geological Prospecting	5	3	4	80.0
水利管理业	Water Conservancy	104	79	60	57.7
交通运输、仓储及邮电通信业	**Transportation, Storage, Postal and Telecommunications Services**	**536**	**385**	**349**	**65.1**
铁路运输业	Railways	4	1	1	25.0
公路运输业	Highways	167	115	105	62.9
管道运输业	Pipelines				
水上运输业	Waterways	7	3	3	42.9
航空运输业	Airways	2			
交通运输辅助业	Subsidiary Transportation	177	141	122	68.9
其他交通运输业	Other Transportation	2			
仓储业	Storage	20	13	11	55.0
邮电通信业	Postal and Telecommunications Services	157	112	107	68.2
批发和零售贸易餐饮业	**Wholesale, Retail Trade and Food Services**	**291**	**199**	**208**	**71.5**
食品饮料烟草和家庭用品批发业	Wholesale Food, Drink, Tobacco and Household Articles	121	89	84	69.4
能源材料和机械电子设备批发业	Wholesale Energy, Material and Electronic Equipment	31	22	26	83.9

续表 2 Continued 2

行业	Sector	施工项目(个) Project under Construction (units)	#新开工 Starting This Year	全部建成投产项目(个) Fully Completed Projest Turn Over for Production (unit)	项目建成投产率(%) Rate of Projests Completed & Put into Use (%)
其他批发业	Other Wholesale	18	10	12	66.7
零售业	Retail	90	61	63	70.0
商业经纪与代理业	Commercial Management and Agencies	6		4	66.7
餐饮业	Food Services	25	17	19	76.0
金融、保险业	**Banking and Insurance**	**110**	**58**	**75**	**68.2**
金融业	Banking	96	50	67	69.8
保险业	Insurance	14	8	8	57.1
房地产业	**Real Estate**	**31**	**22**	**18**	**58.1**
房地产开发与经营业	Real Estate Development and Management	7	3	3	42.9
房地产管理业	Real Estate Management	23	19	15	65.2
房地产代理与经纪业	Real Estate Management and Agencies	1			
社会服务业	**Social Services**	**349**	**268**	**242**	**69.3**
公共设施服务业	Public Facilities Services	264	216	191	72.3
居民服务业	Residential Services	16	9	11	68.8
旅馆业	Hotels	38	26	23	60.5
租赁服务业	Rentals				
旅游业	Touism	5	2	2	40.0
娱乐服务业	Recreational Services	13	7	7	53.8
信息、咨询服务业	Information and Consultancy Services	1	1	1	100.0
计算机应用服务业	Computer Supply Services	1	1		
其他社会服务业	Other Social Services	11	6	7	63.6
卫生体育和社会福利业	**Health Care, Sports and Social Welfare**	**225**	**156**	**133**	**59.1**
卫生	Health Care	203	141	122	60.1
体育	Sports	14	10	5	35.7
社会福利保障业	Social Welfare	8	5	6	75.1
教育、文化艺术和广播电影电视业	**Education, Culture and Arts, Radio, Film and Television**	**1186**	**850**	**860**	**72.5**
教育	Education	1085	796	808	74.5
文化艺术业	Culture and Arts	54	27	29	53.7
广播、电影、电视业	Radio, Film and Television	47	27	23	48.9
科学研究和综合技术服务业	**Scientific Research and Polytechnical Services**	**56**	**29**	**30**	**53.6**
科学研究业	Scientific Research	30	16	11	36.7
综合技术服务业	Polytechnical Services	26	13	19	73.1
国家机关、政党机关和社会团体	**Government Agencies, Party Agencies and Social Organizations**	**838**	**580**	**551**	**65.8**
#国家机关	Government Agencies and Party	813	565	537	66.1
政党机关	Agencies	9	8	3	33.3
其他行业	**Other Sectors**	**38**	**23**	**26**	**68.4**

5-15 更新改造投资主要指标
MAJOR ITEMS OF UPDATING AND TRANSFORMATION INVESTMENT

指标	Items	1990	1995	1997	1998
投资总额 （亿元）	**Total Value of Investment (10^8 yuan)**	**41.53**	**218.78**	**268.77**	**296.01**
按资金来源分	Grouped by Sources of Finance				
国家预算内投资	State Appropriation	0.50	1.98	0.77	2.0
国内贷款	Domestic Loans	13.02	60.21	49.15	45.35
利用外资	Foreign Investment	3.06	35.28	34.91	23.96
自筹投资	Fund Raising	22.33	113.07	177.73	210.98
其他投资	Others	2.62	8.24	6.21	13.72
按构成分	Grouped by Composition				
建筑安装工程	Construction and Installation	16.04	70.40	87.22	98.67
设备工器具购置	Purchase of Equipments and Instruments	21.61	130.99	162.97	174.98
其他费用	Others	3.88	17.39	18.58	22.36
按建设性质分	Grouped by Type of Construction				
#新建	New Construction	1.44	32.91	15.12	18.00
扩建	Expension	22.75	108.02	157.14	170.86
改建	Replacement	16.07	72.19	80.70	91.84
按用途分	Grouped by Function				
增产	Increasing Output	15.04	103.57	108.81	79.78
节约能源	Economize on Energy	1.80	4.88	7.57	10.57
其他节约	Other Economizations	0.09	0.64	1.94	1.14
增加品种	Increasing Varieties	6.98	33.40	38.04	41.43
提高产品质量	Improve the Quality of Products	2.98	14.12	20.47	13.36
三废治理	Waste Water, Waste Gas and Waste Residue Treatment	0.52	4.18	3.44	5.57
其他	Others	14.12	57.99	88.50	144.16
新增固定资产 （亿元）	**Newly Incraesed Fixed Assets (10^8 yuan)**	**36.96**	**174.91**	**232.54**	**264.41**
建设项目个数 （个）	**Number of Projections Under Construction**	**3244**	**3926**	**3418**	**3415**
全部建成投产项目	Total Projects Completed In Use (units)	1871	2963	2662	2609
房屋建筑面积 （万平方米）	**Floor Space of Building (10000 sq·m)**				
施工面积	Floor Space Under Construction	353.62	359.69	295.82	255.91
#住宅	Residential Housing	72.44	29.34	21.91	23.69
竣工面积	Floor Space Completed	200.84	225.11	188.76	168.69
#住宅	Residential Housing	45.88	20.67	13.62	18.85

5-16 国民经济各行业按建设性质分的更新改造投资（1998）
TECHNICAL UPDATES AND TRANSFORMATION OF INVESTMENT OF STATE-OWNED UNITS BY TYPE OF CONSTRUCTION AND SECTOR

单位:亿元 (10^8 yuan)

行业	Sector	投资额 Investment	#新建 New Construction	#扩建 Expension	#改建 Replacement
全省总计	**Provincial**	**296.01**	**18.00**	**170.86**	**91.84**
农、林、牧、渔业	**Farming, Forestry, Animal Husbandry and Fishery**	**1.19**	**0.10**	**0.62**	**0.47**
农业	Farming	0.56		0.14	0.42
林业	Forestry				
畜牧业	Animal Husbandry	0.05	0.05		
渔业	Fishery	0.11	0.05	0.06	
农林牧渔服务业	FFAF Services	0.47		0.42	0.05
采掘业	**Excavation**	**4.65**		**0.62**	**4.03**
煤炭采选业	Coal Mining and Processing	2.72		0.27	2.45
石油和天然气开采业	Petroleum and Natural Gas Extraction	1.28			1.28
黑色金属矿采选业	Ferrous Metals Mining and Processing	0.06		0.01	0.05
有色金属矿采选业	Nonferrous Metals Mining and Processing	0.10		0.10	
非金属矿采选业	Nonmetal Minerals Mining and Processing	0.49		0.24	0.25
其他矿采选业	Other Minerals Mining and Processing				
木材及竹材采运业	Logging and Transport of Timber and Bamboo				
制造业	**Manufacturing**	**131.97**	**10.03**	**65.81**	**46.04**
食品加工业	Food Processing	5.00	0.40	3.32	1.24
食品制造业	Food Production	2.42	0.02	1.60	0.37
饮料制造业	Beverage Production	3.81	0.26	2.16	1.02
烟草加工业	Tobacco Processing	1.55			1.11
纺织业	Textile Industry	8.13	0.04	3.31	4.51
服装及纤维制品制造业	Garments and Other Fiber Products	0.71	0.17	0.28	0.19
皮革毛皮羽绒及制品业	Leather, Furs, Down and Related Products	0.48		0.39	0.06
木材加工及竹藤棕草制品业	Timber Processing, Bamboo, Cane, Palm Fiber and Straw Products	0.50	0.01	0.48	0.01
家具制造业	Furniture Manufacturing	0.13			0.13
造纸及纸制品业	Papermaking and Paper Products	2.10	0.13	1.23	0.74
印刷业记录媒介的复制	Printing and Record Pressing	0.76		0.37	0.36
文教体育用品制造业	Stationery, Education and Sports Goods	0.05	0.02	0.01	0.01
石油加工及炼焦业	Petroleum Processing and Coking Products	5.53		0.56	4.96
化学原料及制品制造业	Raw Chemical Materials and Chemical Products	23.84	2.42	12.49	8.73
医药制造业	Medical and Pharmaceutical Products	3.47	0.15	1.74	1.23
化学纤维制造业	Chemical Fibers	2.77	0.08	2.13	0.56
橡胶制品业	Rubber Products	5.19	0.01	5.11	0.04
塑料制品业	Plastic Products	1.62	0.52	0.74	0.36
非金属矿物制品业	Nonmetal Mineral Products	6.17	0.30	3.23	2.52
黑色金属冶炼及压延加工业	Smelting and Pressing of Ferrous Metals	11.84	0.10	8.66	2.76

续表 1 Continued 1

单位:亿元 (10⁸ yuan)

行业	Sector	投资额 Investment	#新建 New Construction	#扩建 Expension	#改建 Replacement
有色金属冶炼及压延加工业	Smelting and Pressing of Nonferrous Metals	0.50		0.16	0.33
金属制品业	Metal Products	1.76	0.47	1.03	0.17
普通机械制造业	Ordinary Machinery Manufacturing	8.92	0.67	2.85	5.36
专用设备制造业	Special Purposes Equipment Manufacturing	6.00	0.86	2.66	1.96
交通运输设备制造业	Transportation Equipment Manufacturing	13.44	0.45	3.07	3.96
电气机械及器材制造业	Electric Equipment and Machinery	7.01	0.78	5.06	1.15
电子及通信设备制造业	Electronic and Telecommunications	6.75	2.03	2.55	1.49
仪器仪表及文化办公用机械制造业	Instruments, Meters, Cultural and Official Machinery	0.93	0.14	0.34	0.41
其他制造业	Other Manufacturing	0.59		0.28	0.30
电力、煤气及水的生产和供应业	**Electric Power, Gas and Water Production and Supply**	**27.03**	**3.31**	**7.51**	**16.14**
电力、蒸气、热水生产和供应业	Electric Power, Steam and Hot Water Production and Supply	24.24	3.31	6.36	14.50
煤气的生产和供应业	Gas Production and Supply	0.45		0.38	0.07
自来水的生产和供应业	Tap Water Production and Supply	2.34		0.77	1.57
建筑业	**Construction**	**1.06**		**0.30**	**0.02**
土木工程建筑业	Civil Engineering Construction	0.91		0.29	0.02
线路、管道和设备安装业	Circuit, Pipelines and Equipment Installation	0.15		0.01	
建筑物的装修装饰业	Building Fitting up and Decorations				
地质勘查、水利管理业	**Geological Prospecting and Water Conservancy**	**0.66**		**0.59**	**0.07**
地质勘查业	Geological Prospecting				
水利管理业	Water Conservancy	0.66		0.59	0.07
交通运输、仓储及邮电通信业	**Transportation, Storage, Postal and Telecommunications Services**	**102.02**	**3.39**	**82.09**	**13.25**
铁路运输业	Railways	0.10			0.10
公路运输业	Highways	5.31	0.03	0.65	2.41
管道运输业	Pipelines				
水上运输业	Waterways	0.43		0.01	0.09
航空运输业	Airways	0.08			0.08
交通运输辅助业	Subsidiary Transportation	2.55	0.08	0.19	1.63
其他交通运输业	Other Transportation				
仓储业	Storage	0.21			0.21
邮电通信业	Postal and Telecommunications Services	93.34	3.28	81.24	8.73
批发和零售贸易餐饮业	**Wholesale, Retail Trade and Food Services**	**2.45**	**0.29**	**1.21**	**0.88**
食品饮料烟草和家庭用品批发业	Wholesale Food, Drink, Tobacco and Household Articles	0.89	0.27	0.29	0.31
能源材料和机械电子设备批发业	Wholesale Energy, Material and Electronic Equipment	0.16		0.03	0.08

续表2 Continued 2

单位:亿元 (10^8 yuan)

行业	Sector	投资额 Investment	#新建 New Construction	#扩建 Expension	#改建 Replacement
其他批发业	Other Wholesale	0.07		0.07	
零售业	Retail	1.14		0.80	0.34
商业经纪与代理业	Commercial Management and Agencies	0.10	0.02		0.08
餐饮业	Food Services	0.09		0.02	0.07
金融、保险业	**Banking and Insurance**				
金融业	Banking				
保险业	Insurance				
房地产业	**Real Estate**				
房地产开发与经营业	Real Estate Development and Management				
房地产管理业	Real Estate Management				
房地产代理与经纪业	Real Estate Management and Agencies				
社会服务业	**Social Services**	**8.06**		**0.48**	**7.04**
公共设施服务业	Public Facilities Services	7.89		0.48	6.87
居民服务业	Residential Services	0.01			0.01
旅馆业	Hotels	0.16			0.16
租赁服务业	Rentals				
旅游业	Touism				
娱乐服务业	Recreational Services				
信息、咨询服务业	Information and Consultancy Services				
计算机应用服务业	Computer Supply Services				
其他社会服务业	Other Social Services				
卫生体育和社会福利业	**Health Care, Sports and Social Welfare**	**0.66**		**0.45**	**0.06**
卫生	Health Care	0.61		0.40	0.06
体育	Sports				
社会福利保障业	Social Welfare	0.05		0.05	
教育、文化艺术和广播电影电视业	**Education, Culture and Arts, Radio, Film and Television**	**1.38**	**0.08**	**0.73**	**0.25**
教育	Education	0.42		0.32	0.01
文化艺术业	Culture and Arts				
广播、电影、电视业	Radio, Film and Television	0.96	0.08	0.41	0.24
科学研究和综合技术服务业	**Scientific Research and Polytechnical Services**	**0.43**		**0.43**	
科学研究业	Scientific Research	0.43		0.43	
综合技术服务业	Polytechnical Services				
国家机关、政党机关和社会团体	**Government Agencies, Party Agencies and Social Organizations**	**1.92**	**0.10**	**0.89**	**0.90**
#国家机关政党机关	Government Agencies and Party Agencies	1.92	0.10	0.89	0.90
其他行业	**Other Sectors**	**12.53**	**0.70**	**9.13**	**2.69**

5－17 国民经济各行业更新改造施工、投产项目个数（1998）

TECHNICAL UPDATES AND TRANSFORMATION PROJECTS UNDER CONSTRUCTION AND PUT INTO USE BY SECTOR

行业	Sector	施工项目（个） Project under Construction (units)	#新开工 Starting This Year	全部建成投产项目（个） Fully Completed Projest Turn Over for Production (unit)	项目建成投产率（%） Rate of Projests Completed & Put into Use (%)
全省总计	**Provincial**	**3415**	**2650**	**2609**	**76.4**
农、林、牧、渔业	**Farming, Forestry, Animal Husbandry and Fishery**	**43**	**36**	**29**	**67.4**
农业	Farming	24	18	15	62.5
林业	Forestry				
畜牧业	Animal Husbandry	1	1	1	100.0
渔业	Fishery	9	8	5	55.6
农林牧渔服务业	FFAF Services	9	9	8	88.9
采掘业	**Excavation**	**53**	**36**	**29**	**54.7**
煤炭采选业	Coal Mining and Processing	31	22	19	61.3
石油和天然气开采业	Petroleum and Natural Gas Extraction	1			
黑色金属矿采选业	Ferrous Metals Mining and Processing	5	2	1	20.0
有色金属矿采选业	Nonferrous Metals Mining and Processing	1			
非金属矿采选业	Nonmetal Minerals Mining and Processing	15	12	9	60.0
制造业	**Manufacturing**	**1678**	**1196**	**1174**	**70.0**
食品加工业	Food Processing	144	122	125	86.8
食品制造业	Food Production	64	52	54	84.4
饮料制造业	Beverage Production	52	47	40	76.9
烟草加工业	Tobacco Processing	9	1	6	66.7
纺织业	Textile Industry	169	130	133	78.7
服装及纤维制品制造业	Garments and Other Fiber Products	15	13	13	86.7
皮革毛皮羽绒及制品业	Leather, Furs, Down and Related Products	6	1	5	83.3
木材加工及竹藤棕草制品业	Timber Processing, Bamboo, Cane, Palm Fiber and Straw Products	12	11	9	75.0
家具制造业	Furniture Manufacturing	3	3	3	100.0
造纸及纸制品业	Papermaking and Paper Products	32	24	17	53.1
印刷业记录媒介的复制	Printing and Record Pressing	23	17	19	82.6
文教体育用品制造业	Stationery, Education and Sports Goods	3	3	3	100.0
石油加工及炼焦业	Petroleum Processing and Coking Products	57	43	49	86.0
化学原料及制品制造业	Raw Chemical Materials and Chemical Products	330	240	237	71.8
医药制造业	Medical and Pharmaceutical Products	73	60	39	53.4
化学纤维制造业	Chemical Fibers	21	17	12	57.1
橡胶制品业	Rubber Products	17	10	9	52.9
塑料制品业	Plastic Products	23	20	15	65.2
非金属矿物制品业	Nonmetal Mineral Products	87	64	61	70.1
黑色金属冶炼及压延加工业	Smelting and Pressing of Ferrous Metals	54	35	33	61.1
有色金属冶炼及压延加工业	Smelting and Pressing of Nonferrous Metals	12	7	8	66.7
金属制品业	Metal Products	28	17	20	71.4
普通机械制造业	Ordinary Machinery Manufacturing	130	72	61	46.9
专用设备制造业	Special Purposes Equipment Manufacturing	73	41	45	61.6
交通运输设备制造业	Transportation Equipment Manufacturing	90	54	59	65.6
电气机械及器材制造业	Electric Equipment and Machinery	67	36	43	64.2
电子及通信设备制造业	Electronic and Telecommunications	59	38	39	66.1
仪器仪表及文化办公用机械制造业	Instruments, Meters, Cultural and Official Machinery	18	12	13	72.2
其他制造业	Other Manufacturing	7	6	4	57.1
电力、煤气及水的生产和供应业	**Electric Power, Gas and Water Production and Supply**	**369**	**308**	**262**	**71.0**

续表 Continued

行业	Sector	施工项目（个） Project under Construction (units)	#新开工 Starting This Year	全部建成投产项目（个） Fully Completed Projest Turn Over for Production (unit)	项目建成投产率（%） Rate of Projects Completed & Put into Use (%)
电力、蒸气、热水生产和供应业	Electric Power, Steam and Hot Water Production and Supply	334	280	236	70.0
煤气的生产和供应业	Gas Production and Supply	4	2		
自来水的生产和供应业	Tap Water Production and Supply	31	26	26	83.9
建筑业	**Construction**	**13**	**9**	**7**	**53.8**
土木工程建筑业	Civil Engineering Construction	10	7	7	70.0
线路、管道和设备安装业	Circuit, Pipelines and Equipment Installation	3	2		
建筑物的装修装饰业	Building Fitting up and Decorations				
地质勘查、水利管理业	**Geological Prospecting and Water Conservancy**	**8**	**8**	**8**	**100.0**
地质勘查业	Geological Prospecting				
水利管理业	Water Conservancy	8	8	8	100.0
交通运输、仓储及邮电通信业	**Transportation, Storage, Postal and Telecommunications Services**	**893**	**736**	**792**	**88.7**
铁路运输业	Railways	1			
公路运输业	Highways	43	41	39	90.7
管道运输业	Pipelines				
水上运输业	Waterways	5	5	4	80.0
航空运输业	Airways	2	2	1	50.0
交通运输辅助业	Subsidiary Transportation	27	14	18	66.7
其他交通运输业	Other Transportation				
仓储业	Storage	7	7	6	85.7
邮电通信业	Postal and Telecommunications Services	808	667	724	89.6
批发和零售贸易餐饮业	**Wholesale, Retail Trade and Food Services**	**62**	**56**	**51**	**82.3**
食品饮料烟草和家庭用品批发业	Wholesale Food, Drink, Tobacco and Household Articles	29	26	26	89.7
能源材料和机械电子设备批发业	Wholesale Energy, Material and Electronic Equipment	8	5	6	75.0
其他批发业	Other Wholesale	2	2	1	50.0
零售业	Retail	18	18	15	83.3
商业经纪与代理业	Commercial Management and Agencies	2	2	1	50.0
餐饮业	Food Services	3	3	2	66.7
社会服务业	**Social Services**	**113**	**111**	**106**	**93.8**
公共设施服务业	Public Facilities Services	109	107	103	94.5
居民服务业	Residential Services	1	1	1	100.0
旅馆业	Hotels	3	3	2	66.7
卫生体育和社会福利业	**Health Care, Sports and Social Welfare**	**18**	**12**	**13**	**72.2**
卫生	Health Care	17	12	12	70.6
社会福利保障业	Social Welfare	1		1	100.0
教育、文化艺术和广播电影电视业	**Education, Culture and Arts, Radio, Film and Television**	**23**	**13**	**11**	**47.8**
教育	Education	3	2	3	100.0
文化艺术业	Culture and Arts	1			
广播、电影、电视业	Radio, Film and Television	19	11	8	42.1
科学研究和综合技术服务业	**Scientific Research and Polytechnical Services**	**1**		**1**	**100.0**
科学研究业	Scientific Research	1		1	100.0
综合技术服务业	Polytechnical Services				
国家机关、政党机关和社会团体	**Government Agencies, Party Agencies and Social Organizations**	**52**	**48**	**45**	**86.5**
国家机关 政党机关	Government Agencies and Party Agencies	52	48	45	86.5
其他行业	**Other Sectors**	**89**	**81**	**81**	**91.0**

5-18 房地产开发投资主要指标
MAJOR ITEMS OF REAL ESTATE DEVELOPMENT INVESTMENT

指标	Items	1990	1995	1997	1998
投资总额 (亿元)	**Total Value of Investment (10^8 yuan)**	**11.71**	**240.85**	**241.55**	**300.24**
按资金来源分	Grouped by Sources of Finance				
国家预算内投资	State Appropriation	0.02	0.90	0.52	0.32
国内贷款	Domestic Loans	1.73	48.05	61.32	69.05
利用外资	Foreign Investment		24.51	13.57	9.87
自筹投资	Fund Raising	5.44	71.09	59.29	87.01
其他投资	Other	4.52	96.30	106.85	133.99
按构成分	Grouped by Use of Funds				
建筑安装工程	Construction and Installation	9.97	172.76	179.03	214.86
设备工器具购置	Purchase of Equipments and Instruments	0.01	5.96	2.94	5.09
其他费用	Others	1.73	62.13	59.58	80.29
按工程用途分	Grouped by Use of Project				
#住宅	Residential Housing	9.76	139.24	142.40	196.15
第三产业	Tertiary Industry	11.71	240.85	241.55	300.24
新增固定资产 (亿元)	**Newly Increase Fixed Assets (10^8 yuan)**	**9.74**	**145.24**	**200.77**	**229.11**
房屋建筑面积 (万平方米)	**Floor Space of Building (10000 sq·m)**				
施工面积	Floor Space Under Construction	555.45	3510.13	3393.55	3809.78
#住宅	Residential Housing	481.80	2502.75	2382.29	2879.63
竣工面积	Floor Space Completed	293.94	1630.06	1647.60	1824.62
#住宅	Residential Housing	257.12	1339.47	1277.46	1471.62
土地开发投资额 (亿元)	**Value of Investment of Land Development (10^8 yuan)**		**26.70**	**24.12**	**29.06**
土地开发面积 (万平方米)	Area of Land Development (10000 sq·m)		1329.00	761.66	904.52
商品房销售额 (亿元)	**Sales Value of Commodity House (10^8 yuan)**	**14.55**	**107.38**	**155.05**	**210.02**
商品房销售建筑面积 (万平方米)	Sales Space Construction of Commodity House (10000 sq·m)	250.02	798.31	1069.75	1321.40

注：土地开发投资与开发面积从1993年起开始统计。

Note: Investment of land development and space development were counted since 1993.

5-19 城镇集体固定资产投资主要指标
MAIN ITEMS OF FIXED ASSETS BY CITIES AND TOWNS COLLECTIVE UNITS

指　　标	Items	1990	1995	1997	1998
投资总额　（亿元）	**Total Value of Investment　(10^8 yuan)**	**20.79**	**89.30**	**74.01**	**75.81**
按资金来源分	Grouped by Sources of Finance				
国家预算内投资	State Appropriation	0.18	0.27	0.32	0.05
国内贷款	Domestic Loans	7.33	20.06	12.23	10.26
利用外资	Foreign Investment	0.49	3.43	2.53	2.59
自筹投资	Fund Raising	10.87	56.62	50.72	53.42
其他投资	Others	1.92	8.92	8.21	9.49
按构成分	Grouped by Composition				
建筑安装工程	Construction and Installation	10.04	47.45	41.76	41.73
设备工器具购置	Purchase of Equipments and Instruments	9.56	37.38	28.68	28.86
其他投资	Others	1.19	4.47	2.57	5.22
按建设性质分	Grouped by Type of Construction				
#新建	New Construction	2.92	9.40	11.39	18.77
扩建	Expension	11.16	56.88	40.85	33.84
改建	Replacement	5.41	17.85	18.51	19.60
按产业分	Grouped by Industry				
#住宅	Residential Housing	2.17	4.80	5.28	4.40
第一产业	Primary Industry	0.27	0.34	0.55	1.30
第二产业	Secondary Industry	15.62	57.16	42.82	45.42
第三产业	Tertiary Industry	4.90	31.80	30.64	29.09
新增固定资产　（亿元）	**Newly Incraesed Fixed Assets　(10^8 yuan)**	**20.13**	**82.69**	**67.79**	**72.77**
施工项目个数　（个）	**Number of Projections Under Construction**	**2859**	**3417**	**2115**	**2225**
全部建成投产项目	Projects Completed and Put Into Production	1821	2750	1699	1788
房屋建筑面积（万平方米）	**Floor Space of Building (10000 sq·m)**				
施工面积	Floor Space Under Construction	362.37	494.37	392.73	330.53
#住宅	Residential Housing	116.55	96.07	91.11	75.04
竣工面积	Floor Space Completed	232.42	354.02	288.22	259.83
#住宅	Residential Housing	79.67	68.10	66.07	66.34

5-20 农村集体固定资产投资主要指标
MAIN ITEMS OF FIXED ASSETS BY RURAL COLLECTIVE UNITS

指　　标	Items	1990	1995	1997	1998
投资总额　（亿元）	**Total Value of Investment　(10^8 yuan)**	**411.76**	**451.52**	**451.06**	**485.82**
按资金来源分	Grouped by Sources of Finance				
国家预算内投资	State Appropriation	3.67	3.47		
国内贷款	Domestic Loans	72.85	71.09	57.45	35.97
利用外资	Foreign Investment	59.84	61.87	59.21	50.53
自筹投资	Fund Raising	213.02	253.20	278.29	342.32
其他投资	Others	62.38	61.89	56.11	57.00
按构成分	Grouped by Composition				
建筑安装工程	Construction and Installation	172.18	183.17	184.40	223.88
设备工器具购置	Purchase of Equipments and Instruments	218.11	246.01	235.30	225.74
其他投资	Others	21.47	22.34	31.36	36.20
按建设性质分	Grouped by Type of Construction				
#新建	New Construction	171.28	164.79	182.71	169.63
扩建	Expension	166.08	196.13	182.81	230.92
改建	Replacement	55.53	72.64	69.62	64.92
按产业分	Grouped by Industry				
#住宅	Residential Housing	7.03	7.71	12.28	17.00
第一产业	Primary Industry	6.82	12.01	17.77	25.78
第二产业	Secondary Industry	349.10	376.56	358.87	341.24
第三产业	Tertiary Industry	55.84	62.95	74.42	118.80
新增固定资产　（亿元）	**Newly Increased Fixed Assets　(10^8 yuan)**	**337.85**	**380.96**	**388.45**	**416.34**
施工项目个数　（个）	**Number of Projections Under Construction**	**29109**	**31910**	**26079**	**32125**
全部建成投产项目	Projects Completed and Put Into Production	26017	28540	23965	29691
房屋建筑面积　（万平方米）	**Floor Space of Building　(10000 sq·m)**				
施工面积	Floor Space Under Construction	2116.07	2073.83	1779.0	1966.76
#住宅	Residential Housing	184.57	206.73	207.95	310.73
竣工面积	Floor Space Completed	1850.81	1759.28	1539.32	1773.90
#住宅	Residential Housing	156.78	168.30	156.29	274.19

5-21 城镇工矿区私人建房
BUILDING CONSTRUCTION BY PRIVATES IN INDUSTRIAL AND MINING REGIONS OF CITIES AND TOWNS

年份 Year	建房户数（户） Building Construction (Household)	竣工房屋建筑面积（万平方米） Floor Space of Building Completed (10000 sq·m)	#住宅 Residential Housing	竣工房屋价值（万元） Value of Building Completed (10000 yuan)	#住宅 Residential Housing
1985	29111	161.84	142.00	15549	13383
1986	26830	176.95	161.35	20718	18179
1987	35688	261.13	278.09	49474	39976
1988	28549	265.05	223.65	50833	42421
1989	29183	219.48	203.96	46062	39437
1990	23686	191.70	163.50	38276	32502
1991	21374	178.29	155.17	46535	41118
1992	20624	293.79	176.68	58648	49778
1993	27690	265.65	225.27	94147	76902
1994	34906	280.74	220.48	122582	94863
1995	24716	310.72	273.10	144205	122940
1996	25654	293.30	248.14	141910	120729
1997	24167	329.17	272.85	164214	125148
1998	30217	406.62	339.48	200095	154091

注：本表不包括农业户在城镇地域内的建房投资及面积。

Note: Building construction and space investment by rural household in area of cities and towns did not include in this table.

5-22 农村个人固定资产投资
FIXED ASSETS INVESTMENT BY RURAL INDIVIDUALS

年份 Year	投资总额（亿元） Total Investment (10^8 yuan)	非生产性固定资产投资 Non-Productive Fixed Assets Investment	#住宅 Residential Housing	生产性固定资产投资 Investment In Productive Fixed Asseets	竣工房屋建筑面积（万平方米） Floor Space of Building Completed (10000 sq·m)	#住宅 Residential Housing
1985	50.89	46.21	42.75	4.68	6783.57	6104.02
1986	76.91	69.83	64.61	7.08	10252.00	9225.00
1987	103.40	93.34	90.78	10.06	10879.93	10619.65
1988	119.30	105.53	100.64	13.77	10323.35	9432.41
1989	124.20	117.30	103.63	6.90	13771.40	8758.82
1990	142.74	134.87	130.53	7.87	9490.74	9276.26
1991	153.37	141.88	140.03	11.49	9225.00	8902.00
1992	141.68	120.28	120.28	21.40	7220.00	6681.00
1993	151.98	129.02	129.02	22.96	7745.00	7167.00
1994	162.80	149.16	149.16	13.64	8549.00	8237.00
1995	199.80	171.76	171.76	28.04	7032.00	6805.00
1996	261.50	221.48	221.48	40.02	7471.00	7253.00
1997	329.88	275.87	273.37	54.01	8712.00	8240.00
1998	299.17	247.00	243.51	52.17	7294.00	6770.00

5－23 城市房地产市场交易情况
TRANSACTION OF REAL ESTATE MARKET IN CITY

指　标	Items	1995	1996	1997	1998
房产买卖	**Real Estate Buying and Selling**				
成交面积　（万平方米）	Transactional Floor Space　(10000 sq. m)	594.80	1603.10	865.55	1688.50
住　宅	Residence	466.2	1015.75	731.60	1375.84
办公用房	House for Office Use	73.0		59.81	133.96
商业用房	House for Commerce Use	55.6		67.71	119.80
成交金额　（万元）	Transactional Value　(10000 yuan)	388105	722293	961777	2111221
住　宅	Residence	276416	524961	816010	1619867
办公用房	House for Office Use	66748	51939	56913	193847
商业用房	House for Commerce Use	36463	103646	88287	200818
房屋租赁	**House Hiring**				
出租面积　（万平方米）	Hiring Floor Space　(10000 sq. m)	1336.0	835.01	1117.44	1427.26
住　宅	Residence	1124.2	686.68	825.30	747.63
办公用房	House for Office Use	64.4	31.71	66.92	191.75
商业用房	House for Commerce Use	155.4	97.01	176.06	371.05
出租金额　（万元）	Hiring Value　(10000 yuan)	21666	35009	37174	65334
住　宅	Residence	7093	4947	6842	9207
办公用房	House for Office Use	2670	9698	5288	7084
商业用房	House for Commerce Use	1125	14580	23327	33877
向个人出售	**Residence Selling to Individual**				
新建住宅面积　（万平方米）	Floor Space of Newly Built Resicence　(10000 sq. m)	366.78	362.00	385.79	692.07
新建住宅销售额　（万元）	Sales Value of Newly Built Residence　(10000 yuan)	373819	400440	426365	937002
旧住宅面积　（万平方米）	Floor Space of Old Resicence　(10000 sq. m)	95.03	1901.19	422.64	785.51
旧住宅销售额　（万元）	Sales Value of Old Residence　(10000 yuan)	17749	366444	141258	281784

6. 物价

PRICE

6 物　　价
PRICE

1　9　9　8

居民消费价格指数	Resident Consumer Price Index	99.4
#食品	Foods	97.3
商品零售价格指数	Retail Price Index	98.2
工业品出厂价格指数	Industrial Products Producer Price Index	94.5
轻工业	Light Industry	96.1
重工业	Heavy Industry	93.7
原材料、燃料、动力购进价格指数	Raw Material, Fuel, and Motive Power Purchasing Price Index	91.4
固定资产价格指数	Fixed Assets Price Index	98.8
农产品收购价格总指数	Farm Products Purthasing Price Index	94.6

商品零售物价指数
(上年=100)

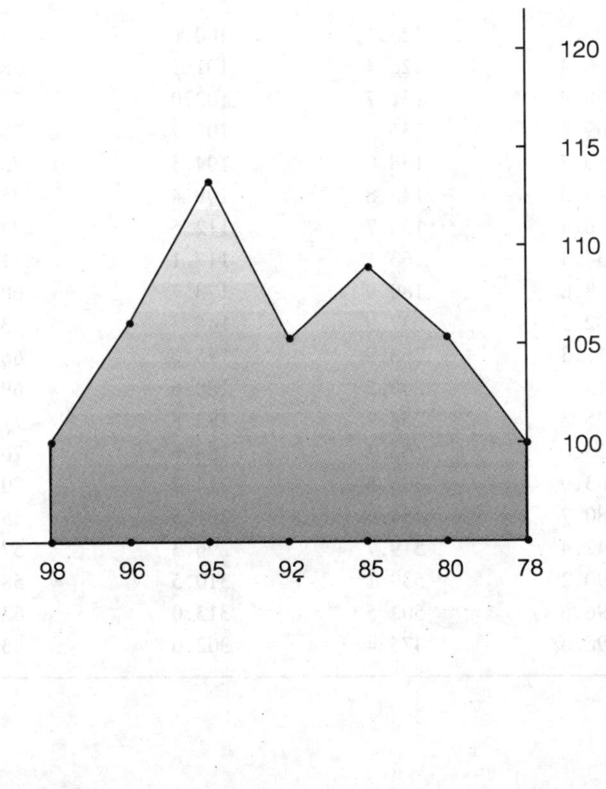

城市居民消费价格指数
(上年=100)

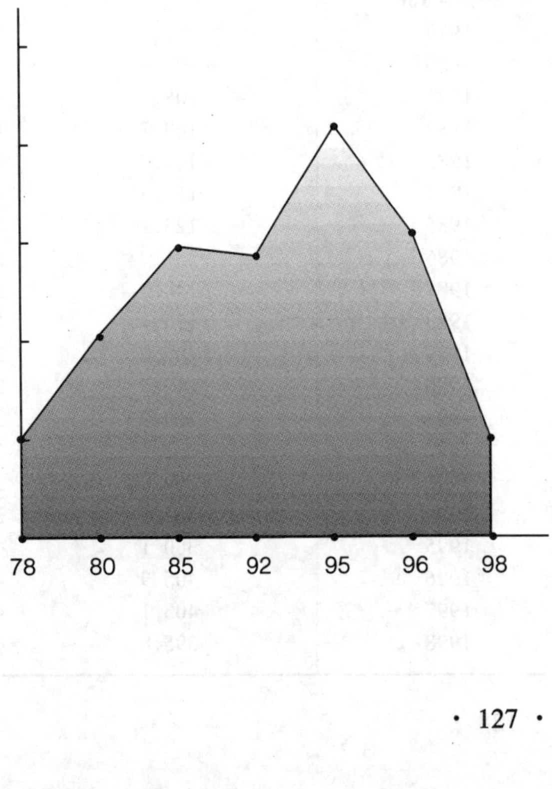

6-1 各种物价总指数
OVERALL PRICE INDICES

年份 Year	全省商品零售价格指数 Retail Price Index	城市居民消费价格总指数 Urban Consumer Price Index	农产品收购价格总指数 Farm Products Purchasing Price Index	农村工业品零售价格总指数 Rural Industrial Products Retail Price Index	工农业商品综合比价指数(以农产品收购价格总指数为100) Industrial and Agricultural Products Price Parity Index
以上年价格为100 **Preceding Year = 100**					
1979	101.3	100.7	123.1	100.6	81.7
1980	105.8	105.7	104.3	100.5	96.4
1981	101.4	102.3	102.6	100.9	98.3
1982	100.9	100.9	102.6	101.7	99.1
1983	100.1	100.8	102.1	100.7	98.6
1984	102.5	104.1	104.2	103.8	99.6
1985	109.5	109.6	106.9	103.7	97.0
1986	107.1	106.4	106.1	104.1	98.1
1987	109.3	110.5	110.9	105.7	95.3
1988	122.3	122.6	126.0	117.6	93.3
1989	116.8	116.0	115.8	120.7	104.2
1990	102.3	103.4	98.7	102.8	104.2
1991	104.8	107.7	99.4	101.8	102.4
1992	105.1	108.8	102.8	102.6	99.8
1993	115.9	118.7	114.8	113.6	99.0
1994	123.6	125.3	148.8	117.4	78.9
1995	114.3	116.2	114.3	117.8	103.1
1996	106.8	110.8	102.0	104.8	102.7
1997	99.3	101.3	94.8	100.8	106.3
1998	98.2	100.0	94.6	96.5	102.0
以1978年价格为100 **1978 = 100**					
1979	101.3	100.7	123.1	100.6	81.7
1980	107.3	106.4	128.4	101.1	78.7
1981	108.7	108.9	131.7	102.0	77.4
1982	109.7	109.9	135.2	103.7	76.7
1983	109.8	110.7	138.0	104.5	75.7
1984	112.5	115.3	143.8	108.4	75.4
1985	123.2	126.4	153.7	112.5	73.2
1986	131.9	134.4	163.1	117.1	71.8
1987	144.2	148.6	180.9	123.7	68.4
1988	176.4	182.1	227.9	145.5	63.8
1989	206.0	211.3	263.9	175.6	66.5
1990	210.7	218.5	260.5	180.6	69.3
1991	220.9	235.3	258.9	183.8	71.0
1992	232.1	256.0	266.2	188.6	70.8
1993	269.0	303.9	305.5	214.2	70.1
1994	332.5	380.7	454.6	251.5	55.3
1995	380.1	442.4	519.7	296.3	57.0
1996	405.9	490.2	530.1	310.5	58.6
1997	403.1	496.6	502.5	313.0	62.3
1998	395.8	496.6	475.4	302.0	63.5

6-2 各种物价总指数(1998)
OVERALL PRICE INDICES

基期 Base Period	全社会零售物价指数 Retail Price Index			城市居民消费价格总指数 Urban Consumer Price Index	农产品收购价格总指数 Farm Products Purchasing Price Index	农村工业品零售价格总指数 Rural Industrial Products Retail Price Index
	全省 Province	城市 Urban	农村 Rural			
以1950年价格为100 1950=100	503.6	557.1	486.4	662.1	818.2	313.7
以1952年价格为100 1952=100	454.3	502.3	422.3	596.7	787.3	310.2
以1957年价格为100 1957=100	425.9	468.0	400.4	543.2	671.7	310.8
以1965年价格为100 1965=100	390.3	422.8	369.7	496.5	539.1	289.5
以1970年价格为100 1970=100	397.0	428.2	377.0	505.1	517.1	301.4
以1978年价格为100 1978=100	395.8	418.6	377.4	496.6	475.4	302.0
以1980年价格为100 1980=100	369.3	392.1	356.5	466.5	370.2	298.7
以1981年价格为100 1981=100	364.2	382.3	352.2	456.0	360.9	296.1
以1982年价格为100 1982=100	361.0	379.5	348.1	452.0	351.7	291.1
以1983年价格为100 1983=100	360.6	378.4	344.6	448.4	344.5	289.1
以1984年价格为100 1984=100	351.8	364.5	333.3	430.7	330.6	278.5
以1985年价格为100 1985=100	321.3	331.7	306.9	393.0	309.3	268.6
以1986年价格为100 1986=100	300.0	311.5	288.4	369.3	291.5	258.0
以1987年价格为100 1987=100	274.5	281.1	267.1	334.2	262.8	244.1
以1988年价格为100 1988=100	224.4	227.6	221.3	272.6	208.6	207.6
以1989年价格为100 1989=100	192.1	196.7	184.9	235.0	180.1	172.0
以1990年价格为100 1990=100	187.8	191.7	181.2	227.3	182.5	167.3
以1991年价格为100 1991=100	179.2	177.9	178.2	211.1	183.6	164.3
以1992年价格为100 1992=100	170.5	165.9	172.5	194.0	178.6	160.2
以1993年价格为100 1993=100	147.1	142.3	150.4	163.4	155.6	141.0
以1994年价格为100 1994=100	119.0	116.9	120.5	130.4	104.6	120.1
以1995年价格为100 1995=100	104.1	103.9	104.5	112.2	91.5	101.9
以1996年价格为100 1996=100	97.5	97.3	97.6	101.3	89.7	97.3
以1997年价格为100 1997=100	98.2	98.2	98.1	100.0	94.6	96.5

6－3 全省商品零售价格分类指数（1998）
RETAIL PRICE INDICES BY CATEGORY

上年＝100 (preceding year＝100)

类别	Category	全省 Province	城市 Urban	农村 Rural
商品零售价格指数	**Retail Price Index**	**98.2**	**98.2**	**98.1**
食品类	Food	98.2	98.4	98.0
饮料、烟酒类	Beverages, Tobacco and Liquor	98.3	98.9	97.7
服装、鞋帽类	Garments, Shoes, Hats	99.6	99.3	100.0
纺织品类	Textiles	99.0	98.6	99.5
中、西药品类	Traditional Chinese and Western Medicines	102.1	101.9	102.5
化妆品类	Cosmetics	100.2	100.4	99.8
书报、杂志	Newspaper and Magazines	108.5	110.6	105.1
文化体育用品类	Stationery and Sports Goods	97.8	96.1	101.0
日用品类	Daily-Use Articles	99.3	99.2	99.4
家用电器类	Household Appliances	95.7	95.0	96.7
首饰类	Jewelery	91.4	91.5	91.3
燃料类	Fuels	95.4	97.9	90.9
建筑装璜材料类	Building Decoration Materials	96.5	97.1	95.8
机电产品类	Mechanical and Electric Products	94.3	93.4	96.2
农业生产资料类	**Means of Agricultural Products**	92.5		92.5
小农具	Small Farm Tools	98.8		98.8
饲料	Forage Grass	100.8		100.8
幼禽家畜	Young Livestock and Fowls	75.6		75.6
大牲畜	Livestock	106.5		106.5
半机械化农具	Semi-mechanized Farm Equipment	99.0		99.0
机械化农具	Mechanized Farm Equipment	95.8		95.8
化学肥料	Chemical Fertilizer	90.9		90.9
农药及农药械	Medicine and Equipment	97.5		97.5
化学农药	Chemical Pesticide	97.5		97.5
农药械	Pasticide Application Equipment	97.8		97.8
农机用油	Oil for Farm Machinies	93.7		93.7
其他	Others	93.0		93.0

6－4 全省居民消费价格分类指数（1998）
RESIDENTS CONSUMER PRICE INDICES BY CATEGORY

上年＝100 (preceding year＝100)

类别	Category	全省 Province	城市 Urban	农村 Rural
居民消费价格总指数	**Resident Consumer Price Index**	**99.4**	**100.0**	**99.0**
食品	Foods	97.3	97.7	96.9
粮食	Grain	103.9	103.7	104.6
淀粉及薯类	Starch and Potato	103.9	104.4	103.6
干豆类及豆制品	Beans and Bean Products	98.7	100.1	97.6
油脂类	Oil or Fat	102.3	103.7	101.3
肉禽及其制品	Meat and Poultry	89.8	89.6	90.2
蛋类	Eggs	105.4	105.2	105.7
水产品类	Aquatic Products	95.1	94.5	95.9
菜类	Vegetable Crops	101.8	103.3	99.9
#鲜菜	Fresh Vegetable	102.0	103.5	99.8
调味品	Flavoring	99.6	100.9	98.8
糖类	Sugar	97.3	98.2	96.9
烟草类	Tobacco	97.6	98.2	97.3
酒和饮料	Liquor	98.7	99.7	98.1
干鲜瓜果类	Dried and Fresh Fruits and Melons	96.4	95.4	97.5
#鲜果	Freshes	96.5	95.3	97.9
糕点类	Cake	101.3	100.7	102.0
奶及奶制品	Milk and Its Products	101.5	102.3	98.9
其他食品	Other	103.1	104.1	99.9
饮食业	Catering Trade	100.8	101.4	99.4
衣着类	Clothing	99.3	98.8	99.7
服装	Carments	98.9	98.5	99.3
衣着材料	Material in Clothing	98.6	97.1	99.0
棉布	Cotton Cloth	100.6	100.4	100.7
棉花化纤混纺布	Blend Cloth	100.3	99.7	100.4
化纤布	Chemical Fiber Cloth	96.8	93.1	98.2
呢绒	Woolen Fabric	99.3	100.4	98.9
绸缎	Silk	101.2	100.0	101.7
毛线	Knitting Wool	97.7	98.1	97.6
鞋袜帽及其他衣着	Shoes, Socks, Hats and Other Clothing	100.9	100.4	101.4
家庭设备及用品	Household Appliance	98.7	98.5	98.9

续表 Continued

上年＝100 (preceding year＝100)

类 别	Category	全 省 Province	城 市 Urban	农 村 Rural
耐用消费品	Durable Consumer Goods	97.6	97.5	97.7
家具	Furniture	96.7	96.4	96.9
家庭设备	Household Equipment	97.9	97.7	98.0
室内装饰品	Room Decoration	101.3	103.9	100.3
床上用品	Bed Articles	100.0	100.1	100.0
家庭日用杂品	Daily-Use Sundries	100.7	100.7	100.7
其他日用品	Others	98.2	97.0	99.4
医疗保健	Medicine and Health Care	102.7	102.2	103.0
医疗器具及保健用品	Medicine and Health Care Articles	101.7	101.7	101.7
中药	Traditional Chinese Medicines	106.1	104.4	106.8
西药	Western Medicines	100.2	100.4	100.1
交通和通讯工具	Traffic and Post	96.1	94.6	97.2
交通工具	Traffic	96.8	96.2	97.1
通讯工具	Post	93.8	91.1	97.8
娱乐教育文化用品	Recreation, Education and Culture Goods	98.5	99.0	98.2
文娱用耐用消费品	Durable Recreation Goods	94.5	90.4	96.4
教材及参考书	Teaching Material and Reference Books	102.3	103.5	100.9
文化娱乐用品	Recreation and Culture Goods	106.3	108.4	103.4
居住	Residence	100.7	109.9	96.2
住房	Housing	99.0	113.7	95.4
建筑材料	Construction Material	93.9	95.1	93.7
房租	Rent	119.6	127.6	109.1
水、电、燃料	Water, Electricity and Fuel	104.0	107.5	99.1
服务项目	Services	108.6	108.0	109.1
电讯费	Telecommunication	98.5	98.5	98.5
邮费	Postage	100.3	101.3	99.9
交通费	Traffic	105.6	108.0	103.7
洗理美容费	Washing, Haircut	107.6	110.4	106.0
文娱费	Recreation	107.6	108.5	105.7
学杂保育费	Tuition and Children Care	110.4	110.0	110.7
修理及其他服务费	Repair and Other Services	104.3	105.4	103.1
医疗保健服务	Health Care	121.2	129.9	119.1

6-5 农产品收购价格分类指数
FARM PRODUCTS PURCHASING PRICE INDICES BY CATEGORY

上年=100　　(preceding year=100)

年份 year	总指数 General Index	粮食 Grain	小麦 Wheat	稻谷 Rice	经济作物 Industrial Crops	食用油 Edide Vegetable Oil	棉花 Cotton	麻 Jute and Ambary Hemp
1979	123.1	131.3	132.6	130.4	124.5	138.7	123.6	100.2
1980	104.3	100.1	100.0	100.5	103.2	87.8	105.3	103.0
1981	102.6	103.3	103.6	103.0	106.2	108.8	105.3	100.0
1982	102.6	103.4	103.8	103.1	102.6	110.8	100.0	102.8
1983	102.1	104.5	104.5	104.5	100.7	85.3	104.5	99.4
1984	104.2	112.0	110.2	109.9	102.2	127.1	100.0	100.6
1985	106.9	97.6	97.7	99.5	99.8	100.1	99.4	95.8
1986	106.1	106.5	102.0	105.5	105.5	108.7	100.0	156.4
1987	110.9	105.6	102.1	113.1	109.2	104.3	113.7	88.7
1988	126.0	113.0	114.8	108.1	107.6	119.1	99.7	125.1
1989	115.8	126.7	117.6	132.2	120.9	103.7	129.5	100.2
1990	98.7	92.7	87.2	102.8	116.3	101.1	125.7	107.9
1991	99.4	97.1	93.9	106.6	101.7	97.3	103.3	90.2
1992	102.8	110.8	116.4	102.1	92.3	95.8	90.9	110.4
1993	114.8	121.4	110.2	148.1	113.5	124.6	110.0	93.9
1994	148.8	151.3	165.6	143.6	161.2	147.4	167.1	174.1
1995	114.3	123.6	129.6	122.7	122.4	100.5	130.0	224.8
1996	102.0	101.2	105.3	93.9	98.7	93.6	100.0	100.0
1997	94.8	85.0	84.4	83.9	101.4	107.1	100.0	91.1
1998	94.6	101.2	101.2	100.5	88.5	92.2	88.3	111.0

续表 1 Continued 1

上年=100 (preceding year=100)

年份 Year	茶叶 Tea	竹木材 Bamboo and Timber	工业用油漆 Paint for Industrial Use	禽畜产品 Livestock Products, Poultry and Eggs	肉畜 Livestock for Slaughtering	#肥猪 Fattened Hogs	禽蛋 Polutry Eggs	#鸡蛋 Chicken Eggs
1979	108.1		100.3	120.9	121.7	121.8	117.5	120.0
1980	100.0		100.4	104.8	104.7	104.3	100.6	100.5
1981	100.0		86.2	100.8	100.0	100.0	108.9	109.0
1982	100.1		100.0	99.9	100.1	100.0	99.2	98.9
1983	80.5		100.0	99.8	100.0	100.0	100.3	100.6
1984	105.6		111.3	102.6	102.8	102.7	102.4	102.5
1985	132.3	111.7	99.9	129.6	120.9	121.0	125.3	123.7
1986	156.8	98.2	100.0	105.9	104.8	104.8	117.3	109.4
1987	109.9	109.5	113.6	116.0	118.5	121.9	142.8	138.1
1988	159.9	114.9	148.5	145.6	165.1	167.0	111.4	116.8
1989	103.3	125.6	148.9	111.3	104.9	104.6	122.5	122.2
1990	101.4	89.1	85.0	94.9	92.0	91.1	119.0	118.2
1991	96.7	109.0	96.9	98.1	102.8	102.7	80.6	77.9
1992	108.2	96.0	79.1	106.1	104.4	102.7	104.0	102.8
1993	119.0	187.1	96.6	109.4	106.7	107.3	107.7	102.9
1994	101.2	105.6	189.0	146.7	158.4	159.8	124.2	121.9
1995	100.6	100.2	111.5	109.9	109.1	108.6	114.2	112.8
1996	133.8	101.1	196.6	106.5	103.3	103.8	115.0	114.3
1997	117.3	99.8	93.5	104.0	112.7	113.8	86.7	81.6
1998	72.3	100.2	54.2	85.6	79.1	76.5	96.0	96.1

续表 2 Continued 2

上年＝100 (preceding year＝100)

年 份 Year	皮 张 Hides and Skins	鬃 毛 Bristles	蚕茧蚕丝 Silkworn Cocoons and Silk	干鲜果 Dried and Fresh Fruits	干鲜菜及调味品 Dried and Fresh Vegetable and Condiments	#鲜 菜 Fresh Vegetable	药 材 Crude Drugs	土副产品 Local Products	水产品 Aquatic Products
1979	100.5	116.5	122.1	100.0	101.5	101.5	98.1	101.5	130.1
1980	126.7	103.5	102.3	109.5	104.0	109.0	97.0	102.6	100.8
1981	110.7	100.0	100.0	103.6	101.5	102.1	101.0	98.3	105.0
1982	97.0	98.1	100.5	97.2	98.3	95.9	98.1	98.1	103.8
1983	95.9	90.7	103.5	109.4	102.1	104.3	108.0	98.2	119.1
1984	91.3	126.4	97.3	112.1	91.3	196.0	99.4	101.8	105.1
1985	157.2	266.3	103.6	161.1	119.5	143.6	121.2	111.2	164.8
1986	184.0	69.0	105.6	116.3	102.6	97.2	49.8	110.0	109.4
1987	111.0	104.2	111.3	104.4	116.8	123.3	98.5	108.7	124.6
1988	124.8	114.6	193.8	223.1	119.9	126.5	234.8	124.8	122.9
1989	88.8	129.4	107.6	70.7	98.9	97.7	98.2	99.5	104.5
1990	84.5	78.5	95.0	101.0	100.0	99.9	97.9	102.5	95.3
1991	110.8	103.1	95.9	118.7	121.4	119.2	173.8	91.3	97.5
1992	120.3	113.1	99.6	100.4	111.9	112.6	109.8	94.5	115.9
1993	125.6	144.7	105.1	102.2	133.2	137.2	62.8	117.3	127.8
1994	132.8	114.7	150.0	138.8	121.2	122.1	109.1	122.2	138.0
1995	99.6	98.0	78.3	108.6	120.5	121.3	192.5	108.0	102.2
1996	106.1	99.6	100.7	90.7	102.0	101.8	109.1	117.1	107.7
1997	94.5	104.3	136.9	76.7	86.1	85.3	88.4	95.0	103.7
1998	84.6	98.2	95.0	104.5	103.4	103.5	85.1	100.8	96.1

6－6 农产品收购价格分类指数
FARM PRODUCTS PURCHASING PRICE INDICES BY CATEGORY

1978＝100

年份 year	总指数 General Index	粮食 Grain	小麦 Wheat	稻谷 Rice	经济作物 Industrial Crops	食用油 Edide Vegetable Oil	棉花 Cotton	麻 Jute and Ambary Hemp
1978	100.0	100.0	100.0	100.0	100.0	100.0	100.0	100.0
1979	123.1	131.3	132.6	130.4	124.5	138.7	123.6	100.2
1980	128.4	131.4	132.6	131.1	128.5	121.8	130.2	103.2
1981	131.7	135.8	137.4	135.0	136.5	132.5	137.0	103.2
1982	135.2	140.4	142.6	139.2	140.0	146.8	137.0	106.1
1983	138.0	146.7	149.0	145.4	141.0	125.2	143.2	105.5
1984	143.8	164.4	164.2	159.8	144.1	159.2	143.2	106.1
1985	153.7	160.5	160.4	159.0	143.8	159.3	142.4	101.7
1986	163.1	170.9	163.6	167.8	151.7	173.2	142.4	159.1
1987	180.9	180.5	167.1	189.8	165.7	180.6	161.9	141.1
1988	227.9	204.0	191.8	205.1	178.3	215.1	161.4	176.5
1989	263.9	258.5	225.6	271.2	215.6	223.1	209.0	176.9
1990	260.5	239.6	196.7	278.8	250.7	225.6	262.7	190.9
1991	258.9	232.7	184.7	297.2	255.0	219.5	271.4	172.2
1992	266.2	257.8	215.0	303.4	235.4	210.3	246.7	190.1
1993	305.5	313.0	236.9	449.3	267.2	262.0	271.4	178.5
1994	454.6	473.6	392.3	645.3	430.7	386.2	453.5	310.8
1995	519.7	585.4	508.5	791.7	527.2	388.1	589.6	698.7
1996	530.1	592.4	535.4	743.4	520.3	363.3	589.6	698.7
1997	502.5	503.5	451.9	623.7	527.6	389.1	589.6	636.5
1998	475.4	509.5	457.3	626.9	466.9	358.8	520.6	706.5

续表 1　Continued 1

1978＝100　　　　(preceding year＝100)

年　份 Year	茶　叶 Tea	竹木材 Bamboo and Timber	工业用油漆 Paint for Industrial Use	禽畜产品 Livestock Products, Poultry and Eggs	肉　畜 Livestock for Slaughtering	#肥　猪 Fattened Hogs	禽　蛋 Polutry Eggs	#鸡　蛋 Chicken Eggs
1978	100.0		100.0	100.0	100.0	100.0	100.0	100.0
1979	108.1		100.3	120.9	121.7	121.8	117.5	120.0
1980	108.1		100.7	126.7	127.4	127.0	118.2	120.6
1981	108.1		86.8	127.7	127.4	127.0	128.7	131.5
1982	108.2		86.8	127.6	127.5	127.0	127.7	130.0
1983	87.1		86.8	127.3	127.5	127.0	128.1	130.8
1984	92.0		96.6	130.6	131.1	130.5	131.2	134.1
1985	121.7	197.3	96.5	169.3	158.4	157.9	164.4	165.8
1986	190.8	193.7	96.5	179.0	166.0	165.4	192.8	181.4
1987	209.7	212.3	109.6	207.6	196.7	201.7	275.3	250.5
1988	335.3	243.9	162.8	302.3	324.8	336.8	306.7	292.6
1989	387.4	306.3	249.0	336.5	340.7	352.3	375.7	357.6
1990	351.2	272.9	206.0	319.3	313.4	320.9	447.1	422.7
1991	339.6	297.5	199.6	313.2	322.2	329.6	360.4	329.3
1992	367.4	285.6	157.9	332.3	336.4	338.5	374.8	338.5
1993	437.2	534.4	156.7	365.2	358.9	363.2	417.4	348.3
1994	442.4	564.3	288.2	533.3	568.5	580.4	501.4	424.6
1995	445.1	565.4	321.3	586.1	620.2	630.3	572.6	478.9
1996	595.5	571.6	631.7	624.2	640.7	654.3	658.5	547.4
1997	698.5	570.5	590.6	649.2	722.1	744.6	570.9	446.7
1998	505.0	571.6	320.1	555.7	571.2	569.6	548.1	429.3

续表 2 Continued 2

1978=100 (preceding year=100)

年份 Year	皮张 Hides and Skins	鬃毛 Bristles	蚕茧蚕丝 Silkworn Cocoons and Silk	干鲜果 Dried and Fresh Fruits	干鲜菜及调味品 Dried and Fresh Vegetable and Condiments	#鲜菜 Fresh Vegetable	药材 Crude Drugs	土副产品 Local Products	水产品 Aquatic Products
1978	100.0	100.0	100.0	100.0	100.0	100.0	100.0	100.0	100.0
1979	100.5	116.5	122.1	100.0	101.5	101.5	98.1	101.5	130.1
1980	127.3	120.6	124.9	109.5	105.6	110.6	95.2	104.1	131.1
1981	141.0	120.6	124.9	113.4	107.1	113.0	96.1	102.4	137.7
1982	136.7	118.3	125.5	110.3	105.3	108.3	94.3	100.4	142.9
1983	131.1	107.3	129.9	120.6	107.5	113.0	101.8	98.6	170.2
1984	119.7	135.6	126.4	135.2	98.2	108.5	101.2	100.4	178.9
1985	188.2	361.1	131.0	217.8	117.3	155.7	122.7	111.6	294.7
1986	346.3	249.2	138.3	253.3	120.3	151.3	61.1	122.8	322.4
1987	384.3	259.7	153.9	264.4	140.5	186.6	60.2	133.5	401.7
1988	479.6	297.6	298.3	589.9	168.5	236.0	141.0	166.6	493.7
1989	425.9	385.1	321.0	417.1	166.7	230.6	138.5	165.8	515.9
1990	360.0	302.3	305.0	421.3	166.7	230.4	135.6	169.9	491.7
1991	398.9	311.7	292.5	500.1	202.4	274.6	235.7	155.1	479.4
1992	479.9	352.5	291.3	502.1	226.5	309.2	258.8	146.6	555.6
1993	603.1	528.0	311.7	527.7	346.1	434.8	168.4	191.3	712.7
1994	800.5	585.1	459.3	712.2	365.7	517.9	177.3	210.2	979.9
1995	797.3	573.4	359.6	773.5	440.7	628.2	341.3	227.0	1001.5
1996	845.9	571.1	362.1	701.6	449.5	639.5	372.4	265.8	1078.6
1997	799.4	595.7	495.7	538.1	387.0	545.5	329.2	252.5	1118.5
1998	676.3	585.0	470.9	562.3	400.2	564.6	280.1	254.5	1074.9

6－7 工业品出厂价格指数
INDUSTRIAL PRODUCTS PRODUCER PRICE INDICES

上年＝100 (preceding year＝100)

分组名称	Group Name	1995	1996	1997	1998
工业品出厂价格总指数	**Industrial Products Producer Price Indices**	**114.2**	**100.6**	**97.9**	**94.5**
轻工业	Light Industry	117.4	100.4	97.6	96.1
以农产品为原料	Using Farm Products as Raw Materials	118.5	102.9	98.7	99.2
以非农产品为原料	Using Non-Farm Products as Raw Materials	115.6	94.7	95.2	90.7
重工业	Heavy Industry	110.7	100.9	98.1	93.7
采掘	Excavation	109.8	105.3	102.1	90.9
原料	Raw Matericals	113.2	100.4	100.4	91.3
加工	Manufacturing	108.9	100.2	95.8	95.7
生产资料	Means of Productions	113.1	100.1	97.4	93.4
采掘	Excavation	109.7	105.3	102.1	90.9
原料	Raw Matericals	116.3	99.3	99.1	91.2
加工	Manufacturing	110.6	99.6	95.6	95.2
生活资料	Consumer Goods	115.4	101.5	98.7	97.0
食品	Food	126.2	105.9	99.0	98.6
衣着	Clothing	115.7	99.6	99.4	100.2
一般日用品	Daily－Use Articles	112.4	101.4	98.6	95.4
耐用消费品	Durable Consumer Goods	100.6	93.5	94.2	89.4

6－8 分行业主要工业品出厂价格指数
INDUSTRIAL PRODUCTS PRODUCER PRICE INDICES

上年＝100 (preceding year＝100)

部门名称	Deparment	1995	1996	1997	1998
冶金工业	Metallurgical Industry	100.3	96.2	96.4	90.0
电力工业	Power	111.6	106.2	105.7	102.0
煤炭及炼焦工业	Coal	111.2	116.9	99.0	90.1
石油工业	Petroleum	119.1	101.9	107.6	89.5
化学工业	Chemical	124.0	100.6	96.3	90.9
机械工业	Machine Building	104.9	97.5	96.4	94.1
建筑材料工业	Building Materials	107.2	97.2	92.9	95.5
森林工业	Forestry	99.6	91.5	97.6	88.3
食品工业	Food Manufacturing	126.2	105.7	98.5	98.1
纺织工业	Textile	119.2	93.7	96.3	96.4
缝纫工业	Trailoring	103.4	118.3	102.8	100.8
皮革工业	Leather	120.0	114.5	100.6	102.3
造纸工业	Paper	137.7	113.3	92.1	91.3
文教艺术用品工业	Cultural, Educational Handicrafts Articles	111.0	100.0	102.3	97.0
其它工业	Other Industries	140.1	101.3	98.1	106.5

6-9 原材料、燃料、动力购进价格指数
RAW MATERIAL, FUEL, POWER PURCHASING PRICE INDICES

上年=100 (preceding year=100)

分组名称	Group Name	1995	1996	1997	1998
总指数	**Overall Index**	**117.3**	**103.9**	**97.9**	**91.4**
燃料、动力类	Fuels, Power	107.7	112.2	105.3	95.1
黑色金属材料类	Ferrous Metal	96.0	100.1	96.7	93.1
有色金属材料和电线类	Non-Ferrous Metal and Wire	124.5	91.2	94.9	84.0
化工原料类	Chemical Materials	131.7	97.1	95.2	86.3
木材及纸浆类	Timber and Pulp	124.8	94.5	99.6	95.7
建筑材料类	Construction Materials	110.8	97.0	98.5	96.3
非金属矿类	Non-Metal Mining Industry	103.2	97.4	91.8	95.8
农副产品类	Farm and Sideline Products	131.9	103.1	97.0	94.6
纺织原料类	Textile Raw Materials	125.7	99.1	91.5	89.5

6-10 固定资产投资价格指数
FIXED ASSETS INVESTMENT PRICE INDICES

上年=100 (preceding year=100)

项目	Item	1995	1996	1997	1998
固定资产投资	Fixed Assets Investment	107.4	103.2	99.2	98.8
建筑安装工程	Construction and Installation	107.1	102.9	100.0	99.7
设备、器具	Equipments and Instruments	105.3	102.6	96.6	95.0
其他费用	Others	113.8	106.4	101.6	102.6

7. 农业

AGRICULTURE

7 农　　业
AGRICULTURE

1 9 9 8

乡村劳动力	Rural Labor Force	2735.91	万人	(10000 persons)
#农林渔业劳动力	Labor Force of Farming, Forestry, Animal Husbandry	1531.46	万人	(10000 persons)
农林牧渔业总产值(现价)	Gross Output Value of Farming, Forestry, Animal Husbandry(current price)	1849.20	亿元	(10^8 yuan)
农作物播种面积	Sown Areas of Farm Crops	8058.28	千公顷	(1000 ha)
粮食产量	Grain Output	3415.12	万吨	(10000 tons)
棉花产量	Cotton Output	46.19	万吨	(10000 tons)
油料产量	Oil-bearing Ouptut	115.63	万吨	(10000 tons)
猪牛羊肉产量	Pork, Beef, Mutton Output	209.31	万吨	(10000 tons)
农业机械总动力	Power of Agricultural Machinery	2594.83	万千瓦	(10000 kilowatt)

农、林、牧、渔业总产值构成和指数

构 成 (%)

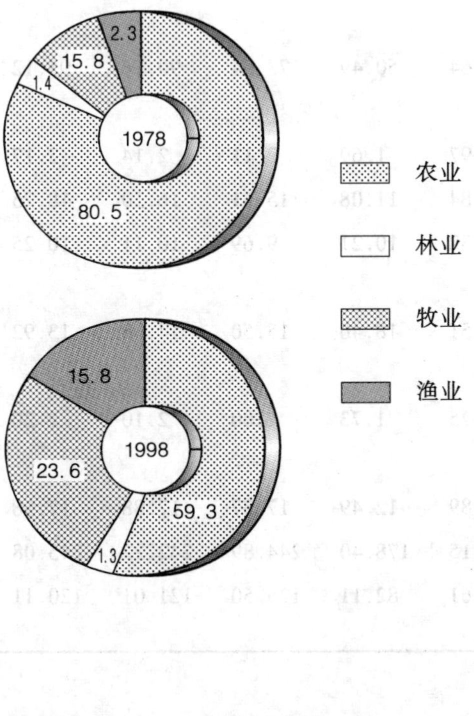

指 数 (1978=100)

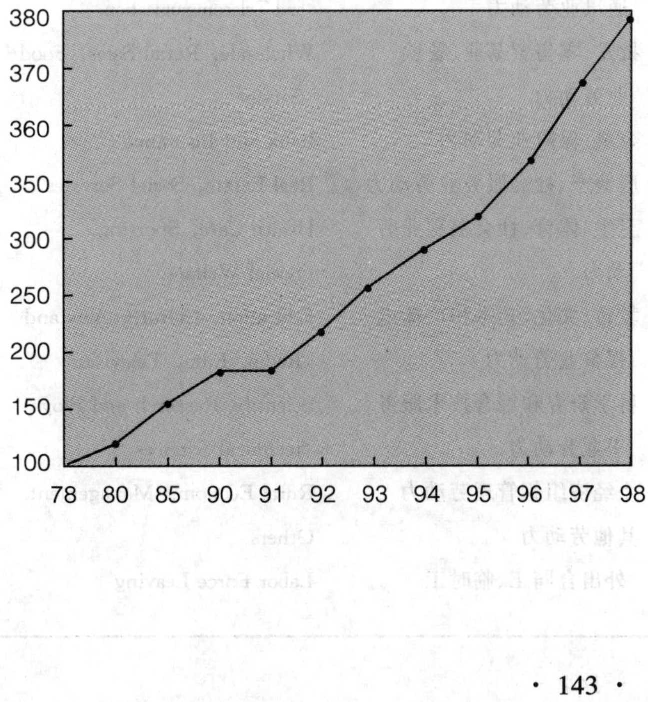

7-1 农村基层组织情况
BASIC RURAL UNITS

单位:万人 (10000 persons)

指标	Items	1985	1990	1995	1997	1998
农村组织情况	**Rural Units**					
乡个数	Township	1810	1452	1046	962	956
镇个数	Town	113	461	799	880	878
村委会个数	Village Committees	36117	36130	35982	35856	35726
村民小组个数	Villager Group	340075	340198	341984	340793	340606
乡村户数、人口	**Households Rural Population**					
乡村户数 (万户)	Households (ten thousand)	1314.04	1508.15	1516.85	1505.35	1503.06
乡村人口	Rural Population	5150.94	5361.80	5321.01	5277.02	5245.18
乡村劳动力合计	**Rural Social Labor Force**	**2598.12**	**2786.86**	**2773.04**	**2750.40**	**2735.91**
按性别分	Grouped by Sex					
男劳动力	Male	1281.06	1440.65	1424.43	1412.00	1402.40
女劳动力	Female	1317.06	1346.21	1348.61	1338.40	1333.51
按行业分	Grouped by Sector					
农林牧渔业劳动力	Farming, Forestry, Animal Husbandary, Fishery	1703.20	1714.49	1541.33	1532.52	1531.46
#农业劳动力	Farming	1522.09	1536.12	1326.54	1325.88	1316.02
工业劳动力	Industry	481.09	520.73	531.78	490.91	462.51
#乡办工业劳动力	Rural Industry	257.13	276.94	271.05	241.51	214.78
建筑业劳动力	Construction	150.18	196.25	227.39	240.86	245.70
交通运输、仓储业和邮电通讯业劳动力	Transportation, Storage, Post and Telecommunication	48.08	70.90	92.33	91.32	91.17
批发、零售贸易业、餐饮业劳动力	Wholesale, Retail Sales, Food Service	33.64	50.49	73.04	90.16	95.12
金融、保险业劳动力	Bank and Insurance	0.97	1.69	2.11	2.14	2.17
房地产、社会服务业劳动力	Real Estate, Social Services	10.84	11.08	15.61	16.10	18.75
卫生、体育、社会福利业劳动力	Health Care, Sporting, Social Welfare	10.32	10.21	9.69	10.11	10.25
教育、文化、艺术和广播电视事业劳动力	Education, Culture, Arts and Radio, Film, Television	19.51	18.40	15.50	14.08	13.92
科学研究和综合技术服务事业劳动力	Scientific Research and Ploy-technical Services	1.25	1.73	2.00	2.10	2.20
乡经济组织管理劳动力	Rural Economic Management	6.89	12.49	17.37	17.88	17.58
其他劳动力	Others	132.15	178.40	244.89	242.22	245.08
#外出合同工、临时工	Labor Force Leaving	47.61	82.11	125.50	121.01	120.11

7-2 历 年 耕 地 面 积
AREAS UNDER CULTIVATION

单位:千公顷　　　　(1000 ha)

年份 Year	年末实有耕地面积 Cultivated Areas (year end)	水田 Paddy Fields	旱地 Dry Fields	年内减少 Decrease in Cultivated Area and Cause	#国家基建占地 Capital Construction	人均占有耕地(平方米) Percapita Cultivated(sq·m) 按乡村人口计算 By Rural Population	按农林牧渔业劳动力计算 By Farming, Forestry, Animal Husbandry, Fishery Labors
1949	5523.40	2199.60	3323.80			1846.68	
1950	5600.40	2233.40	3367.00			1833.34	
1951	5715.40	2257.73	3457.67			1833.34	
1952	5808.47	2273.47	3535.00			1820.00	3580.12
1953	5888.73	2200.40	3688.33			1806.68	3553.35
1954	5934.27	2266.53	3667.74			1780.01	3506.68
1955	5934.73	2332.00	.3602.73			1733.34	3513.35
1956	5884.53	2438.07	3446.46			1673.34	3466.68
1957	5825.20	2545.13	3280.07			1633.34	3960.02
1958	5222.40	2514.13	2708.27			1466.67	4006.69
1959	5086.93	2472.60	2614.33			1440.01	4480.02
1960	5014.00	2341.67	2672.33			1440.01	4040.02
1961	4997.80	2263.73	2734.07			1406.67	3673.35
1962	5016.20	2161.33	2854.87			1360.01	3473.35
1963	5008.40	2161.60	2846.80			1320.01	3300.02
1964	4985.00	2189.80	2795.20			1286.67	3146.68
1965	4947.47	2225.93	2721.54			1246.67	3073.35
1966	4934.40	2289.45	2644.95			1206.67	2906.68
1967	4908.70	2277.65	2631.05			1166.67	2766.68
1968	4870.90	2272.85	2598.05			1126.67	2613.35
1969	4850.36	2334.31	2516.05			1080.01	2466.28
1970	4820.63	2509.13	2311.50			1033.34	2480.01
1971	4784.55	2831.75	1952.80			1006.67	1700.01
1972	4761.97	2865.59	1896.38	26.91	17.23	993.34	2333.35
1973	4737.99	2797.07	1940.92	33.87	16.88	986.67	2300.01
1974	4720.91	2790.15	1930.76	23.13	16.04	966.61	2326.78
1975	4705.53	2484.83	2220.70	23.00	13.39	946.67	2340.01
1976	4689.37	2831.34	1858.03	24.53	17.53	933.34	2293.34
1977	4672.79	2797.36	1875.43	21.81	15.05	920.00	2313.34
1978	4660.79	2743.14	1917.65	20.20	14.60	913.34	2293.34
1979	4650.40	2781.79	1868.61	18.67	13.20	920.00	2360.01
1980	4641.38	2788.62	1852.76	15.27	10.73	913.34	2380.01
1981	4637.01	2775.35	1861.66	11.67	5.67	900.00	2340.01
1982	4631.21	2755.59	1875.62	14.12	4.80	893.34	2326.68
1983	4630.05	2769.02	1861.03	7.67	5.24	893.34	2306.68
1984	4621.09	2837.99	1783.10	15.80	7.13	886.67	2353.35
1985	4604.03	2804.58	1799.45	21.40	5.87	886.67	2700.01
1986	4590.79	2780.11	1810.68	18.59	7.31	893.34	2793.35
1987	4579.81	2770.17	1809.64	18.19	6.21	886.67	2826.68
1988	4568.84	2767.73	1801.11	12.73	5.91	886.67	2820.01
1989	4562.32	2775.97	1786.35	10.43	4.64	886.67	2713.35
1990	4557.86	2804.13	1753.73	8.78	4.63	853.34	2660.01
1991	4549.97	2840.85	1709.12	11.15	4.80	846.67	2613.35
1992	4521.77	2836.81	1684.96	30.96	13.02	840.00	2673.35
1993	4495.66	2711.40	1784.26	28.83	8.71	840.00	2766.68
1994	4464.00	2658.08	1805.92	33.02	11.98	833.34	2806.68
1995	4448.31	2669.68	1778.63	23.69	11.74	833.34	2886.68

7－3 农村社会总产值
GROSS OUTPUT VALUE OF RURAL

单位：亿元 (10[8] yuan)

年份 Year	农村社会总产值 Gross Output of Rural	农林牧渔业总产值 Farming, Forestry, Animal Husbandry, Firshery	农村工业总产值 Rural Industry	农村建筑业总产值 Rural Construction	农村运输业总产值 Rural Transportation	农村批发、零售贸易业、餐饮业总产值 Rural Wholesale, Retail Sale and Food Service
1978	183.97	105.87	62.43	5.81	2.56	7.30
1980	274.13	138.45	109.33	14.55	3.09	8.71
1985	775.71	288.55	385.54	60.75	19.45	21.42
1986	959.73	332.66	497.28	76.96	25.45	27.38
1987	1245.20	380.25	697.41	99.35	33.06	35.13
1988	1703.28	497.95	980.79	132.06	43.58	48.90
1989	1872.41	522.25	1113.84	136.05	46.82	53.45
1990	2072.69	580.53	1251.95	133.99	48.27	57.95
1991	2312.06	580.93	1467.37	149.99	50.45	63.32
1992	3516.37	673.82	2463.26	203.63	69.42	106.24
1993	5650.77	875.37	4192.94	300.79	103.49	178.18
1994	8277.73	1335.23	6099.06	382.14	160.28	301.02
1995	10567.60	1686.78	7703.25	498.77	229.84	448.96
1996	10283.46	1693.76	7182.91	554.88	280.74	571.17
1997	11174.08	1816.37	7856.85	560.12	291.97	648.77
1998	11888.17	1849.20	8438.69	571.95	315.60	712.73

7－4 农村社会总产值指数
INDICES OF GROSS OUTPUT VALUE OF RURAL

按可比价格计算 1978＝100 (At comparable price 1978＝100)

年份 Year	农村社会总产值 Gross Output of Rural	农林牧渔业总产值 Farming, Forestry, Animal Husbandry, Firshery	农村工业总产值 Rural Industry	农村建筑业总产值 Rural Construction	农村运输业总产值 Rural Transportation	农村批发、零售贸易业、餐饮业总产值 Rural Wholesale, Retail Sale and Food Service
1978	100.0	100.0	100.0	100.0	100.0	100.0
1980	127.8	104.8	174.0	214.8	103.5	102.4
1985	317.6	165.3	604.8	787.7	571.7	221.0
1986	385.2	175.6	783.1	978.2	733.4	277.0
1987	471.7	181.1	1035.7	1191.9	899.0	335.3
1988	607.5	193.1	1428.8	1491.6	1115.8	439.5
1989	626.6	193.7	1498.1	1441.8	1124.8	450.8
1990	682.4	198.6	1683.9	1397.4	1141.2	480.9
1991	780.9	196.4	2011.0	1578.4	1205.3	531.0
1992	1212.8	221.9	3476.9	2191.4	1693.6	909.8
1993	1837.3	247.0	5650.0	3051.4	2380.2	1438.4
1994	2537.5	276.8	8065.8	3655.5	3475.8	2291.5
1995	3081.3	314.6	9774.8	4538.2	4740.9	3250.8
1996	3663.7	337.9	11868.0	4884.2	5602.1	4000.9
1997	4172.0	363.8	13660.1	5157.0	6095.1	4753.1
1998	4641.6	378.3	15285.7	5597.9	7003.8	5551.9

注：从 1996 年开始农村工业总产值口径发生变化，故当年数据小于上年数。

Note: The bore of gross output value of rural industry was changed, since 1996, so the year's data were less than preceding year.

7－5　历年农林牧渔业总产值(当年价格)
GROSS OUTPUT VALUE OF FARMING, FORESTRY, ANIMAL HUSBANDRY AND FISHERY (CURRENT PRICE)

单位:亿元　　　　　　　　　　　　　　　　　　　　　　　　　　　　(10⁸ yuan)

年　份 Year	农林牧渔业总产值 Gross Outprt Value of FFAF	农　业 Farming	林　业 Foresty	牧　业 Animal Husbandry	渔　业 Fishery
1949	22.59	19.41	…	3.02	0.16
1952	31.87	26.14	0.03	5.00	0.70
1955	36.22	32.25	0.04	2.81	1.12
1957	36.81	30.10	0.22	5.25	1.24
1962	40.15	34.19	0.32	4.48	1.16
1965	57.27	47.02	0.63	8.25	1.37
1970	71.33	57.08	0.85	11.76	1.64
1975	91.66	72.17	1.47	15.55	2.47
1976	100.71	82.53	1.31	14.86	2.01
1977	89.16	73.05	1.25	12.90	1.96
1978	105.87	85.17	1.48	16.78	2.44
1979	145.25	114.26	2.03	25.77	3.19
1980	138.45	105.98	1.94	26.65	3.88
1981	153.62	119.90	2.00	27.11	4.61
1982	188.11	145.69	1.96	35.80	4.66
1983	206.86	160.38	3.30	36.66	6.52
1984	253.82	193.28	4.33	47.17	9.04
1985	288.55	201.85	4.63	66.54	15.53
1986	332.66	235.07	5.15	69.83	22.61
1987	380.25	257.90	6.02	87.95	28.38
1988	497.95	310.20	7.29	140.49	39.97
1989	522.25	325.02	7.02	148.13	42.08
1990	580.53	362.46	7.94	160.78	49.35
1991	580.93	354.42	7.55	168.30	50.66
1992	673.82	411.33	9.93	188.64	63.92
1993	875.37	518.55	14.61	236.81	105.40
1994	1335.23	777.94	18.38	390.70	148.21
1995	1686.78	986.15	21.42	475.67	203.54
1996	1693.76	1062.39	23.48	368.54	239.35
1997	1816.37	1085.26	22.56	430.57	277.98
1998	1849.20	1096.88	24.16	435.51	292.65

注：从1996年开始有关数据与农业普查接轨，故牧业产值当年数据小于上年数。

Note: The relative targets were in line with the data of agricultural general survey, since 1996, so the output value of animal husbandry (in this year) was less than preceding year.

7－6 历年农林牧渔业总产值指数
INDICES OF GROSS OUTPUT VALUE OF FFAF

按可比价格计算 1949＝100 (At comparable price 1949＝100)

年 份 Year	农林牧渔业总产值 Gross Output Value of Agriculturd	农业 Farming	林业 Foresty	牧业 Animal Husbandry	渔业 Fishery
1949	100.0	100.0		100.0	100.0
1952	144.2	135.7	100.0	166.5	612.2
1955	163.0	174.3	87.5	80.5	522.0
1957	157.4	151.4	900.0	159.0	563.4
1962	134.7	134.1	1387.5	106.8	407.3
1965	201.4	190.7	2162.5	224.6	534.1
1970	239.7	232.5	1487.5	255.0	575.6
1975	294.7	281.6	2487.5	322.3	819.5
1976	306.2	296.1	3012.5	301.1	773.2
1977	275.4	264.9	2987.0	280.1	787.8
1978	334.6	326.8	2525.0	323.9	778.0
1979	371.1	354.7	2650.0	426.8	858.5
1980	350.7	326.0	2637.5	435.8	1014.6
1981	378.4	357.7	2512.5	432.6	1170.7
1982	434.8	404.2	2662.5	535.6	1231.7
1983	460.6	433.3	2950.0	525.9	1226.8
1984	536.3	460.6	3475.0	621.5	1522.0
1985	553.1	456.1	3750.0	727.9	1922.0
1986	587.7	486.4	3650.0	732.5	2592.7
1987	605.9	502.4	3825.0	741.1	2802.4
1988	646.1	526.3	3587.5	847.5	3051.2
1989	648.3	529.4	3387.5	843.1	3102.4
1990	664.6	535.2	3300.5	899.3	3346.3
1991	657.1	513.3	2971.7	946.3	3385.3
1992	742.5	583.6	3538.2	1045.7	3913.7
1993	826.4	619.6	4391.5	1191.6	5275.3
1994	926.3	668.9	4936.8	1400.2	6278.5
1995	1052.7	755.4	5774.3	1551.0	7785.4
1996	1130.6	821.0	6204.0	1599.2	8707.8
1997	1217.1	873.5	5746.0	1773.5	9532.8
1998	1265.6	899.4	6313.9	1847.5	10219.7

注：由于 1952 年以前林业产值很少，故以 1952 年的林业产值为 100。
Note：Forestry：1952＝100.（Because before 1992，the output value of forestry was very small.）

7-7 农林牧渔业分项产值

GROSS OUTPOUT VALUE OF FARMING, FORESTRY, ANIMAL HUSBANDRY AND FISHERY BY BRANCH

单位:亿元 (10⁸ yuan)

指标	Items	总产值(当年价) Gross Output Value (current price)		总产值(1990年不变价) Gross Output Value (1990 fixed price)	
		1997	1998	1997	1998
农林牧渔业总产值	**Total**	**1816.37**	**1849.20**	**994.96**	**1034.61**
农业产值	Farming	1085.26	1096.88	594.94	612.59
种植业产值	Planting	897.15	886.94	408.04	403.96
主产品产值	Main Product	862.63	854.08	384.16	382.11
#粮食	Grain Grops	507.20	496.96	215.54	207.93
棉花	Cotton Grops	82.70	69.20	36.25	33.00
油料	Oil-Bearing Grops	39.75	31.25	20.25	16.71
糖料	Sugar Crops	1.49	1.42	0.34	0.28
蔬菜、瓜类	Vegetables, Melons Grops	145.60	162.33	60.13	68.16
茶、桑、水果	Tea, Mulberry, Fruit	31.55	31.97	21.66	21.78
副产品产值	Sideline Product	34.52	32.86	23.88	21.85
#粮食作物	Grain Grops	30.32	29.19	21.36	19.54
其他农业产值	Other Grops	188.11	209.94	186.90	208.63
野生植物采集	Wild Plant Gathering	3.66	1.12	2.56	3.03
农民家庭兼营商品性工业	Household Handicraft lnductry	184.45	205.82	184.34	205.60
林业产值	Forestry	22.56	24.16	13.80	15.17
营林	Afforestation	5.37	6.05	3.02	3.10
林产品	Forest Products	4.91	3.71	1.84	1.61
村及村以下竹木采伐	Lumbering in Village below	12.28	14.40	8.94	10.46
牧业产值	Animal Husbandry	430.57	435.51	237.04	246.92
牲畜	Animal	237.60	226.93	99.37	102.73
大牲畜繁殖、增长、增重	Large Domestic Animals, Livestock Breeding	4.51	3.48	2.19	1.65
猪	Hogs	206.09	206.26	86.87	95.55
羊	Sheep and Goats	27.00	17.19	10.31	5.53
家禽的饲养	Poultry Raising	69.17	78.45	43.18	45.75
活的畜禽产品	Live Animal and Poultry Products	89.95	94.25	69.15	71.94
其他动物饲养	Others	32.13	33.98	24.05	25.41
捕猎	Hunting	1.72	1.90	1.29	1.09
渔业产值	Fishery	277.98	292.65	149.18	159.93
海水产品	Seawater Aquatic Products	71.40	80.59	44.04	51.22
淡水产品	Freshwater Aquatic Products	206.58	212.06	105.14	108.71

7-8 农作物播种面积

TOTAL SOWN AREAS OF FARM CROPS

单位:千公顷 (1000 ha)

年份 Year	总播种面积 Total Sown Areas	粮食作物 Grain Crops	#小麦 Wheat	#稻谷 Rice	#薯类 Tubers	#玉米 Corn	#大豆 Soybeans
1952	9413.60	8223.93	2003.20	1970.27	383.87	604.87	908.87
1957	9440.87	7982.27	1957.33	2177.27	370.07	589.20	789.60
1962	8589.47	7172.07	1384.00	1795.47	402.13	493.73	665.87
1965	7831.45	6211.31	1531.96	1902.15	481.06	449.41	523.96
1970	8102.59	6244.56	1513.54	2372.12	404.35	464.92	428.89
1975	8758.89	6377.93	1325.27	2971.09	365.05	379.02	281.58
1978	8582.74	6310.93	1412.82	2661.18	478.29	445.01	345.36
1980	8248.93	6090.25	1519.47	2676.15	332.02	386.21	236.47
1985	8557.84	6432.44	2170.39	2431.11	282.45	659.62	317.93
1990	8259.18	6363.02	2399.19	2454.44	221.65	461.01	244.67
1991	8091.70	6202.77	2364.93	2351.40	214.51	426.44	177.81
1992	8234.63	6180.77	2366.23	2447.27	192.59	421.14	192.28
1993	8032.29	6029.66	2281.66	2278.44	201.00	472.37	270.67
1994	7861.76	5748.78	2114.26	2168.36	179.46	458.95	255.41
1995	7909.01	5755.15	2150.35	2250.31	166.71	461.98	201.32
1996	7914.10	5877.42	2216.26	2335.91	180.59	467.83	179.49
1997	7966.78	5994.43	2341.37	2377.62	169.61	439.00	217.44
1998	8058.28	5946.26	2314.95	2369.70	162.67	473.49	220.83

续表 Continued

单位:千公顷 (1000 ha)

年份 Year	经济作物 Economic Crops	#棉花 Cotton Crops	#油菜籽 Rape-seed	#花生 Peanuts	#芝麻 Sesame	#黄红麻 Hemp Crops	#甘蔗 Sugar-cane	#甜菜 Beet-roots	#烤烟 Flue-Cured Tobacco	其他 Others
1952	751.66	454.47	109.37	119.10	29.80	11.51			0.10	438.01
1957	871.73	564.23	93.63	160.26	10.00	14.13				586.87
1962	618.07	416.54	71.79	84.21	13.43	6.21			2.04	799.33
1965	807.39	563.81	72.02	116.47	9.26	11.07	0.14		6.41	812.75
1970	797.58	585.10	83.73	71.50	8.80	11.72	0.08	4.12	5.83	1060.45
1975	869.05	586.97	147.92	72.27	5.03	16.50	0.74	5.69	5.47	1511.91
1978	905.84	589.99	156.46	65.49	10.60	20.71	0.75	6.91	7.05	1365.97
1980	957.04	631.00	169.58	83.79	4.61	11.51	0.35	5.78	2.17	1201.64
1985	1302.77	592.24	442.64	134.11	12.85	24.78	4.11	4.39	3.47	822.63
1990	1188.41	572.13	440.81	108.71	5.85	5.16	3.35	2.23	5.63	707.75
1991	1202.48	550.61	482.80	102.95	4.79	4.57	3.18	0.73	5.16	686.45
1992	1350.29	673.43	483.78	107.36	7.14	3.99	3.83	0.70	7.39	703.57
1993	1143.39	517.65	458.30	125.42	8.65	5.20	5.50	1.31	2.02	859.24
1994	1225.86	534.57	516.59	146.52	6.65	2.15	4.57	0.70	0.87	887.12
1995	1268.75	564.90	530.66	148.66	7.54	1.31	3.95	0.17	1.17	885.11
1996	1132.24	485.91	498.00	123.55	9.19	0.89	3.66	0.87	1.44	904.44
1997	1063.10	438.74	473.93	117.25	13.66	0.79	3.46	1.51	2.61	909.25
1998	1063.32	416.16	468.94	141.39	16.23	0.54	3.25	0.52	0.09	1048.70

7－9 主要农作物播种面积和产量（1998）
TOTAL SOWN AREAS OF FARM CROPS AND OUTPUT

指标	Items	播种面积（千公顷） Sown Areas (1000 ha)	单位面积产量（千克/公顷） Per ha Output (kg)	总产量（吨） Total Output (tons)
农作物总播种面积	**TOTAL SOWN AREAS OF FARM CROPS**	**8058.28**		
粮食、大豆总计	**Total Grain Soybeans**	**5946.26**	**5743**	**34151244**
夏粮	Summer Grain	2696.34	3205	8642251
小麦	Wheat	2314.95	3282	7596788
元麦	Hull-less Barley	29.84	2271	67755
大麦	Barley	241.32	3062	738920
蚕豌豆	Broad and Dea Bean	110.23	2166	238788
秋粮	Autumn Grain	3249.92	7849	25508993
稻谷	Rice	2369.70	8816	20891785
早稻	Early Rice			
中稻	Semilate Rice	1535.73	8676	13323558
单季晚稻	Single late Rice	820.78	9100	7468895
双季后作稻	Late Double-crop Rice	13.19	7531	99332
在稻谷中：杂优稻	Among Rice: Hybrid Fine Rice	653.47	8455	5525041
薯类	Tubers	162.67	6367	1035729
玉米	Corn	473.49	6045	2862270
高粱	Sorghum	0.18	3344	602
谷子	Millet			
其他秋粮	Others	23.05	3118	71859
大豆	Soybeans	220.83	2929	646748
经济作物	**Economic Crops**	**1063.32**		
棉花	Cotton	416.16	1110	461938
油料	Oil-Bearing Crops	626.82	1845	1156344
#花生	Peanuts	141.39	3459	489017
油菜籽	Rapeseed	468.94	1370	642594
芝麻	Sesame	16.23	1460	23703
麻类	Hemp Grops	1.01	3293	3326
#黄麻	Jute	0.39	2615	1020
红麻	Ambary	0.15	3220	483
苎麻	Ramie	0.43	3747	1611
糖类	Sugar Crops	3.77	52094	196394
#甘蔗	Sugarcane	3.25	56556	183807
甜菜	Beetroots	0.52	24206	12587
烟叶	Tobacco Crops	0.32	2553	817
#烤烟	Flue-Cured Tobacco	0.09	1678	151
药材	Crude drugs	7.14		
其他经济作物	Others	8.10		
#薄荷	Mint	8.07		
留兰香	Spearmint	0.03		
其他农作物	**Others**	**1048.70**		
#蔬菜	Vegetable	733.84		
瓜类	Melon Crops	83.57		
绿肥	Organic Fertilizer	76.21		

7-10 主要农产品产量
OUTPUT OF MAJOR FARM CROPS

单位:万吨 (10000 tons)

年份 Year	粮食 Grain	夏粮 Summer Grain	秋粮 Autumn Grain	棉花 Cotton	油料 Oil-Bearing Grops	#花生 Peanuts	#油菜籽 Rapeseed
1949	748.50	217.00	531.50	2.81	15.94	11.82	3.60
1952	997.55	277.85	719.70	9.28	21.68	14.38	6.00
1957	1063.60	274.85	788.75	15.01	25.07	19.81	4.93
1962	965.35	280.65	684.70	8.21	10.27	6.38	3.52
1965	1442.75	379.85	1062.90	26.44	21.68	13.87	7.41
1970	1705.15	415.50	1289.65	32.82	21.67	10.31	10.87
1975	2056.85	524.40	1532.45	45.48	29.64	11.73	17.63
1978	2400.65	677.30	1723.35	47.54	37.44	13.60	23.06
1980	2417.95	873.60	1544.35	41.81	38.64	14.50	23.93
1985	3126.52	1064.46	2062.06	47.91	108.78	34.13	73.11
1990	3264.15	1143.46	2120.69	46.42	112.39	30.12	81.41
1991	3035.51	1032.43	2003.08	55.71	114.06	28.12	85.32
1992	3320.55	1251.19	2069.36	52.74	127.33	30.51	95.88
1993	3279.70	1152.60	2127.10	42.90	125.71	37.66	87.04
1994	3124.05	1105.29	2018.76	45.71	133.59	44.80	87.77
1995	3286.30	1073.46	2212.84	56.16	159.46	48.43	109.54
1996	3476.35	1200.95	2275.40	53.75	147.50	39.65	106.34
1997	3563.79	1226.91	2336.88	50.75	141.93	39.53	100.53
1998	3415.12	864.22	2550.90	46.19	115.63	48.90	64.26

7-11 人均占有主要农产品产量
OUTPUT OF PER PERSON FARM CROPS

单位:千克/人 (kg/person)

年份 Year	粮食产量 Grain	棉花产量 Cotton	油料产量 Oil-Bearing Grops	生猪饲养量(头/人) Output of Raising Hogs	猪、牛、羊肉产量 Output of Pork, Beef and Mutton	水产品产量 Output of Aquatic Products
1952	270.0	2.5	5.9	0.24		4.6
1957	257.0	3.7	6.1	0.34		6.9
1962	225.0	1.9	2.4	0.22		4.5
1965	316.0	5.8	4.8	0.46		5.5
1970	329.0	6.4	4.2	0.50		5.2
1975	367.0	8.1	5.3	0.60		6.5
1978	414.0	8.2	6.5	0.60		6.9
1980	408.5	7.1	6.6	0.70	18.1	7.2
1985	505.0	7.8	17.6	0.64	22.4	10.9
1990	486.0	6.9	16.7	0.59	23.6	17.6
1991	446.1	8.2	16.8	0.59	24.0	17.3
1992	482.8	7.7	18.5	0.61	25.1	19.6
1993	472.6	6.2	18.1	0.62	25.8	22.7
1994	446.7	6.5	19.1	0.65	28.5	25.8
1995	466.6	8.0	22.6	0.69	30.9	31.2
1996	490.4	7.6	20.8	0.51	24.7	34.7
1997	499.9	7.1	19.9	0.57	26.2	37.3
1998	476.6	6.4	16.1	0.63	29.2	39.4

注：从1996年开始，牧业有关数据与农业普查接轨，故小于上年数。

Note: Relative targets of animal husbandry were in line with data of agricultural general survey, since 1996, so they were less than last year.

7-12 蚕、茶、果生产情况
STATISTICS ON SILKWORM COCOONS, TEA, FRUIT

单位:万吨、千公顷 (10000 tons、1000 ha)

指标	Items	1985	1990	1995	1997	1998
蚕茧产量	Silkworm Cocoons	7.31	12.00	18.62	8.64	8.51
茶叶产量	Tea	0.92	1.41	1.06	1.19	1.20
红毛茶	Red Tea	0.46	0.43	0.13	0.15	0.22
绿毛茶	Green Tea	0.45	0.94	0.91	1.02	0.91
其他茶	Others	0.01	0.04	0.02	0.02	0.07
水果产量	Fruits	34.10	49.33	101.35	140.40	144.36
#苹果	Apple	6.56	10.63	32.16	54.92	62.87
柑桔	Citrus Fruit	2.40	3.13	4.57	5.17	3.13
梨	Pear	14.62	15.01	24.30	31.26	30.85
葡萄	Grapes	0.86	2.42	5.79	6.79	7.16
桃子	Peach	3.69	11.27	17.74	17.56	18.35
枇杷	Loquat	0.11	0.20	0.74	0.90	0.68
红枣	Date	0.23	0.19	0.18	0.14	0.16
柿子	Persimmon	0.96	2.96	7.11	12.48	12.44
桑园面积	Mulberry Field Area	110.01	116.33	228.49	80.50	74.04
茶园面积	Tea Field Area	14.31	13.17	19.29	19.05	18.88
#当年采摘面积	Pick Area	9.66	11.04	10.37	13.98	14.36
果园	Orchards Field	46.73	104.86	157.75	140.52	134.09
#苹果园	Apple	14.19	46.30	84.46	67.99	60.79
柑桔园	Citrus	3.53	3.50	2.01	4.82	3.24
梨园	Pear	12.83	14.98	22.89	24.04	22.98
葡萄园	Grapes	2.31	2.59	3.93	4.90	4.23

7-13 林业生产情况
STATISTICS ON FORESTRY

单位:千公顷 (1000 ha)

指标	Items	1985	1990	1995	1997	1998
造林面积	Build Forestry Areas	28.25	19.63	27.20	19.03	15.14
用材林	Material Forest	19.67	11.42	12.44	9.20	7.42
经济林	Economic Forest	3.85	2.10	11.30	5.92	4.83
防护林	Windbreak Forest	4.01	5.80	3.36	3.54	2.70
其他林	Others	0.72	0.31	0.10	0.37	0.19
林产品产量 (吨)	Output of Forestery Products (tons)					
油桐籽	Tung-Oil Seed	192	41	12	16	20
油茶籽	Tea-Oil Seed	81	27	18	25	27
乌桕籽	Oriental Arborviate	4	…	1	1	…
竹笋干	Bamboo Shoots	603	856	1254	890	958
核桃	Walnuts	8	4	1	1	1
板栗	Chestnut	1939	2733	7156	7980	9263
白果	Ginkgo	2525	4037	5303	4961	2592
迹地更新面积	Slash Updateing Areas	0.95	0.68	1.13	1.10	1.97
当年育苗面积	Raise Seedlings Areas	11.94	7.31	8.89	9.87	11.35
幼林抚育作业面积 (千公顷次)	Young Growth Works Areas (1000 ha-T)	94.74	95.03	125.36	112.24	131.65
幼林抚育实际面积	Young Growth Actual Areas	58.29	51.56	61.92	70.36	69.43
成林抚育实际面积	Adult Growth Actual Areas	45.45	58.44	89.87	89.51	101.40
林木种子采集量 (吨)	Output of Forestry Seeds Pick (tons)	426	90	203	2179	339
木材采伐量 (万立方米)	Output of Timber Cut (10000)	47.25	85.68	153.02	132.92	153.05
竹材采伐量(万根)	Bamboo Cut (10000)	257.77	403.07	732.38	780.68	749.94
年末实有林地面积	Actual Forestry Areas(year-end)	438.15	445.82	518.71	567.59	605.78
四旁植树 (万株)	Planting (10000)	17640	14901	14633	13834	12267
林木种子园个数 (个)	Forest Seeds Fields	16	11	16	16	16
林木种子园面积 (公顷)	Forest Seeds Field Areas (ha)	48	101	108	76	82

7-14 畜牧业生产情况
STATISTICS ON LIVESTOCK

指标	Items	1985	1990	1995	1997	1998
牲畜年末头数 （万头）	**Livestock（Year-end） （10000）**					
大牲畜	Large Animals	85.34	92.50	123.27	82.24	84.69
牛	Cattle and Buffalo	68.06	71.48	99.06	67.13	70.77
#良种及改良乳牛	Fine improved Variety Cows	3.15	3.49	2.93	2.74	3.28
马	Horses	3.34	2.11	2.48	1.14	0.87
驴	Donkeys	11.88	16.55	18.79	12.53	11.77
骡	Mules	2.06	2.36	2.94	1.44	1.28
猪	Hogs	1950.96	1851.10	2118.97	1829.80	1961.86
羊 （万只）	Sheep and Goats （10000）	400.56	850.80	1273.89	851.80	904.91
山羊	Goats	351.81	797.45	1211.16	825.73	870.80
绵羊	Sheep	48.75	53.35	62.73	26.07	34.11
畜产品产量	**Livestock Products**					
猪牛羊出栏头数 （万头）	Hogs, Sheep and Goats （10000）					
当年肉猪出栏头数	Hogs	2012.55	2116.62	2754.90	2229.68	2531.23
当年出售和自宰的肉用牛	Ox by Selled and Killed	5.45	12.85	35.62	30.84	28.42
当年出售和自宰的肉用羊 （万只）	Sheep and Goats by Selled and Killed （10000）	326.13	831.81	1724.38	1051.85	1112.81
肉类产量 （万吨）	Output of Meat （10000 tons）					
猪肉	Pork	135.61	149.24	195.82	167.23	189.85
牛肉	Beef	0.65	1.86	5.43	6.17	5.69
羊肉	Mutton	2.64	7.28	16.54	13.02	13.77
禽肉	Poulty	20.45	34.90	84.33	75.69	82.29
其他畜产品产量 （吨）	Others （tons）					
牛奶产量	Cow Milk	74997	86860	99948	110896	121442
羊奶产量	Sheep and Goats Milk	461	2152	4378	6248	2469
绵羊毛产量	Sheep Milk	1179	1853	2305	2232	2290
山羊毛产量	Goats Mik	132	74	71	99	11
羊绒	Cashmere	…	1	2	2	2
蜂蜜	Honey	7632	12186	7275	7022	16440
禽蛋 （万吨）	Poulty Eggs （10000 tons）	60.69	89.72	175.32	151.11	157.06

注：从1996年开始，牧业有关数据与农业普查接轨，故小于上年数。

Note: Relative targets of animal husbandry were in line with data of agricultural general survey, since 1996, so they were less than last year.

7-15 水 产 品 产 量
OUTPUT OF AQUATIC PRODUCTS

单位:万吨 (10000 tons)

指 标	Items	1985	1990	1995	1997	1998
水产品产量	**Output of Aquatic Products**	**67.54**	**118.25**	**219.47**	**265.72**	**282.03**
海水产品产量	Seawater Aquatic Products	24.10	33.85	65.08	85.07	88.21
按生产性质分	Group by Nature					
天然生产	Naturally Grown	22.58	30.68	56.70	71.14	70.78
人工养殖	Artificially Cultured	1.52	3.17	8.38	13.93	17.43
按类别分	Group by Category					
鱼类	Fish	18.32	22.38	37.71	50.50	48.65
虾蟹类	Shrimp, Prawn and Crab	4.00	6.02	10.74	10.49	12.15
贝类	Shell-fish	1.76	5.24	16.23	23.20	26.51
藻类	Algae	0.02	0.21	0.40	0.88	0.90
淡水产品产量	Freshwater Aquatic Products	43.44	84.40	154.39	180.65	193.82
按生产性质分	Group by Nature					
天然生产	Naturally Grown	10.72	16.42	25.47	30.25	31.56
人工养殖	Artificially Cultured	32.72	67.98	128.92	150.40	162.26
按类别分	Group by Category					
鱼类	Fish	41.00	79.58	139.34	161.17	163.95
虾蟹类	Shirmp, Prawn and Crab	1.29	2.64	9.73	15.21	20.28
贝类	Shell fish	1.15	2.18	5.32	4.27	9.59
在海水产品中	**Among Seawater Aquatic**					
大黄鱼	Big Yellow Croaker	598	225	380	605	501
小黄鱼	Small Yellow Croaker	2478	5382	40575	32121	37638
带鱼	Hairtail	41729	57135	142971	76733	86017
墨鱼	Cuttlefish	7650	1671	3118	8820	8928
水产养殖面积	**Aquatic Raise Areas**	**393.59**	**448.14**	**555.23**	**592.43**	**612.26**
(千公顷)	**(1000 ha)**					
淡水养殖面积	Freshwater Raise Areas	345.04	381.27	467.29	486.67	502.21
海水养殖面积	Seawater Raise	48.55	66.87	87.94	105.76	110.05

7-16 农业现代化情况
STATISTICS ON AGRICULTURAL MODERNIZATION

单位:千公顷 (1000 ha)

指标	Items	1985	1990	1995	1997	1998
农业机械化情况	**Statistics on Agricultural Machinery**					
机耕面积	Area Ploughed by Tractors	3244.04	3632.49	3639.43	3820.08	3893.08
机播面积	Seeded Area by Tractors	333.23	1046.41	1730.23	1870.45	1952.24
#机播三麦面积	Wheats Area by Tractors	313.61	1010.26	1661.56	1742.14	1822.29
机械植保面积	Plant Protection Area by Tractors	833.31	1727.52	2730.54	3701.12	4082.10
机械收获面积	Harvest Area by Tractors	78.79	531.93	1194.21	2062.09	2520.76
农村电气化情况	**Electrification of Rural**					
农村用电量 (亿千瓦小时)	Electricity Consumed in Rural Area (10^8 kw/h)	63.57	105.26	238.16	263.12	263.95
农用物资使用情况	**Used Agricultural Product Material**					
化肥施用量 (折纯量)(万吨)	Consumption of Chemical Fertilizers (pure)(10000 tons)	157.80	221.79	292.77	322.68	333.32
每亩耕地施用化肥 (折纯量)(千克)	Per Mu Consumption of Chemical Fertilizers (pure)(kg)	22.8	32.4	43.8	48.5	50.3
农用塑料薄膜使用量 (万吨)	Used Plastic Film (10000 tons)			5.35	5.66	5.44
农用柴油使用量 (万吨)	Used Diesel Oil (10000 tons)		3.12	59.17	72.94	73.16
农药使用量 (万吨)	Used Agricultural Chemical Insecticides (10000 tons)		7.98	8.87	9.66	9.88
农田水利情况	**Irrigation and Water Conservancy**					
有效灌溉面积	Effective Irrigation Area	3587.93	3970.92	3832.78	3839.36	3855.44
#机电排灌面积	Electrical Irrigation Area	3305.60	3518.06	3803.50	3778.99	3795.75
机电排灌面积占有效灌溉面积的比重%	Rate: $\frac{Electrical\ Irrigation\ Area}{Effective\ Irrigatim\ Area}$	92.1	88.6	99.2	98.4	98.5
机电井数 (万眼)	Electrical Well (10000)	4.08	4.89	4.75	5.03	4.81
#已配套 (万眼)	Form a Complete Set (10000)	2.26	3.20	3.11	3.50	3.37

7-17 主要年份农业机械拥有量
POSSESION OF AGRICUITURAL MACHINERY

年份 Year	农业机械总动力(万千瓦) Total Power of Agricultural Machinery (10000 kw)	农用大中型拖拉机(混合台) Large and Medium Agricultural Tractors (mixed)	农用小型及手扶拖拉机(万台) Mini and Walking Agricultural Tractors (10000 sets)	农用排灌动力机械(万千瓦) Machinery for Agricultural Drainage and Irrigation (10000 kw)	农用水泵(万台) Agricultural Water Pump (10000 sets)	喷灌机械(套) Machinery for Sprinkling (sets)
1952	5.59	48		5.05		
1957	13.32	549		9.79		
1962	66.12	1557	…	60.66		
1965	82.64	2203	0.06	70.27		
1978	855.16	11836	19.25	363.73	29.20	8305
1980	1113.05	16238	25.61	442.48	36.18	24856
1985	1675.06	18902	49.16	450.27	37.75	20809
1990	2004.77	19468	71.65	490.83	39.63	9370
1991	1966.61	19952	72.64	492.88	40.73	10687
1992	2016.07	20654	72.41	494.57	41.55	11571
1993	2081.75	21322	73.52	501.35	41.59	12044
1994	2161.40	21458	74.98	507.66	42.63	13068
1995	2226.95	23198	75.04	508.91	43.36	14991
1996	2297.43	30483	76.53	515.99	44.84	15952
1997	2499.69	35928	83.32	538.66	50.63	29946
1998	2594.83	39844	83.87	553.73	52.20	37571

续表 Continued

年份 Year	联合收割机(台) Combine Harvesters (units)	机动脱粒机(万台) Motorized Huller (10000 units)	机动喷雾(粉)器(部) Motorized Duster (units)	饲料粉碎机(万部) Fodder Grinder (10000 units)	农用载重汽车(辆) Trucks for Agricultural Use(units)	渔用机动船(艘) Fishery Motorized Ship (units)
1952					35	
1957	18				34	2
1962	152	0.63			119	413
1965	176	3.60		…	227	401
1978	295	32.96	20126	10.18	1656	3914
1980	478	40.99	43314	11.88	3343	5179
1985	687	68.51	55136	7.30	10395	16602
1990	2411	89.42	94900	6.51	16132	40728
1991	3583	92.29	113542	6.55	15915	43367
1992	5964	93.37	123699	6.29	16164	44788
1993	7279	94.80	126331	6.06	18076	48792
1994	8604	98.32	132776	5.92	21910	50067
1995	12063	105.22	170785	5.27	24390	50548
1996	20074	105.01	196395	6.32	26077	54206
1997	27656	121.42	265523	7.17	27619	60742
1998	33343	123.80	291009	7.64	29093	58431

7－18 农业主要经济效益指标
MAJOR INDICATIONS OF AGRICULTURE

指　　标	Items	1990	1995	1997	1998
每个农村劳动力创造的农村社会总产值（元）	Gross Output Value of Rural Area By Per Rural Labor (yuan)	7437.37	38108.36	40567.45	43337.58
每个农林牧渔业劳动力创造的农林牧渔业总产值（元）	Gross Output Value of FFAF By Per FFAF Labor (yuan)	3386.02	10943.67	11861.16	12070.58
农林牧渔业净产值（元）	Net Output Value of FFAF (yuan)	2017.86	56526.96	6059.71	6143.66
粮食产量（公斤）	Output of Grain (kg)	1903.86	2132.12	2327.21	2229.21
棉花产量（公斤）	Output of Cotton (kg)	27.08	36.44	33.14	30.15
油料产量（公斤）	Output of Oil-Bearing (kg)	65.55	103.46	92.68	75.48
肉类产量（公斤）	Output of Meat (kg)	113.18	198.46	174.10	192.73
水产品产量（公斤）	Output of Aquatic (kg)	68.97	142.39	173.52	184.09
农林牧渔业商品率（%）	Commodity Rate of FFAF	58.92	64.07	69.52	72.87
农业商品率（%）	Commodity Rate of Farming	48.28	52.78	60.20	63.47
林业商品率（%）	Commodity Rate of Forestry	41.44	63.96	76.33	74.32
牧业商品率（%）	Commodity Rate of Animal Husbandry	76.68	78.59	81.31	84.11
渔业商品率（%）	Commodity Rate of Fishery	82.76	84.88	87.08	91.28

注：① 产值均为现行价格。
② 从1996年开始农村工业总产值口径发生变化，故每个农村劳动力创造的农村社会总产值小于上年，如按同口径相比则增长22.1%。

Notes: 1) Gross output value at current price.
2) The bore of gross output value of rural industry was changed, since 1996. The targets of animal husbandry etc. were in line with the data of agricultural general survey, so they were less than last year, if the bore was same, there will be an increase of 22.1 %.

7－19 农村自然灾害情况
BASIC SIATISTICS ON RURAL NATURAL DISASTER

单位：千公顷 (1000 ha)

指　　标	Items	1990	1995	1996	1997	1998
受灾面积	Area Covered	2503.0	1282.0	1613.7	2808.0	3614.0
#旱　灾	Drought	451.0	667.0	624.7	1004.7	604.0
水　灾	Flood	1669.0	269.0	745.0	466.7	443.0
成灾面积	Area Affected	929.0	461.0	395.5	1210.0	1583.0
#旱　灾	Drought	127.0	227.0	29.3	353.3	133.0
水　灾	Flood	580.0	79.0	265.5	200.0	178.0

注：资料来源于国家民政部反馈。

Note: Data were from State Ministry of Civil Adiministration.

7－20 农村乡镇集体企业基本情况
TOWNSHIP AND VILLAGE COLLECTIVE ENTERPRISES

指　　标	Items	1985	1990	1995	1997	1998
乡村集体企业单位数 （个）	**Enterprises**	**98567**	**113159**	**108821**	**93931**	**77561**
按国民经济部门分	Grouped By Economic Sector					
农业企业	Agriculture	2365	878	725	898	1365
工业企业	Industry	81560	99883	93476	78499	64468
建筑企业	Construction	3087	2933	2589	2034	1853
交通运输企业	Transportation	3826	2670	1744	1357	1605
商业、饮食、服务业及其他	Commerce and Other Services	7729	6795	10287	11143	8270
乡村集体企业从业人数 （万人）	**Persons Employed (10000 persons)**	**627.09**	**672.93**	**668.44**	**528.23**	**462.41**
按国民经济部门分	Grouped By Economic Sector					
农业企业	Agriculture	6.62	2.35	3.39	2.49	2.97
工业企业	Industry	511.66	588.12	576.14	457.28	388.31
建筑企业	Construction	83.00	63.20	68.11	50.47	53.84
交通运输企业	Transportation	16.24	11.47	6.60	3.91	3.98
商业、饮食、服务业及其他	Commerce and Other Service	9.57	7.79	14.20	14.08	13.31
乡村集体企业主营业收入 （亿元）	**Total Revenue from Major Business (10^8 yuan)**	**352.12**	**951.36**	**5237.46**	**5419.91**	**5154.71**
按国民经济部门分	Grouped By Economic Sector					
农业企业	Agriculture	2.19	1.88	15.94	11.58	6.06
工业企业	Industry	310.34	876.98	5140.36	5215.38	4827.02
建筑企业	Construction	24.00	42.85	17.20	109.90	153.26
交通运输企业	Transportation	5.80	8.67	2.08	1.69	7.13
商业、饮食、服务业及其他	Commerce and Other Services	9.79	20.98	61.88	81.36	161.24

7－21 乡村集体企业主要经济指标（1998）
MAIN ECONOMIC INDICATORS OF TOWNSHIP AND VILLAGE COLLECTIVE ENTERPRISES

单位：亿元 (10^8 yuan)

指标	Items	合计 Total	#农业企业 Agriculture	#工业企业 Industry	#施工企业 Construction	#交通运输企业 Transportation
主营业收入	Operating Revenue	5154.71	6.06	4827.02	153.27	7.13
#营业成本	Operating Cost	4493.10	4.70	4207.35	134.94	5.89
营业费用	Operating Expenses	147.86	0.46	138.40	2.90	0.33
营业税金及附加	Operating Tax And Added	39.65	0.13	32.73	4.32	0.21
管理费用	Management Cost	247.30	0.25	232.54	7.08	0.39
财务费用	Financial Cost	95.84	0.36	92.57	1.20	0.07
利润总额	Total Profits	151.27	0.20	143.05	3.00	0.33
#应交所得税	Payable Income Taxes	26.55	0.03	25.33	0.58	0.04
实交各种税金	Taxes Paid	132.18	0.15	125.25	3.98	0.26
可供分配的利润	Capable Assign Profits	16.41	3.80	8.18	1.65	0.12
#提取盈余公积	Accumulated Funds	33.78	0.03	32.50	0.52	0.06
应付利润	Payable Profit	69.46	0.11	65.28	1.54	0.11
工资总额	Total Wage Bill	277.22	0.56	240.69	25.52	0.93
固定资产原值年末数	Original Value of Fixed Assets (Year-end)	1794.47	2.36	1715.88	30.57	4.49
累计提取的折旧	Draw Depreciation Funds	476.50	0.57	457.08	9.99	0.87
固定资产净值	Average Balances of Net Value of Fixed Assets	1317.98	1.79	1258.81	20.59	3.62
流动资产年末数	Circulating Funds	2276.37	18.21	2060.84	134.38	1.98
#货币资金	Money Funds	179.06	0.30	166.13	5.10	0.42
存货	Stock	946.94	12.60	852.04	59.05	0.16
本年长短期借款余额	Balance of Long Period and Short Period Lend Money	832.25	13.67	791.81	10.27	0.88
长期负债合计	Total Long Term Loan	282.18	0.26	275.75	2.01	0.19
亏损企业(个)	Deficit Enterprises	8493	10	7994	58	45
亏损余额	Balance of Deficit	25.09	0.01	23.96	0.21	0.07

7-22 农业综合开发主要指标(1988-1998)
MAJOR INDICATORS OF AGRICULTURAL SYNTHETICAL DEVELOPMENT

指标	Items		开发总计 Total	国家立项 State Items	省立丘陵山区 Provincial Items For Hill and Mountain Area	省立高沙土 Provincial Items For High Sand Soil Area
投资总额 (万元)	Total Value of Investment	(10000 yuan)	495494	482992	7692	4810
财政资金	State Appropriation		227333	216442	7692	3200
专项贷款	Special Loans		112111	112111		
自筹资金	Fund Raising		136044	134434		1610
其他资金	Others		20005	20005		
改造中低产田 (千公顷)	Reformation of Medium and Low Production Farm Land	(1000 ha)	1374	1339	22	13
开荒 (千公顷)	Rectamation of Wasteland	(1000 ha)	75	75		
造林 (千公顷)	Afforestration	(1000 ha)	102	101		1

注：省立丘陵山区为1996-1998年数；省立高沙土为1998年数。
Note: Data of provincial items for hill and mountain area refer to 1996-1998; data of provincial items for high sand soil area refer to 1998.

7-23 滩涂开发工程完成情况
PROJECTS OF SHALLOW SEA BEACHES DEVELOPMENT COMPLETED

指标	Items	开发面积(千公顷) Developed Areas (1000 ha)	总投资(万元) Total Investment (10000 yuan)	省级投资 Provincial Level Investment	农业综合开发立项 Agricultural Sunthetical Development Items	社会投资 Social Investment
1996年	**1996**					
围 垦	Cultivation of Tideland	7.4	13098	4100		8998
垦 荒	Reclamation of Wasteland	4.5	2700	990		1710
中低产田改造	Reformation of Medium and Low Production Farm Land					
1997年	**1997**					
围 垦	Cultivation of Tideland	8.4	12165	2992		9173
垦 荒	Reclamation of Wasteland	5.5	17277	2060	1365	13852
中低产田改造	Reformation of Medium and Low Production Farm Land	6.1	1802		1802	
1998年	**1998**					
围 垦	Cultivation of Tideland	7.5	8880	3440		5440
垦 荒	Reclamation of Wasteland	5.0	3960	1910	2050	
中低产田改造	Reformation of Medium and Low Production Farm Land	3.7	1250		1250	

8. 工业、能源

INDUSTRY,ENERGY

8 工 业、能 源
INDUSTRY, ENERGY

1 9 9 8

全部工业总产值(现价)	Gross output Value of Total Industry	13185.70	亿元	(10^8 yuan)
轻工业	Light Industry	6843.38	亿元	(10^8 yuan)
重工业	Heavy Industry	6342.40	亿元	(10^8 yuan)
限额以上工业总产值(现价)	Over-norm Gross Output Value of Industry (current prices)	8053.03	亿元	(10^8 yuan)
限额以上独立核算工业企业	Over-norm Industrial Enterprises with Independent Accounting System			
资产合计	Total Property	9098.51	亿元	(10^8 yuan)
负债合计	Total Liability	5663.88	亿元	(10^8 yuan)
产品销售收入	Revenue of Products Sales	7375.45	亿元	(10^8 yuan)
利税总额	Total Pre-Tax Profit	491.61	亿元	(10^8 yuan)
职工人数	Staff and Workers	578.77	万人	(10000 persons)
煤炭消费量	Total Coal Consumption	7383.09	万吨	(10000 tons)
原油消费量	Total Crude Oil Consumption	1108.44	万吨	(10000 tons)

工业总产值(亿元)

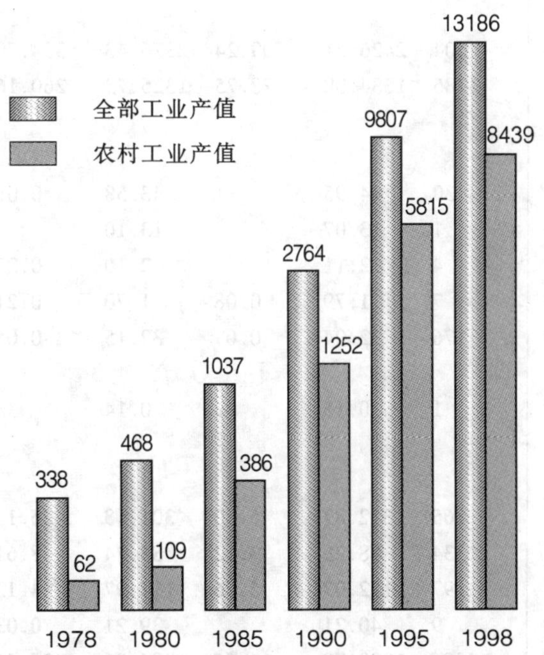

工业总产值指数(上年=100)

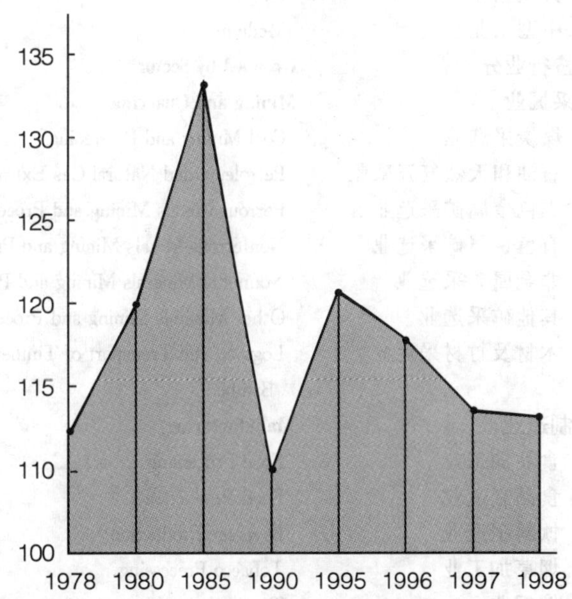

8－1 限额以上工业产销总值（1998）
TOTAL VALUE OF OVER-NORM INDUSTRIAL PRODUCTION AND SALES

单位：亿元 (10⁸ yuan)

指标	Items	企业单位数（个） Number of Enterprises (unit)	工业总产值（现价） Total Output Value (current price)	#新产品产值 Output Value of New Products	工业销售产值（现价） Value of Industrial Products Sales (current price)	#出口交货值 Delivery Value for Export
总　计	**Total**	**17957**	**8053.03**	**870.96**	**7727.33**	**1467.32**
按登记注册类型分	**Grouped by Type of Registeration**					
内资企业	Inner Funded Enterprise	15058	6223.66	620.63	5955.40	800.49
#国有企业	State-Owned Enterprise	2628	1620.29	258.65	1577.46	161.20
集体企业	Collective-Owned Enterprise	6215	2309.94	140.66	2188.65	324.01
有限责任公司	Responsibility Co. Ltd.	848	709.32	84.92	691.77	79.03
股份有限公司	Share Holding Co. Ltd.	337	388.63	77.75	372.39	59.92
港、澳、台商投资企业	Hongkong, Macao and Taiwan Funded Enterprise	1418	709.71	43.82	685.62	201.48
外商投资企业	Foreign Funded Enterprise	1481	1119.66	206.51	1086.31	465.35
按轻重工业分	**Grouped by Light and Heavy Industry**					
轻工业	Light Industry	8890	3709.65	326.89	3546.00	902.45
#以农产品为原料	Using Farm Products as Raw Meterials	5726	2326.19	106.69	2225.83	626.03
重工业	Heavy Industry	9067	4343.38	544.07	4181.33	564.88
#原料工业	Raw Material	2331	1547.25	56.97	1504.14	97.38
加工工业	Manufacturing	6533	2708.13	486.95	2591.37	466.94
按企业规模分	**Grouped by Scale of Enterprise**					
#大型企业	Large	604	2426.61	509.24	2376.43	334.70
中型企业	Medium	1785	1384.38	178.75	1325.73	260.16
按行业分	**Grouped by Sector**					
采掘业	**Mining and Quarring**					
煤炭采选业	Coal Mining and Processing	30	44.95		43.58	0.06
石油和天然气开采业	Petroleum and Natural Gas Extraction	1	13.07		13.10	
黑色金属矿采选业	Ferrous Metals Mining and Processing	4	2.11		2.10	0.25
有色金属矿采选业	Nonferrous Metals Mining and Processing	7	1.79	0.08	1.70	0.21
非金属矿采选业	Nonmetal Minerals Mining and Processing	176	32.04	0.07	32.15	0.05
其他矿采选业	Other Minerals Mining and Processing					
木材及竹材采运业	Logging and Transport of Timber and Bamboo	1	0.15	..	0.14	
制造业	**Manufacturing**					
食品加工业	Food Processing	865	312.87	5.50	301.63	26.16
食品制造业	Food Production	334	88.28	3.12	83.74	8.61
饮料制造业	Beverage Production	197	122.07	5.76	117.97	4.12
烟草加工业	Tobacco Processing	9	40.21		39.21	0.03
纺织业	Textile Industry	2086	1039.79	61.55	994.06	325.46

续表 Continued

单位:亿元 (10[8] yuan)

指 标	Items	企业单位数 Number of Enterprises	工业总产值(现价) Total Output Value (current price)	#新产品产值 Output of New Products	工业销售产值(现价) Value of Industrial Products Sales (current price)	#出口交货值 Delivery Value for Export
服装及纤维制品制造业	Garments and Other Fiber Products	869	334.96	6.77	320.76	166.42
皮革毛皮羽绒及制品业	Leather, Furs, Down and Related Products	316	112.22	8.60	107.47	51.43
木材加工及竹藤棕草制品业	Timber Processing, Bamboo, Cane, Palm Fiber and Straw Products	245	68.19	1.84	63.30	5.04
家具制造业	Furniture Manufacturing	116	27.55	0.42	26.32	4.47
造纸及纸制品业	Papermaking and Paper Products	351	102.95	3.11	96.29	12.04
印刷业记录媒介的复制	Printing and Record Pressing	262	55.96	0.36	53.73	2.50
文教体育用品制造业	Stationery, Education and Sports Goods	270	87.45	4.23	83.50	50.61
石油加工及炼焦业	Petroleum Processing and Coking Products	80	154.42	3.92	157.18	3.34
化学原料及制品制造业	Raw Chemical Materials and Chemical Products	1722	776.30	42.69	742.95	108.17
医药制造业	Medical and Pharmaceutical Products	273	127.94	21.45	120.70	23.51
化学纤维制造业	Chemical Fibers	193	196.30	16.60	187.01	10.74
橡胶制品业	Rubber Products	192	69.57	5.88	66.22	16.78
塑料制品业	Plastic Products	701	235.21	19.63	222.74	33.67
非金属矿物制品业	Nonmetal Mineral Products	1220	314.25	10.77	301.26	24.55
黑色金属冶炼及压延加工业	Smelting and Pressing of Ferrous Metals	329	312.46	26.53	300.16	10.65
有色金属冶炼及压延加工业	Smelting and Pressing of Nonferrous Metals	335	170.35	4.46	162.83	18.06
金属制品业	Metal Products	1064	329.20	18.96	311.61	72.11
普通机械制造业	Ordinary Machinery Manufacturing	1514	567.76	108.86	543.93	69.29
专用设备制造业	Special Purposes Equipment Manufacturing	992	304.72	33.68	288.66	35.11
交通运输设备制造业	Transportation Equipment Manufacturing	692	447.62	133.27	436.20	62.11
电气机械及器材制造业	Electric Equipment and Machinery	1197	537.85	102.03	509.40	46.73
电子及通信设备制造业	Electronic and Telecommunications	527	543.98	203.55	525.19	206.82
仪器仪表及文化办公用机械制造业	Instruments, Meters, Cultural and Official Machinery	201	80.82	12.16	78.75	33.23
其他制造业	Other Manufacturing	361	91.09	4.25	86.90	34.41
电力、煤气及水的生产和供应业	**Electric Power, Gas and Water Production and Supply**					
电力、蒸气、热水生产和供应业	Electric Power, Steam and Hot Water Production and Supply	119	282.34	0.35	281.56	0.17
煤气生产和供应业	Gas Production and Supply	17	7.83	0.00	7.35	0.00
自来水的生产和供应业	Tap Water Production and Supply	86	15.26	0.00	14.86	0.01

注:本表口径为全部国有企业及年产品销售收入 500 万元以上非国有企业。

Note: The bore of this table was state-owned enterprises and nonstate-owned enterprises with 5 million yuan above of revenue of product sales yearly (so did follows).

8-2 历年工业总产值

GROSS OUTPUT VALUE OF INDUSTRY OVER THE YEARS

单位：亿元 (10^8 yuan)

年份 Year	工业总产值 Gross Output Value of Industry (当年价) (current price)	按轻重工业分 Grouped by Light and Heavy Industry		按经济类型分 Grouped by Ownership			在总计中：农村工业 Among Total: Rural Industry
		轻工业 Light Industry	重工业 Heavy Industry	#国有经济 State-Owned	#集体经济 Collective-Owned	#其他经济 Others	
1950	19.00	17.94	1.06	11.93	7.07		
1952	25.53	23.97	1.56	17.39	8.14		
1955	32.82	29.57	3.25	23.43	9.39		
1957	41.01	34.78	6.23	30.21	10.80		
1962	53.36	42.95	10.41	43.76	9.60		
1965	88.08	66.28	21.80	73.10	12.57		3.16
1966	104.19	74.60	29.59	84.41	17.25		4.14
1970	135.47	83.14	52.33	107.68	24.69		7.19
1975	235.28	130.28	105.00	161.62	65.22		23.25
1976	247.59	134.97	112.62	169.03	65.21		33.31
1977	297.12	158.12	139.00	183.45	92.59		50.57
1978	337.65	176.94	160.71	207.52	105.28		62.43
1979	386.05	208.11	177.94	238.58	117.86		72.29
1980	467.82	267.97	199.85	268.11	153.30	2.45	109.33
1981	504.94	307.98	196.96	276.70	175.49	3.74	124.79
1982	534.87	317.54	217.33	297.64	180.79	5.18	132.16
1983	600.70	348.56	252.14	320.79	209.48	8.00	159.59
1984	745.36	433.00	312.36	350.35	283.41	12.12	231.02
1985	1036.67	552.23	484.44	426.24	415.90	18.73	385.54
1986	1235.38	671.24	564.14	482.50	500.01	22.92	497.28
1987	1590.31	859.40	730.91	582.51	644.07	34.92	688.52
1988	2152.93	1151.00	1001.93	747.21	877.54	57.90	980.79
1989	2507.42	1338.53	1168.89	877.21	1002.62	86.04	1113.84
1990	2764.10	1510.57	1253.53	948.40	1094.82	104.66	1251.95
1991	3161.60	1682.76	1478.84	1045.31	1258.55	160.50	1467.37
1992	4673.57	2379.00	2294.57	1319.21	1934.05	263.36	2463.26
1993	7096.46	3439.50	3656.96	1651.04	2781.66	626.46	4192.94
1994	9826.50	5014.54	4811.96	1959.99	3642.09	1206.25	6099.06
1995	9807.19	4785.42	5021.77	2096.69	3559.74	1326.03	5815.30
1996	11555.60	5676.47	5879.13	2244.68	3974.16	1700.41	7182.91
1997	12542.40	6382.96	6159.44	2214.06	3741.00	2267.32	7856.85
1998	13185.70	6843.38	6342.40	1963.80	3056.04	3033.19	8438.62

8-3 历年工业总产值指数
INDICES OF GROSS OUTPUT VALUE OF INDUSTRY OVER THE YEARS

本表按可比价格计算 1949=100　　　　(At comparable price 1949=100)

年份 Year	工业总产值 Gross Output Value of Inductry	按轻重工业分 Grouped by Light and Heavy Industry		按经济类型分 Grouped by Ownership			在总计中：农村工业 Among Total: Rural Industry
		轻工业 Light Industry	重工业 Heavy Industry	#国有经济 State-Owned	#集体经济 Collective-Owned	#其他经济 Others	
1949	100.0	100.0	100.0	100.0	100.0		
1950	119.5	119.2	123.1	122.8	114.4		
1952	160.6	159.1	178.6	179.0	131.7		
1955	208.3	194.9	306.0	236.5	153.3		
1957	266.6	230.2	700.9	321.0	180.8		
1962	334.8	270.6	1102.6	449.1	155.0		
1965	577.0	448.2	2117.1	760.4	248.0		100.0
1966	710.8	488.7	3366.7	921.0	229.7		130.6
1970	1040.8	599.4	6318.8	1358.9	487.9		219.6
1975	1861.2	944.4	12870.8	2120.4	1275.4		720.5
1976	2050.5	1021.0	14475.3	2218.1	1502.2		1064.0
1977	2461.8	1189.7	17929.2	2527.4	1901.7		1641.4
1978	2797.8	1330.2	20707.9	2886.6	2131.7		1999.4
1979	3186.6	1561.8	22875.3	3260.6	2443.5		2410.1
1980	3847.3	2021.4	25552.8	3612.8	3186.4	100.0	3477.9
1981	4171.8	2360.5	25144.9	3797.7	3553.9	153.3	3966.6
1982	4490.8	2474.5	28080.5	4075.4	3858.3	209.2	4233.1
1983	5113.9	2790.0	32420.7	4490.5	4491.5	335.5	5113.3
1984	6304.5	3378.2	40947.6	4843.3	6059.9	541.6	7455.2
1985	8408.9	4425.1	55903.7	5590.1	8496.0	787.8	12092.1
1986	9811.6	5264.6	63611.0	6077.9	10104.0	885.1	15656.5
1987	12151.6	6336.4	81715.9	6936.9	12733.9	1419.8	20989.6
1988	15271.4	7975.7	102496.3	7915.4	16167.5	2165.6	28566.3
1989	15981.9	8303.0	107964.6	8024.5	16846.4	2742.4	29952.4
1990	17583.9	9246.4	117011.0	8632.8	18603.2	3404.2	33667.8
1991	20131.3	10304.4	138466.3	9227.5	21869.1	5499.4	40207.2
1992	30039.9	14934.2	213695.0	11299.1	34050.2	9407.3	69516.5
1993	42668.4	20680.9	312033.2	12394.8	46817.3	21069.9	112965.1
1994	57057.8	28386.0	405576.0	13109.5	59214.4	38081.7	161879.9
1995	69176.9	34693.4	487583.5	14965.8	74870.4	52053.9	196198.4
1996	81725.4	40979.5	576131.6	16435.3	84909.6	69309.5	237774.4
1997	92840.0	47208.4	625678.9	17848.7	93740.2	80260.4	273678.3
1998	105094.9	54431.3	688246.8	18919.6	97958.5	105301.6	3256771.77

8－4 限额以上独立核算工业企业主要经济指标(1998)

单位:亿元

行业	Items	企业单位数(个) Number of Enterprises (units)	全部从业人员年平均人数(人) Annual Average of All Employees (persons)	工业增加值(当年价) Added Value of Industry (current price)
总　计	**Total**	**17957**	**578.77**	**1916.92**
按登记注册类型分	**Grouped by Type of Registeration**			
内资企业	Inner Funded Enterprise	15058	504.84	1493.94
#国有企业	State-Owned Enterprise	2628	163.85	433.58
集体企业	Collective-Owned Enterprise	6215	166.80	510.85
有限责任公司	Responsibility Co. Ltd.	848	63.35	190.72
股份有限公司	Share Holding Co. Ltd.	337	22.31	99.38
港、澳、台商投资企业	Hongkong, Macao and Taiwan Funded Enterprise	1418	34.40	166.53
外商投资企业	Foreign Funded Enterprise	1481	39.54	256.46
按轻重工业分	**Grouped by Light and Heavy Industry**			
轻工业	Light Industry	8890	275.24	854.20
#以农产品为原料	Using Farm Products as Raw Meterials	5726	188.11	533.70
重工业	Heavy Industry	9067	303.53	1062.72
#原料工业	Raw Material	2331	76.51	402.55
加工工业	Manufacturing	6533	203.54	619.27
按企业规模分	**Grouped by Scale of Enterprise**			
#大型企业	Large	604	142.32	658.22
中型企业	Medium	1785	131.27	320.04
按行业分	**Grouped by Sector**			
煤炭采选业	Coal Mining and Processing	30	16.16	24.44
石油和天然气开采业	Petroleum and Natural Gas Extraction	1	2.12	7.93
黑色金属矿采选业	Ferrous Metals Mining and Processing	4	0.63	0.43
有色金属矿采选业	Nonferrous Metals Mining and Processing	7	0.27	0.65
非金属矿采选业	Nonmetal Minerals Mining and Processing	176	7.63	11.33
其他矿采选业	Other Minerals Mining and Processing			
木材及竹材采运业	Logging and Transport of Timber and Bamboo	1	0.01	0.03
食品加工业	Food Processing	865	16.78	52.61
食品制造业	Food Production	334	6.88	20.98
饮料制造业	Beverage Production	197	8.50	35.98

MAJOR ECONOMIC INDICATORS OF OVER-NORM INDUSTRIAL ENTERPRISES WITH INDEPENDENT ACCOUNTING SYSTEMS

(10^8 yuan)

实收资本 Actual Capital	资产合计 Total Property	流动资产合计 Circulating Funds	流动资产年平均余额 Average Balance Circulating Funds	固定资产合计 Fixed Assets	固定资产原价 Original Value of Fixed Assets	固定资产净值年平均余额 Average Balances Net Value of Fixed Asstes
2441.76	**9098.51**	**4355.37**	**4255.81**	**4002.98**	**4936.57**	**3488.93**
1563.93	6836.96	3373.90	3322.57	2904.99	3659.83	2515.58
534.69	2634.31	1178.82	1205.75	1248.00	1576.13	1133.69
441.81	1791.93	999.95	964.23	656.63	813.74	563.20
305.06	1100.36	472.07	452.29	506.71	678.19	408.15
96.60	499.09	240.60	232.66	209.22	218.45	154.97
282.84	845.27	385.00	375.09	406.16	501.79	361.02
594.99	1416.28	596.48	558.15	691.83	774.95	612.32
978.31	3546.48	1730.15	1677.86	1515.90	1846.62	1343.22
553.00	2094.16	1006.15	964.90	911.10	1116.63	821.22
1463.46	5552.03	2625.23	2577.94	2487.08	3089.95	2145.71
623.25	2231.81	818.73	830.61	1261.53	1545.04	1087.77
796.17	3159.20	1742.78	1683.42	1142.78	1417.00	983.86
901.61	3682.05	1593.44	1602.85	1749.25	2198.80	1501.09
392.35	1676.61	848.60	824.33	696.26	879.71	600.92
23.11	92.44	40.77	41.36	43.83	70.60	40.38
11.97	36.50	10.15	9.71	23.56	34.69	19.48
0.91	4.11	1.76	1.74	1.52	2.59	1.48
0.94	2.83	1.20	1.10	1.47	1.76	1.08
13.72	50.43	19.03	20.01	25.15	33.20	22.18
0.01	0.01			0.01	0.01	0.01
48.20	215.73	107.76	106.57	88.24	106.35	79.11
36.46	103.85	44.14	41.97	49.24	59.68	43.23
39.79	145.59	70.12	66.91	65.41	75.07	52.29

续 表 1

单位:亿元

行 业 Items		企业单位数(个) Number of Enterprises (units)	全部从业人员年平均人数(人) Annual Average of All Employees (persons)	工业增加值(当年价) Added Value of Industry (current price)
烟草加工业	Tobacco Processing	9	0.50	23.95
纺织业	Textile Industry	2086	99.14	225.75
服装及纤维制品制造业	Garments and Other Fiber Products	869	26.74	78.84
皮革毛皮羽绒及制品业	Leather, Furs, Down and Related Products	316	8.34	24.89
木材加工及竹藤棕草制品业	Timber Processing, Bamboo, Cane, Palm Fiber and Straw Products	245	4.64	12.41
家具制造业	Furniture Manufacturing	116	1.74	6.25
造纸及纸制品业	Papermaking and Paper Products	351	8.15	21.77
印刷业记录媒介的复制	Printing and Record Pressing	262	5.22	15.51
文教体育用品制造业	Stationery, Education and Sports Goods	270	7.87	20.99
石油加工及炼焦业	Petroleum Processing and Coking Products	80	4.10	24.64
化学原料及制品制造业	Raw Chemical Materials and Chemical Products	1722	45.96	177.12
医药制造业	Medical and Pharmaceutical Products	273	8.43	40.58
化学纤维制造业	Chemical Fibers	193	8.76	41.50
橡胶制品业	Rubber Products	192	7.13	16.21
塑料制品业	Plastic Products	701	12.70	53.53
非金属矿物制品业	Nonmetal Mineral Products	1220	38.28	78.78
黑色金属冶炼及压延加工业	Smelting and Pressing of Ferrous Metals	329	13.66	54.71
有色金属冶炼及压延加工业	Smelting and Pressing of Nonferrous Metals	335	6.35	31.83
金属制品业	Metal Products	1064	21.47	73.25
普通机械制造业	Ordinary Machinery Manufacturing	1514	53.36	137.99
专用设备制造业	Special Purposes Equipment Manufacturing	992	29.90	69.27
交通运输设备制造业	Transportation Equipment Manufacturing	692	26.33	97.81
电气机械及器材制造业	Electric Equipment and Machinery	1197	30.39	129.26
电子及通信设备制造业	Electronic and Telecommunications	527	23.49	108.86
仪器仪表及文化办公用机械制造业	Instruments, Meters, Cultural and Official Machinery	201	6.88	21.76
其他制造业	Other Manufacturing	361	7.30	21.85
电力、蒸气、热水生产和供应业	Electric Power, Steam and Hot Water Production and Supply	119	9.46	146.44
煤气生产和供应业	Gas Production and Supply	17	1.07	0.05
自来水的生产和供应业	Tap Water Production and Supply	86	2.10	6.45

Continued 1

(10[8] yuan)

实收资本 Actual Capital	资产合计 Total Property	流动资产合计 Circulating Funds	流动资产年平均余额 Average Balance Circulating Funds	固定资产合计 Fixed Assets	固定资产原价 Original Value of Fixed Assets	固定资产净值年平均余额 Average Balances Net Value of Fixed Asstes
5.80	28.10	9.60	13.31	14.98	20.09	13.72
237.75	988.74	457.83	433.81	447.21	579.78	407.24
73.10	218.23	120.23	116.93	80.46	98.48	72.00
19.64	75.73	47.83	47.05	22.22	27.93	20.27
12.69	50.23	28.35	28.16	19.08	23.03	16.75
8.83	25.11	13.57	13.19	8.87	10.44	8.41
44.65	154.50	59.42	53.90	84.23	74.94	77.89
15.91	60.29	32.33	30.83	24.46	32.45	26.82
13.73	50.51	31.92	30.64	14.29	17.63	13.58
37.65	134.36	55.88	54.61	69.26	106.38	58.18
259.57	899.11	380.23	355.41	439.79	579.51	350.49
38.95	152.57	83.14	77.19	56.05	66.62	45.63
95.04	321.85	110.96	114.54	187.36	223.51	160.39
28.95	94.41	39.01	38.98	47.31	48.15	38.32
60.93	204.53	100.48	96.51	85.39	108.96	76.38
144.48	451.77	169.45	162.15	235.65	282.36	209.33
133.51	419.47	176.81	171.66	211.08	191.77	137.28
34.16	125.75	68.68	66.59	47.57	57.40	41.59
85.16	299.59	167.96	163.95	108.51	136.48	99.08
165.16	710.53	423.81	409.71	232.13	296.90	197.72
79.85	328.81	194.26	190.11	111.75	149.35	99.24
140.27	527.01	267.20	264.23	205.25	247.98	178.88
150.04	548.79	334.44	328.48	166.37	200.41	140.61
141.55	597.57	355.79	340.04	179.57	231.02	159.07
28.11	87.01	50.16	46.82	30.57	40.74	27.32
17.95	62.24	38.18	36.73	19.29	25.07	18.11
147.47	716.45	214.68	254.81	474.54	585.22	468.68
14.30	31.12	7.42	6.25	22.59	23.61	18.16
30.28	79.55	19.34	18.46	57.24	64.25	47.05

续表 2

单位:亿元

行业	Items	负债合计 Total Liabilities	流动负债合计 Total Circulating Liabilities	所有者权益 Owner's Rights and Interests
总计	**Total**	**5663.88**	**4415.82**	**3434.63**
按登记注册类型分	**Grouped by Type of Registeration**			
#内资企业	Inner Funded Enterprise	4381.19	3441.93	2455.77
国有企业	State-Owned Enterprise	1720.26	1240.47	914.05
集体企业	Collective-Owned Enterprise	1202.50	1029.13	589.44
有限责任公司	Responsibility Co. Ltd.	629.65	470.14	470.70
股份有限公司	Share Co. Ltd.	257.98	202.81	241.11
港、澳、台商投资企业	Hongkong, Macao and Taiwan Funded Enterprise	500.64	372.54	344.64
外商投资企业	Foreign Funded Enterprise	782.05	601.36	634.23
按轻重工业分	**Grouped by Light and Heavy Industry**			
轻工业	Light Industry	2276.48	1871.98	1270.00
#以农产品为原料	Using Farm Products as Raw Meterials	1410.35	1171.66	683.81
重工业	Heavy Industry	3387.39	2543.84	2164.64
#原料工业	Raw Material	1256.69	846.70	975.13
加工工业	Manufacturing	2039.67	1631.80	1119.53
按企业规模分	**Grouped by Scale of Enterprise**			
#大型企业	Large	2082.69	1461.60	1599.37
中型企业	Medium	1136.19	907.21	540.42
按行业分	**Grouped by Sector**			
煤炭采选业	Coal Mining and Processing	57.07	46.07	35.37
石油和天然气开采业	Petroleum and Natural Gas Extraction	17.71	7.24	18.79
黑色金属矿采选业	Ferrous Metals Mining and Processing	3.00	2.48	1.11
有色金属矿采选业	Nonferrous Metals Mining and Processing	1.80	1.10	1.03
非金属矿采选业	Nonmetal Minerals Mining and Processing	23.67	17.36	26.76
其他矿采选业	Other Minerals Mining and Processing			0.00
木材及竹材采运业	Logging and Transport of Timber and Bamboo			0.01
食品加工业	Food Processing	156.65	137.91	59.08
食品制造业	Food Production	65.81	55.30	38.04
饮料制造业	Beverage Production	95.35	84.94	50.25
烟草加工业	Tobacco Processing	13.46	11.81	14.64

Continued 2

(10[8] yuan)

产品销售收入 Revnue of Product Sales	产品销售成本 Costs of Product Sales	产品销售税金及附加 Product Sales Pre-Tax and Related Payments	产品销售利润 Product Sales After-Tax Profits	利润总额 Total After-Tax Profits	本年应交增值税 Added Value Tax	利税总额 Total Pre-Tax Profits
7375.45	**6314.14**	**66.08**	**114.33**	**151.51**	**274.03**	**491.61**
5674.92	4850.58	60.42	70.31	114.50	214.51	389.43
1588.94	1356.91	28.64	34.60	4.47	69.29	102.40
2018.82	1739.89	15.52	19.50	48.02	66.87	130.41
697.52	592.01	5.86	4.94	19.90	30.23	55.98
357.99	293.24	1.72	2.69	19.08	11.99	32.79
647.29	556.95	2.44	9.84	15.59	24.86	42.89
1053.25	906.61	3.22	34.18	21.41	34.66	59.29
3337.80	2860.37	38.23	53.74	61.14	113.28	215.66
2087.33	1816.76	28.48	33.95	28.80	65.88	123.16
4037.65	3453.77	27.85	60.59	87.34	160.76	275.95
1487.57	1327.15	12.55	18.39	29.39	66.28	108.22
2466.56	2063.05	14.20	40.77	57.33	88.76	160.30
2411.72	2047.55	30.95	26.29	78.18	99.22	208.35
1248.84	1050.31	11.79	24.08	14.40	49.96	76.13
43.49	30.96	0.59	1.06	−0.18	3.53	3.94
12.94	10.54	0.16	0.00	0.36	1.13	1.65
1.84	1.70	0.02	0.18	−0.17	0.07	−0.09
1.82	1.31	0.01	0.01	0.04	0.08	0.13
29.58	22.40	0.51	0.25	0.57	1.54	2.62
0.00	0.00	0.00	0.00	0.00	0.00	0.00
0.14	0.14	0.00	0.00	0.00	0.00	0.00
283.72	257.05	0.77	4.13	1.34	3.86	5.97
82.43	68.31	0.35	2.37	0.12	3.39	3.87
116.77	91.09	5.76	3.31	2.88	5.54	14.18
38.42	19.41	13.86	0.00	2.43	3.66	19.95

续 表 3

单位:亿元

行业	Items	负债合计 Total Liabilities	流动负债合计 Total Circulating Liabilities	所有者权益 Owner's Rights and Interests
纺织业	Textile Industry	687.40	540.60	301.34
服装及纤维制品制造业	Garments and Other Fiber Products	129.95	115.36	88.28
皮革毛皮羽绒及制品业	Leather, Furs, Down and Related Products	51.07	47.68	24.67
木材加工及竹藤棕草制品业	Timber Processing, Bamboo, Cane, Palm Fiber and Straw Products	36.18	33.67	14.05
家具制造业	Furniture Manufacturing	15.82	14.41	9.29
造纸及纸制品业	Papermaking and Paper Products	111.47	91.62	43.03
印刷业记录媒介的复制	Printing and Record Pressing	38.20	31.75	22.09
文教体育用品制造业	Stationery, Education and Sports Goods	33.11	31.37	17.40
石油加工及炼焦业	Petroleum Processing and Coking Products	74.46	48.32	59.91
化学原料及制品制造业	Raw Chemical Materials and Chemical Products	546.12	390.82	352.99
医药制造业	Medical and Pharmaceutical Products	93.66	79.07	58.91
化学纤维制造业	Chemical Fibers	170.18	116.77	151.68
橡胶制品业	Rubber Products	65.32	41.89	29.09
塑料制品业	Plastic Products	126.96	99.26	77.57
非金属矿物制品业	Nonmetal Mineral Products	283.59	206.18	168.18
黑色金属冶炼及压延加工业	Smelting and Pressing of Ferrous Metals	243.51	193.39	175.96
有色金属冶炼及压延加工业	Smelting and Pressing of Nonferrous Metals	84.70	68.44	41.05
金属制品业	Metal Products	196.45	167.51	103.14
普通机械制造业	Ordinary Machinery Manufacturing	445.30	383.75	265.23
专用设备制造业	Special Purposes Equipment Manufacturing	214.69	181.68	114.12
交通运输设备制造业	Transportation Equipment Manufacturing	324.47	259.81	202.54
电气机械及器材制造业	Electric Equipment and Machinery	339.10	297.62	209.69
电子及通信设备制造业	Electronic and Telecommunications	408.78	317.11	188.80
仪器仪表及文化办公用机械制造业	Instruments, Meters, Cultural and Official Machinery	50.18	41.11	36.83
其他制造业	Other Manufacturing	39.75	35.27	22.49
电力、蒸气、热水生产和供应业	Electric Power, Steam and Hot Water Production and Supply	374.11	192.47	342.33
煤气生产和供应业	Gas Production and Supply	14.98	9.34	16.14
自来水的生产和供应业	Tap Water Production and Supply	28.51	14.26	51.05

Continued 3

(10^8 yuan)

产 品 销售收入 Revnue of Product Sales	产 品 销售成本 Costs of Product Sales	产品销售税金及附加 Product Sales Pre-Tax and Related Payments	产 品 销售利润 Product Sales After-Tax Profits	利润总额 Total After-Tax Profits	本年应交增值税 Added Value Tax	利税总额 Total Pre-Tax Profits
929.84	835.00	4.27	12.51	7.19	27.68	39.14
286.57	251.28	1.05	2.88	8.68	7.95	17.68
99.92	86.59	0.52	0.95	2.06	3.04	5.62
60.59	55.49	0.34	1.99	-0.13	2.26	2.46
24.76	21.03	0.16	0.09	0.98	0.79	1.93
90.94	79.31	0.46	5.71	-3.07	3.48	0.87
50.34	40.46	0.37	0.80	2.27	2.76	5.40
77.66	66.35	0.28	0.27	3.02	2.06	5.37
172.59	151.59	5.14	1.08	2.41	6.24	13.80
703.44	595.94	5.48	9.37	18.69	26.59	50.75
127.69	89.19	1.20	1.35	8.52	7.92	17.64
182.62	159.68	0.95	5.13	2.81	7.13	10.89
60.69	50.65	0.80	2.08	-0.80	2.54	2.54
211.62	180.62	1.33	2.44	7.11	7.26	15.70
279.59	235.49	2.35	7.68	-0.10	13.47	15.72
294.73	272.61	1.10	4.41	0.82	7.91	9.84
145.86	130.79	0.81	1.20	2.49	3.87	7.17
288.98	247.07	1.66	4.91	5.74	9.79	17.19
516.99	420.26	3.05	6.98	13.75	20.81	37.61
268.37	224.94	1.73	4.89	3.82	9.69	15.25
416.56	358.92	4.77	5.79	9.94	15.87	30.58
474.37	379.22	2.43	7.93	17.89	19.65	39.96
516.88	449.34	1.09	9.31	14.16	13.13	28.38
74.84	61.10	0.25	1.24	1.97	2.62	4.83
79.98	69.46	0.72	0.60	1.87	2.85	5.44
303.95	278.88	1.58	0.45	12.63	22.61	36.82
8.05	9.11	0.03	0.72	-0.67	0.26	-0.38
14.70	10.05	0.12	0.26	0.05	0.96	1.13

8-5 国有独立核算工业企业主要经济指标（1998）

单位:亿元

行业	Items	企业单位数（个） Number of Enterprises (units)	全部从业人员年平均人数（人） Annual Average of All Employees (persons)	工业增加值（当年价） Added Value of Industry (current price)
总计	**Total**	**2628**	**163.85**	**433.58**
按轻重工业分	**Grouped by Light and Heavy Industry**			
轻工业	Light Industry	1392	68.51	141.82
#以农产品为原料	Using Farm Products as Raw Meterials	1043	52.18	109.39
重工业	Heavy Industry	1236	95.34	291.76
#原料工业	Raw Material	269	27.62	153.43
加工工业	Manufacturing	919	60.04	124.85
按企业规模分	**Grouped by Scale of Enterprise**			
#大型企业	Large	265	65.50	266.73
中型企业	Medium	633	57.42	100.87
按行业分	**Grouped by Sector**			
#煤炭采选业	Coal Mining and Processing	16	3.25	2.99
石油和天然气开采业	Petroleum and Natural Gas Extraction	1	2.12	7.93
黑色金属矿采选业	Ferrous Metals Mining and Processing	2	0.61	0.27
有色金属矿采选业	Nonferrous Metals Mining and Processing	3	0.14	0.25
非金属矿采选业	Nonmetal Minerals Mining and Processing	33	1.82	2.36
食品加工业	Food Processing	409	9.85	19.19
食品制造业	Food Production	138	3.06	3.84
饮料制造业	Beverage Production	82	3.94	9.44
烟草加工业	Tobacco Processing	4	0.46	22.95
纺织业	Textile Industry	214	27.31	41.98
服装及纤维制品制造业	Garments and Other Fiber Products	27	1.76	3.30
皮革毛皮羽绒及制品业	Leather, Furs, Down and Related Products	18	0.92	2.16
木材加工及竹藤棕草制品业	Timber Processing, Bamboo, Cane, Palm Fiber and Straw Products	13	0.21	0.25

注：本表口径为内资企业中的国有工业。（下同）

Note: The bore of this table was state-owned industry in inner enterprises.

MAJOR ECONOMIC INDICATORS OF STATE-OWNED INDUSTRIAL ENTERPRISES WITH INDEPENDENT ACCOUNTING SYSTEMS

(10[8] yuan)

实收资本 Actual Capital	资产合计 Total Property	流动资产合计 Total Circulating Funds	流动资产年平均余额 Average Balance Circulating Funds	固定资产合计 Total Fixed Assets	固定资产原价 Original Value of Fixed Assets	固定资产净值年平均余额 Average Balances Net Value of Fixed Asstes
534.69	**2634.31**	**1178.82**	**1205.75**	**1248.00**	**1576.13**	**1133.69**
164.24	800.42	351.90	343.01	379.26	470.30	335.97
99.77	541.72	243.65	237.78	251.07	320.21	224.83
370.45	1833.89	826.92	862.74	868.74	1105.82	797.72
171.45	825.42	306.09	351.38	480.76	606.15	464.48
180.14	939.99	496.92	487.13	349.54	444.07	300.48
322.01	1546.20	672.94	708.77	743.34	953.89	705.33
135.32	692.38	318.87	313.24	324.28	398.97	272.68
3.54	13.53	7.14	8.06	4.89	7.65	4.37
11.97	36.50	10.15	9.71	23.56	34.69	19.48
0.75	3.69	1.43	1.41	1.44	2.50	1.40
0.31	1.18	0.44	0.44	0.61	0.59	0.30
2.51	15.28	5.45	5.27	8.86	11.34	8.13
14.99	95.55	48.57	47.50	41.21	51.12	37.85
6.73	32.00	12.11	11.85	14.82	17.17	13.19
7.05	51.79	26.77	26.67	22.11	25.79	18.13
5.52	26.82	8.67	12.42	14.72	19.73	13.43
50.42	267.53	115.36	107.90	127.51	169.49	116.45
3.13	12.34	5.95	5.77	5.59	5.74	4.31
2.33	9.96	6.43	5.59	3.01	4.20	2.92
0.22	1.49	0.57	0.62	0.80	0.75	0.58

续 表 1

单位:亿元

行业	Items	企业单位数(个) Number of Enterprises (units)	全部从业人员年平均人数(人) Annual Average of All Employees (persons)	工业增加值(当年价) Added Value of Industry (current price)
家具制造业	Furniture Manufacturing	11	0.23	0.60
造纸及纸制品业	Papermaking and Paper Products	30	1.73	2.14
印刷业记录媒介的复制	Printing and Record Pressing	85	2.12	2.93
文教体育用品制造业	Stationery, Education and Sports Goods	7	0.22	0.17
石油加工及炼焦业	Petroleum Processing and Coking Products	7	3.24	20.18
化学原料及制品制造业	Raw Chemical Materials and Chemical Products	229	15.93	29.16
医药制造业	Medical and Pharmaceutical Products	69	3.36	8.65
化学纤维制造业	Chemical Fibers	17	1.46	1.59
橡胶制品业	Rubber Products	11	1.88	2.68
塑料制品业	Plastic Products	22	0.43	0.53
非金属矿物制品业	Nonmetal Mineral Products	186	10.03	14.13
黑色金属冶炼及压延加工业	Smelting and Pressing of Ferrous Metals	24	4.18	8.02
有色金属冶炼及压延加工业	Smelting and Pressing of Nonferrous Metals	16	0.98	4.02
金属制品业	Metal Products	63	2.65	10.48
普通机械制造业	Ordinary Machinery Manufacturing	195	15.26	33.95
专用设备制造业	Special Purposes Equipment Manufacturing	186	8.63	11.61
交通运输设备制造业	Transportation Equipment Manufacturing	115	10.28	31.61
电气机械及器材制造业	Electric Equipment and Machinery	97	4.25	10.57
电子及通信设备制造业	Electronic and Telecommunications	78	7.71	14.12
仪器仪表及文化办公用机械制造业	Instruments, Meters, Cultural and Official Machinery	43	2.67	4.11
其他制造业	Other Manufacturing	31	0.51	0.55
电力、蒸气、热水生产和供应业	Electric Power, Steam and Hot Water Production and Supply	56	7.33	98.66
煤气生产和供应业	Gas Production and Supply	14	1.05	-0.13
自来水的生产和供应业	Tap Water Production and Supply	74	1.99	6.09

Continued 1

(10[8] yuan)

实收资本 Actual Capital	资产合计 Total Property	流动资产合计 Total Circulating Funds	流动资产年平均余额 Average Balance Circulating Funds	固定资产合计 Total Fixed Assets	固定资产原价 Original Value of Fixed Assets	固定资产净值年平均余额 Average Balances Net Value of Fixed Asstes
0.70	3.09	1.66	1.60	0.93	1.43	0.95
2.90	18.73	8.21	8.18	9.68	10.11	7.60
3.42	14.09	5.18	5.07	7.84	10.86	7.34
0.18	1.13	0.81	0.78	0.27	0.37	0.25
26.11	95.95	39.25	42.71	50.44	83.75	41.18
32.29	207.33	84.55	82.90	106.94	130.65	88.04
9.83	41.78	21.36	20.23	15.96	19.30	13.06
4.29	28.00	8.28	8.53	16.72	20.44	14.35
2.08	9.44	4.88	4.69	3.95	4.99	3.63
1.53	6.12	2.28	2.61	3.31	4.20	2.91
16.36	103.81	39.04	38.64	56.22	65.91	48.24
21.41	97.93	43.24	43.77	48.24	42.69	26.78
5.38	26.33	12.16	10.75	12.14	14.89	10.45
11.36	46.79	24.65	22.69	16.92	21.12	16.05
44.57	241.49	141.76	136.86	80.89	97.93	64.04
16.51	91.46	48.39	47.53	37.58	50.89	34.17
56.74	226.73	107.19	104.66	95.67	116.76	87.98
11.42	62.00	37.64	36.79	19.92	23.24	15.94
29.58	183.52	110.59	113.92	42.50	60.16	32.98
5.40	25.61	13.27	12.44	10.37	14.67	9.65
1.02	3.22	1.53	1.52	1.38	1.87	1.24
78.29	423.79	147.86	191.63	262.41	342.26	301.82
14.01	29.72	6.88	5.75	21.99	23.12	17.73
29.07	76.01	17.81	17.15	55.37	61.96	45.58

续 表 2

单位:亿元

行业	Items	负债合计 Total Liabilities	流动负债合计 Total Circulating Liabilities	所有者权益 Owner's Rights and Interests
总计	**Total**	**1720.26**	**1240.47**	**914.05**
按轻重工业分	**Grouped by Light and Heavy Industry**			
轻工业	Light Industry	578.72	438.29	221.70
以农产品为原料	Using Farm Products as Raw Meterials	412.62	319.73	129.10
重工业	Heavy Industry	1141.54	802.19	692.35
原料工业	Raw Material	475.30	312.03	350.12
加工工业	Manufacturing	628.32	466.72	311.67
按企业规模分	**Grouped by Scale of Enterprise**			
大型企业	Large	940.03	638.20	606.16
中型企业	Medium	485.63	374.78	206.75
按行业分	**Grouped by Sector**			
煤炭采选业	Coal Mining and Processing	9.75	8.53	3.77
石油和天然气开采业	Petroleum and Natural Gas Extraction	17.71	7.24	18.79
黑色金属矿采选业	Ferrous Metals Mining and Processing	2.78	2.26	0.91
有色金属矿采选业	Nonferrous Metals Mining and Processing	0.79	0.53	0.38
非金属矿采选业	Nonmetal Minerals Mining and Processing	8.11	5.75	7.17
食品加工业	Food Processing	80.23	70.53	15.32
食品制造业	Food Production	23.16	18.45	8.84
饮料制造业	Beverage Production	42.15	36.41	9.64
烟草加工业	Tobacco Processing	12.74	11.10	14.08
纺织业	Textile Industry	204.47	143.52	63.06
服装及纤维制品制造业	Garments and Other Fiber Products	7.87	6.22	4.47
皮革毛皮羽绒及制品业	Leather, Furs, Down and Related Products	7.86	6.77	2.10
木材加工及竹藤棕草制品业	Timber Processing, Bamboo, Cane, Palm Fiber and Straw Products	1.16	0.74	0.33

Continued 2

(10^8 yuan)

产品销售收入 Revnue of Product Sales	产品销售成本 Costs of Product Sales	产品销售税金及附加 Product Sales Pre-Tax and Related Payments	产品销售利润 Product Sales After-Tax Profits	利润总额 Total After-Tax Profits	本年应交增值税 Added Value Tax	利税总额 Total Pre-Tax Profits
1588.94	**1356.91**	**28.64**	**34.60**	**4.47**	**69.29**	**102.40**
537.89	452.10	18.39	12.97	−3.23	21.80	36.95
406.06	343.29	17.68	9.61	−3.32	15.97	30.33
1051.04	904.81	10.25	21.63	7.70	47.50	65.45
492.74	446.89	6.66	5.45	5.71	25.53	37.89
530.38	435.04	3.28	15.34	2.32	20.04	25.65
947.24	813.86	21.09	12.01	15.34	43.88	80.30
378.47	314.90	6.18	12.88	−6.49	16.40	16.09
8.96	7.72	0.08	0.51	−0.42	0.47	0.14
12.94	10.54	0.16	0.00	0.36	1.13	1.65
1.15	1.05	0.01	0.18	−0.18	0.06	−0.12
0.64	0.42	0.00	0.01	0.00	0.03	0.04
4.88	3.54	0.08	0.17	−0.10	0.31	0.29
104.50	96.33	0.22	2.36	−1.62	1.28	−0.12
14.52	11.68	0.05	0.61	−0.12	0.73	0.67
31.20	23.12	2.87	0.89	−0.37	1.84	4.33
37.71	18.88	13.85	0.00	2.32	3.62	19.79
178.95	160.82	0.57	4.07	−2.79	6.83	4.61
10.87	9.32	0.01	0.16	0.26	0.21	0.49
6.26	4.94	0.02	0.18	−0.07	0.27	0.22
0.69	0.60	0.01	0.04	−0.04	0.02	−0.01

续 表 3

单位:亿元

行 业 Items		负债合计 Total Liabilities	流动负债合计 Total Circulating Liabilities	所有者权益 Owner's Rights and Interests
家具制造业	Furniture Manufacturing	2.46	1.87	0.64
造纸及纸制品业	Papermaking and Paper Products	14.55	10.55	4.18
印刷业记录媒介的复制	Printing and Record Pressing	10.34	7.69	3.75
文教体育用品制造业	Stationery, Education and Sports Goods	1.03	0.97	0.10
石油加工及炼焦业	Petroleum Processing and Coking Products	48.31	26.91	47.63
化学原料及制品制造业	Raw Chemical Materials and Chemical Products	155.76	102.85	51.56
医药制造业	Medical and Pharmaceutical Products	27.63	21.93	14.14
化学纤维制造业	Chemical Fibers	24.38	16.69	3.62
橡胶制品业	Rubber Products	6.53	4.53	2.91
塑料制品业	Plastic Products	5.05	3.38	1.07
非金属矿物制品业	Nonmetal Mineral Products	69.95	46.93	33.86
黑色金属冶炼及压延加工业	Smelting and Pressing of Ferrous Metals	67.03	52.93	30.90
有色金属冶炼及压延加工业	Smelting and Pressing of Nonferrous Metals	18.23	12.11	8.09
金属制品业	Metal Products	28.90	22.99	17.89
普通机械制造业	Ordinary Machinery Manufacturing	146.88	119.28	94.61
专用设备制造业	Special Purposes Equipment Manufacturing	62.20	50.49	29.26
交通运输设备制造业	Transportation Equipment Manufacturing	140.65	97.43	86.07
电气机械及器材制造业	Electric Equipment and Machinery	39.58	33.46	22.43
电子及通信设备制造业	Electronic and Telecommunications	147.53	107.92	35.99
仪器仪表及文化办公用机械制造业	Instruments, Meters, Cultural and Official Machinery	17.12	13.08	8.50
其他制造业	Other Manufacturing	1.87	1.57	1.35
电力、蒸气、热水生产和供应业	Electric Power, Steam and Hot Water Production and Supply	223.73	144.42	200.06
煤气生产和供应业	Gas Production and Supply	13.87	8.62	15.84
自来水的生产和供应业	Tap Water Production and Supply	26.61	12.87	49.40

Continued 3

(10⁸ yuan)

产品销售收入 Revnue of Product Sales	产品销售成本 Costs of Product Sales	产品销售税金及附加 Product Sales Pre-Tax and Related Payments	产品销售利润 Product Sales After-Tax Profits	利润总额 Total After-Tax Profits	本年应交增值税 Added Value Tax	利税总额 Total Pre-Tax Profits
2.32	1.92	0.02	0.00	0.07	0.12	0.21
7.57	6.22	0.03	0.41	−0.25	0.39	0.17
7.37	5.78	0.05	0.39	−0.23	0.50	0.33
0.62	0.49	0.00	0.01	0.01	0.02	0.03
130.79	115.58	4.64	0.40	1.21	4.94	10.80
137.62	117.08	0.70	2.97	−1.14	4.44	4.00
35.99	27.82	0.20	0.25	1.58	1.94	3.72
10.01	9.42	0.04	0.91	−0.88	0.37	−0.47
7.89	6.31	0.16	0.01	0.08	0.49	0.73
1.91	1.65	0.01	0.28	−0.25	0.12	−0.13
42.65	34.54	0.29	2.06	−1.41	2.75	1.63
43.59	40.88	0.15	1.73	−1.55	1.45	0.05
17.01	14.46	0.05	0.15	0.66	0.66	1.37
37.49	31.43	0.11	0.55	0.74	1.72	2.58
133.48	105.30	0.73	2.78	2.16	5.36	8.25
45.63	36.65	0.20	2.09	−0.81	1.75	1.13
137.47	114.51	1.64	1.67	4.66	6.02	12.32
39.61	32.23	0.19	0.67	0.55	1.86	2.59
100.03	87.33	0.21	6.43	−3.90	2.23	−1.46
10.55	7.70	0.04	0.55	−0.31	0.60	0.33
2.29	1.89	0.01	0.08	−0.06	0.07	0.03
201.86	190.39	1.07	0.09	6.93	13.50	21.50
7.08	8.27	0.03	0.71	−0.70	0.25	−0.43
13.85	9.37	0.11	0.23	0.07	0.93	1.11

8－6 限额以上独立核算集体工业企业主要经济指标（1998）

单位:亿元

行业	Items	企业单位数（个） Number of Enterprises (units)	全部从业人员年平均人数（人） Annual Average of All Employees (persons)	工业增加值（当年价） Added Value of Industry (current price)
总计	**Total**	**6215**	**166.80**	**510.85**
按轻重工业分	**Grouped by Light and Heavy Industry**			
轻工业	Light Industry	2862	85.97	267.73
#以农产品为原料	Using Farm Products as Raw Meterials	1792	59.44	170.57
重工业	Heavy Industry	3353	80.83	243.12
#原料工业	Raw Material	863	20.03	73.79
加工工业	Manufacturing	2359	57.91	164.73
按企业规模分	**Grouped by Scale of Enterprise**			
#大型企业	Large	108	14.79	97.14
中型企业	Medium	552	36.06	99.06
按行业分	**Grouped by Sector**			
#煤炭采选业	Coal Mining and Processing	12	0.55	0.54
黑色金属矿采选业	Ferrous Metals Mining and Processing	1	0.02	0.05
有色金属矿采选业	Nonferrous Metals Mining and Processing	1	0.03	0.04
非金属矿采选业	Nonmetal Minerals Mining and Processing	123	2.52	4.38
食品加工业	Food Processing	159	2.39	13.39
食品制造业	Food Production	71	1.81	6.54
饮料制造业	Beverage Production	49	1.18	2.65
烟草加工业	Tobacco Processing	4	0.04	0.97
纺织业	Textile Industry	772	35.09	85.44
服装及纤维制品制造业	Garments and Other Fiber Products	258	8.99	26.54
皮革毛皮羽绒及制品业	Leather, Furs, Down and Related Products	99	2.70	8.71
木材加工及竹藤棕草制品业	Timber Processing, Bamboo, Cane, Palm Fiber and Straw Products	87	1.47	3.74

MAJOR ECONOMIC INDICATORS OF
OVER-NORM COLLECTIVE-OWNEDINDUSTRIAL ENTERPRISES
WITH INDEPENDENT ACCOUNTING SYSTEMS

(10[8] yuan)

实收资本 Actual Capital	资产合计 Total Property	流动资产合计 Total Circulating Funds	流动资产年平均余额 Average Balance Circulating Funds	固定资产合计 Total Fixed Assets	固定资产原价 Original Value of Fixed Assets	固定资产净值年平均余额 Average Balances Net Value of Fixed Asstes
441.81	**1791.93**	**999.95**	**964.23**	**656.63**	**813.74**	**563.20**
222.24	909.83	484.21	467.42	353.21	431.75	304.05
142.94	588.41	298.11	286.65	242.55	298.34	212.72
219.56	882.10	515.73	496.81	303.43	381.99	259.15
72.23	280.48	140.66	136.13	118.15	135.13	93.15
144.56	593.73	370.97	356.72	182.25	242.53	163.53
98.61	370.14	177.73	173.16	158.76	181.69	129.40
105.92	433.90	236.33	226.99	159.47	202.51	135.51
0.58	1.84	0.78	0.66	0.88	1.29	0.55
0.02	0.18	0.10	0.10	0.08	0.10	0.08
0.03	0.16	0.05	0.05	0.11	0.12	0.06
2.46	7.09	3.87	3.78	2.64	3.73	2.40
11.13	40.02	19.65	21.08	13.62	15.57	10.89
8.34	25.60	13.04	10.85	10.74	13.25	10.18
2.33	8.25	4.02	4.17	3.94	4.74	3.23
0.26	1.20	0.84	0.79	0.25	0.36	0.29
72.11	329.39	155.78	146.58	148.30	186.56	133.14
27.54	78.47	43.31	43.45	28.54	33.68	23.19
4.38	23.36	14.13	13.91	6.68	7.73	5.56
2.24	9.25	5.26	5.09	3.50	4.37	3.32

续 表 1

单位:亿元

行业	Items	企业单位数(个) Number of Enterprises (units)	全部从业人员年平均人数(人) Annual Average of All Employees (persons)	工业增加值(当年价) Added Value of Industry (current price)
家具制造业	Furniture Manufacturing	34	0.49	1.35
造纸及纸制品业	Papermaking and Paper Products	141	3.02	6.40
印刷业记录媒介的复制	Printing and Record Pressing	87	1.57	7.20
文教体育用品制造业	Stationery, Education and Sports Goods	86	2.31	6.88
石油加工及炼焦业	Petroleum Processing and Coking Products	30	0.31	1.60
化学原料及制品制造业	Raw Chemical Materials and Chemical Products	650	10.58	47.17
医药制造业	Medical and Pharmaceutical Products	66	1.22	10.94
化学纤维制造业	Chemical Fibers	67	2.36	11.28
橡胶制品业	Rubber Products	63	1.96	4.50
塑料制品业	Plastic Products	255	5.30	15.57
非金属矿物制品业	Nonmetal Mineral Products	494	14.18	29.67
黑色金属冶炼及压延加工业	Smelting and Pressing of Ferrous Metals	126	3.62	19.69
有色金属冶炼及压延加工业	Smelting and Pressing of Nonferrous Metals	131	2.26	11.48
金属制品业	Metal Products	389	8.55	25.71
普通机械制造业	Ordinary Machinery Manufacturing	554	15.91	33.23
专用设备制造业	Special Purposes Equipment Manufacturing	336	9.76	26.59
交通运输设备制造业	Transportation Equipment Manufacturing	264	6.65	25.98
电气机械及器材制造业	Electric Equipment and Machinery	485	11.16	46.07
电子及通信设备制造业	Electronic and Telecommunications	117	3.85	13.71
仪器仪表及文化办公用机械制造业	Instruments, Meters, Cultural and Official Machinery	52	1.51	3.72
其他制造业	Other Manufacturing	121	2.84	7.52
电力、蒸气、热水生产和供应业	Electric Power, Steam and Hot Water Production and Supply	18	0.48	1.22
煤气生产和供应业	Gas Production and Supply	1	0.00	0.01
自来水的生产和供应业	Tap Water Production and Supply	11	0.10	0.35

Continued 1

(10^8 yuan)

实收资本 Actual Capital	资产合计 Total Property	流动资产合计 Total Circulating Funds	流动资产年平均余额 Average Balance Circulating Funds	固定资产合计 Total Fixed Assets	固定资产原价 Original Value of Fixed Assets	固定资产净值年平均余额 Average Balances Net Value of Fixed Asstes
1.04	4.03	2.12	2.21	1.59	1.66	1.26
5.78	29.39	14.32	13.82	13.32	16.03	12.16
6.15	26.53	16.62	16.18	8.57	10.83	7.48
5.08	18.03	11.16	10.50	5.14	6.34	5.04
3.20	10.16	4.13	4.32	4.66	5.84	4.57
34.67	141.87	80.69	79.01	50.52	63.51	44.88
2.85	22.58	13.49	12.00	8.24	8.19	5.60
16.58	58.76	21.31	19.25	31.58	31.79	23.54
2.98	16.18	9.45	9.34	6.02	7.44	5.25
13.50	50.43	28.34	26.91	17.88	23.82	15.69
32.10	110.70	50.52	48.78	49.56	64.36	43.10
22.35	85.89	45.31	44.12	34.84	30.63	21.04
10.37	41.80	23.78	23.34	14.29	16.93	12.00
24.50	92.92	56.26	52.37	29.21	37.96	26.84
28.75	118.48	76.35	74.24	36.34	50.77	32.70
21.43	97.87	61.47	59.52	29.99	39.77	25.49
16.97	77.22	47.89	47.74	23.32	29.18	19.67
40.35	165.99	111.16	108.85	45.80	58.30	40.71
10.59	53.36	36.41	33.61	12.89	19.35	10.74
3.77	13.32	8.71	8.27	3.58	4.89	3.04
4.50	21.73	15.29	14.88	5.12	7.25	4.88
1.75	6.52	2.77	3.10	3.23	5.45	3.37
0.01	0.12	0.08	0.08	0.04	0.04	0.04
1.13	3.23	1.50	1.29	1.60	1.93	1.20

续表 2

单位:亿元

行业	Items	负债合计 Total Liabilities	流动负债合计 Total Circulating Liabilities	所有者权益 Owner's Rights and Interests
总计	**Total**	**1202.50**	**1029.13**	**589.44**
按轻重工业分	**Grouped by Light and Heavy Industry**			
轻工业	Light Industry	607.74	513.26	302.09
#以农产品为原料	Using Farm Products as Raw Meterials	388.04	323.54	200.37
重工业	Heavy Industry	594.76	515.57	287.34
#原料工业	Raw Material	186.50	157.15	93.98
加工工业	Manufacturing	404.09	354.90	189.64
按企业规模分	**Grouped by Scale of Enterprise**			
#大型企业	Large	218.43	170.40	151.72
中型企业	Medium	293.99	249.41	139.91
按行业分	**Grouped by Sector**			
#煤炭采选业	Coal Mining and Processing	1.05	0.85	0.79
黑色金属矿采选业	Ferrous Metals Mining and Processing	0.11	0.11	0.07
有色金属矿采选业	Nonferrous Metals Mining and Processing	0.12	0.01	0.04
非金属矿采选业	Nonmetal Minerals Mining and Processing	3.98	3.38	3.11
食品加工业	Food Processing	25.37	22.76	14.65
食品制造业	Food Production	16.05	13.55	9.56
饮料制造业	Beverage Production	5.91	5.33	2.34
烟草加工业	Tobacco Processing	0.65	0.65	0.54
纺织业	Textile Industry	226.10	182.73	103.30
服装及纤维制品制造业	Garments and Other Fiber Products	46.69	41.02	31.79
皮革毛皮羽绒及制品业	Leather, Furs, Down and Related Products	15.11	14.20	8.24
木材加工及竹藤棕草制品业	Timber Processing, Bamboo, Cane, Palm Fiber and Straw Products	6.55	5.84	2.70
家具制造业	Furniture Manufacturing	2.39	2.13	1.64

Continued 2

(10[8] yuan)

产品销售收入 Revnue of Product Sales	产品销售成本 Costs of Product Sales	产品销售税金及附加 Product Sales Pre-Tax and Related Payments	产品销售利润 Product Sales After-Tax Profits	利润总额 Total After-Tax Profits	本年应交增值税 Added Value Tax	利税总额 Total Pre-Tax Profits
2018.82	**1739.89**	**15.52**	**19.50**	**48.02**	**66.87**	**130.41**
1052.82	914.85	8.66	9.54	27.54	31.98	68.18
675.82	591.72	4.94	6.29	17.85	19.56	42.35
966.00	825.05	6.86	9.96	20.48	34.89	62.23
318.12	282.89	2.28	3.82	4.49	10.45	17.22
630.16	527.23	4.33	6.10	15.34	23.86	43.53
369.25	309.88	2.77	2.28	19.25	10.83	32.85
419.88	362.08	2.94	4.84	6.95	14.68	24.56
1.77	1.49	0.03	0.01	0.07	0.10	0.20
0.21	0.19			0.01		0.01
0.14	0.09			0.01		0.02
16.22	13.45	0.26	0.07	0.54	0.55	1.36
65.08	57.88	0.35	0.30	1.50	1.23	3.08
26.42	22.48	0.17	0.18	0.59	0.88	1.64
10.50	8.83	0.57	0.10	0.16	0.38	1.10
0.61	0.46	0.01		0.09	0.04	0.13
354.79	318.98	2.01	3.52	6.19	8.88	17.08
98.58	85.70	0.50	0.82	3.76	3.15	7.41
34.61	29.06	0.19	0.24	1.01	1.18	2.38
15.06	13.27	0.16	0.35	0.04	0.58	0.78
6.03	5.31	0.05	0.03	0.15	0.20	0.41

续 表 3

单位：亿元

行业	Items	负债合计 Total Liabilities	流动负债合计 Total Circulating Liabilities	所有者权益 Owner's Rights and Interests
造纸及纸制品业	Papermaking and Paper Products	22.08	17.37	7.31
印刷业记录媒介的复制	Printing and Record Pressing	15.81	14.04	10.72
文教体育用品制造业	Stationery, Education and Sports Goods	11.50	10.96	6.53
石油加工及炼焦业	Petroleum Processing and Coking Products	7.21	6.37	2.95
化学原料及制品制造业	Raw Chemical Materials and Chemical Products	92.08	79.00	49.79
医药制造业	Medical and Pharmaceutical Products	12.01	10.26	10.57
化学纤维制造业	Chemical Fibers	38.43	27.84	20.33
橡胶制品业	Rubber Products	12.56	10.80	3.62
塑料制品业	Plastic Products	32.14	26.99	18.29
非金属矿物制品业	Nonmetal Mineral Products	73.41	61.08	37.29
黑色金属冶炼及压延加工业	Smelting and Pressing of Ferrous Metals	55.68	46.75	30.21
有色金属冶炼及压延加工业	Smelting and Pressing of Nonferrous Metals	29.54	25.64	12.26
金属制品业	Metal Products	62.63	56.58	30.29
普通机械制造业	Ordinary Machinery Manufacturing	82.37	74.31	36.11
专用设备制造业	Special Purposes Equipment Manufacturing	66.73	58.76	31.14
交通运输设备制造业	Transportation Equipment Manufacturing	54.19	48.23	23.03
电气机械及器材制造业	Electric Equipment and Machinery	116.03	104.35	49.96
电子及通信设备制造业	Electronic and Telecommunications	37.29	30.95	16.07
仪器仪表及文化办公用机械制造业	Instruments, Meters, Cultural and Official Machinery	9.00	7.88	4.31
其他制造业	Other Manufacturing	15.39	13.69	6.34
电力、蒸气、热水生产和供应业	Electric Power, Steam and Hot Water Production and Supply	4.66	3.59	1.86
煤气生产和供应业	Gas Production and Supply	0.11	0.05	0.01
自来水的生产和供应业	Tap Water Production and Supply	1.57	1.08	1.66

Continued 3

(10^8 yuan)

产品销售收入 Revnue of Product Sales	产品销售成本 Costs of Product Sales	产品销售税金及附加 Product Sales Pre-Tax and Related Payments	产品销售利润 Product Sales After-Tax Profits	利润总额 Total After-Tax Profits	本年应交增值税 Added Value Tax	利税总额 Total Pre-Tax Profits
26.82	22.65	0.17	0.59	0.23	1.04	1.44
24.90	20.02	0.23	0.26	1.64	1.32	3.19
24.27	20.23	0.08	0.03	1.00	0.94	2.02
9.29	8.52	0.23	0.44	−0.29	0.19	0.13
187.56	160.29	1.70	1.56	4.94	6.87	13.51
22.97	14.68	0.68	0.11	2.87	1.28	4.82
54.02	48.48	0.32	0.67	1.43	1.54	3.29
17.32	14.72	0.15	0.21	0.22	0.79	1.17
65.13	56.10	0.47	0.31	2.12	2.02	4.62
110.82	95.07	1.11	1.14	2.09	4.28	7.47
94.41	86.77	0.46	1.02	0.97	2.06	3.49
52.15	46.83	0.34	0.44	0.81	1.27	2.42
99.27	84.55	0.71	1.09	2.09	3.45	6.25
121.42	102.12	0.86	1.36	2.48	5.22	8.56
112.16	98.30	0.66	1.09	1.55	3.35	5.56
102.78	90.72	1.06	0.76	2.52	2.81	6.39
161.31	127.19	1.06	1.89	5.69	7.10	13.85
55.36	45.35	0.38	0.29	1.05	2.25	3.68
12.91	10.78	0.07	0.21	0.18	0.53	0.78
28.52	24.62	0.41	0.23	0.41	1.08	1.90
4.43	3.89	0.03	0.18	−0.08	0.29	0.24
0.05	0.04					
0.80	0.62	0.02	0.02	−0.01	0.03	0.04

8－7 限额以上独立核算全部工业企业主要经济效益指标（1998）

单位：%

行业	Items	企业亏损面 Rate of Loss Making Enterprise	产值利税率 Rate Between Pre-Tax Profit and Output Value	销售利税率 Rate Between Pre-Tax Profit and Sales
总计	**Total**	**24.28**	**6.10**	**6.67**
按登记注册类型分	**Grouped by Type of Registeration**			
内资企业	Inner Funded Enterprise	23.54	6.26	6.86
#国有企业	State-Owned Enterprise	41.13	6.32	6.44
集体企业	Collective-Owned Enterprise	21.16	5.65	6.46
有限责任公司	Responsibility Co. Ltd.	22.41	7.89	8.03
股份有限公司	Share Holding Co. Ltd.	19.58	8.44	9.16
港、澳、台商投资企业	Hongkong, Macao and Taiwan Funded Enterprise	25.32	6.04	6.63
外商投资企业	Foreign Funded Enterprise	30.79	5.30	5.63
按轻重工业分	**Grouped by Light and Heavy Industry**			
轻工业	Light Industry	26.07	5.81	6.46
#以农产品为原料	Using Farm Products as Raw Meterials	27.33	5.29	5.90
重工业	Heavy Industry	22.52	6.35	6.83
#原料工业	Raw Material	24.67	6.99	7.27
加工工业	Manufacturing	21.97	5.92	6.50
按企业规模分	**Grouped by Scale of Enterprise**			
#大型企业	Large	25.33	8.59	8.64
中型企业	Medium	33.00	5.50	6.10
按行业分	**Grouped by Sector**			
煤炭采选业	Coal Mining and Processing	36.67	8.76	9.05
石油和天然气开采业	Petroleum and Natural Gas Extraction		12.64	12.77
黑色金属矿采选业	Ferrous Metals Mining and Processing	50.00	-4.27	-4.89
有色金属矿采选业	Nonferrous Metals Mining and Processing	28.57	7.08	6.94
非金属矿采选业	Nonmetal Minerals Mining and Processing	11.93	8.18	8.86
木材及竹材采运业	Logging and Transport of Timber and Bamboo		1.36	1.41
食品加工业	Food Processing	27.86	1.91	2.10
食品制造业	Food Production	34.73	4.38	4.69
饮料制造业	Beverage Production	30.46	11.62	12.15
烟草加工业	Tobacco Processing		49.61	51.92

MAJOR ECONOMIC RESULTS INDICATORS OF OVER-NORM WHOLE INDUSTRIAL ENTERPRISES WTIH INDEPENDENT ACCOUNTING SYSTEMS

(%)

工业增加率 Rate of Industrial Added Value	资金利税率 Rate Between Pre-Tax Profit and Assets	百元固定资产实现利税 Pre-Tax Profit Per 100 yuan Fixed Assets	百元销售收入实现利润 Profit Per 100 yuan Sales Revenue	成本费用利润率 Rate Between Profit and Cost	流动资产周转次数(次/年) Turnover of Total Circulating Funds (time/year)	全员劳动生产率(元/人) Total Labor Productivity (yuan/person)
21.06	**6.35**	**9.96**	**2.05**	**2.10**	**1.73**	**33121**
21.12	6.67	10.64	2.02	2.06	1.71	29593
23.40	4.38	6.50	0.28	0.28	1.32	26463
19.59	8.54	16.03	2.38	2.44	2.09	30626
23.22	6.51	8.25	2.85	2.89	1.54	30106
22.48	8.46	15.01	5.33	5.64	1.54	44539
20.87	5.83	8.55	2.41	2.47	1.73	48413
20.82	5.07	7.65	2.03	2.06	1.89	64868
20.51	7.14	11.68	1.92	1.97	1.99	31035
20.50	6.90	11.03	1.38	1.41	2.16	28372
21.53	5.84	8.93	2.16	2.20	1.57	35012
22.65	5.64	7.00	1.98	2.01	1.79	52613
20.25	6.01	11.31	2.32	2.37	1.47	30425
23.72	6.71	8.42	3.24	3.35	1.50	154487
20.27	5.34	4.03	1.15	1.17	1.51	67014
46.58	4.82	5.58	-0.42	-0.42	1.05	15120
52.27	5.66	4.76	2.78	3.00	1.33	37460
18.41	-2.80	-3.47	-9.30	-8.47	1.06	6918
32.69	5.79	7.17	1.94	1.97	1.65	24149
32.16	6.22	7.90	1.93	2.00	1.48	14853
18.05	19.80	20.62	1.06	1.07	88.63	35946
15.78	3.22	5.62	0.47	0.47	2.66	31352
20.83	4.54	6.48	0.15	0.15	1.96	30478
25.90	11.90	18.89	2.47	2.60	1.75	42352
52.25	73.82	99.30	6.32	10.94	2.89	475703

续 表 1

单位：%

行 业	Items	企业亏损面 Rate of Loss Making Enterprise	产值利税率 Rate Between Pre-Tax Profit and Output Value	销售利税率 Rate Between Pre-Tax Profit and Sales
纺织业	Textile Industry	29.39	3.76	4.21
服装及纤维制品制造业	Garments and Other Fiber Products	25.89	5.28	6.17
皮革毛皮羽绒及制品业	Leather, Furs, Down and Related Products	16.77	5.01	5.63
木材加工及竹藤棕草制品业	Timber Processing, Bamboo, Cane, Palm Fiber and Straw Products	16.33	3.61	4.06
家具制造业	Furniture Manufacturing	16.38	7.00	7.79
造纸及纸制品业	Papermaking and Paper Products	23.65	0.84	0.95
印刷业记录媒介的复制	Printing and Record Pressing	29.01	9.64	10.72
文教体育用品制造业	Stationery, Education and Sports Goods	10.37	6.14	6.91
石油加工及炼焦业	Petroleum Processing and Coking Products	32.50	8.94	8.00
化学原料及制品制造业	Raw Chemical Materials and Chemical Products	20.50	6.54	7.22
医药制造业	Medical and Pharmaceutical Products	22.34	13.79	13.82
化学纤维制造业	Chemical Fibers	37.31	5.55	5.96
橡胶制品业	Rubber Products	22.40	3.65	4.18
塑料制品业	Plastic Products	22.97	6.67	7.42
非金属矿物制品业	Nonmetal Mineral Products	24.92	5.00	5.62
黑色金属冶炼及压延加工业	Smelting and Pressing of Ferrous Metals	34.95	3.15	3.34
有色金属冶炼及压延加工业	Smelting and Pressing of Nonferrous Metals	20.60	4.21	4.92
金属制品业	Metal Products	21.24	5.22	5.95
普通机械制造业	Ordinary Machinery Manufacturing	22.59	6.63	7.28
专用设备制造业	Special Purposes Equipment Manufacturing	24.70	5.01	5.68
交通运输设备制造业	Transportation Equipment Manufacturing	25.43	6.83	7.34
电气机械及器材制造业	Electric Equipment and Machinery	23.14	7.43	8.42
电子及通信设备制造业	Electronic and Telecommunications	23.91	5.22	5.49
仪器仪表及文化办公用机械制造业	Instruments, Meters, Cultural and Official Machinery	24.88	5.98	6.46
其他制造业	Other Manufacturing	23.27	5.98	6.81
电力、蒸气、热水生产和供应业	Electric Power, Steam and Hot Water Production and Supply	11.76	13.04	12.11
煤气生产和供应业	Gas Production and Supply	58.82	−4.88	−4.75
自来水的生产和供应业	Tap Water Production and Supply	18.60	7.42	7.70

Continued 1

(%)

工业增加率 Rate of Industrial Added Value	资金利税率 Rate Between Pre-Tax Profit and Assets	百元固定资产实现利税 Pre-Tax Profit Per 100 yuan Fixed Assets	百元销售收入实现利润 Profit Per 100 yuan Sales Revenue	成本费用利润率 Rate Between Profit and Cost	流动资产周转次数(次/年) Turnover of Total Circulating Funds (time/year)	全员劳动生产率(元/人) Total Labor Productivity (yuan/person)
19.18	4.65	6.75	0.77	0.78	2.14	22771
21.39	9.36	17.95	3.03	3.11	2.45	29481
19.95	8.35	20.14	2.06	2.11	2.12	29851
16.03	5.48	10.68	-0.22	-0.22	2.15	26785
20.39	8.93	18.47	3.94	4.11	1.88	35980
18.60	0.66	1.16	-3.38	-3.27	1.69	26713
23.95	9.36	16.63	4.51	4.70	1.63	29702
21.64	12.13	30.43	3.89	4.03	2.53	26669
13.49	12.23	12.97	1.40	1.44	3.16	60152
20.17	7.19	8.76	2.66	2.70	1.98	38538
27.55	14.37	26.49	6.67	7.17	1.65	48113
18.45	3.96	4.87	1.54	1.56	1.59	47377
20.61	3.28	5.27	-1.32	-1.32	1.56	22715
20.10	9.08	14.41	3.36	3.48	2.19	42144
22.36	4.23	5.57	-0.04	-0.04	1.72	20578
14.99	3.19	5.13	0.28	0.28	1.72	40038
16.43	6.63	12.50	1.71	1.73	2.19	50159
19.72	6.54	12.60	1.99	2.03	1.76	34114
21.32	6.19	12.67	2.66	2.75	1.26	25858
19.91	5.27	10.21	1.42	1.44	1.41	23165
19.05	6.90	12.33	2.39	2.42	1.58	37148
21.10	8.52	19.94	3.77	3.92	1.44	42534
18.05	5.69	12.28	2.74	2.78	1.52	46350
24.30	6.52	11.86	2.63	2.69	1.60	31649
21.53	9.93	21.71	2.34	2.42	2.18	29952
46.29	5.09	6.29	4.15	4.40	1.19	154823
0.59	-1.57	-1.62	-8.37	-6.28	1.29	496
40.10	1.73	1.76	0.35	0.34	0.80	30716

8-8 独立核算国有工业企业主要经济效益指标（1998）

单位：%

行业	Items	企业亏损面 Rate of Loss Making Enterprise	产值利税率 Rate Between Pre-Tax Profit and Output Value	销售利税率 Rate Between Pre-Tax Profit and Sales
总计	**Total**	**41.13**	**6.32**	**6.44**
按轻重工业分	**Grouped by Light and Heavy Industry**			
轻工业	Light Industry	40.88	6.39	6.87
#以农产品为原料	Using Farm Products as Raw Meterials	41.80	6.87	7.47
重工业	Heavy Industry	41.42	6.28	6.23
#原料工业	Raw Material	37.55	8.17	7.69
加工工业	Manufacturing	42.55	4.65	4.84
按企业规模分	**Grouped by Scale of Enterprise**			
#大型企业	Large	28.68	8.74	8.48
中型企业	Medium	40.92	3.91	4.25
按行业分	**Grouped by Sector**			
#煤炭采选业	Coal Mining and Processing	50.00	1.74	1.51
石油和天然气开采业	Petroleum and Natural Gas Extraction		12.64	12.77
黑色金属矿采选业	Ferrous Metals Mining and Processing	100.00	-9.69	-10.26
有色金属矿采选业	Nonferrous Metals Mining and Processing	66.67	7.13	5.84
非金属矿采选业	Nonmetal Minerals Mining and Processing	30.30	5.33	5.84
食品加工业	Food Processing	39.36	-0.10	-0.11
食品制造业	Food Production	47.10	4.50	4.59
饮料制造业	Beverage Production	40.24	12.56	13.89
烟草加工业	Tobacco Processing		51.08	52.48
纺织业	Textile Industry	44.86	2.44	2.57
服装及纤维制品制造业	Garments and Other Fiber Products	29.63	4.36	4.50
皮革毛皮羽绒及制品业	Leather, Furs, Down and Related Products	22.22	2.75	3.43
木材加工及竹藤棕草制品业	Timber Processing, Bamboo, Cane, Palm Fiber and Straw Products	46.15	-1.21	-1.56

MAJOR ECONOMIC RESULTS INDICATORS OF OVER-NORM WHOLE INDUSTRIAL ENTERPRISES WTIH INDEPENDENT ACCOUNTING SYSTEMS

(%)

工业增加率 Rate of Industrial Added Value	资金利税率 Rate Between Pre-Tax Profit and Assets	百元固定资产实现利税(元) Pre-Tax Profit Per 100 yuan Fixed Assets (yuan)	百元销售收入实现利润(元) Profit Per 100 yuan Sales Revenue (yuan)	成本费用利润率 Rate Between Profit and Cost	流动资产周转次数(次/年) Turnover of Total Circulating Funds (time/year)	全员劳动生产率(元/人) Total Labor Productivity (yuan/person)
23.40	**4.38**	**6.50**	**0.28**	**0.28**	**1.32**	**26463**
21.66	5.44	7.86	−0.60	−0.61	1.57	20701
21.96	6.56	9.47	−0.82	−0.84	1.71	20965
24.35	3.94	5.92	0.73	0.74	1.22	30603
28.75	4.64	6.25	1.16	1.18	1.40	55560
19.72	3.26	5.78	0.44	0.44	1.09	20794
25.18	5.68	8.42	1.62	1.66	1.34	145620
21.45	2.75	4.03	−1.72	−1.70	1.21	69487
34.05	1.09	1.77	−4.72	−4.43	1.11	9202
52.27	5.66	4.76	2.78	3.00	1.33	37460
19.33	−4.21	−4.73	−15.63	−13.34	0.82	4538
40.76	5.09	6.38	0.73	0.71	1.47	18137
39.44	2.13	2.51	−2.12	−2.04	0.93	12944
14.84	−0.14	−0.23	−1.55	−1.52	2.20	19474
22.78	2.66	3.88	−0.80	−0.77	1.23	12555
24.73	9.67	16.80	−1.20	−1.28	1.17	23957
51.86	76.57	100.33	6.15	10.76	3.04	502339
19.10	2.05	2.72	−1.56	−1.52	1.66	15373
26.92	4.85	8.52	2.40	2.41	1.88	18737
24.14	2.53	5.13	−1.11	−1.09	1.12	23417
26.45	−0.89	−1.43	−5.18	−4.84	1.10	12205

续 表 1

单位：%

行 业	Items	企业亏损面 Rate of Loss Making Enterprise	产值利税率 Rate Between Pre-Tax Profit and Output Value	销售利税率 Rate Between Pre-Tax Profit and Sales
家具制造业	Furniture Manufacturing	45.45	9.17	9.22
造纸及纸制品业	Papermaking and Paper Products	56.67	1.99	2.24
印刷业记录媒介的复制	Printing and Record Pressing	42.35	4.07	4.42
文教体育用品制造业	Stationery, Education and Sports Goods	14.29	4.81	5.39
石油加工及炼焦业	Petroleum Processing and Coking Products	71.43	9.46	8.25
化学原料及制品制造业	Raw Chemical Materials and Chemical Products	37.55	2.71	2.91
医药制造业	Medical and Pharmaceutical Products	28.99	12.08	10.34
化学纤维制造业	Chemical Fibers	52.94	−4.42	−4.72
橡胶制品业	Rubber Products	36.36	8.96	9.30
塑料制品业	Plastic Products	45.45	−5.75	−6.65
非金属矿物制品业	Nonmetal Mineral Products	51.08	3.40	3.81
黑色金属冶炼及压延加工业	Smelting and Pressing of Ferrous Metals	66.67	0.13	0.12
有色金属冶炼及压延加工业	Smelting and Pressing of Nonferrous Metals	18.75	7.44	8.07
金属制品业	Metal Products	39.68	6.57	6.87
普通机械制造业	Ordinary Machinery Manufacturing	44.62	6.01	6.18
专用设备制造业	Special Purposes Equipment Manufacturing	45.16	2.35	2.47
交通运输设备制造业	Transportation Equipment Manufacturing	39.13	8.43	8.96
电气机械及器材制造业	Electric Equipment and Machinery	44.33	6.28	6.53
电子及通信设备制造业	Electronic and Telecommunications	46.15	−1.44	−1.46
仪器仪表及文化办公用机械制造业	Instruments, Meters, Cultural and Official Machinery	39.53	3.04	3.17
其他制造业	Other Manufacturing	54.84	1.28	1.27
电力、蒸气、热水生产和供应业	Electric Power, Steam and Hot Water Production and Supply	5.36	11.55	10.65
煤气生产和供应业	Gas Production and Supply	64.29	−6.30	−6.01
自来水的生产和供应业	Tap Water Production and Supply	17.57	7.73	8.00

Continued 1

(%)

工业增加率 Rate of Industrial Added Value	资金利税率 Rate Between Pre-Tax Profit and Assets	百元固定资产实现利税(元) Pre-Tax Profit Per 100 yuan Fixed Assets (yuan)	百元销售收入实现利润(元) Profit Per 100 yuan Sales Revenue (yuan)	成本费用利润率 Rate Between Profit and Cost	流动资产周转次数(次/年) Turnover of Total Circulating Funds (time/year)	全员劳动生产率(元/人) Total Labor Productivity (yuan/person)
23.55	8.39	14.91	3.00	3.09	1.45	25690
21.50	1.07	1.68	-3.30	-3.16	0.93	12380
31.66	2.63	3.00	-3.13	-2.98	1.45	13779
20.54	3.23	9.16	0.97	0.93	0.79	7590
14.82	12.87	12.89	0.93	0.96	3.06	62184
17.61	2.34	3.06	-0.83	-0.82	1.66	18299
23.65	11.18	19.28	4.38	4.59	1.78	25767
12.52	-2.07	-2.31	-8.81	-7.98	1.17	10939
27.13	8.83	14.69	1.08	1.11	1.68	14278
20.30	-2.30	-3.02	-13.35	-11.33	0.73	12139
25.97	1.87	2.47	-3.31	-3.18	1.10	14087
16.30	0.08	0.13	-3.55	-3.41	1.00	19197
18.90	6.47	9.22	3.89	3.95	1.58	40999
22.59	6.65	12.20	1.98	2.02	1.65	39534
21.18	4.11	8.43	1.62	1.66	0.98	22249
20.94	1.38	2.22	-1.78	-1.71	0.96	13452
18.87	6.40	10.55	3.39	3.46	1.31	30744
22.04	4.91	11.13	1.38	1.39	1.08	24893
12.14	-0.99	-2.42	-3.90	-3.68	0.88	18302
33.09	1.51	2.28	-2.97	-2.85	0.85	15412
21.30	1.05	1.56	-2.52	-2.55	1.50	10909
47.80	4.36	6.28	3.43	3.61	1.05	134578
-1.62	-1.81	-1.84	-9.87	-7.17	1.23	-1213
40.23	1.77	1.79	0.53	0.52	0.81	30558

8－9 独立核算集体工业企业主要经济效益指标（1998）

单位：%

行 业	Items	企业亏损面 Rate of Loss Making Enterprise	产值利税率 Rate Between Pre-Tax Profit and Output Value	销售利税率 Rate Between Pre-Tax Profit and Sales
总 计	**Total**	**21.16**	**5.65**	**6.46**
按轻重工业分	**Grouped by Light and Heavy Industry**			
轻工业	Light Industry	24.18	5.69	6.48
#以农产品为原料	Using Farm Products as Raw Meterials	25.89	5.55	6.27
重工业	Heavy Industry	18.58	5.60	6.44
#原料工业	Raw Material	23.41	4.75	5.41
加工工业	Manufacturing	17.42	5.97	6.91
按企业规模分	**Grouped by Scale of Enterprise**			
#大型企业	Large	21.30	7.88	8.90
中型企业	Medium	31.70	5.21	5.85
按行业分	**Grouped by Sector**			
煤炭采选业	Coal Mining and Processing	16.67	9.09	11.55
黑色金属矿采选业	Ferrous Metals Mining and Processing		4.78	4.78
有色金属矿采选业	Nonferrous Metals Mining and Processing		13.25	13.31
非金属矿采选业	Nonmetal Minerals Mining and Processing	8.13	7.49	8.37
食品加工业	Food Processing	11.32	4.43	4.73
食品制造业	Food Production	25.35	5.63	6.20
饮料制造业	Beverage Production	20.41	9.88	10.51
烟草加工业	Tobacco Processing	0.00	9.86	22.24
纺织业	Textile Industry	31.99	4.27	4.82
服装及纤维制品制造业	Garments and Other Fiber Products	27.13	6.47	7.52
皮革毛皮羽绒及制品业	Leather, Furs, Down and Related Products	16.16	6.35	6.86
木材加工及竹藤棕草制品业	Timber Processing, Bamboo, Cane, Palm Fiber and Straw Products	12.64	4.67	5.16

MAJOR ECONOMIC RESULTS INDICATORS OF OVER-NORM WHOLE INDUSTRIALENTERPRISES WTIH INDEPENDENT ACCOUNTING SYSTEMS

(%)

工业增加率 Rate of Industrial Added Value	资金利税率 Rate Between Pre-Tax Profit and Assets	百元固定资产实现利税(元) Pre-Tax Profit Per 100 yuan Fixed Assets (yuan)	百元销售收入实现利润(元) Profit Per 100 yuan Sales Revenue (yuan)	成本费用利润率 Rate Between Profit and Cost	流动资产周转次数(次/年) Turnover of Total Circulating Funds (time/year)	全员劳动生产率(元/人) Total Labor Productivity (yuan/person)
19.59	**8.54**	**16.03**	**2.38**	**2.44**	**2.09**	**30626**
19.89	8.84	15.79	2.62	2.69	2.25	31142
19.93	8.48	14.19	2.64	2.72	2.36	28698
19.27	8.23	16.29	2.12	2.17	1.94	30077
17.78	7.51	12.74	1.41	1.43	2.34	36839
19.96	8.37	17.95	2.43	2.50	1.77	28446
20.66	10.86	18.08	5.21	5.50	2.13	122857
18.38	6.78	12.13	1.65	1.68	1.85	56166
22.14	17.06	15.85	4.18	4.43	2.70	9811
19.87	5.62	10.48	3.64	3.82	2.15	25064
23.45	16.93	16.61	9.98	11.15	2.95	11424
22.58	21.98	36.40	3.35	3.51	4.29	17412
17.86	9.62	19.76	2.31	2.38	3.09	55960
19.62	7.79	12.36	2.21	2.26	2.44	36130
21.22	14.90	23.26	1.51	1.61	2.51	22415
65.97	12.52	37.92	14.37	16.26	0.77	241775
18.97	6.11	9.16	1.74	1.77	2.42	24350
20.63	11.12	22.00	3.81	3.95	2.27	29525
20.44	12.20	30.73	2.91	3.01	2.49	32240
19.42	9.24	17.76	0.25	0.25	2.96	25485

续 表 1

单位：%

行　　业	Items	企业亏损面 Rate of Loss Making Enterprise	产值利税率 Rate Between Pre-Tax Profit and Output Value	销售利税率 Rate Between Pre-Tax Profit and Sales
家具制造业	Furniture Manufacturing	8.82	6.37	6.77
造纸及纸制品业	Papermaking and Paper Products	22.70	4.79	5.35
印刷业记录媒介的复制	Printing and Record Pressing	25.29	11.56	12.80
文教体育用品制造业	Stationery, Education and Sports Goods	10.47	7.48	8.34
石油加工及炼焦业	Petroleum Processing and Coking Products	33.33	1.23	1.36
化学原料及制品制造业	Raw Chemical Materials and Chemical Products	17.69	6.28	7.20
医药制造业	Medical and Pharmaceutical Products	16.67	15.01	20.99
化学纤维制造业	Chemical Fibers	31.34	5.53	6.09
橡胶制品业	Rubber Products	22.22	5.86	6.75
塑料制品业	Plastic Products	20.39	6.32	7.09
非金属矿物制品业	Nonmetal Mineral Products	16.80	5.95	6.75
黑色金属冶炼及压延加工业	Smelting and Pressing of Ferrous Metals	34.92	3.30	3.70
有色金属冶炼及压延加工业	Smelting and Pressing of Nonferrous Metals	22.90	3.94	4.64
金属制品业	Metal Products	18.25	5.37	6.29
普通机械制造业	Ordinary Machinery Manufacturing	18.05	5.85	7.05
专用设备制造业	Special Purposes Equipment Manufacturing	22.02	4.38	4.96
交通运输设备制造业	Transportation Equipment Manufacturing	20.45	5.22	6.22
电气机械及器材制造业	Electric Equipment and Machinery	21.03	7.31	8.58
电子及通信设备制造业	Electronic and Telecommunications	17.09	6.07	6.64
仪器仪表及文化办公用机械制造业	Instruments, Meters, Cultural and Official Machinery	25.00	5.07	6.07
其他制造业	Other Manufacturing	21.49	5.94	6.67
电力、蒸气、热水生产和供应业	Electric Power, Steam and Hot Water Production and Supply	22.22	4.84	5.43
煤气生产和供应业	Gas Production and Supply	100.00	−6.82	−7.01
自来水的生产和供应业	Tap Water Production and Supply	18.18	4.45	4.87

Continued 1

(%)

工业增加率 Rate of Industrial Added Value	资金利税率 Rate Between Pre-Tax Profit and Assets	百元固定资产实现利税(元) Pre-Tax Profit Per 100 yuan Fixed Assets (yuan)	百元销售收入实现利润(元) Profit Per 100 yuan Sales Revenue (yuan)	成本费用利润率 Rate Between Profit and Cost	流动资产周转次数(次/年) Turnover of Total Circulating Funds (time/year)	全员劳动生产率(元/人) Total Labor Productivity (yuan/person)
18.68	11.74	24.64	2.51	2.57	2.72	27589
18.95	5.53	8.96	0.84	0.85	1.94	21200
22.27	13.47	29.43	6.60	7.08	1.54	45932
22.30	13.02	31.94	4.14	4.33	2.31	29744
13.57	1.42	2.17	-3.17	-3.11	2.15	50938
19.47	10.91	21.27	2.63	2.71	2.37	44585
31.31	27.40	58.90	12.49	14.77	1.91	89952
16.63	7.69	10.35	2.66	2.71	2.81	47736
19.84	8.01	15.73	1.29	1.32	1.85	22918
18.87	10.84	19.38	3.26	3.37	2.42	29356
21.19	8.14	11.61	1.89	1.93	2.27	20929
15.99	5.36	11.40	1.03	1.04	2.14	54386
16.43	6.85	14.30	1.55	1.58	2.23	50912
19.52	7.89	16.46	2.10	2.15	1.90	30068
20.05	8.00	16.85	2.04	2.09	1.64	20881
18.28	6.54	13.98	1.39	1.40	1.88	27240
18.94	9.48	21.90	2.45	2.53	2.15	39082
21.54	9.26	23.76	3.53	3.66	1.48	41263
19.77	8.29	19.00	1.89	1.93	1.65	35577
21.32	6.93	16.02	1.36	1.38	1.56	24670
21.06	9.63	26.24	1.43	1.48	1.92	26538
21.67	3.72	4.42	-1.78	-1.79	1.43	25249
14.31	-3.07	-8.42	-7.46	-6.99	0.67	34000
38.30	1.56	2.02	-0.84	-0.84	0.62	33683

8－10 限额以上农村独立核算工业企业基本情况（1998）

BASIC SITUATION OF RURAL OVER-NORM INDIUSTRIAL ENTERPRISES WITH INDEPENDENT ACCOUNTING SYSTEMS

单位：亿元 (10^8 yuan)

指标	Items	实绩	农村工业占全省比重(%) Rate of Rural Industry in Whole Province (%)
企业单位数 (个)	Number of Enterprsises	11308	62.97
年末全部职工人数 (万人)	Total Employees (year-end 10000 person)	233.32	40.31
工业总产值 (当年价)	Gross Output Value of Industry (current price)	3826.37	47.52
产品销售收入	Revenue of Product Sales	3270.94	44.35
#产品销售税金及附加	Product Sales Pre-Tax and Related Payments	24.40	36.93
利税总额	Total Pre-Tax Profits	222.91	45.34
年末固定资产原价	Year End Original Value of Fixed Assets	1271.42	25.76
年末固定资产净值	Year End Net Value of Fixed Assets	936.21	26.83
全部流动资产年平均余额	Average Balance Circulating Funds	1435.34	33.73
本年应交增值税	Added Value Tax Payable This Year	104.52	38.14
本年进项税额	Tax Value of Income Items	373.88	45.60
本年销项税额	Tax Value of Sales Items	467.92	44.61

8－11 限额以下非国有工业及个体经营基本情况（1998）

BASIC BUSINESS INDICATION OF BELOW-NORM NONSTATE-OWNED INDUSTRY AND INDIVIDUALS

单位：亿元 (10^8 yuan)

指标	Items	企业单位数（个） Number of Enterprises (unit)	工业总产值 Total Industrial Output Value	上交税金 Tax Payment	年末全部从业人员（万人） Year End Total Employment (10000 persons)
总计	**Total**	**498608**	**5132.67**	**107.81**	**483.62**
按轻重工业分	Grouped by Light and Heavy Industry				
轻工业	Light Industry	345100	3133.73	61.59	295.34
重工业	Heavy Industry	153508	1998.93	46.22	188.28
按登记注册类型分	Grouped by Type of Registeration				
集体企业	Collective Enterprise	45528	1550.62	34.85	156.26
股份合作制企业	Share Holding Cooperative Enterprise	18506	639.60	15.17	54.23
私营企业	Private Enterprise	72452	1298.90	26.42	105.08
联营企业	Joint Owned Enterprise	2131	56.84	1.50	4.41
个体经营	Individual Business	352736	1374.86	20.96	141.55
外商及港澳台投资企业	Foreign Funded and Hongkong, Macao and Taiwan Funded Enterprise	2733	119.61	5.24	12.97
其他企业	Other Enterprise	4522	92.23	3.68	9.11
在总计中：	Among Total:				
农村工业	Rural Industry	464088	4612.32	93.17	425.12

8－12 主要工业产品产量
OUTPUT OF MAJOR INDUSTRIAL PRODUCTS

单位:万吨 (10000 tons)

产品名称	Items	1985	1990	1995	1997	1998
钢	Steel	98.97	190.18	360.40	475.01	523.78
生铁	Pig Iron	98.59	154.35	253.71	267.52	291.29
成品钢材	Rolled-steel Final Products	145.18	203.01	787.89	856.79	933.63
#优质钢型材	Quality Rolled	2.85	3.86	41.52	49.36	56.21
线材	Wire Rod Steel	36.97	55.64	210.77	230.33	258.69
薄钢板	Low Gauge Plate	2.84	5.37	21.97	21.03	25.26
无缝钢管	Seamless Steel Pipe	6.22	10.36	33.69	30.67	25.39
铁矿石(原矿)	Iron Mineral (original)	172.27	129.06	238.16	139.37	65.51
发电量 (亿千瓦小时)	Electricity (10^8 kwh)	234.48	404.47	700.41	777.00	763.49
#火力发电	Fire Power	233.92	403.95	686.99	776.54	753.97
原煤	Coal	2193.85	2407.79	2650.72	2506.01	2378.53
洗精煤	Washing Coal	405.76	434.60	432.63	310.64	287.89
原油	Crude Oil	55.81	86.00	101.41	117.23	125.82
原油加工量	Volume of Crude Oil Processing	499.23	808.66	976.51	1087.88	1098.72
汽油	Gasoline	67.98	93.34	108.07	122.00	91.64
煤油	Keroseme	22.13	43.52	50.64	55.77	51.88
燃料油	Fuel Oil	156.08	274.82	162.04	99.26	123.73
硫酸(折 100%)	Sulphuric Acid (100%)	97.70	122.47	171.63	189.40	175.82
浓硝酸	Concentrated Nitric Acid	2.14	2.46	4.64	4.08	5.57
盐酸	Hydrochloric Acid	22.70	37.49	46.71	52.16	49.11
烧碱(氢氧化钠)	Caustic Ash (sodium Hydroxide)	24.09	32.87	51.85	59.59	58.57
纯碱(无水碳酸钠)	Soda Ash (Anhydrous Sodium Carbonate)	2.69	17.57	58.10	90.37	102.97
合成氨	Synthetc Ammonia	153.45	164.25	202.93	202.15	195.03
农用化肥(折 100%)	Chemical Fertilizers (100%)	121.71	145.90	191.85	187.98	170.12
氮肥	Nitrogen	100.64	110.85	125.87	122.72	122.89
磷肥	Phosphate	20.76	34.83	63.87	62.75	38.78
钾肥	Potassium	0.31	0.22	2.11	2.51	8.46
化学农药(含生物农药)	Chimecal Pesticide	4.27	4.51	12.18	9.27	8.59
乙烯	Ethylene	1.16	27.97	27.67	39.96	40.91
肥皂	Soap	7.12	4.02	3.92	2.91	2.97
合成洗涤剂	Synthetic Detergents	8.12	14.39	38.26	22.29	17.93
塑料制品	Plastic Products	32.97	43.35	246.27	118.08	95.93
#农用薄膜	Rural Use Membrane	1.27	1.95	4.99	2.32	4.82
内燃机生产量 (万千瓦)	Output of Internal Combustion Engines (10000 kw)	633.79	931.35	4361	5042.56	5086.70

注：1998 年为全部国有企业及年产品销售收入为 500 万元以上非国有企业。

Note: The figure of 1998 was nonstate-owned enterprise with 5million yuan over of revenue of products sales.

续 表 continued

单位:万吨 (10000 tons)

产品名称		Items		1985	1990	1995	1997	1998
金属切削机床	(台)	Metal-cutting Machines		18583	15894	44606	30101	25068
#数控机床		Digital (computer-controled) Machine Tools		8719	871	2785	3261	2313
高精度机床		High Precision Machine Tools		73	181	235	129	124
大型机床		Large Machine Tools		54	89	76	61	28
锻压机械	(台)	Forging Press Machines		15167	9590	40487	25350	897
化工设备	(吨)	Chemical Industry Equipment	(tons)	16691	24781	102576	56637	36930
汽车	(辆)	Motor Vehicals		24474	46291	125197	104801	89828
#载货汽车		Trucks		15715	32092	59799	38968	27253
客车	(辆)	Passenger Carriage		655	1930	28243	31005	31061
大中型拖拉机	(台)	Large and Medium Tractors		413	1084	2138	4236	2909
小型拖拉机	(万台)	Mini-tractors	(10000)	9.16	14.13	28.92	24.32	20.93
缝纫机	(万架)	Sewing Machines	(10000)	97.93	67.24	67.56	65.91	63.83
自行车	(万辆)	Bicycles	(10000)	375.08	400.21	718.20	486.59	425.45
照相机	(万架)	Cameras	(10000)	35.76	18.17	33.34	31.64	27.27
电风扇	(万台)	Electric Fans	(10000)	463.93	969.47	2083.24	710.46	631.30
家用电冰箱	(万台)	Household Refrigerators	(10000)	14.87	36.64	11.45	59.81	68.71
家用洗衣机	(万台)	Household Washing Machines	(10000)	75.07	8.77	90.24	143.00	149.36
电视机	(万台)	Television Sets	(10000)	276.45	296.61	475.89	379.93	466.28
#彩色电视机		Color TV Sets	(10000)	25.87	83.18	250.72	282.06	394.14
录放音机	(万台)	Recorders	(10000)	213.91	483.69	466.70	203.16	159.39
收音机	(万台)	Radio	(10000)	559.77	702.29	315.74	38.13	15.70
表	(万只)	Watches	(10000)	447.18	420.31	481.76	430.99	309.45
水泥		Cement		1116.90	1532.89	3966.42	4031.73	3856.30
平板玻璃	(万重量箱)	Plate Glass	(10000 wt. cases)	301.26	323.96	868.73	1380.13	1629.27
原盐		Salt		167.10	184.54	345.47	388.91	110.48
罐头		Canned Food		10.16	8.42	7.04	5.56	3.62
卷烟	(万箱)	Cigaretes	(10000 cases)	87.55	89.45	78.98	85.24	90.3
化学纤维		Chemical Fibers		12.52	40.76	102.20	139.11	140.94
纱		Yarn		46.28	69.46	86.25	96.57	90.58
布	(亿米)	Cloth	(10^8 m)	21.05	28.91	48.90	40.46	31.72
#纯棉布		Pure Cotton Cloth		10.76	16.06	25.31	22.98	18.69
纯化纤布	(万米)	Pure Fiber Cloth	(10000 m)	3.55	3.86	13.67	7.37	5.53
毛线	(吨)	Knitting Wool	(tons)	18783	83134	185345	149944	127418
呢绒	(万米)	Woolen Piece Goods	(10000 m)	4574	7316	28212	17034	13330
丝	(吨)	Silk	(tons)	8562	13329	29073	19070	14537
丝织品	(亿米)	Knitting Silk	(10^8 m)	3.25	4.45	11.21	11.07	10.94

8-13 主要工业企业能源消费量
ENERGY CONSUMPTION OF MAJOR INDUSTIAL ENTERPRISES

单位:万吨 (10000 tons)

名　称	Item	1995	1996	1997	1998
煤　炭	Coal	5980.45	5988.90	6588.27	7383.09
焦　炭	Coke	252.27	229.76	239.79	279.48
原　油	Crude Oil	1027.52	996.43	1091.64	1108.44
汽　油	Gasoline	17.93	33.28	16.61	30.39
煤　油	Kerasene	1.27	1.21	9.26	10.42
柴　油	Diesel Oil	29.97	31.84	30.78	57.84
燃料油	Fuel Oil	122.27	230.45	115.22	165.58
液化石油气	LPG	29.26	34.07	26.44	21.76

8-14 平均每天各种能源消费量
AVERAGE DAILY ENERGY CONSUMPTION BY TYPE IN MAIN YEARS

单位:万吨 (10000 tons)

名　称	Item	1980	1995	1996	1997	1998
煤　炭	Coal	17.05	16.51	16.55	18.17	20.23
焦　炭	Coke	0.63	0.63	0.69	0.66	0.77
原　油	Crude Oil	2.26	2.76	2.84	3.02	3.04
燃料油	Fuel Oil	0.52	0.65	0.36	0.33	0.45
汽　油	Gasoline	0.25	0.15	0.12	0.11	0.08
煤　油	Kerasene	0.03	0.01	0.01	0.04	0.03
柴　油	Diesel Oil	0.48	0.20	0.21	0.19	0.16

9. 建筑及地质勘查业

CONSTRUCTION AND GEOLOGICAL PROSPECTING

9 建筑及地质勘查业
CONSTRUCTION AND GEOLOGICAL PROSPECTING

1 9 9 8

建筑施工企业个数	Construction Enterprises	3587	个	(units)
建筑施工企业职工平均人数	Staff (annual average)	232.32	万人	(10000 persons)
建筑业总产值	Construction Enterprises Output Value	1224.42	亿元	(10^8 yuan)
房屋建筑竣工面积	Floor Space of Building Completed	9958.9	万平方米	(10000 sq·m)
建筑业全员劳动生产率	Overall Labor Produtivity	52704	元/人	(yuan/person)
建筑业技术装备率	Per Capital Machinery Value	4462	元/人	(yuan/person)

建筑业总产值 (亿元)

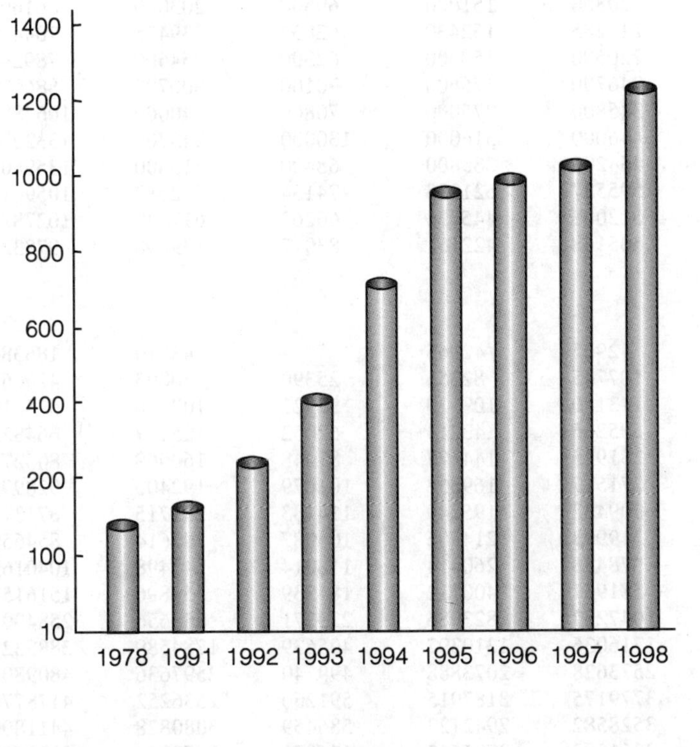

建筑业产值构成 (%)
(1998 年)

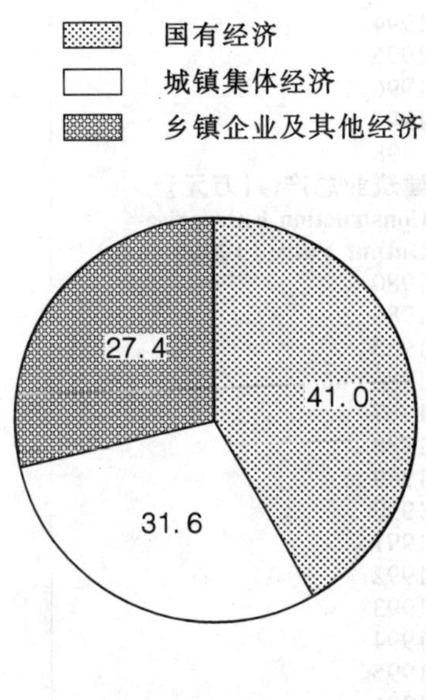

9-1 建筑施工企业概况

MAJOR ECONOMIC INDICATORS OF CONSTRUCTION ENTERPRISES

年份 Year	总计 Total	国有经济 State-Owned	地方 Local-Owned	部属 Central-Owned	城镇集体经济 Collective-Owned	乡镇企业及其它经济 Rural and Township Industry and Others
一、企业单位个数(个) Number of Enterprises						
1980	2022	28	26	2	100	1894
1984	2282	97	82	15	131	2054
1985	2360	114	86	28	148	2098
1986	2445	147	123	24	149	2149
1987	2532	160	135	25	179	2193
1988	2614	164	136	28	187	2263
1989	2408	175	144	31	204	2029
1990	2284	162	138	24	201	1921
1991	2316	173	147	26	209	1934
1992	2417	203	176	27	251	1963
1993	2810	308	273	35	429	2073
1994	3348	389	353	36	513	2446
1995	3426	406	370	36	505	2515
1996	3528	589	554	35	868	2071
1997	3546	564	525	39	884	2098
1998	3587	573	535	38	881	2133
二、全部职工平均人数(人) Staff and Workers (person)						
1980	681831	80158	80158		103539	498134
1984	1064044	159793	127447	32346	124946	779305
1985	1240855	175997	138211	37786	140470	924388
1986	1352039	204519	158109	47410	150957	996563
1987	1442535	214782	150799	63983	169628	1058125
1988	1426444	212518	146239	66279	175373	1038553
1989	1285491	220800	151000	69800	203000	861691
1990	1243129	215285	152430	62855	239425	784419
1991	1264447	220600	158300	62300	254600	789247
1992	1434373	246700	176600	70100	300700	886973
1993	1750600	345800	275000	70800	340000	1064800
1994	2121720	446000	316000	130000	343700	1332020
1995	2329400	454200	385800	68400	515600	1359600
1996	2207128	595527	521393	74134	552582	1059019
1997	2156870	512003	445736	66267	617040	1027827
1998	2323186	505168	422151	83017	839698	978320
三、建筑业总产值(万元) Construction Enterprise-Output Value (10000 yuan)						
1980	273259	42965	42965		43910	186384
1984	598409	107745	82355	25390	70003	420661
1985	826349	143150	109228	33922	107980	575219
1986	995215	205266	143214	62052	125127	664822
1987	1196168	231925	144477	87448	160969	803274
1988	1392911	271517	169838	101679	192403	928991
1989	1420518	309432	195249	114183	239715	871371
1990	1472266	319993	214906	105087	297614	854659
1991	1762091	378428	260414	118014	343498	1040165
1992	2657999	581951	400712	181239	559896	1516152
1993	4499913	1047257	823986	223271	868656	2584000
1994	7385950	1716036	1310397	405639	1784589	3885325
1995	9981064	2573628	2073888	499740	2597636	4809800
1996	10494202	3779175	3187915	591260	2536252	4178775
1997	11021210	3528582	2942122	586459	3080828	4411800
1998	12244219	3351593	2725542	626051	3872938	5019689

续表 Continued

年份 Year	总计 Total	国有经济 State-Owned	地方 Local-Owned	部属 Central-Owned	城镇集体经济 Collective-Owned	乡镇企业及其它经济 Rural and Township Industry and Others
四、施工房屋面积(万平方米) **Floor Space of Building Under Construction** **(10000 sq·m)**						
1980	3189.80	467.30	467.30		588.50	2134.00
1984	4662.14	558.65	507.99	50.66	594.77	3508.72
1985	5570.32	619.94	536.58	83.36	690.92	4259.46
1986	5934.61	638.72	557.69	81.03	706.20	4589.69
1987	6521.55	687.40	556.80	130.60	807.19	5026.96
1988	6545.10	650.76	535.68	155.08	868.28	5026.06
1989	5447.35	672.60	547.40	125.20	927.70	3847.05
1990	5240.98	699.10	580.30	118.80	1070.40	3471.48
1991	5711.13	778.71	660.44	118.27	1143.12	3789.30
1992	7780.32	1049.90	901.00	148.90	1688.30	5042.12
1993	10229.96	1801.32	1573.13	228.19	2045.54	6383.10
1994	13201.21	2356.00	2062.20	293.90	3269.60	7575.61
1995	16646.14	3470.96	3135.28	335.68	4621.48	8553.70
1996	15672.95	5032.00	4663.09	368.91	3723.69	6917.26
1997	16191.85	4407.38	4031.04	376.34	4344.53	7439.94
1998	17803.33	3831.67	3593.61	238.06	5887.35	8084.31
五、竣工房屋面积(万平方米) **Floor Space of Building Completed (10000 sq·m)**						
1980	2296.09	233.70	233.70		352.83	1709.56
1984	3033.59	280.56	260.67	19.89	357.71	2395.23
1985	3527.20	272.55	245.03	27.52	382.94	2871.71
1986	3926.24	306.44	281.46	24.98	403.02	3216.78
1987	4083.20	328.32	263.87	64.45	416.08	3338.80
1988	3858.50	265.09	226.77	38.32	429.67	3163.74
1989	3446.47	284.50	246.40	38.10	502.10	2659.87
1990	3307.93	354.40	302.20	52.20	617.00	2336.53
1991	3422.75	361.35	322.27	39.08	618.49	2442.91
1992	4387.99	446.60	395.90	50.70	837.40	3103.99
1993	5767.78	772.59	705.11	67.48	1077.09	3918.10
1994	9336.28	903.20	838.60	64.60	1620.00	6813.08
1995	8739.38	1304.03	1243.04	60.99	2056.55	5378.80
1996	8252.13	1946.38	1872.36	74.02	2141.69	4164.06
1997	8787.36	1678.84	1601.39	77.46	2600.34	4508.18
1998	9958.90	1748.46	1686.40	62.05	3497.35	4713.10
六、房屋建筑面积竣工率(%) **Rate of Building Completed (percent)**						
1980	72.0	50.0	50.0		60.0	80.1
1984	63.3	50.2	51.3	39.3	60.1	68.3
1985	66.2	44.0	45.7	33.0	55.4	67.4
1986	62.6	48.0	50.1	30.8	57.1	70.1
1987	62.6	47.8	47.4	49.3	51.5	66.4
1988	59.0	40.7	42.3	33.3	49.5	62.9
1989	63.3	42.3	45.0	30.4	54.1	69.1
1990	63.1	50.7	52.1	43.9	57.6	67.3
1991	59.9	46.4	48.8	33.0	54.1	64.5
1992	56.4	42.5	43.9	34.0	49.6	61.6
1993	56.4	42.9	44.8	29.6	52.7	61.4
1994	70.7	38.3	40.7	22.0	49.5	89.9
1995	52.5	34.9	39.6	18.2	44.5	62.9
1996	52.7	38.7	40.2	20.1	57.5	60.2
1997	54.3	38.1	39.7	20.6	59.9	60.6
1998	55.9	45.6	46.9	26.1	59.4	58.3

9－2 建筑施工企业主要经济指标（1998）

MAJOR ECONOMIC IINDICATORS OF CONSTRUCTION ENTERPRISES

指标	Items	合计 Total	国有经济 State-Owned	城镇集体经济 Collective-Owned	乡镇企业及其它经济 Rural and Township Industry and Others
施工企业个数（个）	Number of Construction Enterprises (units)	3587	573	881	2133
建筑业总产值（亿元）	Construction Enterprises Gross Output Value (10^8 yuan)	1224.42	335.16	387.29	501.97
#建筑工程	Construction	1080.77	285.87	341.18	453.72
安装工程	Construction and Installation	122.63	44.49	40.19	37.96
建筑业增加值	Construction Added-Value	244.65	67.46	76.31	100.87
#固定资产折旧	Depreciation on Fixed Assers	15.20	5.58	4.03	5.59
应付工资	Wages Payable	184.28	46.74	63.92	73.62
应付福利	Walfare Costs Payable	17.99	5.55	5.92	6.52
工程结算税金及附加	Taxes and Added Taxes of Settle Accounts	26.79	7.96	7.52	11.30
竣工产值（亿元）	Buildings Completed Output Value (10^8 yuan)	949.60	252.59	310.92	386.09
单位工程施工个数（个）	Number of Projects Under Construction (units)	65841	17574	21981	26286
#本年新开工	Beginning Projects in this Year	48338	12341	16366	19631
投标承包个数	Projects of Biding System	29293	8160	9120	12013
单位工程竣工个数（个）	Number of Projects Completed (units)	48322	12174	16541	19607
#优良工程个数	High Quality	15961	4690	5150	6121
房屋建筑施工面积（万平方米）	Floor Space of Buildings Under Construction (10000 sq·m)	17803.33	3831.67	5887.35	8084.31
#本年新开工	Beginning Projects in this Year	10920.82	1905.36	3923.80	5091.67
投标承包的面积	Floor Space of Biding System	10495.01	2783.85	3303.64	4407.53
房屋建筑竣工面积（万平方米）	Floor Space of Buildings Completed (10000 sq·m)	9958.90	1748.46	3497.35	4713.10
#优良工程面积	Floor Space of High Quality Projects	4119.76	914.51	1135.46	2069.79
自有机械设备总台数（万台）	Number of Machines Owned (10000 sets)	60.55	15.26	18.42	26.86
自有机械设备总功率（万千瓦）	Capacity of Machines Owned (10000 kw)	686.90	277.04	175.41	234.46
自有机械设备净值（亿元）	Machinery Owned Net Value (10^8 yuan)	103.66	36.77	24.89	42.00
职工平均人数（万人）	Staff and Workers Annual Average (10000 persons)	232.32	50.52	83.97	97.83
全员劳动生产率（元/人）	Overall Labor Productivity (yuan/person)	52704	66346	46123	51309
技术装备率（元/人）	Per Capita Machinery Value (yuan/person)	4462	7280	2964	4293
动力装备率（千瓦/人）	Per Capita Machinery Value (kw/person)	2.96	5.48	2.09	2.40
利润总额（亿元）	Total Profits (10^8 yuan)	14.07	2.71	4.29	7.06

9-3 建筑施工企业按行业类别分主要经济指标(1998)
MAJOR ECONOMIC INDICATORS BY SPECIALIZE SUBJECT OF CONSTRUCTION ENTERPRISES

指标	Items	土木工程建筑业 Civil Engineering	#房屋建筑业 Building	线路管道设备安装业 Line and Equipment Installation	装修装饰业 Building Decoration
施工企业个数 (个)	Number of Construction Enterprises (units)	2860	2399	340	387
建筑业总产值 (亿元)	Construction Enterprises Gross Output Value (10^8 yuan)	1090.79	964.35	94.24	39.39
#建筑工程	Construction	1022.26	902.89	24.46	34.06
安装工程	Construction and Installation	50.83	45.63	67.36	4.44
建筑业增加值	Construction Added-Value	215.97	191.65	21.96	6.72
#固定资产折旧	Depreciation on Fixed Assers	12.91	9.86	1.70	0.59
应付工资	Wages Payable	166.47	151.74	13.82	3.99
应付福利	Walfare Costs Payable	15.81	13.51	1.76	0.42
工程结算税金及附加	Taxes and Added Taxes of Settle Accounts	23.20	20.54	2.43	1.16
竣工产值 (亿元)	Buildings Completed Output Value (10^8 yuan)	840.49	741.19	78.18	30.92
单位工程施工个数 (个)	Number of Projects Under Construction (units)	53640	44557	12201	
#本年新开工	Beginning Projects in this Year	39397	32085	8941	
投标承包个数	Projects of Biding System	27100	23944	2193	
单位工程竣工个数 (个)	Number of Projects Completed (units)	38492	31328	9830	
#优良工程个数	High Quality	12588	10383	3373	
房屋建筑施工面积 (万平方米)	Floor Space of Buildings Under Construction (10000 sq·m)	17698.89	17449.53	104.44	
#本年新开工	Beginning Projects in this Year	10854.63	10707.96	66.19	
投标承包的面积	Floor Space of Biding System	10441.58	10325.59	53.43	
房屋建筑竣工面积 (万平方米)	Floor Space of Buildings Completed (10000 sq·m)	9911.43	9753.01	47.47	
#优良工程面积	Floor Space of High Quality Projects	4099.88	4043.26	19.89	
自有机械设备总台数 (万台)	Number of Machines Owned (10000 sets)	52.97	45.77	4.91	2.67
自有机械设备总功率 (万千瓦)	Capacity of Machines Owned (10000 kw)	609.39	442.42	66.46	11.05
自有机械设备净值(亿元)	Machinery Owned Net Value (10^8 yuan)	92.47	70.13	7.88	3.31
职工平均人数 (万人)	Staff and Workers Annual Average (10000 persons)	214.15	195.23	12.95	5.23
全员劳动生产率 (元/人)	Overall Labor Productivity (yuan/person)	50937	49395	72787	75369
技术装备率 (元/人)	Per Capita Machinery Value (yuan/person)	4318	3592	6083	6340
动力装备率 (千瓦/人)	Per Capita Machinery Value (kw/person)	2.85	2.27	5.13	2.12
利润总额 (亿元)	Total Profits (10^8 yuan)	11.27	9.30	2.06	0.73

注：装修装饰业1998年起免填单位工程施工个数。

Note: The number of building decorative projects under construction didn't ask to count, since 1998.

9-4 建筑业企业财务状况（1998）
CONSTRUCTION FINANCIAL INDICATOERS

单位：万元　　　　(10000 yuan)

指标	Items	合计 Total	#国有经济 State-Owned	#地方企业 Local-Owned	#城镇集体经济 Collective-Owned
资本金合计	**Total Capital Assets**	**2161162**	**646776**	**529286**	**627426**
年末资产负债	**Total Liability (year-end)**				
流动资产合计	Circulating Funds	9779661	3472566	2761899	3081610
#存货	Stock	4352589	1160067	979485	1573469
#在建工程	Under Construction Project	3382335	848619	773998	1312072
固定资产合计	Total Fixed	2023537	789630	599517	509741
固定资产原价合计	Total Original Value of Fixed Assets	2760286	1106724	828556	708934
#生产经营用	Used by Production	2133303	811966	629060	552686
累计折旧	Total Depreciation Drawn Accumulated	841661	336768	244519	213694
#本年折旧	Draw Depreciation This Year	151986	55778	41008	40279
资产总计	Total Property	12256505	4455204	3494693	3724559
流动负债合计	Total Circulating Liability	9088113	3342607	2613199	2888717
长期负债合计	Total Long-term Liability	302150	167326	115667	56171
所有者权益合计	Right and Interests of Owner's	2866242	945271	765827	779672
损益与分配	**Loss-profit and Allocation**				
工程结算收入	Project Avenue	8093638	2768487	2105737	2773423
工程结算成本	Project Cost	7143668	2453378	1877270	2011914
工程结算税金及附加	Project Taxes-added	267851	79571	60771	75234
工程结算利润	Project Profit	682118	235538	167696	186276
其他业务利润	Other Profit	53690	23633	16916	17386
管理费用	Management Fee	524049	202264	141198	147617
#税金	Taxes	18540	4441	3769	6698
利润总额	Total Profit	140673	27106	25246	42919
应交所得税	Payable Income Taxes	43646	10932	8533	13054
应付利润	Payable Profit	36824	4634	4337	10835
工资、福利费	**Wages, Walfare**				
本年应付工资总额	Payable Total Wages This Year	1842800	467390	366467	639248
本年应付福利费	Payable Total Walfare This Year	179878	55493	43536	59235
建筑业增加值	**Construction Added-Value**	2446461	674643	518405	763134
亏损企业个数	**Number of Loss-Making Enterprises**	600	105	94	181

9－5 建筑业按行业类别分财务状况（1998）
CONSTRUCTION FINANCIAL INDICATOERS BY SPECIALIZED SUBJECT

单位：万元 （10000 yuan）

指标	Items	土木工程建筑业 Civil Engineering	#房屋建筑业 Building	线路管道设备安装业 Line and Equipment Installation	装修装饰业 Building Decoration
资本金合计	**Total Capital Assets**	**1803826**	**1468319**	**228465**	**128872**
年末资产负债	**Total Liability (year-end)**				
流动资产合计	Circulating Funds	8554746	7197177	879447	345468
#存货	Stock	3924062	3475249	285363	143164
#在建工程	Under Construction Project	3125841	2799976	180271	76223
固定资产合计	Total Fixed	1708408	1288959	228214	86915
固定资产原价合计	Total Original Value of Fixed Assets	2328880	1748209	324342	107063
#生产经营用	Used by Production	1796331	1358790	252067	84905
累计折旧	Total Depreciation Drawn Accumulated	713211	539847	99479	28971
#本年折旧	Draw Depreciation This Year	129078	98650	17041	5867
资产总计	Total Property	10652120	8782729	1154463	449921
流动负债合计	Total Circulating Liability	7994793	6737796	816222	277098
长期负债合计	Total Long-term Liability	265757	160690	22397	13997
所有者权益合计	Right and Interests of Owner's	2391571	1884243	315845	158826
损益与分配	**Loss-profit and Allocation**				
工程结算收入	Project Avenue	7040623	5895339	730140	322876
工程结算成本	Project Cost	6266981	5256418	606869	269818
工程结算税金及附加	Project Taxes-added	231974	205399	24325	11552
工程结算利润	Project Profit	541667	433521	98945	41506
其他业务利润	Other Profit	46843	39726	5942	905
管理费用	Management Fee	414090	328030	79415	30544
#税金	Taxes	15148	13474	1338	2055
利润总额	Total Profit	112743	93000	20645	7284
应交所得税	Payable Income Taxes	34104	28665	7443	2100
应付利润	Payable Profit	28807	24947	6045	1972
工资、福利费	**Wages, Walfare**				
本年应付工资总额	Payable Total Wages This Year	1664745	1517389	138157	39898
本年应付福利费	Payable Total Walfare This Year	158076	135140	17600	4203
建筑业增加值	**Construction Added-Value**	2159720	1916497	219564	67177
亏损企业个数	**Number of Loss-Making Enterprises**	440	361	61	99

9-6 地质勘查基本情况
BASIC STATISTICS ON GEOLOGICAL PROSPECTING

项 目	Item	1995	1996	1997	1998
机构单位数 （个）	Number of Institutions	26	26	27	25
#野外队(大队级)	Field Groups	6	6	6	6
局实验室	Laboratories of Bureau	1	1	1	1
科研单位	Scientific Research Institutions	1	1	1	1
工业企业	Industry Enterprises	2	2	2	2
地质院校	Geological Colleges	1	1	1	1
新发现或新证实的主要矿产地 （处）	Main Mining Areas Newly Discovered and Confirmed (unit)	缺	1	5	4
年末职工人数 （人）	Number of Staff and Workers (year-end) (person)	8355	8393	8421	8050
平均人数 （人）	Average Number of Staff and Workers (person)	8469	8465	8336	7954
工资总额 （万元）	Total Wages (10000 yuan)	5905	6195	6335	6293
地勘费	Geological Prospecting Expense	6201	6987	7068	8082
机械岩心钻探 （米）	Dring Completed (metre)	64802	24693	15131	26518
预算内	Budgetary	18011	9660	5743	4600
地质市场	Geological Market	46791	15033	9388	21918
基本建设投资 （万元）	Investment in Capital Construction (10000 yuan)	3747	4181	1537	1704
总收入 （万元）	Total Income (10000 yuan)	35119	40312	46607	48114
净收入 （万元）	Net Income (10000 yuan)	281	354	630	760
增加值 （万元）	Added Value (10000 yuan)		14053	14856	16506
总产值 （万元）	Total Output Value (10000 yuan)		44143	51575	54657

10. 交通运输、邮电业

TRANSPORTATION, POSTAL AND TELECOMMUNICATION SERVICES

10 交通运输、邮电业
TRANSPORTATION, POSTAL AND TELECOMMUNICATION SERVICES

1 9 9 8

全社会客运量	Total Passenger Traffic	97033	万人	(10000 persons)
#公　　路	Highway	92215	万人	(10000 persons)
全社会货运量	Total Freight Traffic	80429	万吨	(10000 tons)
#公　　路	Highway	54328	万吨	(10000 tons)
邮电业务总量	Total Volume of Postal and Telecommunication Services	167.81	亿元	(10^8 yuan)
#函　　件	Letters	5.16	亿件	(10^8)
年末电话用户	Residential Telephone (Year-end)	749.59	万户	(10000)
年末移动电话用户	Residential Mobile Telephone (Year-end)	140.10	万户	(10000)

全 社 会 客 货 运 量

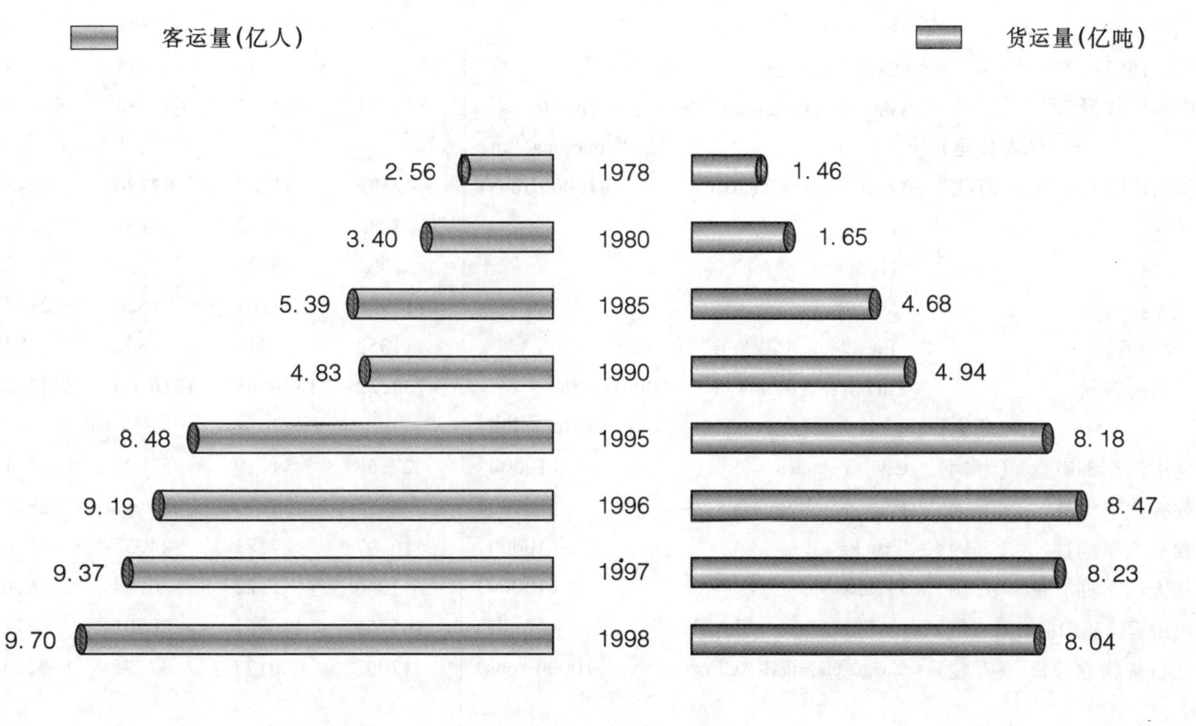

10－1 交通运输业基本情况
TRANSPORTATION

指 标 Items		1990	1995	1997	1998
运输线路长度 （公里）	**Length of Transportation Routes**				
铁路营业里程	Total Railways Length in Operation	748	747	751	753
铁路正线延展长度	Mainline Railways Length Completed	1250	1290	1307	1436
公路通车里程	Total Highway in Operation	24772	25970	27102	27331
#有路面里程	Paved	23582	25352	26590	26860
内河航道里程	Navigable Inland Waterways	23665	23803	23911	23908
#水深1米以上	Depth Above 1 Meter	20340	22466	22496	22601
输油管道里程	Petroleum Pipelines	334	334	334	334
公路桥梁 （座）	Highway Bridges	8886	9793	10624	10936
（米）	(m)	283948	337978	408891	423250
#危险桥 （座）	Dangerous Bridges	144	163	176	131
（米）	(m)	4360	5374	5700	812
通航河流上永久性水利闸坝 （座）	Permanent Floodgates and Dams Over Navigable Rivers	481	436	439	421
#碍航闸坝 （座）	Floodgates and Dams For Abstruct	118	123	137	106
客运量总计 （万人）	**Total passenger Traffie (10000 persons)**	**48339**	**84803**	**93684**	**97033**
铁路	Railway	4788	5185	4433	4451
公路	Highway	41850	78947	88826	92215
水运	Waterway	1701	623	341	273
民用航空	Civil Aviation		48	84	94
旅客周转量 （亿人公里）	**Turnover Volume of Passenger Traffic (10^8 persons/km)**	**324.94**	**630.56**	**657.93**	**680.02**
货物运输量总计 （万吨）	**Total Freight Traffic (10000 tons)**	**49399**	**81830**	**82290**	**80429**
铁路	Railway	4235	4143	4131	3793
公路	Highway	27904	49578	52441	54328
水运	Waterway	15908	27161	24826	21363
输油管道	Petroleum Pipelines	1352	948	892	945
货物周转量 （亿吨公里）	**Turnover Volume of Freight Traffic (10^8 tons/km)**	**730.22**	**1376.88**	**1370.63**	**1353.23**
民用汽车拥有量 （万辆）	Civil Vehicles (10000)	27.68	51.19	51.99	56.11
载客汽车辆数 （万辆）	Passenger vehicals (10000)	9.55	21.99	26.36	29.52
载货汽车辆数 （万辆）	Trucks (10000)	16.97	27.83	24.32	25.44
私人汽车拥有量 （万辆）	Private Vehicals (10000)	1.40	5.22	6.64	8.03
民用运输船舶拥有量（艘）	Civil Transport Vessels (units)	165762	140961	88501	88724
港口货物吞吐量 （万吨）	Cargo Handled At Ports (10000 tons)	17002	20177	32795	32885

10－2 客 运 量
PASSENGER TRAFFIC

单位:万人 (10000 persons)

年份 Year	总计 Total	铁路 Railway	公路 Highway	#交通系统 Department of Communication	水运 Waterway	#内河 Inland Waterway	民用航空 Civil Aviation
1978	25621	2752	18694	18694	4175	4175	
1980	34002	3364	26463	26463	4175	4175	
1985	53935	4819	45751	42342	3365	3365	
1986	58598	4927	50784	40914	2887	2887	
1987	54817	5372	46793	40902	2652	2652	
1988	54845	5983	46307	38985	2555	2555	
1989	52073	5421	44439	36233	2213	2213	
1990	48339	4788	41850	33822	1701	1701	
1991	50264	4932	43764	34316	1568	1568	
1992	55400	5035	48748	34414	1617	1617	
1993	59666	5533	53331	27573	797	797	5
1994	61104	5471	54930	21414	677	677	26
1995	84803	5185	78947	21273	623	623	48
1996	91870	4502	86801	22168	499	499	68
1997	93684	4433	88826	24609	341	341	84
1998	97033	4451	92215	24168	273	273	94

注：民用航空客运量从1993年起仅指省内航空公司完成数，不包括航空港的旅客发出量。

Note: Passenger traffic by civil aviation refered to fulfillment in our province only, excluded passengers sent out by air harbour, since 1993.

10－3 旅 客 周 转 量
TURNOVER VOLUME OF PASSENGER TRAFFIC

单位:亿人公里 (10^8 persons/km)

年份 Year	总计 Total	铁路 Railway	公路 Highway	#交通系统 Department of Communication	水运 Waterway	#内河 Inland Waterway	民用航空 Civil Aviation
1978	105.29	46.35	49.93	49.93	9.01	9.01	
1980	140.15	61.60	68.25	68.25	10.30	10.30	
1985	273.76	107.46	156.30	156.30	10.00	10.00	
1986	297.19	117.59	170.60	170.60	9.00	9.00	
1987	323.36	129.37	185.70	166.45	8.29	8.29	
1988	351.89	146.99	196.78	170.90	8.12	8.12	
1989	346.43	138.51	200.90	169.17	7.02	7.02	
1990	324.94	124.13	195.24	157.81	5.57	5.57	
1991	342.12	132.57	204.11	167.32	5.44	5.44	
1992	515.08	147.53	361.28	181.00	6.27	6.27	
1993	520.86	161.36	355.50	166.01	3.42	3.42	0.58
1994	641.09	166.94	367.98	135.62	3.28	3.28	2.89
1995	630.56	163.69	459.08	137.66	3.42	3.42	4.37
1996	647.73	143.85	459.70	143.58	2.51	2.51	5.67
1997	657.93	144.68	504.05	153.13	1.64	1.64	7.56
1998	680.02	141.15	527.62	154.15	1.12	1.12	10.13

10－4 货 运 量
FREIGHT TRAFFIC

单位:万吨 (10000 tons)

年份 Year	总 计 Total	铁 路 Railway	公 路 Highway	#交通系统 Department of Communication	水 运 Waterway	#内 河 Inland Waterway	海 运 Sea-shipping	输油管道 Petroleum Pipeline
1978	14626	3224	4488	4488	6557	6657		357
1980	16527	3420	4427	4427	6482	6452	30	2198
1985	46842	4037	23255	4797	18117	18067	73	1433
1986	48264	4143	20682	5027	22012	21953	85	1427
1987	55937	4241	30525	4938	19758	19698	61	1413
1988	55863	4289	29246	4733	20847	20755	92	1481
1989	55086	4489	30599	4480	18665	18578	108	1333
1990	49399	4235	27904	4238	15908	15809	110	1352
1991	49298	4078	27948	4438	16064	15884	190	1208
1992	56953	4343	30730	4841	20751	20533	218	1129
1993	66339	4344	35060	4535	25915	25610	305	1020
1994	69470	4318	36899	4342	27279	26920	351	974
1995	81830	4143	49578	4294	27161	26728	432	948
1996	84666	4361	50571	4077	28819	28429	391	915
1997	82290	4131	52441	3694	24826	24424	402	892
1998	80429	3793	54328	3122	21363	21059	304	945

10－5 货 物 周 转 量
TURNOVER VOLUME OF FREIGHT TRAFFIC

单位:亿吨公里 (10^8 tons/km)

年份 Year	总 计 Total	铁 路 Railway	公 路 Highway	#交通系统 Department of Communication	水 运 Waterway	#内 河 Inland Waterway	海 运 Sea-shipping	输油管道 Petroleum Pipeline
1978	283.85	172.72	11.24	11.24	87.97	87.97		11.92
1980	382.77	186.31	11.45	11.45	93.56	91.51	2.05	91.45
1985	575.58	240.48	81.30	19.99	205.90	194.83	11.07	47.90
1986	616.22	260.85	62.60	21.31	240.30	227.80	12.50	47.67
1987	715.74	271.22	128.50	22.21	261.40	252.50	8.90	47.15
1988	742.05	279.31	143.91	24.46	269.40	253.21	16.19	49.43
1989	776.51	292.40	174.92	22.70	264.70	238.73	25.97	44.49
1990	730.22	297.44	154.01	20.70	233.65	209.53	24.12	45.12
1991	788.41	301.73	166.21	21.89	280.59	240.23	40.36	39.88
1992	963.94	333.85	179.92	24.60	400.78	361.87	38.91	49.39
1993	1193.87	346.49	235.07	23.07	578.01	520.51	57.50	34.30
1994	1246.12	372.13	243.33	21.16	598.02	523.21	74.81	32.65
1995	1376.88	393.51	281.04	19.63	670.75	585.84	84.91	31.58
1996	1412.56	380.09	289.44	17.74	712.33	635.20	77.13	30.70
1997	1370.63	355.73	303.40	15.57	681.42	617.18	64.24	30.08
1998	1353.23	343.41	316.14	13.18	661.85	579.51	82.34	31.71

10－6 直属港口货物吞吐量（1998）
CARGO HANDLED AT PORTS DIRECTLY UNDER PROVINCE

单位：万吨 (10000 tons)

指标	Items	连云港 Liangyungang	南京 Nanjing	南通 Nantong	镇江 Zhengjiang	张家港 Zhangjiagang
货物吞吐量合计	**Total Cargo Handled**	**1776**	**5279**	**2017**	**1680**	**1363**
外贸吞吐量	Foreign Trade Handled	1007	623	364	289	442
进口	Import	372	433	249	147	264
出口	Export	635	190	115	142	178
内贸吞吐量	Domestic Trade Handled	769	4656	1653	1391	921
进口	Import	61	2215	1154	817	608
出口	Export	708	2441	499	574	313

10－7 直属港口码头泊位和库场能力（1998）
ABILITIES OF BERTH AND STOREGROUND AT PORTS DIRECTLY UNDER PROVINCE

指标	Items	连云港 Liangyungang	南京 Nanjing	南通 Nantong	镇江 Zhengjiang	张家港 Zhangjiagang
码头泊位个数(个)	Berths of Dacks	26	47	42	30	16
码头泊位长度(米)	Lengh of Harbor (m)	5073	5585	4390	3097	2931
#万吨级以上(个)	10000 Tonnage Above	21	14	9	8	13
库场堆存能力	Ability of Storeground Store Up					
总面积(平方米)	Total Area (sq·m)	752321	569565	341755	342988	386594
总容量(吨)	Total Capacity (tons)	1527785	2625837	1225821	605774	1494598
仓库面积(平方米)	Area of Warehouse (sq·m)	170589	58136	24195	37850	56816
容量(吨)	Capacity (tons)	120316	99081	22924	56689	100538
堆场面积(平方米)	Space of Storeground (sq·m)	581732	511429	317560	305138	329778
容量(吨)	Capacity (tons)	1407469	2526756	1202897	549085	1394060

10－8 全省民用车辆拥有量
CIVIL VEHICLES BY WHOLE PROVINCE

单位:辆 (unit)

指 标	Items	1990	1995	1997	1998
民用汽车	Civil Vehicles	276813	511903	519930	561129
载货汽车	Trucks	169665	278295	243248	254395
#大 型	Large-Scale	130505	198300	161841	159261
载客汽车	Passenger Vehicles	95549	219875	263610	295237
#大 型	Large Scale	17944	22355	21603	24002
特种汽车	Particular Cars	7658	10960	8363	7267
其他专用汽车	Other Vehicles for Special Use	3941	2773	4709	4230
轮胎式拖拉机	Tyre Shapes Tractors	308017	441198	371290	344453
# 手扶拖拉机	Hand Tractors	264452	327553	289024	241388
摩托车	Motor	235898	1295475	2070436	2403792
# 两轮摩托车	Motorcycle	228051	1242212	2007901	2328750
其他机动车	Other Motor Vehicles	51472	101560	168414	180259
载货挂车	Cargo Trailers	9589	11420	7535	7247

10－9 全省民用运输船舶拥有量
CIVIL TRANSPORT VESSELS BY WHOLE PROVINCE

指 标 Items	1990		1995		1998	
	艘 Tankers	万吨(客)位千瓦 10000 tons (seat) kw	艘 Tankers	万吨(客)位千瓦 10000 tons (seat) kw	艘 Tankers	万吨(客)位千瓦 10000 tons (seat) kw
货 船 Cargo Ships	126244	314.41	111898	544.81	65825	453.52
客 船 Passenger Ships	1029	8.04	919	6.73	671	4.78
拖 船 Tugboats	4421	37.66	3953	36.69	2751	38.76
货运驳船 Cargo Barges	34068	205.58	24191	196.55	19447	259.64

10－10 运输邮电企业财务状况（1998）
FINANCIAL AFFAIRS OF TRANSPORTATION POST AND TELECOMMUNICATION ENTERPRISES

单位：万元 （10000 yuan）

指标	Items	铁路 Railway	公路 Highway	水运 Waterway	港口 Port
企业个数	Number of Enterprises	3	168	111	77
#亏损企业(个)	Loss Making Enterprises	2	60	71	42
资本金合计	Total Capital Funds	1149217	634984	84907	226468
流动资产年末合计	Total Circulation Funds (Year end)	112320	111956	226311	257775
#存货	Inventory	28438	5981	8003	11646
固定资产年末合计	Total Fixed Assets (Year end)	1191249	523028	204946	574959
固定资产原价合计	Orginal Value of Fixed Assets	1600127	654029	256278	723069
#生产经营用	For the Use of Production and Business	1569887	531307	208190	582371
累计折旧	Depreciation Accumulated	485090	284276	111392	209558
#本年提取的	Drawed in this Year	39206	24004	9406	24153
资产总计	Total Assets	1318873	634984	431257	832734
流动负债年末合计	Total Circulation Liabilities (Year end)	198150	293684	154477	257682
长期负债年末合计	Total Long Term Liabilities (Year end)	37583	97895	67177	273400
负债合计	Total Liabilities	253733	391579	221654	531082
营运业务收入	Revenue	304795	224188	105378	201590
营业成本	Costs	248652	172364	93381	154992
营业税金及附加	Pre-tax and Related Payment	9370	7269	2893	6387
营运费用	Business Expenditures				
管理费用	Management Expenditures	27339	59871	33650	49204
#税金	Tax	151	633	356	258
营业利润	Product Sales After-Tax Profit	15398	13379	18878	21545
利润总额	Total Profit After-Tax	708	－3405	－21633	－7165
应交所得税	Income Tax Payable	4	1067	453	191
转作奖金的利润	Profit Transfered to Bonus				
应付利润	Profit Payable	3706		12	
#已分配股利	Share Hold Profit Distributed				

10－11 运输邮电企业财务状况（1998）
FINANCIAL AFFAIRS OF TRANSPOTATION, POST AND TELECOMMUNICATION ENTERPRISES

单位:万元 (10000 yuan)

指标	Items	民航 Civil Aviation	管道 Pipeline	邮政 Posts	电信 Telecommunications
企业个数	Number of Enterprises	4	1	67	195
#亏损企业(个)	Loss Making Enterprises	3		29	87
资本金合计	Total Capital Funds	229060	76313	26638	894107
流动资产年末合计	Total Circulation Funds (Year end)	78526	224627	23385	510877
#存货	Inventory	20296	4399	862	64012
固定资产年末合计	Total Fixed Assets (Year end)	342728	140839	91862	3809598
固定资产原价合计	Orginal Value of Fixed Assets	299021	314578	120852	4232418
#生产经营用	For the Use of Production and Business	279546	269309	120318	4065028
累计折旧	Depreciation Accumulated	28810	180421	38841	1311869
#本年提取的	Drawed in this Year	8082	18350	12071	452425
资产总计	Total Assets	437800	375189	115247	5401176
流动负债年末合计	Total Circulation Liabilities (Year end)	90353	189705	40723	1756650
长期负债年末合计	Total Long Term Liabilities (Year end)	114043	9214	67033	265861
负债合计	Total Liabilities	204396	198919	107756	2022511
营运业务收入	Revenue	82173	83450	29182	1435654
营业成本	Costs	67520	73611	29446	989062
营业税金及附加	Pre-tax and Related Payment	2678	2732	12499	50783
营运费用	Business Expenditures	10999	72		130331
管理费用	Management Expenditures	8755	7536	11820	256574
#税　金	Tax	72	83	78	3812
营业利润	Product Sales After-Tax Profit	－15033	1451	－36076	140378
利润总额	Total Profit After-Tax	－13659	506	－35098	151156
应交所得税	Income Tax Payable	114	140	3052	11375
转作奖金的利润	Profit Transfered to Bonus				
应付利润	Profit Payable	－1800	91		2669
#已分配股利	Share Hold Profit Distributed				

10－12 邮电业务基本情况
POSTS AND TELECOMMUNCATIONS SERVICES

指标	Items	1993	1994	1995	1996	1997	1998
邮电业务总量（亿元）	Revenue from Posts & Telecommunication Services (10^8 yuan)	34.51	51.78	72.24	96.03	132.52	167.81
函件（亿件）	Letters (10^8)	4.03	4.60	5.31	5.41	5.26	5.16
包件（万件）	Parcels (10000)	1375	1638	1619	1569	641	574
邮政快件（万件）	Express Mail (10000)	3043	2950	2809	2646	1883	840
特快专递（万件）	Special Express (10000)	421	701	870	919	696	700
报刊期发数（万份）	Newspapers and Magazines Circulation (10000)	2115	1829	1655	1567	1646	1762
电报（万份）	Telegrams (10000)	1502	1009	693	480	304	235
传真（份）	Faxs	187951	234552	277823	319180	439452	531690
长途电话（万张）	Distance Telephone Calls	45484	64506	85937	92157	118775	133904
年末市内电话（万户）	Urban Telephones (10000 subscribers)	103.11	165.70	226.54	283.42	336.47	386.11
#住宅电话（万户）	Residencial Telephones (10000)	66.35	122.48	176.47	226.22	270.21	311.46
年末无线寻呼电话用户（万户）	Wireless Telephones (10000)	29.81	60.67	109.55	200.08	298.79	303.95
年末移动电话用户（户）	Mobile Telephones (subscribers)	23842	98797	231897	450238	880229	1400954
国际互联网用户（户）	International Exchange Network Users (household)			105	2283	17928	69856
年末农村电话（户）	Rural Telephones (subscribers)	288480	527551	1036261	1674868	2573586	3634812
邮电局所（处）	Post Offices	2981	3017	3218	3297	3384	4720
邮路及农村投递路线总长度（公里）	Length of Postal Routes and Rural Delivery Routes (km)	295088	296175	302648	309816	313800	327780
#汽车邮路	Highway Routes	34190	36942	43766	48657	48007	50334
铁路邮路	Railway Routes	4413	4421	4198	4399	4919	4796
长话电路（路）	Long Distance Telephone Lines (line)	47933	71461	64117	88175	113820	180168
邮电通信工具拥有量（部、门）	Telecommunications Facilites (unit)						
市话交换机容量（万门）	City Switchboards Capacity (10000)	165.87	269.44	382.11	489.35	719.64	772.35
农话交换机容量（万部）	Rural Switchboards Capacity (10000)	88.19	133.74	214.66	335.64	335.84	519.88
长途光缆长度（波长公里）	Length of Distance Light Cable (wavelength/km)	2313	3218	2959	3188	6316	6828
电话机（万部）	Telephones (10000)	210.82	340.56	491.98	681.20	900.64	1160.42
城市电话（万部）	Urban Telephones (10000)	162.65	245.46	333.90	431.97	516.27	601.22
农村电话（万部）	Rural Telephones (10000)	48.17	95.10	158.08	249.23	384.37	559.20

10-13 邮电通信水平
LEVEL OF POSTS AND TELECOMMUNCATIONS SERVICES

指标	Items	1995	1997	1998
邮电通信水平	Level of Post and Telecommunication			
每局所服务面积 (平方公里)	Per Breau (Office) Service Area (sq.m)	32	30	22
每百人平均函件量 (件/百人)	Per 100 Persons Volume of Letters (units/100 persons)	777	773	739
每百人平均订阅报刊量 (份/百人)	Per 100 Persons Volume of Newspaper Subscribing (units/100 persons)	24	24	25
每百人平均包件 (件/百人)	Per 100 Persons Parcels (units/100 persons)	24	9	8
每百人平均汇票量 (张/百人)	Per 100 Persons Volume of Money Order (units/100 persons)	17	18	18
每百人平均电报量 (份/百人)	Per 100 Persons Volume of Telegrams (units/100 persons)	10	4	3
每百人长话量 (张/百人)	Per 100 Persons Volume of Distance Telephones (units/100 persons)	1258	1719	1917
电话普及率 (部/百人)	Rate of Popularization of Telephones (units/100 persons)	7.54	14.31	18.72
市话普及率	Urban Telephones	22.85	37.53	43.80
农话普及率	Rural Telephones	3.00	7.26	10.64
人均用邮量 (元/人)	Per Capita Volume of Post Business (yuan/person)	105.75	194.65	240.26
开通无线寻呼的市县 (个)	Number of Cities and Counties with Wireless Telephones Opened (units)	74	76	76
开通移动电话的市县 (个)	Number of Cities and Counties with Mobile Telephones Opened (units)	74	76	76
设有局所的乡(镇)比重 (%)	Percentage of Countries (Towns) with Breau (Office) Established (%)	99.3	98.9	98.5
通邮路的乡(镇)比重 (%)	Percentage of Townships (Towns) with Postal Routs Opened (%)	100	99.4	99.1
开办特快专递业务的市县 (个)	Number of Cities and Countries with Special Express Mail (units)	74	76	76

11. 国内贸易

DOMESTIC TRADE

11 国 内 贸 易
DOMESTIC TRADE

1 9 9 8

社会消费品零售总额	Total Retail Sales of Consumer Goods	2238.01	亿元	(10^8 yuan)
批发零售贸易业商品销售总额	Total Sales Value of Wholesale and Retail Trade	5202.90	亿元	(10^8 yuan)
批发零售贸易业商品批发总额	Total Wholesale Value of Wholesale and Retail Trade	3662.45	亿元	(10^8 yuan)
批发零售贸易业商品零售总额	Total Retail Sales Value of Wholesale and Retail Trade	1540.45	亿元	(10^8 yuan)
全省商品交易市场个数	Number of Transaction Markets	6018	个	(unit)
城市	Ubran	1856		
农村	Rural	4162		
全省商品交易成交额	Transaction Value	3182.36	亿元	(10^8 yuan)
城市	Ubran	1637.79		
农村	Rural	1544.57		

社会消费品零售总额(亿元)

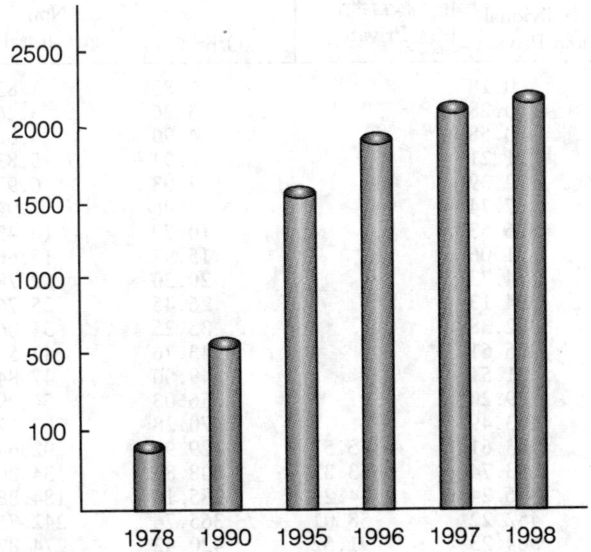

社会消费品零售额构成(%)

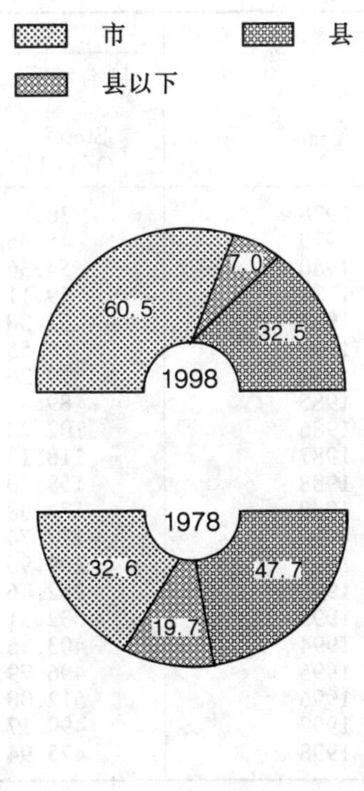

11－1 社会消费品零售总额(按地区分)

TOTAL RETAIL SALES OF CONSEUMER GOODS BY REGION

单位:亿元 (10⁸ yuan)

年份 Year	社会消费品零售总额 Total Retail Sales of Consumer Goods	按地区分 By Region 市 City	县 Country	县以下 Below Country Level
1978	84.79	27.65	16.68	40.46
1979	99.16	32.57	19.27	47.32
1980	122.56	41.21	23.28	58.07
1981	134.79	47.12	24.74	62.93
1982	150.01	50.91	27.29	71.81
1983	169.12	58.61	29.55	80.96
1984	205.05	74.45	36.42	94.18
1985	262.57	99.96	45.32	117.29
1986	304.58	111.92	51.13	141.53
1987	360.74	134.65	60.23	165.86
1988	471.83	198.46	66.28	207.09
1989	509.56	221.01	68.33	220.22
1990	515.43	231.26	67.05	217.12
1991	578.12	281.69	67.37	229.06
1992	704.52	364.47	74.59	265.46
1993	967.77	540.19	86.09	341.49
1994	1287.86	748.97	91.13	447.76
1995	1650.00	961.71	124.21	564.08
1996	1932.89	1157.95	131.14	643.80
1997	2118.12	1273.54	146.38	698.20
1998	2238.01	1353.44	156.17	728.40

注：1996 年及以后社会消费品零售总额及各分组指标中不含售给城乡居民生活用住房的零售额。
Note：In 1996，the residential house was not included in the total retail sales of consumer goods and all the tagets by trips.

11－2 社会消费品零售总额(按经济类型分)

TOTAL RETAIL SALES OF CONSEUMER GOODS BY OWNERSHIP

单位:亿元 (10⁸ yuan)

年份 Year	按经济类型分 By Ownership 国有经济 State-Owned	集体经济 Collective-Owned	个体和私营经济 Individual and Private	#私营经济 Private	其他各种经济 Other	农民对非农业居民的零售额 Agricultural to Non-agricultural
1978	38.66	44.12	0.18		1.83	1.83
1979	45.96	49.66	0.28		3.26	3.26
1980	54.36	62.72	0.58		4.90	4.82
1981	59.11	68.53	1.21		5.94	5.83
1982	62.38	78.21	2.39		7.03	6.97
1983	68.55	84.77	7.74		8.06	7.92
1984	79.26	98.56	16.53		10.70	10.43
1985	89.86	125.68	31.06		15.97	15.66
1986	102.20	147.45	34.73		20.20	19.78
1987	118.18	171.98	44.13		26.45	25.76
1988	158.20	216.00	62.38		35.25	34.06
1989	174.98	215.21	75.61		43.76	42.57
1990	177.74	207.18	81.51		49.00	47.84
1991	209.96	222.93	89.20		56.03	54.09
1992	262.06	258.69	113.49		70.28	67.17
1993	332.51	341.72	163.61	5.57	129.93	92.64
1994	403.36	441.91	233.74	13.33	208.85	134.20
1995	496.79	531.81	336.24	34.21	285.16	184.88
1996	512.08	602.83	452.22	58.01	365.76	242.75
1997	499.17	634.30	564.23	91.52	420.42	274.82
1998	475.94	616.61	694.22	136.98	451.24	289.02

11－3 社会消费品零售总额(按行业分)
TOTAL RETAIL SALES OF CONSEUMER GOODS BY SECTOR

单位:亿元 (10^8 yuan)

年 份 Year	批发零售贸易业 Wholesales and Retail Sales Trade	餐 饮 业 Catering Trade	制 造 业 Manutacturing	其他行业 Others
1978	71.03	3.24	6.32	4.20
1979	81.52	3.90	6.83	6.91
1980	98.50	4.72	11.03	8.31
1981	104.47	5.17	14.86	10.29
1982	114.90	5.49	17.00	12.62
1983	127.66	6.14	20.70	14.62
1984	150.68	7.61	27.69	19.07
1985	188.03	10.45	37.00	27.09
1986	214.97	12.53	44.50	32.58
1987	250.16	15.84	53.39	41.35
1988	327.17	20.33	70.83	53.50
1989	353.63	22.47	70.91	62.55
1990	358.12	24.17	66.76	66.38
1991	402.90	27.86	72.95	74.41
1992	486.09	33.64	91.35	93.44
1993	665.72	44.74	129.88	127.43
1994	877.67	67.67	161.08	181.44
1995	1125.77	90.19	179.35	254.69
1996	1337.15	126.02	186.71	283.01
1997	1446.31	154.60	196.37	320.84
1998	1540.46	175.59	184.53	337.43

11－4 社会消费品零售总额分类
TOTAL RETAIL SALES OF CONSEUMER GOODS BY CATEGORY

单位:亿元 (10^8 yuan)

年 份 Year	社会消费品零售总额 Total Retail Sales of Consumer Goods	食品类 Foods	衣着类 Clothing	日用品类 Daily Use Goods	文化娱乐用品类 Goods of Culture and Entertain-ment	书报杂志类 Newspaper and Magzines	药和医疗用品类 Medicine and Medical Goods	房屋及建筑材料类 Houses and Building Material	燃料类 Fuel
1978	84.79	43.25	20.00	7.60	3.25	0.71	3.89	2.99	3.10
1979	99.16	50.37	23.01	8.77	4.36	0.97	3.98	4.41	3.29
1980	122.56	62.04	28.76	10.14	5.66	1.49	4.30	6.00	4.17
1981	134.79	68.63	31.68	11.76	5.75	1.52	4.41	6.59	4.45
1982	150.01	77.71	32.28	12.73	6.84	1.72	5.32	8.73	4.68
1983	169.12	87.19	36.32	14.02	7.54	2.01	6.10	10.96	4.98
1984	205.05	104.23	45.41	17.03	10.03	2.51	6.41	13.62	5.81
1985	262.57	135.03	56.52	21.55	16.39	3.28	6.91	16.13	6.76
1986	304.58	156.87	59.45	25.52	20.62	3.78	8.67	20.97	8.70
1987	360.74	189.35	71.46	29.20	23.46	3.86	10.17	24.31	8.93
1988	471.83	246.23	89.09	45.81	34.64	4.28	12.75	27.09	11.94
1989	509.56	266.71	99.87	42.19	36.42	5.94	15.04	30.54	12.85
1990	515.43	285.13	91.53	38.12	34.47	6.68	18.55	26.88	14.07
1991	578.12	315.11	102.33	47.41	35.26	8.24	22.73	32.95	14.09
1992	704.52	360.71	126.11	76.09	42.98	11.41	30.51	39.45	17.26
1993	967.77	492.59	167.43	105.58	64.84	15.26	45.49	55.16	21.42
1994	1287.86	655.52	217.65	156.96	78.56	20.61	55.38	79.85	23.33
1995	1650.00	841.50	277.20	199.65	99.00	26.40	69.30	108.90	28.05
1996	1932.89	1005.10	324.35	245.48	117.90	35.20	90.84	78.84	35.18
1997	2118.12	1077.70	342.50	284.46	147.84	42.15	113.32	73.72	36.43
1998	2238.01	1146.98	312.43	300.56	166.96	54.83	133.16	83.25	39.84

11－5　批发零售贸易业商品购销存总额（1998）

TOTAL PURCHASE SALES AND INVENTORY OF WHOLESALE AND RETAIL SALES TRADE

单位：亿元　　　　　　　　　　　　　　　　　　　　　　　　　　　　　　　　　　(10^8 yuan)

项　　目	Item	商品购进总额 Total Goods Purchase	商品销售总额 Total Sales	批发 Whole-sales	零售 Retail Sales	商品库存总额 Total Inventory
总　　计	**Total**		**5202.90**	**3662.45**	**1540.45**	
限额以上企业和单位	**Over-Norm Enterprises and Units**	**2315.76**	**2609.74**	**2098.64**	**511.10**	**300.17**
#国有及国有控股	State-Owned and State Share Holding	1662.06	1855.19	1497.97	357.22	176.94
按登记注册类型分	**Grouped by Type of Registeration**					
内资企业	Inner Enterprises	2292.70	2584.06	2094.17	489.89	297.55
国有企业	State-Owned Enterprises	1226.59	1360.89	1131.92	228.97	139.39
集体企业	Collective-Owned Enterprises	514.83	602.78	497.81	104.97	106.05
股份合作企业	Share Holding Cooperative Enterprises	26.65	30.68	22.84	7.84	3.91
联营企业	Joint-Owned Enterprises	16.28	17.87	11.94	5.93	1.81
有限责任公司	Responsibility Co. Ltd.	240.38	262.67	208.31	54.36	18.15
股份有限公司	Share Holding Co. Ltd.	264.22	305.12	217.70	87.42	27.77
私营企业	Private Enterprises	3.75	4.05	3.65	0.40	0.47
港澳台商投资企业	Hongkong, Macao and Taiwan Funded	10.36	11.58	3.22	8.36	1.54
#合资经营企业	Joint Funded Enterprises	8.86	10.07	3.22	6.85	1.40
合作经营企业	Cooperative Operation Enterprises	1.50	1.51		1.51	0.14
外商投资企业	Foreign Invested Enterprises	12.70	14.10	1.25	12.85	1.08
#中外合资经营企业	Sino-Foreign Joint Funded Enterprises	7.61	9.14	1.25	7.89	0.96
中外合作经营企业	Sino-Foreign Cooperative Operation Enterprises	0.75	0.72		0.72	0.02
外资企业	Foreign Funded Enterprises	4.34	4.24		4.24	0.10
按行业分	**Grouped by Sectors**					
批发业	Wholesale Trade	1941.57	2169.90	1987.10	182.80	234.37
食品饮料烟草批发业	Food. Beverage and Tabacco	388.15	486.18	443.56	42.62	47.80
棉麻土畜产品批发业	Cotton, Jute, Native and Livestock Products	92.39	89.20	85.41	3.79	54.83
纺织品服装鞋帽批发业	Textile Products, Garments, Shoes and Hats	217.84	232.84	231.62	1.22	11.16
日用百货批发业	Daily Use Goods	112.18	129.54	99.61	29.93	13.81
日用杂品批发业	Daily Use Articles	10.73	12.04	9.61	2.43	1.83
五金交电化工批发业	Hardware, Electric Appliance and Chemicals	148.70	152.40	127.84	24.56	21.93
药品及医疗器械批发业	Medicine and Medical Appliance	68.55	80.91	39.87	41.04	10.89
能源批发业	Energy	238.93	257.61	250.26	7.35	14.60
化工材料批发业	Chemical Materials	68.43	73.67	72.21	1.46	6.25
木材批发业	Timber	6.14	6.75	6.46	0.29	0.57
建筑材料批发业	Building Materials	10.61	13.13	12.42	0.71	1.11
矿产品批发业	Ore Products	1.53	1.64	1.64		0.05
金属材料批发业	Metal Material	196.23	208.83	203.95	4.88	15.23
机械电子设备批发业	Machine and Electric Equipment	60.56	79.29	77.68	1.61	4.41
汽车摩托车及零配件批发业	Spare and Component Parts for Automobiles, Motocycles	70.76	75.14	61.12	14.02	6.08
再生物资回收批发业	Recycled Material Collection	52.67	54.96	54.58	0.38	1.89
工艺美术品批发业	Handicraft Article	12.99	12.99	12.99		0.28
图书报刊批发业农业生	Books and Newspapers	20.71	21.28	20.64	0.64	2.88
产资料批发业	Agricultural Means of Production	116.56	131.13	125.29	5.84	13.45
其他类未包括的批发业	Others	46.91	50.37	50.34	0.03	5.32

续表 Continued

单位:亿元 (10[8] yuan)

项目	Item	商品购进总额 Total Goods Purchase	商品销售总额 Total Sales	批发 Whole-sales	零售 Retail Sales	商品库存总额 Total Inventory
零售业	Retail Sales Trade	374.19	439.84	111.54	328.30	65.80
食品饮料烟草零售业	Foods, Beverage and Tabacco	24.97	29.72	8.02	21.70	6.12
日用百货零售业	Daily Use Goods	278.65	333.87	85.11	248.76	46.04
纺织品服装鞋帽零售业	Textile Products, Garments, Shoes, and Hats	7.61	9.44	2.66	6.78	1.84
日用杂品零售业	Daily Use Articles	1.44	1.45	0.53	0.92	0.22
五金交电化工零售业	Hardwares, Electric Appliance and Chemicals	17.22	17.78	3.13	14.65	2.86
药品及医疗器械零售业	Medicine and Medical Appliance	16.20	19.59	5.79	13.80	3.15
图书报刊零售业	Books and Newspaper	22.71	22.12	3.08	19.04	4.51
其他零售业	Others	5.39	5.87	3.22	2.65	1.06
限额以下企业和单位按行业分	**Below-Norm Enterprises and Units Grouped by Sectors**		**1779.65**	**1204.20**	**575.45**	
批发业	Wholesale Trade		1237.26	1032.66	204.60	
食品饮料烟草批发业	Food. Beverage and Tabacco		290.11	222.83	67.28	
棉麻土畜产品批发业	Cotton, Jute, Native and Livestock Products		32.09	29.40	2.69	
纺织品服装鞋帽批发业	Textile Products, Garments, Shoes and Hats		98.63	80.14	18.49	
日用百货批发业	Daily Use Goods		67.72	48.93	18.79	
日用杂品批发业	Daily Use Articles		23.71	18.58	5.13	
五金交电化工批发业	Hardware, Electric Appliance and Chemicals		92.77	75.58	17.19	
药品及医疗器械批发业	Medicine and Medical Appliance		15.10	12.84	2.26	
能源批发业	Energy		86.34	74.61	11.73	
化工材料批发业	Chemical Materials		56.39	52.13	4.26	
木材批发业	Timber		18.39	15.13	3.26	
建筑材料批发业	Building Materials		84.67	69.43	15.24	
矿产品批发业	Ore Products		0.68	0.62	0.06	
金属材料批发业	Metal Material		149.28	141.22	8.06	
机械电子设备批发业	Machine and Electric Equipment		39.55	33.99	5.56	
汽车摩托车及零配件批发业	Spare and Component Parts for Automobiles, Motocycles		36.22	29.29	6.93	
再生物资回收批发业	Recycled Material Collection		22.42	21.44	0.98	
工艺美术品批发业	Handicraft Article		1.07	0.79	0.28	
图书报刊批发业	Books and Newspapers		2.90	1.89	1.01	
农业生产资料批发业	Agricultural Means of Production		56.74	48.88	7.86	
其他类未包括的批发业	Others		62.48	54.94	7.54	
零售业	Retail Sales Trade		542.39	171.54	370.85	
食品饮料烟草零售业	Foods, Beverage and Tabacco		129.89	39.33	90.56	
日用百货零售业	Daily Use Goods		161.83	65.67	96.16	
纺织品服装鞋帽零售业	Textile Products, Garments, Shoes, and Hats		48.64	11.52	37.12	
日用杂品零售业	Daily Use Articles		23.70	3.89	19.81	
五金交电化工零售业	Hardwares, Electric Appliance and Chemicals		48.23	16.07	32.16	
药品及医疗器械零售业	Medicine and Medical Appliance		17.69	6.49	11.20	
图书报刊零售业	Books and Newspaper		9.24	1.40	7.84	
其他零售业	Others		103.17	27.17	76.00	
个　体	**Individual**		**813.51**	**359.61**	**453.90**	

11－6 大中型批发零售贸易业主要商品销售数量
SALES VOLUME OF MAJOR COMMODITIES BY LARGE AND MEDIUM SIZED WHOLESALE AND RETAIL TRADE

品名		Items		1995	1996	1997	1998
粮食	（万吨）	Grain	（10000 tons）	313.48	276.11	253.46	215.17
食用植物油	（万吨）	Edible Vegetable Oil	（10000 tons）	32.12	34.79	17.50	16.74
猪和猪肉	（万吨）	Pigs and Pork	（10000 tons）	31.69	40.92	29.48	36.68
食糖	（万吨）	Sugar	（10000 tons）	55.83	56.03	58.94	42.81
棉花	（万吨）	Cotton	（10000 tons）	75.62	73.67	71.35	51.67
布	（万米）	Clothing	（10000 m）	86953.12	64385.32	58429.52	48570.77
#棉布		Cotton Clothing		35665.48	22763.52	22078.27	16484.05
呢绒	（万米）	Wollen Fabric	（10000 m）	1262.40	949.69	828.67	608.92
绸缎	（万米）	Silk and Stins	（10000 m）	8187.45	5816.04	5554.56	4171.24
各种服装	（万件）	Garments	（10000 units）	34817.83	25045.31	22199.18	22551.89
鞋	（万双）	Shoes	（10000 pairs）	25534.07	23611.21	15083.43	9559.89
#皮鞋		Leather Shoes		5724.11	4258.87	3058.40	1949.93
黄金饰品	（亿元）	Gold Jewelry	（10^8 yuan）	16.42	13.66	15.69	13.31
照相机	（万架）	Cameras	（10000 units）	46.85	36.69	36.29	27.82
自行车	（万辆）	Bicycles	（10000 units）	406.84	348.22	307.80	190.11
摩托车	（万辆）	Motor-cycles	（10000 units）	69.62	81.46	86.12	56.45
电视机	（万台）	Television Sets	（10000 units）	265.24	236.91	246.84	212.46
#彩色电视机		Color TV		175.45	174.91	177.44	187.38
录音机	（万台）	Recorders	（10000 units）	132.49	106.45	75.03	54.54
#组合音响		Hi－Fi Systems			16.19	16.00	7.57
摄像相	（万台）	TV Camera	（10000 units）		17.97	0.74	0.65
录像机	（万台）	Videorecorders	（10000 units）	57.38	45.58	17.68	4.20
影碟机	（万台）	VCD	（10000 units）	·		9.58	41.73
#进口影碟机		Import VCD				0.67	1.25
家用电脑	（万台）	Computer	（10000 units）		7.41	3.75	0.59
家用电风扇	（万台）	Electric Fans	（10000 units）	827.31	645.00	420.55	230.00
家用洗衣机	（万台）	Washing Machines	（10000 units）	139.66	135.59	132.85	110.65
家用电冰箱	（万台）	Refrigerators	（10000 units）	95.01	95.06	91.19	95.16
房间空调器	（万台）	Air Conditioners	（10000 units）	222.45	199.32	209.79	171.71
微波炉	（万台）	Microwave Stove	（10000 units）			33.70	61.30
抽油烟机	（万台）	Rang Hoods	（10000 units）	66.98	57.55	51.59	40.61

续表 Continued

单位:万吨 (10000 tons)

品名	Items	1995	1996	1997	1998
化学肥料	Chemical Fertilizers	1010.83	844.21	771.89	698.35
化学农药	Chemical Pesticide	15.14	15.70	13.42	7.58
农用塑料薄膜	Plastic Film for Agricultural Use	5.82	6.59	3.69	2.38
汽车 (万辆)	Motor Vehicals (10000 units)	8.24	8.65	9.08	6.41
#轿车	Coaches (10000 units)	3.21	3.33	3.61	2.73
生铁	Pig Iron	139.74	120.87	125.83	95.37
钢材	Steel	865.81	655.59	613.38	521.44
#普通中型钢材	Middle Common Steel	93.64	70.38	69.25	36.15
普通小型钢材	Small Common Steel	171.69	139.90	160.18	119.20
钢带	Steel Tape	9.64	10.47	12.55	7.44
线材	Wire Rod	168.88	73.16	78.30	64.59
中厚钢板	Thicker Steel Plate	155.50	111.17	111.73	100.50
薄钢板	Thin Steel Plate	139.67	111.77	82.80	74.57
硅钢片	Silicon Steel	6.10	6.02	3.71	4.07
铜	Copper	6.47	4.02	5.04	1.52
铝	Aluminium	10.10	5.99	11.83	5.64
铅	Lead	1.22	0.91	2.81	0.72
锌	Zinc	3.44	2.53	4.00	2.82
锡	Tin	0.23	0.29	0.35	0.11
铜材	Copper Material	1.07	0.64	0.94	0.62
铝材	Aluminium Material	1.11	1.27	2.12	1.35
硫酸	Sulphuric Acid	1.83	2.28	1.88	2.87
烧碱	Caustic Soda	3.60	2.54	2.26	2.19
纯碱	Soda Ash	5.65	6.20	9.86	9.25
天然橡胶	Natural Rubber	4.54	4.57	3.12	2.42
合成橡胶	Synthetic Rubber	3.49	3.00	2.66	1.55
水泥	Cement	191.52	147.52	104.20	69.31
平板玻璃 (万箱)	Plate Glass (10000 weight box)	143.00	158.32	89.09	56.49
原木 (万立方米)	Log (10000 cubic meters)	80.15	49.71	31.68	31.45
锯材 (万立方米)	Sawed (10000 cubic meters)	28.44	14.84	8.54	14.62
煤炭	Coal	3924.00	3749.00	2917.00	2462.00
焦炭	Coke	37.15	28.45	37.19	10.74
原油	Crude Oil	53.00	17.25	19.58	9.72
汽油	Gosoline	234.09	278.43	387.21	373.34
柴油	Diesel	330.55	348.64	492.67	504.95
煤油	Kerosene	12.74	11.58	11.65	11.97
燃料油	Fuel Oil	71.35	42.72	95.45	50.44

11－7 限额以上批发零售贸易企业财务状况（1998）
FINANCIAL AFFAIRS OF OVER-NORM WHOLESALE AND RETAIL TRADE ENTERPRISES

单位:亿元 (10[8] yuan)

项目	Item	商品销售收入 Revenue of Product Sales	商品销售成本 Cost of Product Sales	主营业务利润 Profits of Major Vocational Work	其他业务利润 Profits of Other Vocational Work	利润总额 Total Profits
总计	**Total**	**2318.85**	**2092.63**	**90.89**	**10.29**	**5.38**
#国有及国有控股	State-Owned and State Share Holding	1657.14	1487.16	71.91	7.63	9.87
按登记注册类型分	**Grouped by Type of Registeration**					
内资企业	Inner Enterprises	2300.57	2077.38	89.24	10.13	6.01
国有企业	State-Owned Enterprises	1226.45	1098.89	51.40	5.31	4.90
集体企业	Collective-Owned Enterprises	533.03	487.48	13.76	1.99	－4.12
股份合作企业	Share Holding Cooperative Enterprises	26.42	24.20	0.86	0.11	－0.23
联营企业	Joint-Owned Enterprises	15.58	14.51	0.54	0.28	－0.08
有限责任公司	Responsibility Co. Ltd.	230.21	212.56	7.55	1.36	1.27
股份有限公司	Share Holding Co. Ltd.	265.10	236.22	15.02	1.06	4.25
私营企业	Private Enterprises	3.78	3.52	0.11	0.02	0.02
港澳台商投资企业	Hongkong, Macao and Taiwan Funded	10.37	8.55	0.83	0.07	－0.27
#合资经营企业	Jointly Funded Enterprises	8.97	7.42	0.77	0.04	－0.08
合作经营企业	Cooperative Operation Enterprises	1.40	1.13	0.06	0.03	－0.19
外商投资企业	Foreign Invested Enterprises	7.91	6.70	0.82	0.09	－0.36
#中外合资经营企业	Sino-Foreign Jointly Funded Enterprises	7.91	6.70	0.82	0.09	－0.36
按经济组织类型分	**Grouped by type of Economic Organization**					
独资企业	Solely Funded Enterprises	1760.03	1586.89	65.16	7.34	0.79
合作合伙企业	Cooperation and Partnership Enterprises	43.40	39.85	1.46	0.41	－0.50
股份有限公司	Share Holding Co. Ltd.	265.56	236.63	15.03	1.06	4.26
有限责任公司	Responsibility Co. Ltd.	249.86	229.26	9.24	1.48	0.83
按行业分	**Grouped by Sectors**					
批发业	Wholesale Trade	1947.36	1778.21	68.63	8.04	8.54
食品饮料烟草和家庭用品批发业	Food, Beverage, Tobacco and Family Appliances	1052.05	940.44	47.36	3.87	9.89
能源材料和机械电子设备批发业	Energy Material and Machinery, Electronic Equipment	697.57	658.87	14.21	3.56	－1.95
其他类批发业	Others	197.74	178.90	7.06	0.61	0.60
零售业	Retail Sales Trade	371.49	314.42	22.26	2.25	－3.16

续表 Continued

单位:亿元 (10^8 yuan)

项目	Item	资产总计 Total Assets	#流动资产 Circulation	#固定资产 Fixed Asset	负债合计 Total Liabilities	#流动负债 Circulational Liabilities	#长期负债 Long Term Liabilities	所有者权益合计 Ownership Rights and Interests
总计	**Total**	**1341.28**	**854.52**	**371.06**	**1056.57**	**936.06**	**120.51**	**284.71**
#国有及国有控股	State-Owned and State Share Holding	910.39	562.81	270.63	701.64	624.66	76.98	208.75
按登记注册类型分	**Grouped by Type of Registeration**							
内资企业	Inner Enterprises	1323.20	849.05	362.96	1043.74	927.19	116.55	279.46
国有企业	State-Owned Enterprises	664.00	425.72	190.75	523.15	472.35	50.80	140.85
集体企业	Collective-Owned Enterprises	342.72	239.80	74.16	285.50	253.00	32.50	57.22
股份合作企业	Share Holding Cooperative Enterprises	11.97	7.64	3.23	10.83	9.14	1.69	1.14
联营企业	Joint-Owned Enterprises	12.89	6.87	4.38	9.85	8.58	1.27	3.04
有限责任公司	Responsibility Co. Ltd.	119.20	75.95	31.46	93.29	80.81	12.48	25.91
股份有限公司	Share Holding Co. Ltd.	171.13	92.09	58.75	120.15	102.35	17.80	50.98
私营企业	Private Enterprises	1.29	0.98	0.23	0.97	0.96	0.01	0.32
港澳台商投资企业	Hongkong, Macao and Taiwan Funded	8.31	3.44	2.00	6.50	5.09	1.41	1.81
#合资经营企业	Jointly Funded Enterprises	7.16	2.97	1.94	5.63	4.39	1.24	1.53
合作经营企业	Cooperative Operation Enterprises	1.15	0.47	0.06	0.87	0.70	0.17	0.28
外商投资企业	Foreign Invested Enterprises	9.77	2.03	6.10	6.33	3.78	2.55	3.44
#中外合资经营企业	Sino-Foreign Jointly Funded Enterprises	9.77	2.03	6.10	6.33	3.78	2.55	3.44
按经济组织类型分	**Grouped by type of Economic Organization**							
独资企业	Solely Funded Enterprises	1007.19	665.88	265.04	809.02	725.72	83.30	198.17
合作合伙企业	Cooperation and Partnership Enterprises	26.02	14.98	7.67	21.55	18.42	3.13	4.47
股份有限公司	Share Holding Co. Ltd.	171.33	92.23	58.80	120.25	102.45	17.80	51.08
有限责任公司	Responsibility Co. Ltd.	136.74	81.43	39.55	105.75	89.47	16.28	30.99
按行业分	**Grouped by Sectors**							
批发业	Wholesale Trade	1044.58	723.80	229.78	830.32	749.65	80.67	214.26
食品饮料烟草和家庭用品批发业	Food, Beverage, Tobacco and Family Appliances	612.40	428.74	130.08	485.90	430.52	55.38	126.50
能源材料和机械电子设备批发业	Energy Material and Machinery, Electronic Equipment	346.98	233.86	82.56	279.09	256.44	22.65	67.89
其他类批发业	Others	85.20	61.20	17.14	65.33	62.69	2.64	19.87
零售业	Retail Sales Trade	296.70	130.72	141.28	226.25	186.41	39.84	70.45

11－8 限额以上餐饮企业财务状况(1998)

FINANCIAL AFFAIRS OF OVER-NORM CATERING ENTERPRISES

单位:亿元 (10^8 yuan)

项目	Item	营业收入 Business Revenue	营业成本 Business Cost	主营业务利润 Profits of Major Vocational Work	其他业务利润 Profits of Other Vocational Work	利润总额 Total Profits
总计	**Total**	**24.19**	**11.18**	**3.70**	**0.11**	**-1.35**
#国有及国有控股	State-Owned and State Share Holding	14.71	6.84	2.20	0.05	-0.82
按登记注册类型分	**Grouped by Type of Registeration**					
内资企业	Inner Enterprises	14.98	7.23	2.00	0.07	-1.09
国有企业	State-Owned Enterprises	9.54	4.82	1.08	0.03	-0.83
集体企业	Collective-Owned Enterprises	2.73	1.20	0.50		-0.20
股份合作企业	Share Holding Cooperative Enterprises	0.58	0.26	0.13		0.02
联营企业	Joint-Owned Enterprises	0.08	0.04	0.01		-0.01
有限责任公司	Responsibility Co. Ltd.	1.29	0.62	0.18		-0.09
股份有限公司	Share Holding Co. Ltd.	0.72	0.26	0.10	0.04	0.02
私营企业	Private Enterprises	0.04	0.03			
港澳台商投资企业	Hongkong, Macao and Taiwan Funded	1.90	0.96	0.19	0.03	-0.34
合资经营企业	Jointly Funded Enterprises	1.63	0.80	0.23	0.02	-0.28
合作经营企业	Cooperative Operation Enterprises	0.14	0.07	-0.01	0.01	-0.04
港澳台商独资经营企业	Hongkgong, Macao and Taiwan Solely Funded	0.06	0.04	-0.03		-0.02
港澳台商投资股份有限公司	Hongkong, Macao and Taiwan Solely Funds Share Holding Co. Ltd.	0.07	0.05			
外商投资企业	Foreign Invested Enterprises	7.31	2.99	1.51	0.01	0.08
中外合资经营企业	Sino-Foreign Joint Funded Enterprises	3.80	1.29	1.01		-0.13
中外合作经营企业	Sino-Foreign Cooperative Operation Enterprises	0.12	0.07			-0.02
外资企业	Foreign Funded Enterprises	3.39	1.63	0.50	0.01	0.23
外商投资股份有限公司	Foreign Invested Share Holding Co. Ltd.					
按经济组织类型分	**Grouped by type of Economic Organization**					
独资企业	Solely Funded Enterprises	15.72	7.68	2.05	0.04	-0.81
合作合伙企业	Cooperation and Partnership Enterprises	0.91	0.45	0.14	0.02	-0.05
股份有限公司	Share Holding Co. Ltd.	0.79	0.31	0.10	0.04	0.02
有限责任公司	Responsibility Co. Ltd.	6.77	2.74	1.41	0.01	-0.51
按行业分	**Grouped by Sectors**					
正餐	Dinner	18.20	8.55	2.61	0.10	-1.82
快餐	Fast Food	5.32	2.27	1.00	0.01	0.44
其他餐饮业	Other Catering	0.67	0.36	0.09		0.03

续表 Continued

单位:亿元 (10[8] yuan)

项目	Item	资产总计 Total Assets	#流动资产 Circulation	#固定资产 Fixed Asset	负债合计 Total Liabilities	#流动负债 Circulational Liabilities	#长期负债 Long Term Liabilities	所有者权益合计 Ownership Rights and Interests
总计	**Total**	**56.03**	**11.82**	**32.62**	**32.56**	**22.89**	**9.67**	**23.47**
#国有及国有控股	State-Owned and State Share Holding	37.13	7.66	22.57	21.38	15.93	5.45	15.75
按登记注册类型分	**Grouped by Type of Registeration**							
内资企业	Inner Enterprises	40.44	6.53	27.02	23.23	15.91	7.32	17.21
国有企业	State-Owned Enterprises	27.08	4.69	18.47	15.17	11.54	3.63	11.91
集体企业	Collective-Owned Enterprises	5.21	0.68	3.31	4.18	2.44	1.74	1.03
股份合作企业	Share Holding Cooperative Enterprises	1.86	0.31	1.36	0.73	0.62	0.11	1.13
联营企业	Joint-Owned Enterprises	0.16	0.09	0.06	0.12	0.12		0.04
有限责任公司	Responsibility Co. Ltd.	3.52	0.53	2.37	1.53	0.95	0.58	1.99
股份有限公司	Share Holding Co. Ltd.	2.57	0.20	1.44	1.46	0.20	1.26	1.11
私营企业	Private Enterprises	0.04	0.03	0.01	0.04	0.04		
港澳台商投资企业	Hongkong, Macao and Taiwan Funded	5.97	3.05	1.89	3.72	2.31	1.41	2.25
合资经营企业	Jointly Funded Enterprises	5.09	2.89	1.28	3.44	2.10	1.34	1.65
合作经营企业	Cooperative Operation Enterprises	0.80	0.14	0.58	0.23	0.16	0.07	0.57
港澳台商独资经营企业	Hongkong, Macao and Taiwan Solely Funded	0.05	0.01	0.01	0.04	0.04		0.01
港澳台商投资股份有限公司	Hongkong, Macao and Taiwan Solely Funded Share Holding Co. Ltd.	0.03	0.01	0.02	0.01	0.01		0.02
外商投资企业	Foreign Invested Enterprises	9.62	2.24	3.71	5.61	4.67	0.94	4.01
中外合资经营企业	Sino-Foreign Jointly Funded Enterprises	6.76	1.54	2.42	3.81	2.95	0.86	2.95
中外合作经营企业	Sino-Foreign Cooperative Operation Enterprises	0.22	0.13	0.08	0.19	0.12	0.07	0.03
外资企业	Foreign Funded Enterprises	2.64	0.57	1.21	1.61	1.60	0.01	1.03
外商投资股份有限公司	Foreign Invested Share Holding Co. Ltd.							
按经济组织类型分	**Grouped by type of Economic Organization**							
独资企业	Solely Funded Enterprises	34.97	5.95	23.00	21.00	15.61	5.39	13.97
合作合伙企业	Cooperation and Partnership Enterprises	3.04	0.66	2.08	1.27	1.03	0.24	1.77
股份有限公司	Share Holding Co. Ltd.	2.61	0.21	1.46	1.47	0.21	1.26	1.14
有限责任公司	Responsibility Co. Ltd.	15.41	5.00	6.08	8.82	6.04	2.78	6.59
按行业分	**Grouped by Sectors**							
正餐	Dinner	51.78	10.93	30.77	30.10	20.50	9.60	21.68
快餐	Fast Food	3.61	0.73	1.50	1.93	1.88	0.05	1.68
其他餐饮业	Other Catering	0.64	0.16	0.35	0.53	0.51	0.02	0.11

11－9 商品交易市场情况
TRANSACTION MARKETS

品　名 Items		1990	1995	1996	1997	1998
商品交易市场数（个）	**Number of Transations Markets (units)**	**4720**	**5111**	**5353**	**5708**	**6018**
按地区分	Grouped by Area					
城市	Urban	574	1293	1314	1521	1856
农村	Rural	4146	3818	4039	4187	4162
按市场类型分	Grouped by Type of Market					
消费品市场	Consumer Goods Market		4711	4849	5107	5322
生产资料市场	Means of Production Market		400	504	601	696
商品交易市场成交额（亿元）	**Transaction Value (10^8 yuan)**	**141.53**	**1464.68**	**2120.50**	**2668.11**	**3182.36**
按地区分	Grouped by Area					
城市	Urban	46.12	703.12	1024.92	1335.19	1637.79
农村	Rural	95.41	761.56	1095.58	1332.95	1544.57
按市场类型分	Grouped by Type of Market					
消费品市场	Consumer Goods Market		1087.39	1571.88	2002.13	2372.72
生产资料市场	Means of Production Market		377.29	548.62	665.98	809.64
按商品类别分	Grouped by Category of Commodities					
消费品	Consumer Goods		1087.39	1571.88	2002.13	2372.72
#粮油类	Grain and Edible Oil	11.18	71.47	94.69	119.43	146.66
肉食禽蛋类	Meat, Poultry and Eggs	38.32	189.49	279.58	369.20	428.83
水产品类	Aquatic Products	20.62	116.55	183.38	249.81	303.57
蔬菜类	Fresh Vegetable	19.67	102.73	173.60	211.86	260.20
干鲜果类	Dried and Fresh Fruits	10.42	64.06	93.13	112.83	141.10
工业品类	Industrial Products	23.70	465.31	647.21	829.41	938.45
生产资料	Means of Production		377.29	548.62	665.98	809.64
#钢材	Steel		128.97	150.26	178.53	236.58
木材	Timber		21.55	27.17	42.48	49.92

12. 对外经济贸易和旅游

FOREIGN ECONOMY, TRADE AND TOURISM

12 对外经济贸易和旅游

FOREIGN ECONOMY, TRADE AND TOURISM

1 9 9 8

对外贸易进出口总额	Total Value of Imports and Exports	264.26	亿美元	(USD 10^8)
#出口	Exports	156.51	亿美元	(USD 10^8)
利用外资签订合同金额	Utilization of Foreign Capital Signed Value	76.86	亿美元	(USD 10^8)
#外商直接投资	Direct Foreign Investments	75.68	亿美元	(USD 10^8)
实际利用外资	Value of Foreign Capital Actually Used	69.57	亿美元	(USD 10^8)
#外商直接投资	Direct Foreign Investments	66.52	亿美元	(USD 10^8)
旅游人数	Number of Tourists	115.40	万人次	(10000 person-times)
国际旅游收入	Foreign Exchange Income from Tourism	5.29	亿美元	(USD 10^8)

外贸进出口总额(亿美元)

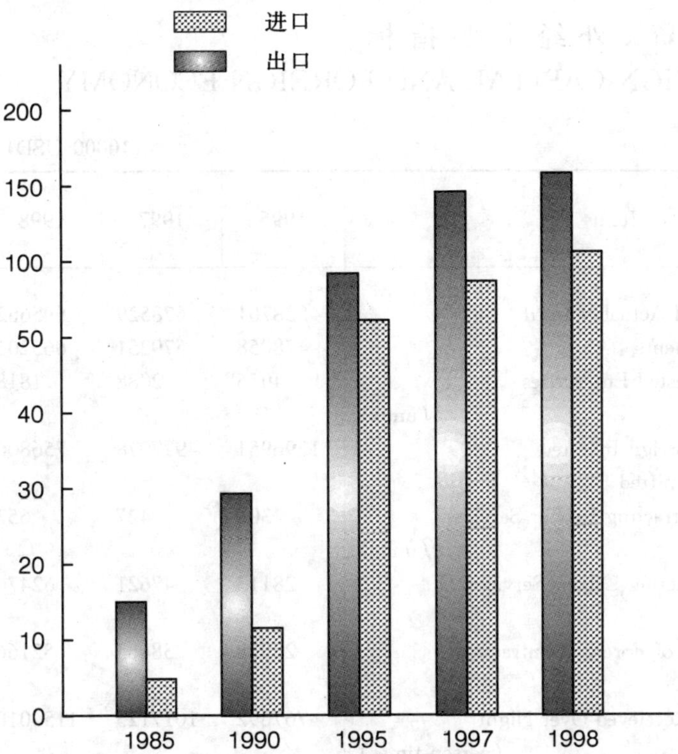

外商直接投资构成(%)

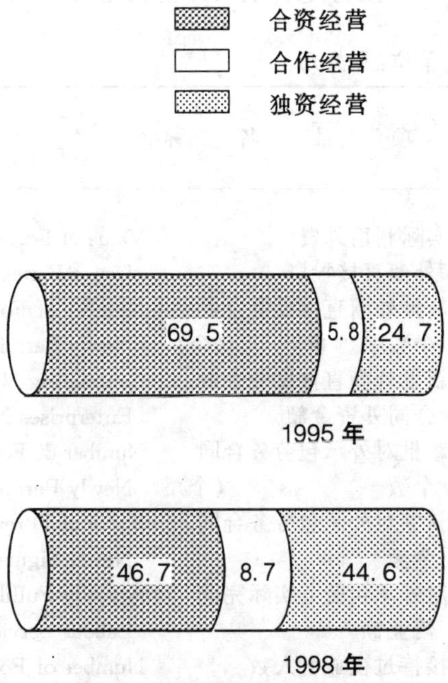

12－1 对外贸易进出口总额
TOTAL IMPORT AND EXPORT VAULE OF FOREIGN TRADE

单位:万美元 (10000 USD)

年 份 Year	海关进出口总额(经营单位) Total Import and Export Value by Customs (Running Unit)			海关进出口总额(收发货地) Total Import and Export Value by Customs (Goods Receiving and Dispatching Place)		
	合 计 Total	进 口 Import	出 口 Export	合 计 Total	进 口 Import	出 口 Export
1985	198685	40107	158578			
1986	241212	54241	186971			
1987	287307	75608	211699			
1988	345812	104062	241750			
1989	384311	130704	253607			
1990	413910	119528	294382			
1991	531019	188518	342501			
1992	696204	296037	400167			
1993	912892	447665	465227	1077540	598161	479379
1994	1175907	507280	668627	1324730	628578	696152
1995	1627803	649637	978166	1800490	794189	1006301
1996	2068789	908691	1160098	2221652	1029213	1192439
1997	2362060	953158	1408902	2529318	1088184	1441134
1998	2642608	1077499	1565109	2816639	1220908	1595731

注：对外贸易系海关统计数据(下同)。

Note：Foreign trade figures all were custom's statistics (so did follows).

12－2 外资、外经主要指标
MAJOR INDICATORS OF FOREIGN CAPITAL AND FOREIGN ECONOMY

单位:万美元 (10000 USD)

项 目 名 称	Items	1995	1997	1998
实际利用外资	Value of Foreign Capital Actuallly Used	528701	678529	695662
#外商直接投资	Direct Foreign Investments	478058	579251	665201
新批外商直接投资企业个数 (个)	Number of Foreign Invested Enterprises Newly Permitted (units)	4056	2088	1818
新批外商直接投资企业合同外资金额	Contracting Value of Foreign Invested Enterprises Newly Permitted	1296951	927078	756806
新批对外承包劳务合同个数 (个)	Number of Foreign Contracting Labour Services Newly Permitted (units)	309	427	652
新签对外承包劳务合同金额	Value of Foreign Contracting Labour Services Newly Signed	28113	47621	62476
对外承包劳务实际完成营业额	Actually Fulfilled Value of Foreign Contracting Labour Services	25928	38465	52166
接待过夜旅游人数 (人次)	Number of Foreigners Receieved Over Night (person-times)	767692	1017125	1154010

12－3　省级主要外贸企业进出口总额(1998)
TOTAL IMPORT AND EXPORT VAULE OF MAJOR PROVINCIAL LEVEL FOREIGN TRADE ENTERPRISE

单位:万美元　　　　(10000 USD)

名　称	Item	进出口总额 Total Improt and Export Value	出口 Export	进口 Import
江苏省服装进出口集团公司	Jiangsu Province Garments Import and Export Group Co.	26412	4499	21913
江苏省针棉织品进出口集团公司	Jiangsu Province Kintting and Cotton Texile Goods Import and Export Group Co.	14386	853	13533
江苏省畜产进出口集团公司	Jiangsu Province Animal Products Import and Export Group Co.	9554	1325	8229
江苏省陶瓷进出口集团公司	Jiangsu Province Pottery and Porcelain Import and Export Group Co.	2319	124	2195
江苏省粮油食品进出口集团公司	Jiangsu Province Grain and Edible Oil Foods Import and Export Group Co.	11278	2373	8905
江苏省纺织进出口集团股份公司	Jiangsu Province Texile Products Import and Export Group Stock Co.	18505	1316	17189
江苏省土产进出口集团股份公司	Jiangsu Province Local Products Import and Export Group Stock Co.	5964	174	5790
江苏省轻工进出口集团股份公司	Jiangsu Province Light Industrial Products Import and Export Group Stock Co.	21756	3487	18269
江苏省工艺品进出口集团公司	Jiangsu Province Handicraft Import and Export Group Co.	12127	462	11665
江苏省五矿进出口集团公司	Jiangsu Province Hardware and Minerals Import and Export Group Co.	5528	483	5045
中化江苏进出口公司	China Chemical Co. Jiangsu Import and Export Co.	12648	2212	10436
江苏省机械进出口集团公司	Jiangsu Province Machinery Import and Export Group Co.	24073	12606	11467
江苏省技术进出口公司	Jiangsu Province Technology Import and Export Co.	14381	4009	10372
江苏省医保进出口集团公司	Jiangsu Province Medicine and Medical Products Import and Export Group Co.	4832	75	4757
中国包装进出口江苏公司	China Package Import and Export Co. Jiangsu Co.	2754	1051	1703
中国出口商品基地建设江苏公司	China Base Construction of Export Commodities Jiangsu Co.	1537	95	1442
江苏省丝绸进出口集团股份有限公司	Jiangsu Province Silk and Satins Import and Export Group Stock Co.	22272	1413	20859
江苏省机械设备进出口集团公司	Jiangsu Province Machinery Equipment Import and Export Group Co.	46387	16962	29425
有色金属进出口公司江苏分公司	China Ferrous Metals Import and Export Co. Jiangsu Co.	3002	119	2883
中国电子进出口总公司江苏公司	China Electronic Import and Export General Co. Jiangsu Co.	1545	62	1483
江苏省图书进出口公司	Jiangsu Province Books Import and Export Co.	2740	2339	401
中化建设总公司江苏公司	China Construction General Co. Jiangsu Co.	7764	1866	5898
江苏省冶金进出口公司	Jiangsu Province Metallurgical Products Import and Export Co.	2225	915	1310
江苏省纺织工业对外贸易公司	Jiangsu Province Textile Inductry Foreign Trade Co.	3400	672	2728
江苏省对外贸易公司	Jiangsu Province Foreign Trade Co.	30166	14021	16145
华宁国际技术贸易公司	Huaning International Technical Trade Co.			
江苏省新时代工贸公司	Jiangsu Province New Era Industrial and Trade Co.	3999	583	3416
江苏省国际经济技术合作公司	Jiangsu Province International Economic	1330	68	1262
	Technical Cooperative Co.	15332	326	15006
中国石化事业金陵公司	China Petrolic and Chemical Cause Jingling Co.	1878	1152	726
中国石化国际事业扬子公司	China Petrolic and Chemical International			
	Cause Yangtze Co.	6359	3175	3184
江苏省江海粮油贸易公司	Jiangsu Province Jiang Hai Grain and Oil Trade Co.	2964	2738	226
江苏省物资集团总公司	Jiangsu Province Material Group General Co.			
江苏省机电产品总公司	Jiangsu Province Machinical and Electronic	1669	772	897
	Products General Co.	479	64	415
江苏省汽车工业销售总公司	Jiangsu Province Motor Industry Sales General Co.	801	33	768
江苏省国际经贸实业总公司	Jiangsu Province International Economic and Trade Industrial General Co.	3044	1037	2007
江苏省商业发展有限公司	Jiangsu Province Commercial Development Co. Ltd.	926	392	534

12－4 进口总额（按贸易方式分）
TOTAL VAULE OF IMPORT (BY TYPE OF TRADE)

单位:万美元 (10000 USD)

项　　目	Items	1990	1997	1998
总　　计	**Total**	**119528**	**953159**	**1077499**
一般贸易	General Trade	51375	184793	266578
国家间、国际组织无偿援助和赠送的物资	Material of Gratuilously Supporting and Contributing by Interstate and International Organizations	117	1335	375
华侨、港澳台同胞、外籍华人捐赠物资	Material Contributed by Overseas Chinese, Hongkong, Macao, Taiwan and Foreign Chinese	72	68	15
补偿贸易	Compensating Trade	1545	4	
来料加工装配贸易	Processing and Assembling Trade Provided with Raw Material	7357	112113	105314
进料加工贸易	Raw Material Input Processing Trade	31825	403840	422577
寄售、代销贸易	Consign and Commission Trade	16		
边境小额贸易	Frontier Small Value Trade			
来料加工装配进口设备	Processing and Assembling Import Equipment Provided with Material	194	23	3274
对外承包工程	Projects Contracted to Foreign Country			
租赁贸易	Rent Trade	1		
外商投资企业作为投资进口的设备、物品	Goods as Invested for Import Equipments and Articals by Foreign Invested Enterprises	25327	237876	259254
出料加工贸易	Raw Material Output Processing Trade	17	67	
易货贸易	Replace Goods with Goods Trade		1	
免税外汇贸易	Tax Free Foreign Exchange Trade		190	159
保税仓库进出境贸易	Import and Export Goods of Protective Tariff Storage		4993	14099
保税区仓储转口货物	Transit Goods of Storage in Protcetive Tariff Area		7041	7965
其他	Others	1682	815	835

12－5 出口总额（按贸易方式分）
TOTAL VAULE OF EXPORT (BY TYPE OF TRADE)

单位:万美元 (10000 USD)

项　　目	Item	1990	1997	1998
总　　计	**Total**	**294382**	**1408902**	**1565109**
一般贸易	General Trade	214024	668753	717587
国家间、国际组织无偿援助和赠送的物资	Material of Gratuilously Supporting and Contributing by Interstate and International Organizations	83	4	
华侨、港澳台同胞、外籍华人捐赠物资	Material Contributed by Overseas Chinese, Hongkong, Macao, Taiwan and Foreign Chinese			
补偿贸易	Compensating Trade	1454	362	11
来料加工装配贸易	Processing and Assembling Trade Provided with Raw Material	9334	139204	151441
进料加工贸易	Raw Material Input Processing Trade	69429	598859	694332
寄售、代销贸易	Consign and Commission Trade			
边境小额贸易	Frontier Small Value Trade	3		
来料加工装配进口设备	Processing and Assembling Import Equipment Provided with Material			
对外承包工程	Projects Contracted to Foreign Country	18	95	100
租赁贸易	Rent Trade			
外商投资企业作为投资进口的设备、物品	Goods as Invested for Import Equipments and Articals by Foreign Invested Enterprises			
出料加工贸易	Raw Material Output Processing Trade	1		91
易货贸易	Replace Goods with Goods Trade			
免税外汇贸易	Tax Free Foreign Exchange Trade			
保税仓库进出境贸易	Import and Export Goods of Protective Tariff Storage		860	1059
保税区仓储转口货物	Transit Goods of Storage in Protcetive Tariff Area		707	460
其他	Others	36	58	28

12－6 进口总额（按企业类型及经营所在地分）
TOTAL VAULE OF IMPORT (BY OWNERSHIP AND REGIONS)

单位：万美元 (10000 USD)

项　　目	Item	1997	1998
总　　计	**Total**	**953159**	**1077499**
按经济类型分	Grouped by Ownership		
#国有企业	State-owned Enterprise	189887	192966
集体企业	Collective-owned Enterprise	13295	16924
中外合资经营企业	Sino-foreign Joint Venture Enterprise	412587	433773
中外合作经营企业	Sino-foreign Cooperative Enterprise	15237	13740
外资企业	Foreign Funded Enterprise	320271	413857
按经营企业所在地分	Grouped by Regions		
#南京市	Nanjing City	80859	72665
无锡市	Wuxi City	153514	183482
徐州市	Xuzhou City	6006	7398
常州市	Changzhou City	42361	36711
苏州市	Suzhou City	398845	444194
南通市	Nantong City	96129	85251
连云港市	Liangyungang City	8510	6291
淮阴市	Huaiying City	2130	3971
盐城市	Yancheng City	8587	7303
扬州市	Yangzhou City	41489	32999
镇江市	Zhenjiang City	27136	94801
泰州市	Taizhou City	3737	5789
宿迁市	Suqian City	674	572

12－7 出口总额（按企业类型及经营所在地分）
TOTAL VAULE OF EXPORT(BY OWNERSHIP AND REGIONS)

单位：万美元 (10000 USD)

项　　目	Item	1997	1998
总　　计	**Total**	**1408902**	**1565109**
按经济类型分	Grouped by Ownership		
#国有企业	State-owned Enterprise	676003	682197
集体企业	Collective-owned Enterprise	61918	77067
中外合资经营企业	Sino-foreign Joint Venture Enterprise	358810	378522
中外合作经营企业	Sino-foreign Cooperation Enterprise	14588	13532
外资企业	Foreign Funded Enterprise	297408	413614
按经营企业所在地分	Grouped by Regions		
#南京市	Nanjing City	87337	90353
无锡市	Wuxi City	214348	259212
徐州市	Xuzhou City	13784	14632
常州市	Changzhou City	94854	105482
苏州市	Suzhou City	464658	520736
南通市	Nantong City	124129	133125
连云港市	Liangyungang City	19614	26523
淮阴市	Huaiying City	7750	10058
盐城市	Yancheng City	24716	19622
扬州市	Yangzhou City	45768	48696
镇江市	Zhenjiang City	30140	36437
泰州市	Taizhou City	8052	14511
宿迁市	Suqian City	1343	1549

12－8 进口商品分类总额
TOTAL VAULE OF IMPORT COMMODITIES BY CATEGORY

单位:万美元 (10000 USD)

项　　目	Item	1997	1998
总　　计	**Total**	**953158**	**1077499**
活动物;动物产品	Live Animal, Animal Products	2276	1665
植物产品	Vegetable Fruits and Ceredals	10604	16883
动、植物油、脂及其分解产品;精制的食用油脂;动、植物蜡	Animal and Vegetable Oil, Fats and Resolved Products Refined Elible Oil and Fats, Animal and Botanical Wax	7437	4729
食品;饮料、酒及醋;烟草及烟草代用品的制品	Food, Beverages, Liquor and Vinegar, Tobacco and Tobacco Substitures	9883	9516
矿产品	Minerals	25323	26937
化学工业及其相关工业的产品	Chemical and Related Products	73900	89160
塑料及其制品;橡胶及其制品	Plastic, Rubber and Related Products	38714	43386
生皮、皮革、毛皮及其制品;鞍具及挽具;旅行用品、手提包及类似品等	Raw Hides, Leather, Furs and Related Products, Saddle and Drawing Articals, Travelling Articals, Handbag and the Like	17849	11761
木及木制品;木炭;软木及软木制品;稻草、秸秆、篮筐及柳条等制品	Wood and Woonden Products, Charcoal, Cork and Cork Products, Rice Straw, Plaited, Basket and Wicker Products	21328	18743
木浆及其纤维状纤维素浆;纸及纸板的废碎品;纸、纸板及其制品	Paper Pulp and Fibre Shaped Cellulose Pulp, Wasted and Broken Material of Paper and Paperboard, Paper, Paperboard and Products	19052	34642
纺织原料及纺织制品	Textile Raw Materials and Products	182288	145788
鞋、帽、伞、杖、鞭及零件;羽毛及制品;人造花;人造制品	Footwear, Headwear, Umbrellas, Canes, Whip and Spare Parts, Feather and Related Products Man-made Flowers, Man-made Products	2569	3218
石料、石膏、水泥、石棉、云母及材料制品;陶瓷产品;玻璃及其制品	Raw Stone, Gypsum, Cement, Asbestos, Mica and Related Products, Ceramical Products, Glass and Related Products	9586	12716
天然或养殖珍珠、宝石或半宝石、贵金属及其制品;仿首饰;硬币	Natural or Cultivated Pearls, Gem or Semigem, Precious Metal and Related Products, Modelled Jewelry, Coin	1583	1399
贱金属及其制品	Base Metals and Related Products	70676	69215
机器、机械器具、电气设备及零件;电视图像、声音录放设备及其零附件	Machinary, Mechanical Implements, Electrical Equipment and Spare Parts, TV Pictures, Voice Recording and Broadcasting Equipment and Spare Parts	414765	540755
车辆、航空器、船舶及有关运输设备	Locomotives, Aircraft, Ship and Related Transportation Equipment	8765	8211
光学、电影、检验、医疗或外科等仪器设备;钟表;乐器及其零附件	Optical, Film, Examining, Medical or Surgical Instruments and Equipment, Clocks and Watches, Instruments and Spare Parts and Appendix	32694	35460
杂项制品	Sundry and Goods Related Products	3864	3314
艺术品、收藏品及古物	Work of Art, Collection and Antique	1	
特殊交易品及未分类商品	Special Trade Products and Others		

12－9 出口商品分类总额
TOTAL VAULE OF EXPORT COMMODITIES BY CATEGORY

单位:万美元 (10000 USD)

项　目	Item	1997	1998
总　计	**Total**	**1408902**	**1565109**
活动物;动物产品	Live Animal, Animal Products	15868	15578
植物产品	Vegetable Fruits and Ceredals	14343	16148
动、植物油、脂及其分解产品;精制的食用油脂;动、植物蜡	Animal and Vegetable Oil, Fats and Resolved Products Refined Elible Oil and Fats, Animal and Botanical Wax	6350	2771
食品;饮料、酒及醋;烟草及烟草代用品的制品	Food, Beverages, Liquor and Vinegar, Tobacco and Tobacco Substitures	29302	20395
矿产品	Minerals	9549	15955
化学工业及其相关工业的产品	Chemical and Related Products	130105	135034
塑料及其制品;橡胶及其制品	Plastic, Rubber and Related Products	26809	35570
生皮、皮革、毛皮及其制品;鞍具及挽具;旅行用品、手提包及类似品等	Raw Hides, Leather, Furs and Related Products, Saddle and Drawing Articals, Travelling Articals, Handbag and the Like	35010	32968
木及木制品;木炭;软木及软木制品;稻草、秸秆、篮筐及柳条等制品	Wood and Woonden Products, Charcoal, Cork and Cork Products, Rice Straw, Plaited, Basket and Wicker Products	11052	7973
木浆及其纤维状纤维素浆;纸及纸板的废碎品;纸、纸板及其制品	Paper Pulp and Fibre Shaped Cellulose Pulp, Wasted and Broken Material of Paper and Paperboard, Paper, Paperboard and Products	4403	4619
纺织原料及纺织制品	Textile Raw Materials and Products	497757	490332
鞋、帽、伞、杖、鞭及零件;羽毛及制品;人造花;人造制品	Footwear, Headwear, Umbrellas, Canes, Whip and Spare Parts, Feather and Related Products Man-made Flowers, Man-made Products	44468	51229
石料、石膏、水泥、石棉、云母及材料制品;陶瓷产品;玻璃及其制品	Raw Stone, Gypsum, Cement, Asbestos, Mica and Related Products, Ceramical Products, Glass and Related Products	13268	15195
天然或养殖珍珠、宝石或半宝石、贵金属及其制品;仿首饰;硬币	Natural or Cultivated Pearls, Gem or Semigem, Precious Metal and Related Products, Modelled Jewelry, Coin	4173	4331
贱金属及其制品	Base Metals and Related Products	92836	90424
机器、机械器具、电气设备及零件;电视图像、声音录放设备及其零附件	Machinary, Mechanical Implements, Electrical Equipment and Spare Parts, TV Pictures, Voice Recording and Broadcasting Equipment and Spare Parts	302787	397887
车辆、航空器、船舶及有关运输设备	Locomotives, Aircraft, Ship and Related Transportation Equipment	45130	77457
光学、电影、检验、医疗或外科等仪器设备;钟表;乐器及其零附件	Optical, Ffilm, Examining, Medical or Surgical Instruments and Equipment, Clocks and Watches, Instruments and Spare Parts and Appendix	46386	59006
杂项制品	Sundry and Goods Related Products	79161	92094
艺术品、收藏品及古物	Work of Art, Collection and Antique	102	91
特殊交易品及未分类商品	Special Trade Products and Others	44	

12－10 进口商品主要国别和地区

IMPORT VAULE OF MAJOR COMMODITIES

(BY COUNTRIES AND REGIONS)

单位:万美元 (10000 USD)

项　　目	Items	1990	1997	1998
总　　计	**Total**	**119528**	**953158**	**1077499**
亚洲地区	Asia		616644	692387
#香　港	Hongkong	9122	32587	32695
马来西亚	Malaysia	1603	13019	18475
新加坡	Singapore	2436	46594	68920
韩　国	Korea		97576	101056
台　湾	Taiwan		117177	124134
日　本	Japan	27093	255565	251892
印度尼西亚	Indonesia	478	14401	25780
泰　国	Thailand	1015	24846	40240
非洲地区	Africa		17987	11513
#埃　及	Egypt		35	145
欧洲地区	Europe		171993	244527
#欧洲共同体	European Union		132588	
#英　国	United Kingdom	1260	8106	12273
德　国	Germany	6915	50352	80547
法　国	France	849	8386	10815
意大利	Italy	3654	29042	28881
荷　兰	Netherland	6074	23963	12745
#东　欧	Estern Europe		11008	
#俄罗斯	Russia		8071	4143
乌克兰	Ukraine		868	27
拉丁美洲	Latin America		20810	16298
#阿根廷	Argentina		3253	2414
墨西哥	Mexico		2746	1308
巴　西	Brazil	570	9526	9981
智　利	Chile	5	1135	1397
北美洲	North America		100092	94855
#加拿大	Canada	1167	7220	10676
美　国	United States	28944	92872	84179
大洋洲	Oceanian		25621	17876
#澳大利亚	Austrilia	2346	21631	14296
新西兰	Newzealand	363	3990	3005

12－11 出口商品主要国别和地区
EXPORT VAULE OF MAJOR COMMODITIES
(BY COUNTRIES AND REGIONS)

单位:万美元 (10000 USD)

项　　目	Items	1990	1997	1998
总　　计	**Total**	**294382**	**1408902**	**1565109**
亚洲地区	Asia		793502	778799
#香　港	Hongkong	53437	153577	138273
马来西亚	Malaysia	1518	13903	12585
新加坡	Singapore	8542	45628	50839
韩　国	Korea		73241	53312
台　湾	Taiwan		23587	31352
日　本	Japan	66101	367644	372598
印度尼西亚	Indonesia	2619	15602	9013
泰　国	Thailand	5366	14102	11022
非洲地区	Africa		20368	24624
#埃　及	Egypt	589	4495	5410
欧洲地区	Europe		262611	351746
#欧洲共同体	European Union		230400	
#英　国	United Kingdom	5390	27787	39854
德　国	Germany	18862	61753	76957
法　国	France	6791	20327	27389
意大利	Italy	10173	25065	28351
荷　兰	Netherland	5313	61004	91866
#东　欧	Estern Europe		17385	
#俄罗斯	Russia		4857	5455
乌克兰	Ukraine		328	473
拉丁美洲	Latin America		43743	52799
#阿根廷	Argentina		5925	7436
墨西哥	Mexico		4231	6422
巴　西	Brazil	147	9045	9852
智　利	Chile	293	6006	5468
北美洲	North America		267908	333336
#加拿大	Canada	5511	21291	21761
美　国	United States	39463	246617	311561
大洋洲	Oceanian		20771	23807
#澳大利亚	Austrilia	3660	17477	20333
新西兰	Newzealand	313	2885	3192

12－12 主要商品进口数量和总额
VOLUME AND VAULE OF MAJOR IMPORT COMMODITIES

单位：数量：万吨　　(10000 tons)
　　　金额：万美元　　(10000 USD)

商品名称		Sectors		1997 数量 Volume	1997 金额 Value	1998 数量 Volume	1998 金额 Value
谷物及谷物粉		Grain and Grain Powder		5	1057	6	794
食用植物油(包括棕榈油)		Edible Vegetable Oil		11	6257	6	3749
饲料用鱼粉	(吨)	Fish Powder Used for Forage	(tons)	61985	4545	20202	1694
原木	(万立方米)	Log	(10000 m^3)	60	13584	61	11565
纸浆		Paper Pulp		14	7942	42	17775
羊毛	(吨)	Wool	(tons)	40830	20198	30515	13498
纺织用合成纤维		Synthetic Fibre for Textile		12	19934	10	13956
纺织用人造纤维	(吨)	Man-made Fibre for Textile	(tons)	33108	4692	22024	2765
成品油		Finished Oil		26	6488	39	7271
医药品	(吨)	Medicinal Products	(tons)	920	1975	407	6087
合成有机染料	(吨)	Synthetic Organic Dyeing	(tons)	1444	1311	1703	1121
初级形状的塑料		Primary Shaped Plastic		22	24491	30	26590
农药	(吨)	Chemical Pesticide	(tons)	987	630	1874	1129
牛皮革及马皮革	(吨)	Cattle Leather and Horse Leather	(tons)	6297	8705	7176	8434
纸及纸板(未切成形的)		Paper and Paperboard (Uncutting into Shapes)		11	7190	21	12128
毛纱线	(吨)	Wool Yarn Thread	(tons)	507	7292	358	619
合成纤维纱线	(吨)	Synthetic Fibre Yarn Thread	(tons)	36944	9351	35812	8397
丝绸	(万米)	Silk and Satins	(10000 m)	321	1433	235	1077
棉机织物	(万米)	Cotton Textiles	(10000 m)	6236	16845	5751	14630
合成纤维长丝机织物	(万米)	Synthetic Fibre Filament Textiles	(10000 m)	17594	33942	14319	27696
针织或钩编织物	(吨)	Knitting or Crochet Products	(tons)	13324	11343	16978	13798
钢材		Rolled Steel		55	33754	50	30955
未锻造的铜及铜材	(吨)	Unforging Copper and Copper Meterial	(tons)	29000	10079	24436	8347
废铜	(吨)	Waste Copper	(tons)	4183	1747	2020	1037
食品加工机械		Food Processing Machines			2627		1172
纺织机械		Textile Machines			31132		22209
工业用缝纫机	(台)	Industrial Use Sewing Machine	(units)	5593	912	6256	476
电视、收音机及无线电通讯设备的零附件	(吨)	TV Sets, Radio and Spare Parts of Wireless Dispatch Equipments	(tons)	4543	11723	2967	9217
集成电路及微电子组件	(万个)	Integrated Circuit and Micro-electronic Sets	(10000 units)	24526	12887	30283	22096
汽车和汽车底盘	(辆)	Vechicals and Vechical Chassis	(units)	119	868	362	1106
医疗仪器及器械		Medical Instruments and Apparatus			1668		1027
印刷品	(吨)	Printed Matter	(tons)	470	380	739	342

12－13 主要商品出口数量和总额
VOLUME AND VAULE OF MAJOR EXPORT COMMODITIES

单位：数量：万吨　金额：万美元　(10000 tons) (10000 USD)

商品名称		Sectors		1997 数量 Volume	1997 金额 Value	1998 数量 Volume	1998 金额 Value
冻鸡	（吨）	Frozen Chicken	(tons)	2561	478	1610	286
谷物及谷物粉		Grain and Grain Power		3	829	8	1943
蔬菜		Vegetables		7	8247	9	8873
干豆		Dry Beans		1	313		139
鲜、干水果及坚果		Flesh, Dried Fruits and Nuts			664		494
食用油籽		Edible Oil Seeds			216		201
食用油（包括棕榈油）	（吨）	Edible Oil (Including Palm Oil)	(tons)	84359	5768	25909	2120
食糖	（吨）	Sugar	(tons)	18489	581	6976	144
天然蜂蜜	（吨）	Natural Honey	(tons)	7326	1000	16547	1709
茶叶	（吨）	Tea	(tons)	3632	606	3167	546
猪肉罐头	（吨）	Pork Can	(tons)	3886	626	3378	537
药材	（吨）	Crude Drugs	(tons)	14789	1299	17487	2114
煤		Coal				200	6531
氧化锌及过氧化锌	（吨）	Zinc Oxide and Zinc Peroxide	(tons)	1459	135	1606	150
合成有机染料	（吨）	Synthetic Organic Dye	(tons)	23503	10838	24148	10358
医药品	（吨）	Medicines	(tons)	22876	21842	24645	24906
美容化妆品及护肤品	（吨）	Cosmetological Goods and Skin Protector	(tons)	337	196	242	245
烟花、爆竹	（吨）	Fireworks and Fire-crackers	(tons)	84	15	127	27
家用或装饰用木制品	（吨）	Wooden Products for Household and Decorated Use	(tons)	2197	852	1959	695
纺织纱线、织物及制品		Textile Yarn Thread, Woven Goods and Related Products	(tons)		193783		185678
亚麻及苎麻机织物	（万米）	Flax and Raime Machine Woven Products	(10000 m)	836	1576	1422	2381
人造纤维短纤机织物	（万米）	Man-made Fiber Short-shape Machine Woven Products	(10000 m)	20338	10706	23164	10609
平板玻璃	（万平方米）	Plate Glass	(10000 sq. m)	293	842	192	1067
钢材		Rolled Steal	(10000 sq. m)	12	8074	7	5701
金属加工机床	（万台）	Metal Processing Machine Tools	(10000 units)	77	5187	71	3963
轴承	（万套）	Bearing	(10000 units)	10950	4241	11997	5619
原电池	（万个）	Crude Battery	(10000 units)	4173	228	11630	862
收音机	（万台）	Radio Sets	(10000 units)	27	32	19	884
电视机	（万台）	TV Sets	(10000 units)	52	4154	72	5270
集装箱	（个）	Container	(unit)	13449	4964	78751	23814
汽车和汽车底盘	（辆）	Vehicals and Vehical Chasis	(unit)	1644	826	1608	1001
自行车	（万辆）	Bicycles	(10000 units)	116	5614	164	7322
服装及衣着附件		Gaments and Related Cloting Appendix			320658		322827

12－14 新签利用外资协议项目

UTILIZATION OF FOREIGN CAPITAL THROUGH NEWLY SIGNED AGREEMENT BY ITEMS

单位:个 (units)

指　　标	Item	1978－1998	1990	1995	1997	1998
总　计	**Total**	**38554**	**490**	**4292**	**2108**	**1843**
对外借款	Foreign Loans	560	42	19		
外国政府贷款	Government Loans	127	23	16		
国际金融组织贷款	Loans from International Monetary Organizations	367	14	2		
外国银行商业贷款	Loans from Foreign Commerical Bank	29	3			
买方信贷	Buyer Credit Loans	12	2	1		
对外发行证券	Issue Negotatial Securities to Foreign Country	25				
外商直接投资	Direct Foreign Investments	36175	395	4056	2088	1818
中外合资经营企业	Joint Venture	29118	358	2827	1100	908
中外合作经营企业	Cooperative Operation	1900	8	265	168	139
外资企业	Foreign Funded	5154	29	964	819	769
外商投资股份制企业	Share Holding with Foreign Investment	3			1	2
外商其他投资	Other Foreign Investment	1819		217	20	25
对外发行股票	Issuing Share Certificate to Foreign Country	6	53		2	1
补偿贸易中外商作价提供设备	Providing with Equipment in Compensation Trade Priced by Travelling Trade	552	33	22	3	3
加工装配中外商作价提供设备	Providing with Equipment and Assembling Priced by Travelling Trade	960	3	195	12	19
国际租赁	International Rent	301	17		3	2

12－15 新签利用外资协议金额

UTILIZATION OF FOREIGN CAPITAL THROUGH NEWLY SIGNED AGREEMENT BY VALUE

单位:万美元 (10000 USD)

指　　标	Item	1978－1998	1990	1995	1997	1998
总　计	**Total**	**7144822**	**36241**	**1302271**	**981316**	**768625**
对外借款	Foreign Loans	202156	9758	3688		
外国政府贷款	Government Loans	56944	7144	3116		
国际金融组织贷款	Loans from International Monetary Organizations	92908	1877	348		
外国银行商业贷款	Loans from Foreign Commerical Bank	46774	326			
买方信贷	Buyer Credit Loans	3994	411	224		
对外发行证券	Issue Negotatial Securities to Foreign Country	1536				
外商直接投资	Direct Foreign Investments	6795112	24416	1296951	927078	756806
中外合资经营企业	Joint Venture	3943302	14478	662155	452767	241152
中外合作经营企业	Cooperative Operation	619103	6640	67518	90074	66273
外资企业	Foreign Funded	2223671	3298	567278	383460	441122
外商投资股份制企业	Share Holding with Foreign Investment	9036			777	8259
外商其他投资	Other Foreign Investment	147554	2066	1632	54238	11819
对外发行股票	Issuing Share Certificate to Foreign Country	73776			52160	5199
补偿贸易中外商作价提供设备	Providing with Equipment in Compensation Trade Priced by Travelling Trade	29782	454	427	315	62
加工装配中外商作价提供设备	Providing with Equipment and Assembling Priced by Travelling Trade	15138	56	1205	1235	5749
国际租赁	International Rent	28858	1556		528	809

12-16 实际利用外资
VALUE OF FOREIGN CAPITAL ACTUALLY USED

单位:万美元 (10000 USD)

指标	Item	1995-1998	1990	1991	1993
总计	**Total**	**3606073**	**43861**	**47498**	**328735**
对外借款	Foreign Loans	320046	27696	20515	27239
外国政府贷款	Government Loans	54852	12660	5792	5533
国际金融组织贷款	Loans from International Monetary Organizations	115135	1360	5200	12299
外国银行商业贷款	Loans from Foreign Commerical Bank	114388	11580	8658	7842
买方信贷	Buyer Credit Loans	33760	2096	865	1565
对外发行证券	Issue Negotatial Securities to Foreign Country	1911			
外商直接投资	Direct Foreign Investments	3153033	14110	23324	300185
中外合资经营企业	Joint Venture	1953805	13787	20099	230438
中外合作经营企业	Cooperative Operation	234588	249	896	27520
外资企业	Foreign Funded	957731	74	2329	42227
外商投资股份制企业	Share Holding with Foreign Investment	6909			
外商其他投资	Other Foreign Investment	132994	2055	3659	1311
对外发行股票	Issuing Share Certificate to Foreign Country	73776			
补偿贸易中外商作价提供设备	Providing with Equipment in Compensation Trade Priced by Travelling Trade	18382	876	577	1247
加工装配中外商作价提供设备	Providing with Equipment and Assembling Priced by Travelling Trade	17782	36	151	
国际租赁	International Rent	23054	1143	2931	64

续表 Continued

指标	Item	1995	1996	1997	1998
总计	**Total**	**528701**	**550292**	**678529**	**695662**
对外借款	Foreign Loans	41816	25258	44373	18806
外国政府贷款	Government Loans	3067	3643	5541	4645
国际金融组织贷款	Loans from International Monetary Organizations	22371	10572	26909	3028
外国银行商业贷款	Loans from Foreign Commerical Bank	4386	10174	11240	7218
买方信贷	Buyer Credit Loans	11992	869	683	3915
对外发行证券	Issue Negotatial Securities to Foreign Country				
外商直接投资	Direct Foreign Investments	478058	507208	579251	665201
中外合资经营企业	Joint Venture	332166	313368	297197	310539
中外合作经营企业	Cooperative Operation	27684	32857	39431	57872
外资企业	Foreign Funded	118208	160983	242447	290057
外商投资股份制企业	Share Holding with Foreign Investment			176	6733
外商其他投资	Other Foreign Investment	8827	17826	54905	11655
对外发行股票	Issuing Share Certificate to Foreign Country		16417	52160	5199
补偿贸易中外商作价提供设备	Providing with Equipment in Compensation Trade Priced by Travelling Trade	681	821	541	62
加工装配中外商作价提供设备	Providing with Equipment and Assembling Priced by Travelling Trade	8017	588	1676	5585
国际租赁	International Rent	129		528	809

12－17 对外承包工程和劳务合作(国际公司)

CONTRACTED PROJECTS AND LABOR SERVICES CO-OPERATION WITH FOREIGN COUNTRIES (INTERNATIONAL CORPORATION)

年份 Year	合同数(份) Number of Contracts	合同金额(万美元) Contracted Value (USD 10000)	实际完成营业额(万美元) Fulfilled Value (USD 10000)	年末在外人数(人) Number of Persons Abroad By the End of Year (persons)
总计 Total				
1978－1980	5	617		
1981	12	921		
1982	18	895		
1983	21	1914		
1984	41	1003		
1985	88	2966		
1986	30	2935		
1987	28	2713		
1988	45	4101		
1989	125	7725		
1990	77	4046	4046	1271
1991	107	7331	6531	3068
1992	97	6854	6323	3094
1993	148	10794	8692	5296
1994	204	24756	13035	7779
1995	309	28113	25928	8206
1996	312	36379	29048	12372
1997	427	47621	38465	15046
1998	652	62476	52166	23223
对外承包工程 Contracted Projects				
1978－1980	2	262		
1981				
1982				
1983	2	785		
1984	4	715		
1985	13	262		
1986	11	1776		
1987	11	396		
1988	20	2373		
1989	17	2081		
1990	32	3571	3521	881
1991	40	5843	6157	1677
1992	38	5473	5719	1270
1993	38	6900	5848	2150
1994	70	19868	10694	3786
1995	101	19495	19774	2946
1996	148	24040	22725	3298
1997	239	34599	31011	5997
1998	224	38224	34878	5784
对外劳务合作 Labor Services				
1978－1980	3	355		
1981	12	921		
1982	18	895		
1983	19	1129		
1984	37	288		
1985	75	2704		
1986	19	1159		
1987	17	2317		
1988	25	1728		
1989	108	5644		
1990	45	475	525	390
1991	67	1488	373	1391
1992	59	1381	604	1824
1993	110	3895	2844	3146
1994	134	4887	2342	3993
1995	205	8591	6120	5260
1996	163	12253	6287	9068
1997	188	13022	7454	9049
1998	427	24250	17271	17439

12－18 国际旅游人数和收入
THE NUMBER OF INTERNATIONAL TOURISTS AND EXCHANGE INCOME

指　　标	Item	1990	1995	1996	1997	1998
接待人数　（人次）	**Number of Receptive Persons**	**724826**	**767692**	**837013**	**1017125**	**1154010**
#南京市	Nanjing City	263345	231704	225342	292510	305234
无锡市	Wuxi City	142873	150553	154461	184085	194866
徐州市	Xuzhou City	4325	4988	5233	6184	25211
常州市	Changzhou City	6570	19474	20501	23935	34046
苏州市	Suzhou City	261601	245700	251143	275656	304335
南通市	Nantong City	9594	29556	54996	89543	80687
连云港市	Liangyungang City	2400	4488	4932	4958	12075
淮阴市	Huaiying City	797	2513	1733	3282	10632
盐城市	Yancheng City	1206	3017	4296	4586	12614
扬州市	Yangzhou City	15701	38177	52583	61542	74529
镇江市	Zhenjiang City	16414	37522	53628	65756	83427
泰州市	Taizhou City			7803	4788	13294
宿迁市	Suqian City			362	300	3060
接待天数　（人天）	**Number of Receptive Person-days**	**1090121**	**1734032**	**1927684**	**2347492**	**3959041**
#南京市	Nanjing City	462279	554895	533790	661159	782235
无锡市	Wuxi City	187801	324836	356359	365010	584984
徐州市	Xuzhou City	10318	19749	17832	21746	272571
常州市	Changzhou City	17506	80119	99179	103410	246029
苏州市	Suzhou City	319285	475323	516176	594841	766809
南通市	Nantong City	33093	100342	124362	276635	366748
连云港市	Liangyungang City	11746	18290	20385	21069	121096
淮阴市	Huaiying City	1938	6262	7687	6440	101516
盐城市	Yancheng City	3555	11667	14599	14083	66960
扬州市	Yangzhou City	22190	82199	122873	160845	246591
镇江市	Zhenjiang City	20410	60350	94051	102064	233083
泰州市	Taizhou City			19898	19727	135229
宿迁市	Suqian City			493	463	35190
国际旅游收入（万美元）	**Foreign Exchange Income from Tourism (10000 USD)**	**7064**	**25988**	**31705**	**42341**	**52880**

12－19　接待外国和港澳台旅游人数和人天数
RECEPTION OF THE TOURISTS FROM ABROAD, HONGKONG, MACAO AND TAIWAN REGIONS

单位：人次、人天　　　　person-times / person-days

指　标	Item	1990	1995	1996	1997	1998
接待人数	**Number of Receptive Persons**	**724826**	**767692**	**837013**	**1017125**	**1154010**
外国人	Foreigners	219215	486794	550890	642686	695537
亚　洲	Asia			346124	426114	401349
#日　本	Japan	82559	175849	217946	248467	248295
菲律宾	Philippines	1577	2591	3905	4694	5907
新加坡	Singapore	9057	37170	34884	43462	39138
泰　国	Thailand	5197	6494	7823	6192	7275
印度尼西亚	Indonesia	1390	8308	7597	8063	4000
马来西亚	Malaysia		21893	37232	74088	63165
韩　国	Korea		23560	27527	31239	21512
蒙　古	Mongolia			120	86	160
印　度	India			1696	1829	1805
其　他	Others			7394	7994	10092
美　洲	America			57696	70198	73022
#美　国	United States	17681	40815	46233	57987	57734
加拿大	Canada	3726	7402	9026	9035	13325
其　他	Others			2437	3176	3963
欧　洲	Europe			112515	110730	129753
#英　国	United Kingdom	6081	19590	22476	19046	24536
法　国	France	6397	22091	19221	17484	17797
德　国	Germany	9158	27052	25431	26739	30481
意大利	Italy	4448	16103	12972	15483	20739
瑞　士	Switzerland			5978	4063	4349
瑞　典	Sweden			4276	3943	4051
荷　兰	Netherland			5701	6662	7758
俄罗斯	Russia	1568	1668	1838	1712	2420
西班牙	Spain		8112	5702	4944	5027
其　他	Others			8920	10654	12595
大洋洲	Oceanian			10810	12383	20365
#澳大利亚	Australia	3016	6533	7296	9619	16065
新西兰	Newzealand	456	978	1636	1434	2876
其　他	Others			1878	1330	1424
华　侨	Overseas Chinese	16505	16484	22398	18269	30585
港澳同胞	Hongkong and Macao Chinese	82481	146636	140594	197111	221355
台湾同胞	Taiwan Chinese	406625	117778	123131	159059	206533
接待人天数	**Number of Receptive Person-days**	**1090121**	**1734032**	**1927684**	**2347492**	**3959041**
外国人	Foreigners	376128	1158294	1349361	1598617	2249033
华　侨	Overseas Chinese	23022	34941	44012	36289	132213
港澳同胞	Hongkong and Maoco Chinese	142527	281358	257041	330280	761278
台湾同胞	Taiwan Chinese	548444	259439	277270	382306	816517

13. 财政、金融、保险

FINANCE ,BANKING AND INSURANCE

13 财政、金融、保险
FINANCE, BANKING AND INSURANCE

1 9 9 8

财政收入	Financial Revenue	579.90	亿元	(10^8 yuan)
#地方财政收入	Local Financial Revenue	308.20	亿元	(10^8 yuan)
财政支出	Financial Expenditure	434.17	亿元	(10^8 yuan)
金融机构存款额	Deposits Balance of Banking Institutions	6578.80	亿元	(10^8 yuan)
金融机构贷款额	Loans Balance of Banking Institutions	5063.57	亿元	(10^8 yuan)
银行现金收入	Bank Cash Revenue	10539.06	亿元	(10^8 yuan)
银行现金支出	Bank Cash	10449.24	亿元	(10^8 yuan)
承保额	Insurance Amount	16420.99	亿元	(10^8 yuan)
赔款支出	Settlement	18.61	亿元	(10^8 yuan)

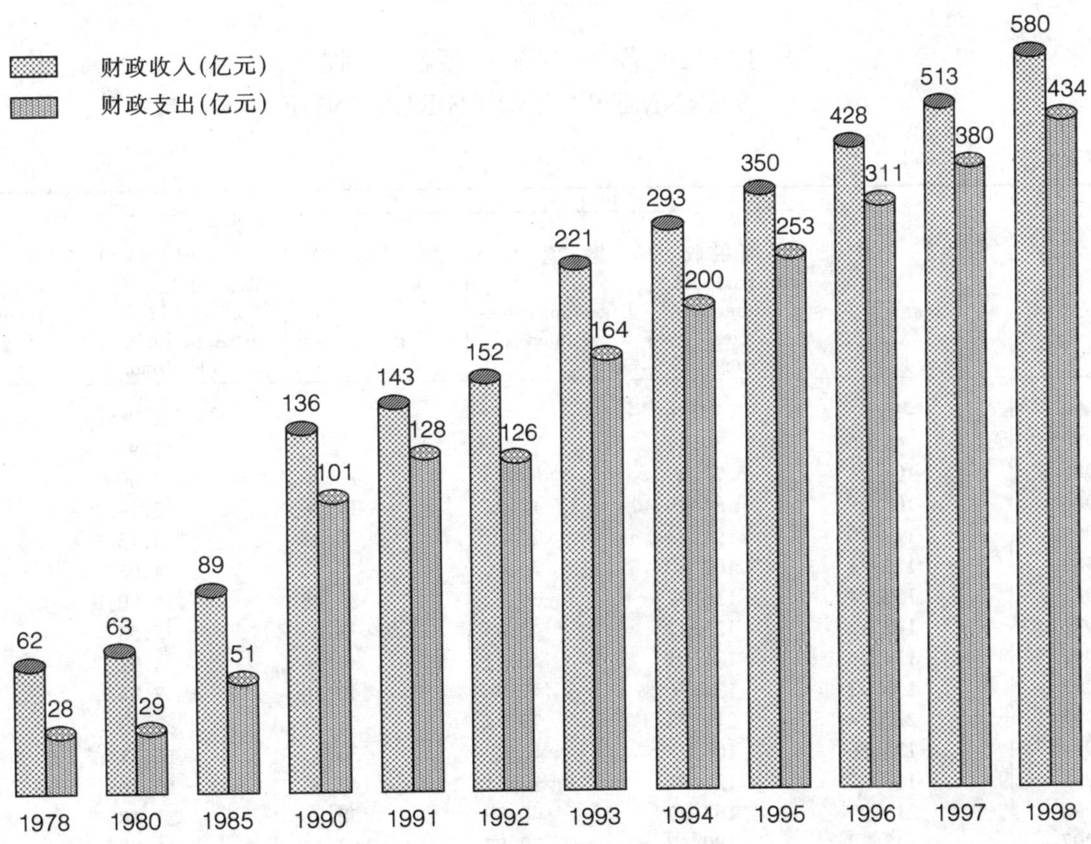

13-1 财　政　收　入
FINANCIAL REVENUE

单位:亿元　(10^8 yuan)

年份 Year	财政收入 Financial Revenue	#地方财政收入 Local Financial Revenue	#各项税收 Taxes	#上交利润 Profits Turned Over	#企业亏损补贴 Subsidies to Loss-Making Enterprise	#其他收入 Others
1978	61.09		35.93	25.04	-1.81	0.13
1980	62.45		41.36	24.57	-1.30	0.09
1985	89.00		101.74	0.24	-14.38	0.21
1986	98.73		103.69	1.44	-8.31	0.48
1987	107.17		112.70	2.74	-9.49	0.55
1988	117.96		123.41	2.09	-15.27	1.00
1989	126.39		137.64	1.32	-22.94	1.92
1990	136.20		143.12	1.81	-20.14	2.48
1991	143.29		134.24	1.28	-17.46	1.64
1992	152.31		153.92	1.40	-12.60	1.70
1993	221.30		227.24	1.06	-16.70	2.23
1994	293.41	136.62	135.86	0.56	-11.90	4.28
1995	350.08	172.64	166.97	0.30	-11.75	1.01
1996	427.99	223.17	213.00	0.49	-10.46	1.44
1997	512.90	273.20	248.39	0.53	-8.81	3.17
1998	579.90	308.20	275.64	0.57	-9.15	2.45

13-2 各　项　税　收
GOVERNMENT TAXES REVENUE

单位:亿元　(10^8 yuan)

年份 Year	合计 Total	#工商税收 Industrial and Commercial Taxes	#增值税 Taxes on Value-Added	#营业税 Run Taxes	#农牧和耕地占用税 Taxes on Use of Cultivated Land and Agriculture, Animal Husbandry	#企业所得税 Enterprise Income Taxes
1978	35.93	33.86			2.06	
1980	41.36	39.42			1.94	
1985	101.74	77.29	7.58	13.70	3.00	18.00
1986	103.69	84.10	17.26	17.38	3.19	14.96
1987	112.70	91.23	22.27	20.45	3.73	16.21
1988	123.41	102.80	35.40	27.83	4.93	14.53
1989	137.64	116.92	38.62	33.48	5.90	13.75
1990	143.12	125.42	43.45	33.83	5.55	11.13
1991	134.24	121.01	40.71	34.66	4.91	7.74
1992	153.92	137.76	47.46	40.46	7.74	7.89
1993	227.24	212.73	79.74	59.91	7.33	6.87
1994	135.86	106.74	46.10	34.27	14.31	14.81
1995	166.97	129.94	52.61	42.31	16.46	20.57
1996	213.00	163.47	60.89	58.96	21.18	28.35
1997	248.39	189.47	70.83	62.15	21.09	37.83
1998	275.64	221.52	79.06	74.85	22.68	31.45

13－3 地 方 财 政 支 出
LOCAL FINANCIAL EXPENDITURE

单位:亿元 (10⁸ yuan)

年份 Year	地方财政支出 Local Expenditure	#基本建设 Capital-Construction	#企业挖潜改造资金 Technical Updates and Tranformation of Enterprise	#科技三项费用 New Products Promotion Funds	#城市维护费 City Maintenance	#科教文卫事业费 Culture, Education Science and Health Care	#行政管理费 Adiministration
1978	28.38	9.26	1.37		0.39	4.98	1.80
1980	28.95	8.67	1.76	0.49	0.67	6.79	2.33
1985	50.53	7.22	1.68	0.71	3.43	14.70	4.88
1986	66.14	6.98	2.13	0.58	4.80	17.61	6.07
1987	68.00	5.91	1.52	0.79	4.27	18.78	6.57
1988	81.45	5.35	2.47	0.67	5.09	22.72	8.53
1989	92.25	5.25	1.80	0.82	5.98	26.16	10.25
1990	100.97	5.70	1.91	1.00	6.12	29.65	11.85
1991	128.18	6.91	2.86	1.31	6.78	32.83	13.30
1992	125.86	7.20	2.59	1.44	6.93	38.28	16.75
1993	163.87	10.18	13.94	2.27	12.70	49.62	22.54
1994	200.17	13.81	12.68	1.59	12.84	72.78	33.99
1995	253.49	18.69	14.62	2.33	17.29	82.69	40.75
1996	310.94	21.00	19.13	3.29	20.31	103.19	52.45
1997	379.51	25.88	26.30	4.34	25.08	118.96	57.81
1998	434.17	30.67	27.21	4.99	28.35	136.75	68.77

13－4 用 于 农 业 的 财 政 支 出
SUPPORTING AGRICULTURAL PRODUCTION

单位:亿元 (10⁸ yuan)

年份 Year	农业支出 Agricultural Expenditure	支援农业生产支出 Expeditures for Sopporting Agricultural Production	农林水气象等部门事业费 Agriculture, Forestry, Irrigation, Meteorology Expenditures	农业基础建设支出 Expenditures of Agricultural Infrastructure Construction	#科技三项费用 New Products Promotion Funds	其他 Others
1978	7.11	1.37	2.78	1.97		0.99
1980	6.39	1.31	2.29	1.89	0.04	0.86
1985	4.62	2.04	2.01	0.44	0.07	0.06
1986	5.46	2.46	2.48	0.41	0.08	0.03
1987	5.69	2.58	2.47	0.53	0.08	0.03
1988	6.92	3.59	2.64	0.59	0.06	0.04
1989	8.50	5.11	2.67	0.63	0.07	0.02
1990	9.20	5.47	2.98	0.63	0.10	0.02
1991	11.42	6.19	4.27	0.81	0.11	0.04
1992	11.85	7.15	3.74	0.82	0.12	0.02
1993	19.19	13.83	4.13	1.08	0.11	0.04
1994	17.14	10.52	5.33	1.10	0.13	0.06
1995	14.99	7.17	6.34	1.28	0.19	0.01
1996	25.57	8.62	8.42	1.65	0.35	0.53
1997	30.09	10.44	10.74	1.77	0.52	6.62
1998	31.21	11.45	12.62	6.20	0.55	0.39

13-5 用于文教、卫生、科学部门的财政支出
FINANCIAL EXPENDITURE ON EDUCATION, HEALTH AND SCIENCE

单位:亿元 (10^8 yuan)

年 份 Year	合 计 Total	#教 育 Education	#卫 生 Health	#公费医疗 Free Medical Services	#科 学 Science	#通讯广播 Communication and Broadcast	#计划生育 Birth Control
1978	4.98	3.07	1.35	0.21	0.06	0.11	0.09
1980	6.79	4.31	1.48	0.29	0.07	0.14	0.12
1985	14.70	9.24	2.67	0.81	0.24	0.36	0.24
1986	17.61	10.66	3.31	0.99	0.27	0.47	0.30
1987	18.78	11.25	3.05	1.22	0.68	0.44	0.31
1988	22.72	14.14	3.37	1.68	0.74	0.49	0.34
1989	26.16	15.95	3.75	2.28	0.79	0.56	0.37
1990	29.65	18.24	4.13	2.69	0.94	0.68	0.49
1991	32.83	19.52	4.72	3.37	1.06	0.76	0.58
1992	38.28	23.31	5.17	3.79	1.22	0.85	0.82
1993	49.62	30.33	6.27	5.47	1.43	1.13	1.00
1994	72.78	47.58	8.95	6.61	2.03	1.26	1.17
1995	82.69	52.91	9.62	8.57	2.26	1.41	1.45
1996	103.19	66.68	11.69	10.65	2.86	1.71	1.75
1997	118.96	75.59	26.88	12.62	3.53	1.88	2.10
1998	136.75	89.73	28.63	13.92	4.01	1.88	2.42

13-6 财 政 价 格 补 贴
FINANCIAL PRICE SUBSIDIES

单位:亿元 (10^8 yuan)

年 份 Year	合 计 Total	粮棉油价格补贴 Grain, Cotton, Oil Price Subsidies	平抑物价等补贴 Subsidies for Price Increases	肉食价格补贴 Subsidies for Increases in Meat Price	其他价格补贴 Others
1980	4.55	2.21			2.34
1985	8.17			1.38	6.79
1986	15.55	10.36	0.89	1.95	2.35
1987	16.94	11.00	2.19	1.51	2.24
1988	18.16	10.80	3.17	1.66	2.53
1989	19.38	11.84	3.36	1.79	2.39
1990	20.37	12.57	3.25	1.74	2.81
1991	18.41	7.32	3.34	2.10	5.65
1992	22.90	12.03	2.00	1.95	6.92
1993	5.48	0.41	0.69	1.61	2.77
1994	6.65	0.41	0.62	1.55	4.07
1995	11.15	0.08	0.16	1.23	9.68
1996	13.00	0.73	0.38	1.21	10.68
1997	10.90	0.09	0.11	1.12	9.58
1998	14.14	0.46	0.13	1.13	12.42

13－7 主要年份全社会存贷款年末余额
TOTAL DEPOSIT AND LOANS BALANCE (YEAR-END)

单位:亿元 (10⁸ yuan)

年 份 Year	全社会年末存款余额 Deposit Balance	#银行系统 Bank System	全社会年末贷款余额 Loans Balance	#银行系统 Bank System
1952	3.28	3.28	1.31	1.31
1957	6.03	6.03	12.53	12.53
1962	13.13	13.13	30.82	30.82
1965	20.47	20.47	33.52	33.52
1970	34.01	34.01	56.39	56.39
1975	48.89	48.89	83.74	83.74
1978	60.72	59.87	115.29	112.75
1980	95.55	90.46	159.11	151.97
1981	124.54	122.20	195.33	191.43
1982	146.21	140.91	217.87	212.86
1983	171.12	160.71	242.28	228.76
1984	221.68	194.12	333.40	303.02
1985	247.12	218.39	387.06	354.89
1986	372.62	311.49	528.83	481.80
1987	443.44	363.35	659.29	571.68
1988	517.81	395.02	742.10	616.34
1989	640.84	481.43	835.56	688.93
1990	860.33	645.65	1013.45	822.70
1991	1136.51	915.36	1230.49	1043.21
1992	1422.61	1141.82	1480.80	1242.36
1993	1797.33	1456.96	1777.80	1469.35
1994	2481.10	1876.21	2218.15	1775.37
1995	3500.49	2606.45	2875.39	2191.72
1996	4706.36	3582.25	3840.74	3023.59
1997	5674.94	4276.37	4452.46	3646.58
1998	6578.80	5131.45	5063.57	4264.77

注:1996 年末全省金融机构资金来源和资金运用各项目余额数含有关金融机构违规经营和帐外经营资金并帐数据。

1997 年起银行机构口径为:国有独资商业银行,其他商业银行、农业发展银行和城市合作银行。

Notes: 1) The balance of fund and utilization of fund in financial institutions in 1996 included statistics of fund from unlawful and extra-account operations in some financial institutions.

2) The bore of banking institutions since 1997 is: state-run commercial banks with sole investment, other commercial banks, agricultural development banks and city cooperative banks.

13－8 银行存贷款年末余额
BANK DEPOSITS AND LOANS BALANCE (YEAR－END)

单位:亿元 (10⁸ yuan)

指标	Items	1985	1990	1995	1997	1998
各项存款	**Deposits**	**218.39**	**645.65**	**2606.45**	**4276.37**	**5131.45**
#企业存款	Enterprises Deposits	80.61	188.21	1021.29	2065.42	2384.90
财政性存款	Treasury Deposits	6.49	10.37	49.97	21.29	17.22
城镇储蓄存款	Urban Savings Deposits	57.81	324.37	1447.10	2163.08	2620.76
#定期储蓄	Deposits for A Fixed Term		297.57	1236.03	1838.34	2211.53
农业存款	Rural Deposits	31.50	57.63	13.28	16.83	17.98
各项贷款	**Loans**	**354.89**	**822.70**	**2191.72**	**3646.58**	**4264.77**
#短期贷款	Loans for A Short Term	286.17	685.73	1697.69	3019.76	3473.18
#工业贷款	Industrial Loans	100.31	277.02	606.19	1027.58	1173.23
商业贷款	Commersial Loans	177.06	350.25	736.47	1030.74	1100.25
乡镇企业贷款	Rural and Town Enterprises Loans		44.78	86.22	158.14	186.01
农业贷款	Agricultural Loans	24.10	20.10	45.31	89.24	119.21
中长期贷款	Long/Middle Term Loans	31.46	84.49	391.19	576.83	640.22

13－9 农村信用合作社存贷款年末余额
RURAL CREDIT ASSOCIATION DEPOSITS AND LOANS BALANCE (YEAR－END)

单位:亿元 (10⁸ yuan)

指标	Items	1985	1990	1995	1997	1998
各项存款	**Deposits**	**55.86**	**167.14**	**522.30**	**792.56**	**887.60**
#农业存款	Agriculture Deposits	6.32	9.51		125.18	141.29
企业存款	Enterprise Deposits	6.85	13.65		16.04	25.15
农民个人储蓄存款	Individual Deposits	41.54	140.13	434.37	639.25	709.75
各项贷款	**Loans**	**33.81**	**106.65**	**403.62**	**527.46**	**569.94**
#农业贷款	Agriculture Loans	2.35	11.36	44.86	75.46	115.19
企业贷款	Enterprise Loans	27.65	85.77	281.31	350.68	369.39
私营企业及个体贷款	Private Enterprise and Individual Loans	0.07	0.07			

13－10 银 行 现 金 收 入
CASH REVENUE OF NATIONAL BANKING SYSTEM

单位：亿元 (10⁸ yuan)

项 目	Items	1980	1985	1990	1995	1997	1998
收入总计	**Total**	**143.74**	**463.82**	**1240.65**	**6960.65**	**9304.27**	**10539.06**
商品销售收入	Commodity Sales	94.66	222.14	477.31	1650.22	1949.10	2148.38
服务事业收入	Service Trade	8.69	19.62	58.64	256.82	400.07	637.08
税款收入	Taxes	0.20	1.84	7.79	32.33	40.89	53.67
农村信用社收入	Rural Credit Cooperatives		1.40	223.63	722.87	112.66	
乡镇企事业收入	Township Enterprises and Nonprofit Institutions	2.57	37.29	44.16	389.92	553.53	
城乡个体经营收入	Individual Business		19.93	3.72	90.21	215.54	339.04
储蓄存款收入	Saving Deposits	14.63	140.81	343.01	2932.99	4851.42	6166.19
其他金融机构收入	Other Banking Institutions			9.74	196.50	258.90	138.81
汇兑收入	Remittances	1.44	3.55	12.34	101.94	108.58	145.94
债券收入	Debts			9.18	524.85	82.33	107.95
其他收入	Others	3.24	17.25	51.13	62.70	751.25	722.73

13－11 银 行 现 金 支 出
CASH EXPENDITURES OF NATIONAL BANKING SYSTEM

单位：亿元 (10⁸ yuan)

项 目	Items	1980	1985	1990	1995	1997	1998
支出总计	**Total**	**149.14**	**478.55**	**1251.41**	**7040.95**	**9487.61**	**10449.24**
工资及对个人其他支出	Wages and Other Payments to Individuals	46.85	106.52	262.01	890.20	1057.02	1244.52
农副产品采购支出	Purchases of Agricultural and Sideline Products	22.76	75.01	132.74	242.31	225.41	173.75
行政企业管理费支出	Government and Enterprises Overhead	7.17	21.05	79.51	488.54	647.25	967.71
农村信用社支出	Rural Credit Cooperatives		0.35	317.33	1018.64	338.87	
乡镇企事业支出	Township Enterprises and Nonprofit Institutions	5.79	78.80	84.45	598.29	791.58	
个体经营支出	Individual Business		34.40	8.26	107.18	238.10	421.13
储蓄存款支出	Saving Deposits	11.47	131.58	261.61	2697.12	4781.02	6068.72
其他金融机构支出	Other Banking Institutions				169.18	246.45	96.20
汇兑支出	Remittances	3.03	7.80	18.86	104.82	106.34	111.66
工矿产品收购支出	Purchase of Industrial and Mineral Products		2.15	6.76	42.07	64.82	328.98
债券支出	Debts			7.33	52.45	62.57	103.83
其他支出	Others	4.05	20.89	64.68	629.66	898.28	848.31

13－12 银行现金投放回笼差额

CASH STATISTICS OF NATIONAL BANKING SYSTEM

单位：亿元 (10^8 yuan)

年份 Year	现金收入 Cash Revenue	现金支出 Cash Expenditures	投放 Monetary Issues
1952	30.05	28.49	－1.56
1962	37.20	34.64	－2.56
1965	40.18	40.41	0.23
1970	46.31	44.46	－1.85
1975	68.56	68.93	0.37
1978	85.29	88.98	3.19
1980	143.74	149.14	5.40
1985	463.82	478.55	14.73
1986	531.49	546.12	14.67
1987	696.64	713.69	17.25
1988	966.24	1031.70	65.50
1989	1109.90	1132.10	22.20
1990	1240.65	1251.41	10.76
1991	1533.50	1570.28	36.78
1992	2220.31	2313.48	93.17
1993	3470.96	3586.97	116.01
1994	5149.10	5289.50	140.40
1995	6960.65	7040.95	80.30
1996	7935.11	8074.89	139.78
1997	9304.27	9487.61	183.34
1998	10539.06	10449.24	－89.82

注：投放栏中的负数表示现金回笼。

Note: Withdrawal of currency is the negative number in monetary issue.

13－13 信用社现金收支

CASH EXPENDITURES OF RURAL CREDIT COOPERATIVES

单位：亿元 (10^8 yuan)

项目	Items	1990	1995	1997	1998
农村信用社	**Rural Credit Cooperatives**				
现金收入	Cash Revenue	311.61	1421.69	2346.15	2572.44
#个体存款收入	Individual Savings Deposits	216.37	952.49	1347.18	1425.45
现金支出	Cash Expenditures	403.33	1709.41	2622.12	2855.79
#个体存款支出	Individual Savings Deposits	213.35	969.17	1360.79	1368.42
城市信用社	**Urban Credit Cooperatives**				
现金收入	Cash Revenue	26.38	426.49	509.02	296.84
#商品销售收入	Commodity Sales	14.45	180.17	166.16	91.70
服务事业收入	Service Trade	2.48	33.70	43.22	24.71
现金支出	Cash Expenditures	24.77	390.78	459.47	290.10
#集体单位工资支出	Wages to Collective Units	6.01	43.77	37.08	31.51
行政管理费支出	Government and Enterprises Overhead	2.54	51.86	46.78	32.45

13－14 保险业务主要指标（1998）
MAJOR INDICATORS OF INSURANCE BUSINESS

单位：万元 (10000 yuan)

指标	Items	保额 Insurance Value	保费收入 Premiums	储金收入 Deposit Business	赔款支出 Indemnite Expenditure
总计	**Total**	**164209912**	**1041131**	**40321**	**186101**
财产险	Property Insurance	94293005	348315.4	12809	162536
企业财产险	Enterprise Property Insurance	54993807	107286.8		40141
机动车辆险	Machine Driving Cars Insurance	15307751	177033.1		95714
船舶险	Ships Insurance	541459	6482		4745
货运险	Freight Transport Insurance	13060004	30207.78		10349
工程责任险	Projects Responsibility Insurance	4355036	13024	48	5080
家庭财产险	Family Property Insurance	5123038	9760.81	12727	4693
农业险	Agricultural Insurance	133571	737	4	435
其他险	Others	778339	3784	30	1379
人寿险	Personal Insurance	69916907	692816	27512	23565
意外险	Accident Insurance	17966434	29166.93	5385	8576
健康险	Healthy Insurance	45358971	19651		11390
养老金险	Pension Insurance	111588	292084		226
子女教育婚嫁金险	Education and Marriage Insurance for Children	198349	61359		581
其他寿险	Others	6281565	290555	22127	2792
中保财产保险公司	**PICC (Property)**				
财产险	Property Insurance	64174905	251782	9908	117269
企业财产险	Enterprise Property Insurance	34167131	74203		29162
机动车辆险	Machine Driving Cars Insurance	13073963	129796		68349
船舶险	Ships Insurance	358132	4657		2914
货运险	Freight Transport Insurance	8481642	21954		7031
工程责任险	Projects Responsibility Insurance	3662816	11740	48	4946
家庭财产险	Family Property Insurance	4156208	8094	9856	4218
农业险	Agricultural Insurance	133571	737	4	435
其他险	Others	141442	601		214
中保人寿保险公司	**PICC (Life)**				
人寿险	Personal Insurance	56887939	463394		22891
意外险	Accident Insurance	9396998	23956	22127	8111
健康险	Healthy Insurance	45116864	18241		11181
养老金险	Pension Insurance	21679	176284		226
子女教育婚嫁金险	Education and Marriage Insurance for Children	34377	34268		581
其他寿险	Others	2318021	210645	22127	2791
中国平安财产保险公司	**PAICC (Property)**				
财产险	Property Insurance	8039249	24569		13165
企业财产险	Enterprise Property Insurance	5927922	8416		2893
机动车辆险	Machine Driving Cars Insurance	482905	11890		7989
船舶险	Ships Insurance	41517	355		291
货运险	Freight Transport Insurance	1331241	2647		1602
工程责任险	Projects Responsibility Insurance				
家庭财产险	Family Property Insurance	189155	441		41
农业险	Agricultural Insurance				
其他险	Others	66509	820		349

续表 Continued

单位：万元 (10000 yuan)

指 标	Items	保 额 Insurance Value	保费收入 Premiums	储金收入 Deposit Business	赔款支出 Indemnite Expenditure
中国平安人寿保险公司	**PAICC (Life)**				
人寿险	Personal Insurance	2866458	73436	1639	581.1
意外险	Accident Insurance	2315804	1147	1639	372.1
健康险	Healthy Insurance	77326	335		209.0
养老金险	Pension Insurance	89909	14792		
子女教育婚嫁金险	Education and Marriage Insurance for Children	163972	23091		
其他寿险	Others	219447	30071		
中国太平洋保险公司	**CPIC**				
财产险	Property Insurance	20483117	66209	2307	30479
企业财产险	Enterprise Property Insurance	13790591	22887		7548
机动车辆险	Machine Driving Cars Insurance	1612941	32197		18434
船舶险	Ships Insurance	138430	1450		1540
货运险	Freight Transport Insurance	3049393	5194		1610
工程责任险	Projects Responsibility Insurance	692220	1284		134
家庭财产险	Family Property Insurance	724843	1160	2277	409
农业险	Agricultural Insurance				
其他险	Others	474699	2037	30	804
人寿险	Personal Insurance	9427844	155728	2394	
意外险	Accident Insurance	5518966	3806	2394	
健康险	Healthy Insurance	164781	1075		
养老金险	Pension Insurance		101008		
子女教育婚嫁金险	Education and Marriage Insurance for Children				
其他寿险	Others	3744097	49839		
大众保险公司	**MIC**				
财产险	Property Insurance	80174	781.43		
企业财产险	Enterprise Property Insurance	37956	40.78		
机动车辆险	Machine Driving Cars Insurance	25887	690.06		
船舶险	Ships Insurance	3380	20		
货运险	Freight Transport Insurance	11383	24.78		
工程责任险	Projects Responsibility Insurance				
家庭财产险	Family Property Insurance	1568	5.81		
农业险	Agricultural Insurance				
其他险	Others				
人寿险	Personal Insurance	4835993	11945.95	2540	3877
意外险	Accident Insurance	39695	40.95		
天安保险公司	**TAIC**				
财产险	Property Insurance	1515560	4974	594	1623
企业财产险	Enterprise Property Insurance	1070207	1740		538
机动车辆险	Machine Driving Cars Insurance	112055	2460		942
船舶险	Ships Insurance				
货运险	Freight Transport Insurance	186345	388		106
工程责任险	Projects Responsibility Insurance				
家庭财产险	Family Property Insurance	51264	60	594	25
农业险	Agricultural Insurance				
其他险	Others	95689	326		12
人寿险	Personal Insurance	694971	217	1352	93
意外险	Accident Insurance	694971	217	1352	93

14. 科技教育

SCIENCE AND TECHNOLOGY, EDUCATION

14 科技 教育
SCIENCE AND TECHNOLOGY, EDUCATION

1 9 9 8

科技机构数	Number of Scientific and Technical Research Institutions	2166	个	(unit)
科技活动人数	Number of Persons Engaged in Scientific and Technical Activities	23.35	万人	(10000 persons)
各类专业技术人员	Scientific Technical Personnel in State-Owned Units	202.15	万人	(10000 persons)
高等学校	Institutions of Higher Education	66	所	(number)
研究生在读人数	Graduate Student Enrollment	1.52	万人	(10000 persons)
普通高校在校学生	Student Enrollment of Regular Institutions of Higher Education	27.32	万人	(10000 persons)
成人高校在校学生	Student Enrollment of Adult Institutions of Higher Education	20.01	万人	(10000 persons)
普通中学在校学生	Student Enrollment of Regular Secondary Schools	324.24	万人	(10000 persons)
高校专任教师	Full-time Teachers of Institutions of Higher Education	2.86	万人	(10000 persons)

各类专业技术人员(万人)

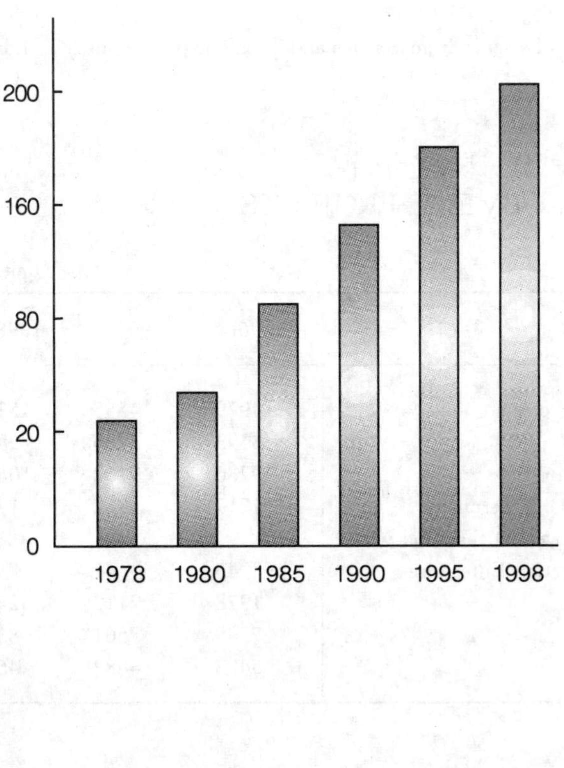

各类技术人员构成(%)

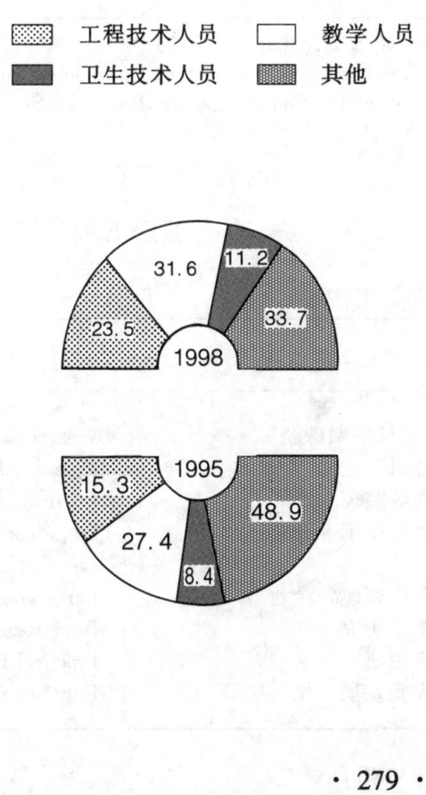

14－1 科技活动基本情况
BASIC STATISTICS FOR SCIENTIFIC AND TECHNICAL ACTIVITIES

单位:亿元 (10[8] yuan)

指标	Items	1996	1997	1998
科技机构数 (个)	**Number of Scientific and Technical Research Institutions**	**2533**	**2136**	**2166**
#科研单位	Research Institutions	334	402	394
大中型工业企业	Large and Medium Industrial Enterprises	1504	1360	1403
大中型建筑企业	Large and Medium Construction Enterprises	28	28	
高等院校	Institutions of Higher Education	383	346	369
科技活动人员数 (万人)	**Persons Engaged in Scientific and Technical Activities (10000 persons)**	**25.19**	**25.24**	**23.35**
#科学家、工程师	Scientific and Engineering	15.11	15.42	13.11
科技活动经费收入总额	**Funding for Scientific and Technical Research**	**86.42**	**98.16**	**106.70**
上级拨款	Apropriations	13.15	14.48	22.03
自筹资金	Private	55.97	67.57	62.02
银行贷款	Loans	12.81	12.22	15.80
其他收入	Others	4.49	3.89	6.85
科技活动经费支出总额	**Expenditures of Scientific and Technical Research Funds**	**78.26**	**87.33**	**97.97**
#内部支出	Internal Expenses	72.14	82.38	92.22
#劳务费	Service Fees	11.88	13.35	18.48
业务费	Professional Fees	23.43	29.56	34.35
其他	Others	18.47	20.18	11.87
固定资产购建支出	Purchasing Fixed Assets	18.36	19.29	27.52
研究与发展经费支出	Research and Development Expenses	25.00	25.17	32.52
研究与发展经费支出占国内生产总值比重 (%)	Proportion of Research and Development Expenses to GDP	0.41	0.38	0.45

注：本表数据根据科委、教委和统计局科技统计年报综合汇总。

Note: Figures in the table are based on statistical annual report of science from Science and Techlonogy Commission, Education Commission and Provincial Statistical Bureau.

14－2 研究与发展课题情况
RESEARCH AND DEVELOPMENT PROJECTS

单位:项 (units)

指标	Items	1996	1997	1998
研究与发展课题	Research and Development Projects	14979	14555	15394
#科研单位	Research Institutins	3393	2785	2860
高等院校	Institutes of Higher Education	9786	9762	10609
大中型工业企业 (万元以上)	Large and Medium Industrial Enterprises (over 10 thousand yuan)	1717	1967	1925
大中型建筑企业	Large and Medium Construction Enterprises	45	41	
#基础研究	Basic Research	1978	2112	2420
应用研究	Practical Research	7599	7561	8314
实验发展	Experiment Development	5402	4882	4660

14－3 县级以上政府部门所属研究与开发机构基本情况
BASIC STATISTICS ON GOVERNMENTAL DEPARTMENT RESEARCH AND DEVELOPMENT INSTITUTIONS ABOVE COUNTY LEVEL

项 目	Items	1990	1995	1997	1998
机构数 （个）	Number of Institutions	326	337	328	321
职工总数 （人）	Personnel (person)	55987	53090	50211	47926
#科学家工程师	Scientists and Engineers	24269	24428	34227	22415
其他科技人员	Others	11103	10796	21524	8617
经费收入总额 （万元）	Revenues (10000 yuan)	107958.1	285637.6	440632.8	507722.6
#政府拨款	Appropriations from Government	33774.7	68776.0	113842.8	142552.4
经费支出总额 （万元）	Expenditures (10000 yuan)	93615.5	285725.4	410324.3	429746.6
#基本建设支出	Capital Construction	7426.3	24379.1	22050.5	19575.7

注：县级以上政府部门所属研究与开发机构1991、1992年不包括国防科工委归口管理的研究机构，以下表同。
Note: The Institution excluded the National Defence Council's Institutions in 1991, 1992, the same as next figures.

14－4 县级以上政府部门所属研究与开发机构(1998)
GOVERNMENTAL DEPARTMENT RESEARCH AND DEVELOPMENT INSTITUTIONS ABOVE COUNTY LEVEL

项 目	Items	机构数（个） Institution	职工总数（人） Personnal	#科学家工程师 Scientist and Engineers	经费收入总额（万元） Revenues (10000yuan)	#政府拨款 Appropriations	经费支出总额（万元） Expenditures (10000yuan)
总 计	**Total**	**321**	**47926**	**22415**	**507722.6**	**142552.4**	**429746.6**
按隶属关系分	By Administrative Relationship						
国务院部门属	Departments of the State Council	55	25669	13407	343693.7	107851.5	283862.5
省 属	Departments of Province	77	11915	5158	88149.0	28647.3	80754.0
省辖市属	Departments of City under Province	189	10342	3850	75879.9	6053.6	65130.1
按国民经济行业分	By Sector						
农、林、牧、渔、水利业	Farming, Forestry, Animal Husbandry, Fishery and Water-Conservancy	52	5099	1869	36223.6	15218.8	34179.2
制造业	Manufacturing	138	28166	12041	275960.7	94820.6	235853.9
地质普查和勘探业	Geological Prospeting	14	2576	1626	18999.7	8275.1	17822.6
建筑业	Construction	16	1322	889	9783.4	671.3	8377.1
交通运输、邮电通讯业	Transportation, Postal and Telecommunications	4	307	190	4839.8	1837.9	4058.9
房地产管理、公用事业、居民服务和咨询业	Real Estate Managment, Public Facilities Services, Residential Service and Consultancy Services	8	484	241	1801.5	638.8	1733.9
卫生、体育和社会福利事业	Health Care, Sporting and Social Welfare	22	2216	1065	24103.0	3858.8	22209.5
教育、文化艺术和广播电视业	Education, Culture and Arts, Radio, Film and Television	2	37	30	857.6	153.3	761.0
科学研究和综合技术服务事业	Scientific Research and Polytechnical Services	54	4508	2621	27986.2	13591.8	23390.6
其他	Others	11	3211	1843	107167.1	3486.0	81359.9

14－5　县级以上政府部门所属研究与开发机构成果
PROJECTS OF GOVERNMENTAL DEPARTMENT RESEARCH AND DEVELOPMENT INSTITUTIONS ABOVE COUNTY LEVEL

年　份 Year	科学著作(万字) Scientific Works (10000 words)	科学论文(篇) Papers	获奖成果(项) Prized Achievements
1987	2138	2532	559
1988	1915	2561	511
1989	1717	3265	495
1990	2540	3728	579
1991	2454	3392	525
1992	2086	3962	477
1993	2273	4629	532
1994	2783	4049	494
1995	4196	4662	468
1996	107(部 Book)	4378	490
1997	93(种 Book)	4906	529
1998	92(种 Book)	4798	361

14－6　县级以上政府部门所属研究与开发机构课题情况（1998）
PROJECTS OF TECHNOLOGY DEVELOPMENT ORGANIZATIONS OF ABOVE COUNTY LEVEL GOVERNMENTAL DEPARTMENT

项　目	Items	课题数(项) Projects (item)	投入人员(人年) Labor Force (person/year)	#科学家工程师 Scientist	投入经费(万元) Funds Input (10000 yuan)	课题平均经费(万元) Per Funds by Project (10000 yuan/item)
总　计	**Total**	**5159**	**15315.2**	**11752.4**	**461623.2**	**89.5**
按课题来源分	By Sources					
国　家	National	1797	6823.3	5435.6	304818.8	169.6
地　方	Local	1399	2751.2	2110.0	14948.9	10.7
企业委托	Enterprises	842	2367.1	1698.7	94204.6	111.9
自　选	Self-selected	710	2028.6	1409.4	25150.1	35.4
国际合作	International coorperate	90	169.9	125.2	3310.6	36.8
其　他	Others	321	1175.1	973.3	19190.2	59.8
按活动类型分	By Type					
基础研究	Basic Research	267	525.2	479.8	6318.0	23.7
应用研究	Practical Research	1051	3047.5	2609.9	61783.5	58.8
实验发展	Experiment Development	1542	4026.5	3201.9	86064.9	55.8
研究与实验发展成果应用	Used by Research and Experiment Development Projects	1433	5171.6	3647.2	219022.9	152.8
科技服务	Seientific and Technical Service	773	1723.0	1331.8	17479.9	22.6
生产性活动	Product Activities	93	821.4	481.6	70954.0	763.0

14－7 大中型工业企业科技情况
BASIC STATISTICS FOR SCIENCE AND TECHNOLOGY OF LARGE AND MEIUM INDUSTRIAL ENTERPRISES

单位:亿元 (10⁸ yuan)

指标	Items	1995	1997	1998
企业数	**Number of Enterprise**	**2329**	**2485**	**2389**
#有科技机构的企业数	Enterprises Having Technical Development Institutions	1068	876	938
企业办科技机构数(个)	**Science and Technology Institutions of Enterprises**	**1599**	**1360**	**1403**
从事科技的人员数(万人)	**Science and Technology Personnel**	**11.48**	**15.31**	**14.18**
#工程技术人员	Technical Personnel	6.86	9.34	8.95
#具有高、中级职称或大学本科及以上学历的人员	Personnel with Senior, Medium, Professional Titles or University and over Education	3.67	7.85	5.89
大专及以下学历具有初级职称的或未评定职称的大、中专人员	Personnel with or without Junior Professional Titles and with Second or university Education	4.10		
总计中:科技机构中的人员	Personnel in Science and Technology Institutions	3.66	3.73	4.19
#有高、中级职称或大学本科以上学历人员	Personnel with Senior, Medium, Junior Professional or over University Record	1.78	2.38	2.39
科技经费筹集额	**Funds of Science and Technology**	**45.80**	**57.48**	**64.00**
#上级拨款	Appropriations from Higher Authorities	1.76	2.08	3.07
专项贷款	Special Loans	7.49	10.23	11.86
本企业自筹	Private Funds	35.14	42.33	47.42
接受外单位委托	Entrusting Funds from Other Unites	0.89	1.09	
科技经费支出总额	**Expenditures of Science and Technology**	42.25	53.83	61.79
内部支出中	Internal Expenses			
#科技人员劳务费	Expenses for Science and Technology Personnel	6.81	7.80	9.44
原材料费	Services and Raw Materials	13.86	18.93	19.82
设计、实验、调研费	Design, Experiment, Investigation and Research	14.70		
固定资产购建费	Purchasing of Fixed Assets		17.03	21.20
用于开发新产品经费	New Product Development Expenditures	20.78	33.57	33.95
外部支出经费	External Funds	2.36		5.43
其他	**Others**			
技术改造支出总额	Total Technical Updating Expenditures	**92.21**	**101.23**	**77.22**
技术引进支出总额	Total Technical Introduced	23.37	21.91	24.49
#引进设计、图纸、工艺、专利用款	Design, Blueprint, Technology and Patent Expenditures	1.85	14.48	15.74
用于消化吸收的经费	Digesting and Absorbing Expenditures	1.17	1.78	1.36
购买国内技术用款	Purchasing Domestic Technology	1.36	2.05	2.76
科技活动产出	**Science and Technology Expenditures**			
新产品销售收入合计	Total New Product Revenue	329.10	514.24	652.65
新产品实现利税	Tax and Profit of New Products	37.45	64.93	81.28
对外转让本企业开发技术成果收入	Revenue of Scientific and Transfering Technical of the Possession	0.41	6.42	
企业对外提供技术咨询及服务收入	Revenue of Enterprises to Other Unit of Technical Service	1.16	1.07	
企业科技成果获奖数	Number for Achievements Prizes in Enterprises	1313	1352	1210
企业专利申请数	Total Patent Application	405	703	510
企业专利获准数	Total Patent Application Certified	224	229	369

14－8 高等学校科技活动情况

BASIC STATISTICS FOR SCIENTIFIC AND TECHNICAL ACTIVITIES IN INSTITUTIONS OF HIGHER EDUCATION

项　　目	Items	1995	1996	1997	1998
参加科技统计的高校　（所）	**Institutions of Higher Education in Statistics**	**47**	**47**	**47**	**47**
从事科技活动人数　（人）	**Personnel in Scientific and Technical Activities**	**57787**	**57358**	**57226**	**57802**
教师	Teachers	28270	27969	27478	28112
其他技术人员	Other Teachnical Persons	27073	26974	27275	27590
辅助人员	Assistants	2444	2415	2473	2100
从事研究与发展活动人数（人）	**Perssonnel in Research and Development**	**20295**	**21052**	**20560**	**20009**
#正教授	Professors	1908	1935	1947	1995
副教授	Associate Professors	4507	4344	4460	4397
讲　师	Lecturers	4849	4650	4579	4239
助　教	Assistants	1563	1783	1726	1656
研究与发展机构　（个）	**Institution of Research and Development**	**408**	**383**	**354**	**369**
机构中研究与发展人员	Personnel	5496	5350	5013	6304
当年研究与开发经费收入（万元）	**Funds Revenue of Research and Development (10000 yuan)**	**50695**	**59525**	**72779**	**86438**
#科技事业费	Scientific and Technical Funds	4958	8392	8785	3794
主管部门专项费	Speical Funds of Department Responsible for the Work	7398	7313	8978	12585
国务院各部门专项费	Speical Funds of State Council Department	2728	2892	2219	2874
省专项费	Provincial Special Funds	3215	3607	5778	7484
企事业单位委托经费	Entrusting Funds of Enterprises	24705	25145	33211	43980
国家自然科学基金	State Natural Sciences Funds	1654	1628	3802	4485
各种收入转入科研经费	Funds from Other Revenues	1179	5545	1082	3334
研究与发展课题　（项）	**Projects**	**9810**	**9786**	**9762**	**10609**
#基础研究	Basic	1710	1783	1835	2081
应用研究	Practical	6177	6084	6377	6797
实验发展	Experiment Development	1923	1919	1550	1731
研究与发展成果	**Achievements of Research and Development**				
出版科学专著　（部）	Publishing Scientific Works	558	856	435	491
发表学术论文　（篇）	Publishing Papers	19153	20564	20899	23180
#国外发表	Abroad	2277	2294	2382	2750
全国性学术刊物发表	National Journals	11199	11797	12404	14704
地方性学术刊物发表	Local Journals	5727	6473	6133	5726
鉴定科技成果　（项）	Appraisal Scientific Achievenments (projects)	641	718	608	648
#国际水平	International	189	195	202	210
国内首创	Original at Home	159	196	143	151
国内先进	Domestically Advanced Level	261	289	241	244
科技成果转让　（项）	**Scientific Achievements Transfered (projects)**	**660**	**716**	**509**	**718**
获奖成果数　（项）	**Prized Achievements (projects)**	**743**	**784**	**704**	**741**
#国家级	National Level	35	28	21	33
部省级	Provincial Level	383	484	421	476

注：研究与发展机构仅指学校上级主管部门批准的机构。

Note: The institutions of research and development were certified only by management department of the school.

14－9 各类专业技术人员数
SCIENTIFC AND TECHNICAL PERSONNEL

单位:万人 (10000 persons)

年份 Year	各类专业技术人员总计 Total	工程技术人员 Engineering	农业技术人员 Agriculture	科学研究人员 Scientific Research	卫生技术人员 Health Care	教学人员 Teaching
1980	43.87	9.63	1.13	1.47	9.02	17.13
1985	83.41	20.70	1.76	1.59	13.35	35.90
1986	89.31	32.33	1.95	1.85	13.80	35.42
1987	102.79	25.68	2.01	1.75	14.29	41.57
1988	125.81	29.06	2.16	1.71	15.74	45.57
1989	150.56	34.08	2.37	1.86	17.42	49.88
1990	158.86	31.84	2.35	1.84	13.87	44.50
1991	166.02	25.86	2.39	0.67	13.54	44.57
1992	174.70	27.36	2.53	0.73	14.17	44.98
1993	172.71	41.72	2.50	2.19	19.90	50.83
1994	179.94	27.88	2.21	0.60	14.99	47.57
1995	184.97	28.38	2.65	0.60	15.48	50.72
1996	189.49	44.82	3.68	1.90	21.75	59.15
1997	193.46	44.51	3.90	1.94	22.13	62.46
1998	202.15	47.53	4.45	1.74	22.72	63.83

注:各类专业技术人员分类指标中,1991年、1992年和1994年、1995年为地方国有单位的各类专业技术人员数。
Note: Numbers of the scientific and technical personnel, in 1991, 1992, 1994 and 1995 referred to local state-owned personnel.

14－10 地方国有经济单位各类专业技术人员分行业情况
SCIENTIFC AND TECHNICAL PERSONNEL IN LOCAL STATE-OWNED UNITS BY SECTOR

单位:万人 (10000 persons)

行业	Items	1990	1995	1997	1998
总计	**Total**	**112.20**	**130.07**	**140.28**	**141.12**
农、林、牧、渔、水利业	Farming, Forestry, Animal Husbandry, Fishery and Water-Conservancy	3.63	5.50	6.26	9.23
制造业	Manufacturing	25.60	30.05	24.91	21.44
地质普查和勘探业	Geological Prospecting	0.12	0.10	1.66	1.84
建筑业	Construction	2.51	3.62	2.69	2.61
交通运输、邮电通讯	Transportation, Post and Teleommunications	2.35	3.45	4.74	5.01
商业、公共饮食业、物资供销和仓储业	Commerce, Catering Trade, Material Supply and Storge	9.94	10.30	8.74	7.91
房地产管理、公用事业、居民服务和咨询服务业	Real Estate Managment, Public Facilities Services, Residential Service and Consultancy Services	2.25	4.85	7.48	6.78
卫生、体育和社会福利事业	Health Care, Sporting and Social Welfare	10.98	14.42	15.63	16.40
教育文化艺术和广播电视事业	Education, Culture and Arts, Radio, Film and Television	44.17	53.93	62.67	64.17
科学研究和综合技术服务事业	Scientific Research and Polytechnical Services	2.31	3.23	3.79	3.75
金融保险事业	Financial and Insurance Business	0.02	0.07	0.30	0.48
国家机关、政党机关和社会团体	Govermant Agencies, Party Agencies and Social Organization	8.20			
其他行业	Others	0.12	0.55	0.14	0.14
电力煤气和水的生产和供应业	Electric Power, Gas and Water Production and Supply			1.27	1.36

14－11 地方国有经济单位各类专业技术人员基本情况
SCIENTIFIC AND TECHNICAL PERSONNEL IN LOCAL STATE-OWNED UNITS

行 业	Items	1990	1995	1996	1997	1998
总 计	**Total**	**112.20**	**130.07**	**136.04**	**140.28**	**141.12**
#高级职称	Senior Professional	3.49	5.77	5.81	6.38	6.59
中级职称	Medium Titles	25.29	34.64	37.24	38.93	40.66
初级职称	Junior Titles	68.46	78.92	79.84	81.50	80.16
工程技术人员	Engineering	24.10	28.38	28.59	28.13	27.65
农业技术人员	Agriculture	2.32	2.65	3.24	3.46	3.79
科学研究人员	Scientific Research	0.79	0.60	0.54	0.53	0.56
卫生技术人员	Health Care	12.74	15.48	15.79	16.11	16.21
教学人员	Teaching	41.70	50.72	54.80	58.95	60.38
民航飞行技术人员	Civil Aviation				0.01	0.01
船舶技术人员	Shipping	0.13	0.16	0.16	0.16	0.18
经济人员	Economic	16.40	13.06	13.03	12.76	12.27
会计人员	Financial Accounting	8.83	8.95	9.55	9.84	9.96
统计人员	Statistical	1.87	1.57	1.54	1.47	1.37
翻译人员	Translator	0.21	0.21	0.21	0.20	0.19
图书、档案、文博人员	Book, Archive, Curture and Nature	1.62	1.74	1.75	1.71	1.78
新闻、出版人员	News Publisher and Announcer	0.54	0.71	0.80	0.85	0.89
律师、公证人员	Lawyer	0.19	0.16	0.17	0.16	0.16
播音人员	Broadcasting	0.03	0.05	0.07	0.08	0.09
工艺美术人员	Crafts Arts	0.20	0.23	0.23	0.23	0.22
体育人员	Sporting	0.14	0.14	0.14	0.15	0.15
艺术人员	Art	0.39	0.44	0.42	0.43	0.44
政工人员	Political Work		4.82	5.01	5.05	4.82

14－12 技术市场交易情况
TECHNICAL MARKET

单位：项目：万项 (10000 projects)
金额：亿元 (10^8 yuan)

项目	Items	1995	1996	1997	1998
技术买方合计	**Technical Buyer Total**				
项目	Projects	2.26	3.11	4.31	4.44
金额	Value	18.16	23.81	28.83	33.07
工业企业	Industrial Enterprises				
项目	Projects	1.48	2.24	3.16	3.23
金额	Value	9.98	13.14	13.63	19.33
科研机构	Scientific Research Institutions				
项目	Projects	0.11	0.13	0.13	0.09
金额	Value	1.38	1.80	1.90	1.27
各级管理部门	Department of Management at All Levels				
项目	Projects	0.24	0.25	0.28	0.29
金额	Value	3.30	4.05	4.98	5.13
技术贸易机构	Technical Trade Organizations				
项目	Projects	0.12	0.14	0.13	0.12
金额	Value	0.81	0.99	1.66	1.28
个人及个人合伙及其他	Individual, Individual Partner and Other				
项目	Projects	0.31	0.35	0.61	0.71
金额	Value	2.69	3.83	6.66	6.06
技术卖方合计	**Technical Seller Total**				
项目	Projects	2.26	3.11	4.31	4.44
金额	Value	18.16	23.81	28.83	33.07
工业企业	Industrial Enterprises				
项目	Projects	0.29	0.83	0.54	0.37
金额	Value	1.68	1.90	1.89	2.18
科研机构	Scientific Research Institutions				
项目	Projects	0.62	0.68	0.69	0.88
金额	Value	8.23	10.16	10.67	13.80
各级管理部门	Department of Management at All Levels				
项目	Projects	0.27	0.49	0.72	0.51
金额	Value	2.04	5.46	7.12	7.69
技术贸易机构	Technical Trade Organizations				
项目	Projects	0.72	0.79	1.52	1.94
金额	Value	3.48	4.73	7.49	7.19
个人及个人合伙及其他	Individual, Individual Partner and Other				
项目	Projects	0.36	0.32	0.84	0.74
金额	Value	2.73	1.56	1.66	2.21

14-13 三种专利申请受理量
THREE KINDS OF PATENT APPLICATIONS RECEIVED

项　　目	Items	1990	1995	1996	1997	1998
申请受理量合计	Total	2706	4078	4980	5339	5828
发　明	Invention	384	538	561	587	767
实用新型	Utility Model	2085	2708	3209	3275	3499
外观设计	Design	237	832	1210	1477	1562
非职务	Non-service	1620	2665	3180	3160	3512
大专院校	Universities and Colleges	135	164	159	131	109
科研单位	Scientific Resarch Institutions	112	104	112	116	139
工矿企业	Industrial and Mineral Enterprises	522	887	1503	1897	2035
机关团体	Organizations	117	258	26	35	33

14-14 三种专利授权量
THREE KINDS OF PATENTS GRANTED

项　　目	Items	1990	1995	1996	1997	1998
申请授权量合计	Total	1455	2413	2578	2960	3787
发　明	Invention	69	72	98	106	85
实用新型	Utility Model	1236	1884	1781	1814	2289
外观设计	Design	150	457	699	1040	1413
非职务	Non-service	916	1506	1487	1635	2009
大专院校	Universities and Colleges	104	112	107	94	103
科研单位	Scientific Research Institutions	78	73	71	80	86
工矿企业	Industrial and Mineral Enterprises	297	447	739	1110	1554
机关团体	Organizations	60	275	175	41	35

14-15 各级各类教育事业(1998)
BASIC STATISTICS FOR EDUCATION BY LEVEL AND TYPE

单位:万人　　　　(10000 persons)

指标	Items	学校数(所) School	毕业生数 Graduates	招生数 New Student Enrollment	在校学生数 Number of Students in schools	教职工数 Staff and Teachers	#专任教师 Fulltime Teachers
普通高等学校	Institutions of Higher Education	66	6.07	9.05	28.84	7.21	2.86
研究生	Postgraduates		0.34	0.56	1.52		
本专科学生	Undergraduate and Students of College for Prefessional Training		5.73	8.49	27.32		
中等专业学校	Specialized Secondary Schools	218	12.34	14.67	48.11	2.93	1.52
中等技术学校	Technical Schools	182	10.96	12.92	43.05	2.38	1.22
中等师范学校	Teacher Training Schools	36	1.38	1.75	5.06	0.55	0.30
#幼儿师范	Children Teacher Training Schools	4	0.11	0.11	0.31	0.04	0.02
普通中学	Regular Secondary Schools	3870	105.63	117.68	324.24	26.08	19.69
高中	Senior	895	17.68	25.92	69.32		4.63
初中	Junior	2975	87.95	91.76	254.92		15.06
#小学附设初中班	Junior Class in Primary Schools		0.01	0.01	0.04		
职业中学	Vocational Schools	445	8.62	8.05	22.91	3.32	2.36
#普中附设职业班	Vocational Class in Regular Secondary Schools		1.40	1.11	3.38		
高中	Senior	444	8.59	8.03	22.86		2.35
初中	Junior	1	0.03	0.02	0.05		0.01
技工学校	Technical Schools	185	3.61	3.68	11.16	1.43	0.78
小学	Primary Schools	23213	94.16	117.86	751.82	31.78	28.20
特殊教育学校	Special Schools	127	0.38	0.53	4.25	0.40	0.30
#盲、聋哑学校	Schools for the Blind, Deaf and Deafmute	72	0.10	0.13	0.79	0.27	0.18
幼儿园	Kindergartens	15888		90.78	168.95	9.13	7.48
工读学校	Missed Children Schools	4			0.02	0.01	0.01
成人高等学校	Adult Education Schools	48	5.14	7.05	20.01	1.32	0.71
#教育学院	Pedagogical College	10	0.24	0.31	0.93	0.21	0.11
成人中等专业学校	Secondary Schools for Adults	246	5.61	5.37	17.39	1.37	0.70
#教师进修学校	Teachers Training Schools	80	1.14	0.90	4.09	0.47	0.24
成人中学	Middle Schools for Adults	1098	7.40	9.97	10.79	0.88	0.52
成人技术培训学校	Technical Training Schools for Adults	30713	609.47	615.77	535.86	2.73	1.55
成人初等学校	Primary Schools for Adults	6643	17.16	19.49	19.06	0.44	0.20

附:1998年在研究生中有14个科研机构招收的研究生86人,毕业57人,在读256人,导师336人。
注:1. 1998年小学附设初中班15个,普中附设职业班993个。
2. 在成人高校毕业、招生、在读人数中,包括普通高校函授部、夜大学和成人脱产班学生数。

Notes: In 1998, fourteen research institutions had 86 new postgraduates persons, 57 persons graduated, 256 persons were in entrollment, and there were 336 teachers.
1. There were 15 junior classes in primary schools, 993 vocational classes in regular secondary schools.
2. Adult education schools include correspondence department or evening universities and class of adult released from production run by institution of higher education.

14－16 主要年份各级各类学校数
SCHOOLS BY LEVEL AND TYPE IN MAIN YEARS

单位:所 (number)

年份 Year	普通高等学校 Institutions of Higher Education	中等学校 Secondary Schools	中等专业学校 Specialized Secondary Schools	中等技术学校 Technical Schools	中等师范学校 Teacher Training Schools	普通中学 Regular Secondary Schools
1952	17	466	119	60	59	347
1957	15	1250	80	47	33	1170
1962	35	2196	58	37	21	1859
1965	29	6389	268	248	20	1618
1970	30	4810	47	37	10	4763
1975	25	4938	86	63	23	4852
1978	35	5959	93	70	23	5866
1980	46	5236	116	91	25	4994
1985	70	6881	163	125	38	6255
1990	70	6377	195	161	34	5808
1991	71	6184	194	159	35	5588
1992	72	5934	195	160	35	5349
1993	72	5660	207	172	35	5054
1994	67	5420	213	177	36	4761
1995	67	5093	213	177	36	4439
1996	66	4884	213	177	36	4230
1997	65	4721	212	176	36	4051
1998	66	4533	218	182	36	3870

续表 Continued

单位:所 (number)

年份 Year	高中 Senior	初中 Junior	职业中学 Vocational Schools	小学 Primary Schools	幼儿园 Kindergartens	盲、聋哑学校 Schools for the Blind Deaf and Deafmutes
1952	81	266		27070	843	8
1957	159	1011		31757	1415	10
1962	374	1485	279	37712	1994	12
1965	361	1257	4503	41369	1760	10
1970	1198	3565		45504		
1975	2433	2419		44464	6526	14
1978	2942	2924		39703	10240	25
1980	2110	2884	126	38143	14472	25
1985	1078	5177	263	33988	25779	28
1990	1017	4791	374	30557	22799	59
1991	995	4593	402	29770	21329	64
1992	981	4368	390	28753	20699	68
1993	968	4086	399	28183	20283	71
1994	967	3794	446	27636	20287	72
1995	963	3676	441	27062	19716	73
1996	936	3294	441	25836	18763	72
1997	919	3132	458	24761	17476	72
1998	895	2975	445	23213	15888	72

14－17 主要年份各级各类学校招生数
NEW STUDENT ENROLLMENT BY LEVEL AND TYPE OF SCHOOL IN MAIN YEARS

单位:万人 (10000 persons)

年份 Year	普通高等学校 Institutions of Higher Education	中等学校 Secondary Schools	中等专业学校 Specialized Secondary Schools	中等技术学校 Technical Schools	中等师范学校 Teacher Training Schools	普通中学 Regular Secondary Schools
1952	0.53	12.66	1.59	1.31	0.28	11.07
1957	0.71	21.35	0.78	0.27	0.51	20.57
1962	0.65	23.82	0.16	0.11	0.05	22.53
1965	0.92	47.48	3.36	3.04	0.32	23.39
1970	0.11	69.24	0.67	0.57	0.10	68.57
1975	0.99	140.00	0.88	0.37	0.51	139.12
1978	3.41	174.65	2.03	1.39	0.64	172.62
1980	1.92	121.44	2.17	1.32	0.85	118.25
1985	4.53	103.84	4.36	3.31	1.05	93.37
1990	4.33	109.51	4.28	3.45	0.83	99.08
1991	4.41	112.37	4.61	3.76	0.85	100.50
1992	5.17	117.63	5.12	4.22	0.90	104.14
1993	6.85	118.81	8.42	7.05	1.37	101.53
1994	6.61	129.98	9.97	8.63	1.34	110.45
1995	6.75	136.80	12.27	10.87	1.40	114.03
1996	7.43	132.35	15.38	13.81	1.57	107.75
1997	7.83	133.30	15.73	13.98	1.75	108.38
1998	8.49	140.40	14.67	12.92	1.75	117.68

续表 Continued

单位:万人 (10000 persons)

年份 Year	高中 Senior	初中 Junior	职业中学 Vocational Schools	小学 Primary Schools	盲、聋哑学校 Schools for the Blind, Deaf and Deafmutes
1952	1.09	9.98		76.49	
1957	2.71	17.86		76.58	
1962	3.43	19.10	1.13	89.93	0.01
1965	3.76	19.63	20.73	207.59	
1970	12.60	55.97		149.62	
1975	37.93	101.19		180.33	0.05
1978	49.73	122.89		160.41	0.06
1980	18.80	99.45	1.02	129.91	0.07
1985	14.96	78.41	6.11	105.85	0.08
1990	13.95	85.13	6.15	90.12	0.11
1991	14.20	86.30	7.26	89.51	0.13
1992	14.81	89.33	8.37	98.95	0.11
1993	14.43	87.10	8.86	113.83	0.11
1994	15.83	94.62	9.56	126.03	0.12
1995	18.47	95.56	10.50	130.42	0.15
1996	20.60	87.15	9.22	135.31	0.13
1997	24.04	84.34	9.19	134.25	0.13
1998	25.92	91.76	8.05	117.86	0.13

注：普通高校的毕业生数不包括研究生人数。

Note: The graduates in regular institutions of higher education did not include post-graduates. (so did follows)

14-18 主要年份各级各类学校毕业生数

GRADUATES BY LEVEL AND TYPE OF SCHOOLS IN MAIN YEARS

单位:万人 (10000 persons)

年份 Year	普通高等学校 Institutions of Higher Education	中等学校 Secondary Schools	中等专业学校 Specialized Secondary Schools	中等技术学校 Technical Schools	中等师范学校 Teacher Training Schools	普通中学 Regular Secondary Schools
1952	0.17	3.34	0.59	0.43	0.16	2.75
1957	0.29	11.12	1.07	0.73	0.34	10.05
1962	1.58	24.96	2.84	1.59	1.25	21.04
1965	1.17	17.77	0.44	0.38	0.06	16.85
1970	1.60	53.15	0.64	0.57	0.07	52.51
1975	0.79	99.69	0.90	0.40	0.50	98.79
1978	1.51	161.96	0.24	0.18	0.06	161.72
1980	1.07	117.99	1.25	0.60	0.65	116.04
1985	2.19	83.37	2.39	1.65	0.74	78.42
1990	4.34	85.27	3.84	2.85	0.99	76.45
1991	4.42	89.07	4.30	3.40	0.90	79.89
1992	4.26	92.79	4.28	3.40	0.88	83.46
1993	4.02	96.21	4.18	3.36	0.82	86.75
1994	4.47	99.29	4.28	3.43	0.85	88.29
1995	5.95	105.40	5.17	4.24	0.93	92.62
1996	6.12	109.51	8.56	7.26	1.30	92.69
1997	5.88	121.36	10.43	9.07	1.36	102.71
1998	5.73	126.59	12.34	10.96	1.38	105.63

续表 Continued

单位:万人 (10000 persons)

年份 Year	高中 Senior	初中 Junior	职业中学 Vocational Schools	小学 Primary Scholls	盲、聋哑学校 Schools for the Blind, Deaf and Deafmutes
1952	0.44	2.31		14.29	
1957	1.57	8.48		35.91	
1962	4.05	16.99	1.08	40.88	0.01
1965	3.09	13.76	0.48	40.82	
1970	6.56	45.95		100.66	
1975	29.50	69.29		110.10	0.02
1978	39.23	122.49		136.12	0.01
1980	42.16	73.88	0.70	122.25	0.04
1985	12.82	65.60	2.56	105.68	0.05
1990	13.77	62.68	4.98	103.78	0.04
1991	12.67	67.22	4.88	102.50	0.05
1992	12.71	70.75	5.05	104.06	0.06
1993	13.72	73.03	5.28	99.15	0.06
1994	13.36	74.93	6.72	101.31	0.08
1995	13.65	78.97	7.61	99.03	0.08
1996	13.59	79.10	8.26	90.23	0.09
1997	15.18	87.53	8.22	86.86	0.09
1998	17.68	87.95	8.62	94.16	0.10

14－19 主要年份各级各类学校在校学生数
STUDENT ENROLLMENT BY LEVEL AND TYPE OF SCHOOLS IN MAIN YEARS

单位:万人 (10000 persons)

年份 Year	普通高等学校 Institutions of Higher Education	中等学校 Secondary Schools	中等专业学校 Specialized Secondary Schools	中等技术学校 Technical Schools	中等师范学校 Teacher Training Schools	普通中学 Regular Secondary Schools
1952	1.13	27.47	4.23	2.38	1.85	23.24
1957	2.91	56.33	5.24	3.49	1.75	51.09
1962	5.25	70.11	2.41	1.73	0.68	65.20
1965	3.90	100.56	6.12	5.60	0.52	67.98
1970	0.11	148.82	0.67	0.57	0.10	148.15
1975	3.00	250.23	2.23	1.21	1.02	248.00
1978	6.05	389.69	3.84	2.22	1.62	385.85
1980	8.41	328.83	6.11	3.99	2.12	320.49
1985	11.96	305.89	9.25	6.88	2.37	284.73
1990	14.69	311.50	13.99	11.42	2.57	281.97
1991	14.47	319.86	14.18	11.66	2.52	288.64
1992	15.27	329.40	14.94	12.41	2.53	294.64
1993	18.02	335.30	19.18	16.08	3.10	293.98
1994	20.15	353.70	24.71	21.23	3.48	304.66
1995	20.86	374.86	31.87	27.91	3.96	316.75
1996	22.06	390.39	40.99	36.70	4.29	323.55
1997	23.90	391.64	45.88	41.21	4.67	320.69
1998	27.32	395.26	48.11	43.05	5.06	324.24

续表 Continued

单位:万人 (10000 persons)

年份 Year	高中 Senior	初中 Junior	职业中学 Vocational Schools	小学 Primary Scholls	幼儿园 Kindergartens	盲、聋哑学校 Schools for the Blind, Deaf and Deafmutes
1952	2.22	21.02		335.20	4.75	0.05
1957	7.32	43.77		412.80	8.88	0.07
1962	11.83	53.37	2.50	448.30	13.73	0.09
1965	10.83	57.15	26.46	698.68	15.49	0.12
1970	21.18	126.97		664.18		
1975	71.59	176.41		925.42	42.98	0.22
1978	101.81	284.04		868.90	67.27	0.32
1980	46.08	274.01	2.23	836.90	123.71	0.36
1985	44.72	240.01	11.91	677.92	165.99	0.43
1990	40.76	241.21	15.54	612.29	165.65	0.63
1991	41.61	247.03	17.04	594.80	187.72	0.68
1992	42.79	251.85	19.82	585.01	201.47	0.67
1993	42.36	251.62	22.14	594.94	206.89	0.68
1994	43.85	260.81	24.33	616.17	208.25	0.80
1995	47.71	269.04	26.24	644.77	214.70	0.86
1996	54.08	269.47	25.85	687.82	206.14	0.82
1997	62.10	258.59	25.07	732.35	187.35	0.80
1998	69.32	254.92	22.91	751.82	168.95	0.79

14-20 主要年份各级各类学校教职工数

STAFF AND WORKERS BY LEVEL AND TYPE OF SCHOOL IN MAIN YEARS

单位:万人 (10000 persons)

年份 Year	普通高等学校 Institutions of Higher Education	中等学校 Secondary Schools	中等专业学校 Specialized Secondary Schools	中等技术学校 Technical Schools	中等师范学校 Teacher Training Schools
1952	0.46	2.04	0.62	0.30	0.32
1957	0.98	4.01	0.98	0.79	0.19
1962	2.11	6.12	0.81	0.70	0.11
1965	1.96	7.48	1.13	1.03	0.10
1970	2.18	7.69	0.14	0.09	0.05
1975	2.34	14.14	0.68	0.50	0.18
1978	2.99	21.51	1.00	0.76	0.24
1980	3.92	21.83	1.34	1.03	0.31
1985	5.94	24.04	2.03	1.67	0.36
1990	6.96	28.21	2.45	1.98	0.47
1991	7.02	28.88	2.47	2.00	0.47
1992	7.07	29.44	2.48	2.01	0.47
1993	7.10	29.93	2.53	2.05	0.48
1994	7.14	30.59	2.62	2.12	0.50
1995	7.16	31.56	2.67	2.16	0.51
1996	7.08	32.38	2.82	2.30	0.52
1997	7.11	32.67	2.91	2.37	0.54
1998	7.21	32.33	2.93	2.38	0.55

续表 Continued

单位:万人 (10000 persons)

年份 Year	普通中学 Senior	职业中学 Vocational Schools	小学 Primary Scholls	幼儿园 Kindergartens	盲、聋哑学校 Schools for the Blind, Deaf and Deafmutes
1952	1.42		9.79	0.16	0.01
1957	3.03		12.15	0.59	0.01
1962	5.11	0.20	16.26	0.98	0.01
1965	5.06	1.29	24.63	0.90	0.02
1970	7.55		22.44		
1975	13.46		29.79	1.79	0.04
1978	20.51		29.23	2.94	0.06
1980	20.35	0.14	31.35	5.10	0.08
1985	21.08	0.93	29.44	7.48	0.10
1990	23.94	1.82	30.57	8.71	0.18
1991	24.53	1.88	30.83	8.90	0.22
1992	24.88	2.08	30.78	8.95	0.23
1993	25.05	2.35	30.75	8.91	0.24
1994	25.40	2.57	31.08	9.58	0.25
1995	25.97	2.92	31.35	9.73	0.26
1996	26.37	3.19	31.85	9.90	0.25
1997	26.41	3.35	32.05	9.36	0.26
1998	26.08	3.32	31.78	9.13	0.27

14-21 主要年份各级各类学校专任教师数
FULL-TIME TEACHERS BY LEVEL AND TYPE OF SCHOOL IN MAIN YEARS

单位:万人　　　　(10000 persons)

年份 Year	普通高等学校 Institutions of Higher Education	中等学校 Secondary Schools	中等专业学校 Specialized Secondary Schools	中等技术学校 Technical Schools	中等师范学校 Teacher Training Schools	普通中学 Regular Secondary Schools
1952	0.17	1.07	0.28	0.12	0.16	0.79
1957	0.46	2.09	0.39	0.30	0.09	0.17
1962	0.98	3.69	0.37	0.31	0.06	3.20
1965	0.87	4.98	0.48	0.43	0.05	3.31
1970	0.98	6.03	0.11	0.08	0.03	5.92
1975	1.01	10.81	0.30	0.20	0.10	10.51
1978	1.34	16.75	0.44	0.31	0.13	16.31
1980	1.59	16.83	0.63	0.47	0.16	15.20
1985	2.30	16.53	0.90	0.72	0.18	14.98
1990	2.76	19.63	1.20	0.97	0.23	17.25
1991	2.76	20.06	1.18	0.95	0.23	17.66
1992	2.70	20.32	1.18	0.95	0.23	17.79
1993	2.70	20.71	1.19	0.96	0.23	18.02
1994	2.73	21.28	1.26	1.01	0.25	18.35
1995	2.73	22.16	1.30	1.04	0.26	18.91
1996	2.74	22.82	1.39	1.13	0.26	19.28
1997	2.79	23.26	1.46	1.18	0.28	19.52
1998	2.86	23.57	1.52	1.22	0.30	19.69

续表　Continued

单位:万人　　　　(10000 persons)

年份 Year	高中 Senior	初中 Junior	职业中学 Vocational Schools	小学 Primary Scholls	幼儿园 Kindergartens	盲、聋哑学校 Schools for the Blind, Deaf and Deafmutes
1952				8.84	0.13	0.01
1957	0.28	1.42		11.50	0.40	0.01
1962	0.66	2.54	0.12	15.66	0.45	0.01
1965	0.64	2.67	1.19	24.02	0.52	0.01
1970				20.94		
1975	3.16	7.35		28.01	1.24	0.02
1978	4.58	11.73		27.07	2.32	0.04
1980	2.86	12.34	0.10	27.97	4.41	0.05
1985	2.88	12.10	0.65	25.91	6.06	0.06
1990	3.27	13.98	1.18	26.95	7.21	0.11
1991	3.36	14.30	1.22	27.00	7.48	0.12
1992	3.38	14.41	1.35	26.66	7.47	0.13
1993	3.39	14.63	1.50	25.59	7.40	0.14
1994	3.42	14.93	1.67	26.95	7.99	0.15
1995	3.59	15.32	1.95	27.35	8.14	0.16
1996	3.88	15.40	2.15	27.96	8.31	0.16
1997	4.24	15.29	2.28	28.32	7.69	0.16
1998	4.63	15.06	2.36	28.20	7.48	0.18

14－22 全省研究生数
POSTGRADUATES IN MAIN YEARS

单位：人 (person)

项目	Items	1990	1995	1997	1998
高等学校	**Institutions of Higher Education**				
招生数	New Students Enrollment	2214	3730	4831	5554
在读人数	Students Enrollment	6718	10700	13317	15233
#女性	Female	1175	2384	3432	4063
毕业生数	Graduates	2626	2202	3565	3440
研究所(院)	**Research Institutions (Academies)**				
招生数	New Students Enrollment	62	65	78	86
在读人数	Students Enrollment	191	191	237	256
#女性	Female	20	27	27	23
毕业生数	Graduates	91	45	58	57

注：1990年研究所(院)女性研究生在读人数系推算。

Note: The number of female postgraduates in 1990 was calculated from that in enrollment.

14－23 主要年份各级各类学校女学生和女教师数
FEMALE STUDENTS ENROLLMENT AND TEACHERS BY LEVEL AND TYPE OF SCHOOLS IN MAIN YEARS

单位：人 (person)

项目	Items	1990	1995	1997	1998
女学生数	**Female Students**				
高等学校	Institutions of Higher Education	4.30	6.79	8.01	9.58
中等专业学校	Specialized Secondary Schools	6.04	16.19	24.00	26.60
普通中学	Regular Secondary Schools	117.64	139.72	141.16	142.81
农业、职业中学	Agricultural and Professional Secondary Schools	6.69	12.30	11.39	10.32
小学	Primary Schools	288.49	306.29	348.65	357.15
女学生占学生总数(%)	**Percentage of Female Students (percent)**				
高等学校	Institutions of Higher Education	29.3	32.6	33.5	35.1
中等专业学校	Specialized Secondary Schools	43.1	50.8	52.3	55.3
普通中学	Regular Secondary Schools	41.7	44.1	44.0	44.0
农业、职业中学	Agricultural and Professional Secondary Schools	43.1	46.9	45.4	45.0
小学	Primary Schools	47.1	47.5	47.6	47.5
女教师数	**Female Teachers**				
高等学校	Institutions of Higher Education	0.71	0.76	0.86	0.92
中等专业学校	Specialized Secondary Schools	0.42	0.52	0.59	0.62
普通中学	Regular Secondary Schools	4.28	5.58	6.23	6.51
农业、职业中学	Agricultural and Professional Secondary Schools	0.28	0.63	0.82	0.88
小学	Primary Schools	10.34	11.64	12.57	12.80
女教师占教师总数(%)	**Percentage of Female Teachers (percent)**				
高等学校	Institutions of Higher Education	25.8	27.8	30.7	32.1
中等专业学校	Specialized Secondary Schools	35.2	39.9	40.5	41.2
普通中学	Regular Secondary Schools	24.8	29.5	31.9	33.1
农业、职业中学	Agricultural and Professional Secondary Schools	24.7	32.4	35.8	37.2
小学	Primary Schools	38.4	42.5	44.4	45.4

15. 文化、体育、卫生、环保

CULTURE, SPORTS, PUBLIC HEALTH AND ENVIRONMENTAL PROTECTION

15 文化、体育、卫生、环保

CULTURE, SPORTS, PUBLIC HEALTH AND ENVIRONMENTAL PROTECTION

1 9 9 8

文化产业机构数	Cultural Institutions	18902	个	(unit)
艺术表演团体	Art Performance Troupes	132	个	(unit)
图书出版量	Books Published	4.68	亿册	(10^8)
杂志出版量	Magazines Published	0.92	亿册	(10^8)
报纸出版量	Newspaper Published	18.60	亿册	(10^8)
等级运动员发展人数	Certified Athletes	3640	人	(person)
等级裁判员发展人数	Certified Referees	1303	人	(person)
卫生机构数	Health Care Institutions	14572	个	(unit)
#医院、卫生院	Hospitals	2610		
医院床位数	Hospital Beds	15.91	万张	(10000 beds)
卫生技术人员	Medical Technical Personnel	25.67	万人	(10000 persons)
工业废水排放总量	Total Volume of Industrial Waste Water Discharged	202943	万吨	(10000 tons)
工业废气排放总量	Total Volume of Industrial Waste Gas Discharged	7488	亿标立方米	(10^8 m^3)
污染治理资金使用额	Total Funds for Pollution Treatment	23.33	亿元	(10^8 yuan)

卫生技术人员(万人)

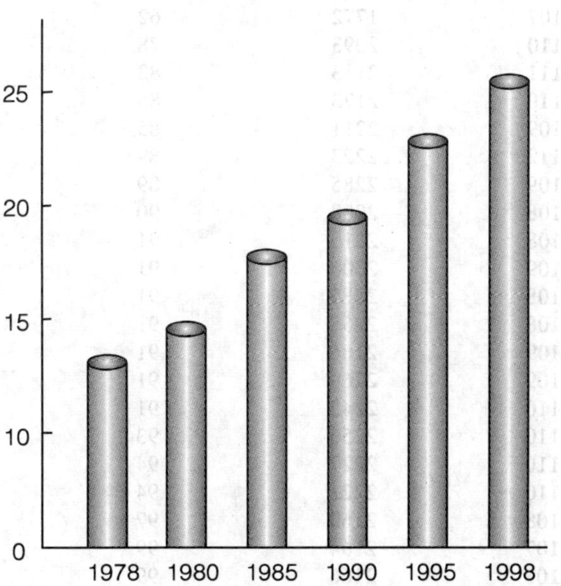

图书、杂志、报纸出版量 (1998 年)

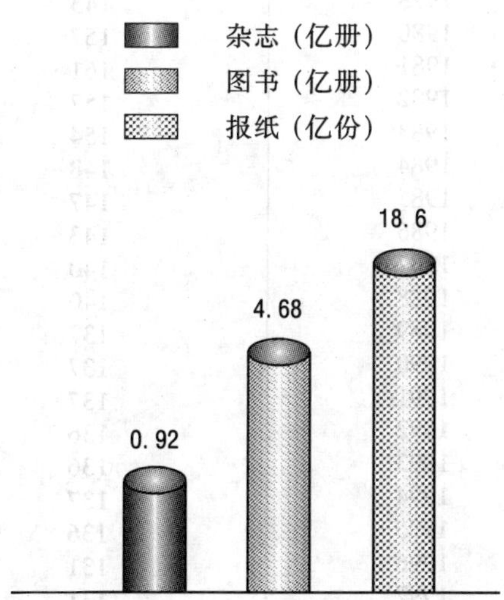

15－1 文化产业机构数、从业人员数（1998）
CULTURAL INSTITUTION AND PERSONNEL

单位：机构：个 人员：人 (number、person)

指标	Items	总计 Total 机构 Institution	总计 Total 人员 Personnel	文化部门 Cultural Department 机构 Institution	文化部门 Cultural Department 人员 Personnel	其他部门 Others 机构 Institution	其他部门 Others 人员 Personnel
总计	**Total**	**18902**	**90654**	**8404**	**41473**	**10498**	**49181**
艺术业	Art	352	10347	352	10347		
图书馆业	Libraries	99	2087	99	2087		
群众文化业	Masses Culture	2287	8078	2287	8078		
艺术教育业	Art Education	21	969	21	969		
娱乐业	Entertainment	11652	55614	1735	7842	9917	47772
文艺科研	Art Research Institutions	10	68	10	68		
文物业	Cultural Relics	151	2260	151	2260		
其他文化产业	Others	4330	11231	3749	9822	581	1409

15－2 主要年份文化艺术、文物事业单位
NUMBER OF INSTITUTIONS FOR CULTURE, ART AND CULTURAL RELICS

单位：个 (number)

年份 Year	艺术表演团体 Art Performance Groups	文化馆 Cultural Centers	文化站 Cultural Stations	公共图书馆 Public Libraries	博物馆 Museums
1952	172	108	651	12	3
1957	218	97	543	25	5
1962	217	99	489	39	12
1965	195	99	889	35	14
1970	113	71	1141	26	15
1975	121	107	1772	62	13
1978	143	110	2093	78	19
1980	157	111	2153	82	19
1981	161	110	2173	85	19
1982	157	109	2211	85	19
1983	154	112	2223	89	21
1984	148	109	2285	89	21
1985	147	108	2308	90	31
1986	143	108	2310	91	34
1987	140	109	2300	91	37
1988	140	108	2285	91	45
1989	137	108	2258	91	50
1990	137	109	2166	91	51
1991	137	109	2269	91	58
1992	136	110	2245	91	62
1993	136	110	2256	93	66
1994	137	110	2227	94	68
1995	136	110	2221	94	72
1996	131	108	2160	97	73
1997	131	107	2164	99	76
1998	132	108	2166	99	79

15－3　艺术表演事业机构和人员数（1998）
ART PERFORMANCE INSTITUTION AND PERSONNEL

单位：机构：个　人员：人　　　　(number、person)

指　标	Items	总计 Total 机构 Institution	总计 Total 人员 Personnel	文化部门 Cultural Department 国有单位 State-Owned 机构 Institution	国有单位 State-Owned 人员 Personnel	集体单位 Collective-Owned 机构 Institution	集体单位 Collective-Owned 人员 Personnel
总　计	**Total**						
艺术表演团体	Art Performance Groups	132	6257	28	2805	104	3452
#话剧、儿童剧、滑稽剧团	Drama, Children's Play and Comedy Groups	7	373	4	247	3	126
歌舞团、轻音乐团	Song and Dance, Light Music Groups	16	1445	10	1159	6	286
乐队、合唱团	Philharmonic and Chorus Groups	1	20	1	20		
文工团、文宣队	Cultural and Performance Groups	1	34			1	34
戏曲剧团	Local Opera Groups	85	3807	12	1291	73	2516
艺术表演场所	Art Centers	137	3489	130	3337	6	93
#剧场、影剧院	Theaters and Music Halls	129	3378	126	3252	2	67

15－4　艺术教育及其他文化产业机构和人员数（1998）
ART EDUCATION AND OTHER CULTURE INSTITUTION AND PERSONNEL

单位：机构：个　人员：人　　　　(number、person)

指　标	Items	总计 Total 机构 Institution	总计 Total 人员 Personnel	文化部门 Cultural Department 国有单位 State-Owned 机构 Institution	国有单位 State-Owned 人员 Personnel	集体单位 Collective-Owned 机构 Institution	集体单位 Collective-Owned 人员 Personnel
教育事业	**Education**	**21**	**969**	**17**	**912**	**4**	**57**
高等艺术学校	Higher Art Education Schools						
中等艺术学校	Secondary Art Schools	9	775	9	775		
文化干部学校	Cultural Cardre Schools	2	8	2	8		
其他艺术教育机构	Others	10	186	6	129	4	57
其他文化产业	**Culture**	**16075**	**67514**	**817**	**4316**	**3646**	**10735**
艺术创作机构	Art Creating Institutions	70	418	68	411	2	7
艺术研究机构	Art Research Institutions	10	68	10	68		
艺术展览机构	Art Exhibition Agency	9	170	9	170		
文化艺术经纪与代理业	Performance Companies	12	53	11	51	1	2
其他	Others	15974	66805	719	3616	3643	10726

15－5 公共图书馆、群众文化事业机构和人员数(1998)
PUBLIC LIBRARIES, MASS CULTURE INSTITUTION AND PERSONNEL

单位：机构：个 人员：人 (number、person)

指标	Items	总计 Total 机构 Institution	总计 Total 人员 Personnel	文化部门 Cultural Department 机构 Institution	文化部门 Cultural Department 人员 Personnel
图书馆事业	Libraries	99	2087	99	2087
#儿童图书馆	Children's Libraries	4	30	4	30
群众文化事业	Mass Culture	2287	8078	2287	8078
群众艺术馆	Mass Art Centers	13	420	13	420
文化馆	Cultural Centers	108	1868	108	1868
文化站	Cultural Stations	2166	5790	2166	5790
#乡镇文化站	Rural Cultural Stations	2002	4269	2002	4269

15－6 文物事业机构和人员数
NUMBER OF INSTITUTIONS AND PERSONNEL IN CULTURAL RELICS

单位：机构：个 人员：人 (number、person)

指标	Items	机构 Institution 1997	机构 Institution 1998	人员 Personnel 1997	人员 Personnel 1998
总计	**Total**	**144**	**151**	**2260**	**2260**
文物单位	Cultural Relics Units	57	61	353	305
文物保护管理单位	Cultural Relics Management	55	58	300	256
其他文物单位	Others	2	3	53	49
博物馆	Museums	76	79	1492	1553
综合性	Synthesized	38	39	909	889
专门性	Special	21	20	324	381
纪念性	Memorial Hall	17	20	259	283
文物商店	Cultural Relics Shops	11	11	415	402

15－7 报纸、杂志出版情况(1998)
BASIC STATISTICS FOR NEWSPAPER AND MAGAZINES PUBLISHED

指标	Items	种数(种) Number of Publications	总印数(万册、万份) Printed Copies (10000)	总印张(万印张) Printed Signatures (10000)
报纸	Newspaper	86	186035	241127
杂志	Magazines	381	9240	26489
综合	Comprehensiveness	11	690	2846
哲学、社会科学	Philosophy and Social Sciences	78	3090	10478
自然科学、技术	Natural Sciences and Technology	247	1451	4454
文化、教育	Culture and Education	20	3420	6292
文学、艺术	Literature and Art	22	227	1663
少年儿童	Children's Reading Material	3	362	756

15－8 图书出版情况(1998)
BASIC STATISTICS FOR BOOKS PUBLISHED

指标	Items	出版图书种数(种) Number of Publication	#租型图书 Rented Books	总印数(万册、万份) Printed Copies (10000)	总印张(万印张) Printed Signatures (10000)
总计	**Total**	**4859**	**346**	**46792**	**222699**
书籍合计	Books	4762	346	46694	222353
哲学、社会科学	Philosophy and Social Sciences	397	9	300	3432
文化、教育	Culture and Education	2475	337	42554	197302
文学、艺术	Literature and Art	993		3181	13625
自然科学、技术	Natural Sciences and Technology	800		596	7253
其他	Others	97		63	741
图片	Pictures	97		98	301

注:总印张数中,含不使用《中国标准书号》的活页文选、活页歌篇等45万印张数。

Note: The total printed signatures included 450000 printed signatures of loose-leaf selected works and song, etc.

15－9 广播、电视事业发展情况
BASIC STATISTICS ON BROADCASTING AND TELEVISION STATIONS

指标		Items		1995	1997	1998
职工人数	（人）	Number of Staff and Workers	(person)	21505	26087	26587
广播电台	（座）	Number of Broadcasting Stations	(set)	61	80	14
发射台及转播台	（座）	Number of Broadcasting Transmission Stations and Relaying Stations	(set)	21	21	21
发射机功率	（千瓦）	Broadcast Power of Transmitters	(kw)	457.5	445.5	526.5
广播人口覆盖率	（%）	Listener Rating	(%)	86.9	88.5	97.7
电视台	（座）	Number of Television Stations	(set)	52	57	14
电视发射及转播台	（座）	Television Transmission Stations and Relaying Stations	(set)	153	154	150
发射机功率	（千瓦）	Power of Transmitters	(kw)	418.5	433.6	438.4
电视人口覆盖率	（%）	Viewer Rating	(%)	93.5	94.7	97.8

15－10 广播、电视节目制作时间
PRODUCTION OF BROADCASTING AND TV PROGRAMS

单位：小时 (hours)

指标	Items	1995	1996	1997	1998
广播节目制作	Production of Broadcasting Programs	197793	248814	298652	282212
#新闻	News Programs	24574	34248	47770	43540
专题	Special Subject Programs	40465	45487	49895	45642
教育	Educational Programs	6168	13241	10634	7518
文艺	Programs of Entertainment	90838	108185	122603	117680
服务性	Service Programs	35746	47653	67750	67832
电视节目制作	Production of TV Programs	28738	41692	47533	53276
#新闻	News Programs	4659	6029	6747	7215
专题	Special Subject Programs	3854	4850	4524	5307
教育	Educational Programs	7450	861	1420	520
文艺	Programs of Entertainment	544	17849	20498	24680
服务性	Service Programs	12231	12103	14344	15554

15－11 体委系统职工人数(1998)
PERSONNEL OF PHYSICAL CULTURE AND SPORTS COMMISSIONS

单位:人 (person)

指标	Items	总计 Total	#优秀运动队 Accom-plished Athlete Team	#体育运动学校 Physical Cultural and Sports School	#重点业余体校 Key Part-Time Sports School	#普通业余体校 Ordinary Part-TimeSports Shools	#公共体育场(馆) Public Stadiums and Gym-nasiums
总计	**Total**	**7381**	**1545**	**654**	**412**	**1168**	**1335**
专职教练员	Full-time coaches	1245	233	193	199	594	
运动员	Athletes	880	880				
管理干部	Adiministrative Staff	2387	181	129	72	268	563
专职教师	Full-time Teachers	650	125	232	89	151	
科技人员	Scientific and Technical Personnel	72	5	13			24
医务人员	Medical Personnel	76	17	10	4	10	3
其他	Others	2071	104	77	48	145	745

15－12 等级运动员、裁判员发展人数
CERTIFIED ATHLETES AND REFEREES BY TYPE OF SPORTS

单位:人 (person)

指标	Items	1985	1990	1995	1997	1998
等级运动员发展人数	Certified Athletes	3009	3199	3359	3439	3640
运动健将	Master Athletes	35	40	54	41	77
一级	First Grade	61	54	88	169	293
二级	Second Grade	283	318	441	693	576
三级	Third Grade	1335	1307	1600	1614	1295
少年级	Juvenile Grade	1295	1480	1176	922	1399
等级裁判员发展人数	Certified Referees	2019	1428	1471	1333	1303
国家(际)级	National (International) Referees	25	7	16	6	21
一级	First Grade	242	86	157	218	32
二级	Second Grade	503	384	408	461	416
三级	Third Grade	1249	951	890	648	834

15－13 群众体育活动情况
MASS SPORTS ACTIVITIES

单位:万人 (10000 persons)

指标	Items	1990	1995	1997	1998
全省各级体委举办运动会情况	**Sports Meeting**				
运动会次数 (次)	Times (time)	1771	1008	994	936
参加运动会的运动员人数	Persons	68.52	30.44	42.45	51.12
达到国家体育锻炼标准的学生	Students Passed "NPTPS"	656.20	704.87	745.66	796.47
大专院校	Institution of Higher Education		13.18	14.90	17.20
中专、中技	Specialized Secondary and Technical School	3.07	15.73	24.12	24.45
中　　学	Secondary School	262.08	294.11	312.25	310.18
小　　学	Primary School	391.05	381.85	394.39	444.64

注:"NPTPS"指国家体育锻炼标准。

Note:"NPTPS" means National Physical Training Program Standards.

15－14 运动员在各级比赛中获奖牌情况(1998)
AWARDS FOR ATHLETES IN COMPETITIONS OF ALL LEVELS

单位:枚 (units)

指标	Items	冠　军 Champion	亚　军 Second Place	第 三 名 Third Place
世界最高比赛	World Highest Competition	10	14	9
亚洲最高比赛	Asian Highest Competition	36	15	8
全国最高比赛	National Highest Competition	30	27	20

15-15 卫生事业基本情况(1998)
BASIC STATISTICS FOR HEALTH CARE

指标	Items	机构数（个） Institutions	床位数（万张） Hospital Beds (10000 bed)	卫生工作人员（万人） Personnel (10000 persons)	#卫生技术人员 Medical Technical Personnel	#医生 Doctors
总计	**Total**	**14572**	**17.01**	**32.61**	**25.67**	**11.61**
医院、卫生院合计	Total Hospitals	2610	15.91	25.76	20.38	8.49
县及县以上医院小计	Hospitals at County Level and Above	458	9.20	14.45	10.91	4.22
综合医院	Comprehensive Hospitals	260	5.77	9.31	7.08	2.74
中医医院	Hospitals of Chinese Medicines	84	1.21	2.17	1.69	0.72
医学院附属医院	Hospital Attached to Medical Colleges	8	0.42	0.76	0.58	0.22
传染病院	Infections Diseases Hospitals	13	0.39	0.42	0.30	0.09
精神病院	Mental Hospitals	44	0.69	0.65	0.43	0.15
结核病院	Tuberculosis Hospitals	4	0.05	0.05	0.03	0.01
妇幼保健院	Hospitals for Maternity and Child Care	11	0.19	0.33	0.25	0.08
儿童医院	Children's Hospitals	3	0.08	0.17	0.13	0.04
职业病院	Vocational Hospitals	5	0.05	0.06	0.03	0.01
肿瘤医院	Tumor Hospitals	3	0.12	0.16	0.12	0.04
其他专科医院	Other Specialized Hospitals	23	0.23	0.37	0.27	0.12
其他医院	Other Hospitals	131	0.44	0.72	0.56	0.24
区、乡(镇)卫生院	Rural Township Hospitals	2021	6.27	10.59	8.91	4.03
疗养院、所	Sanatoriums	30	0.59	0.25	0.10	0.04
门诊部、诊所、医务室	Clinics	8035	0.02	3.06	3.03	1.83
专科防治所、站	Specialized Stations	120	0.12	0.30	0.21	0.12
#结核病防治所、站	Tuberculosis Prevention Stations	8		0.01	0.01	…
职业病防治所、站	Occupational Diseases Control Stations	3	0.02	0.03	0.02	0.01
卫生防疫站	Sanatation and Diseases Control Stations	144	0.02	0.92	0.68	0.50
妇幼保健所、站	Meternity and Child Care Centers	114	0.01	0.26	0.20	0.13
药品检验所、室	Medicines and Chemical Reagent	75		0.09	0.07	
医学科学研究机构	Institutions of Medical Sciences Test Labs	18	0.06	0.17	0.10	0.04
其他卫生机构	Other Health Care Institutions	170	0.28	1.47	0.57	0.30
个体开业	Individual-Run Medical Units	3256		0.33	0.33	0.16

15－16 主要年份卫生机构数
HEALTH CARE INSTITUTIONS IN MAIN YEARS

单位：个　　　　(number)

年份 Year	总计 Total	医院卫生院 Hospitals	#县级以上医院 Hospitals at County Level Above	疗养院、所 Sanatoriums	门诊部、所 Clinics	专科防治所、站 Specialized Stations
1949	259	115	71	3	141	
1952	2896	117	114	16	2688	20
1957	6145	138	135	32	5460	45
1962	11726	490	208	55	10832	50
1965	12253	472	201	39	11418	48
1970	6899	2340	207	5	4231	70
1975	7894	2327	240	5	5212	8
1976	8262	2353	252	6	5521	7
1977	8621	2385	304	6	5738	6
1978	9277	2428	334	7	6301	9
1979	9650	2453	369	9	6639	13
1980	9943	2457	371	11	6910	17
1981	10563	2483	390	16	7495	19
1982	10787	2502	397	20	7689	21
1983	10745	2515	407	22	7628	25
1984	11154	2523	415	24	8004	56
1985	11515	2460	426	32	8405	84
1986	11743	2470	448	32	8609	95
1987	11934	2482	462	35	8777	98
1988	12248	2472	467	36	9105	96
1989	12325	2483	478	34	9159	95
1990	12366	2491	483	35	9178	108
1991	12377	2495	477	36	9187	112
1992	12277	2493	481	36	9082	114
1993	12074	2483	486	36	8867	120
1994	12067	2559	494	36	8785	121
1995	12039	2534	490	35	8784	122
1996	14944	2617	489	35	8410	121
1997	13386	2620	488	33	8071	121
1998	14572	2610	458	30	8035	120

注：1998 年卫生机构总数中含个体开业 3256 个。

Note: The total of health care institutions included individual-run 3256 units in 1998.

续表 Continued

年份 Year	卫生防疫站 Sanatation and Diseases Control Stations	妇幼保健所、站 Meternity and Child Care Centers	药品检验所、站 Medicines and Chemical Reagent	医学科学研究机构 Institutions of Medical Sciences Labs	其他卫生机构 Other Health Care Institutions
1952	4	31			20
1957	67	174		3	226
1962	97	98	11	4	89
1965	95	85	12		84
1970	70	47	9	2	125
1975	104	71	13	7	147
1976	104	75	22	7	167
1977	106	82	64	9	225
1978	107	84	83	12	246
1979	114	92	82	14	234
1980	119	99	82	11	237
1981	119	98	79	15	239
1982	124	95	79	15	242
1983	123	95	73	15	249
1984	124	100	73	16	234
1985	127	105	72	16	214
1986	129	109	72	16	211
1987	128	112	72	18	212
1988	131	112	72	18	206
1989	135	114	73	16	216
1990	135	114	73	16	216
1991	137	114	74	14	208
1992	135	115	75	14	213
1993	141	117	75	18	217
1994	141	117	75	17	216
1995	141	117	75	17	214
1996	142	115	75	18	172
1997	143	114	75	18	172
1998	144	114	75	18	170

15－17 主要年份卫生机构人员数

PERSONNEL OF HEALTH CARE INSTITUTIONS IN MAIN YEARS

单位:万人 (10000 persons)

年份 Year	总计 Total	卫生技术人员 Medical Technical Personnel	#医生 Doctors	中医 Traditional Chinses Medicine	西医师 Western Medicine Senior	西医士 Western Medicine Junior	#护师、护士 Senior and Junior Nurses	每万人口医生数(人) Doctors of Per 10000 Population
1949	…	…	…	…	…	…	…	…
1952	6.28	5.24	2.62	1.72	0.25	0.64	0.34	7.00
1957	10.32	9.27	3.31	1.98	0.36	0.97	0.61	7.90
1962	9.97	8.47	4.20	1.95	0.65	1.60	1.09	9.60
1965	10.15	8.56	4.52	1.88	0.99	1.65	1.21	9.70
1970	8.50	6.78	3.41	0.97	1.20	1.24	1.59	6.40
1975	13.48	10.79	4.75	1.31	1.63	1.81	1.84	8.40
1976	14.49	11.54	4.96	1.30	1.67	1.99	2.03	8.70
1977	16.45	13.29	5.61	1.49	1.69	2.44	1.83	9.70
1978	17.45	14.00	5.70	1.48	1.90	2.32	1.79	9.70
1979	18.45	14.58	5.71	1.43	2.02	2.26	1.86	9.60
1980	19.03	15.04	6.10	1.42	2.45	2.23	2.08	10.20
1981	20.53	16.23	6.52	1.48	2.84	2.19	2.64	10.80
1982	21.44	16.93	7.16	1.54	3.25	2.37	3.04	11.70
1983	21.92	17.22	7.36	1.49	3.39	2.48	3.27	11.90
1984	22.64	17.68	7.50	1.48	3.48	2.53	3.38	12.10
1985	23.68	18.28	7.65	1.48	3.55	2.62	3.61	12.30
1986	24.53	18.90	7.88	1.47	3.68	2.73	3.78	12.50
1987	25.06	19.18	7.84	1.42	3.65	2.77	3.89	12.30
1988	25.96	20.05	8.60	1.47	4.87	2.26	4.52	13.30
1989	26.82	20.75	9.67	1.50	6.19	1.98	5.06	14.70
1990	27.58	21.35	9.94	1.50	6.29	2.15	5.34	14.60
1991	28.63	22.22	10.20	1.49	6.41	2.30	5.61	14.90
1992	29.39	22.89	10.43	1.49	6.59	2.36	5.76	15.10
1993	30.20	23.44	10.63	1.50	6.80	2.33	5.99	15.30
1994	30.85	24.05	10.94	1.53	7.08	2.33	6.28	15.60
1995	31.57	24.55	11.22	1.52	7.31	2.39	6.44	15.90
1996	31.90	25.02	11.34	1.53	7.46	2.35	6.69	15.95
1997	32.42	25.48	11.58	1.49	7.72	2.37	6.95	16.20
1998	32.61	25.67	11.61	1.47	7.88	2.26	7.13	16.20

15－18 主要年份卫生机构床位数
HOSPITAL BEDS IN MAIN YEARS

单位：万张　　(10000 beds)

年份 Year	总计 Total	医院 Hospitals	#县及县以上医院 County Level and Above	疗养院、所 Sanatoriums	其他卫生机构 Other Health Care Institutions	每万人口医院床位数(张) Hospital Beds of Per 10000 Population
1949	0.46	0.45	0.26	0.01		1.30
1952	1.75	0.83	0.83	0.12	0.80	2.20
1957	2.21	1.32	1.31	0.33	0.56	3.10
1962	5.85	3.71	3.01	0.57	1.57	8.60
1965	6.52	3.98	3.13	0.46	2.08	8.60
1970	7.89	6.88	3.16	0.08	0.93	13.10
1975	10.79	9.57	4.06	0.09	1.13	17.00
1976	11.13	9.88	4.15	0.11	1.14	17.30
1977	11.60	10.43	4.68	0.12	1.05	18.10
1978	12.29	11.07	4.96	0.13	1.09	19.00
1979	12.54	11.40	5.27	0.16	0.98	19.30
1980	12.75	11.62	5.48	0.23	0.90	19.60
1981	13.28	11.96	5.83	0.29	1.03	19.90
1982	13.21	12.01	5.92	0.34	0.86	19.70
1983	13.49	12.25	6.20	0.39	0.85	20.00
1984	13.93	12.50	6.42	0.42	1.01	20.30
1985	14.29	12.65	6.71	0.55	1.09	20.40
1986	14.71	13.07	7.07	0.56	1.08	20.80
1987	15.38	13.59	7.44	0.64	1.15	21.40
1988	15.94	14.06	7.79	0.69	1.19	21.80
1989	16.08	14.22	8.02	0.64	1.22	21.80
1990	16.45	14.54	8.32	0.67	1.24	21.50
1991	16.77	14.85	8.52	0.74	1.18	21.70
1992	17.02	15.07	8.68	0.73	1.22	21.80
1993	17.33	15.29	8.94	0.73	1.31	21.90
1994	17.45	15.42	9.07	0.72	1.31	22.00
1995	17.46	15.48	9.15	0.71	1.27	21.90
1996	17.03	15.78	9.23	0.69	0.56	22.19
1997	17.03	15.90	9.31	0.62	0.51	22.24
1998	17.01	15.91	9.20	0.59	0.51	22.15

15－19　医院、卫生院诊疗人次及入院人数（1998）
NUMBER OF HOSPITAL PATIENTS

指　标	Items	诊疗人次（万人次）Treatmental Person times (10000 person times)	#门、急诊 Out Patients Emergency	入院人次（万人）Number of Persons Admitted to Hospital (10000 persons)	每百诊次的入院人数（人）Per 100 Treatmental Times of Persons Admitted to Hospital
医院、卫生院合计	**Total**	**13097**	**12868**	**275**	**2**
县及县以上医院合计	County Level and Above	6284	6135	155	3
#卫生部门	Department of Sanitation	4973	4869	135	3
工业及其他部门	Department of Industry and Others	912	893	144	2
集体所有制	Collective Owned	399	373	5	1
其他医院	Other Hospital	517	501	3	1
卫 生 院	Commune Hospital	6296	6232	117	2

15－20　县及县以上医院病床使用情况
UTILIZATION OF HOSPITAL BEDS AT AND ABOVE COUNTY LEVEL

指　标	Items	1995	1996	1997	1998
病床周转次数（次）	Turnover Time of Hospital Beds (times)	16	16	16	17
病床工作日（日）	Work Day of Hospital Beds (days)	269	268	259	251
病床使用率（%）	Rate of Utilization (%)	74	73	71	69
出院者平均住院日（日）	Average Hospitalized Day of the People Leaving Hospital (days)	17	16	16	15

15－21 主要年份环境保护情况
ENVIRONMENTAL PROTECITION IN MAIN YEARS

指标	Items	1995	1997	1998
工业废水量	**Industrial Waste Water**			
工业废水排放量 (万吨)	Industrial Waste Water Discharged (10000 tons)	220184	220071	202943
# 符合排放标准的	According to Standard	144090	143292	153854
工业废水排放的污染物	**Pollution of Industrial Waste Water Discharged**			
汞及其无机化合物 (公斤)	Mercury and Inorganic Compound (kg)	75	710	10
镉及其无机化合物 (公斤)	Cadmium and Inorganic Compound (kg)	656	660	580
六价铬化合物 (公斤)	6-valence Chromium Compound (kg)	58805	45430	41420
砷及其无机化合物 (公斤)	Arsenic and Inorganic Compound (kg)	166274	133180	134400
铅及其无机化合物 (公斤)	Aluminium and Inorganic Compound (kg)	9021	38610	13370
酚 (公斤)	Phenol (kg)	462699	392820	317100
氰化物 (公斤)	Cyanide (kg)	97199	111170	104560
石油类 (吨)	Petroleum Type (tons)	4697	4467	2964
工业废气排放总量 (亿标立米)	Industrial Waste Gas Discharged (10^8 cu. m)	7872.11	8164.24	7487.85
#生产工艺排放的	Waste Gas in the Process of Production	1888.00	2093.90	1876.68
# 净化处理的	Gas Purified	1547.87	1698.22	1495.39
二氧化硫排放量 (万吨)	Sulphur Dioxide (10000 tons)	104.47	133.49	124.02
烟尘排放量 (万吨)	Soot (10000 tons)	54	62	54
工业粉尘产生量 (万吨)	Industrial Dust Produced (10000 tons)	139	244	200
排放量 (万吨)	Volume Discharged (10000 tons)	27	81	55
回收量 (万吨)	Volume Retrieved (10000 tons)	112	163	145
工业粉尘回收率 (%)	Rate of Industrial Dust Discharged	80.6	66.8	72.5
固体废物产生量 (万吨)	Solid Waste Residue Produced (10000 tons)	2883	2857	2944
蒸汽锅炉 (台/万蒸吨)	Steam Boiler (10000 Steam tons)	6012/5.9	7002/7.4	6862/8.4
工业炉窑 (座)	Industrial Stove	3202	4786	4522
其他	**Others**			
"三废"综合利用产品产值 (万元)	Output Value of Products Made from Waste Gas, Waste Water and Waste Residue (10000 yuan)	93208	242814	161299
"三废"综合利用产品利润 (万元)	Profits Obtained from Waste Gas, Waste Water and Waste Residue (10000 yuan)	32159	37932	33624

注：自1997年起，本表及以下各表调查范围含乡镇企业。

Note: Survey scrope of this table and follows covered township enterprises since 1997.

15－22 工业"三废"排放及处理情况（1998）

行业名称	Items	工业企业数（个） Number of Enterprises (unit)	工业废水排放总量（万吨） Industrial Waste Water Discharged (10000 tons)	#直接排入海的 Discharged Directly to Sea
总计	**Total**	**6984**	**202943**	**2033**
#重点调查企业	Key Sunvey Enterprises	6984	196606	2033
采掘业	Mining and Quarrying	89	2645	3
食品、烟草加工及食品、饮料制造业	Food, Tobacco and Beverage Processing	643	6907	39
纺织业	Textile Industry	1017	21905	238
皮革、毛皮、羽绒及其制品业	Leather, Furs, Feather and Related Products	82	692	…
造纸及纸制品业	Papermaking and Paper Products	164	12231	
印刷业、记录媒介的复制	Printing and Record Pressing	49	107	2
石油加工及炼焦业	Petroleum Processing and Coking	34	2168	
化工原料及化学制品制造业	Raw Chemical Materials and Chemical Products	938	70416	642
医药制造业	Medical and Pharmaceutical Products	173	4517	53
化学纤维制造业	Chemical Fiber	38	4124	64
橡胶制品业	Rubber Products	63	655	
塑料制品业	Plastic Products	107	1212	…
非金属矿物制造业	Nonmetal Mineral Industry	914	3219	65
#水泥制造业	Cement Manufacturing	172	756	
黑色金属冶炼及压延工业	Smelting and Pressing of Ferrous Metals	158	28508	
有色金属冶炼及压延工业	Smelting and Pressing of Nonferrous Metals	94	1007	
金属制品业	Metal Products	604	1060	28
机械、电气、电子设备制造业	Machine, Electric and Electronic Equipment Manufacturing	1193	11058	51
电力、煤气及水的生产和供应业	Production and Supply of Power, Coal Gas and Tap Water	126	27986	839
其它行业	Other Industries	498	2526	9

DISCHARGE AND TREATMENT OF INDUSTRIAL WASTE WATER, WASTE GAS AND RESIDUE

工业废水排放达标量（万吨） Industrial Waste Water Reaching Discharged (Standards 10000 tons)	工业废气排放总量（亿标立方米） Industrial Waste Gas Discharged (Standards 10^8 cu. m)	燃料燃烧过程废气排放总量（亿标立方米） Waste Gas Dischanged From Fuel (Standards 10^8 cu. m)	#经过消烟除尘的 Soot and Dust Removed	生产工艺过程废气排放总量（亿标立方米） Waste Gas Discharged in the Process of Production (Standards 10^8 cu. m)	#经过净化处理的 Gas Purified	工业二氧化硫排放量（吨） Industrial Sulphur Dioxide Discharged (tons)	#生产工艺过程中排放的 Sulphur Dioxide Discharged in the Process of Production
153854	**7488**	**5611**	**5271**	**1877**	**1495**	**1240151**	**77480**
153854	7488	5611	5271	1877	1495	1056317	77479
2434	30	25	21	5	5	4511	1279
4373	113	92	90	20	19	14987	1
12442	299	271	253	29	28	52248	220
296	3	4	3			768	
7441	90	88	83	2	…	11958	
47	1	…	…	…		56	
1957	72	48	45	24	19	5164	3120
51134	942	749	729	194	168	124362	12305
2949	34	33	33	1	1	7467	24
3099	270	124	115	146	30	24895	
484	12	12	10	…	…	2516	
1096	26	15	15	11	11	4307	
2967	1175	410	311	765	619	130110	28724
717	745	170	159	575	466	49251	24330
24572	699	270	184	428	420	54279	30735
702	54	52	44	2	1	4807	159
805	34	17	8	17	16	6040	92
9702	330	144	97	186	116	18746	783
25624	3217	3209	3196	8	7	630707	11
1730	87	48	34	39	35	142223	27

续表 1

行业名称	Items	工业二氧化硫去除总量（吨） Industrial Sulphur Dioxide Removed (tons)	#生产工艺过程去除的 Removed in the Process of Production	工业烟尘排放量（吨） Industrial Soot Discharged (tons)	工业烟尘去除量（吨） Industrial Soot Removed (tons)
总计	**Total**	**171213**	**70278**	**536291**	**7329276**
#重点调查企业	Key Sunvey Enterprises	171213	70278	385271	7329276
采掘业	Mining and Quarrying	1140	1012	2045	5986
食品、烟草加工及食品、饮料制造业	Food, Tobacco and Beverage Processing	1899	1	5620	26450
纺织业	Textile Industry	9089	17	21551	86065
皮革、毛皮、羽绒及其制品业	Leather, Furs, Feather and Related Producets	49		285	1025
造纸及纸制品业	Papermaking and Paper Products	641		4853	29869
印刷业、记录媒介的复制	Printing and Record Pressing	1		42	373
石油加工及炼焦业	Petroleum Processing and Coking	26031	25972	688	627
化工原料及化学制品制造业	Raw Chemical Materials and Chemical Products	53839	30402	48036	610566
医药制造业	Medical and Pharmaceutical Products	3129	13	2423	9858
化学纤维制造业	Chemical Fiber	1274		3724	69708
橡胶制品业	Rubber Products	268	2	895	7109
塑料制品业	Plastic Products	994		762	2798
非金属矿物制造业	Nonmetal Mineral Industry	15105	7927	122655	139251
#水泥制造业	Cement Manufacturing	11202	5126	29457	106698
黑色金属冶炼及压延工业	Smelting and Pressing of Ferrous Metals	5379	2869	14067	71110
有色金属冶炼及压延工业	Smelting and Pressing of Nonferrous Metals	287		5627	75166
金属制品业	Metal Products	51		2828	2399
机械、电气、电子设备制造业	Machine, Electric and Electronic Equipment Manufacturing	15311	173	10150	28195
电力、煤气及水的生产和供应业	Production and Supply of Power, Coal Gas and Tap Water	36023	1883	192071	6149705
其它行业	Other Industries	703	7	97969	13016

Continued 1

工业粉尘排放量（吨）Industrial Dust Discharged (tons)	工业粉尘回收量（吨）Industrial Dust Retrieved (tons)	工业固体废物产生量（万吨）Industrial Waste Residue Produced (10000 tons)	工业固体废物综合利用量（万吨）Industrial Waste Residue Used (10000 tons)	工业固体废物贮存量（万吨）Industrial Waste Residue Stored (10000 tons)	工业固体废物处置量（万吨）Industrial Waste Residue Treated (10000 tons)	工业固体废物排放量（万吨）Industrial Waste Residue Discharged (10000 tons)	历年累计堆存量（万吨）Volume of Waste Residue Accumulated Over the Years (10000 tons)
550547	**1451962**	**2944**	**2259**	**443**	**86**	**19**	**9896**
306158	1451962	2713	2259	443	86	12	9896
392	525	534	332	144	9	5	5591
558	11889	86	83	…	1	1	
144	576	87	82	…	4	…	
		2	1	…	…	…	
	18	46	39	1	2	4	
		45	44				
1439	878	8	7	…	…		
2229	21268	412	340	52	29	2	236
	2	15	14		1		
	32	41	26	7	8		181
9	22	4	3		1		
366	362	8	7		…		
505345	1108853	63	62		1		
460820	782482	27	26				
22739	222309	453	408	35	9	…	274
445	119	17	9	8	…		76
7133	84	6	5		1	…	
8319	70778	68	63	1	4	1	
193	3204	867	708	195	15		3534
1236	11043	182	26		1	6	4

续 表 2

行 业 名 称	Items	三废综合利用产品产值（万元）Output Value of Products Made from Waste Gas Waste Water and Waste Residues (10000 yuan)	三废综合利用产品利润（万元）Profits Obtained From Waste Water, Waste Gas and Waste Residue (10000 yuan)
总 计	**Total**	**161299**	**33624**
#重点调查企业	Key Sunvey Enterprises	161299	33624
采掘业	Mining and Quarrying	2124	307
食品、烟草加工及食品、饮料制造业	Food, Tobacco and Beverage Processing	3455	1335
纺织业	Textile Industry	2103	940
皮革、毛皮、羽绒及其制品业	Leather, Furs, Feather and Related Producets	101	1
造纸及纸制品业	Papermaking and Paper Products	5193	765
印刷业、记录媒介的复制	Printing and Record Pressing	2	1
石油加工及炼焦业	Petroleum Processing and Coking	14816	5750
化工原料及化学制品制造业	Raw Chemical Materials and Chemical Products	54679	14546
医药制造业	Medical and Pharmaceutical Products	5088	478
化学纤维制造业	Chemical Fiber	1224	518
橡胶制品业	Rubber Products	22	7
塑料制品业	Plastic Products	1759	107
非金属矿物制造业	Nonmetal Mineral Industry	34904	3443
#水泥制造业	Cement Manufacturing	20664	1374
黑色金属冶炼及压延工业	Smelting and Pressing of Ferrous Metals	23807	2459
有色金属冶炼及压延工业	Smelting and Pressing of Nonferrous Metals	818	376
金属制品业	Metal Products	105	136
机械、电气、电子设备制造业	Machine, Electric and Electronic Equipment Manufacturing	4507	1094
电力、煤气及水的生产和供应业	Production and Supply of Power, Coal Gas and Tap Water	5639	1095
其它行业	Other Industries	953	266

Continued 2

工业锅炉 Industrial Boiler		#烟尘排放达标的 Soot Discharge Standardized		工业窑炉数（座） Number of Industrial Store (unit)	#烟尘排放达标的（座） Soot Discharge Standardized (unit)
（台） (unit)	（蒸吨） (Steam tons)	（台） (unit)	（蒸吨） (Steam tons)		
6862	**84491**	**5214**	**71556**	**4522**	**2437**
6862	84491	5214	71556	4522	2437
259	915	194	723	59	45
689	2427	495	1874	35	20
1501	6194	1216	5255	179	156
76	215	50	146	1	1
243	2266	181	966	16	1
24	43	18	33	262	
33	568	24	546	79	67
1088	8469	783	6624	501	356
226	865	179	688	15	5
94	2083	78	1998	6	6
81	314	62	247	6	5
78	253	63	226	10	5
259	585	181	491	1242	474
75	182	61	173	337	174
161	1290	128	1113	404	258
61	764	49	739	135	72
220	264	141	226	260	124
951	3830	743	3339	1153	777
319	52027	258	45403	22	18
499	1119	371	919	137	47

15-23 企事业污染治理情况
TREATMENT OF WASTE WATER, WASTE GAS AND RESIDUE BY ENTERPRISES AND INSTITUTIONS

单位:万元 (10000 yuan)

指标	Items	1990	1995	1997	1998
汇总单位数 (个)	**Number of Units Converaged**	**3796**	**1117**	**935**	**1481**
污染治理资金来源合计	**Source of Funds for Pollution Treatment**	**24784**	**54187**	**80616**	**233256**
基本建设资金	Capital Construction	5615	2665	1354	3974
更新改造资金	Technical Updating and Transformation	5901	20882	8354	4810
综合利用利润留成资金	Retained Profits	417	4863	8911	21075
环境保护补助资金	Environment Protection Subsidy Funds	7003	4935	4577	8193
贷款	Loans	3859	2694	12072	23008
其它资金	Others	1989	17578	45348	172196
污染治理资金使用额	**Use of Funds**	**24781**	**54187**	**80616**	**233256**
治理废水	Waste Water	14309	33410	61531	180029
治理废气	Waste Gas	6358	13428	14189	31250
治理固体废物	Waste Residue	2368	4554	1784	13829
治理噪声	Noice Abatement	521	1940	939	592
其它	Others	1225	855	21732	7556
当年安排治理项目 (个)	**Projects Arranged for Treatment in This Years**	**1382**	**919**	**738**	**2524**
治理废水 (个)	Waste Water	567	357	399	1789
治理废气 (个)	Waste Gas	597	359	235	521
治理固体废物 (个)	Solid Waste Residue	49	38	18	32
治理噪声 (个)	Noice Abatement	133	127	58	58
其它 (个)	Others	36	38	28	124
当年竣工项目 (个)	**Projects Completed**	**1307**	**776**	**786**	**1897**
治理废水 (个)	Waste Water	533	278	433	1455
治理废气 (个)	Waste Gas	565	310	245	275
治理固体废物 (个)	Solid Waste Residue	41	38	20	16
治理噪声 (个)	Noice Abatement	130	121	60	40
其它 (个)	Others	38	29	28	111
当年竣工项目设计处理利用"三废"能力	**Capacities of Projects Completed for the Treatment and Utilization of Waste Water, Waste Gas and Residue by Design**				
处理废水量 (万吨/日)	Waste Water (10000 tons/day)	9.77	22.62	129.15	151.30
处理废气量 (万标立米/时)	Waste Gas (10000 standards cu·m/hour)	366.99	187.00	302.21	201.45
处理利用固体废物量 (万吨/日)	Solid Waste Residue (10000 tons/day)	24.00	44.00	11.22	22.90

注:1990年、1995年处理利用固体废物量计量单位为(万吨/年)。

Note: The measure unit of solid waste residue treatment and utilization was (10000 tons/year) in 1990 and 1995.

16. 档案、司法、社会福利、其他

ARCHIVES,JUDGEMENT,SOCIAL WELFARE AND OTHER

16 档案、司法、社会福利、其他
ARCHIVES, JUDGEMENT, SOCIAL WELFARE AND OTHER

1 9 9 8

档案事业机构	Number of Archive Institutions	1396	个	(unit)
馆藏档案案卷	Files Stored	689	万卷	
档案资料利用人次	Number of Person-times Using Archive Material	9.31	万人次	(10000)
律师事务所	Lawyer Offices	522	个	(unit)
律师所工作人员	Number of Personnels in Lawyer Offices	5922	人	(person)
人民调解委员会	Number of People's Mediation Committees	55081	个	(unit)
调解民事纠纷	Number of Civil Disputes Mediated	30.30	万件	(10000)
社会救济福利事业费	Funds For Social Relief and Welfare	63207	万元	(10000 yuan)
自然灾害救济费	Funds For Natural Calamities Relief	10803	万元	(10000 yuan)

社会救济福利事业费（亿元）

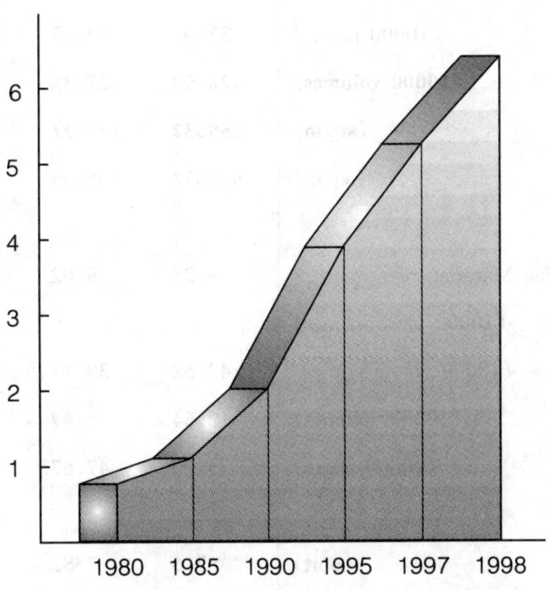

国内公证文书分类构成(%)

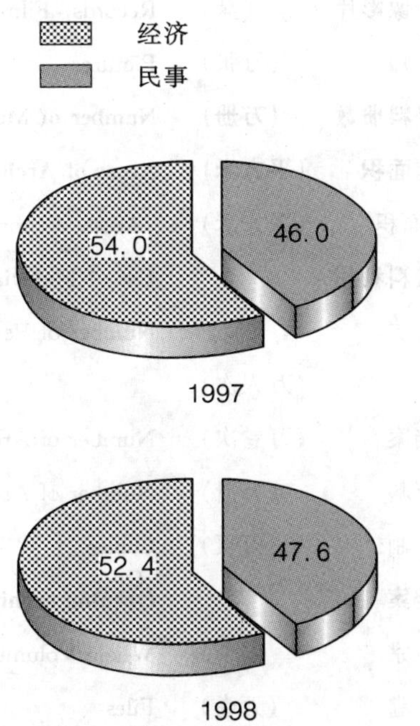

16－1　档案事业机构和人员数（1998）
NUMBER OF PERSONS AND INSTITUTIONS OF ARCHIVES

指　标	Item	机构数（个）Number of Institutions (unit)	专职人员数（人）Full-Time Persons (person)	#女　性 Female	#大专以上文化程度 College and Higher Level
总　计	**Total**	**1396**	**4703**	**3016**	**2570**
档案行政管理部门	Adiministrative Department of Archives	111	668	215	434
档案馆	Archives	158	1531	852	989
档案室(处、科)	Archives Offices (Sections)	1127	2504	1949	1147

16－2　档案馆档案资料馆藏和利用情况
CONDITIONS OF FILES STORED AND USED IN THE ARCHIVES

指　标	Item	1995	1997	1998
馆藏档案	**Archives Stored**			
全　宗　（个）	Whole Volume　(unit)	13018	13733	13932
案　卷　（万卷）	Files　(10000 volumes)	569.60	659.47	689.08
录音录像影片　（盘）	Records, Films of Videotape　(copy)	10002	13249	16933
照　片　（万张）	Pictures　(10000 pieces)	37.05	42.43	44.42
馆藏资料册数　（万册）	**Number of Material Stored　(10000 volumes)**	**128.00**	**127.38**	**130.92**
档案馆面积　（平方米）	**Areas of Archives　(sq.m)**	**159532**	**175921**	**193935**
#库房面积　（平方米）	Areas of Storerooms　(sq.m)	918532	105195	108149
档案资料利用	**Use of Material**			
利用人次　（万人次）	Number of Person-times Using Material　(10000 person-times)	9.28	9.02	9.31
利用档案　（万卷次）	Number of Archives Used　(10000 volume-times)	42.52	39.14	37.53
利用资料　（万册）	Number of Archives Used　(10000 volumes)	12.54	5.47	5.54
复　制　（万页）	Copies　(10000 pages)	75.20	47.67	49.71
开放档案	**Opening archives**			
全　宗　（个）	Whole Volume　(unit)	6716	7582	7766
案　卷　（万卷）	Files　(10000 volumes)	97.61	139.83	156.61

16－3 律师、公证及调解工作基本情况 BASIC STATISTICS ON LAWYERS, NOTARIZATION AND MEDIATION

指 标		Item		1990	1995	1997	1998
律师工作		**Lawyers**					
律师事务所	（个）	Number of Lawyer Offices	(unit)	139	414	532	522
律师所工作人员	（人）	Number of Personnels in Lawyer Offices	(person)	1696	3150	5503	5922
聘请担任常年法律顾问单位	（处）	Number of Units with Permanent Legal Advisors	(unit)	7298	22054	24826	23378
民事诉讼代理	（件）	Agent of Civil Cases	(case)	14000	9236	33984	38050
刑事辩护	（件）	Defending of Criminal Cases	(case)	12060	13254	17421	17325
经济诉讼代理	（件）	Agent of Economic Cases	(case)		25822	31831	31266
非诉讼法律事务	（件）	Agent of Non-Litigious Legal Affairs	(case)	2472	52002	40376	29451
解答法律咨询	（人次）	Legal Advisory Services	(person-times)	119148	272809	234685	231386
代写法律事务文书	（件）	Agent of Legal Document Written on Behalf of Clients	(case)	17760	39390	62548	62548
公证工作		**Notarization**					
公证处	（个）	Number of Notary Offices	(unit)	102	110	120	117
公证人员	（人）	Notarial Personnel	(person)	674	654	742	754
#公证员	（人）	Notaries		386	526	564	628
助理公证员	（人）	Assistant Notaries	(person)		43	47	35
办理国内公证文书	（件）	Number of Domestic Notarized Documents	(case)	222988	302248	295311	332293
#经济合同公证	（件）	Notarized Business Contracts	(case)	150725	156650	159583	174011
人民调解工作		**People's Mediation**					
专职司法助理员	（人）	Number of Full-Time Judicial Assistants	(person)	2320	2212	2173	2105
人民调解委员会	（个）	Number of People's Mediation Committees	(unit)	56293	57607	55508	55081
调解人员	（人）	Number of Mediators	(person)	860677	1003238	949731	822945
调解民事纠纷	（件）	Number of Civil Disputes Mediated	(case)	320426	303718	300915	302973

16-4 涉外公证文书分类
FOREIGN-RELATED NOTARIAL DOCUMENTS BY TYPE

单位:件 (case)

指标	Item	1997	1998
合计	**Total**	**59749**	**69039**
出生	Births	10963	10927
学历	Schooling	6275	8860
经历	Personal Histories	2722	5242
生存、居住	Survial and Residence	1226	130
死亡	Deaths	359	83
收养子女	Children Adoption	572	718
亲属关系	Kinship	3788	4526
婚姻状况	Marriages	6104	6447
继承权	Rights of Inheritance	174	203
遗嘱	Testaments	224	81
委托书	Trust Deeds	509	1098
声明书	Declarations	652	343
受、未受刑事处分	Criminal Records & Uncriminal Records	7696	8210
文本相符	Confirmation of Copies and Photo-Offset Copies to Originals	5825	5494
其他	Others	12660	16677

16-5 调解民事纠纷分类
CIVIL DISPUTES MEDIATED BY TYPE

单位:件 (case)

指标	Item	1990	1995	1997	1998
合计	**Total**	320426	303718	300915	302973
婚姻	Marriages	49328	54167	49112	47142
继承	Rights of Inheritance	10034	13006	11192	12383
赡、抚、扶养	Family Fostering	24298	29195	26119	28745
其他婚姻家庭	Other Marriage Family	46855	38268	34617	36246
房屋、宅基地	Housing and Housing Sites	46197	52350	45502	50388
邻里	Neighbor Disputes	21920	26137	29686	29964
债务	Debts	22893	29325	30883	29632
生产经营	Business	24154	22345	22440	22959
损害赔偿	Compensation for Damages	25749	23160	26665	21017
其他	Others	48998	15765	24699	21419

16-6 国内公证文书分类
DOMESTIC NOTARIAL DOCUMENTS BY TYPE

单位:件 (unit)

项 目	Item	1997	1998
总 计	**Total**	**295311**	**332293**
经济公证	**Notarized Documents on Economic Affairs**	**159583**	**174011**
购 销	Purchases and Sales of Products	990	1151
联 营	Joint Business	722	871
拍 卖	Auctions	1074	2080
贷 款	Loans	39647	38398
担 保	Guarantees	2857	4068
招标、投标	Bidding	4962	5597
科技协作	Coordination of Science and Technology	107	84
供用电	Supply and Use of Electric Power	1754	1126
劳务合同	Labor Contracts	23303	18776
建筑工程承包	Construction Project Contracts	2813	1966
工商服务业承包	Industrial and Commercial Service Contracts	4977	6403
农林牧副渔业承包	Farming, Forestry, Animal Husbandry, Sideline Production and Fishery Contracts	10337	4756
财产租赁	Property Leases	5282	5192
企业租赁	Enterprise Leases	1814	2223
资产经营责任制	System of Assets Business Responsibility	1072	781
其他经济合同	Other Business Contracts	14123	22212
法人(代表人)资格	Legal Person (agent) Identification	4469	1901
法人委托书	Legal Person Trust Deeds	9735	5473
公司章程	Corporation Constitutions	91	214
执行许可证明	Operating Permits	808	541
其 他	Others	28646	50198
民事公证	**Notarized Documents on Civil Relations**	**135728**	**158282**
收 养	Child Adoption	1509	1192
解除收养	Adoption Renouncements	89	415
继承权	Rights of Inheritance	1801	3099
遗 嘱	Testaments	2680	3674
产 权	Property Rights	1017	1263
亲属关系	Kinship	530	1158
死 亡	Death Certificates	63	36
房屋买卖	Purchases and Sales of Houses	5683	7790
房屋租赁	House Leases	3214	4150
留学协议	Foreign Study Contracts	253	773
遗赠扶养协议	Donations and Family Fostering	592	573
其他民事协议	Other Civil Agreements	25547	44453
委托书	Trust Deeds	1760	2498
赠与书	Presentaton Documents	3061	5259
声明书	Declarations	4973	6806
现场监督	Field Supervision	12696	10665
文本相符	Confirmation of Copies and Photo-Offset Copies to Originals	459	605
宅基地使用权	Rights to Housing Site	2066	812
证据保全	Evidence Preservation	919	962
计划生育协议	Birth Control Contracts	16016	15561
其 他	Others	50800	46538

16－7 主要年份社会抚恤及社会救济福利费用情况
PERSONS ENJOYING REGULAR SUBSIDY AND COMMISERATE OF COUNTRY IN MAIN YEARS

单位：万元 (10000 yuan)

年份 Year	合计 Total	抚恤事业费 Commiserate	社会救济福利事业费 Subsidies of Welfare	自然灾害救济费 Subsidies of Natural Calamity	在合计中：由集体单位供给的 Among Total: Collletive Funds
1980	15208	5138	7188	2882	6176
1981	18054	6778	7230	4046	7578
1982	18551	8158	8009	2385	9013
1983	22360	8901	10101	3359	10182
1984	24966	9804	12548	2615	11237
1985	24095	11115	10976	2004	11922
1986	29015	13514	11989	3513	13175
1987	29866	12722	14206	2939	14106
1988	34903	15536	16207	3161	17427
1989	40778	18265	18310	4203	20082
1990	46657	20676	20333	5648	21595
1991	69567	20530	27005	22032	27730
1992	60808	22548	23267	14993	23433
1993	60972	25920	27448	7605	27022
1994	72276	31933	34078	6265	32392
1995	87470	38966	39544	8961	38558
1996	104278	48874	46470	8935	47955
1997	119396	57247	52304	9846	54823
1998	141192	67183	63207	10803	64214

16－8 享受补助救济人员情况
PERSONS RECEIVING SUBSIDIES OR RELIEF FUNDS

指标	Items	1995	1997	1998
散居孤老残幼人数 （万人）	Persons in Children, Elderly and Disabled Staff Receiving Relief Funds (10000 person)	15.30	15.41	16.20
得到国家定期定量救济人数 （人）	Persons Receiving Periodical and Fixed Government Relief Funds (person)	9063	8841	8326
得到集体给予补助人数 （万人）	Persons Recieving Collective Subsidies (10000 person)	12.85	10.36	10.45
农村困难户得到救济人数 （万人次）	Rural Poor Households Receiving Relief Funds and Subsidies (10000 person-times)	193.13	158.90	162.45
城镇困难户得到救济补助人数 （万人次）	Persons in Urban Poor Households Recieving Relief Funds and Subsidies (10000 person-times)	31.96	23.87	26.47
城镇困难户得到国家定期定量救济人数 （人）	Persons in Urban Poor Households Recieving Periodical and Fixed Government Relief Funds (person)	10103	8113	6437
精减退职老职工得到救济人数 （万人）	Laid-Off, Retired, Elderly Staff Recieving Relief Funds (10000 person)	3.67	3.61	3.55
本年新增扶贫户数 （万户）	Increase Poor Households (10000 household)	11.62	8.81	7.47
本年脱贫户数 （万户）	Households Leaving the Poor Household Support Program (10000 household)	10.39	11.91	10.00

16-9 社会福利事业单位和工作人员数
SOCIAL WELFARE INSTITUTIONS AND STAFF

指标	Items	1997 机构(个) Institutions	1997 工作人员(人) Staff	1998 机构(个) Institutions	1998 工作人员(人) Staff
总计	**Total**	**10713**	**457614**	**9827**	**417697**
社会福利事业单位	Social Welfare Institutions	3147	15879	2918	15134
民政部门办	Run by Civil Adiministration Departments	86	5026	88	4987
社会办	Run by Communities	3061	10853	2830	10147
社会福利企业单位	Social Welfare Enterprises	7424	438956	6768	399698
民政部门办	Run by Civil Adiministration Departments	433	31351	437	28403
#假肢厂(站)	Artificial Limb Factories	1	117	2	121
#安置农场	Settle Down Farm	1	204	1	197
社会办	Run by Communities	6991	407605	6331	371295
收容遣送站	Collecting and Repatriation Units	25	402	26	410
殡葬事业单位	Funeral and Interment Institution	117	2377	115	2455

16-10 社会福利事业基本情况(1998)
BASIC STATISTICS ON SOCIAL WELFARE INSTITUTIONS

指标	Items	院数(个) Homes	工作人员(人) Staff	床位(张) Beds	年末收养人员(人) Persons Housed (year-end)
总计	**Total**	**3090**	**15671**	**80435**	**66299**
民政部门办社会福利事业单位	Run by Civil Administration Departments	88	4987	11456	8915
优抚休、疗养院	Convalescent Homes	18	768	1230	1000
城市福利院	Urban Social Welfare Homes	70	4219	10226	7915
城镇集体办光荣院、敬老院	Run by Urban Collective Units	1430	5682	35256	28389
光荣院	Homes for Disabled Veterans	2	7	25	15
敬老院	Rural Homes for the Elderly	1428	5675	35231	28374
农村集体办光荣院、敬老院	Run by Rural Collective	1572	5002	33723	28995
光荣院	Homes for Disabled Veterans	3	6	25	24
敬老院	Urban Homes for the Elderly	1569	4996	33698	28971

16－11 工会、妇联基本情况
BASIC CONDITION OF LABOUR UNION AND WOMEN'S FEDERATION

指标	Items	1995	1997	1998
工会基本情况	**Basic Condition of Labour Union**			
基层工会组织数（个）	Number of Basic Level Labour Union Organizations (units)	36215	31662	31741
职工人数（人）	Number of Staff and Workers (persons)	7142585	5723621	5490828
#女职工人数（人）	Women Workers (persons)	3055349	2390799	2180087
会员人数（人）	Number of Members (persons)	6454813	5246421	5096394
#女会员人数（人）	Women Members (persons)	2758135	2154479	1994473
女职工工作委员会（个）	Number of Women Workers Working Committees (units)	22843	19264	21459
建立职工代表大会制度的单位（个）	Number of Units Established with Workers Delegating Congress System (units)	23194	19329	23746
建立劳动争议调解委员会的单位（个）	Number of Units Established with Labour Disputation Mediating Committees (units)	18292	12255	15978
建立工会劳动保护监督检查委员会（个）	Number of Units Established with Labour Protection Supervisting and Examing Committees (units)		11397	12830
建立工会劳动法律监督检查组织（个）	Number of Organizations Established with Law of Labour Supervising and Examing Committees By Labour Union (units)		8370	9649
开展扶贫帮困送温暖活动的单位（个）	Number of Units Carried Out Supporting Poverty and Providing Warmth Activities (units)		10132	25812
开展合理化建议活动的单位（个）	Number of Units Carried Out Rationalization Proposal Activities (units)	26209	12893	
开展劳动竞赛的单位（个）	Number of Units Carried Out Labour Competition (units)	26388	9435	
妇联基本情况	**Basic Condition of Women's Federation**			
妇女脱盲人数（万人）	Numer of Women Free from Illiteracy (10000 persons)	27.32	5.40	
参加技术培训人数（万人）	Number of Persons Took Part in Technical Training (10000 persons)	337.19	650.00	500.01
妇联干部数（人）	Number of Cadres of Women's Federation (persons)	3265	3230	3231

17. 城市经济与建设

URBAN ECONOMY AND CONSTRUCTION

17 城市经济与建设
URBAN ECONOMY AND CONSTRUCTION

1 9 9 8

城市基础设施投资总额	Total Investment Value of Urban Infrastructure	123.39	亿元	(10^8 yuan)
全年供水总量	Total Annual Supply of Tap Water	35.90	亿吨	(10000 tons)
城市气化率	Population With Access to Urban Gas	92.7	%	(%)
城市实有道路长度	Length of Urban Roads	9618	公里	(km)
人均居住面积	Per Capita Living Space	9.9	平方米/人	(sp. m/person)
公交营运车辆	Operating Public Transtport Vehicles	12411	辆	(unit)
人均公共绿地面积	Public Green Areas Per Capita	7.7	平方米/人	(sp. m/person)

城市用气普及率(%)

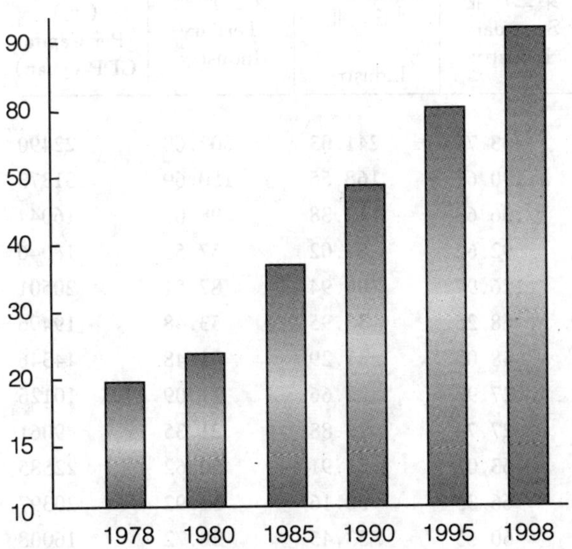

建城区绿化覆盖率(%)

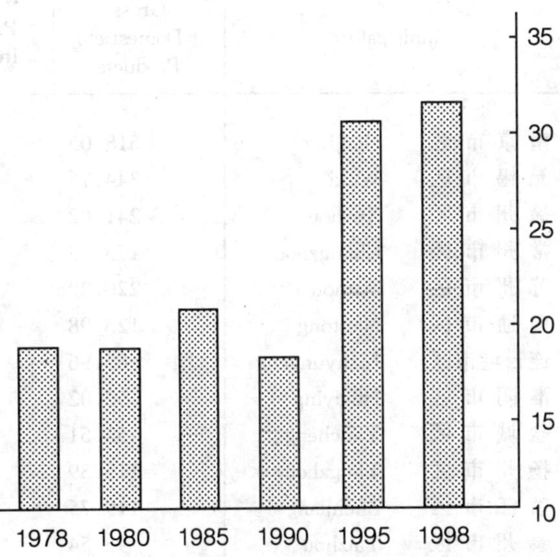

17－1 主要城市人口、劳动力(1998)
POPULATION AND EMPLOYMENT OF MAJOR MUNICIPALITY

单位:万人 (10000 persons)

市名 Municipality		年末总人口 Total Population (year-end)	#非农业人口 Nonagricultural Population	当年出生人口(人) Births	当年死亡人口(人) Deaths	年末从业人数 Employment (year-end)	#在岗职工人数 Staff and Workers Employed
南京市区	Nanjing	276.36	238.89	16564	16693	142.27	100.05
无锡市区	Wuxi	110.21	94.09	9805	7852	56.56	36.67
徐州市区	Xuzhou	151.86	104.47	14758	8273	74.39	44.71
常州市区	Changzhou	85.61	77.26	9444	4829	49.90	27.31
苏州市区	Suzhou	107.75	84.57	6442	7367	54.19	30.49
南通市区	Nantong	63.96	46.83	5807	3430	40.48	21.66
连云港市区	Lianyungang	60.45	44.79	6616	2530	31.83	18.64
淮阴市区	Huaiying	52.18	32.09	10467	3219	29.27	13.69
盐城市区	Yancheng	59.88	33.22	6395	2770	24.17	14.65
扬州市区	Yangzhou	51.35	39.50	4995	3219	27.84	19.81
镇江市区	Zhenjiang	59.27	47.00	6427	2940	32.77	18.72
泰州市区	Taizhou	58.80	22.00	5317	4089	32.30	11.76
宿迁市区	Suqian	23.70	11.54	2705	917	8.47	3.49

17－2 主要城市国内生产总值(1998)
GROSS DOMESTIC PRODUCTS OF MAJOR MUNICIPALITY

单位:亿元 (10^8 yuan)

市名 Municipality		国内生产总值 Gross Domestic Products	第一产业 Primary Industry	第二产业 Secondary Industry	#工业 Industry	第三产业 Tertiary Industry	人均国内总产值(元) Per Capita GDP (yuan)
南京市区	Nanjing	618.05	6.74	303.71	241.03	307.60	22490
无锡市区	Wuxi	344.76	3.44	190.63	168.55	150.69	31373
徐州市区	Xuzhou	241.62	6.92	136.63	113.38	98.07	16044
常州市区	Changzhou	153.73	3.58	92.62	87.02	57.53	18046
苏州市区	Suzhou	220.20	5.72	126.97	106.94	87.51	20501
南通市区	Nantong	123.98	2.24	68.26	55.95	53.48	19496
连云港市区	Lianyungang	85.96	6.45	48.03	41.29	31.48	14346
淮阴市区	Huaiying	52.02	3.00	27.93	22.66	21.09	10126
盐城市区	Yancheng	53.51	4.41	27.74	23.88	21.35	9061
扬州市区	Yangzhou	115.39	1.75	63.02	51.91	50.62	22585
镇江市区	Zhenjiang	119.75	1.48	66.35	50.16	51.92	20397
泰州市区	Taizhou	93.54	4.17	60.65	53.45	28.72	16008
宿迁市区	Suqian	13.43	1.06	6.97	4.04	5.40	5715

17－3 主要城市工业总产值(1998)
GROSS OUTPUT VALUE OF INDUSTRY OF MAJOR MUNICIPALITY

单位:亿元 (10⁸ yuan)

市名 Municipality		全部工业总产值(当年价) Gross Output Value of Total Industry (current price)	限额以上工业产值 Over Norm Industrial Output Value	国有经济 State-owned	集体经济 Collective -owned	其他经济 Others	限额以下工业产值 Below Norm Industrial Output Value
南京市区	Nanjing	925.61	851.65	344.05	81.12	426.49	73.96
无锡市区	Wuxi	614.84	470.61	133.69	39.91	297.00	144.23
徐州市区	Xuzhou	323.97	246.04	102.23	37.84	105.97	77.93
常州市区	Changzhou	393.69	320.09	78.45	78.13	163.51	73.60
苏州市区	Suzhou	454.77	374.03	63.69	63.90	246.43	80.74
南通市区	Nantong	203.85	179.68	40.14	11.28	128.25	24.17
连云港市区	Lianyungang	160.43	89.34	28.74	15.08	45.52	71.09
淮阴市区	Huaiying	94.52	76.48	34.33	7.21	34.94	18.04
盐城市区	Yancheng	92.44	68.26	38.22	6.97	23.07	24.18
扬州市区	Yangzhou	196.22	157.36	66.76	32.05	58.55	38.85
镇江市区	Zhenjiang	167.34	133.55	74.83	16.94	41.77	33.80
泰州市区	Taizhou	174.40	140.24	34.04	56.40	49.80	34.16
宿迁市区	Suqian	19.35	7.56	1.33	4.60	2.18	11.79

17－4 主要城市限额以上工业企业主要指标(1998)
MAJOR INDICATORS OF OVER NORM INDUSTRIAL ENTERPRISES WITH INDEPENDENT ACCOUMING SYSTEMS OF MAJOR MUNICIPALITY

单位:亿元 (10⁸ yuan)

市名 Municipality		企业单位数(个) Number of Enterprises (units)	#亏损企业 Loss Making Enterprises	资产合计 Total Property	负债合计 Total Liabilities	产品销售收入 Revenue of Product Sales	利税总额 Total Pre-Tax Profits
南京市区	Nanjing	896	200	1345.14	780.89	880.11	80.62
无锡市区	Wuxi	682	153	735.58	434.54	482.33	37.23
徐州市区	Xuzhou	266	79	365.21	254.78	201.86	19.79
常州市区	Changzhou	695	179	424.44	259.23	301.58	13.96
苏州市区	Suzhou	611	151	577.56	351.25	344.76	11.96
南通市区	Nantong	353	122	296.74	148.49	164.78	14.99
连云港市区	Lianyungang	304	88	141.87	87.02	73.78	6.40
淮阴市区	Huaiying	122	26	122.68	84.50	71.28	8.94
盐城市区	Yancheng	123	33	126.10	79.17	60.98	4.26
扬州市区	Yangzhou	254	74	227.78	138.37	133.92	7.45
镇江市区	Zhenjiang	239	104	186.72	123.88	94.87	4.14
泰州市区	Taizhou	194	42	155.35	82.22	130.31	22.49
宿迁市区	Suqian	21	8	16.29	11.86	6.80	0.43

17－5 主要城市固定资产投资(1998)
FIXED ASSETS INVESTMENT OF MAJOR MUNICIPALITY

单位:亿元 (10⁸ yuan)

市名	Municipality	全社会固定资产投资完成额 Value of Fixed Assets Investment Fulfiled	基本建设投资完成 Value of Capital Construction Fulfilled	更新改造投资完成 Technical Updating and Transformation	房地产开发投资完成 Investment of Real Estate Development Fulfiled	商品房屋销售建筑面积(万平方米) Construction Space by Sale of Commodity Building (10000 sq.m)	#住宅 Housing
南京市区	Nanjing	316.53	133.19	57.17	97.13	156.29	128.94
无锡市区	Wuxi	142.54	30.37	13.70	20.36	83.28	73.30
徐州市区	Xuzhou	110.40	48.19	20.73	14.26	54.24	51.05
常州市区	Changzhou	69.94	18.77	17.78	12.44	42.34	38.29
苏州市区	Suzhou	195.43	34.55	24.11	35.28	131.42	113.87
南通市区	Nantong	89.93	36.98	10.02	10.95	58.56	54.77
连云港市区	Lianyungang	44.87	23.12	9.30	4.00	33.09	30.44
淮阴市区	Huaiying	34.34	16.11	10.40	2.91	21.92	21.28
盐城市区	Yancheng	23.32	9.43	4.71	5.13	33.50	31.40
扬州市区	Yangzhou	63.97	42.54	10.72	5.99	36.28	33.36
镇江市区	Zhenjiang	105.98	89.85	7.28	4.55	24.66	23.83
泰州市区	Taizhou	35.87	17.05	6.58	3.82	14.56	13.50
宿迁市区	Suqian	12.00	8.99	0.09	1.26	3.15	3.14

17－6 主要城市财政收支(1998)
FINANCIAL REVENUE AND EXPENDITURE OF MAJOR MUNICIPALITY

单位:亿元 (10⁸ yuan)

市名	Municipality	财政收入 Financial Revenue	#地方财政收入 Local Financial Revenue	#各项税收 Taxes	财政支出 Financial Expenditure	#文教科卫事业费 Culture, Edication, Science and Health Care	#支农支出 Expenditures Supporting Agriculture
南京市区	Nanjing	96.45	43.99	40.82	49.64	9.87	2.13
无锡市区	Wuxi	37.53	19.40	17.37	18.55	4.16	0.51
徐州市区	Xuzhou	25.42	10.08	8.92	11.92	3.41	0.76
常州市区	Changzhou	25.00	13.11	12.05	11.52	2.60	0.20
苏州市区	Suzhou	27.05	15.84	14.60	16.87	3.27	0.32
南通市区	Nantong	15.27	8.31	7.19	9.08	2.08	0.10
连云港市区	Lianyungang	8.76	5.39	4.28	7.10	1.63	0.09
淮阴市区	Huaiying	11.73	3.97	3.21	4.91	1.31	0.20
盐城市区	Yancheng	6.12	3.65	2.89	5.42	1.46	0.12
扬州市区	Yangzhou	8.14	4.30	3.74	6.19	1.61	0.08
镇江市区	Zhenjiang	10.05	4.80	4.40	6.25	1.71	0.13
泰州市区	Taizhou	12.58	6.72	6.21	8.74	1.49	0.34
宿迁市区	Suqian	1.07	0.69	0.54	2.73	0.42	0.10

17－7 主要城市国内外贸易（1998）
DOMESTIC AND FOREIGN TRADE OF MAJOR MUNICIPALITY

单位：万美元　　　　(10000 USD)

市名 Municipality		社会消费品零售总额（亿元）Total Retail Sales of Consumer Goods (10^8 yuan)	外贸自营出口总额 Total Export Value of Foreign Trade (Self-management)	协议合同外资金额 Foreign Capital Value Through Contract and Agreement	#外商直接投资 Direct Foreign Investment	实际利用外资 Actual Utilization of Foreign Capital Value	#外商直接投资 Direct Foreign Investment
南京市区	Nanjing	311.19	89476	27909	27909	65928	57183
无锡市区	Wuxi	137.05	192664	65506	62976	56610	49144
徐州市区	Xuzhou	90.97	18964	22545	17383	19204	19204
常州市区	Changzhou	72.66	79183	52734	17277	38731	24042
苏州市区	Suzhou	77.79	155856	206461	206461	140146	140146
南通市区	Nantong	47.75	101453	35139	33179	53939	30654
连云港市区	Lianyungang	38.63	29165	9259	7130	8982	6145
淮阴市区	Huaiying	33.87	12630	1486	300	6452	5263
盐城市区	Yancheng	35.42	18515	3021	1551	2695	2695
扬州市区	Yangzhou	45.65	37998	4936	4446	14847	4647
镇江市区	Zhenjiang	41.47	33690	18542	18542	60658	60658
泰州市区	Taizhou	29.38	6335	2899	2177	3669	3397
宿迁市区	Suqian	7.68	390	163	163	459	459

17－8 主要城市邮电业务（1998）
REVENUE FROM POSTS AND TELECOMMUNICATION OF MAJOR MUNICIPALITY

市名 Municipality		邮电业务总量（亿元）Revenue From Posts and Telecommunication Services (10^8 yuan)	年末电话机数（万部）Telephones (10000)	年末无线寻呼用户（万户）Wireless Telephones (10000)	年末移动电话用户（万户）Mobile Telephones (10000)	全年用电量（亿千瓦小时）Power Consumption (10^8 kwh)	#城乡居民用电 Urban and Rural Power Consumption
南京市区	Nanjing	23.71	127.65	30.20	20.11	99.46	9.75
无锡市区	Wuxi	13.30	73.74	38.56	12.82	38.99	4.55
徐州市区	Xuzhou	6.07	37.16	11.84	5.78	36.78	2.52
常州市区	Changzhou	10.57	64.90	30.54	9.56	27.78	3.38
苏州市区	Suzhou	13.78	67.48	19.61	11.23	30.45	3.55
南通市区	Nantong	4.41	23.09	12.70	4.56	19.67	2.44
连云港市区	Lianyungang	2.73	12.28	7.79	2.23	12.68	1.11
淮阴市区	Huaiying	2.14	12.91	7.22	1.46	12.15	0.90
盐城市区	Yancheng	2.91	17.15	6.90	2.20	7.60	1.41
扬州市区	Yangzhou	4.60	24.22	13.14	4.30	11.14	1.64
镇江市区	Zhenjiang	3.97	29.26	10.27	3.16	19.88	1.26
泰州市区	Taizhou	1.92	18.46	5.00	1.42	7.77	1.12
宿迁市区	Suqian	0.74	5.61	1.51	0.60	4.40	1.24

17－9　主要城市环境保护（1998）
ENVIRONMENT PROTECTION OF MAJOR MUNICIPALITY

单位：万吨　　(10000 tons)

市名	Municipality	工业废水排放总量 Industrial Waste Water Discharged	工业废水处理排放达标量 Industrial Waste Water Reaching Discharge Standards	工业废水处理量 Industrial Waste Water Treated	生活污水排放量 Domestic Sewage Discharged	工业废气排放量（亿标米）Industrial Waste Gas Discharged (Standards 10^8 cu.m)	环境噪声达标面积（平方公里）Standardized Space of Environmental Noise (sq.km)
南京市区	Nanjing	64391	16719	56245	42498	1672.48	106
无锡市区	Wuxi	6296	5704	4000	18605	159.12	60
徐州市区	Xuzhou	2062	917	7154	7682	202.74	58
常州市区	Changzhou	5305	4582	2325	10148	198.10	50
苏州市区	Suzhou	8531	3030	7458	16116	240.60	60
南通市区	Nantong	4799	3450	2103	2632	390.60	52
连云港市区	Lianyungang	3185	3107	4709	2410	179.04	35
淮阴市区	Huaiying	1667	691	1483	2258	71.82	27
盐城市区	Yancheng	1709	148	841	1898	100.86	18
扬州市区	Yangzhou	3572	857	981	2300	136.23	37
镇江市区	Zhenjiang	6017	2656	4691	7560	477.52	38
泰州市区	Taizhou	9908	7968	2334	4857	128.80	19
宿迁市区	Suqian	1616	1605	858	402	21.24	3

17－10　主要城市居民生活(一)（1998）
PEOPLE'S LIVELIHOOD OF MAJOR MUNICIPALITY（Ⅰ）

单位：元　　(yuan)

市名	Municipality	在岗职工平均工资 Average Wage Bill of Employed Staff and Workers	#国有经济 State-owned	城镇居民人均可支配收入 Per Capita Allocatable Income of Urban Residents	城镇居民人均消费支出 Per Capita Living Expenditures of Urban Residents	#食品 Food	#衣着用品 Clothing Articals
南京市区	Nanjing	11316	11482	7018	6056	2735	598
无锡市区	Wuxi	10465	10960	7178	6220	2766	460
徐州市区	Xuzhou	9000	9234	6011	4381	2011	465
常州市区	Changzhou	10288	11022	7107	5282	2721	367
苏州市区	Suzhou	10595	11087	7812	6289	2816	433
南通市区	Nantong	9075	9213	6899	5701	2614	521
连云港市区	Lianyungang	7457	8400	5458	3945	1862	498
淮阴市区	Huaiying	7477	8039	5193	3692	1684	401
盐城市区	Yancheng	7335	7883	5173	4131	1999	434
扬州市区	Yangzhou	8786	9637	6101	4432	2421	441
镇江市区	Zhenjiang	8949	9594	6019	4701	2291	495
泰州市区	Taizhou	6982	8097	6057	4726	2269	446
宿迁市区	Suqian	6007	7460	3896	2984	1450	367

17－11　主要城市居民生活(二)(1998)
PEOPLE'S LIVELIHOOD OF MAJOR MUNICIPALITY (Ⅱ)

单位:元　　　　(yuan)

市　　名 Municipality		城镇居民人均消费支出 Per Capita Consumptive Expenditure of Urban Residents				居民消费价格指数(%) Consumer Price Index (%)	商品零售价格指数(%) Retail Price Index (%)
		#家庭设备、用品及服务 Family Facilities, Articals and Services	#医疗保健 Medicine and Medical Services	#娱乐、教育、文化服务 Cultural, Educational Recreational Artical and Services	#居　住 Residence		
南京市区	Nanjing	497	225	841	552	100.0	98.2
无锡市区	Wuxi	709	266	661	718	100.9	99.0
徐州市区	Xuzhou	365	206	565	341	100.0	98.3
常州市区	Changzhou	417	196	525	591	101.6	98.8
苏州市区	Suzhou	872	192	840	488	99.0	97.0
南通市区	Nantong	540	139	593	640	99.9	97.5
连云港市区	Lianyungang	153	144	415	557	99.6	98.1
淮阴市区	Huaiying	338	117	565	260	100.1	99.1
盐城市区	Yancheng	332	93	429	519	98.0	96.4
扬州市区	Yangzhou	333	76	405	402	100.5	99.1
镇江市区	Zhenjiang	251	92	561	551	99.5	97.2
泰州市区	Taizhou	341	161	421	371	100.1	98.7
宿迁市区	Suqian	167	128	237	292	99.3	98.6

17－12　主要城市教育、科技、卫生(1998)
CULTURE, SCIENCE AND TECHNOLOGY, PUBLIC HEALTH OF MAJOR MUNICIPALITY

市　　名 Municipality		高等学校在校学生数(万人) Number of Students in Education of High Institutions (10000 persons)	各类专业技术人员数(万人) Number of Scientific and Technical Personnel (10000 persons)	公共图书馆(个) Public Libraries	医院、卫生院数(个) Hospitals and Commune Hospitals	医院、卫生院床位数(张) Hospital Beds	医生数(人) Doctors
南京市区	Nanjing	13.24	27.56	13	192	16224	12980
无锡市区	Wuxi	1.25	11.12	5	42	6490	2484
徐州市区	Xuzhou	2.48	10.68	1	46	7906	5567
常州市区	Changzhou	1.43	9.09	1	31	4804	2268
苏州市区	Suzhou	2.92	8.18	4	33	5682	2717
南通市区	Nantong	0.99	3.70	2	28	4783	2410
连云港市区	Lianyungang	0.94	4.99	2	32	2845	1478
淮阴市区	Huaiying	0.71	3.27	1	17	2595	1124
盐城市区	Yancheng	0.82	5.13	1	16	1416	721
扬州市区	Yangzhou	2.31	5.22	1	21	3393	1368
镇江市区	Zhenjiang	1.69	5.11	1	22	3365	2634
泰州市区	Taizhou	0.19	3.69	1	22	1858	1136
宿迁市区	Suqian		0.56	1	5	377	219

17－13 城市公用事业基本情况
BASIC STATISICS ON URBAN PUBLIC UTILITIES

指标	Items	1990	1995	1997	1998
自来水年供水量（万吨）	Annual Supply of Tap Water (10000 tons)	256664	382325	343106	358999
#生活用水量	Residential Consumption	62369	105192	131650	137663
平均每人日生活用水（升）	Per Capita Day (litres)	176.4	225.6	267.94	273.3
用水普及率（%）	Population with Access to Tap Water (%)	91.3	98.9	99.3	99.2
公共汽(电)车营运车辆（辆）	Operating Public Transportation Vehicles (Buses and Trolley Buses)	2827	8101	9665	12411
平均每万人拥有公共交通车辆（标台）	Public Vehicles per 10000 Population (standard unit)	3.6	7.1	7.0	8.7
年末实有道路长度（公里）	Length of Road (year end) (km)	5812	8163	9440	9618
平均每万人拥有（公里）	Length of Road per 10000 Population (km)	6.5	8.3	8.4	8.7
年末实有道路面积（万平方米）	Area of Road (year end) (10000 sq.m)	5672	8669	10438	11336
每万人拥有（万平方米）	Area of Paved Road Per 10000 Population (10000 sq.m)	6.3	8.3	9.3	9.8
排水道长度（公里）	Length of Sewer Pipelines (km)	4099	8262	8812	9574
平均每万人拥有（公里）	Length of Sewer Pipelines Per 10000 Population (km)	4.6	7.9	7.8	8.3
人工煤气供气量（万立方米）	Coal Gas Supply (10000 cu.m)	142681	282227	274853	331580
#家庭用量	Residential Use	15902	30877	34055	34797
煤气管道长度（公里）	Length of Gas Pipelines (km)	1118	2041	2939	3470
液化气家庭用量（吨）	Residential Consumption of Liquefied Gas (tons)	122691	436131	392574	430131
用气普及率（%）	Population with Access to Gas (%)	36.8	81.8	87.8	92.7
城市绿化	Landscaping in Cities				
公共绿地面积（公顷）	Public Green Areas (hectare)	3447	7402	8175	8891
人均公共绿地面积（平方米）	Public Green Areas Per Capita (sq.m)	3.8	6.9	7.3	7.7
公园面积（公顷）	Area of Parks (Hectare)	2991	5648	4831	4920
环境卫生	Sanitation and Hygiene				
清运垃圾（万吨）	Garbage Disposal (10000 tons)	288	398	479	486
清运粪便（万吨）	Disposal of Night Soil (10000 tons)	221	209	196	302
每万人拥有公厕（座）	Public Restrooms Per 10000 Population	9.0	7.0	6.8	6.5

注：人均拥有指标按城市人口中非农业人口计算。

Note: Figrues for public utilities per 10000 persons were based on nonagricultural population in urban areas.

17－14 城市房屋面积情况
FLOOR SPACE OF URBAN BUILDINGS

单位:万平方米 (10000 sq.m)

年份 市名 Year Ctites	年末实有房屋建筑面积 Floor Space of Building (Year End)	#住宅 Rseidential Housing	本年房屋竣工面积 Floor Space of Building Completed Within the Year	#住宅 Rseidential Housing	年末实有房屋减少面积 Decreased Floor Space of Buiding (Year End)	#住宅 Rseidential Housing
1978	7655	3397	451	195		
1979	8554	3791	569	307	117	65
1980	9224	4127	663	386	59	31
1981	10032	4588	782	493	76	41
1982	10772	5043	778	469	71	37
1983	12002	5791	926	575	66	38
1984	12808	6249	894	507	84	53
1985	13811	6722	1039	557	131	87
1986	18000	8592	1203	632	132	85
1987	19139	9139	1189	589	160	109
1988	22552	10565	1433	691	187	125
1989	27898	14735	1457	774	173	131
1990	27179	13460	1169	651	160	119
1991	31523	15785	1317	702	203	144
1992	34899	17632	1635	850	363	260
1993	36890	19378	2261	1331	458	379
1994	34556	17362	2058	1207	361	272
1995	38320	19878	2415	1469	427	288
1996	40865	21386	2495	1443	447	263
1997	42778	22140	2629	1477	391	284
1998	45598	23467	2865	1596	456	350
市区 **Urban District**						
南京市区 Nanjing	8607	4267	633	310	63	46
无锡市区 Wuxi	3988	1756	176	95	38	29
徐州市区 Xuzhou	3104	1514	157	90	37	23
常州市区 Changzhou	2758	1360	97	43	19	17
苏州市区 Suzhou	3738	1857	267	163	47	47
南通市区 Nantong	1775	781	142	69	51	42
连云港市区 Lianyungang	1651	798	76	60	18	11
淮阴市区 Huaiying	1129	587	68	55	13	11
盐城市区 Yancheng	978	550	42	30	6	5
扬州市区 Yangzhou	1700	709	76	45	17	14
镇江市区 Zhenjiang	1650	845	49	35	11	11
泰州市区 Taizhou	825	448	70	38	17	17
宿迁市区 Suqian	352	217	32			

续表 Continued

年份 市名 Year Cities	年末实有住宅使用面积（万平方米） Floor space of Residential Housing in Use (Year-end 10000 sq. m)	年末实有住宅居住面积（万平方米） Floor space of Residential Housing for Living (Year-end 10000 sq. m)	人均使用面积（平方米/人） Per Capita Floorspace in Use (sq. m/person)	人均居住面积（平方米/人） Per Capita Floorspace for Living (sq. m/person)	解决缺房户（户） Number of Homeless Households Acquiring Housing (Household)
1978		1746		4.3	
1979		1917		4.0	
1980		2097		4.2	
1981		2330		4.5	
1982		2595		4.9	
1983		2950		5.2	
1984		3207		5.4	
1985		3460		5.6	
1986	6263	4064	9.9	6.4	17589
1987	6710	4380	9.9	6.5	29885
1988	7870	5009	10.4	6.6	10789
1989	11053	7113	12.0	7.7	12614
1990	9936	6564	10.8	7.2	14497
1991	11783	7802	11.7	7.7	13587
1992	12998	8714	11.9	8.0	13340
1993	14123	9550	12.3	8.3	7424
1994	12681	8470	12.0	8.0	17189
1995	14670	10118	12.3	8.5	14021
1996	15491	10391	13.5	9.0	20963
1997	16073	10740	13.9	9.3	20503
1998	17251	11535	14.7	9.9	14320
市 区 Urban District					
南京市区 Nanjing	3051	2212	12.8	9.3	
无锡市区 Wuxi	1370	878	14.6	9.3	
徐州市区 Xuzhou	1088	692	12.4	7.9	
常州市区 Changzhou	953	555	15.9	9.2	
苏州市区 Suzhou	1235	802	14.6	9.5	4676
南通市区 Nantong	580	354	13.5	8.2	1000
连云港市区 Lianyungang	599	399	13.4	8.9	1550
淮阴市区 Huaiying	460	282	14.7	9.0	1298
盐城市区 Yancheng	408	272	13.1	8.7	540
扬州市区 Yangzhou	616	382	15.6	9.7	1600
镇江市区 Zhenjiang	617	440	13.1	9.4	–
泰州市区 Taizhou	326	225	14.8	10.2	81
宿迁市区 Suqian	187	167	12.1	10.8	–

17－15 城市自来水情况
INDICATOR OF URBAN TAP WATER SUPPLY

年份 市名 Year Ctites	综合生产能力（万吨/日） General Production Capacity 10000 tons/Day	全年供水总量（万吨） Total Aunual Supply of Tap Water (10000 tons)	#生产用水量 Productive Use	#生活用水量 Residential Use	用水人口（万人） Residents With Access to Tap Water (10000 persons)	人均日生活用水量（升） Daily Per Capita Residential Tap Water Comsuption (liter)	城市人口用水普及率（%） Population With Access to Tap Water (%)
1978	112.3	35056	20073	12013	347.2	94.8	83.6
1979	125.1	39163	22408	14271	433.2	102.8	89.5
1980	142.6	45221	26005	16323	463.0	89.0	92.2
1981	157.7	49822	28768	16965	471.8	90.0	91.4
1982	165.0	56319	31149	20627	496.5	112.9	94.4
1983	175.1	62552	34831	22303	532.0	114.9	94.0
1984	212.6	68627	37380	24650	550.1	122.8	92.3
1985	218.9	76609	40908	29280	585.4	137.0	89.0
1986	602.9	177764	128259	39666	691.4	158.0	95.4
1987	706.6	204727	148378	42299	706.1	172.1	90.2
1988	734.9	220433	156689	51146	829.0	169.0	87.2
1989	856.3	233848	167472	54326	896.6	166.0	88.3
1990	941.7	256664	181543	62369	968.0	176.4	91.3
1991	1056.1	282691	201088	68287	1049.2	178.3	93.8
1992	1191.4	317812	224575	77010	1158.6	182.1	96.0
1993	1299.5	342780	239520	83041	1238.6	183.7	97.1
1994	1368.9	358696	243332	93030	1212.3	210.2	98.7
1995	1388.7	382325	190471	105192	1277.5	225.6	98.9
1996	1424.4	349423	192948	135429	1300.7	285.3	99.0
1997	1457.1	343106	189889	131650	1346.1	267.9	99.3
1998	1543.6	358999	199055	137663	1388.0	271.8	99.2
市区 Urban District							
南京市区 Nanjing	492.2	152964	99739	53168	276.4	527.1	100.0
无锡市区 Wuxi	109.6	23521	12246	8816	110.2	219.2	100.0
徐州市区 Xuzhou	74.5	13498	6132	7366	102.5	196.9	100.0
常州市区 Changzhou	66.0	15310	7192	7024	82.6	232.9	100.0
苏州市区 Suzhou	75.0	22819	6316	9664	97.3	272.3	100.0
南通市区 Nantong	50.7	10033	5217	3615	55.2	179.4	100.0
连云港市区 Lianyungang	31.1	7587	3266	3779	54.1	191.5	98.0
淮阴市区 Huaiying	35.0	5472	2554	2070	39.2	144.7	100.0
盐城市区 Yancheng	28.8	7388	3069	2903	33.1	240.4	100.0
扬州市区 Yangzhou	40.0	10790	4794	3724	51.4	198.7	100.0
镇江市区 Zhenjiang	50.0	12033	6450	4370	54.5	219.7	100.0
泰州市区 Taizhou	33.9	5024	2385	2114	31.0	187.0	96.0
宿迁市区 Suqian	5.4	1550	805	324	10.8	81.9	72.9

17－16 城市煤气、液化石油气情况
URBAN COAL GAS AND LIQUEFIED PETROLEUM

年份 市名 Year Ctites	全年供气总量 Total Gas Supply		家庭用气量 Residential Use		用气人口(万人) Population with Access to Gas (10000 person)		城市气化率(%) Percentage of Population Using Gas for Household Use (%)
	人工煤气(万立方米) Coal Gas (10000 cu. m)	液化石油气(吨) Liquefied Petroleum (tons)	人工煤气(万立方米) Coal Gas (10000 cu. m)	液化石油气(吨) Liquefied Petroleum (tons)	人工煤气 Coal Gas	液化石油气 Liquefied Petroleum	
1978	11756	23666	1592	22043	15.7	48.4	15.7
1979	11631	29381	1837	27656	17.5	61.0	16.2
1980	11401	32591	2215	31350	20.0	69.6	17.8
1981	10808	36387	2571	35439	21.8	74.0	18.6
1982	11358	37974	2740	37067	21.2	68.6	17.1
1983	11588	39725	2830	38841	23.4	68.5	16.2
1984	12468	40011	3122	38389	28.5	71.1	16.7
1985	13155	42495	3851	38834	39.9	76.2	17.9
1986	15951	118160	5394	60917	51.3	121.4	27.2
1987	109401	129880	7346	73511	73.8	141.1	31.6
1988	108438	178855	10704	92662	81.7	166.9	32.9
1989	140497	190471	13429	105671	93.0	186.1	32.5
1990	142681	216936	15902	122691	101.2	219.3	36.8
1991	142665	252342	17750	137780	116.3	261.2	41.9
1992	147625	337456	20943	190861	131.0	373.1	53.3
1993	153994	442089	23774	258003	150.6	498.0	63.5
1994	184552	574191	26281	337126	180.3	558.8	74.1
1995	282227	436131	30877	361990	213.4	637.3	81.8
1996	271852	543989	35837	468838	243.3	701.2	86.6
1997	274853	468106	34055	392574	244.1	746.2	87.8
1998	331580	620344	34797	430131	271.1	798.3	92.7
市区 Urban District							
南京市区 Nanjing	303537	101687	12774	80914	78.3	151.7	96.3
无锡市区 Wuxi	4806	29281	3310	28252	23.3	60.5	89.2
徐州市区 Xuzhou	4888	24788	2891	21062	30.3	46.9	87.9
常州市区 Changzhou	3533	31175	2861	30070	22.8	47.9	91.5
苏州市区 Suzhou	5184	72061	4114	29551	34.7	47.4	97.0
南通市区 Nantong	2575	17828	2562	14851	23.0	22.0	96.1
连云港市区 Lianyungang	547	14154	547	14154	3.8	33.3	82.6
淮阴市区 Huaiying	410	16950	388	8965	4.1	25.1	90.9
盐城市区 Yancheng		13532		13232		25.6	90.5
扬州市区 Yangzhou	1918	11845	1625	9605	17.9	18.7	92.5
镇江市区 Zhenjiang	2906	52584	2520	9554	22.4	20.0	90.1
泰州市区 Taizhou		16236		16236		20.2	91.8
宿迁市区 Suqian		1070		1006		9.6	72.2

17－17 城市市政工程情况
URBAN CIVIL FACILITIES

年份 市名 Year Ctites	年末实有道路长度（公里） Length of Roads (Year-end) (km)	年末实有道路面积（万平方米） Area of Roads (10000 sq. m)	排水管道长度（公里） Length of Drainage Pipelines (km)	城市污水日处理能力（万吨） Day Capacity of Sewerage Disposal (10000 tons)	城市路灯盏数（盏） Street Lights (units)	人均拥有道路面积（平方米/人） Per Capita of Road Areas (sq. m/person)	排水管道密度（公里）（平方米/人） Density of Drainage Pipelines (km) (sq. m/person)	污水处理率（%） Rate of Sewerage Disposal (%)
1978	1893	1154	1503					
1979	1837	1118	1513		10455	2.3		
1980	1881	1160	1650	0.1	48338	2.3		0.2
1981	1960	1225	1735	0.6	57669	2.4	4.8	0.2
1982	2174	1324	1852	0.8	54851	2.5	4.9	0.3
1983	2302	1458	2025	1.3	61983	2.6	5.1	0.4
1984	2368	1534	2161	1.7	67320	2.6	5.3	0.5
1985	2437	1623	2277	1.8	71362	2.5	5.3	0.6
1986	4144	3867	2676	83.2	84991	6.2	5.9	1.2
1987	4526	4224	3005	78.0	101472	6.2	6.2	1.0
1988	3998	3878	3522	89.7	110072	5.1	5.9	1.3
1989	6872	6607	3782	91.3	122170	7.7	5.3	23.0
1990	5812	5672	4099	103.5	128647	6.3	5.7	16.4
1991	5658	5216	4872	133.2	143658	5.8	5.4	13.4
1992	6781	6587	5721	155.5	164828	7.0	5.6	16.7
1993	7090	7581	6653	160.7	194088	7.4	4.7	22.9
1994	6150	7094	7019	236.7	193930	7.1	6.0	31.8
1995	8163	8669	8262	273.5	215234	8.3	7.5	38.7
1996	8552	9711	8860	390.3	255695	8.9	7.5	42.7
1997	9440	10438	8812	434.3	289689	9.3	7.1	47.5
1998	9618	11336	9574	589.3	328270	9.8	7.6	49.3
市　区 Urban District								
南京市区 Nanjing	1591	1889	1257	301.6	37867	7.9	7.0	53.7
无锡市区 Wuxi	809	771	1113	43.0	26991	8.2	11.8	50.0
徐州市区 Xuzhou	593	863	403	20.6	20393	9.8	6.2	45.2
常州市区 Changzhou	648	713	818	28.5	19353	9.2	12.0	46.0
苏州市区 Suzhou	652	875	1022	46.0	28366	10.3	12.9	65.3
南通市区 Nantong	249	256	228	6.0	11542	5.5	3.8	15.2
连云港市区 Lianyungang	482	461	347	…	9464	10.3	6.9	48.4
淮阴市区 Huaiying	194	235	188	13.5	7203	7.3	5.2	62.3
盐城市区 Yancheng	174	194	177	10.0	7001	6.8	7.0	46.7
扬州市区 Yangzhou	232	368	378	7.9	15022	9.3	8.1	28.5
镇江市区 Zhenjiang	554	546	323	20.2	17097	11.6	5.8	66.5
泰州市区 Taizhou	177	256	206	0.7	9476	11.6	6.1	4.7
宿迁市区 Suqian	70	145	59		3498	10.9	3.5	

17-18 城市园林绿化情况
URBAN PARKS, GARDENS AND GREEN AREAS

年份市名 Year Ctites	园林绿地面积（公顷）Total Area of Parks, Gardens and Green Areas in Cities (hectares)	#公共绿地 Public Green Areas	建成区绿化覆盖面积（公顷）Coverage Space of Green Areas Developed (hectares)	公园 Park 个数（个）Number (unit)	面积（公顷）Area (hectares)	游人量（万人次）Visitors to Park and Zoos (10000 person-times)	人均公共绿地面积（平方米）Per Capita Public Green Areas (sq.m)	建成区绿化覆盖率（%）Coverage Rate of Green Area Developed (%)
1978	7303			59	786			
1979	6434			65	842			
1980	6582	1341		72	944		2.7	19.3
1981	7187	1122		73	931	4614	2.3	19.5
1982	7379	1150		73	959	5042	2.2	19.8
1983	8709	1287		75	966	6192	2.3	21.8
1984	7837	1263		78	946	6533	2.1	22.1
1985	7998	1450		83	1030	7003	2.3	20.6
1986	15650	2395	8379	122	1940	7725	3.7	18.3
1987	19424	3530	12074	134	2096	8667	5.1	25.0
1988	18100	3058	11717	158	2540	8727	4.0	19.7
1989	21654	3214	12804	172	2725	8034	3.7	19.2
1990	20337	3447	14112	184	2991	8556	3.8	19.5
1991	19096	3841	16423	201	3071	8247	4.3	18.4
1992	20898	4283	21726	217	2958	8028	4.5	21.4
1993	30174	5882	31133	242	5179	8816	5.8	22.1
1994	33089	6124	34728	241	5396	6610	6.1	29.6
1995	48564	7226	34093	264	5648	7746	6.9	30.8
1996	50558	7528	35964	283	5263	6154	6.9	30.3
1997	52349	8175	38356	287	4831	6959	7.3	30.9
1998	54756	8891	40513	295	4920	6109	7.7	32.3
市区 Urban District								
南京市区 Nanjing	9808	1928	7142	40	1706	1248	8.1	40.0
无锡市区 Wuxi	3067	691	3187	17	540	1036	7.4	33.9
徐州市区 Xuzhou	3048	869	2180	13	650	450	9.9	33.7
常州市区 Changzhou	1277	389	2077	12	112	535	5.0	30.5
苏州市区 Suzhou	2117	401	2152	36	315	978	4.7	27.2
南通市区 Nantong	813	256	1706	7	41	230	5.5	28.5
连云港市区 Lianyungang	15128	271	1550	8	88	121	6.1	30.8
淮阴市区 Huaiying	966	168	1147	5	62	76	5.2	31.7
盐城市区 Yancheng	561	157	648	6	75	102	5.6	25.5
扬州市区 Yangzhou	1512	324	1658	16	205	117	8.2	35.7
镇江市区 Zhenjiang	2309	297	1824	14	196	191	6.3	32.8
泰州市区 Taizhou	629	88	841	7	44	94	4.0	24.7
宿迁市区 Suqian	218	20	218	2	11	21	1.5	13.1

17-19 城市环境卫生情况
URBAN ENVIRONMENT SANITATION

年份 市名 Year Ctites	清扫面积（万平方米） Sweeping Areas (10000 sq.m)	生活垃圾清运量（万吨） Residential Garbages Disposal Cleared (10000 tons)	粪便清运量（万吨） Night Soil Disposal Cleared (10000 tons)	无害化处理厂日处理能力（吨） Day Disposal Capacities of No Harmful Disposal Factory (tons)	垃圾粪便年处理量（万吨） Annual Garbages and Night Soil Disposal Cleared (10000 tons)	环卫机械（辆） Machines of Environment Sanitation (Set)	公共厕所（座） Public Toilet
1979	503	79	229			223	3545
1980	601	158	232			296	3712
1981	687	88	229			408	4032
1982	777	99	221			539	4036
1983	793	116	197			605	4497
1984	985	125	180			665	4593
1985	1078	159	147	20		734	4700
1986	1372	190	202	20		920	5448
1987	1676	198	196	120		1067	5556
1988	2056	231	260	120		1181	6912
1989	2136	262	260	162		1735	7910
1990	2445	288	221	385		1322	8072
1991	3068	341	271	1588	357.3	1604	9974
1992	3432	409	419	7622	531.7	1785	9265
1993	4095	408	441	14014	654.1	1998	9162
1994	4240	360	388	16442	658.8	1736	7095
1995	5429	398	209	13810	532.5	2072	7263
1996	6252	426	198	13125	523.9	2144	6932
1997	7085	479	196	15813	606.0	2351	7675
1998	7589	486	302	18570	721.4	2407	7486
市 区 Urban District							
南京市区 Nanjing	1058	89	120	2539	180.8	528	945
无锡市区 Wuxi	538	32	27	1613	58.9	196	484
徐州市区 Xuzhou	360	28	1	800	29.4	154	258
常州市区 Changzhou	406	24	8	840	30.0	176	696
苏州市区 Suzhou	832	45	30	1483	74.9	210	358
南通市区 Nantong	314	13	3	1500	12.7	57	228
连云港市区 Lianyungang	259	20	2	1154	21.2	98	674
淮阴市区 Huaiying	164	15	3	550	17.5	39	153
盐城市区 Yancheng	101	12	6	500	17.5	52	152
扬州市区 Yangzhou	185	75	14	372	20.0	50	278
镇江市区 Zhenjiang	232	22	4	950	25.6	43	206
泰州市区 Taizhou	172	8	9	230	14.8	39	246
宿迁市区 Suqian	110	8	3	287	10.5	8	88

17-20 城市公共汽(电)车、出租汽车情况
URBAN PUBLIC TRANST AND TAXI

年份 市名 Year Ctites	年末实有公共汽(电)车营运车数(辆) Operating Public Transt Vehicles (Year-end)	实有公共汽(电)车营运标准车台(标台) Operating Standard Public Transt Vehicles (Standardized)	公共汽(电)车营运线路长度(公里) Length of Public Transt Route (km)	公共汽(电)车客运总量(万人次) Passengers Carried by Transt (10000 person times)	每万人拥有公共交通车辆(标台) Vehicale Per 10000 Population (Standardized)	出租汽车营运车数(辆) Operating Taxis
1978	1407		1772			
1979	1503		1860	98880		90
1980	1605		1920	100671		150
1981	1771		1876	120794		175
1982	1962		1963	126384		208
1983	2010		2212	131313		215
1984	2128		2739	137097		324
1985	2237		2904	143146		605
1986	2642	2937	3385	145399	4.5	2927
1987	2711	3089	3963	151393	4.3	2980
1988	2844	3186	3780	145027	3.9	3869
1989	2826	3167	4603	135947	3.7	4555
1990	2827	3210	3991	130641	3.6	5775
1991	2968	3727	4229	124409	4.1	5005
1992	4578	4855	6939	120282	5.1	8133
1993	6384	5954	7570	109248	5.8	9838
1994	7367	6808	10127	110921	6.8	12307
1995	8019	7215	13642	95362	7.1	18073
1996	7962	7144	3544	104583	6.6	25403
1997	9665	7916	5684	124805	7.0	32493
1998	12411	10080	5198	157600	8.7	34661
市区 Urban District						
南京市区 Nanjing	2872	2678	830	76611	11.2	8378
无锡市区 Wuxi	758	758	380	13692	8.1	2493
徐州市区 Xuzhou	932	626	343	11197	7.1	3875
常州市区 Changzhou	1048	877	344	11490	11.4	1173
苏州市区 Suzhou	804	847	292	12952	10.0	2332
南通市区 Nantong	184	210	175	4508	4.5	1215
连云港市区 Lianyungang	647	502	157	3560	11.2	2169
淮阴市区 Huaiying	1007	378	48	1298	11.8	873
盐城市区 Yancheng	332	268	120	2965	9.5	617
扬州市区 Yangzhou	498	358	213	3485	9.1	1581
镇江市区 Zhenjiang	502	414	213	5390	8.8	1268
泰州市区 Taizhou	122	93	38	695	4.2	660
宿迁市区 Suqian	11	11	60	30	0.8	340

注：从1996年起，公共汽(电)车营运线路长度改为运营线路网长度(下同)。
Note: The length of public transport route had changed into the length of public transport route net (so did follows), since 1996.

18. 区域经济

REGIONAL ECONOMY

苏南苏中苏北经济主要指标 (1998)
MAJOR ECONOMIC INDICATORS OF SOUTH JIANGSU MIDDLE JIANGSU AND NORTH JIANGSU

单位:万元 (10000yuan)

分市名称 Municipality	国内生产总值(当年价) Gross Domestic Product (current price)	第一产业 Primary Industry	第二产业 Secondery Industry	#工业 Industry	第三产业 Tertiary Industry	人均国内生产总值(元) Percapita GDP	工农业总产值(当年价) Total Ontput Value of Industry and Agriculture
苏南合计 Southern Jiangsu Total	**28066187**	**1788665**	**15922411**	**14510063**	**10355111**	**20830**	**62989362**
苏州市 Suzhou Municipality	12500133	880069	7019538	6324814	4600526	21733	27812037
无锡市 Wuxi Municipality	10520080	464244	6092594	5658326	3963242	24338	24230313
常州市 Changzhou Municipality	5045974	444352	2810279	2526923	1791343	14842	10947012
苏中合计 Mid Jiangsu Total	**25838475**	**3274534**	**12709077**	**10683283**	**9854864**	**10223**	**51833456**
南京市 Nanjing Municipality	8251263	496943	4104724	3356788	3649596	15537	15092303
镇江市 Zhenjiang Municipality	3905572	320265	2176817	1853591	1408490	14709	8566971
扬州市 Yangzhou Municipality	4015906	594082	1941695	1680136	1480129	8997	8536785
泰州市 Taizhou Municipality	3420817	616903	1568511	1336338	1235403	6873	7044275
南通市 Nantong Municipality	6244917	1246341	2917330	2456430	2081246	7936	12593122
苏北合计 Northern Jiangsu Total	**16697340**	**4987162**	**6664195**	**5699140**	**5045983**	**5402**	**37062152**
徐州市 Xuzhou Municipality	5551461	1124458	2542282	2171680	1884721	6370	10955294
淮阴市 Huaiying Municipality	2197767	790758	785283	641551	621726	4422	4694616
盐城市 Yancheng Municipality	4646832	1548250	1760148	1558851	1338434	5879	11214918
连云港市 Lianyungang Municipality	2646654	804150	1046871	893297	795633	6010	6715066
宿迁市 Suqian Municipality	1654626	719546	529611	433761	405469	3366	3482258

单位:万人 续表 1 Continued 1 (10000persons)

分市名称 Municipality	土地面积(平方公里) Land Area (sq·km)	年末总人口 Year-end Population	年末从业人员 Year-end Employment	#在岗职工人数 Staff and Workers Employed	#国有经济 State-Owned Units	乡村劳动力 Rural Labor Force	#农林牧渔业 Farming, Forestry, Animal, Husbandry and Fishery
苏南合计 Southern Jiangsu Total	**17513**	**1348.31**	**737.18**	**187.75**	**107.08**	**512.96**	**170.79**
苏州市 Suzhou Municipality	8488	575.35	307.52	78.88	44.87	223.14	66.53
无锡市 Wuxi Municipality	4650	432.21	228.51	62.20	35.40	158.48	50.88
常州市 Changzhou Municipality	4375	340.75	201.15	46.67	26.81	131.34	53.38
苏中合计 Mid Jiangsu Total	**30869**	**2530.59**	**1394.27**	**320.24**	**187.28**	**1011.44**	**526.37**
南京市 Nanjing Municipality	6597	532.31	278.63	117.85	76.75	138.42	74.14
镇江市 Zhenjiang Municipality	3843	265.64	156.44	37.36	22.73	102.54	47.22
扬州市 Yangzhou Municipality	6638	446.59	235.78	51.91	31.25	178.01	90.17
泰州市 Taizhou Municipality	5790	498.56	263.58	44.04	21.96	217.54	111.47
南通市 Nantong Municipality	8001	787.49	459.84	69.08	34.59	374.93	203.37
苏北合计 Northern Jiangsu Total	**52885**	**3104.19**	**1459.04**	**251.30**	**179.05**	**1210.84**	**834.12**
徐州市 Xuzhou Municipality	11258	875.78	421.09	77.72	63.66	332.36	240.05
淮阴市 Huaiying Municipality	10645	498.98	253.46	41.21	29.53	211.71	145.37
盐城市 Yancheng Municipality	14983	791.64	330.07	71.16	44.33	283.04	179.40
连云港市 Lianyungang Municipality	7444	443.53	212.45	36.85	24.62	166.40	118.49
宿迁市 Suqian Municipality	8555	494.26	241.97	24.36	16.91	217.33	150.81

单位:万元　　　　续表 2　Continued 2　　　　(10000yuan)

分市名称 Municipality	农林牧渔业总产值(当年价) Total Output Value of Farming, Forestry, Animal Husbandry and Fishery (current price)	农业 Farming	林业 Forestry	牧业 Animal Husbandry	渔业 Fishery	农作物播种面积(千公顷) Sown Areas of Farm crops (1000 hectares)	#粮食作物(千公顷) Grain crops (1000 hectares)
苏南合计 Southern Jiangsu Total	**3352944**	**2121371**	**28354**	**562735**	**640484**	**1134.65**	**841.52**
苏州市 Suzhou Municipality	1654137	1047069	8789	239493	358786	532.80	371.31
无锡市 Wuxi Municipality	858727	566547	13757	181653	96770	286.20	233.82
常州市 Changzhou Municipality	840080	507755	5808	141589	184928	315.65	236.39
苏中合计 Mid Jiangsu Total	**6329511**	**3673168**	**78236**	**1383676**	**1194431**	**2654.75**	**1955.75**
南京市 Nanjing Municipality	979644	586628	16834	247533	128649	429.99	284.18
镇江市 Zhenjiang Municipality	610137	434302	10980	94925	69930	265.13	205.33
扬州市 Yangzhou Municipality	1183066	641035	16326	286857	238848	493.41	385.70
泰州市 Taizhou Municipality	1200881	729913	20553	263664	186751	563.98	451.27
南通市 Nantong Municipality	2355783	1281290	13543	490697	570253	902.24	629.27
苏北合计 Northern Jiangsu Total	**9911331**	**5859748**	**183326**	**2460844**	**1407413**	**4268.88**	**3148.99**
徐州市 Xuzhou Municipality	2176720	1398487	63185	593604	121444	1014.34	745.58
淮阴市 Huaiying Municipality	1587154	945535	24283	429097	188239	717.91	562.12
盐城市 Yancheng Municipality	3299121	1751644	43866	878581	625030	1307.28	834.17
连云港市 Lianyungang Municipality	1504006	903002	20046	266244	314714	553.25	429.51
宿迁市 Suqian Municipality	1344330	861080	31946	293318	157986	676.10	577.61

续表 3　Continued 3

分市名称 Municipality	粮食产量（万吨）Output of Grain (10000tons)	油料产量（吨）Output of Oil-Bearing Crop (tons)	棉花产量（吨）Output of Cotton (tons)	肉类总产量（吨）Output of Animal Meat (tons)	水产品产量（吨）Output of Aquatic (tons)	农业机械总动力（万千瓦）Total Motive Power of Machinery for Agriculture (1000kwh)	农村用电量（万千瓦小时）Electricity Consumed in Rural Arear (10000kwh)
苏南合计 Southern Jiangsu Total	**542.68**	**112804**	**25484**	**334240**	**461607**	**614.00**	**1453798**
苏州市 Suzhou Municipality	239.63	56462	24284	143463	284113	283.00	603035
无锡市 Wuxi Municipality	149.77	20297		103270	71714	173.00	545517
常州市 Changzhou Municipality	153.28	36045	1200	87507	105780	158.00	305246
苏中合计 Mid Jiangsu Total	**1135.01**	**435191**	**135313**	**871219**	**1036885**	**808.00**	**708324**
南京市 Nanjing Municipality	176.91	106504	4838	155912	96903	164.00	118155
镇江市 Zhenjiang Municipality	126.87	33869	3137	57940	58975	109.00	111671
扬州市 Yangzhou Municipality	231.51	51808	24681	202975	180687	168.00	116322
泰州市 Taizhou Municipality	273.35	53976	28691	176778	152432	174.00	134835
南通市 Nantong Municipality	326.36	189034	73966	277614	547888	193.00	227341
苏北合计 Northern Jiangsu Total	**1785.72**	**608349**	**316516**	**1492307**	**1392118**	**1172.00**	**476582**
徐州市 Xuzhou Municipality	386.00	95495	39189	345585	120174	286.00	163385
淮阴市 Huaiying Municipality	345.96	133533	8946	221399	205728	201.00	61238
盐城市 Yancheng Municipality	485.41	172039	191866	544508	595046	293.00	157797
连云港市 Lianyungang Municipality	251.93	124767	56001	170428	323643	195.00	51892
宿迁市 Suqian Municipality	316.42	82515	20514	210387	147527	197.00	42270

单位:万元　　　　　　　　　　续表 4　Continued 4　　　　　　　　　　(10000yuan)

分市名称 Municipality	全部工业产值(现价) Output Value of Total Industry (current prise)	#限额以上工业企业 Over- Norm Industrial Enterprises	#国有控股企业 State Owned Shareholding Enterprises	限额以上独立核算工业企业 Over- Norm Industrial Enterprises with Independent Accounting 资产合计 Total Capital Assets	流动资产年平均余额 Average Annual Balance Circulating Funds	产品销售收入 Revenue of Product Sales	利税总额 Total Pre- tax Profits
苏南合计 Southern Jiangsu Total	**59636418**	**37799802**	**8409810**	**42200229**	**19773598**	**34376093**	**2148589**
苏州市 Suzhou Municipality	26157900	16256934	3610004	18824205	7930999	14720068	832170
无锡市 Wuxi Municipality	23371586	14608603	3037591	16028630	7828148	13303822	956584
常州市 Changzhou Municipality	10106932	6934265	1762215	7347394	4014451	6352203	359835
苏中合计 Mid Jiangsu Total	**45503945**	**30406550**	**12056367**	**35273426**	**16161930**	**27246870**	**2078485**
南京市 Nanjing Municipality	14112659	11795863	6437752	15296710	6679770	11624475	975515
镇江市 Zhenjiang Municipality	7956834	4583456	1421352	4376747	2092664	3657393	226233
扬州市 Yangzhou Municipality	7353719	4966325	2028307	5949495	2835572	4319233	227516
泰州市 Taizhou Municipality	5843394	3670673	914802	3865791	2087781	3171524	350454
南通市 Nantong Municipality	10237339	5390233	1254154	5784683	2466143	4474245	298767
苏北合计 Northern Jiangsu Total	**27150821**	**12323948**	**6037592**	**13511464**	**6622536**	**10735856**	**830015**
徐州市 Xuzhou Municipality	8778574	4074137	2721121	5070971	2215972	3478097	295628
淮阴市 Huaiying Municipality	3107462	1670726	906997	2006798	888912	1470635	137643
盐城市 Yancheng Municipality	7915797	3907665	1289587	3644093	2269001	3438387	213277
连云港市 Lianyungang Municipality	5211060	1890695	803299	2028244	839843	1645745	106060
宿迁市 Suqian Municipality	2137928	780725	316588	761358	408808	702992	77407

注:限额以上工业企业是指全部国有及年销售收入 500 万元以上非国有企业。
Note: Over- norm industrial enterpriser: refer to all of the state- owned enterprises and non- state- owned enterprises with500 thousand yuan above of annual revenue of product sales.

单位:万美元 续表5 Continued 5 (10000USD)

分市名称 Municipality	社会消费品零售总额(万元) Total Retail Sales of Consumer Goods (10000yuan)	外贸进出口总额 Total Value of Foreign Trade Import and Export	#出口 Export	利用外资新签协议合同数(个) Number of Agreements of Foreign Capital Utilization Through Newly Signed Contracts	协议合同外资金额 Total Value of Foreign Capital Utilization Through Newly Signed Contracts	实际利用外资金额 Foreign Capital Actually Used	#客商直接投资 Direct Foreign Investment
苏南合计 Southern Jiangsu Total	**7719614**	**1517182**	**991092**	**988**	**611122**	**444972**	**425954**
苏州市 Suzhou Municipality	2978952	924974	564535	518	408694	284180	284180
无锡市 Wuxi Municipality	3001362	432828	295522	205	120101	105111	91146
常州市 Changzhou Municipality	1739300	159380	131035	265	82327	55681	50628
苏中合计 Mid Jiangsu Total	**9490745**	**719954**	**472121**	**690**	**155527**	**247520**	**203935**
南京市 Nanjing Municipality	3823853	171282	117422	371	54247	83590	74845
镇江市 Zhenjiang Municipality	1066005	150898	80436	100	29669	75738	74655
扬州市 Yangzhou Municipality	1320357	83267	56166	43	6384	17029	6829
泰州市 Taizhou Municipality	1146795	37356	29567	54	12045	10086	9814
南通市 Nantong Municipality	2133735	277151	188530	122	53182	61077	37792
苏北合计 Northern Jiangsu Total	**5298595**	**153847**	**126351**	**365**	**59718**	**61335**	**53444**
徐州市 Xuzhou Municipality	1606304	37801	27474	83	27817	22816	22816
淮阴市 Huaiying Municipality	830892	18470	15447	53	3729	8559	5635
盐城市 Yancheng Municipality	1504284	55283	45165	95	15307	15347	14184
连云港市 Lianyungang Municipality	844668	39273	35245	117	11390	13145	10308
宿迁市 Suqian Municipality	512447	3020	3020	17	1475	1468	501

单位:万元　　　　续表 6　Continued 6　　　　(10000yuan)

分市名称 Municipality	财政收入 Total Financial Revenue	#地方财政收入 Local Financial Revenue	财政支出 Financial Expenditure	金融机构存款余额 Deposits Balance of Bankig Institutions	金融机构贷款余额 Loans Balance of Banking Institutions	金融机构现金收入 Cash Revenue of Banking Institutions	金融机构现金支出 Cash Expenditure of Banking Institutions
苏南合计 Southern Jiangsu Total	**2087160**	**1040995**	**1035979**	**24409467**	**16824061**	**53989679**	**54492004**
苏州市 Suzhou Municipality	876327	457830	463983	11124378	7242834	25143490	25440237
无锡市 Wuxi Municipality	759896	356592	347882	8487089	6159927	18275036	18188056
常州市 Changzhou Municipality	450937	226573	224114	4798000	3421300	10571153	10863711
苏中合计 Mid Jiangsu Total	**2242730**	**1100065**	**1400044**	**30836174**	**23571743**	**48778722**	**49746859**
南京市 Nanjing Municipality	1082397	507798	596533	15438096	12773141	17741415	17280379
镇江市 Zhenjiang Municipality	228823	110794	142362	2608337	2201036	5664587	6031224
扬州市 Yangzhou Municipality	255303	122882	183200	3416000	2595120	6656887	7210402
泰州市 Taizhou Municipality	273506	144100	207216	3170934	2313596	6145452	6624448
南通市 Nantong Municipality	402701	214491	270733	6202807	3688850	12570381	12600406
苏北合计 Northern Jiangsu Total	**1097762**	**595407**	**965205**	**10767987**	**10220604**	**30287337**	**30653015**
徐州市 Xuzhou Municipality	395108	194247	283443	3768104	3226763	10061390	10120620
淮阴市 Huaiying Municipality	196221	91258	148825	1469452	1635405	4417089	4332440
盐城市 Yancheng Municipality	243237	147838	253695	3182079	2981838	9315929	9680115
连云港市 Lianyungang Municipality	164713	111058	155341	1610654	1649442	3932121	3932522
宿迁市 Suqian Municipality	98483	51006	123901	737698	727156	2560808	2587318

单位:万元　　　　续表 7　Continued 7　　　　(10000yuan)

分市名称 Municipality	全社会固定资产投资完成额 Total Value of Fixed Assets Fulfilled	#基本建设 Capital Construction	更新改造 Updating and Trans-formation	房地产投资 Real Estate Investment	公路客运量(万人) Highway Passenger Traffic (10000 person)	公路货运量(万吨) Highway Freight Traffic (10000 tons)	邮电业务总量 Revenue From Postal and Telecommunication Services
苏南合计 Southern Jiangsu Total	**8593945**	**1393963**	**866486**	**1149070**	**36848**	**11107**	**679464**
苏州市 Suzhou Municipality	4508810	734843	367793	585447	14255	3060	330275
无锡市 Wuxi Municipality	2772222	390032	255857	340423	15067	4707	217270
常州市 Changzhou Municipality	1312913	269088	242836	223200	7526	3340	131919
苏中合计 Mid Jiangsu Total	**10132754**	**3852634**	**1356801**	**1448384**	**33203**	**17133**	**669966**
南京市 Nanjing Municipality	3766000	1483499	623350	1010571	12523	6368	271030
镇江市 Zhenjiang Municipality	1633619	972846	152101	87390	4909	3054	86145
扬州市 Yangzhou Municipality	1277511	595851	172579	107871	5874	2638	104784
泰州市 Taizhou Municipality	957995	267817	168060	70031	3127	1174	88235
南通市 Nantong Municipality	2497629	532621	240711	172521	6770	3899	119772
苏北合计 Northern Jiangsu Total	**5115785**	**1578042**	**736338**	**404840**	**19963**	**11810**	**309642**
徐州市 Xuzhou Municipality	1882611	591413	270144	185631	6048	4608	96046
淮阴市 Huaiying Municipality	811283	236164	156452	42470	2287	1129	52298
盐城市 Yancheng Municipality	1126038	260876	119252	114272	5479	2708	86812
连云港市 Lianyungang Municipality	838307	316190	153773	45400	4303	2583	50769
宿迁市 Suqian Municipality	457546	173399	36717	17067	1846	782	23717

单位:万元　　续表 8　Continued 8　　(10000yuan)

分市名称 Municipality	在岗职工工资总额 Gross Wage Bill of Employed Staff and Workers	#国有经济 State Owned Units	居民人均可支配收入(元) Annual Allocatable Income Per Capita of Residents (yuan)	居民人均消费支出(元) Annual Living Expenditure Per Capita of Residents (yuan)	农民人均纯收入(元) Annual Net Income Perccapita of Peasants (yuan)	保险福利费用总额 Total Funds of Insurance and Welfare	城乡居民储蓄存款余额 Deposit Saving Balance of Urban and Rural Residents
苏南合计 Southern Jiangsu Total	**1846724**	**1125582**				**762475**	**14006402**
苏州市 Suzhou Municipality	775708	473809	7812	6289	5347	321793	6490389
无锡市 Wuxi Municipality	615360	371197	7178	6220	5018	261447	4674613
常州市 Changzhou Municipality	455656	280576	7107	5282	4289	179235	2841400
苏中合计 Mid Jiangsu Total	**2803705**	**1798952**				**1113055**	**15479588**
南京市 Nanjing Municipality	1281584	860696	7018	6056	3937	562527	5052485
镇江市 Zhenjiang Municipality	311082	206908	6019	4701	3931	106969	1595645
扬州市 Yangzhou Municipality	405677	274057	6101	4432	3257	124164	2172694
泰州市 Taizhou Municipality	284426	170242	6057	4726	3251	110336	2157298
南通市 Nantong Municipality	520936	287049	6899	5701	3504	209059	4501466
苏北合计 Northern Jiangsu Total	**1630011**	**1290701**				**556342**	**7046041**
徐州市 Xuzhou Municipality	592951	514527	6011	4381	3102	225621	2438696
淮阴市 Huaiying Municipality	253277	199981	5193	3692	2851	82164	879148
盐城市 Yancheng Municipality	404690	294733	5173	4131	3186	129077	2267595
连云港市 Lianyungang Municipality	243057	175689	5458	3945	2938	89951	969186
宿迁市 Suqian Municipality	136036	105771	3896	2984	2630	29529	491416

续表 9 Continued 9

分 市 名 称 Municipality	高等学校在校学生数（人） Student Enrollment of Institutions of Higher Education (person)	普通中学学生数（万人） Regular Secondary Schools (10000 persons)	各类专业技术人员数（万人） Scientific and Technical Personnel (10000 persons)	#中级技术职称以上人员 Technical Personnels With Middle Title Level and Over	医院、卫生院（个） Hospitals	医院卫生院床位数（张） Hospital Beds	医生数（人） Doctors
苏 南 合 计 Southern Jiangsu Total	**59099**	**57.11**	**56.52**	**17.34**	**533**	**42655**	**20699**
苏 州 市 Suzhou Municipality	32375	23.00	20.32	6.21	212	17663	8779
无 锡 市 Wuxi Municipality	12473	19.41	19.42	5.82	160	14179	6414
常 州 市 Changzhou Municipality	14251	14.69	16.78	5.31	161	10813	5506
苏 中 合 计 Mid Jiangsu Total	**186469**	**100.15**	**82.76**	**28.78**	**1121**	**68190**	**44783**
南 京 市 Nanjing Municipality	132439	21.80	31.23	13.29	303	20618	15745
镇 江 市 Zhenjiang Municipality	19111	11.33	9.71	3.72	117	7399	5638
扬 州 市 Yangzhou Municipality	23095	16.62	14.56	4.32	196	10679	5870
泰 州 市 Taizhou Municipality	1905	19.98	12.51	3.25	176	10546	6421
南 通 市 Nantong Municipality	9919	30.41	14.75	4.20	329	18948	11109
苏 北 合 计 Northern Jiangsu Total	**49554**	**166.98**	**63.92**	**17.73**	**956**	**48234**	**30663**
徐 州 市 Xuzhou Municipality	24763	51.25	21.62	6.84	233	15703	11756
淮 阴 市 Huaiying Municipality	7125	22.05	8.94	3.05	195	7900	4094
盐 城 市 Yancheng Municipality	8238	41.63	18.54	3.74	247	12940	7855
连云港市 Lianyungang Municipality	9428	26.52	10.17	2.71	147	6739	4072
宿 迁 市 Suqian Municipality		25.53	4.65	1.39	134	4952	2886

19. 市县社会经济

CITY (COUNTY) SOCIAL ECONOMY

19—1 国民经济综合指标（1998）
INDICATORS OF NATIONAL ECONOMIC GENERAL SURVEY

单位：万元 （10000yuan）

市县名称 City and County	国内生产总值（当年价）Gross Domestic Product (current price)	第一产业 Primary Industry	第二产业 Secondery Industry	#工业 Industry	第三产业 Tertiary Industry	人均国内生产总值（元）Percapita GDP
南京市 Nanjing Municipality	**8251263**	**496943**	**4104724**	**3356788**	**3649596**	**15537**
江宁县 Jiangning County	861038	117831	547070	492901	196137	11545
江浦县 Jiangpu County	206922	58620	71808	61773	76494	6925
六合县 Liuhe County	361294	105539	143966	125546	111789	5291
溧水县 Lishui County	337170	62030	179307	162548	95833	8311
高淳县 Gaochun County	304292	85513	125445	103692	93334	7088
无锡市 Wuxi Municipality	**10520080**	**464244**	**6092594**	**5658326**	**3963242**	**24338**
江阴市 Jiangyin City	2722380	141954	1647143	1572012	933283	23807
宜兴市 Yixing City	1650069	165241	905531	837899	579297	15152
锡山市 Xishan City	2700015	122622	1633648	1562923	943745	27243
徐州市 Xuzhou Municipality	**5551461**	**1124458**	**2542282**	**2171680**	**1884721**	**6370**
丰县 Fengxian County	328523	144287	93564	82029	90672	3131
沛县 Peixian County	515887	177464	182736	161540	155687	4510
铜山县 Tongshan County	788169	214374	395254	363868	178541	5969
睢宁县 Shuining County	326869	145753	90869	75986	90247	2643
新沂市 Xinyi City	432953	161824	143474	120736	127655	4529
邳州市 Pizhou City	532064	229869	163401	127046	138794	3541
常州市 Changzhou Municipality	**5045974**	**444352**	**2810279**	**2526923**	**1791343**	**14842**
溧阳市 Liyang City	686818	118152	324662	239818	244004	8869
金坛市 Jintan City	513019	93034	239571	189648	180414	9472
武进市 Wujin City	1960023	193667	1110083	1032193	656273	15909
苏州市 Suzhou Municipality	**12500133**	**880069**	**7019538**	**6324814**	**4600526**	**21733**
常熟市 Changshu City	2053696	149815	1067422	940600	836459	19700
张家港市 Zhangjiagang City	2350109	104031	1399165	1312861	846913	27525
昆山市 Kunshan City	1505347	116018	868949	798475	520380	25675
吴江市 Wujiang City	1750653	147622	942510	867447	660521	22604

单位:万元　　　　续表 1　Continued 1　　　　(10000yuan)

市县名称 City and County		国内生产总值(当年价) Gross Domestic Product (current price)	第一产业 Primary Industry	第二产业 Secondery Industry	#工业 Industry	第三产业 Tertiary Industry	人均国内生产总值(元) Percapita GDP
太仓市	Taicang City	1205387	127828	655595	605001	421964	26810
吴县市	Wuxian City	1649511	179939	864881	799714	604691	16990
南通市	**Nantong Municipatity**	**6244917**	**1246341**	**2917330**	**2456430**	**2081246**	**7936**
海安县	Haian County	593865	179012	202109	160624	212744	5997
如东县	Rudong County	685048	256638	220645	175675	207765	6078
启东市	Qidong City	1020060	254471	415582	358247	350007	8743
如皋市	Rugao City	654320	165102	262111	212165	227107	4483
通州市	Tongzhou City	1117074	206423	520643	429595	390008	7682
海门市	Haimen City	988486	162363	457138	397200	368985	9549
连云港市	**Lianyungang Municipality**	**2646654**	**804150**	**1046871**	**893297**	**795633**	**6010**
赣榆县	Ganyu County	569811	213315	218715	195994	137781	5583
东海县	Donghai County	521276	223098	166018	142227	132160	4808
灌云县	Guanyun County	485011	192813	129501	99617	162697	4836
灌南县	Guannan County	210964	110447	52343	42513	48174	3028
淮阴市	**Huaiyin Municipality**	**2197767**	**790758**	**785283**	**641551**	**621726**	**4422**
淮阴县	Huaiyin County	298132	133119	101115	85056	63898	3651
涟水县	Lianshui County	267354	147611	63800	43000	55943	2676
洪泽县	Hongze County	147855	68149	41715	35525	37991	3993
盱眙县	Xuyi County	282200	129800	69517	57550	82883	3973
金湖县	Jinhu County	237411	87409	87493	71048	62509	6791
淮安市	Huaian City	444635	194666	142328	122820	107641	3674
盐城市	**Yancheng Municipality**	**4646832**	**1548250**	**1760148**	**1558851**	**1338434**	**5879**
响水县	Xiangshui County	201609	92480	46914	39256	62215	3650
滨海县	Binhai County	366000	160821	101179	83772	104000	3424
阜宁县	Funing County	427932	152760	153657	130690	121515	3980
射阳县	Sheyang County	623310	240028	231113	212061	152169	6018

单位:万元 续表 2 Continued 2 (10000yuan)

市县名称 City and County	国内生产总值(当年价) Gross Domestic Product (current price)	第一产业 Primary Industry	第二产业 Secondery Industry	#工业 Industry	第三产业 Tertiary Industry	人均国内生产总值(元) Percapita GDP
建湖县 Jianhu County	470636	130549	218078	202783	122009	5915
盐都县 Yandou County	628501	197566	256739	231297	174196	7227
东台市 Dongtai City	748106	296000	244988	210907	207118	6371
大丰市 Dafeng City	645679	233900	230086	209255	181693	8709
扬州市 Yangzhou Municipality	**4015906**	**594082**	**1941695**	**1680136**	**1480129**	**8997**
宝应县 Baoying County	480338	167860	158657	134306	153821	5286
邗江县 Hanjiang County	599807	72000	320362	299205	207445	10888
仪征市 Yizheng City	410796	56370	223844	200096	130582	6949
高邮市 Gaoyou City	520790	155058	210194	180240	155538	6253
江都市 Jiangdu City	825859	125252	374033	322765	326574	7725
镇江市 Zhenjiang Municipality	**3905572**	**320265**	**2176817**	**1853591**	**1408490**	**14709**
丹徒县 Dantu County	460731	55160	259287	240480	146284	12052
丹阳市 Danyang City	1202636	130386	663911	605107	408339	14908
扬中市 Yangzhong City	503981	34626	305413	237588	163942	18234
句容市 Jurong City	540727	85318	284693	268801	170716	8970
泰州市 Taizhou Municipality	**3420817**	**616903**	**1568511**	**1336338**	**1235403**	**6873**
兴化市 Xinghua City	639462	259200	166340	129845	213922	4166
靖江市 Jingjiang City	581876	63423	265000	230000	253453	8775
泰兴市 Taixing City	759098	145012	313700	253601	300386	5957
姜堰市 Jiangyan City	505010	107606	216994	188426	180410	5487
宿迁市 Suqian Municipality	**1654626**	**719546**	**529611**	**433761**	**405469**	**3366**
宿豫县 Suyu County	325329	129834	130930	118213	64565	3494
沭阳县 Shuyang County	492636	237432	132082	97011	123122	3004
泗阳县 Siyang County	330817	154591	95657	87532	80569	2945
泗洪县 Sihong County	371540	187085	101244	90587	83211	3768

19—2 人　　口 (1998)
POPULATION

市县名称 City and County		年末总人口(万人) Year-end Total Population (10000 persons)	#非农业人口 Non-Agriculture	平均人口(万人) Average Population (10000 persons)	出生人数(人) Birth (person)	死亡人数(人) Death (person)	人口自然增长率(‰) Natural Growth Rate
南京市	**Nanjing Municipality**	**532.31**	**276.23**	**531.06**	**37804**	**32506**	**1.00**
江宁县	Jiangning County	74.69	11.99	74.58	6385	4692	2.27
江浦县	Jiangpu County	29.73	5.49	29.88	2833	1934	3.01
六合县	Liuhe County	68.22	9.57	68.29	5123	3729	2.04
溧水县	Lishui County	40.50	5.23	40.57	3816	2482	3.29
高淳县	Gaochun County	42.81	5.06	42.93	3083	2976	0.25
无锡市	**Wuxi Municipality**	**432.21**	**171.04**	**432.25**	**43635**	**30497**	**3.04**
江阴市	Jiangyin City	114.44	33.94	114.35	10071	7892	1.91
宜兴市	Yixing City	108.40	25.88	108.90	15219	7680	6.92
锡山市	Xishan City	99.16	17.13	99.11	8540	7073	1.48
徐州市	**Xuzhou Municipality**	**875.78**	**188.42**	**871.47**	**91325**	**41298**	**5.74**
丰县	Fengxian County	105.57	9.95	104.92	14315	4776	9.09
沛县	Peixian County	115.16	19.05	114.39	10985	3918	6.18
铜山县	Tongshan County	132.77	15.73	132.05	17884	7260	8.05
睢宁县	Shuining County	124.25	10.55	123.67	10981	6259	3.82
新沂市	Xinyi City	96.15	12.75	95.60	7872	4507	3.52
邳州市	Pizhou City	150.02	15.92	150.24	14530	6305	5.47
常州市	**Changzhou Municipality**	**340.75**	**130.43**	**339.99**	**40230**	**22255**	**5.29**
溧阳市	Liyang City	77.76	29.25	77.44	16364	5026	14.64
金坛市	Jintan City	54.16	9.77	54.16	3697	3532	0.30
武进市	Wujin City	123.22	14.15	123.20	10725	8868	1.51
苏州市	**Suzhou Municipality**	**575.35**	**192.88**	**575.17**	**40487**	**42125**	**-0.28**
常熟市	Changshu City	104.18	26.45	104.25	7606	8403	-0.76
张家港市	Zhangjiagang City	85.40	16.85	85.38	6724	5928	0.93
昆山市	Kunshan City	58.75	17.70	58.63	4273	3893	0.65
吴江市	Wujiang City	77.33	17.65	77.45	5551	5846	-0.38

续表 1 Continued 1

市县名称 City and County	年末总人口（万人）Year－end Total Population (10000 persons)	#非农业人口 Non－Agricul－ture	平均人口（万人）Average Population (10000 persons)	出生人数（人）Birth (person)	死亡人数（人）Death (person)	人口自然增长率（‰）Natural Growth Rate
太仓市 Taicang City	44.94	11.99	44.96	3098	3874	－1.73
吴县市 Wuxian City	97.00	17.67	97.09	6793	6814	－0.02
南通市 Nantong Municipatity	**787.49**	**247.21**	**786.90**	**72031**	**59291**	**1.62**
海安县 Haian County	98.90	32.93	99.03	6530	7683	－1.16
如东县 Rudong County	112.52	44.67	112.71	7852	9567	－1.52
启东市 Qidong City	116.54	23.16	116.67	11630	7692	3.38
如皋市 Rugao City	146.55	27.60	145.96	13848	11582	1.55
通州市 Tongzhou City	145.23	36.50	145.42	9932	11361	－0.98
海门市 Haimen City	103.79	35.52	103.52	16432	7976	8.17
连云港市 Lianyungang Municipality	**443.53**	**84.37**	**440.39**	**60995**	**20238**	**9.25**
赣榆县 Ganyu County	102.56	8.87	102.07	12007	5012	6.85
东海县 Donghai County	109.18	9.12	108.42	19263	5193	12.98
灌云县 Guanyun County	101.38	14.06	100.30	15558	4237	11.29
灌南县 Guannan County	69.96	7.53	69.68	7551	3266	6.15
淮阴市 Huaiyin Municipality	**498.98**	**88.28**	**496.99**	**57345**	**26440**	**6.22**
淮阴县 Huaiyin County	82.18	8.15	81.66	10721	4672	7.41
涟水县 Lianshui County	100.03	8.71	99.91	7752	4972	2.78
洪泽县 Hongze County	37.21	7.56	37.03	3898	1605	6.19
盱眙县 Xuyi County	70.97	8.71	71.03	5194	3177	2.84
金湖县 Jinhu County	35.06	7.49	34.96	3497	2036	4.18
淮安市 Huaian City	121.35	15.57	121.03	15816	6759	7.48
盐城市 Yancheng Municipality	**791.64**	**156.06**	**790.38**	**79111**	**50472**	**3.62**
响水县 Xiangshui County	55.47	8.79	55.24	5478	2332	5.70
滨海县 Binhai County	106.60	12.96	106.89	8324	5401	2.73
阜宁县 Funing County	107.35	14.47	107.53	8673	6841	1.70
射阳县 Sheyang County	104.11	16.26	103.58	11157	6446	4.55

续表 2 Continued 2

市县名称 City and County		年末总人口（万人）Year-end Total Population (10000 persons)	#非农业人口 Non-Agriculture	平均人口（万人）Average Population (10000 persons)	出生人数（人）Birth (person)	死亡人数（人）Death (person)	人口自然增长率（‰）Natural Growth Rate
建湖县	Jianhu County	79.61	15.15	79.56	9561	6265	4.14
盐都县	Yandou County	86.94	16.76	86.96	11452	6890	5.25
东台市	Dongtai City	117.62	23.14	117.43	11864	8641	2.74
大丰市	Dafeng City	74.06	15.31	74.14	6207	4886	1.78
扬州市	**Yangzhou Municipality**	**446.59**	**107.85**	**446.37**	**40411**	**31891**	**1.91**
宝应县	Baoying County	90.89	13.43	90.87	8093	6395	1.87
邗江县	Hanjiang County	55.07	6.49	55.09	4314	4143	0.31
仪征市	Yizheng City	59.13	16.64	59.12	6151	4045	3.56
高邮市	Gaoyou City	83.23	13.57	83.29	6975	6192	0.94
江都市	Jiangdu City	106.92	18.22	106.91	9883	7897	1.86
镇江市	**Zhenjiang Municipality**	**265.64**	**91.92**	**265.53**	**22845**	**18474**	**1.65**
丹徒县	Dantu County	38.03	4.78	38.23	2597	3088	-1.28
丹阳市	Danyang City	80.43	21.19	80.67	6152	6188	-0.04
扬中市	Yangzhong City	27.62	8.10	27.64	3551	2284	4.58
句容市	Jurong City	60.29	10.85	60.28	4118	3974	0.24
泰州市	**Taizhou Municipality**	**498.56**	**89.02**	**497.69**	**42330**	**34411**	**1.59**
兴化市	Xinghua City	153.42	19.90	153.48	9971	10036	-0.04
靖江市	Jingjiang City	66.36	13.62	66.31	6015	4192	2.75
泰兴市	Taixing City	127.93	18.53	127.44	13627	9366	3.34
姜堰市	Jiangyan City	92.05	14.97	92.03	7400	6728	0.73
宿迁市	**Suqian Municipality**	**494.26**	**53.14**	**491.53**	**56349**	**23849**	**6.61**
宿豫县	Suyu County	93.41	3.90	93.11	9996	5184	5.17
沭阳县	Shuyang County	165.18	13.78	163.97	21344	7343	8.54
泗阳县	Siyang County	112.92	10.71	112.34	13656	5685	7.10
泗洪县	Sihong County	99.05	13.21	98.61	8648	4720	3.98

19—3 劳 动 力 资 源（1998）
RESOURCE OF LABOR FORCE

单位:万人　　(10000persons)

市县名称	City and County	年末全部从业人员数 Year-end Total Employment	在岗职工人数 Staff and Workers Employed	#国有经济 State-Owned Units	城镇个体和私营企业劳动者 Rural Individual Laborer	乡村劳动力 Labor Force in Rural Area	#农林牧渔业 Farming, Forestry, Animal Husbandry and Fishery
南京市	**Nanjing Municipality**	**278.63**	**117.85**	**76.75**	**26.28**	**138.42**	**74.14**
江宁县	Jiangning County	43.62	5.46	2.79	2.67	36.80	17.31
江浦县	Jiangpu County	12.87	2.37	1.43	0.52	10.66	5.49
六合县	Liuhe County	33.68	3.89	2.61	0.70	30.85	17.76
溧水县	Lishui County	20.51	3.42	1.66	0.23	17.89	9.99
高淳县	Gaochun County	25.68	2.66	1.53	0.14	23.37	15.43
无锡市	**Wuxi Municipality**	**228.51**	**62.20**	**35.40**	**7.75**	**158.48**	**50.88**
江阴市	Jiangyin City	61.52	9.05	4.75	3.35	50.61	13.71
宜兴市	Yixing City	57.31	8.50	5.40	0.99	48.43	24.03
锡山市	Xishan City	53.12	7.98	5.43	0.03	45.96	10.73
徐州市	**Xuzhou Municipality**	**421.09**	**77.72**	**63.66**	**17.33**	**332.36**	**240.05**
丰县	Fengxian County	50.93	3.86	2.65	0.74	46.62	39.10
沛县	Peixian County	51.45	5.61	4.73	1.83	44.34	31.53
铜山县	Tongshan County	58.22	7.11	4.94	0.20	51.13	35.20
睢宁县	Shuining County	61.28	4.65	3.70	0.82	58.26	44.24
新沂市	Xinyi City	47.10	5.14	3.66	1.55	41.51	28.64
邳州市	Pizhou City	77.72	6.64	5.06	1.67	71.09	51.32
常州市	**Changzhou Municipality**	**201.15**	**46.67**	**26.81**	**11.45**	**131.34**	**53.38**
溧阳市	Liyang City	43.98	5.00	2.82	0.79	34.40	17.82
金坛市	Jintan City	34.78	5.99	4.14	2.83	25.26	12.35
武进市	Wujin City	72.49	8.37	4.86	2.40	57.10	20.14
苏州市	**Suzhou Municipality**	**307.52**	**78.88**	**44.87**	**10.42**	**223.14**	**66.53**
常熟市	Changshu City	60.01	11.31	6.20	1.15	48.67	15.88
张家港市	Zhangjiagang City	40.10	8.82	5.43	0.15	31.90	8.20
昆山市	Kunshan City	34.07	9.04	3.88	1.32	24.73	8.17
吴江市	Wujiang City	43.30	6.91	3.93	1.42	35.63	11.58

单位:万人 续表1 Continued 1 (10000persons)

市县名称 City and County		年末全部从业人员数 Year-end Total Employment	在岗职工人数 Staff and Workers Employed	#国有经济 State-Owned Units	城镇个体和私营企业劳动者 Rural Individual Laborer	乡村劳动力 Labor Force in Rural Area	#农林牧渔业 Farming, Forestry, Animal Husbandry and Fishery
太仓市	Taicang City	24.62	5.59	3.27	0.69	19.05	7.48
吴县市	Wuxian City	51.23	6.72	4.16	0.59	44.96	10.18
南通市	**Nantong Municipatity**	**459.84**	**69.08**	**34.59**	**6.66**	**374.93**	**203.37**
海安县	Haian County	54.57	7.82	3.69	0.83	45.10	27.45
如东县	Rudong County	64.01	7.95	3.94	0.40	54.96	27.63
启东市	Qidong City	79.13	7.96	4.04	0.92	69.23	37.59
如皋市	Rugao City	77.35	8.00	4.52	0.58	66.88	38.15
通州市	Tongzhou City	79.87	8.99	4.46	1.00	69.04	40.14
海门市	Haimen City	64.43	6.70	3.06		57.01	28.74
连云港市	**Lianyungang Municipality**	**212.45**	**36.85**	**24.62**	**8.32**	**166.40**	**118.49**
赣榆县	Ganyu County	47.48	4.05	3.12	1.13	42.24	27.68
东海县	Donghai County	54.75	5.21	4.15	0.76	48.48	36.03
灌云县	Guanyun County	43.68	5.83	4.33	2.11	35.52	27.55
灌南县	Guannan County	34.71	3.12	2.30	0.75	30.81	22.53
淮阴市	**Huaiyin Municipality**	**253.46**	**41.21**	**29.53**	**8.95**	**211.71**	**145.37**
淮阴县	Huaiyin County	37.85	3.96	3.04	0.96	35.75	23.90
涟水县	Lianshui County	50.19	5.35	3.97	1.16	46.88	35.48
洪泽县	Hongze County	19.83	2.83	2.02	0.59	16.84	11.17
盱眙县	Xuyi County	35.73	4.62	3.81	0.74	32.06	24.93
金湖县	Jinhu County	18.37	3.65	2.67	0.59	14.66	9.73
淮安市	Huaian City	62.22	7.11	3.98	2.02	53.82	33.85
盐城市	**Yancheng Municipality**	**330.07**	**71.16**	**44.33**	**12.27**	**283.04**	**179.40**
响水县	Xiangshui County	21.45	4.81	3.11	0.79	18.60	14.49
滨海县	Binhai County	39.38	5.51	3.02	1.14	37.19	27.07
阜宁县	Funing County	43.37	5.69	3.26	1.18	40.72	28.56
射阳县	Sheyang County	39.77	9.40	5.42	1.58	33.51	23.20

单位:万人　　　　续表 2　Continued 2　　　　(10000persons)

市县名称 City and County		年末全部从业人员数 Year-end Total Employment	在岗职工人数 Staff and Workers Employed	#国有经济 State-Owned Units	城镇个体和私营企业劳动者 Rural Individual Laborer	乡村劳动力 Labor Force in Rural Area	#农林牧渔业 Farming, Forestry, Animal Husbandry and Fishery
建湖县	Jianhu County	34.79	7.51	3.96	1.18	29.77	12.99
盐都县	Yandou County	37.05	6.32	3.53	1.20	32.94	18.09
东台市	Dongtai City	52.54	9.77	5.78	1.69	47.22	28.28
大丰市	Dafeng City	37.55	7.50	4.87	1.78	31.53	21.14
扬州市	**Yangzhou Municipality**	**235.78**	**51.91**	**31.25**	**4.48**	**178.01**	**90.17**
宝应县	Baoying County	49.82	5.83	3.39	0.53	43.14	27.54
邗江县	Hanjiang County	28.30	3.81	1.74	0.11	24.37	7.61
仪征市	Yizheng City	32.37	8.73	4.87	1.10	22.53	11.26
高邮市	Gaoyou City	44.20	6.26	3.36	0.82	37.06	22.67
江都市	Jiangdu City	53.25	7.47	4.35	0.42	45.26	19.40
镇江市	**Zhenjiang Municipality**	**156.44**	**37.36**	**22.73**	**6.98**	**102.54**	**47.22**
丹徒县	Dantu County	26.10	3.54	2.16	0.54	20.39	9.14
丹阳市	Danyang City	48.91	7.27	4.64	1.28	36.58	16.52
扬中市	Yangzhong City	18.64	3.51	1.74	1.03	13.70	4.23
句容市	Jurong City	30.02	4.32	2.62	0.89	25.46	15.02
泰州市	**Taizhou Municipality**	**263.58**	**44.04**	**21.96**	**3.43**	**217.54**	**111.47**
兴化市	Xinghua City	77.44	7.18	4.26	0.33	70.68	45.73
靖江市	Jingjiang City	39.73	8.84	3.89	0.48	29.50	10.99
泰兴市	Taixing City	63.62	9.50	4.98	0.96	54.02	25.92
姜堰市	Jiangyan City	50.49	6.76	2.90	0.48	44.70	21.45
宿迁市	**Suqian Municipality**	**241.97**	**24.36**	**16.91**	**15.43**	**217.33**	**150.81**
宿豫县	Suyu County	48.92	3.70	2.49	4.40	45.12	27.81
沭阳县	Shuyang County	78.13	5.00	3.69	3.26	72.98	51.32
泗阳县	Siyang County	55.75	6.46	4.86	4.88	49.26	33.05
泗洪县	Sihong County	50.70	5.71	3.85	1.93	44.99	36.30

19—4 农林牧渔业总产值 (1998)
TOTAL OUTPUT VALUE OF FARMING FORESTRY ANIMAL HUSBANDRY AND FISHERY

单位:万元 (10000yuan)

市县名称 City and County		农林牧渔业总产值(当年价) Total Output Value of Farming, Forestry, Animal Husbandry and Fishery (current price)	#农业产值 Output Value of Farming	#林业产值 Output Value of Forestry	农林牧渔业总产值(1990年不变价格) Total Output Value of Farming, Forestry, Animal Husbamdry and Fishery (1990 con-stant price)	#农业产值 Output Value of Farming	#林业产值 Output Value of Forestry
南京市	**Nanjing Municipality**	**979644**	**586628**	**16834**	**464707**	**258151**	**10163**
江宁县	Jiangning County	236965	148680	5620	111213	64411	2495
江浦县	Jiangpu County	115321	63733	4943	60026	28578	4560
六合县	Liuhe County	203862	130120	3293	97319	57938	1575
溧水县	Lishui County	117694	83724	830	56581	39640	352
高淳县	Gaochun County	161042	86664	534	72987	40031	234
无锡市	**Wuxi Municipality**	**858727**	**566547**	**13757**	**457381**	**327306**	**4818**
江阴市	Jiangyin City	264351	176313	810	152733	112722	332
宜兴市	Yixing City	298440	210958	11440	159320	121687	3711
锡山市	Xishan City	228915	152055	764	116855	83036	487
徐州市	**Xuzhou Municipality**	**2176720**	**1398487**	**63185**	**1106069**	**684462**	**30129**
丰县	Fengxian County	266865	192122	5310	156018	114302	3284
沛县	Peixian County	348366	228933	6720	178424	108911	3871
铜山县	Tongshan County	401055	267717	9345	207608	132546	5719
睢宁县	Shuining County	282536	191797	4721	137521	88184	2863
新沂市	Xinyi City	303556	166828	8446	151139	80535	5367
邳州市	Pizhou City	450727	268311	26275	211745	119373	7707
常州市	**Changzhou Municipality**	**840080**	**507755**	**5808**	**429659**	**260778**	**2725**
溧阳市	Liyang City	221527	142642	4012	98672	64768	1800
金坛市	Jintan City	178964	89261	1163	78416	39773	605
武进市	Wujin City	363206	234412	543	210366	137324	256
苏州市	**Suzhou Municipality**	**1654137**	**1047069**	**8789**	**897880**	**619633**	**4270**
常熟市	Changshu City	273218	196696	758	142046	106886	332
张家港市	Zhangjiagang City	193258	140761	1062	110275	82559	720
昆山市	Kunshan City	229695	126873	1260	120989	72221	941
吴江市	Wujiang City	270903	125393	1281	131634	63875	558

单位:万元　　　　续表 1　Continued 1　　　　(10000yuan)

市县名称 City and County		农林牧渔业总产值(当年价) Total Output Value of Farming, Forestry, Animal Husbandry and Fishery (current price)	#农业产值 Output Value of Farming	#林业产值 Output Value of Forestry	农林牧渔业总产值(1990年不变价格) Total Output Value of Farming, Forestry, Animal Husbamdry and Fishery (1990 constant price)	#农业产值 Output Value of Farming	#林业产值 Output Value of Forestry
太仓市	Taicang City	231139	167720	704	131129	106856	342
吴县市	Wuxian City	345920	227236	3513	208340	153919	1292
南通市	**Nantong Municipatity**	**2355783**	**1281290**	**13543**	**1414868**	**821795**	**6525**
海安县	Haian County	325569	145238	883	199205	81467	386
如东县	Rudong County	468642	227570	4423	268254	131040	1964
启东市	Qidong City	517848	227300	973	302264	151916	601
如皋市	Rugao City	303074	183866	1825	167081	101869	953
通州市	Tongzhou City	383337	275148	3852	247165	195748	1751
海门市	Haimen City	303182	179072	1114	192520	127639	566
连云港市	**Lianyungang Municipality**	**1504006**	**903002**	**20046**	**826718**	**496163**	**12278**
赣榆县	Ganyu County	414089	180112	6587	220688	101208	3773
东海县	Donghai County	405489	282463	6437	225075	152839	3660
灌云县	Guanyun County	356969	248743	724	189463	128226	413
灌南县	Guannan County	201178	137236	5165	117785	84633	3674
淮阴市	**Huaiyin Municipality**	**1587154**	**945535**	**24283**	**906816**	**513377**	**19459**
淮阴县	Huaiyin County	260820	137682	1055	141710	71633	710
涟水县	Lianshui County	312212	209863	5235	182536	121661	4445
洪泽县	Hongze County	153684	66876	6892	99007	33971	5658
盱眙县	Xuyi County	250954	154409	2023	126038	73241	1380
金湖县	Jinhu County	159513	76473	5221	94337	37023	4496
淮安市	Huaian City	391006	259336	3552	232522	155832	2548
盐城市	**Yancheng Municipality**	**3299121**	**1751644**	**43866**	**2044387**	**1048187**	**30411**
响水县	Xiangshui County	199700	132840	1795	119640	79624	1353
滨海县	Binhai County	310033	180601	5851	177926	103863	4403
阜宁县	Funing County	327237	152791	2994	190105	92097	1904
射阳县	Sheyang County	531684	281868	7130	342663	169402	5465

单位:万元　　　　续表 2　Continued 2　　　　(10000yuan)

市县名称 City and County		农林牧渔业总产值(当年价) Total Output Value of Farming, Forestry, Animal Husbandry and Fishery (current price)	#农业产值 Output Value of Farming	#林业产值 Output Value of Forestry	农林牧渔业总产值(1990年不变价格) Total Output Value of Farming, Forestry, Animal Husbamdry and Fishery (1990 constant price)	#农业产值 Output Value of Farming	#林业产值 Output Value of Forestry
建湖县	Jianhu County	272091	129124	1792	164538	77600	819
盐都县	Yandou County	417090	180566	7395	258050	107790	4510
东台市	Dongtai City	639116	315323	8924	419915	187443	6986
大丰市	Dafeng City	511948	337796	7571	320348	208976	4719
扬州市	**Yangzhou Municipality**	**1183066**	**641035**	**16326**	**666700**	**364664**	**12429**
宝应县	Baoying County	325657	158151	5345	168613	84880	3969
邗江县	Hanjiang County	156693	81737	3262	99500	54967	3135
仪征市	Yizheng City	104652	71271	672	54694	36161	410
高邮市	Gaoyou City	314382	165581	2953	185226	94957	2209
江都市	Jiangdu City	240391	139778	3914	135981	80031	2607
镇江市	**Zhenjiang Municipality**	**610137**	**434302**	**10980**	**346236**	**242744**	**6345**
丹徒县	Dantu County	106981	73773	1019	57356	38189	569
丹阳市	Danyang City	237931	161804	1102	139255	92168	805
扬中市	Yangzhong City	79552	61740	2420	57110	47168	1387
句容市	Jurong City	156132	117153	6177	79339	57191	3454
泰州市	**Taizhou Municipality**	**1200881**	**729913**	**20553**	**663692**	**408231**	**8920**
兴化市	Xinghua City	517903	303422	2900	273356	162935	1600
靖江市	Jingjiang City	122609	77006	2596	71626	45718	1928
泰兴市	Taixing City	263678	157249	7824	145442	88401	2731
姜堰市	Jiangyan City	216602	137070	4261	125729	78043	1447
宿迁市	**Suqian Municipality**	**1344330**	**861080**	**31946**	**759645**	**489748**	**25939**
宿豫县	Suyu County	244156	146501	1815	141322	86163	1051
沭阳县	Shuyang County	439778	302638	12948	248229	171004	10367
泗阳县	Siyang County	292203	197057	12101	173564	117610	10394
泗洪县	Sihong County	348611	201164	5001	185951	107751	4083

19—5 农业机械化和现代化 (1998)
MACHANIZATTON AND MODERNIZARION OF AGRICULTURE

市县名称 City and County	机耕地面积（千公顷） Areas of Mortorized Cultivation (10000 hectares)	有效灌溉面积（千公顷） Available Irrigated Areas (1000 hectares)	农业机械总动力(万千瓦小时) Total Power of Agricltural Machinery (1000kwh)	农用化肥施用量(吨) Comsuption of Chemical Fertilizers (tons)	农村用电量(万千瓦小时) Electricity Comsumed in Rural Areas (10000kwh)
南京市 Nanjing Municipality	**178.77**	**197.99**	**164.00**	**182134**	**118155**
江宁县 Jiangning County	44.12	48.56	43.00	36961	37068
江浦县 Jiangpu County	13.91	20.52	14.00	14893	5288
六合县 Liuhe County	48.32	48.89	35.00	58390	13447
溧水县 Lishui County	33.74	28.37	20.00	14398	13095
高淳县 Gaochun County	22.15	30.39	33.00	42276	7823
无锡市 Wuxi Municipality	**133.79**	**169.44**	**173.00**	**122389**	**545517**
江阴市 Jiangyin City	38.14	49.87	55.00	31500	169817
宜兴市 Yixing City	52.63	62.08	55.00	53796	132987
锡山市 Xishan City	37.20	49.84	54.00	28844	183884
徐州市 Xuzhou Municipality	**558.31**	**461.27**	**286.00**	**537636**	**163385**
丰县 Fengxian County	83.33	73.34	48.00	78236	5610
沛县 Peixian County	74.58	70.30	42.00	65282	17910
铜山县 Tongshan County	102.00	95.11	58.00	109401	56870
睢宁县 Shuining County	89.34	62.71	30.00	67694	10687
新沂市 Xinyi City	79.27	70.18	33.00	81313	11053
邳州市 Pizhou City	101.67	65.84	41.00	99941	19339
常州市 Changzhou Municipality	**146.60**	**360.59**	**158.00**	**112792**	**305246**
溧阳市 Liyang City	48.33	55.69	41.00	34937	40681
金坛市 Jintan City	33.00	40.60	26.00	24030	25019
武进市 Wujin City	57.63	79.05	80.00	40631	189848
苏州市 Suzhou Municipality	**247.25**	**303.91**	**283.00**	**217907**	**603035**
常熟市 Changshu City	63.86	63.63	42.00	35970	103219
张家港市 Zhangjiagang City	38.33	44.17	41.00	27358	134101
昆山市 Kunshan City	37.08	46.90	41.00	33360	69710
吴江市 Wujiang City	46.80	46.27	50.00	35526	76950

续表 1　　Continued 1

市县名称 City and County		机耕地面积（千公顷）Areas of Mortorized Cultivation (10000 hectares)	有效灌溉面积（千公顷）Available Irrigated Areas (1000 hectares)	农业机械总动力（万千瓦小时）Total Power of Agricltural Machinery (1000kwh)	农用化肥施用量（吨）Comsuption of Chemical Fertilizers (tons)	农村用电量（万千瓦小时）Electricity Comsumed in Rural Areas (10000kwh)
太仓市	Taicang City	37.73	37.58	30.00	30511	49823
吴县市	Wuxian City	44.81	50.96	66.00	41765	135281
南通市	**Nantong Municipatity**	**264.88**	**340.16**	**193.00**	**260047**	**227341**
海安县	Haian County	43.63	45.74	41.00	31125	27539
如东县	Rudong County	54.67	80.80	38.00	65214	28172
启东市	Qidong City	10.79	39.60	29.00	28372	26214
如皋市	Rugao City	64.97	57.02	32.00	51160	30379
通州市	Tongzhou City	66.00	80.39	31.00	37057	48829
海门市	Haimen City	17.64	29.15	16.00	39305	41940
连云港市	**Lianyungang Municipality**	**336.14**	**523.24**	**195.00**	**268980**	**51892**
赣榆县	Ganyu County	66.00	49.48	46.00	42685	13841
东海县	Donghai County	111.25	93.57	65.00	86805	18720
灌云县	Guanyun County	93.33	74.66	35.00	76307	8534
灌南县	Guannan County	53.57	37.24	28.00	47865	5492
淮阴市	**Huaiyin Municipality**	**362.29**	**315.07**	**201.00**	**285101**	**61238**
淮阴县	Huaiyin County	58.13	49.07	21.00	41882	9591
涟水县	Lianshui County	82.44	69.69	22.00	45272	9095
洪泽县	Hongze County	26.30	27.76	35.00	29868	2852
盱眙县	Xuyi County	70.75	59.73	38.00	46830	7964
金湖县	Jinhu County	34.03	30.53	33.00	38766	6766
淮安市	Huaian City	76.37	66.06	38.00	68398	20935
盐城市	**Yancheng Municipality**	**619.65**	**588.08**	**293.00**	**498961**	**157797**
响水县	Xiangshui County	41.43	40.80	21.00	35126	7623
滨海县	Binhai County	70.80	58.24	37.00	41205	12179
阜宁县	Funing County	73.95	73.02	26.00	39920	13641
射阳县	Sheyang County	100.57	98.76	52.00	106852	18481

续表 2　　Continued 2

市县名称 City and County		机耕地面积(千公顷) Areas of Mortorized Cultivation (10000 hectares)	有效灌溉面积(千公顷) Available Irrigated Areas (1000 hectares)	农业机械总动力(万千瓦小时) Total Power of Agricltural Machinery (1000kwh)	农用化肥施用量(吨) Comsuption of Chemical Fertilizers (tons)	农村用电量(万千瓦小时) Electricity Comsumed in Rural Areas (10000kwh)
建湖县	Jianhu County	60.36	60.36	31.00	29795	17721
盐都县	Yandou County	64.11	66.50	34.00	52310	21745
东台市	Dongtai City	102.89	83.86	54.00	78403	31760
大丰市	Dafeng City	89.93	85.73	31.00	100320	26560
扬州市	**Yangzhou Municipality**	**312.06**	**256.24**	**168.00**	**164586**	**116322**
宝应县	Baoying County	83.00	56.20	29.00	36500	15169
邗江县	Hanjiang County	35.00	29.16	37.00	16278	27796
仪征市	Yizheng City	32.00	35.34	28.00	21629	11794
高邮市	Gaoyou City	74.73	61.30	30.00	45032	22861
江都市	Jiangdu City	83.33	68.99	41.00	43331	30329
镇江市	**Zhenjiang Municipality**	**145.60**	**136.27**	**109.00**	**103267**	**111671**
丹徒县	Dantu County	32.47	30.26	20.00	20884	22228
丹阳市	Danyang City	55.36	53.06	37.00	40691	41433
扬中市	Yangzhong City	10.62	10.56	12.00	6949	16962
句容市	Jurong City	41.08	38.81	29.00	27912	19568
泰州市	**Taizhou Municipality**	**270.98**	**295.00**	**174.00**	**271840**	**134835**
兴化市	Xinghua City	105.42	129.83	66.00	128527	32126
靖江市	Jingjiang City	28.78	29.65	25.00	28982	30312
泰兴市	Taixing City	63.90	71.87	39.00	30264	38114
姜堰市	Jiangyan City	53.90	54.77	32.00	61547	19576
宿迁市	**Suqian Municipality**	**247.34**	**315.52**	**197.00**	**307444**	**42270**
宿豫县	Suyu County	69.19	63.17	38.00	49946	16476
沭阳县	Shuyang County	11.70	106.25	59.00	97543	10804
泗阳县	Siyang County	62.34	58.98	32.00	53576	7113
泗洪县	Sihong County	99.99	82.26	64.00	102467	6316

19—6 农 产 品 产 量（1998）
OUTPUT OF AGRICULTURAL PRODUCTS

市县名称 City and County	粮食产量（万吨）Output of Grain (10000tons)	油料产量（吨）Output of Oil-Bearing Crops (tons)	棉花产量（吨）Output of Cotton (tons)	肉类总产量（吨）Output of Animal Meat (tons)	水产品产量（吨）Output of Aquati (tons)	肥猪出栏头数（万头）Slaughtered Fattened Hogs (10000head)
南京市 Nanjing Municipality	**176.91**	**106504**	**4838**	**155912**	**96903**	**130.00**
江宁县 Jiangning County	47.60	20385	715	29145	27128	26.00
江浦县 Jiangpu County	18.46	8877	225	22525	13067	14.00
六合县 Liuhe County	44.13	19733	2810	34728	11022	28.00
溧水县 Lishui County	27.26	20495	396	14326	11000	13.00
高淳县 Gaochun County	27.55	29915	85	21549	21135	22.00
无锡市 Wuxi Municipality	**149.77**	**20297**		**103270**	**71714**	**117.00**
江阴市 Jiangyin City	43.85	1941		35914	14801	38.00
宜兴市 Yixing City	58.24	10384		24034	39923	25.00
锡山市 Xishan City	42.19	6561		26541	18050	36.00
徐州市 Xuzhou Municipality	**386.00**	**95495**	**39189**	**345585**	**120174**	**212.00**
丰县 Fengxian County	44.19	11769	7144	47640	2516	35.00
沛县 Peixian County	51.91	10070	2272	56701	15052	32.00
铜山县 Tongshan County	75.87	2344	10240	45518	22576	27.00
睢宁县 Shuining County	64.62	21148	5737	48167	15501	32.00
新沂市 Xinyi City	49.79	40324		55785	30704	36.00
邳州市 Pizhou City	73.00	6115	10728	72612	25200	43.00
常州市 Changzhou Municipality	**153.28**	**36045**	**1200**	**87507**	**105780**	**88.00**
溧阳市 Liyang City	47.82	21365	952	14843	28780	11.00
金坛市 Jintan City	33.43	9492	248	17933	26263	18.00
武进市 Wujin City	63.89	4599		43322	43000	50.00
苏州市 Suzhou Municipality	**239.63**	**56462**	**24284**	**143463**	**284113**	**192.00**
常熟市 Changshu City	44.04	6545	8348	26123	35008	39.00
张家港市 Zhangjiagang City	32.93	4336	10824	20819	15318	21.00
昆山市 Kunshan City	37.46	11030	33	20264	55000	27.00
吴江市 Wujiang City	38.44	18104		26858	66560	37.00

续表 1　Continued 1

市县名称 City and County		粮食产量（万吨） Output of Grain (10000tons)	油料产量（吨） Output of Oil-Bearing Crops (tons)	棉花产量（吨） Output of Cotton (tons)	肉类总产量（吨） Output of Animal Meat (tons)	水产品产量（吨） Output of Aquati (tons)	肥猪出栏头数（万头） Slaughtered Fattened Hogs (10000head)
太仓市	Taicang City	26.66	4621	5079	15327	14554	19.00
吴县市	Wuxian City	48.55	8716		23288	73508	33.00
南通市	**Nantong Municipatity**	**326.36**	**189034**	**73966**	**277614**	**547888**	**235.00**
海安县	Haian County	54.75	10767	4385	60435	17525	50.00
如东县	Rudong County	70.42	24058	23745	62769	156558	47.00
启东市	Qidong City	40.11	51054	15850	22160	254545	12.00
如皋市	Rugao City	67.16	20374	7420	67196	15918	75.00
通州市	Tongzhou City	58.34	36389	12442	33617	28059	36.00
海门市	Haimen City	27.82	42667	9970	24422	64190	8.00
连云港市	**Lianyungang Municipality**	**251.93**	**124767**	**56001**	**170428**	**323643**	**149.00**
赣榆县	Ganyu County	48.69	61691	643	24585	155000	24.00
东海县	Donghai County	89.02	60231	1710	58900	50000	50.00
灌云县	Guanyun County	60.99	578	40018	47054	33691	42.00
灌南县	Guannan County	42.37	2228	7627	23848	27305	26.00
淮阴市	**Huaiyin Municipality**	**345.96**	**133533**	**8946**	**221399**	**205728**	**258.00**
淮阴县	Huaiyin County	45.94	35390	58	55515	12472	66.00
涟水县	Lianshui County	68.05	22512	4442	50860	21072	63.00
洪泽县	Hongze County	30.06	3750		15357	41368	13.00
盱眙县	Xuyi County	71.46	52978	130	31454	36217	28.00
金湖县	Jinhu County	35.18	7214	4164	11706	44795	13.00
淮安市	Huaian City	83.78	10428	152	47261	46189	62.00
盐城市	**Yancheng Municipality**	**485.41**	**172039**	**191866**	**544508**	**595046**	**480.00**
响水县	Xiangshui County	35.41	9676	16902	28931	38142	30.00
滨海县	Binhai County	60.45	19837	14478	52729	54971	51.00
阜宁县	Funing County	62.09	13552	7400	109412	29751	108.00
射阳县	Sheyang County	73.36	22785	51044	61092	179080	54.00

续表 2　Continued 2

市县名称 City and County		粮食产量（万吨）Output of Grain (10000tons)	油料产量（吨）Output of Oil-Bearing Crops (tons)	棉花产量（吨）Output of Cotton (tons)	肉类总产量（吨）Output of Animal Meat (tons)	水产品产量（吨）Output of Aquati (tons)	肥猪出栏头数（万头）Slaughtered Fattened Hogs (10000head)
建湖县	Jianhu County	49.91	6728	7066	26746	55300	28.00
盐都县	Yandou County	53.41	9286	16263	82660	69743	75.00
东台市	Dongtai City	82.57	57248	31176	102912	80657	61.00
大丰市	Dafeng City	56.18	30539	41219	58563	81991	42.00
扬州市	**Yangzhou Municipality**	**231.51**	**51808**	**24681**	**202975**	**180687**	**186.00**
宝应县	Baoying County	54.09	11292	8735	37707	65325	32.00
邗江县	Hanjiang County	28.61	8960	191	31024	16066	30.00
仪征市	Yizheng City	30.53	4436	37	18331	5009	19.00
高邮市	Gaoyou City	62.57	13850	11723	61815	69292	54.00
江都市	Jiangdu City	52.79	11803	3995	43885	24995	39.00
镇江市	**Zhenjiang Municipality**	**126.87**	**33869**	**3137**	**57940**	**58975**	**57.00**
丹徒县	Dantu County	25.47	6965	123	9861	11071	10.00
丹阳市	Danyang City	50.69	7955	222	25411	22822	25.00
扬中市	Yangzhong City	11.39	23		6156	4789	6.00
句容市	Jurong City	35.59	17591	2790	12882	15478	12.00
泰州市	**Taizhou Municipality**	**273.35**	**53976**	**28691**	**176778**	**152432**	**191.00**
兴化市	Xinghua City	114.00	18411	23578	48357	102158	46.00
靖江市	Jingjiang City	30.10	3593	1683	25392	8211	29.00
泰兴市	Taixing City	60.36	14343		53833	13672	65.00
姜堰市	Jiangyan City	51.25	14287	3398	36602	22872	38.00
宿迁市	**Suqian Municipality**	**316.42**	**82515**	**20514**	**210387**	**147527**	**237.00**
宿豫县	Suyu County	58.63	5238	2838	44298	25848	50.00
沭阳县	Shuyang County	104.35	24061	9147	79210	23000	99.00
泗阳县	Siyang County	57.38	16863	5407	39811	41000	42.00
泗洪县	Sihong County	92.06	36164	3039	43795	55479	42.00

19—7 工业企业单位数 (1998)

NUMBER OF TOWNSHIP LEVEL AND ABOVE INDUSTRIAL ENTERPRISES

单位:个

市县名称 City and County	工业企业单位数 Number of Enterprises	#限额以上工业企业 Over-Norm Industrial Enterprises	#国有企业 State-Owned Enterprises	#集体企业 Collective-Owned Enterprises	#私营企业 Private-Run Enterprises	#股份合作企业 Share-holding Cooperative Enterprises
南京市 Nanjing Municipality	**11284**	**1831**	**273**	**709**	**114**	**130**
江宁县 Jiangning County	3414	541	20	279	55	49
江浦县 Jiangpu County	683	101	18	28	4	21
六合县 Liuhe County	1354	97	15	48		7
溧水县 Lishui County	1520	112	15	26	35	10
高淳县 Gaochun County	773	84	21	21	3	24
无锡市 Wuxi Municipality	**34135**	**2756**	**222**	**889**	**346**	**636**
江阴市 Jiangyin City	10821	743	25	340	85	127
宜兴市 Yixing City	6602	462	36	68	46	240
锡山市 Xishan City	11500	869	64	309	194	130
徐州市 Xuzhou Municipality	**53838**	**638**	**206**	**263**	**37**	**46**
丰县 Fengxian County	9140	60	18	10	8	10
沛县 Peixian County	8235	65	25	24	4	3
铜山县 Tongshan County	6559	80	12	58	5	2
睢宁县 Shuining County	7957	33	19	8	3	1
新沂市 Xinyi City	8387	50	21	14	1	4
邳州市 Pizhou City	7910	84	24	30	9	15
常州市 Changzhou Municipality	**17425**	**2016**	**193**	**614**	**230**	**588**
溧阳市 Liyang City	1700	282	36	132	87	6
金坛市 Jintan City	2836	156	17	52	33	25
武进市 Wujin City	8853	883	40	204	53	474
苏州市 Suzhou Municipality	**82263**	**2994**	**300**	**859**	**327**	**448**
常熟市 Changshu City	39758	367	34	130	17	84
张家港市 Zhangjiagang City	9580	402	27	86	9	201
昆山市 Kunshan City	3498	513	39	84	49	31
吴江市 Wujiang City	14999	379	42	170	55	27

单位:个 续表 1 Continued 1

市县名称 City and County	工业企业单位数 Number of Enterprises	#限额以上工业企业 Over-Norm Industrial Enterprises	#国有企业 State-Owned Enterprises	#集体企业 Collective-Owned Enterprises	#私营企业 Private-Run Enterprises	#股份合作企业 Shareholding Cooperative Enterprises
太仓市 Taicang City	3033	293	32	81	33	23
吴县市 Wuxian City	7438	429	29	89	141	55
南通市 Nantong Municipatity	**70780**	**1578**	**174**	**286**	**64**	**461**
海安县 Haian County	8338	175	15	27	8	82
如东县 Rudong County	12021	187	12	51	8	55
启东市 Qidong City	7104	203	18	21	6	60
如皋市 Rugao City	11544	143	23	41	17	17
通州市 Tongzhou City	9211	271	14	43	5	112
海门市 Haimen City	20676	246	40	36	14	91
连云港市 Lianyungang Municipality	**43925**	**768**	**235**	**341**	**27**	**17**
赣榆县 Ganyu County	10062	138	27	80	7	4
东海县 Donghai County	9219	161	48	88	6	
灌云县 Guanyun County	13010	111	41	63		
灌南县 Guannan County	6939	54	19	9	13	3
淮阴市 Huaiyin Municipality	**33546**	**534**	**198**	**141**	**104**	**22**
淮阴县 Huaiyin County	2757	69	12	24	23	
涟水县 Lianshui County	4034	51	23	18	8	1
洪泽县 Hongze County	1971	55	26	8	16	2
盱眙县 Xuyi County	6545	46	30	8	2	
金湖县 Jinhu County	3959	83	22	17	28	11
淮安市 Huaian City	11768	108	39	35	22	3
盐城市 Yancheng Municipality	**47710**	**1049**	**205**	**351**	**61**	**235**
响水县 Xiangshui County	5734	37	13	15	3	3
滨海县 Binhai County	3827	59	10	16	8	11
阜宁县 Funing County	3965	111	13	59		16
射阳县 Sheyang County	7400	94	28	33	2	18

单位:个　　　　续表 2　Continued 2

市县名称 City and County	工业企业单位数 Number of Enterprises	#限额以上工业企业 Over-Norm Industrial Enterprises	#国有企业 State-Owned Enterprises	#集体企业 Collective-Owned Enterprises	#私营企业 Private-Run Enterprises	#股份合作企业 Share-holding Cooperative Enterprises
建湖县 Jianhu County	4403	118	16	53	1	19
盐都县 Yandou County	3906	157	30	59	15	35
东台市 Dongtai City	9316	199	32	38	13	92
大丰市 Dafeng City	7741	151	25	46	3	32
扬州市 Yangzhou Municipality	**24788**	**1262**	**188**	**518**	**150**	**149**
宝应县 Baoying County	2777	118	26	33	22	7
邗江县 Hanjiang County	3451	270	12	63	98	45
仪征市 Yizheng City	1983	124	28	32	12	20
高邮市 Gaoyou City	5006	199	31	93	8	44
江都市 Jiangdu City	8343	297	24	193	6	27
镇江市 Zhenjiang Municipality	**19319**	**1230**	**246**	**689**	**69**	**40**
丹徒县 Dantu County	3914	105	25	59	5	5
丹阳市 Danyang City	7160	408	72	291	8	3
扬中市 Yangzhong City	2626	234	38	144	10	12
句容市 Jurong City	4212	244	28	136	43	6
泰州市 Taizhou Municipality	**27502**	**956**	**112**	**400**	**59**	**201**
兴化市 Xinghua City	5840	157	13	60	25	26
靖江市 Jingjiang City	2604	225	29	133	14	22
泰兴市 Taixing City	10187	223	24	43	7	104
姜堰市 Jiangyan City	5105	157	15	61	9	47
宿迁市 Suqian Municipality	**50249**	**340**	**72**	**155**	**73**	**7**
宿豫县 Suyu County	13393	75	11	37	14	5
沭阳县 Shuyang County	18854	104	18	25	58	1
泗阳县 Siyang County	3309	89	23	52	1	1
泗洪县 Sihong County	12410	51	12	32		

19—8 全部工业总产值（1998）
GROSS OUTPUT VALUE OF TOTAL INDUSTRY

单位:万元　　　　(10000yuan)

市县名称 City and County	全部工业总产值(当年价) Gross Output Value of Total Industry (current price)	#限额以上工业企业 Over-Norm Industrial Enterprises	#国有企业 State-Owned Enterprises	#集体企业 Collective-Owned Enterprises	#私营企业 Private-Run Enterprises	#股份合作企业 Share-holding Cooperative Enterprises
南京市 Nanjing Municipality	**14112659**	**11795863**	**3691802**	**2151646**	**298584**	**344658**
江宁县 Jiangning County	2353268	1815628	119187	718364	126894	107611
江浦县 Jiangpu County	356622	225653	19572	48008	6496	55417
六合县 Liuhe County	661115	259439	47688	141239		17341
溧水县 Lishui County	900729	661925	22879	375049	107581	36841
高淳县 Gaochun County	584814	316671	41999	57828	11910	72349
无锡市 Wuxi Municipality	**23371586**	**14608603**	**1986812**	**5273224**	**500164**	**2012992**
江阴市 Jiangyin City	6912453	4883142	274769	2838571	115970	522796
宜兴市 Yixing City	3605524	1631856	103251	289667	68742	797684
锡山市 Xishan City	6705226	3387505	271858	1745841	290038	426150
徐州市 Xuzhou Municipality	**8778574**	**4074137**	**1456330**	**846420**	**58665**	**104062**
丰县 Fengxian County	654532	155428	32775	10395	12259	18269
沛县 Peixian County	857787	184576	43800	85967	7779	8543
铜山县 Tongshan County	2322760	879429	192455	258279	5478	3835
睢宁县 Shuining County	432720	74415	26283	24416	3856	764
新沂市 Xinyi City	610724	160438	92858	24280	600	3253
邳州市 Pizhou City	660380	159449	45853	64720	12617	18391
常州市 Changzhou Municipality	**10106932**	**6934265**	**1188512**	**2091252**	**320680**	**1257306**
溧阳市 Liyang City	1059200	683277	137182	325406	129914	28366
金坛市 Jintan City	950465	465728	76765	135546	51196	52947
武进市 Wujin City	4160390	2584387	190111	848974	70352	1004242
苏州市 Suzhou Municipality	**26157900**	**16256934**	**1888211**	**4196177**	**679290**	**1307542**
常熟市 Changshu City	4078000	2101273	363840	672170	29685	207475
张家港市 Zhangjiagang City	4720555	3072288	189946	1014421	15844	603878
昆山市 Kunshan City	3051788	2420097	121862	268767	113963	55510
吴江市 Wujiang City	3551356	1665121	248210	860513	99016	73064

单位:万元　　　　续表 1　Continued 1　　　　(10000yuan)

市县名称 City and County		全部工业总产值(当年价) Gross Output Value of Total Industry (current price)	#限额以上工业企业 Over-Norm Industrial Enterprises	#国有企业 State-Owned Enterprises	#集体企业 Collective-Owned Enterprises	#私营企业 Private-Run Enterprises	#股份合作企业 Share-holding Cooperative Enterprises
太仓市	Taicang City	2402006	1326787	163569	270773	108004	99642
吴县市	Wuxian City	3806500	1931103	163868	470497	283471	213490
南通市	**Nantong Municipatity**	**10237339**	**5390233**	**695847**	**707621**	**113300**	**920679**
海安县	Haian County	844906	361393	38105	54969	11813	149629
如东县	Rudong County	836738	455195	31882	102638	8325	57036
启东市	Qidong City	1675804	682770	41860	55412	11494	150739
如皋市	Rugao City	1096580	387203	79441	145420	27793	34074
通州市	Tongzhou City	2144911	1026047	19506	132378	9875	237692
海门市	Haimen City	1599922	680869	83619	103970	28064	210355
连云港市	**Lianyungang Municipality**	**5211060**	**1890695**	**561420**	**636812**	**43061**	**37517**
赣榆县	Ganyu County	1606911	326294	63798	171576	17520	13306
东海县	Donghai County	1081310	289657	53185	171870	7384	
灌云县	Guanyun County	664156	281223	126525	108722		
灌南县	Guannan County	254394	100125	30515	33823	15396	4493
淮阴市	**Huaiyin Municipality**	**3107462**	**1670726**	**686461**	**299663**	**157219**	**44526**
淮阴县	Huaiyin County	444557	211734	38284	52498	24962	
涟水县	Lianshui County	214042	115096	74499	27876	8144	1308
洪泽县	Hongze County	227329	122080	53983	18207	34181	5611
盱眙县	Xuyi County	291993	105364	70495	24564	1738	
金湖县	Jinhu County	325664	157652	40994	39892	33778	27604
淮安市	Huaian City	658656	194004	64886	64568	40710	3638
盐城市	**Yancheng Municipality**	**7915797**	**3907665**	**972825**	**1340397**	**73194**	**610832**
响水县	Xiangshui County	260007	106079	54467	37531	3044	3147
滨海县	Binhai County	446000	120271	42371	30475	7214	12589
阜宁县	Funing County	865986	401144	76007	169672		43965
射阳县	Sheyang County	966026	437297	163738	128648	2825	34570

单位:万元 续表 2 Continued 2 (10000yuan)

市县名称 City and County		全部工业总产值(当年价) Gross Output Value of Total Industry (current price)	#限额以上工业企业 Over-Norm Industrial Enterprises	#国有企业 State-Owned Enterprises	#集体企业 Collective-Owned Enterprises	#私营企业 Private-Run Enterprises	#股份合作企业 Share-holding Cooperative Enterprises
建湖县	Jianhu County	973501	467659	35725	310410	760	35164
盐都县	Yandou County	1114887	587948	48424	314177	24268	80905
东台市	Dongtai City	1230206	518750	68260	88963	13391	245838
大丰市	Dafeng City	1134786	585949	101602	190856	1978	109147
扬州市	**Yangzhou Municipality**	**7353719**	**4966325**	**1020596**	**1388442**	**363966**	**350031**
宝应县	Baoying County	680670	355432	75440	80489	22403	14286
邗江县	Hanjiang County	1310083	908934	55757	286531	297792	97716
仪征市	Yizheng City	1019835	844459	86730	44680	13274	31486
高邮市	Gaoyou City	933877	550208	70148	245523	11592	124859
江都市	Jiangdu City	1447093	733666	64880	410729	7963	76078
镇江市	**Zhenjiang Municipality**	**7956834**	**4583456**	**1180567**	**2314185**	**149487**	**89443**
丹徒县	Dantu County	1102171	469258	82764	337117	7318	11041
丹阳市	Danyang City	2726322	1396662	238963	947849	15204	7145
扬中市	Yangzhong City	955866	666008	59333	500512	13330	24656
句容市	Jurong City	1499057	716074	51177	359274	109260	29778
泰州市	**Taizhou Municipality**	**5843394**	**3670673**	**662286**	**1558341**	**75919**	**353471**
兴化市	Xinghua City	765502	344239	53595	112880	22796	29875
靖江市	Jingjiang City	1192269	795008	134165	454457	21791	60989
泰兴市	Taixing City	1181452	621061	98342	190011	13923	174787
姜堰市	Jiangyan City	960142	507921	35764	236947	9032	86211
宿迁市	**Suqian Municipality**	**2137928**	**780725**	**211215**	**295232**	**86249**	**27957**
宿豫县	Suyu County	681705	179718	33603	79153	20605	23204
沭阳县	Shuyang County	555418	158961	47399	36098	64234	2281
泗阳县	Siyang County	376601	190106	93816	76561	1410	2472
泗洪县	Sihong County	330689	176316	23093	62869		

19—9 限额以上独立核算工业企业主要财务指标 (1998)
INDICATORS OF OVER－NORM INDUSTRIAL ENTERPRISES WITH INDEPENDENT ACCONTING SYSTEMS

单位:万元 (10000yuan)

市县名称 City and County		资产合计 Total Capital Assets	流动资产年平均余额 Annual Average Balance Circulating Funds	固定资产原价合计 Original Value of Fixed Assets	产品销售收入 Revenue of Product Sales	利税总额 Total Pre－tax Profits	从业人员年平均人数(万人) Year End Employments (10000 persons)
南京市	**Nanjing Municipality**	**15296710**	**6679770**	**9130697**	**11624475**	**975515**	**74.97**
江宁县	Jiangning County	969517	455062	498905	1705019	125274	10.10
江浦县	Jiangpu County	212318	104344	106383	183190	6283	2.60
六合县	Liuhe County	174917	95536	85619	199724	4366	2.31
溧水县	Lishui County	313694	172427	135877	513613	15611	2.75
高淳县	Gaochun County	174892	87890	75980	221835	17800	2.00
无锡市	**Wuxi Municipality**	**16028630**	**7828148**	**7838219**	**13303822**	**956584**	**80.07**
江阴市	Jiangyin City	4061535	1889124	1941413	4374809	380261	21.82
宜兴市	Yixing City	1330292	662909	721455	1394249	93031	9.87
锡山市	Xishan City	3281052	1813675	1448589	2711485	110997	18.92
徐州市	**Xuzhou Municipality**	**5070971**	**2215972**	**3103698**	**3478097**	**295628**	**49.24**
丰县	Fengxian County	123750	56669	71999	137860	6654	1.83
沛县	Peixian County	202647	89173	96732	151483	10021	2.19
铜山县	Tongshan County	594985	257057	260105	837798	67158	5.12
睢宁县	Shuining County	88247	43308	46845	61014	－413	1.00
新沂市	Xinyi City	244935	88179	145585	135734	2789	3.69
邳州市	Pizhou City	164318	79749	92361	135609	11542	3.02
常州市	**Changzhou Municipality**	**7347394**	**4014451**	**3433978**	**6352203**	**359835**	**50.69**
溧阳市	Liyang City	589773	306378	300057	637265	38019	5.53
金坛市	Jintan City	381525	194629	177456	392024	20962	4.10
武进市	Wujin City	2131733	1362213	843126	2307099	161280	16.34
苏州市	**Suzhou Municipality**	**18824205**	**7930999**	**10151690**	**14720068**	**832170**	**89.78**
常熟市	Changshu City	2453440	1112536	1156606	1927939	179536	12.41
张家港市	Zhangjiagang City	3300168	1360031	1782083	2906883	155405	14.14
昆山市	Kunshan City	2870609	1161295	1673823	2312674	149805	12.24
吴江市	Wujiang City	1775319	755826	962915	1450992	78325	10.63

单位:万元　　续表1　Continued 1　　(10000yuan)

市县名称 City and County		资产合计 Total Capital Assets	流动资产年平均余额 Annual Average Balance Circulating Funds	固定资产原价合计 Original Value of Fixed Assets	产品销售收入 Revenue of Product Sales	利税总额 Total Pre-tax Profits	从业人员年平均人数(万人) Year End Employments (10000 persons)
太仓市	Taicang City	1212168	508228	649281	1063232	58384	6.33
吴县市	Wuxian City	1436942	667942	794471	1610765	91161	11.31
南通市	**Nantong Municipatity**	**5784683**	**2466143**	**3357584**	**4474245**	**298767**	**45.99**
海安县	Haian County	288244	144196	181151	309288	12115	5.08
如东县	Rudong County	490086	234902	272375	387191	23340	4.84
启东市	Qidong City	429971	225418	218176	554127	29202	4.52
如皋市	Rugao City	360858	199177	198985	326900	8382	4.95
通州市	Tongzhou City	705112	392427	332729	706843	48756	6.87
海门市	Haimen City	543021	278382	262214	542115	27122	5.18
连云港市	**Lianyungang Municipality**	**2028244**	**839843**	**1238391**	**1645745**	**106060**	**18.30**
赣榆县	Ganyu County	141684	73804	82987	302482	14234	2.20
东海县	Donghai County	217381	90905	107323	262826	9990	2.58
灌云县	Guanyun County	161606	84015	75806	258440	9437	2.40
灌南县	Guannan County	88916	46045	43009	84171	8449	1.45
淮阴市	**Huaiyin Municipality**	**2006798**	**888912**	**1195882**	**1470635**	**137643**	**17.51**
淮阴县	Huaiyin County	194352	77689	145389	131362	6327	1.73
涟水县	Lianshui County	128130	78516	62047	115086	7749	1.89
洪泽县	Hongze County	83830	35419	55644	107079	6741	1.28
盱眙县	Xuyi County	109642	50613	60248	94865	4516	1.54
金湖县	Jinhu County	122563	59539	66191	143478	12178	1.41
淮安市	Huaian City	141438	79340	76848	165949	10771	2.83
盐城市	**Yancheng Municipality**	**3644093**	**2269001**	**1896716**	**3438387**	**213277**	**35.60**
响水县	Xiangshui County	94043	51292	47115	81178	3704	1.11
滨海县	Binhai County	99664	46087	54621	99757	5818	1.51
阜宁县	Funing County	219139	106075	118680	383007	19440	2.58
射阳县	Sheyang County	382584	192466	190458	348862	17772	3.61

单位:万元 续表2 Continued 2 (10000yuan)

市县名称 City and County		资产合计 Total Capital Assets	流动资产年平均余额 Annual Average Balance Circulating Funds	固定资产原价合计 Original Value of Fixed Assets	产品销售收入 Revenue of Product Sales	利税总额 Total Pre-tax Profits	从业人员年平均人数(万人) Year End Employments (10000 persons)
建湖县	Jianhu County	334672	172795	131743	450846	32751	3.83
盐都县	Yandou County	403798	229066	205681	547358	36500	4.63
东台市	Dongtai City	413824	212201	232010	450172	29044	6.16
大丰市	Dafeng City	435355	211444	247526	467444	25661	5.00
扬州市	**Yangzhou Municipality**	**5949495**	**2835572**	**3511525**	**4319233**	**227516**	**41.19**
宝应县	Baoying County	308252	170868	144277	304980	15362	3.58
邗江县	Hanjiang County	593705	306385	261949	813313	68028	6.10
仪征市	Yizheng City	1632648	695745	1225262	791248	17317	6.31
高邮市	Gaoyou City	423109	220342	174095	473331	20435	4.93
江都市	Jiangdu City	714026	408664	326320	597123	31835	6.96
镇江市	**Zhenjiang Municipality**	**4376747**	**2092664**	**2340225**	**3657393**	**226233**	**32.76**
丹徒县	Dantu County	292723	170286	125468	389899	25973	2.55
丹阳市	Danyang City	1009659	544990	448651	1190725	73288	11.13
扬中市	Yangzhong City	671562	426413	235819	499997	57117	4.80
句容市	Jurong City	535602	169309	366713	628036	28486	4.34
泰州市	**Taizhou Municipality**	**3865791**	**2087781**	**1762641**	**3171524**	**350454**	**31.93**
兴化市	Xinghua City	388742	181654	213175	315724	18242	4.08
靖江市	Jingjiang City	716631	385804	366925	570293	35289	7.38
泰兴市	Taixing City	681036	339661	352229	544591	43011	8.28
姜堰市	Jiangyan City	525874	299796	225994	437798	28992	4.67
宿迁市	**Suqian Municipality**	**761358**	**408808**	**404460**	**702992**	**77407**	**11.05**
宿豫县	Suyu County	86273	40068	49214	163158	6272	1.96
沭阳县	Shuyang County	85721	53306	40940	135749	9264	1.86
泗阳县	Siyang County	208242	124773	97698	172234	23401	2.86
泗洪县	Sihong County	218225	119699	101747	163840	34214	2.83

19—10 国有独立核算工业企业主要财务指标 (1998)
MAJOR FINANCIAL AFFAIR INDICATORS OF STATE-OWNED INDUSTRIAL ENTERPRISES WITH INDEPENDENT ACCOUNTING SYSTEMS

单位:万元 (10000yuan)

市县名称 City and County		资产合计 Total Capital Assets	流动资产年平均余额 Annual Average Balance Circulating Funds	固定资产原价合计 Original Value of Fixed Assets	产品销售收入 Revenue of Product Sales	利税总额 Total Pre-tax Profits	从业人员年平均人数(万人) Year End Employments (10000 persons)
南京市	**Nanjing Municipality**	**5966115**	**2858512**	**3234091**	**4014451**	**357330**	**27.79**
江宁县	Jiangning County	102117	48798	57931	82000	1413	0.81
江浦县	Jiangpu County	42887	22613	21563	18769	-72	0.25
六合县	Liuhe County	55900	27307	31673	48050	36	0.53
溧水县	Lishui County	18961	10056	11235	15216	-382	0.17
高淳县	Gaochun County	33385	14148	18733	22558	526	0.33
无锡市	**Wuxi Municipality**	**3531754**	**1601130**	**1915333**	**1922848**	**75327**	**17.42**
江阴市	Jiangyin City	306705	132550	166885	271620	10992	1.48
宜兴市	Yixing City	213883	84693	136903	95241	-498	2.52
锡山市	Xishan City	391072	195478	208705	227859	5820	2.42
徐州市	**Xuzhou Municipality**	**2082021**	**913810**	**1376087**	**1029788**	**107527**	**18.79**
丰县	Fengxian County	48261	18506	35713	22419	-540	0.76
沛县	Peixian County	95265	34645	49760	36939	1871	0.99
铜山县	Tongshan County	172032	84757	79946	181970	6925	1.53
睢宁县	Shuining County	50745	23863	28952	21132	-2040	0.66
新沂市	Xinyi City	152859	53033	93015	73780	630	2.61
邳州市	Pizhou City	81942	38425	54634	34833	2422	1.44
常州市	**Changzhou Municipality**	**2157226**	**1030042**	**1233276**	**1041052**	**44142**	**11.80**
溧阳市	Liyang City	184882	91991	91279	132877	9256	1.23
金坛市	Jintan City	84030	40133	44704	71597	3405	0.63
武进市	Wujin City	261444	195937	77656	180910	7357	1.35
苏州市	**Suzhou Municipality**	**3544339**	**1270552**	**2333107**	**1670357**	**114696**	**17.42**
常熟市	Changshu City	604461	221807	448533	331667	48676	2.11
张家港市	Zhangjiagang City	188068	83625	116105	174429	14826	1.17
昆山市	Kunshan City	167932	66729	118105	133837	5034	1.08
吴江市	Wujiang City	374440	134715	257339	247460	9819	2.10

单位:万元 续表 1 Continued 1 (10000yuan)

市县名称 City and County		资产合计 Total Capital Assets	流动资产年平均余额 Annual Average Balance Circulating Funds	固定资产原价合计 Original Value of Fixed Assets	产品销售收入 Revenue of Product Sales	利税总额 Total Pre－tax Profits	从业人员年平均人数(万人) Year End Employments (10000 persons)
太仓市	Taicang City	247278	99124	149263	145500	5509	1.54
吴县市	Wuxian City	224665	106588	128293	137894	924	2.32
南通市	**Nantong Municipatity**	**953214**	**359242**	**668150**	**584882**	**15602**	**9.33**
海安县	Haian County	45190	19974	35795	34941	－418	0.70
如东县	Rudong County	65741	24259	41599	24530	320	0.79
启东市	Qidong City	81752	24233	63454	32618	907	1.02
如皋市	Rugao City	89303	44052	59805	75917	－1270	1.41
通州市	Tongzhou City	26215	13273	17619	19768	－512	0.44
海门市	Haimen City	86544	34785	60772	64433	1509	1.04
连云港市	**Lianyungang Municipality**	**879576**	**325148**	**647903**	**415124**	**14225**	**7.16**
赣榆县	Ganyu County	58543	29302	36287	49527	1430	0.86
东海县	Donghai County	86859	36345	53136	45478	－2572	1.09
灌云县	Guanyun County	74299	41730	37665	97365	3365	1.10
灌南县	Guannan County	42839	18385	21116	26397	5833	0.56
淮阴市	**Huaiyin Municipality**	**1037744**	**488554**	**626057**	**615358**	**87596**	**9.12**
淮阴县	Huaiyin County	46652	20741	29159	32020	537	0.66
涟水县	Lianshui County	104088	67138	47176	74431	6203	1.25
洪泽县	Hongze County	55606	25351	39836	46578	3924	0.84
盱眙县	Xuyi County	82657	37623	46562	61265	2118	1.12
金湖县	Jinhu County	58363	24462	36927	40347	4896	0.73
淮安市	Huaian City	61028	34403	35166	44050	1409	0.96
盐城市	**Yancheng Municipality**	**1534264**	**1196699**	**860749**	**839041**	**34996**	**12.57**
响水县	Xiangshui County	51374	28717	26608	45227	1675	0.57
滨海县	Binhai County	44723	23130	22936	33605	924	0.52
阜宁县	Funing County	65691	23155	51373	71708	2463	0.78
射阳县	Sheyang County	163444	85530	76876	130118	4280	1.60

单位:万元　　　　续表 2 Continued 2　　　　(10000yuan)

市县名称 City and County		资产合计 Total Capital Assets	流动资产年平均余额 Annual Average Balance Circulating Funds	固定资产原价合计 Original Value of Fixed Assets	产品销售收入 Revenue of Product Sales	利税总额 Total Pre-tax Profits	从业人员年平均人数(万人) Year End Employments (10000 persons)
建湖县	Jianhu County	62676	29329	31405	29685	291	0.84
盐都县	Yandou County	77525	39829	49813	39145	352	0.83
东台市	Dongtai City	112523	50807	75320	65158	2760	1.32
大丰市	Dafeng City	127994	55290	87070	94479	5221	1.60
扬州市	**Yangzhou Municipality**	**1944131**	**798902**	**1237746**	**907160**	**40273**	**12.53**
宝应县	Baoying County	79746	42765	42019	73216	2179	0.90
邗江县	Hanjiang County	52370	19065	25522	54822	3038	0.41
仪征市	Yizheng City	206370	65488	142803	64132	223	1.30
高邮市	Gaoyou City	68875	36374	28299	60691	682	1.09
江都市	Jiangdu City	147804	76472	67036	53814	936	1.12
镇江市	**Zhenjiang Municipality**	**1436487**	**614055**	**915282**	**776566**	**54992**	**8.70**
丹徒县	Dantu County	53327	26095	30268	61732	3269	0.67
丹阳市	Danyang City	327173	134328	166994	221197	15360	2.34
扬中市	Yangzhong City	69520	45688	25761	53143	3838	0.54
句容市	Jurong City	76483	31114	53993	46462	1951	0.85
泰州市	**Taizhou Municipality**	**966255**	**451934**	**523428**	**681420**	**98734**	**7.10**
兴化市	Xinghua City	93790	48381	51195	51066	184	1.08
靖江市	Jingjiang City	172696	70030	97970	122486	3162	1.73
泰兴市	Taixing City	129455	62526	81575	83462	5009	1.47
姜堰市	Jiangyan City	38649	17320	24676	33665	-819	0.55
宿迁市	**Suqian Municipality**	**309950**	**148888**	**190060**	**184296**	**18856**	**4.13**
宿豫县	Suyu County	18973	8152	8910	31564	900	0.33
沭阳县	Shuyang County	25770	13471	17457	34521	801	0.54
泗阳县	Siyang County	136999	73392	75052	85921	15532	1.63
泗洪县	Sihong County	47930	21879	26197	20155	593	1.14

19—11 限额以上集体独立核算工业企业主要财务指标 (1998)

MAJOR FINANCIAL AFFAIR INDICATORS OF OVER - NORM COLLECTIVE - OWNED INDUSTRIAL ENTERPRISES WITH INDEPENDENT ACCOUNTING SYSTEMS

单位:万元 (10000yuan)

市县名称	City and County	资产合计 Total Capital Assets	流动资产年平均余额 Annual Average Balance Circulating Funds	固定资产原价合计 Original Value of Fixed Assets	产品销售收入 Revenue of Product Sales	利税总额 Total Pre - tax Profits	从业人员年平均人数(万人) Year End Employments (10000 persons)
南京市	**Nanjing Municipality**	**1230744**	**681335**	**557951**	**1893579**	**106364**	**16.63**
江宁县	Jiangning County	297749	152462	160671	686038	48272	4.71
江浦县	Jiangpu County	36196	19979	18986	39366	1981	1.59
六合县	Liuhe County	63914	36874	30711	95645	3037	0.98
溧水县	Lishui County	177489	96509	64433	322604	6608	0.90
高淳县	Gaochun County	25183	11312	13732	40117	1117	0.50
无锡市	**Wuxi Municipality**	**4309697**	**2272894**	**1916697**	**4543852**	**308904**	**27.03**
江阴市	Jiangyin City	2096700	1028458	979685	2516839	214747	13.18
宜兴市	Yixing City	236429	121726	113541	252400	18509	1.36
锡山市	Xishan City	1544746	887953	608856	1384381	51316	8.43
徐州市	**Xuzhou Municipality**	**605413**	**267915**	**323818**	**742297**	**45629**	**9.51**
丰县	Fengxian County	12486	5412	7677	9553	263	0.20
沛县	Peixian County	53585	31362	19666	71406	5551	0.78
铜山县	Tongshan County	182872	76134	102019	230896	13374	2.33
睢宁县	Shuining County	12672	4849	7323	18311	915	0.22
新沂市	Xinyi City	39129	15598	23572	19306	759	0.44
邳州市	Pizhou City	50568	25455	24207	57890	4131	1.01
常州市	**Changzhou Municipality**	**1693813**	**968907**	**757745**	**1959252**	**103546**	**16.12**
溧阳市	Liyang City	224426	121892	119794	301728	16137	2.62
金坛市	Jintan City	112804	64902	48188	111201	7298	1.34
武进市	Wujin City	709366	425002	281279	793331	50452	5.31
苏州市	**Suzhou Municipality**	**3951202**	**1899013**	**1927919**	**3797433**	**204274**	**26.54**
常熟市	Changshu City	686131	379223	323626	612507	47004	4.69
张家港市	Zhangjiagang City	1035506	441203	559876	972408	43084	4.64
昆山市	Kunshan City	267635	141483	113041	260066	25443	2.02
吴江市	Wujiang City	908243	363266	461672	751967	37708	5.38

单位:万元　　　　　　　　　　续表 1　　Continued 1　　　　　　　　　　(10000yuan)

市县名称 City and County		资产合计 Total Capital Assets	流动资产年平均余额 Annual Average Balance Circulating Funds	固定资产原价合计 Original Value of Fixed Assets	产品销售收入 Revenue of Product Sales	利税总额 Total Pre-tax Profits	从业人员年平均人数(万人) Year End Employments (10000 persons)
太仓市	Taicang City	188452	98538	84407	218399	12393	1.31
吴县市	Wuxian City	240477	136266	103052	397598	17834	2.36
南通市	**Nantong Municipatity**	**656538**	**368532**	**310587**	**572028**	**30290**	**7.62**
海安县	Haian County	36763	14825	23703	44534	-129	0.62
如东县	Rudong County	132387	71219	67150	82041	8003	1.29
启东市	Qidong City	48654	27174	21175	38219	1583	0.57
如皋市	Rugao City	123473	74400	58529	123282	3460	1.27
通州市	Tongzhou City	97874	59223	45384	98265	5607	1.10
海门市	Haimen City	101587	58066	40030	85240	6107	0.95
连云港市	**Lianyungang Municipality**	**261224**	**136299**	**128194**	**587842**	**35694**	**4.32**
赣榆县	Ganyu County	49570	28813	26535	163517	8972	0.94
东海县	Donghai County	50241	22728	26517	159787	11222	1.08
灌云县	Guanyun County	65183	30314	28606	109766	5248	0.99
灌南县	Guannan County	23315	14762	10308	26381	1159	0.39
淮阴市	**Huaiyin Municipality**	**227434**	**97818**	**126323**	**275787**	**14724**	**3.50**
淮阴县	Huaiyin County	15264	8714	6063	44722	3434	0.43
涟水县	Lianshui County	16349	7920	9578	28234	995	0.44
洪泽县	Hongze County	5742	2978	2475	18089	1056	0.16
盱眙县	Xuyi County	16131	4773	7415	23829	2028	0.26
金湖县	Jinhu County	29415	15208	13786	39186	2211	0.33
淮安市	Huaian City	44270	26881	23134	60343	3338	1.03
盐城市	**Yancheng Municipality**	**843339**	**449453**	**405164**	**1218152**	**77701**	**10.46**
响水县	Xiangshui County	32800	17028	16072	24236	1652	0.45
滨海县	Binhai County	21977	10250	11634	27842	2017	0.39
阜宁县	Funing County	78410	41838	39615	162298	7614	0.99
射阳县	Sheyang County	107917	45784	67942	107687	4071	1.16

单位:万元　　　　续表 2　Continued 2　　　　(10000yuan)

市县名称 City and County	资产合计 Total Capital Assets	流动资产年平均余额 Annual Average Balance Circulating Funds	固定资产原价合计 Original Value of Fixed Assets	产品销售收入 Revenue of Product Sales	利税总额 Total Pre-tax Profits	从业人员年平均人数(万人) Year End Employments (10000 persons)
建湖县 Jianhu County	186682	103437	61511	301595	25708	1.97
盐都县 Yandou County	183308	111073	87602	300568	20417	2.15
东台市 Dongtai City	70368	36834	43075	80055	5160	1.37
大丰市 Dafeng City	108482	51488	59357	151017	7197	1.35
扬州市 Yangzhou Municipality	**1067581**	**620289**	**452332**	**1206541**	**78482**	**12.18**
宝应县 Baoying County	69176	42961	29964	69883	3775	1.05
邗江县 Hanjiang County	189592	111653	70581	260615	29645	1.64
仪征市 Yizheng City	28790	14735	15762	38418	1222	0.62
高邮市 Gaoyou City	185740	100353	74904	216053	11137	2.12
江都市 Jiangdu City	342955	218665	146851	331021	17871	3.93
镇江市 Zhenjiang Municipality	**1587879**	**954007**	**626824**	**1898930**	**133165**	**16.10**
丹徒县 Dantu County	205161	127372	79086	292261	20741	1.51
丹阳市 Danyang City	548227	332939	227041	786197	43800	7.44
扬中市 Yangzhong City	501607	317590	166494	365946	46387	3.32
句容市 Jurong City	125418	66504	67149	314673	15697	2.07
泰州市 Taizhou Municipality	**1319210**	**826515**	**528590**	**1221816**	**138582**	**13.31**
兴化市 Xinghua City	95545	51994	48675	89224	6883	1.33
靖江市 Jingjiang City	338922	211483	146532	287012	22320	4.13
泰兴市 Taixing City	204186	110735	107287	181237	16152	3.20
姜堰市 Jiangyan City	255286	145978	102543	197124	17047	1.83
宿迁市 Suqian Municipality	**165242**	**102493**	**75263**	**270673**	**26781**	**3.49**
宿豫县 Suyu County	29221	13635	16905	71648	3018	0.66
沭阳县 Shuyang County	21575	12863	11231	29225	2435	0.54
泗阳县 Siyang County	52843	39728	16102	68082	6191	0.97
泗洪县 Sihong County	30197	21030	10709	63134	11795	0.59

19—12 限额以上独立核算工业企业经济效益 (1998)
ECCNOMIC RESULTS OF OVER－NORM INDUSTRIAL ENTERPRISES WITH INDEPENDENT ACCOUNTING SYSTEMS

市县名称 City and County	销售利税率(%) Pre－tax Profits/Product Sales			资金利税率(%) Pre－tax Profits/Total Assets		
	合计 Total	国有工业企业 State－Owned	集体工业企业 Collective－Owned	合计 Total	国有工业企业 State－Owned	集体工业企业 Collective－Owned
南京市 Nanjing Municipality	**8.39**	**8.90**	**5.62**	**7.84**	**7.28**	**9.99**
江宁县 Jiangning County	7.35	1.72	7.04	15.41	1.54	18.44
江浦县 Jiangpu County	3.43	－0.38	5.03	3.35	－0.19	5.96
六合县 Liuhe County	2.19	0.07	3.18	2.84	0.08	5.14
溧水县 Lishui County	3.04	－2.51	2.05	5.74	－2.04	4.58
高淳县 Gaochun County	8.02	2.33	2.78	12.65	1.89	5.18
无锡市 Wuxi Municipality	**7.19**	**3.92**	**6.80**	**7.25**	**2.59**	**8.57**
江阴市 Jiangyin City	8.69	4.05	8.53	11.69	4.50	12.42
宜兴市 Yixing City	6.67	－0.52	7.33	7.78	－0.25	8.95
锡山市 Xishan City	4.09	2.55	3.71	3.91	1.63	3.96
徐州市 Xuzhou Municipality	**8.50**	**10.44**	**6.15**	**6.93**	**6.04**	**9.23**
丰县 Fengxian County	4.83	－2.41	2.75	5.85	－1.16	2.23
沛县 Peixian County	6.62	5.07	7.77	6.16	2.66	11.67
铜山县 Tongshan County	8.02	3.81	5.79	14.77	4.77	9.33
睢宁县 Shuining County	－0.68	－9.65	5.00	－0.50	－4.27	8.28
新沂市 Xinyi City	2.05	0.85	3.93	1.42	0.52	2.13
邳州市 Pizhou City	8.51	6.95	7.14	8.27	3.33	10.18
常州市 Changzhou Municipality	**5.66**	**4.24**	**5.28**	**5.70**	**2.39**	**7.13**
溧阳市 Liyang City	5.97	6.97	5.35	7.33	5.85	7.98
金坛市 Jintan City	5.35	4.76	6.56	6.49	4.76	7.62
武进市 Wujin City	6.99	4.07	6.36	8.43	2.97	8.46
苏州市 Suzhou Municipality	**5.65**	**6.87**	**5.38**	**5.35**	**4.00**	**6.27**
常熟市 Changshu City	9.31	14.68	7.67	8.50	9.06	7.85
张家港市 Zhangjiagang City	5.35	8.50	4.43	5.85	9.20	5.31
昆山市 Kunshan City	6.48	3.76	9.78	6.09	3.27	11.43
吴江市 Wujiang City	5.40	3.97	5.01	5.35	3.26	5.23

续表 1　Continued 1

市县名称 City and County	销售利税率（%）Pre－tax Profits/Product Sales			资金利税率（%）Pre－tax Profits/Total Assets		
	合计 Total	国有工业企业 State－Owned	集体工业企业 Collective－Owned	合计 Total	国有工业企业 State－Owned	集体工业企业 Collective－Owned
太仓市 Taicang City	5.49	3.79	5.67	5.94	2.68	7.89
吴县市 Wuxian City	5.66	0.67	4.49	7.16	0.48	8.12
南通市 Nantong Municipatity	**6.68**	**2.67**	**5.30**	**6.37**	**1.91**	**5.34**
海安县 Haian County	3.92	－1.20	－0.29	4.67	－0.98	－0.41
如东县 Rudong County	6.03	1.30	9.75	5.57	0.57	7.35
启东市 Qidong City	5.27	2.78	4.14	7.55	1.36	3.57
如皋市 Rugao City	2.56	－1.67	2.81	2.54	－1.55	3.00
通州市 Tongzhou City	6.90	－2.59	5.71	7.89	－1.96	6.49
海门市 Haimen City	5.00	2.34	7.16	5.76	1.94	7.13
连云港市 Lianyungang Municipality	**6.44**	**3.43**	**6.07**	**6.05**	**1.80**	**15.31**
赣榆县 Ganyu County	4.71	2.89	5.49	10.86	2.66	19.29
东海县 Donghai County	3.80	－5.66	7.02	5.73	－3.51	25.03
灌云县 Guanyun County	3.65	3.46	4.78	6.61	4.85	9.75
灌南县 Guannan County	10.04	22.10	4.39	10.77	17.24	5.00
淮阴市 Huaiyin Municipality	**9.36**	**14.23**	**5.34**	**7.70**	**9.58**	**7.62**
淮阴县 Huaiyin County	4.82	1.68	7.68	3.41	1.26	25.69
涟水县 Lianshui County	6.73	8.33	3.52	6.18	6.04	6.54
洪泽县 Hongze County	6.30	8.42	5.84	8.88	7.66	20.70
盱眙县 Xuyi County	4.76	3.46	8.51	5.06	3.12	20.95
金湖县 Jinhu County	8.49	12.13	5.64	11.43	9.68	9.06
淮安市 Huaian City	6.49	3.20	5.53	7.98	2.46	7.78
盐城市 Yancheng Municipality	**6.20**	**4.17**	**6.38**	**4.75**	**1.31**	**10.42**
响水县 Xiangshui County	4.56	3.70	6.82	4.26	3.44	5.68
滨海县 Binhai County	5.83	2.75	7.24	6.60	2.28	10.36
阜宁县 Funing County	5.08	3.43	4.69	9.97	4.01	10.46
射阳县 Sheyang County	5.09	3.29	3.78	5.47	3.16	4.36

续表2 Continued 2

市县名称 City and County	销售利税率(%) Pre－tax Profits/Product Sales 合计 Total	国有工业企业 State－Owned	集体工业企业 Collective－Owned	资金利税率(%) Pre－tax Profits/Total Assets 合计 Total	国有工业企业 State－Owned	集体工业企业 Collective－Owned
建湖县 Jianhu County	7.26	0.98	8.52	11.94	0.55	17.15
盐都县 Yandou County	6.67	0.90	6.79	9.66	0.46	11.59
东台市 Dongtai City	6.45	4.24	6.45	7.79	2.79	7.35
大丰市 Dafeng City	5.49	5.53	4.77	6.70	4.50	7.85
扬州市 Yangzhou Municipality	**5.27**	**4.44**	**6.50**	**4.35**	**2.49**	**8.42**
宝应县 Baoying County	5.04	2.98	5.40	5.54	2.92	5.72
邗江县 Hanjiang County	8.36	5.54	11.38	13.95	10.55	18.24
仪征市 Yizheng City	2.19	0.35	3.18	1.11	0.13	4.85
高邮市 Gaoyou City	4.32	1.12	5.15	5.98	1.25	7.14
江都市 Jiangdu City	5.33	1.74	5.40	5.04	0.75	5.64
镇江市 Zhenjiang Municipality	**6.19**	**7.08**	**7.01**	**6.11**	**4.65**	**9.58**
丹徒县 Dantu County	6.66	5.30	7.10	9.78	6.77	11.16
丹阳市 Danyang City	6.15	6.94	5.57	8.41	5.94	8.82
扬中市 Yangzhong City	11.42	7.22	12.68	9.69	5.96	10.70
句容市 Jurong City	4.54	4.20	4.99	6.00	3.10	13.88
泰州市 Taizhou Municipality	**11.05**	**14.49**	**11.34**	**10.57**	**12.20**	**11.72**
兴化市 Xinghua City	5.78	0.36	7.71	5.46	0.22	7.86
靖江市 Jingjiang City	6.19	2.58	7.78	5.55	2.27	7.35
泰兴市 Taixing City	7.90	6.00	8.91	7.27	4.27	8.72
姜堰市 Jiangyan City	6.62	－2.43	8.65	6.30	－2.39	7.78
宿迁市 Suqian Municipality	**11.01**	**10.23**	**9.89**	**10.94**	**6.54**	**16.36**
宿豫县 Suyu County	3.84	2.85	4.21	8.21	6.12	11.31
沭阳县 Shuyang County	6.82	2.32	8.33	10.87	3.15	11.08
泗阳县 Siyang County	13.59	18.08	9.09	11.94	12.08	12.22
泗洪县 Sihong County	20.88	2.94	18.68	17.40	1.46	40.21

19—13 交 通 邮 电 事 业 (1998)
TRANSPOTATION, POSTAL AND TELECOMMUNICATION SERVICES

市县名称 City and County		公路客运量（万人）Highway Passenger Traffic (10000 persons)	公路货运量（万吨）Highway Freight Traffic (10000tons)	水运客运量（万人）Waterway Passenger Traffic (10000 persons)	水运货运量（万吨）Waterway Freight Traffic (10000tons)	邮电业务总量（万元）Revenue from Posts and Telecom－munication (10000yuan)	全年用电量（万千瓦时）Annual Electricity Consumed (10000kuh)
南京市	**Nanjing Municipality**	**12523**	**6368**		**3703**	**271030**	**1157151**
江宁县	Jiangning County	399	136		1	10046	72175
江浦县	Jiangpu County	613	4		2	5948	17005
六合县	Liuhe County	499	7		14	7968	29199
溧水县	Lishui County	58	3			5344	26454
高淳县	Gaochun County	93	10			4579	17686
无锡市	**Wuxi Municipality**	**15067**	**4707**	**56**	**1339**	**217270**	**1090232**
江阴市	Jiangyin City	3126	1268		212	45591	301526
宜兴市	Yixing City	2808	552		541	38722	150507
锡山市	Xishan City	2674	1115		218		248301
徐州市	**Xuzhou Municipality**	**6048**	**4608**		**514**	**96046**	**636504**
丰县	Fengxian County	213	243		23	5851	19390
沛县	Peixian County	410	556		113	6986	75974
铜山县	Tongshan County	873	1369		24		74870
睢宁县	Shuining County	236	299		3	6756	22709
新沂市	Xinyi City	233	490		73	7227	38278
邳州市	Pizhou City	307	733		212	8534	37500
常州市	**Changzhou Municipality**	**7526**	**3340**	**1**	**1666**	**131919**	**601148**
溧阳市	Liyang City	1440	637		738	14063	72457
金坛市	Jintan City	636	371		416	12163	52584
武进市	Wujin City	2485	1218		235		198356
苏州市	**Suzhou Municipality**	**14255**	**3060**	**36**	**3142**	**330275**	**1327589**
常熟市	Changshu City	1836	543	3	343	49688	169880
张家港市	Zhangjiagang City	1972	443		422	41440	284733
昆山市	Kunshan City	1555	193	2	440	40501	143298
吴江市	Wujiang City	1127	288	1	389	37738	165091

续表 1　　Continued 1

市县名称 City and County		公路客运量（万人）Highway Passenger Traffic (10000 persons)	公路货运量（万吨）Highway Freight Traffic (10000tons)	水运客运量（万人）Waterway Passenger Traffic (10000 persons)	水运货运量（万吨）Waterway Freight Traffic (10000tons)	邮电业务总量（万元）Revenue from Posts and Telecom-munication (10000yuan)	全年用电量（万千瓦时）Annual Electricity Consumed (10000kuh)
太仓市	Taicang City	874	279		110	23064	91844
吴县市	Wuxian City	1663	425	12	908		168206
南通市	**Nantong Municipatity**	**6770**	**3899**	**43**	**1361**	**119772**	**554720**
海安县	Haian County	252	479		576	11287	49700
如东县	Rudong County	383	575		134	9672	62908
启东市	Qidong City	850	372		68	16114	48013
如皋市	Rugao City	498	565	9	185	11770	59639
通州市	Tongzhou City	540	616		272	14061	76013
海门市	Haimen City	973	414		28	12736	61748
连云港市	**Lianyungang Municipality**	**4303**	**2583**		**236**	**50769**	**219686**
赣榆县	Ganyu County	70	21		56	6928	27001
东海县	Donghai County	287	77		12	7098	33167
灌云县	Guanyun County	25	32		64	5671	21457
灌南县	Guannan County	90	30		15	3794	11303
淮阴市	**Huaiyin Municipality**	**2287**	**1129**	**13**	**1506**	**52298**	**249590**
淮阴县	Huaiyin County	112	92		12	3820	18100
涟水县	Lianshui County	366	98			4490	20941
洪泽县	Hongze County	142	97	13	132	3708	14847
盱眙县	Xuyi County	251	188		90	4872	28011
金湖县	Jinhu County	145	99		51	5520	18814
淮安市	Huaian City	284	252		57	8501	27353
盐城市	**Yancheng Municipality**	**5479**	**2708**	**10**	**4411**	**86812**	**360415**
响水县	Xiangshui County	730	60		312	3921	19128
滨海县	Binhai County	46	158		59	6304	21787
阜宁县	Funing County	90	791		194	7097	33216
射阳县	Sheyang County		99		512	9478	43184

续表 2　Continued 2

市县名称 City and County	公路客运量（万人） Highway Passenger Traffic (10000 persons)	公路货运量（万吨） Highway Freight Traffic (10000tons)	水运客运量（万人） Waterway Passenger Traffic (10000 persons)	水运货运量（万吨） Waterway Freight Traffic (10000tons)	邮电业务总量（万元） Revenue from Posts and Telecom－munication (10000yuan)	全年用电量（万千瓦时） Annual Electricity Consumed (10000kuh)
建湖县 Jianhu County	197	830		1442	7867	29490
盐都县 Yandou County	466	61		488		26528
东台市 Dongtai City	686	57		571	12819	51712
大丰市 Dafeng City	154	20		211	10260	59364
扬州市 Yangzhou Municipality	**5874**	**2638**	**54**	**1164**	**104784**	**399641**
宝应县 Baoying County	525	192	19	393	11134	35398
邗江县 Hanjiang County	736	475		69		41213
仪征市 Yizheng City	415	475	18	12	13480	109486
高邮市 Gaoyou City	351	238	17	243	11369	34574
江都市 Jiangdu City	1750	705		294	22756	67536
镇江市 Zhenjiang Municipality	**4909**	**3054**	**28**	**1069**	**86145**	**392338**
丹徒县 Dantu County	349	316	23	59	1989	32463
丹阳市 Danyang City	861	781		121	21601	93717
扬中市 Yangzhong City	378	184		3	14793	25701
句容市 Jurong City	597	537		31	8099	41618
泰州市 Taizhou Municipality	**3127**	**1174**	**188**	**1576**	**88235**	**312706**
兴化市 Xinghua City	397	169	131	105	14357	56857
靖江市 Jingjiang City	927	367		332	17954	66514
泰兴市 Taixing City	819	185	11	85	21489	71274
姜堰市 Jiangyan City	634	245	28	769	15202	40337
宿迁市 Suqian Municipality	**1846**	**782**		**353**	**23717**	**118795**
宿豫县 Suyu County	176	119				
沭阳县 Shuyang County	744	137		45	6085	25158
泗阳县 Siyang County	260	118		92	5231	26039
泗洪县 Sihong County	402	132		108	4979	23556

19—14 固定资产投资完成额 (1998)
VALUE OF FIXED ASSETS INVESTMENT FULFILLED

单位:万元 (10000yuan)

市县名称 City and County	全社会固定资产投资完成额 Value of Total Fixed Assets Investment Fulfilled	#基本建设 Capital Construction	#更新改造 Updating and Trans-formation	#房地产开发投资 Investment of Real Estate Development	#城镇集体经济 Urban Collective-Owned	#农村集体经济 Rural Collective-Owned
南京市 Nanjing Municipality	**3766000**	**1483499**	**623350**	**1010571**	**71763**	**363385**
江宁县 Jiangning County	300958	73194	26242	24599	9397	139290
江浦县 Jiangpu County	57976	26875	705	2150	2930	17011
六合县 Liuhe County	83255	7695	15322	7239	1161	17877
溧水县 Lishui County	80129	25162	2685	3139	8499	13346
高淳县 Gaochun County	78415	18637	6743	2111	7204	17187
无锡市 Wuxi Municipality	**2772222**	**390032**	**255857**	**340423**	**82287**	**972792**
江阴市 Jiangyin City	574802	15753	67483	62825	22047	325653
宜兴市 Yixing City	322021	33919	29056	34690	27363	168565
锡山市 Xishan City	450018	36638	22270	39354	14948	254160
徐州市 Xuzhou Municipality	**1882611**	**591413**	**270144**	**185631**	**87044**	**458197**
丰县 Fengxian County	96895	14460	7200	800	2318	34218
沛县 Peixian County	112588	16787	19448	4560	2871	30495
铜山县 Tongshan County	211505	16938	8788	29457	5234	98215
睢宁县 Shuining County	76037	19111	10720	624	550	20450
新沂市 Xinyi City	144030	19418	13738	6280	10268	38079
邳州市 Pizhou City	137538	22785	2941	1350	200	53165
常州市 Changzhou Municipality	**1312913**	**269088**	**242836**	**223200**	**77642**	**358589**
溧阳市 Liyang City	176284	19698	28215	30859	17547	55376
金坛市 Jintan City	125686	13685	22398	23139	14142	46832
武进市 Wujin City	311517	47975	14408	44767	12013	157745
苏州市 Suzhou Municipality	**4508810**	**734843**	**367793**	**585447**	**66155**	**862366**
常熟市 Changshu City	506488	32260	28977	52125	19478	75865
张家港市 Zhangjiagang City	444715	44475	28552	30884	25149	119124
昆山市 Kunshan City	579897	50764	17710	52099	645	275932
吴江市 Wujiang City	264224	24717	28597	19755	14291	114394

单位:万元　　　　续表 1　Continued 1　　　　(10000yuan)

市县名称 City and County	全社会固定资产投资完成额 Value of Total Fixed Assets Investment Fulfilled	#基本建设 Capital Construction	#更新改造 Updating and Trans-formation	#房地产开发投资 Investment of Real Estate Development	#城镇集体经济 Urban Collective-Owned	#农村集体经济 Rural Collective-Owned
太仓市 Taicang City	407118	204265	12861	27330	2578	62060
吴县市 Wuxian City	352052	32818	9977	50446	950	157921
南通市 Nantong Municipatity	**2497629**	**532621**	**240711**	**172521**	**73048**	**400769**
海安县 Haian County	156898	16422	20356	5151	23481	30927
如东县 Rudong County	208250	11707	30627	1049	1656	43719
启东市 Qidong City	271205	24022	28729	15145	7011	84249
如皋市 Rugao City	223416	24631	15912	9571	12148	43752
通州市 Tongzhou City	425297	54879	25312	16311	10414	77217
海门市 Haimen City	313280	31184	19536	15776	11085	90949
连云港市 Lianyungang Municipality	**838307**	**316190**	**153773**	**45400**	**64167**	**156721**
赣榆县 Ganyu County	107848	27693	11999	2160	3359	32301
东海县 Donghai County	101222	22152	18626	888	4420	35204
灌云县 Guanyun County	101366	20184	21562	890	11976	29378
灌南县 Guannan County	79221	14988	8542	1419	3716	34278
淮阴市 Huaiyin Municipality	**811283**	**236164**	**156452**	**42470**	**32226**	**153751**
淮阴县 Huaiyin County	98277	16322	10630	4900	1672	29000
涟水县 Lianshui County	91288	14631	8452	1779	1972	17965
洪泽县 Hongze County	40527	5589	6361	1028	1164	10060
盱眙县 Xuyi County	73763	12388	7600	2023	1070	20406
金湖县 Jinhu County	53920	13847	5250	1747	3576	11372
淮安市 Huaian City	110136	12285	14198	1855	6916	48000
盐城市 Yancheng Municipality	**1126038**	**260876**	**119252**	**114272**	**76624**	**254694**
响水县 Xiangshui County	60210	17665	6245	1780	7341	9164
滨海县 Binhai County	77534	16868	7537	2179	2162	15903
阜宁县 Funing County	128445	24130	13841	20075	10917	35022
射阳县 Sheyang County	102692	17736	7816	10319	11933	27801

单位:万元 　　续表 2 　Continued 2 　　(10000yuan)

市县名称 City and County		全社会固定资产投资完成额 Value of Total Fixed Assets Investment Fulfilled	#基本建设 Capital Construction	#更新改造 Updating and Trans－formation	#房地产开发投资 Investment of Real Estate Development	#城镇集体经济 Urban Collective－Owned	#农村集体经济 Rural Collective－Owned
建湖县	Jianhu County	89007	25737	3955	3271	9547	28707
盐都县	Yandou County	124034	26105	3317	4154	4378	51708
东台市	Dongtai City	177678	13186	15527	12201	8654	35949
大丰市	Dafeng City	133236	25113	13932	8974	9832	31539
扬州市	**Yangzhou Municipality**	**1277511**	**595851**	**172579**	**107871**	**30985**	**161109**
宝应县	Baoying County	83581	10988	14432	6039	1175	17224
邗江县	Hanjiang County	115726	15920	5460	13229	1832	40960
仪征市	Yizheng City	173233	109230	9771	4911	6739	5419
高邮市	Gaoyou City	106759	6085	11360	8087	5104	34888
江都市	Jiangdu City	158512	28234	24325	15717	10737	35810
镇江市	**Zhenjiang Municipality**	**1633619**	**972846**	**152101**	**87390**	**28710**	**262232**
丹徒县	Dantu County	100156	15898	17245	10991	1013	32109
丹阳市	Danyang City	226612	26986	46854	11988	10100	100710
扬中市	Yangzhong City	134113	18920	8618	16321	3809	61987
句容市	Jurong City	112925	12579	6557	2561	9552	41536
泰州市	**Taizhou Municipality**	**957995**	**267817**	**168060**	**70031**	**60824**	**146189**
兴化市	Xinghua City	166894	22978	25269	9231	2130	31835
靖江市	Jingjiang City	106978	22069	24470	4651	21275	11917
泰兴市	Taixing City	205400	30347	39266	8734	9537	35122
姜堰市	Jiangyan City	120029	21946	13235	9220	4348	34717
宿迁市	**Suqian Municipality**	**457546**	**173399**	**36717**	**17067**	**13500**	**55049**
宿豫县	Suyu County	61190	14018	5365		946	12451
沭阳县	Shuyang County	131998	39567	7603	2247	1679	14000
泗阳县	Siyang County	62079	11484	14023	100	1127	10076
泗洪县	Sihong County	82240	18466	8820	2086	3226	13160

19—15 国 内 贸 易（1998）
DOMESTIC TRADE

单位：万元 （10000yuan）

市县名称 City and County		批发零售贸易业商品销售总额 Total Sales Invwholesale and Retail Trade	社会消费品零售总额 Total Retail Sales of Consumer Goods	#批发零售贸易业 Wholesale and Retail Trade	#餐饮业 Catering Trade	#制造业 Manufactu－ring	#农业生产者 Agriculture to Non Agriculture
南 京 市	**Nanjing Municipality**	**9757238**	**3823853**	**2573901**	**277658**	**193914**	**679655**
江 宁 县	Jiangning County	255029	175032	92288	9995	26217	45508
江 浦 县	Jiangpu County	294388	83867	51108	6080	12584	13760
六 合 县	Liuhe County	140964	179260	97689	12318	14132	53769
溧 水 县	Lishui County	160531	118888	84749	10147	5368	18250
高 淳 县	Gaochun County	85697	154952	82606	5048	18170	40688
无 锡 市	**Wuxi Municipality**	**9654507**	**3001362**	**2184014**	**364294**	**189284**	**201225**
江 阴 市	Jiangyin City	2138667	606472	392878	77432	43361	83799
宜 兴 市	Yixing City	2498985	516486	374354	38887	32377	52245
锡 山 市	Xishan City	1639189	507949	425739	51677	19716	6895
徐 州 市	**Xuzhou Municipality**	**2729152**	**1606304**	**1048472**	**145036**	**135393**	**248773**
丰 县	Fengxian County	163799	115033	74406	10019	17494	13109
沛 县	Peixian County	159915	128715	93968	2472	19402	11882
铜 山 县	Tongshan County	363773	135971	95470	10679	17932	11890
睢 宁 县	Shuining County	138182	76110	57008	6341	6042	6520
新 沂 市	Xinyi City	235593	110139	83234	8191	9843	8498
邳 州 市	Pizhou City	224027	130665	90429	12669	11521	11740
常 州 市	**Changzhou Municipality**	**3835830**	**1739300**	**1212496**	**109700**	**138602**	**239969**
溧 阳 市	Liyang City	442186	341290	222609	22165	38422	44616
金 坛 市	Jintan City	324506	254046	136906	10997	69537	33400
武 进 市	Wujin City	1260708	417328	314482	21727	18713	54544
苏 州 市	**Suzhou Municipality**	**8754153**	**2978952**	**2168166**	**251620**	**201786**	**257946**
常 熟 市	Changshu City	1941845	650138	445099	47796	66556	38618
张家港市	Zhangjiagang City	1252165	371298	277422	30008	17078	23560
昆 山 市	Kunshan City	730491	305066	221065	39765	17671	17584
吴 江 市	Wujiang City	934122	290077	227190	9078	18224	29282

单位:万元 续表 1 Continued 1 (10000yuan)

市县名称 City and County		批发零售贸易业商品销售总额 Total Sales Invwholesale and Retail Trade	社会消费品零售总额 Total Retail Sales of Consumer Goods	#批发零售贸易业 Wholesale and Retail Trade	#餐饮业 Catering Trade	#制造业 Manufactu－ring	#农业生产者 Agriculture to Non Agriculture
太仓市	Taicang City	510515	216158	160533	19111	31388	5126
吴县市	Wuxian City	1079578	368298	274117	50843	19547	19857
南通市	**Nantong Municipatity**	**4377319**	**2133735**	**1504152**	**106982**	**307290**	**162186**
海安县	Haian County	455424	172169	111195	7205	33331	17544
如东县	Rudong County	318888	244227	171878	5782	28765	24000
启东市	Qidong City	551120	330164	232639	11510	58590	16600
如皋市	Rugao City	393568	247169	160594	10594	43706	24757
通州市	Tongzhou City	763512	331591	216174	29284	56306	26913
海门市	Haimen City	574292	330887	229901	9867	60263	23890
连云港市	**Lianyungang Municipality**	**1806094**	**844668**	**561985**	**74723**	**82990**	**114346**
赣榆县	Ganyu County	236932	139546	78610	11501	30832	13257
东海县	Donghai County	248283	135635	103201	12781	10805	7840
灌云县	Guanyun County	277531	117797	71979	9587	21875	12811
灌南县	Guannan County	123851	65353	45709	7398	6969	5277
淮阴市	**Huaiyin Municipality**	**1650268**	**830892**	**546143**	**57701**	**74181**	**142127**
淮阴县	Huaiyin County	111547	64130	35604	5764	4032	18730
涟水县	Lianshui County	106680	83067	56026	2956	14350	9735
洪泽县	Hongze County	109387	63575	46353	4721	3849	7345
盱眙县	Xuyi County	113696	83365	45446	10128	14720	11146
金湖县	Jinhu County	154048	76731	54226	3361	9981	6494
淮安市	Huaian City	243557	121368	87471	10929	10962	11850
盐城市	**Yancheng Municipality**	**3027618**	**1504284**	**1146210**	**76437**	**106364**	**165595**
响水县	Xiangshui County	143535	60296	47377	3201	3911	4070
滨海县	Binhai County	205389	98592	68086	6412	6944	16743
阜宁县	Funing County	217275	126315	81038	8603	16181	14918
射阳县	Sheyang County	292874	173601	131669	10268	13845	17819

单位:万元　　　　续表 2　Continued 2　　　　(10000yuan)

市县名称 City and County	批发零售贸易业商品销售总额 Total Sales Invwholesale and Retail Trade	社会消费品零售总额 Total Retail Sales of Consumer Goods	#批发零售贸易业 Wholesale and Retail Trade	#餐饮业 Catering Trade	#制造业 Manufactu－ring	#农业生产者 Agriculture to Non Agriculture
建湖县 Jianhu County	262730	148770	120435	9596	10054	8285
盐都县 Yandou County	315733	140779	106066	8420	10330	15963
东台市 Dongtai City	381938	239952	181988	9284	21092	27583
大丰市 Dafeng City	320051	161828	123259	7226	6328	24723
扬州市 Yangzhou Municipality	**2273399**	**1320357**	**855272**	**98783**	**116689**	**215115**
宝应县 Baoying County	218644	135871	96235	3990	19081	14721
邗江县 Hanjiang County	211398	106029	65430	13359	16305	2740
仪征市 Yizheng City	245400	197356	79546	11559	7701	94272
高邮市 Gaoyou City	264151	140229	98611	13431	11268	15700
江都市 Jiangdu City	492308	284396	177472	15339	43190	32992
镇江市 Zhenjiang Municipality	**1587945**	**1066005**	**665823**	**93807**	**97077**	**209298**
丹徒县 Dantu County	136294	108116	58051	4982	19313	25770
丹阳市 Danyang City	498904	282246	193284	28587	22440	37935
扬中市 Yangzhong City	208021	123664	88994	5510	16068	13092
句容市 Jurong City	114280	137295	77892	12070	24420	22913
泰州市 Taizhou Municipality	**2191888**	**1146795**	**712511**	**76660**	**105289**	**237996**
兴化市 Xinghua City	321131	172628	87576	3914	24583	53800
靖江市 Jingjiang City	389496	227091	146837	14841	19863	43294
泰兴市 Taixing City	283354	250245	169074	15471	24740	35597
姜堰市 Jiangyan City	292009	203025	135498	17038	20242	27950
宿迁市 Suqian Municipality	**692458**	**512447**	**321129**	**27161**	**101712**	**57942**
宿豫县 Suyu County	138792	91951	65009	4523	21910	453
沭阳县 Shuyang County	196312	141644	84347	5515	32461	19272
泗阳县 Siyang County	143716	121702	75317	4774	25933	14045
泗洪县 Sihong County	107190	80347	54179	2130	13915	7372

19—16 对外经济贸易(1998)
UTILIZATION OF FOREIGN CAPITAL

单位:万美元 (10000USD)

市县名称	City and County	外贸进出口总额 Total Value of Foreign Trade Import and Export	#出口 Export	协议合同外资金额 Foreign Funds of Signed Contracts	#客商直接投资 Direct Foreign Investments	实际利用外资 Foreign Capital Actually Used	#客商直接投资 Direct Foreign Investments
南京市	**Nanjing Municipality**	**171282**	**117422**	**54247**	**54247**	**83590**	**74845**
江宁县	Jiangning County	19595	17840	23898	23898	15183	15183
江浦县	Jiangpu County	3090	3069	601	601	1328	1328
六合县	Liuhe County	2507	2470	1241	1241	814	814
溧水县	Lishui County	2505	2006	469	469	240	240
高淳县	Gaochun County	2579	2561	129	129	97	97
无锡市	**Wuxi Municipality**	**432828**	**295522**	**120101**	**113212**	**105111**	**91146**
江阴市	Jiangyin City	68494	52449	30260	25901	26407	22048
宜兴市	Yixing City	25194	22133	6014	6014	6084	6084
锡山市	Xishan City	34889	28276	18321	18321	16010	13870
徐州市	**Xuzhou Municipality**	**37801**	**27474**	**27817**	**22655**	**22816**	**22816**
丰县	Fengxian County	1080	1079	270	270	426	426
沛县	Peixian County	1275	1264	986	986	759	759
铜山县	Tongshan County	4035	3101	2347	2347	1294	1294
睢宁县	Shuining County	373	373	230	230	91	91
新沂市	Xinyi City	1660	1467	881	881	762	762
邳州市	Pizhou City	1288	1226	558	558	280	280
常州市	**Changzhou Municipality**	**159380**	**131035**	**82327**	**37948**	**55681**	**50628**
溧阳市	Liyang City	6197	5616	6286	6028	3499	3241
金坛市	Jintan City	12233	9077	3684	1682	3704	3598
武进市	Wujin City	40694	37159	19623	12961	9747	9747
苏州市	**Suzhou Municipality**	**924974**	**564535**	**408694**	**408694**	**284180**	**284180**
常熟市	Changshu City	95356	67542	20472	20472	20010	20010
张家港市	Zhangjiagang City	144432	81104	37372	37372	32002	32002
昆山市	Kunshan City	196805	125996	98061	98061	50005	50005
吴江市	Wujiang City	49300	34195	8467	8467	7003	7003

单位:万美元　　　　　　　　　　　　续表 1　　Continued 1　　　　　　　　　　　　(10000USD)

市县名称 City and County		外贸进出口总额 Total Value of Foreign Trade Import and Export	#出口 Export	协议合同外资金额 Foreign Funds of Signed Contracts	#客商直接投资 Direct Foreign Investments	实际利用外资 Foreign Capital Actually Used	#客商直接投资 Direct Foreign Investments
太 仓 市	Taicang City	70145	46449	18755	18755	18012	18012
吴 县 市	Wuxian City	74912	53393	19106	19106	17002	17002
南 通 市	**Nantong Municipatity**	**277151**	**188530**	**53182**	**51222**	**61077**	**37792**
海 安 县	Haian County	11034	10500	1218	1218	505	505
如 东 县	Rudong County	15705	12595	3294	3294	932	932
启 东 市	Qidong City	18987	15799	3050	3050	2022	2022
如 皋 市	Rugao City	12717	11952	1175	1175	211	211
通 州 市	Tongzhou City	32040	24714	1184	1184	2506	2506
海 门 市	Haimen City	14030	11517	8122	8122	962	962
连云港市	**Lianyungang Municipality**	**39273**	**35245**	**11390**	**9261**	**13145**	**10308**
赣 榆 县	Ganyu County	1830	1830	468	468	1035	1035
东 海 县	Donghai County	1820	1820	115	115	2015	2015
灌 云 县	Guanyun County	2186	1858	1288	1288	908	908
灌 南 县	Guannan County	572	572	260	260	205	205
淮 阴 市	**Huaiyin Municipality**	**18470**	**15447**	**3729**	**805**	**8559**	**5635**
淮 阴 县	Huaiyin County	556	556	303	58	432	186
涟 水 县	Lianshui County	588	502	115	15	115	15
洪 泽 县	Hongze County	191	191	626	276	407	58
盱 眙 县	Xuyi County	310	310	242	2	240	
金 湖 县	Jinhu County	591	587	434	42	389	
淮 安 市	Huaian City	676	671	523	112	524	113
盐 城 市	**Yancheng Municipality**	**55283**	**45165**	**15307**	**13725**	**15347**	**14184**
响 水 县	Xiangshui County	358	358	1823	1823	427	427
滨 海 县	Binhai County	1172	909	294	294	107	107
阜 宁 县	Funing County	2842	2774	2549	2549	1977	1977
射 阳 县	Sheyang County	6891	4467	2436	2436	2012	1204

单位:万美元　　　　续表 2　Continued 2　　　　(10000USD)

市县名称 City and County		外贸进出口总额 Total Value of Foreign Trade Import and Export	#出口 Export	协议合同外资金额 Foreign Funds of Signed Contracts	#客商直接投资 Direct Foreign Investments	实际利用外资 Foreign Capital Actually Used	#客商直接投资 Direct Foreign Investments
建湖县	Jianhu County	4451	3922	292	180	1577	1465
盐都县	Yandou County	7314	4848	389	389	2297	2297
东台市	Dongtai City	5578	4025	1431	1431	2034	1791
大丰市	Dafeng City	6270	5347	3072	3072	2221	2221
扬州市	**Yangzhou Municipality**	**83267**	**56166**	**6384**	**5894**	**17029**	**6829**
宝应县	Baoying County	9591	7214	835	835	825	825
邗江县	Hanjiang County	3450	2828	172	172	405	405
仪征市	Yizheng City	2507	2007	211	211	21	21
高邮市	Gaoyou City	5630	5101	20	20	50	50
江都市	Jiangdu City	1153	1018	210	210	881	881
镇江市	**Zhenjiang Municipality**	**150898**	**80436**	**29669**	**28044**	**75738**	**74655**
丹徒县	Dantu County	9928	7886	4021	4021	2532	2532
丹阳市	Danyang City	21297	20430	2905	1527	1537	559
扬中市	Yangzhong City	11630	10773	3478	3231	2502	2397
句容市	Jurong City	7773	7657	723	723	8509	8509
泰州市	**Taizhou Municipality**	**37356**	**29567**	**12045**	**10323**	**10086**	**9814**
兴化市	Xinghua City	831	686	1919	1919	980	980
靖江市	Jingjiang City	13382	11029	2428	2428	1200	1200
泰兴市	Taixing City	7792	6551	3683	2683	3108	3108
姜堰市	Jiangyan City	6392	4966	1116	1116	1129	1129
宿迁市	**Suqian Municipality**	**3020**	**3020**	**1475**	**1475**	**1468**	**501**
宿豫县	Suyu County	2322	2322	44	44	704	
沭阳县	Shuyang County	15	15	616	616	83	42
泗阳县	Siyang County	103	103	320	320	123	
泗洪县	Sihong County	190	190	332	332	99	

19—17 财 政 主 要 指 标 (1998)
MAJOR INDICATORS OF FINANCE

单位:万元 (10000yuan)

市县名称 City and County	财政收入 Total Financial Revenue	#地方财政收入 Local Financial Revenue	财政支出 Financial Expenditure	#基本建设支出 Capital Construction	#支农支出 Farming and Rural Water Conservancy Funds	#教育事业费支出 Educational Services Funds
南京市 Nanjing Municipality	**1082397**	**507798**	**596533**	**33083**	**37113**	**79163**
江宁县 Jiangning County	46046	25530	34968	653	5223	9672
江浦县 Jiangpu County	20026	10090	13885	280	1857	3259
六合县 Liuhe County	16512	10051	16560	245	2933	3975
溧水县 Lishui County	19219	11363	17698	89	3220	4195
高淳县 Gaochun County	16138	10820	17050	668	2608	3667
无锡市 Wuxi Municipality	**759896**	**356592**	**347882**	**19622**	**11526**	**68277**
江阴市 Jiangyin City	145765	62411	61222	4871	1756	13937
宜兴市 Yixing City	87276	37204	39792	2886	1484	12365
锡山市 Xishan City	151601	62936	61323	123	3193	15363
徐州市 Xuzhou Municipality	**395108**	**194247**	**283443**	**3257**	**22987**	**78634**
丰县 Fengxian County	16586	11890	26558	446	3513	8480
沛县 Peixian County	28004	17284	27162	52	2530	9204
铜山县 Tongshan County	38507	23507	35526	165	3019	13769
睢宁县 Shuining County	15360	11683	23762	58	2365	9192
新沂市 Xinyi City	18204	12432	21683	132	1619	7191
邳州市 Pizhou City	24271	16622	29529	30	2316	11262
常州市 Changzhou Municipality	**450937**	**226573**	**224114**	**14095**	**7503**	**47519**
溧阳市 Liyang City	40630	20378	27012	238	883	9679
金坛市 Jintan City	33642	17615	20604	33	791	7033
武进市 Wujin City	126703	57479	61316	1837	3823	16052
苏州市 Suzhou Municipality	**876327**	**457830**	**463983**	**34901**	**13964**	**79461**
常熟市 Changshu City	159545	77444	75710	9382	2293	14202
张家港市 Zhangjiagang City	130249	66021	63863	675	3019	12186
昆山市 Kunshan City	86128	44371	44949	35	1069	9399
吴江市 Wujiang City	73743	35866	34555	82	789	8307

单位:万元 续表 1 Continued 1 (10000yuan)

市县名称 City and County		财政收入 Total Financial Revenue	#地方财政收入 Local Financial Revenue	财政支出 Financial Expenditure	#基本建设支出 Capital Construction	#支农支出 Farming and Rural Water Conservancy Funds	#教育事业费支出 Educational Services Funds
太仓市	Taicang City	60046	29978	28542	790	370	5367
吴县市	Wuxian City	96094	45746	47621	114	3264	10615
南通市	**Nantong Municipatity**	**402701**	**214491**	**270733**	**10680**	**3627**	**64750**
海安县	Haian County	31131	16730	26881	262	444	7896
如东县	Rudong County	35986	20145	29187	82	423	8825
启东市	Qidong City	48788	26210	32176	218	419	9202
如皋市	Rugao City	32178	17062	26369	216	381	8991
通州市	Tongzhou City	55286	26652	34242	145	581	9987
海门市	Haimen City	46666	24558	31101	100	359	8805
连云港市	**Lianyungang Municipality**	**164713**	**111058**	**155341**	**6119**	**4859**	**35985**
赣榆县	Ganyu County	24389	19346	24813	329	1158	7935
东海县	Donghai County	22211	17407	23561	84	1589	7635
灌云县	Guanyun County	19488	14793	21050	8	663	6542
灌南县	Guannan County	11031	5578	14921	508	566	4203
淮阴市	**Huaiyin Municipality**	**196221**	**91258**	**148825**	**2372**	**5883**	**38579**
淮阴县	Huaiyin County	13711	8728	16789	56	304	4597
涟水县	Lianshui County	13294	8453	21053	275	653	7593
洪泽县	Hongze County	10166	6998	11754	45	752	3044
盱眙县	Xuyi County	12316	8431	15452	70	988	4574
金湖县	Jinhu County	12371	7118	11840	25	781	2931
淮安市	Huaian City	17030	11841	22804	192	412	8310
盐城市	**Yancheng Municipality**	**243237**	**147838**	**253695**	**5218**	**5261**	**80640**
响水县	Xiangshui County	9716	6246	14007	80	429	4808
滨海县	Binhai County	13520	8316	25168	127	393	9028
阜宁县	Funing County	19415	13257	24840	45	683	10047
射阳县	Sheyang County	24983	15859	26698	137	331	9545

单位:万元　　　　　　　　　　　续表 2　Continued 2　　　　　　　　　　　(10000yuan)

市县名称 City and County		财政收入 Total Financial Revenue	#地方财政收入 Local Financial Revenue	财政支出 Financial Expenditure	#基本建设支出 Capital Construction	#支农支出 Farming and Rural Water Conservancy Funds	#教育事业费支出 Educational Services Funds
建湖县	Jianhu County	23436	13371	26989	48	610	9402
盐都县	Yandou County	25014	15338	27101	59	651	9222
东台市	Dongtai City	35932	21330	30050	172	726	11368
大丰市	Dafeng City	30031	17579	24684	155	271	8176
扬州市	**Yangzhou Municipality**	**255303**	**122882**	**183200**	**5676**	**5328**	**45912**
宝应县	Baoying County	22281	10780	21688	66	427	7411
邗江县	Hanjiang County	26974	11931	17850	494	535	5177
仪征市	Yizheng City	49771	21368	27815	107	2463	6317
高邮市	Gaoyou City	21722	10908	21459	66	609	7948
江都市	Jiangdu City	53137	24892	32466	530	538	9890
镇江市	**Zhenjiang Municipality**	**228823**	**110794**	**142362**	**2899**	**2766**	**35340**
丹徒县	Dantu County	20570	10778	15885	20	187	5458
丹阳市	Danyang City	59389	27606	30407	666	429	11247
扬中市	Yangzhong City	28771	13750	16774	35	231	3967
句容市	Jurong City	19608	10684	16817	128	628	4841
泰州市	**Taizhou Municipality**	**273506**	**144100**	**207216**	**6271**	**12554**	**52250**
兴化市	Xinghua City	26232	14765	31264	917	1638	12571
靖江市	Jingjiang City	41157	22178	27702	339	1998	8093
泰兴市	Taixing City	46048	22150	35246	168	3403	12977
姜堰市	Jiangyan City	34220	17824	25629	107	2164	8514
宿迁市	**Suqian Municipality**	**98483**	**51006**	**123901**	**8891**	**4762**	**37624**
宿豫县	Suyu County	11004	7622	20375	1407	480	7120
沭阳县	Shuyang County	17084	12992	27035	91	661	11954
泗阳县	Siyang County	28872	10816	24238	83	570	8588
泗洪县	Sihong County	30870	12714	24932	6	2093	6708

19—18 金融主要指标（1998）
MAJOR INDICATORS OF BANKING

单位：万元 (10000yuan)

市县名称 City and County		年末金融机构存款余额 Year-end Deposits Balance of Banking Institutions	年末金融机构贷款余额 Year-end Loans Balance of Banking Institutions	城乡居民储蓄余额 Savings Deposit of Urban and Rural Residents	金融机构现金收入 Cash Revenue of Banking Institutions	金融机构现金支出 Cash Expenditure of Banking Institutions
南京市	**Nanjing Municipality**	**15438096**	**12773141**	**5052485**	**17741415**	**17280379**
江宁县	Jiangning County	488256	446440	311620	831854	968010
江浦县	Jiangpu County	182330	155452	91355	299587	320078
六合县	Liuhe County	234133	232057	175023	469795	501644
溧水县	Lishui County	167856	166928	119486	384091	423599
高淳县	Gaochun County	162176	162864	117158	387467	398528
无锡市	**Wuxi Municipality**	**8487089**	**6159927**	**4674613**	**18275036**	**18188056**
江阴市	Jiangyin City	1751100	1355000	952800	4033458	4244122
宜兴市	Yixing City	1134123	762162	719635	4025557	4044732
锡山市	Xishan City	1623466	1114865	1032378	3244263	3625775
徐州市	**Xuzhou Municipality**	**3768104**	**3226763**	**2438696**	**10061390**	**10120620**
丰县	Fengxian County	202842	177176	165461	794532	802159
沛县	Peixian County	375402	290329	314558	1085287	1150750
铜山县	Tongshan County	479798	389318	344175	1347697	1345966
睢宁县	Shuining County	176429	174750	147203	544251	531361
新沂市	Xinyi City	189829	214116	136191	663560	653914
邳州市	Pizhou City	290241	228154	220552	592315	654066
常州市	**Changzhou Municipality**	**4798000**	**3421300**	**2841400**	**10571153**	**10863711**
溧阳市	Liyang City	535474	399349	388509	1436684	1467562
金坛市	Jintan City	342877	292929	251590	1082334	1155434
武进市	Wujin City	1454908	876363	912041	3305602	3774953
苏州市	**Suzhou Municipality**	**11124378**	**7242834**	**6490389**	**25143490**	**25440237**
常熟市	Changshu City	2002901	937700	1412262	6224904	5955761
张家港市	Zhangjiagang City	1527827	1062289	1018310	3013219	3079124
昆山市	Kunshan City	1096669	707080	581477	2096863	2297775
吴江市	Wujiang City	1018529	715105	614061	3134777	3267036

单位:万元　　　　续表 1　Continued 1　　　　(10000yuan)

市县名称 City and County	年末金融机构存款余额 Year-end Deposits Balance of Banking Institutions	年末金融机构贷款余额 Year-end Loans Balance of Banking Institutions	城乡居民储蓄余额 Savings Deposit of Urban and Rural Residents	金融机构现金收入 Cash Revenue of Banking Institutions	金融机构现金支出 Cash Expenditure of Banking Institutions
太仓市 Taicang City	788211	484517	535276	1604916	1660742
吴县市 Wuxian City	1281485	735761	875988	2978676	3225877
南通市 Nantong Municipatity	**6202807**	**3688850**	**4501466**	**12570381**	**12600406**
海安县 Haian County	670276	310945	541376	1371445	1322565
如东县 Rudong County	564160	427311	456251	1165451	1190449
启东市 Qidong City	843659	453420	724274	1901366	1999126
如皋市 Rugao City	571171	357733	464325	1574011	1639292
通州市 Tongzhou City	911938	459778	720653	1755654	1856584
海门市 Haimen City	799496	384758	647568	1498067	1589642
连云港市 Lianyungang Municipality	**1610654**	**1649442**	**969186**	**3932121**	**3932522**
赣榆县 Ganyu County	203755	182727	153257	777713	788776
东海县 Donghai County	207469	237356	149644	863897	848114
灌云县 Guanyun County	155529	231536	116795	695338	930191
灌南县 Guannan County	81690	119888	60360	320428	338766
淮阴市 Huaiyin Municipality	**1469452**	**1635405**	**879148**	**4417089**	**4332440**
淮阴县 Huaiyin County	121116	118912	83334	463842	445907
涟水县 Lianshui County	128810	173682	100649	524591	530519
洪泽县 Hongze County	104310	120406	81577	582180	596491
盱眙县 Xuyi County	111133	174527	79464	331452	346777
金湖县 Jinhu County	135047	147091	93428	396216	414407
淮安市 Huaian City	198468	216823	152779	472683	493413
盐城市 Yancheng Municipality	**3182079**	**2981838**	**2267595**	**9315929**	**9680115**
响水县 Xiangshui County	98631	138342	77901	432909	460980
滨海县 Binhai County	193737	189707	152945	747824	803530
阜宁县 Funing County	244772	218108	201279	872367	846680
射阳县 Sheyang County	325328	430724	245510	1147541	1249551

单位:万元　　　　续表 2　Continued 2　　　　(10000yuan)

市县名称 City and County		年末金融机构存款余额 Year-end Deposits Balance of Banking Institutions	年末金融机构贷款余额 Year-end Loans Balance of Banking Institutions	城乡居民储蓄余额 Savings Deposit of Urban and Rural Residents	金融机构现金收入 Cash Revenue of Banking Institutions	金融机构现金支出 Cash Expenditure of Banking Institutions
建湖县	Jianhu County	277078	264193	224456	922858	991839
盐都县	Yandou County	311767	276183	238254	90339	98564
东台市	Dongtai City	606646	397880	491863	1345772	1355848
大丰市	Dafeng City	373234	326765	284055	173077	190756
扬州市	**Yangzhou Municipality**	**3416000**	**2595120**	**2172694**	**6656887**	**7210402**
宝应县	Baoying County	266347	273665	210575	789253	860661
邗江县	Hanjiang County	329632	244957	231737	755261	920131
仪征市	Yizheng City	382725	287231	239872	771737	867214
高邮市	Gaoyou City	324148	283368	247635	933044	1048618
江都市	Jiangdu City	857698	529074	660747	1463803	1632011
镇江市	**Zhenjiang Municipality**	**2608337**	**2201036**	**1595645**	**5664587**	**6031224**
丹徒县	Dantu County	284213	292260	172780	608513	649949
丹阳市	Danyang City	643370	476687	476450	1558452	1654418
扬中市	Yangzhong City	380516	229481	281402	947780	1156914
句容市	Jurong City	248238	185831	182913	704398	746378
泰州市	**Taizhou Municipality**	**3170934**	**2313596**	**2157298**	**6145452**	**6624448**
兴化市	Xinghua City	519666	484645	420292	1608988	1713610
靖江市	Jingjiang City	518617	391443	408417	947770	1094536
泰兴市	Taixing City	614498	437082	484095	1379040	1493490
姜堰市	Jiangyan City	528006	335381	400710	974118	1033971
宿迁市	**Suqian Municipality**	**737698**	**727156**	**491416**	**2560808**	**2587318**
宿豫县	Suyu County					
沭阳县	Shuyang County	162002	193933	128887	670916	673789
泗阳县	Siyang County	142217	142088	106995	525048	526232
泗洪县	Sihong County	174652	141986	113397	657095	652210

19—19 人 民 生 活（1998）
PEOPLE'S LIVELIHOOD

市县名称 City and County	在岗职工工资总额（万元）Gross Wage Bill of Employed Staff and Workers	#国有经济 State-Owned Units	在岗职工平均工资（元）Average Wage of Employed Staff and Workers	#国有经济 State-Owned Units	农民人均纯收入（元）Per Capita Net Income of Peasants
南京市 Nanjing Municipality	**1281584**	**860696**	**10661**	**11005**	**3937**
江宁县 Jiangning County	40509	23123	7247	8258	3787
江浦县 Jiangpu County	17616	11511	7626	8050	3674
六合县 Liuhe County	24619	18346	6264	7002	3476
溧水县 Lishui County	22282	12352	6421	7441	3591
高淳县 Gaochun County	20012	12626	7385	8252	3585
无锡市 Wuxi Municipality	**615360**	**371197**	**9744**	**10383**	**5018**
江阴市 Jiangyin City	85798	47196	9041	9853	5308
宜兴市 Yixing City	72204	49816	8357	9208	4326
锡山市 Xishan City	71500	54005	8773	9891	5342
徐州市 Xuzhou Municipality	**592951**	**514527**	**7717**	**8149**	**3102**
丰县 Fengxian County	21755	17435	5621	6579	2807
沛县 Peixian County	34171	29986	6113	6380	3109
铜山县 Tongshan County	47062	32312	6675	6635	3428
睢宁县 Shuining County	23397	20398	5142	5666	2551
新沂市 Xinyi City	30835	23803	5976	6575	2857
邳州市 Pizhou City	39118	33044	5972	6635	2847
常州市 Changzhou Municipality	**455656**	**280576**	**9571**	**10330**	**4289**
溧阳市 Liyang City	39365	25205	7905	8970	3687
金坛市 Jintan City	51014	37958	8446	9213	4015
武进市 Wujin City	75786	47789	8969	9874	5034
苏州市 Suzhou Municipality	**775708**	**473809**	**9616**	**10260**	**5347**
常熟市 Changshu City	107056	62854	9325	9993	5282
张家港市 Zhangjiagang City	80212	53113	8912	9710	5405
昆山市 Kunshan City	83000	38506	9232	9798	5351
吴江市 Wujiang City	61116	37583	8608	9467	5463

续表 1　　Continued 1

市县名称 City and County	在岗职工工资总额（万元） Gross Wage Bill of Employed Staff and Workers	#国有经济 State-Owned Units	在岗职工平均工资（元） Average Wage of Employed Staff and Workers	#国有经济 State-Owned Units	农民人均纯收入（元） Per Capita Net Income of Peasants
太仓市 Taicang City	52021	32288	9273	9638	5336
吴县市 Wuxian City	56665	38807	8321	9306	5294
南通市 Nantong Municipatity	**520936**	**287049**	**7438**	**8215**	**3504**
海安县 Haian County	48501	28465	6010	7570	3415
如东县 Rudong County	53789	29767	6783	7498	3117
启东市 Qidong City	54828	31800	6914	7930	4124
如皋市 Rugao City	52017	34239	6344	7411	2743
通州市 Tongzhou City	63675	35392	7013	7882	3771
海门市 Haimen City	47576	25400	7069	8411	4177
连云港市 Lianyungang Municipality	**243057**	**175689**	**6548**	**7104**	**2938**
赣榆县 Ganyu County	24655	20521	6148	6620	3065
东海县 Donghai County	28355	23714	5391	5700	2999
灌云县 Guanyun County	33342	27164	5759	6377	2951
灌南县 Guannan County	15997	12727	5015	5510	2506
淮阴市 Huaiyin Municipality	**253277**	**199981**	**6133**	**6774**	**2851**
淮阴县 Huaiyin County	21485	17371	5467	5752	2644
涟水县 Lianshui County	26010	21601	4853	5469	2604
洪泽县 Hongze County	15321	11919	5395	5930	3103
盱眙县 Xuyi County	27212	23508	5941	6219	2568
金湖县 Jinhu County	22499	17648	6147	6561	3208
淮安市 Huaian City	37268	26664	5256	6733	3175
盐城市 Yancheng Municipality	**404690**	**294733**	**5722**	**6691**	**3186**
响水县 Xiangshui County	20636	15628	4400	5209	2760
滨海县 Binhai County	24381	17921	4425	5974	2845
阜宁县 Funing County	29564	20671	5298	6283	2950
射阳县 Sheyang County	52359	35261	5558	6506	3344

续表 2　　Continued 2

市县名称 City and County	在岗职工工资总额（万元）Gross Wage Bill of Employed Staff and Workers	#国有经济 State-Owned Units	在岗职工平均工资（元）Average Wage of Employed Staff and Workers	#国有经济 State-Owned Units	农民人均纯收入（元）Per Capita Net Income of Peasants
建湖县 Jianhu County	40244	25285	5395	6450	3187
盐都县 Yandou County	34403	23895	5418	6675	3387
东台市 Dongtai City	50036	34204	5106	5918	3542
大丰市 Dafeng City	47225	33654	6305	6910	3642
扬州市 Yangzhou Municipality	**405677**	**274057**	**7669**	**8626**	**3257**
宝应县 Baoying County	36965	25787	6319	7629	3160
邗江县 Hanjiang County	25390	14396	6412	8133	3450
仪征市 Yizheng City	74075	41937	8314	8371	3053
高邮市 Gaoyou City	39684	25695	6401	7670	3192
江都市 Jiangdu City	50322	32482	6639	7416	3445
镇江市 Zhenjiang Municipality	**311082**	**206908**	**8184**	**8899**	**3931**
丹徒县 Dantu County	25968	17167	7315	7948	3640
丹阳市 Danyang City	57034	39291	7697	8289	4084
扬中市 Yangzhong City	26011	14898	7348	8562	4509
句容市 Jurong City	30703	20806	7042	7851	3490
泰州市 Taizhou Municipality	**284426**	**170242**	**6390**	**7731**	**3251**
兴化市 Xinghua City	44048	31602	6169	7506	3090
靖江市 Jingjiang City	54246	30050	6143	7805	3436
泰兴市 Taixing City	58847	37208	6130	7442	3186
姜堰市 Jiangyan City	44268	22879	6279	7703	3060
宿迁市 Suqian Municipality	**136036**	**105771**	**5621**	**6236**	**2630**
宿豫县 Suyu County	20891	16694	5662	6704	2608
沭阳县 Shuyang County	27468	22376	5664	6164	2692
泗阳县 Siyang County	34129	28779	5211	5767	2552
泗洪县 Sihong County	32704	23151	5799	5982	2649

19—20 文 教 卫 生 事 业 (1998)
CULTURE EDUCATION AND HEALTH CARE SERVICES

单位:万元 (10000yuan)

市县名称 City and County	高等学校在校学生(人) Student Enrollment in Institutions of Higher Education (person)	普通中学在校学生(万人) Student Enrollment in Primary Schools (10000 persons)	小学在校学生数(万人) Student Enrollment in Primary Schools (10000 persons)	卫生机构数(个) Health Care Institutions	医院卫生院床位数(张) Hospital Beds	医生数(人) Doctors (person)
南京市 Nanjing Municipality	**132439**	**21.80**	**48.11**	**1285**	**20618**	**15745**
江宁县 Jiangning County		3.31	8.02	73	1188	802
江浦县 Jiangpu County		1.14	3.67	89	502	385
六合县 Liuhe County		2.69	7.84	79	1089	699
溧水县 Lishui County		1.41	4.35	64	598	421
高淳县 Gaochun County		1.60	3.90	59	1017	458
无锡市 Wuxi Municipality	**12473**	**19.41**	**41.98**	**1441**	**14179**	**6414**
江阴市 Jiangyin City		4.97	12.85	255	2846	1428
宜兴市 Yixing City		4.31	10.50	333	2257	1272
锡山市 Xishan City		4.72	9.41	173	2586	1230
徐州市 Xuzhou Municipality	**24763**	**51.25**	**130.99**	**1261**	**15703**	**11756**
丰县 Fengxian County		6.25	14.38	94	1050	932
沛县 Peixian County		7.22	17.41	169	1731	1428
铜山县 Tongshan County		9.53	17.98	136	1463	986
睢宁县 Shuining County		6.73	20.29	67	1150	901
新沂市 Xinyi City		5.70	16.00	67	1140	960
邳州市 Pizhou City		7.67	27.95	86	1263	982
常州市 Changzhou Municipality	**14251**	**14.69**	**31.24**	**833**	**10813**	**5506**
溧阳市 Liyang City		3.20	7.49	104	1704	901
金坛市 Jintan City		2.48	5.50	92	1336	801
武进市 Wujin City		5.26	11.40	163	2969	1536
苏州市 Suzhou Municipality	**32375**	**23.00**	**48.88**	**1440**	**17663**	**8779**
常熟市 Changshu City	1599	3.88	7.87	239	3099	1469
张家港市 Zhangjiagang City	1528	3.86	8.43	207	2337	1149
昆山市 Kunshan City		2.35	5.27	111	1722	841
吴江市 Wujiang City		2.73	6.52	86	1595	776

单位:万元　　　　　　　　　　续表 1　　Continued 1　　　　　　　　　　(10000yuan)

市县名称 City and County		高等学校在校学生(人) Student Enrollment in Institutions of Higher Education (person)	普通中学在校学生(万人) Student Enrollment in Primary Schools (10000 persons)	小学在校学生数(万人) Student Enrollment in Primary Schools (10000 persons)	卫生机构数(个) Health Care Institutions	医院卫生院床位数(张) Hospital Beds	医生数(人) Doctors (person)
太仓市	Taicang City		1.55	3.17	75	1459	697
吴县市	Wuxian City		3.82	9.09	112	1769	1130
南通市	**Nantong Municipatity**	**9919**	**30.41**	**65.36**	**2093**	**18948**	**11109**
海安县	Haian County		4.22	8.12	189	1988	1234
如东县	Rudong County		3.96	9.00	295	2269	1467
启东市	Qidong City		4.68	9.60	308	2388	1559
如皋市	Rugao City		5.93	13.60	280	2588	1589
通州市	Tongzhou City		5.06	12.02	354	2636	1578
海门市	Haimen City		4.03	8.07	301	2296	1272
连云港市	**Lianyungang Municipality**	**9428**	**26.52**	**65.75**	**838**	**6739**	**4072**
赣榆县	Ganyu County		6.84	15.91	72	954	816
东海县	Donghai County		7.22	17.24	105	1039	729
灌云县	Guanyun County		5.92	13.69	126	1138	660
灌南县	Guannan County		3.12	10.81	96	763	389
淮阴市	**Huaiyin Municipality**	**7125**	**22.05**	**55.40**	**606**	**7900**	**4094**
淮阴县	Huaiyin County		4.19	9.74	50	544	389
涟水县	Lianshui County		5.25	11.64	82	1096	559
洪泽县	Hongze County		1.26	3.44	63	595	311
盱眙县	Xuyi County		2.74	9.07	72	910	542
金湖县	Jinhu County		1.54	3.45	72	712	369
淮安市	Huaian City		4.86	12.48	89	1448	800
盐城市	**Yancheng Municipality**	**8238**	**41.63**	**87.63**	**881**	**12940**	**7855**
响水县	Xiangshui County		3.12	8.27	55	828	489
滨海县	Binhai County		6.35	12.91	79	1045	887
阜宁县	Funing County		6.72	12.17	81	1094	989
射阳县	Sheyang County		6.14	10.68	75	1597	981

单位:万元　　　　　　续表 2　Continued 2　　　　　　(10000yuan)

市县名称 City and County		高等学校在校学生(人) Student Enrollment in Institutions of Higher Education (person)	普通中学在校学生(万人) Student Enrollment in Primary Schools (10000 persons)	小学在校学生数(万人) Student Enrollment in Primary Schools (10000 persons)	卫生机构数(个) Health Care Institutions	医院卫生院床位数(张) Hospital Beds	医生数(人) Doctors (person)
建湖县	Jianhu County		3.70	9.28	168	1420	783
盐都县	Yandou County		5.11	10.18	90	1388	754
东台市	Dongtai City		4.45	11.57	127	2515	1366
大丰市	Dafeng City		3.11	6.85	80	1637	885
扬州市	**Yangzhou Municipality**	**23095**	**16.62**	**38.71**	**936**	**10679**	**5870**
宝应县	Baoying County		3.21	8.13	116	1294	808
邗江县	Hanjiang County		2.35	4.93	83	848	622
仪征市	Yizheng City		1.88	5.78	133	1409	767
高邮市	Gaoyou City		2.83	6.92	111	1474	948
江都市	Jiangdu City		4.07	8.95	158	2261	1357
镇江市	**Zhenjiang Municipality**	**19111**	**11.33**	**24.18**	**850**	**7399**	**5638**
丹徒县	Dantu County		1.83	3.32	95	773	441
丹阳市	Danyang City		3.57	7.84	157	1544	1250
扬中市	Yangzhong City		1.27	2.62	70	670	578
句容市	Jurong City	2207	2.44	5.94	90	1047	735
泰州市	**Taizhou Municipality**	**1905**	**19.98**	**46.38**	**674**	**10546**	**6421**
兴化市	Xinghua City		5.80	16.12	131	2382	1196
靖江市	Jingjiang City		3.40	5.33	107	2186	1187
泰兴市	Taixing City		5.09	11.85	139	2410	1829
姜堰市	Jiangyan City		3.36	8.00	94	1710	1073
宿迁市	**Suqian Municipality**		**25.53**	**67.19**	**474**	**4952**	**2886**
宿豫县	Suyu County		4.87	12.53	38	844	565
沭阳县	Shuyang County		8.68	23.04	145	1359	728
泗阳县	Siyang County		5.60	14.69	83	1201	799
泗洪县	Sihong County		4.82	14.15	125	1171	575

20. 县(市)社会经济序列

COUNTY (CITY) SOCIAL ECONOMIC ALIGNMENT

20－1 年 末 总 人 口 (1998)
YEAR END TOTAL POPULATION

位次 No.	县（市）名称 County (City)		指标值（万人）Value (10000 persons)	位次 No.	县（市）名称 County (City)		指标值（万人）Value (10000 persons)
1	沭阳县	Shuyang County	165.18	33	新沂市	Xinyi City	96.15
2	兴化市	Xinghua City	153.42	34	宿豫县	Suyu County	93.41
3	邳州市	Pizhou City	150.02	35	姜堰市	Jiangyan City	92.05
4	如皋市	Rugao City	146.55	36	宝应县	Baoying County	90.89
5	通州市	Tongzhou City	145.23	37	盐都县	Yandou County	86.94
6	铜山县	Tongshan County	132.77	38	张家港市	Zhangjiagang City	85.40
7	泰兴市	Taixing City	127.93	39	高邮市	Gaoyou City	83.23
8	睢宁县	Shuining County	124.25	40	淮阴县	Huaiyin County	82.18
9	武进市	Wujin City	123.22	41	丹阳市	Danyang City	80.43
10	淮安市	Huaian City	121.35	42	建湖县	Jianhu County	79.61
11	东台市	Dongtai City	117.62	43	溧阳市	Liyang City	77.76
12	启东市	Qidong City	116.54	44	吴江市	Wujiang City	77.33
13	沛县	Peixian County	115.16	45	江宁县	Jiangning County	74.69
14	江阴市	Jiangyin City	114.44	46	大丰市	Dafeng City	74.06
15	泗阳县	Siyang County	112.92	47	盱眙县	Xuyi County	70.97
16	如东县	Rudong County	112.52	48	灌南县	Guannan County	69.96
17	东海县	Donghai County	109.18	49	六合县	Liuhe County	68.22
18	宜兴市	Yixing City	108.40	50	靖江市	Jingjiang City	66.36
19	阜宁县	Funing County	107.35	51	句容市	Jurong City	60.29
20	江都市	Jiangdu City	106.92	52	仪征市	Yizheng City	59.13
21	滨海县	Binhai County	106.60	53	昆山市	Kunshan City	58.75
22	丰县	Fengxian County	105.57	54	响水县	Xiangshui County	55.47
23	常熟市	Changshu City	104.18	55	邗江县	Hanjiang County	55.07
24	射阳县	Sheyang County	104.11	56	金坛市	Jintan City	54.16
25	海门市	Haimen City	103.79	57	太仓市	Taicang City	44.94
26	赣榆县	Ganyu County	102.56	58	高淳县	Gaochun County	42.81
27	灌云县	Guanyun County	101.38	59	溧水县	Lishui County	40.50
28	涟水县	Lianshui County	100.03	60	丹徒县	Dantu County	38.03
29	锡山市	Xishan City	99.16	61	洪泽县	Hongze County	37.21
30	泗洪县	Sihong County	99.05	62	金湖县	Jinhu County	35.06
31	海安县	Haian County	98.90	63	江浦县	Jiangpu County	29.73
32	吴县市	Wuxian City	97.00	64	扬中市	Yangzhong City	27.62

20-2 国内生产总值（1998）
GROSS DOMESTIC PRODUCT

位次 No.	县（市）名称 County（City）	指标值（万元）Value (10000 yuan)	位次 No.	县（市）名称 County（City）	指标值（万元）Value (10000 yuan)
1	江阴市 Jiangyin City	2722380	33	东海县 Donghai County	521276
2	锡山市 Xishan City	2700015	34	高邮市 Gaoyou City	520790
3	张家港市 Zhangjiagang City	2350109	35	沛县 Peixian County	515887
4	常熟市 Changshu City	2053696	36	金坛市 Jintan City	513019
5	武进市 Wujin City	1960023	37	姜堰市 Jiangyan City	505010
6	吴江市 Wujiang City	1750653	38	扬中市 Yangzhong City	503981
7	宜兴市 Yixing City	1650069	39	沭阳县 Shuyang County	492636
8	吴县市 Wuxian City	1649511	40	灌云县 Guanyun County	485011
9	昆山市 Kunshan City	1505347	41	宝应县 Baoying County	480338
10	太仓市 Taicang City	1205387	42	建湖县 Jianhu County	470636
11	丹阳市 Danyang City	1202636	43	丹徒县 Dantu County	460731
12	通州市 Tongzhou City	1117074	44	淮安市 Huaian City	444635
13	启东市 Qidong City	1020060	45	新沂市 Xinyi City	432953
14	海门市 Haimen City	988486	46	阜宁县 Funing County	427932
15	江宁县 Jiangning County	861038	47	仪征市 Yizheng City	410796
16	江都市 Jiangdu City	825859	48	泗洪县 Sihong County	371540
17	铜山县 Tongshan County	788169	49	滨海县 Binhai County	366000
18	泰兴市 Taixing City	759098	50	六合县 Liuhe County	361294
19	东台市 Dongtai City	748106	51	溧水县 Lishui County	337170
20	溧阳市 Liyang City	686818	52	泗阳县 Siyang County	330817
21	如东县 Rudong County	685048	53	丰县 Fengxian County	328523
22	如皋市 Rugao City	654320	54	睢宁县 Shuining County	326869
23	大丰市 Dafeng City	645679	55	宿豫县 Suyu County	325329
24	兴化市 Xinghua City	639462	56	高淳县 Gaochun County	304292
25	盐都县 Yandou County	628501	57	淮阴县 Huaiyin County	298132
26	射阳县 Sheyang County	623310	58	盱眙县 Xuyi County	282200
27	邗江县 Hanjiang County	599807	59	涟水县 Lianshui County	267354
28	海安县 Haian County	593865	60	金湖县 Jinhu County	237411
29	靖江市 Jingjiang City	581876	61	灌南县 Guannan County	210964
30	赣榆县 Ganyu County	569811	62	江浦县 Jiangpu County	206922
31	句容市 Jurong City	540727	63	响水县 Xiangshui County	201609
32	邳州市 Pizhou City	532064	64	洪泽县 Hongze County	147855

20-3 人均国内生产总值（1998）
PER CAPITA GROSS DOMESTIC PRODUCT

位次 No.	县（市）名称 County（City）	指标值（元）Value（yuan）	位次 No.	县（市）名称 County（City）	指标值（元）Value（yuan）
1	张家港市 Zhangjiagang City	27525	33	如东县 Rudong County	6078
2	锡山市 Xishan City	27243	34	射阳县 Sheyang County	6018
3	太仓市 Taicang City	26810	35	海安县 Haian County	5997
4	昆山市 Kunshan City	25675	36	铜山县 Tongshan County	5969
5	江阴市 Jiangyin City	23807	37	泰兴市 Taixing City	5957
6	吴江市 Wujiang City	22604	38	建湖县 Jianhu County	5915
7	常熟市 Changshu City	19700	39	赣榆县 Ganyu County	5583
8	扬中市 Yangzhong City	18234	40	姜堰市 Jiangyan City	5487
9	吴县市 Wuxian City	16990	41	六合县 Liuhe County	5291
10	武进市 Wujin City	15909	42	宝应县 Baoying County	5286
11	宜兴市 Yixing City	15152	43	灌云县 Guanyun County	4836
12	丹阳市 Danyang City	14908	44	东海县 Donghai County	4808
13	丹徒县 Dantu County	12052	45	新沂市 Xinyi City	4529
14	江宁县 Jiangning County	11545	46	沛县 Peixian County	4510
15	邗江县 Hanjiang County	10888	47	如皋市 Rugao City	4483
16	海门市 Haimen City	9549	48	兴化市 Xinghua City	4166
17	金坛市 Jintan City	9472	49	洪泽县 Hongze County	3993
18	句容市 Jurong City	8970	50	阜宁县 Funing County	3980
19	溧阳市 Liyang City	8869	51	盱眙县 Xuyi County	3973
20	靖江市 Jingjiang City	8775	52	泗洪县 Sihong County	3768
21	启东市 Qidong City	8743	53	淮安市 Huaian City	3674
22	大丰市 Dafeng City	8709	54	淮阴县 Huaiyin County	3651
23	溧水县 Lishui County	8311	55	响水县 Xiangshui County	3650
24	江都市 Jiangdu City	7725	56	邳州市 Pizhou City	3541
25	通州市 Tongzhou City	7682	57	宿豫县 Suyu County	3494
26	盐都县 Yandou County	7227	58	滨海县 Binhai County	3424
27	高淳县 Gaochun County	7088	59	丰县 Fengxian County	3131
28	仪征市 Yizheng City	6949	60	灌南县 Guannan County	3028
29	江浦县 Jiangpu County	6925	61	沭阳县 Shuyang County	3004
30	金湖县 Jinhu County	6791	62	泗阳县 Siyang County	2945
31	东台市 Dongtai City	6371	63	涟水县 Lianshui County	2676
32	高邮市 Gaoyou City	6253	64	睢宁县 Shuining County	2643

20-4 工农业总产值（1998）
TOTAL OUTPUT VALUE OF INDUSTRY AND AGRICUTURE

位次 No.	县（市）名称 County (City)		指标值（万元）Value (10000 yuan)	位次 No.	县（市）名称 County (City)		指标值（万元）Value (10000 yuan)
1	江阴市	Jiangyin City	7176804	33	建湖县	Jianhu County	1245592
2	锡山市	Xishan City	6934141	34	丹徒县	Dantu County	1209152
3	张家港市	Zhangjiagang City	4913813	35	沛县	Peixian County	1206153
4	武进市	Wujin City	4523596	36	阜宁县	Funing County	1193223
5	常熟市	Changshu City	4351218	37	姜堰市	Jiangyan City	1176744
6	吴县市	Wuxian City	4152420	38	海安县	Haian County	1170475
7	宜兴市	Yixing City	3903964	39	金坛市	Jintan City	1129429
8	吴江市	Wujiang City	3822259	40	仪征市	Yizheng City	1124487
9	昆山市	Kunshan City	3281483	41	邳州市	Pizhou City	1111107
10	丹阳市	Danyang City	2964253	42	淮安市	Huaian City	1049662
11	铜山县	Tongshan County	2723815	43	扬中市	Yangzhong City	1035418
12	太仓市	Taicang City	2633145	44	灌云县	Guanyun County	1021125
13	江宁县	Jiangning County	2590233	45	溧水县	Lishui County	1018423
14	通州市	Tongzhou City	2528248	46	宝应县	Baoying County	1006327
15	启东市	Qidong City	2193652	47	沭阳县	Shuyang County	995196
16	赣榆县	Ganyu County	2021000	48	宿豫县	Suyu County	925861
17	海门市	Haimen City	1903104	49	丰县	Fengxian County	921397
18	东台市	Dongtai City	1869322	50	新沂市	Xinyi City	914280
19	江都市	Jiangdu City	1687484	51	六合县	Liuhe County	864977
20	句容市	Jurong City	1655189	52	滨海县	Binhai County	756033
21	大丰市	Dafeng City	1646734	53	高淳县	Gaochun County	745856
22	盐都县	Yandou County	1531977	54	睢宁县	Shuining County	715256
23	射阳县	Sheyang County	1497710	55	淮阴县	Huaiyin County	705377
24	东海县	Donghai County	1486799	56	泗洪县	Sihong County	679300
25	邗江县	Hanjiang County	1466776	57	泗阳县	Siyang County	668804
26	泰兴市	Taixing City	1445130	58	盱眙县	Xuyi County	542947
27	如皋市	Rugao City	1399654	59	涟水县	Lianshui County	526254
28	靖江市	Jingjiang City	1314878	60	金湖县	Jinhu County	485177
29	如东县	Rudong County	1305380	61	江浦县	Jiangpu County	471943
30	兴化市	Xinghua City	1283405	62	响水县	Xiangshui County	459707
31	溧阳市	Liyang City	1280727	63	灌南县	Guannan County	455572
32	高邮市	Gaoyou City	1248259	64	洪泽县	Hongze County	381013

20－5 人均工农业总产值（1998）

PERCAPITA TOTAL OUTPUT VALUE OF INDUSTRY AND AGRICULTURE

位次 No.	县（市）名称 County (City)	指标值（元） Value (yuan)	位次 No.	县（市）名称 County (City)	指标值（元） Value (yuan)
1	锡山市 Xishan City	69964	33	建湖县 Jianhu County	15656
2	江阴市 Jiangyin City	62762	34	高邮市 Gaoyou City	14987
3	太仓市 Taicang City	58566	35	射阳县 Sheyang County	14459
4	张家港市 Zhangjiagang City	57552	36	金湖县 Jinhu County	13878
5	昆山市 Kunshan City	55969	37	东海县 Donghai County	13713
6	吴江市 Wujiang City	49351	38	姜堰市 Jiangyan City	12787
7	吴县市 Wuxian City	42769	39	六合县 Liuhe County	12666
8	常熟市 Changshu City	41738	40	海安县 Haian County	11819
9	扬中市 Yangzhong City	37461	41	如东县 Rudong County	11582
10	丹阳市 Danyang City	36745	42	泰兴市 Taixing City	11340
11	武进市 Wujin City	36718	43	阜宁县 Funing County	11097
12	宜兴市 Yixing City	35849	44	宝应县 Baoying County	11074
13	江宁县 Jiangning County	34731	45	沛县 Peixian County	10544
14	丹徒县 Dantu County	31628	46	洪泽县 Hongze County	10289
15	句容市 Jurong City	27458	47	灌云县 Guanyun County	10181
16	邗江县 Hanjiang County	26625	48	宿豫县 Suyu County	9944
17	溧水县 Lishui County	25103	49	如皋市 Rugao City	9589
18	大丰市 Dafeng City	22211	50	新沂市 Xinyi City	9564
19	金坛市 Jintan City	20854	51	丰县 Fengxian County	8782
20	铜山县 Tongshan County	20627	52	淮安市 Huaian City	8673
21	靖江市 Jingjiang City	19829	53	淮阴县 Huaiyin County	8638
22	赣榆县 Ganyu County	19800	54	兴化市 Xinghua City	8362
23	仪征市 Yizheng City	19020	55	响水县 Xiangshui County	8322
24	启东市 Qidong City	18802	56	盱眙县 Xuyi County	7644
25	海门市 Haimen City	18384	57	邳州市 Pizhou City	7396
26	盐都县 Yandou County	17617	58	滨海县 Binhai County	7073
27	通州市 Tongzhou City	17386	59	泗洪县 Sihong County	6889
28	高淳县 Gaochun County	17374	60	灌南县 Guannan County	6538
29	溧阳市 Liyang City	16538	61	沭阳县 Shuyang County	6069
30	东台市 Dongtai City	15919	62	泗阳县 Siyang County	5953
31	江浦县 Jiangpu County	15795	63	睢宁县 Shuining County	5784
32	江都市 Jiangdu City	15784	64	涟水县 Lianshui County	5267

20－6 粮 食 产 量 (1998)
OUTPUT OF GRAIN

位次 No.	县（市）名称 County (City)	指标值（万吨） Value (10000tn)	位次 No.	县（市）名称 County (City)	指标值（万吨） Value (10000tn)
1	兴化市 Xinghua City	114.00	33	建湖县 Jianhu County	49.91
2	沭阳县 Shuyang County	104.35	34	新沂市 Xinyi City	49.79
3	泗洪县 Sihong County	92.06	35	赣榆县 Ganyu County	48.69
4	东海县 Donghai County	89.02	36	吴县市 Wuxian City	48.55
5	淮安市 Huaian City	83.78	37	溧阳市 Liyang City	47.82
6	东台市 Dongtai City	82.57	38	江宁县 Jiangning County	47.60
7	铜山县 Tongshan County	75.87	39	淮阴县 Huaiyin County	45.94
8	射阳县 Sheyang County	73.36	40	丰县 Fengxian County	44.19
9	邳州市 Pizhou City	73.00	41	六合县 Liuhe County	44.13
10	盱眙县 Xuyi County	71.46	42	常熟市 Changshu City	44.04
11	如东县 Rudong County	70.42	43	江阴市 Jiangyin City	43.85
12	涟水县 Lianshui County	68.05	44	灌南县 Guannan County	42.37
13	如皋市 Rugao City	67.16	45	锡山市 Xishan City	42.19
14	睢宁县 Shuining County	64.62	46	启东市 Qidong City	40.11
15	武进市 Wujin City	63.89	47	吴江市 Wujiang City	38.44
16	高邮市 Gaoyou City	62.57	48	昆山市 Kunshan City	37.46
17	阜宁县 Funing County	62.09	49	句容市 Jurong City	35.59
18	灌云县 Guanyun County	60.99	50	响水县 Xiangshui County	35.41
19	滨海县 Binhai County	60.45	51	金湖县 Jinhu County	35.18
20	泰兴市 Taixing City	60.36	52	金坛市 Jintan City	33.43
21	宿豫县 Suyu County	58.63	53	张家港市 Zhangjiagang City	32.93
22	通州市 Tongzhou City	58.34	54	仪征市 Yizheng City	30.53
23	宜兴市 Yixing City	58.24	55	靖江市 Jingjiang City	30.10
24	泗阳县 Siyang County	57.38	56	洪泽县 Hongze County	30.06
25	大丰市 Dafeng City	56.18	57	邗江县 Hanjiang County	28.61
26	海安县 Haian County	54.75	58	海门市 Haimen City	27.82
27	宝应县 Baoying County	54.09	59	高淳县 Gaochun County	27.55
28	盐都县 Yandou County	53.41	60	溧水县 Lishui County	27.26
29	江都市 Jiangdu City	52.79	61	太仓市 Taicang City	26.66
30	沛县 Peixian County	51.91	62	丹徒县 Dantu County	25.47
31	姜堰市 Jiangyan City	51.25	63	江浦县 Jiangpu County	18.46
32	丹阳市 Danyang City	50.69	64	扬中市 Yangzhong City	11.39

20－7 油 料 产 量（1998）
OUTPUT OF OIL－BEARING CROPS

位次 No.	县（市）名称 County（City）	指标值（吨）Value（tn）	位次 No.	县（市）名称 County（City）	指标值（吨）Value（tn）
1	赣榆县 Ganyu County	61691	33	丰县 Fengxian County	11769
2	东海县 Donghai County	60231	34	宝应县 Baoying County	11292
3	东台市 Dongtai City	57248	35	昆山市 Kunshan City	11030
4	盱眙县 Xuyi County	52978	36	海安县 Haian County	10767
5	启东市 Qidong City	51054	37	淮安市 Huaian City	10428
6	海门市 Haimen City	42667	38	宜兴市 Yixing City	10384
7	新沂市 Xinyi City	40324	39	沛县 Peixian County	10070
8	通州市 Tongzhou City	36389	40	响水县 Xiangshui County	9676
9	泗洪县 Sihong County	36164	41	金坛市 Jintan City	9492
10	淮阴县 Huaiyin County	35390	42	盐都县 Yandou County	9286
11	大丰市 Dafeng City	30539	43	邗江县 Hanjiang County	8960
12	高淳县 Gaochun County	29915	44	江浦县 Jiangpu County	8877
13	沭阳县 Shuyang County	24061	45	吴县市 Wuxian City	8716
14	如东县 Rudong County	24058	46	丹阳市 Danyang City	7955
15	射阳县 Sheyang County	22785	47	金湖县 Jinhu County	7214
16	涟水县 Lianshui County	22512	48	丹徒县 Dantu County	6965
17	溧阳市 Liyang City	21365	49	建湖县 Jianhu County	6728
18	睢宁县 Shuining County	21148	50	锡山市 Xishan City	6561
19	溧水县 Lishui County	20495	51	常熟市 Changshu City	6545
20	江宁县 Jiangning County	20385	52	邳州市 Pizhou City	6115
21	如皋市 Rugao City	20374	53	宿豫县 Suyu County	5238
22	滨海县 Binhai County	19837	54	太仓市 Taicang City	4621
23	六合县 Liuhe County	19733	55	武进市 Wujin City	4599
24	兴化市 Xinghua City	18411	56	仪征市 Yizheng City	4436
25	吴江市 Wujiang City	18104	57	张家港市 Zhangjiagang City	4336
26	句容市 Jurong City	17591	58	洪泽县 Hongze County	3750
27	泗阳县 Siyang County	16863	59	靖江市 Jingjiang City	3593
28	泰兴市 Taixing City	14343	60	铜山县 Tongshan County	2344
29	姜堰市 Jiangyan City	14287	61	灌南县 Guannan County	2228
30	高邮市 Gaoyou City	13850	62	江阴市 Jiangyin City	1941
31	阜宁县 Funing County	13552	63	灌云县 Guanyun County	578
32	江都市 Jiangdu City	11803	64	扬中市 Yangzhong City	23

20－8 肉类总产量(1998)
OUTPUT OF ANIMAL MEAT

位次 No.	县(市)名称	County (City)	指标值(吨) Value (tn)	位次 No.	县(市)名称	County (City)	指标值(吨) Value (tn)
1	阜宁县	Funing County	109412	33	六合县	Liuhe County	34728
2	东台市	Dongtai City	102912	34	通州市	Tongzhou City	33617
3	盐都县	Yandou County	82660	35	盱眙县	Xuyi County	31454
4	沭阳县	Shuyang County	79210	36	邗江县	Hanjiang County	31024
5	邳州市	Pizhou City	72612	37	江宁县	Jiangning County	29145
6	如皋市	Rugao City	67196	38	响水县	Xiangshui County	28931
7	如东县	Rudong County	62769	39	吴江市	Wujiang City	26858
8	高邮市	Gaoyou City	61815	40	建湖县	Jianhu County	26746
9	射阳县	Sheyang County	61092	41	锡山市	Xishan City	26541
10	海安县	Haian County	60435	42	常熟市	Changshu City	26123
11	东海县	Donghai County	58900	43	丹阳市	Danyang City	25411
12	大丰市	Dafeng City	58563	44	靖江市	Jingjiang City	25392
13	沛县	Peixian County	56701	45	赣榆县	Ganyu County	24585
14	新沂市	Xinyi City	55785	46	海门市	Haimen City	24422
15	淮阴县	Huaiyin County	55515	47	宜兴市	Yixing City	24034
16	泰兴市	Taixing City	53833	48	灌南县	Guannan County	23848
17	滨海县	Binhai County	52729	49	吴县市	Wuxian City	23288
18	涟水县	Lianshui County	50860	50	江浦县	Jiangpu County	22525
19	兴化市	Xinghua City	48357	51	启东市	Qidong City	22160
20	睢宁县	Shuining County	48167	52	高淳县	Gaochun County	21549
21	丰县	Fengxian County	47640	53	张家港市	Zhangjiagang City	20819
22	淮安市	Huaian City	47261	54	昆山市	Kunshan City	20264
23	灌云县	Guanyun County	47054	55	仪征市	Yizheng City	18331
24	铜山县	Tongshan County	45518	56	金坛市	Jintan City	17933
25	宿豫县	Suyu County	44298	57	洪泽县	Hongze County	15357
26	江都市	Jiangdu City	43885	58	太仓市	Taicang City	15327
27	泗洪县	Sihong County	43795	59	溧阳市	Liyang City	14843
28	武进市	Wujin City	43322	60	溧水县	Lishui County	14326
29	泗阳县	Siyang County	39811	61	句容市	Jurong City	12882
30	宝应县	Baoying County	37707	62	金湖县	Jinhu County	11706
31	姜堰市	Jiangyan City	36602	63	丹徒县	Dantu County	9861
32	江阴市	Jiangyin City	35914	64	扬中市	Yangzhong City	6156

20－9 限额以上独立核算工业利税总额 （1998）
PRE－TAX PROFITS OF OVER－NORM INDUSTRIAL ENTERPRISES WITH INDEPENDENT ACCOUNTING SYSTEM

位次 No.	县（市）名称 County（City）	指标值（万元） Value (10000 yuan)	位次 No.	县（市）名称 County（City）	指标值（万元） Value (10000 yuan)
1	江阴市 Jiangyin City	380261	33	金坛市 Jintan City	20962
2	常熟市 Changshu City	179536	34	高邮市 Gaoyou City	20435
3	武进市 Wujin City	161280	35	阜宁县 Funing County	19440
4	张家港市 Zhangjiagang City	155405	36	兴化市 Xinghua City	18242
5	昆山市 Kunshan City	149805	37	高淳县 Gaochun County	17800
6	江宁县 Jiangning County	125274	38	射阳县 Sheyang County	17772
7	锡山市 Xishan City	110997	39	仪征市 Yizheng City	17317
8	宜兴市 Yixing City	93031	40	溧水县 Lishui County	15611
9	吴县市 Wuxian City	91161	41	宝应县 Baoying County	15362
10	吴江市 Wujiang City	78325	42	赣榆县 Ganyu County	14234
11	丹阳市 Danyang City	73288	43	金湖县 Jinhu County	12178
12	邗江县 Hanjiang County	68028	44	海安县 Haian County	12115
13	铜山县 Tongshan County	67158	45	邳州市 Pizhou City	11542
14	太仓市 Taicang City	58384	46	淮安市 Huaian City	10771
15	扬中市 Yangzhong City	57117	47	沛县 Peixian County	10021
16	通州市 Tongzhou City	48756	48	东海县 Donghai County	9990
17	泰兴市 Taixing City	43011	49	灌云县 Guanyun County	9437
18	溧阳市 Liyang City	38019	50	沭阳县 Shuyang County	9264
19	盐都县 Yandou County	36500	51	灌南县 Guannan County	8449
20	靖江市 Jingjiang City	35289	52	如皋市 Rugao City	8382
21	泗洪县 Sihong County	34214	53	涟水县 Lianshui County	7749
22	建湖县 Jianhu County	32751	54	洪泽县 Hongze County	6741
23	江都市 Jiangdu City	31835	55	丰县 Fengxian County	6654
24	启东市 Qidong City	29202	56	淮阴县 Huaiyin County	6327
25	东台市 Dongtai City	29044	57	江浦县 Jiangpu County	6283
26	姜堰市 Jiangyan City	28992	58	宿豫县 Suyu County	6272
27	句容市 Jurong City	28486	59	滨海县 Binhai County	5818
28	海门市 Haimen City	27122	60	盱眙县 Xuyi County	4516
29	丹徒县 Dantu County	25973	61	六合县 Liuhe County	4366
30	大丰市 Dafeng City	25661	62	响水县 Xiangshui County	3704
31	泗阳县 Siyang County	23401	63	新沂市 Xinyi City	2789
32	如东县 Rudong County	23340	64	睢宁县 Shuining County	－413

20－10 社会消费品零售额（1998）
TOTAL RETAIL SALES OF CONSUMER GOODS

位次 No.	县（市）名称 County (City)	指标值（万元） Value (10000 yuan)	位次 No.	县（市）名称 County (City)	指标值（万元） Value (10000 yuan)
1	常熟市 Changshu City	650138	33	沭阳县 Shuyang County	141644
2	江阴市 Jiangyin City	606472	34	盐都县 Yandou County	140779
3	宜兴市 Yixing City	516486	35	高邮市 Gaoyou City	140229
4	锡山市 Xishan City	507949	36	赣榆县 Ganyu County	139546
5	武进市 Wujin City	417328	37	句容市 Jurong City	137295
6	张家港市 Zhangjiagang City	371298	38	铜山县 Tongshan County	135971
7	吴县市 Wuxian City	368298	39	宝应县 Baoying County	135871
8	溧阳市 Liyang City	341290	40	东海县 Donghai County	135635
9	通州市 Tongzhou City	331591	41	邳州市 Pizhou City	130665
10	海门市 Haimen City	330887	42	沛县 Peixian County	128715
11	启东市 Qidong City	330164	43	阜宁县 Funing County	126315
12	昆山市 Kunshan City	305066	44	扬中市 Yangzhong City	123664
13	吴江市 Wujiang City	290077	45	泗阳县 Siyang County	121702
14	江都市 Jiangdu City	284396	46	淮安市 Huaian City	121368
15	丹阳市 Danyang City	282246	47	溧水县 Lishui County	118888
16	金坛市 Jintan City	254046	48	灌云县 Guanyun County	117797
17	泰兴市 Taixing City	250245	49	丰县 Fengxian County	115033
18	如皋市 Rugao City	247169	50	新沂市 Xinyi City	110139
19	如东县 Rudong County	244227	51	丹徒县 Dantu County	108116
20	东台市 Dongtai City	239952	52	邗江县 Hanjiang County	106029
21	靖江市 Jingjiang City	227091	53	滨海县 Binhai County	98592
22	太仓市 Taicang City	216158	54	宿豫县 Suyu County	91951
23	姜堰市 Jiangyan City	203025	55	江浦县 Jiangpu County	83867
24	仪征市 Yizheng City	197356	56	盱眙县 Xuyi County	83365
25	六合县 Liuhe County	179260	57	涟水县 Lianshui County	83067
26	江宁县 Jiangning County	175032	58	泗洪县 Sihong County	80347
27	射阳县 Sheyang County	173601	59	金湖县 Jinhu County	76731
28	兴化市 Xinghua City	172628	60	睢宁县 Shuining County	76110
29	海安县 Haian County	172169	61	灌南县 Guannan County	65353
30	大丰市 Dafeng City	161828	62	淮阴县 Huaiyin County	64130
31	高淳县 Gaochun County	154952	63	洪泽县 Hongze County	63575
32	建湖县 Jianhu County	148770	64	响水县 Xiangshui County	60296

20－11 财 政 收 入（1998）
FINANCIAL REVENIE

位次 No.	县（市）名称 County（City）	指标值（万元）Value（10000 yuan）	位次 No.	县（市）名称 County（City）	指标值（万元）Value（10000 yuan）
1	常熟市 Changshu City	159545	33	邗江县 Hanjiang County	26974
2	锡山市 Xishan City	151601	34	兴化市 Xinghua City	26232
3	江阴市 Jiangyin City	145765	35	盐都县 Yandou County	25014
4	张家港市 Zhangjiagang City	130249	36	射阳县 Sheyang County	24983
5	武进市 Wujin City	126703	37	赣榆县 Ganyu County	24389
6	吴县市 Wuxian City	96094	38	邳州市 Pizhou City	24271
7	宜兴市 Yixing City	87276	39	建湖县 Jianhu County	23436
8	昆山市 Kunshan City	86128	40	宝应县 Baoying County	22281
9	吴江市 Wujiang City	73743	41	东海县 Donghai County	22211
10	太仓市 Taicang City	60046	42	高邮市 Gaoyou City	21722
11	丹阳市 Danyang City	59389	43	丹徒县 Dantu County	20570
12	通州市 Tongzhou City	55286	44	江浦县 Jiangpu County	20026
13	江都市 Jiangdu City	53137	45	句容市 Jurong City	19608
14	仪征市 Yizheng City	49771	46	灌云县 Guanyun County	19488
15	启东市 Qidong City	48788	47	阜宁县 Funing County	19415
16	海门市 Haimen City	46666	48	溧水县 Lishui County	19219
17	泰兴市 Taixing City	46048	49	新沂市 Xinyi City	18204
18	江宁县 Jiangning County	46046	50	沭阳县 Shuyang County	17084
19	靖江市 Jingjiang City	41157	51	淮安市 Huaian City	17030
20	溧阳市 Liyang City	40630	52	丰县 Fengxian County	16586
21	铜山县 Tongshan County	38507	53	六合县 Liuhe County	16512
22	如东县 Rudong County	35986	54	高淳县 Gaochun County	16138
23	东台市 Dongtai City	35932	55	睢宁县 Shuining County	15360
24	姜堰市 Jiangyan City	34220	56	淮阴县 Huaiyin County	13711
25	金坛市 Jintan City	33642	57	滨海县 Binhai County	13520
26	如皋市 Rugao City	32178	58	涟水县 Lianshui County	13294
27	海安县 Haian County	31131	59	金湖县 Jinhu County	12371
28	泗洪县 Sihong County	30870	60	盱眙县 Xuyi County	12316
29	大丰市 Dafeng City	30031	61	灌南县 Guannan County	11031
30	泗阳县 Siyang County	28872	62	宿豫县 Suyu County	11004
31	扬中市 Yangzhong City	28771	63	洪泽县 Hongze County	10166
32	沛县 Peixian County	28004	64	响水县 Xiangshui County	9716

20-12 在岗职工平均工资 (1998)
AVERAGE WAGE OF EMPLOYED STAFF AND WORKERS

位次 No.	县(市)名称 County (City)	指标值(元) Value (yuan)
1	常熟市 Changshu City	9325
2	太仓市 Taicang City	9273
3	昆山市 Kunshan City	9232
4	江阴市 Jiangyin City	9041
5	武进市 Wujin City	8969
6	张家港市 Zhangjiagang City	8912
7	锡山市 Xishan City	8773
8	吴江市 Wujiang City	8608
9	金坛市 Jintan City	8446
10	宜兴市 Yixing City	8357
11	吴县市 Wuxian City	8321
12	仪征市 Yizheng City	8314
13	溧阳市 Liyang City	7905
14	丹阳市 Danyang City	7697
15	江浦县 Jiangpu County	7626
16	高淳县 Gaochun County	7385
17	扬中市 Yangzhong City	7348
18	丹徒县 Dantu County	7315
19	江宁县 Jiangning County	7247
20	海门市 Haimen City	7069
21	句容市 Jurong City	7042
22	通州市 Tongzhou City	7013
23	启东市 Qidong City	6914
24	如东县 Rudong County	6783
25	铜山县 Tongshan County	6675
26	江都市 Jiangdu City	6639
27	溧水县 Lishui County	6421
28	邗江县 Hanjiang County	6412
29	高邮市 Gaoyou City	6401
30	如皋市 Rugao City	6344
31	宝应县 Baoying County	6319
32	大丰市 Dafeng City	6305
33	姜堰市 Jiangyan City	6279
34	六合县 Liuhe County	6264
35	兴化市 Xinghua City	6169
36	赣榆县 Ganyu County	6148
37	金湖县 Jinhu County	6147
38	靖江市 Jingjiang City	6143
39	泰兴市 Taixing City	6130
40	沛县 Peixian County	6113
41	海安县 Haian County	6010
42	新沂市 Xinyi City	5976
43	邳州市 Pizhou City	5972
44	盱眙县 Xuyi County	5941
45	泗洪县 Sihong County	5799
46	灌云县 Guanyun County	5759
47	沭阳县 Shuyang County	5664
48	宿豫县 Suyu County	5662
49	丰县 Fengxian County	5621
50	射阳县 Sheyang County	5558
51	淮阴县 Huaiyin County	5467
52	盐都县 Yandou County	5418
53	洪泽县 Hongze County	5395
54	建湖县 Jianhu County	5395
55	东海县 Donghai County	5391
56	阜宁县 Funing County	5298
57	淮安市 Huaian City	5256
58	泗阳县 Siyang County	5211
59	睢宁县 Shuining County	5142
60	东台市 Dongtai City	5106
61	灌南县 Guannan County	5015
62	涟水县 Lianshui County	4853
63	滨海县 Binhai County	4425
64	响水县 Xiangshui County	4400

20－13 农民人均纯收入（1998）
PER CAPITA NET INCOME OF PEASANTS

位次 No.	县（市）名称 County（City）	指标值（元） Value（yuan）	位次 No.	县（市）名称 County（City）	指标值（元） Value（yuan）
1	吴江市 Wujiang City	5463	33	射阳县 Sheyang County	3344
2	张家港市 Zhangjiagang City	5405	34	金湖县 Jinhu County	3208
3	昆山市 Kunshan City	5351	35	高邮市 Gaoyou City	3192
4	锡山市 Xishan City	5342	36	建湖县 Jianhu County	3187
5	太仓市 Taicang City	5336	37	泰兴市 Taixing City	3186
6	江阴市 Jiangyin City	5308	38	淮安市 Huaian City	3175
7	吴县市 Wuxian City	5294	39	宝应县 Baoying County	3160
8	常熟市 Changshu City	5282	40	如东县 Rudong County	3117
9	武进市 Wujin City	5034	41	沛县 Peixian County	3109
10	扬中市 Yangzhong City	4509	42	洪泽县 Hongze County	3103
11	宜兴市 Yixing City	4326	43	兴化市 Xinghua City	3090
12	海门市 Haimen City	4177	44	赣榆县 Ganyu County	3065
13	启东市 Qidong City	4124	45	姜堰市 Jiangyan City	3060
14	丹阳市 Danyang City	4084	46	仪征市 Yizheng City	3053
15	金坛市 Jintan City	4015	47	东海县 Donghai County	2999
16	江宁县 Jiangning County	3787	48	灌云县 Guanyun County	2951
17	通州市 Tongzhou City	3771	49	阜宁县 Funing County	2950
18	溧阳市 Liyang City	3687	50	新沂市 Xinyi City	2857
19	江浦县 Jiangpu County	3674	51	邳州市 Pizhou City	2847
20	大丰市 Dafeng City	3642	52	滨海县 Binhai County	2845
21	丹徒县 Dantu County	3640	53	丰县 Fengxian County	2807
22	溧水县 Lishui County	3591	54	响水县 Xiangshui County	2760
23	高淳县 Gaochun County	3585	55	如皋市 Rugao City	2743
24	东台市 Dongtai City	3542	56	沭阳县 Shuyang County	2692
25	句容市 Jurong City	3490	57	泗洪县 Sihong County	2649
26	六合县 Liuhe County	3476	58	淮阴县 Huaiyin County	2644
27	邗江县 Hanjiang County	3450	59	宿豫县 Suyu County	2608
28	江都市 Jiangdu City	3445	60	涟水县 Lianshui County	2604
29	靖江市 Jingjiang City	3436	61	盱眙县 Xuyi County	2568
30	铜山县 Tongshan County	3428	62	泗阳县 Siyang County	2552
31	海安县 Haian County	3415	63	睢宁县 Shuining County	2551
32	盐都县 Yandou County	3387	64	灌南县 Guannan County	2506

20－14 城乡居民储蓄存款（1998）
SAVINGS DEPOSIT BALANCE OF URBAN AND RURAL RESIDENTS

位次 No.	县（市）名称 County（City）	指标值（万元）Value (10000 yuan)	位次 No.	县（市）名称 County（City）	指标值（万元）Value (10000 yuan)
1	常熟市 Changshu City	1412262	33	仪征市 Yizheng City	239872
2	锡山市 Xishan City	1032378	34	盐都县 Yandou County	238254
3	张家港市 Zhangjiagang City	1018310	35	邗江县 Hanjiang County	231737
4	江阴市 Jiangyin City	952800	36	建湖县 Jianhu County	224456
5	武进市 Wujin City	912041	37	邳州市 Pizhou City	220552
6	吴县市 Wuxian City	875988	38	宝应县 Baoying County	210575
7	启东市 Qidong City	724274	39	阜宁县 Funing County	201279
8	通州市 Tongzhou City	720653	40	句容市 Jurong City	182913
9	宜兴市 Yixing City	719635	41	六合县 Liuhe County	175023
10	江都市 Jiangdu City	660747	42	丹徒县 Dantu County	172780
11	海门市 Haimen City	647568	43	丰县 Fengxian County	165461
12	吴江市 Wujiang City	614061	44	赣榆县 Ganyu County	153257
13	昆山市 Kunshan City	581477	45	滨海县 Binhai County	152945
14	海安县 Haian County	541376	46	淮安市 Huaian City	152779
15	太仓市 Taicang City	535276	47	东海县 Donghai County	149644
16	东台市 Dongtai City	491863	48	睢宁县 Shuining County	147203
17	泰兴市 Taixing City	484095	49	新沂市 Xinyi City	136191
18	丹阳市 Danyang City	476450	50	沭阳县 Shuyang County	128887
19	如皋市 Rugao City	464325	51	溧水县 Lishui County	119486
20	如东县 Rudong County	456251	52	高淳县 Gaochun County	117158
21	兴化市 Xinghua City	420292	53	灌云县 Guanyun County	116795
22	靖江市 Jingjiang City	408417	54	泗洪县 Sihong County	113397
23	姜堰市 Jiangyan City	400710	55	泗阳县 Siyang County	106995
24	溧阳市 Liyang City	388509	56	涟水县 Lianshui County	100649
25	铜山县 Tongshan County	344175	57	金湖县 Jinhu County	93428
26	沛县 Peixian County	314558	58	江浦县 Jiangpu County	91355
27	江宁县 Jiangning County	311620	59	淮阴县 Huaiyin County	83334
28	大丰市 Dafeng City	284055	60	洪泽县 Hongze County	81577
29	扬中市 Yangzhong City	281402	61	盱眙县 Xuyi County	79464
30	金坛市 Jintan City	251590	62	响水县 Xiangshui County	77901
31	高邮市 Gaoyou City	247635	63	灌南县 Guannan County	60360
32	射阳县 Sheyang County	245510	64	宿豫县 Suyu County	

附录 1.

部分省市经济主要指标

APPENDIX Ⅰ
MAJOR ECONOMIC INDICATORS OF SOME PROVINCES AND MUNICIPALITIES

附录1-1 人口主要指标(1998)
MAJOR INDICATORS OF POPULATION

地区 Region			年末总人口(万人) Year-end Total Population (10000 persons)	出生率(‰) Birth Rate (‰)	死亡率(‰) Death Rate (‰)	自然增长率(‰) Natural Growth Rate (‰)
全	国	Country	124810	16.03	6.50	9.53
北	京	Beijing	1246	6.00	5.30	0.70
天	津	Tianjin	957	9.89	6.49	3.40
辽	宁	Liaoning	4157	11.39	6.81	4.58
上	海	Shanghai	1464	5.20	7.00	-1.80
江	苏	Jiangsu	7182	10.97	6.84	4.13
浙	江	Zhejiang	4456	11.15	6.33	4.82
安	徽	Anhui	6184	15.74	6.54	9.20
福	建	Fujian	3299	11.53	6.20	5.33
江	西	Jiangxi	4191	16.85	7.05	9.80
山	东	Shandong	8838	11.58	6.12	5.46
湖	北	Hubei	5907	12.58	6.70	5.88
湖	南	Hunan	6502	12.31	7.10	5.21
广	东	Guangdong	7143	16.51	5.61	10.90
四	川	Sichuan	8493	14.62	7.14	7.48
陕	西	Shanxi	3596	13.56	6.43	7.13

附录1-2 国内生产总值(1998)
GROSS DOMESTIC PRODUCTS

地区 Region			国内生产总值(亿元) Gross Domestic Products (10^8 yuan)	第一产业 Primary Industry	第二产业 Secondary Industry	#工业 Industry	第三产业 Tertiary Industry	#交通运输仓储邮电通信业 Transportation, Storage, Postal and Telecommunication Services	人均国内生产总值(元) Per Capita GDP (yuan)
全	国	Country	79552.8	14298.7	39149.8	33540.9	26104.3	5029.3	6404
北	京	Beijing	2009.9	87.0	790.8	614.0	1132.1	156.6	18423
天	津	Tianjin	1340.7	78.0	658.1	586.2	604.6	133.0	14041
辽	宁	Liaoning	3805.6	540.0	1867.3	1677.2	1398.3	246.9	9176
上	海	Shanghai	3688.2	78.5	1847.2	1646.7	1762.5	259.5	28236
江	苏	Jiangsu	7200.0	1016.3	3640.1	3157.7	2543.6	435.8	10021
浙	江	Zhejiang	4980.0	620.0	2720.0	2450.0	1640.0	325.9	11202
安	徽	Anhui	2828.3	735.0	1330.0	1201.8	763.3	160.9	4595
福	建	Fujian	3330.2	623.6	1444.7	1208.8	1261.8	347.3	10121
江	西	Jiangxi	1850.2	451.4	742.6	615.7	656.2	135.3	4436
山	东	Shandong	7162.2	1230.0	3456.9	3052.6	2475.3	440.3	8128
湖	北	Hubei	3704.2	748.2	1752.9	1579.3	1203.1	186.8	6289
湖	南	Hunan	3211.4	831.4	1291.1	1114.8	1088.9	216.5	4953
广	东	Guangdong	7937.2	1010.5	3997.9	3477.8	2928.8	681.3	11184
四	川	Sichuan	3580.3	941.2	1528.3	1273.6	1110.8	152.8	4231
陕	西	Shanxi	1410.5	281.0	592.2	468.0	537.3	124.6	3937

注:本部分资料摘自《中国统计摘要—1999》。(下同)
Note: These data were adopted from "Statistical Summary of China, 1999" (so did follows).

附录 1－3 在岗职工工资总额及平均工资（1998）
TOTAL AND AVERAGE WAGE BILL OF STAFF AND WORKERS (ON POST)

地区 Region		工资总额（亿元）Total Wage Bill (10^8 yuan)	#国有经济 State-owned Units	#集体经济 Collective-owned Units	#外商投资单位 Foreign Investment Units	平均工资（元）Average (yuan)	#国有经济 State-owned Units	#集体经济 Collective-owned Units	#外商投资单位 Foreign Investments Units
全国	Country	9296.5	6812.5	1021.6	327.0	7479	7668	5331	11767
北京	Beijing	530.3	378.6	39.5	40.5	12451	12348	8567	20951
天津	Tianjin	218.0	142.3	22.5	23.4	9946	10237	6121	13756
辽宁	Liaoning	504.5	372.8	68.7	18.9	7161	7604	4972	9951
上海	Shanghai	491.0	317.9	39.6	53.3	13580	13746	9344	17975
江苏	Jiangsu	628.5	422.3	99.5	25.6	8256	8872	6033	10246
浙江	Zhejiang	414.2	252.2	72.9	11.8	9759	10480	7882	11030
安徽	Anhui	262.8	197.2	34.6	2.4	6117	6628	4166	7372
福建	Fujian	282.1	162.4	27.2	30.8	8531	8682	6662	8905
江西	Jiangxi	173.9	140.0	15.2	2.0	5384	5473	3720	8735
山东	Shandong	575.4	444.4	61.6	20.4	6854	7469	4558	7419
湖北	Hubei	387.8	311.8	40.5	4.3	6436	6783	4748	9864
湖南	Hunan	311.9	259.9	34.1	2.9	6558	6797	5034	8949
广东	Guangdong	890.7	523.7	104.3	55.0	11032	11264	7663	14373
四川	Sichuan	378.6	290.7	42.4	3.0	6577	7044	4639	8023
陕西	Shanxi	204.5	171.0	13.9	1.3	6029	6257	3823	7837

附录 1－4 固定资产投资完成额（1998）
TOTAL INVESTMENT IN FIXED ASSETS

地区 Region		投资总额（亿元）Total Value of Investment (10^8 yuan)	#地方项目 Local Item	#基本建设 Capital Construction	#更新改造 Updating and Transformation	#房地产开发 Real Estate Development
全国	Country	21102.3	14595.3	11904.3	4467.2	3579.6
北京	Beijing	1048.3	667.7	415.6	252.4	377.4
天津	Tianjin	500.4	377.0	261.2	120.7	106.7
辽宁	Liaoning	870.0	511.4	435.6	260.4	148.7
上海	Shanghai	1798.7	1498.0	819.6	365.6	598.9
江苏	Jiangsu	1602.7	1281.8	747.2	296.0	300.2
浙江	Zhejiang	1067.4	787.6	613.1	175.3	218.4
安徽	Anhui	427.9	344.3	249.4	106.9	54.8
福建	Fujian	773.5	709.5	328.8	168.2	164.9
江西	Jiangxi	259.6	203.2	158.5	62.0	27.0
山东	Shandong	1185.4	841.3	663.1	281.5	130.1
湖北	Hubei	891.6	555.0	517.5	227.0	131.2
湖南	Hunan	473.9	288.9	305.1	114.8	40.8
广东	Guangdong	2036.6	1686.1	1035.3	312.9	594.0
四川	Sichuan	863.5	604.2	536.2	182.4	119.6
陕西	Shanxi	421.0	285.2	254.0	84.0	50.6

注：本表不包括城乡集体和个人投资。

Note: In this table, investments by urban and rural collective units and individuals were excluded.

附录1－5 地方财政收入与支出(1998) LOCAL FINANCIAL REVENUE AND EXPENDITURE

地区 Region		地方财政收入(亿元) Local Financial Revenue (10^8 yuan)	#增值税 Added Value Taxes	#企业所得税 Enterprise Income Taxes	地方财政支出(亿元) Local Financial Expenditure (10^8 yuan)	#基本建设 Capital Construction	#支农支出 Supporting Agriculture	#教育事业费 Culture, Education and Science
全国	Country	4983.95	908.44	515.14	7672.58	778.24	205.96	1214.78
北京	Beijing	229.45	37.58	26.98	280.68	32.50	5.95	41.31
天津	Tianjin	101.40	18.99	12.79	137.93	24.16	1.35	21.74
辽宁	Liaoning	264.62	48.49	25.41	390.29	46.86	12.27	48.94
上海	Shanghai	380.70	75.58	50.88	470.05	97.77	6.34	67.46
江苏	Jiangsu	308.20	79.06	31.45	434.17	30.67	11.45	89.73
浙江	Zhejiang	198.10	58.43	36.10	286.81	15.81	8.49	53.79
安徽	Anhui	159.19	23.27	17.67	242.07	23.75	6.57	39.23
福建	Fujian	187.92	24.58	14.41	254.87	25.10	7.05	45.93
江西	Jiangxi	97.16	12.31	6.92	175.26	12.50	5.53	27.85
山东	Shandong	352.39	70.14	46.81	487.82	31.85	11.10	88.62
湖北	Hubei	168.95	29.36	15.25	280.12	26.06	6.28	43.29
湖南	Hunan	156.77	22.98	8.44	273.64	28.75	6.75	39.33
广东	Guangdong	640.75	92.75	70.50	825.61	124.29	17.89	109.11
四川	Sichuan	197.29	29.57	22.54	320.93	27.34	9.36	48.31
陕西	Shanxi	93.33	16.34	5.62	166.20	14.79	7.62	26.16

附录1－6 居民消费和商品零售价格指数(1998) RESIDENTS CONSUMER PRICE INDEX AND RETAIL PRICE INDEX

地区 Region		居民消费价格指数(上年＝100) Residents Consumer Price Index(1997＝100)			商品零售价格指数(上年＝100) Retail Price Index (1997＝100)		
		全省 Province	城市 Urban	农村 Rural	全省 Province	城市 Urban	农村 Rural
全国	Country	99.2	99.4	99.0	97.4	97.4	97.6
北京	Beijing	102.4			98.3		
天津	Tianjin	99.5			96.6		
辽宁	Liaoning	99.3	99.8	98.7	97.6	97.6	97.4
上海	Shanghai	100.0			95.1		
江苏	Jiangsu	99.4	100.0	99.0	98.2	98.2	98.1
浙江	Zhejiang	99.7	100.5	99.3	98.4	98.4	98.4
安徽	Anhui	100.0	100.3	99.9	98.1	98.4	98.0
福建	Fujian	99.7	100.0	99.5	98.5	98.3	98.9
江西	Jiangxi	101.0	101.0	101.0	98.8	98.5	98.9
山东	Shandong	99.4	99.7	99.0	97.1	97.1	97.2
湖北	Hubei	98.4	97.9	99.0	97.1	96.3	98.0
湖南	Hunan	100.2	100.5	100.1	97.9	98.3	97.4
广东	Guangdong	98.2	98.3	98.1	97.0	96.9	97.2
四川	Sichuan	99.6	99.8	99.5	97.7	97.7	97.6
陕西	Shanxi	98.4	97.7	99.3	96.2	95.6	97.5

附录1-7　城镇居民家庭人均收支(1998)
URBAN HOUSEHOLD PER CAPITA INCOME AND EXPENDITURE

单位:元　　(yuan)

地区 Region		全部收入 Total Income	#可支配收入 Allocatable Income	实际支出 Actual Expenditure	消费性支出 Living Expenditure	非消费性支出 Non-Living Expenditure	恩格尔系数(%) Engle Coefficient (%)
全　国	Country	5458.34	5425.05	5322.95	4331.61	987.17	44.48
北　京	Beijing	8520.61	8471.98	8216.90	6970.83	1246.03	41.11
天　津	Tianjin	7126.23	7110.54	6522.51	5471.01	1051.50	43.56
辽　宁	Liaoning	4646.41	4617.24	4802.00	3890.74	907.66	44.60
上　海	Shanghai	8825.26	8773.10	7520.93	6866.41	654.52	50.51
江　苏	Jiangsu	6064.45	6017.85	6047.70	4889.43	1155.92	45.11
浙　江	Zhejiang	7883.77	7836.76	7363.25	6217.93	1144.15	42.53
安　徽	Anhui	4798.76	4770.47	4924.12	3777.41	1144.12	49.53
福　建	Fujian	6544.81	6485.63	6409.16	5181.45	1221.48	51.82
江　西	Jiangxi	4274.32	4251.42	4061.01	3266.81	791.33	49.25
山　东	Shandong	5414.17	5380.08	5225.99	4143.96	1079.40	39.63
湖　北	Hubei	4849.43	4826.36	4903.13	4074.38	822.61	43.88
湖　南	Hunan	5474.55	5434.26	5724.00	4370.95	1348.76	43.64
广　东	Guangdong	8904.83	8839.68	8245.29	7054.09	1188.95	44.12
四　川	Sichuan	5159.97	5127.08	5309.43	4382.59	923.97	44.92
陕　西	Shanxi	4243.76	4220.24	4271.80	3538.52	732.14	41.10

附录1-8　农民家庭人均收支(1998)
RURAL HOUSEHOLD PER CAPITA INCOME AND EXPENDITURE

单位:元　　(yuan)

地区 Region		总收入 Total Income	#现金 Cash	纯收入 Net Income	总支出 Total Expenditure	#生活消费 Living Expenditure	现金支出 Cash Expenditure	恩格尔系数(%) Engle Coefficient (%)
全　国	Country	3018.48	2163.61	2161.98	2457.17	1590.33	1930.98	53.43
北　京	Beijing	4593.57	4369.92	3952.32	3667.26	2873.20	3573.36	42.29
天　津	Tianjin	4558.80	3684.23	3395.7	3227.86	1976.70	2930.08	46.11
辽　宁	Liaoning	3635.71	2543.86	2579.79	2805.77	1702.68	2370.45	52.79
上　海	Shanghai	5964.55	5582.47	5406.84	4923.53	4206.89	4954.07	42.19
江　苏	Jiangsu	4258.15	4014.20	3376.78	3261.75	2336.78	3562.70	47.80
浙　江	Zhejiang	4864.70	4338.22	3814.56	4011.62	2890.65	3691.81	47.11
安　徽	Anhui	2538.28	1795.17	1862.86	2012.59	1333.05	1576.91	54.92
福　建	Fujian	3597.13	2983.96	2946.37	2740.42	2025.09	2403.51	54.40
江　西	Jiangxi	2799.29	1980.14	2048.00	2323.03	1538.24	1709.51	58.47
山　东	Shandong	3561.87	2460.00	2452.83	2766.77	1595.09	2161.81	50.44
湖　北	Hubei	2917.66	1887.38	2172.24	2493.61	1699.43	1765.95	54.07
湖　南	Hunan	2988.21	2163.04	2064.85	2829.87	1889.17	2185.14	58.61
广　东	Guangdong	4462.15	3692.86	3527.14	3677.53	2683.18	3130.22	51.08
四　川	Sichuan	2738.39	1731.76	1789.17	2382.31	1440.77	1610.02	60.51
陕　西	Shanxi	1928.48	1300.67	1405.59	1740.78	1181.38	1324.06	49.50

附录1－9 农林牧渔业总产值和指数（1998）
GROSS OUTPUT VALUE AND INDEX OF FARMING, FORESTRY, ANIMAL HUSBANDRY, FISHERY

单位:亿元 (10^8 yuan)

地区 Region		农林牧渔业总产值	Gross Output Value of Farming, Forestry, Animal Husbandry and Fishery				农林牧渔业总产值指数(上年=100) Index of Gross Output Value of Farming, Forestry, Animal Husbandry and Fishery (1997=100)
			农业 Farming	林业 Forestry	牧业 Animal Husbandry	渔业 Fishery	
全国	Country	25103.4	14099.3	848.8	7729.8	2425.5	104.6
北京	Beijing	174.6	89.3	3.0	75.7	6.5	101.9
天津	Tianjin	156.2	98.8	1.2	38.1	18.1	107.3
辽宁	Liaoning	997.8	505.8	17.2	322.7	152.2	109.5
上海	Shanghai	203.6	86.6	0.8	87.5	28.6	101.1
江苏	Jiangsu	1849.2	1096.9	24.2	435.5	292.7	106.4
浙江	Zhejiang	997.2	534.3	59.3	173.8	229.8	100.0
安徽	Anhui	1229.6	658.7	56.8	386.3	127.8	102.3
福建	Fujian	985.4	405.8	77.8	207.3	294.6	107.0
江西	Jiangxi	730.0	355.0	47.0	240.0	88.0	97.0
山东	Shandong	2242.0	1122.4	51.2	745.6	322.9	106.0
湖北	Hubei	1222.6	688.0	41.3	371.4	121.9	101.1
湖南	Hunan	1304.1	654.0	48.9	519.5	81.8	101.5
广东	Guangdong	1705.4	862.0	54.5	441.6	347.3	105.3
四川	Sichuan	1448.4	819.2	43.8	554.0	31.4	104.3
陕西	Shanxi	458.6	322.2	19.8	113.6	3.0	106.5

附录1－10 主要农产品产量（1998）
OUTPUT OF MAJOR FARM PRODUCTS

单位:万吨 (10000 tons)

地区 Region		棉花 Cotton	油料 Oil-Bearing Crops	糖料 Sugar Crops	水产品 Aquatic Products	肉猪出栏头数(万头) Hogs (10000 Head)
全国	Country	450.1	2313.9	9790.4	3906.4	45077.2
北京	Beijing	0.2	2.8		7.6	353.5
天津	Tianjin	0.6	3.8		21.4	155.9
辽宁	Liaoning	1.8	23.4	41.6	312.7	1131.0
上海	Shanghai	0.5	6.8	7.1	26.8	450.0
江苏	Jiangsu	46.2	115.6	19.6	282.0	2531.2
浙江	Zhejiang	6.5	35.5	61.9	422.7	1126.1
安徽	Anhui	29.0	176.5	24.4	146.2	1835.3
福建	Fujian		24.6	219.3	475.9	1295.8
江西	Jiangxi	7.6	84.3	186.4	118.3	2040.0
山东	Shandong	41.3	335.6	0.3	650.5	2454.0
湖北	Hubei	32.5	216.7	110.0	218.3	2513.3
湖南	Hunan	19.2	120.7	188.4	116.8	4792.8
广东	Guangdong		79.3	1756.9	554.3	2221.1
四川	Sichuan	10.2	146.4	161.7	42.3	5090.3
陕西	Shanxi	2.3	35.5	5.0	5.0	786.5

附录1－11 工业总产值及指数(1998)
TOTAL OUTPUT VALUE AND INDEX OF INDUSTRY

单位:亿元 (10^8 yuan)

地区 Region		工业总产值 Gross Industrial Output Value and Index	#国有及国有控投企业 State-owned and State-owned Shareholding Enterprises	#集体企业 Collective-owned Enterprises	#股份制企业 Shareholding Enterprises	#外商及港澳台投资企业 Foreign, Hongkong, Macao and Taiwan Invested Enterprises	工业总产值指数(上年=100) Index of Gross Industrial Output Value (1997=100)
全国	Country	70092.39	34109.62	18897.07	5281.06	15531.91	110.70
北京	Beijing	1715.57	1218.72	173.13	71.69	552.43	110.90
天津	Tianjin	2087.14	731.40	626.92	45.44	816.03	108.30
辽宁	Liaoning	3231.42	2065.27	486.96	212.49	501.12	108.50
上海	Shanghai	5897.34	2932.91	1114.81	406.34	2288.68	110.80
江苏	Jiangsu	8053.03	2653.00	2309.94	388.63	1829.37	112.50
浙江	Zhejiang	4632.07	1214.89	2211.29	508.50	695.44	110.33
安徽	Anhui	1569.24	974.89	363.55	207.33	131.94	110.30
福建	Fujian	2041.23	576.03	255.04	110.32	1220.20	113.90
江西	Jiangxi	860.55	681.90	151.64	13.18	46.82	111.12
山东	Shandong	6398.14	2744.87	2778.98	437.36	761.55	115.65
湖北	Hubei	3059.81	1789.02	1015.41	337.19	250.16	113.97
湖南	Hunan	1387.47	945.90	294.50	51.13	78.34	112.25
广东	Guangdong	9978.49	2772.05	2116.15	638.48	5004.44	113.83
四川	Sichuan	1911.68	1253.30	322.18	315.28	112.44	113.51
陕西	Shanxi	947.09	751.61	122.61	61.60	105.40	107.43

注：本表口径为全部国有企业及年产品销售收入500万元以上的非国有企业。

Note: The bore of this table was state-owned enterprises and nonstate-owned enterprises with 5 million yuan above of revenue of product sales yearly (so did follows)

附录1－12 主要工业产品产量(1998)
OUT PUT OF MAJOR INDUSTRIAL PRODUCTS

地区 Region		钢(万吨) Steel (10000 tons)	成品钢材(万吨) Rolled-steel Finalproducts (10000 tons)	原煤(万吨) Coal (10000 tons)	发电量(亿千瓦小时) Electricity (10^8 kwh)	水泥(万吨) Cement (10000 tons)	农用化肥(万吨) Chemical Fertilizers (10000 tons)	汽车(万辆) (10000units)
全国	Country	11559.0	10518.0	125000.0	11670.0	53600.0	3010.0	163.0
北京	Beijing	803.2	676.1	989.5	144.5	763.0	11.3	8.5
天津	Tianjin	254.9	189.4		165.3	183.0	7.7	15.6
辽宁	Liaoning	1406.5	1149.2	5785.7	608.1	1663.7	76.8	4.3
上海	Shanghai	1603.8	1417.3		483.2	331.0	12.7	23.6
江苏	Jiangsu	523.8	933.6	2378.5	763.5	3856.3	170.1	9.00
浙江	Zhejiang	147.4	258.2	91.5	492.1	3435.9	71.8	0.9
安徽	Anhui	405.8	325.1	4502.2	308.8	1928.7	162.0	7.1
福建	Fujian	113.3	188.0	726.5	321.9	1458.3	63.5	0.6
江西	Jiangxi	222.9	179.2	2107.5	181.1	1133.4	52.2	12.2
山东	Shandong	579.3	490.6	8976.9	823.8	5411.7	312.2	3.4
湖北	Hubei	808.8	712.6	1326.3	510.1	2269.9	226.9	17.9
湖南	Hunan	270.6	250.8	4352.1	345.7	2338.5	153.7	0.8
广东	Guangdong	263.7	318.5	299.9	1004.4	5091.9	54.0	1.0
四川	Sichuan	567.9	465.9	5696.4	455.6	2462.6	245.6	2.0
陕西	Shanxi	52.5	48.9	2278.2	246.0	859.0	75.3	1.6

附录1－13 工业企业主要经济效益指标（1998）
MAJOR ECONOMIC RESULT INDICATORS OF INDUSTRIAL ENTERPRISES

地 区 Region		总资产贡献率（%） Rate of Total Funds Contribution（%）	资本保值增值率（%） Rate Between Value-Added and Assets（%）	资 产 负债率（%） Rate of Capital Liabilities	流动资产周转次数（次） Turnover of Circulating Funds（time）	成本费用利润率（%） Rate Between Cost and Profit（%）	全员劳动生产率（元/人） Labor Productivity（yuan/person）	产品销售率（%） Rate of Product Sales（%）
全 国	Country	7.72	108.11	64.02	1.41	2.41	25154	96.49
北 京	Beijing	6.51	97.26	61.00	1.13	2.75	37472	98.22
天 津	Tianjin	6.91	110.56	63.47	1.41	3.44	24624	96.98
辽 宁	Liaoning	4.73	105.84	64.92	1.13	－0.82	17657	96.47
上 海	Shanghai	7.41	113.76	54.77	1.35	3.81	44789	97.89
江 苏	Jiangsu	8.39	108.16	62.63	1.73	2.10	33121	95.99
浙 江	Zhejiang	10.39	114.14	59.93	1.76	3.77	29470	95.82
安 徽	Anhui	7.06	104.14	65.13	1.32	－0.27	17168	95.32
福 建	Fujian	9.23	110.10	58.47	1.64	2.90	26048	96.56
江 西	Jiangxi	5.72	108.25	73.70	1.08	－0.43	12345	97.32
山 东	Shandong	9.34	111.03	64.75	1.68	4.10	24642	96.79
湖 北	Hubei	7.66	114.35	64.69	1.44	2.33	25274	96.77
湖 南	Hunan	9.48	107.53	66.69	1.34	0.04	15647	97.59
广 东	Guangdong	7.57	105.34	63.23	1.70	2.65	39304	96.26
四 川	Sichuan	7.30	114.49	64.56	1.11	2.37	21391	94.02
陕 西	Shanxi	5.06	106.80	72.16	1.01	－1.88	15190	95.78

附录1－14 全社会货物运量及周转量（1998）
TOTAL FREIGHT TRAFFIC AND TURNOVER VOLUME

地 区 Region		货运量（万吨） Freight Traffic（10000 tons）	#铁 路 Railway	#公 路 Highway	#水 运 Waterway	货物周转量（亿吨公里） Turnover Volume of Freight Traffic（10^8 tons/km）	#铁 路 Railway	#公 路 Highway	#水 运 Waterway
全 国	Country	1271758	161243	976004	109555	37855.1		5483.4	19405.8
北 京	Beijing	30120	2630	27490		333.8	255.4	78.3	
天 津	Tianjin	21489	2467	18584	438	362.7	229.9	60.3	72.6
辽 宁	Liaoning	78535	12483	65481	571	1229.9	901.7	206.5	121.7
上 海	Shanghai	31026	1152	26352	3522	206.3	40.3	49.5	116.6
江 苏	Jiangsu	80429	4204	54328	21363	1353.2	344.7	316.1	661.9
浙 江	Zhejiang	60404	1761	45338	13305	897.9	173.3	257.1	467.5
安 徽	Anhui	36184	5204	27198	3782	887.2	543.9	214.2	129.2
福 建	Fujian	31425	2325	25400	3700	674.1	141.9	164.6	367.6
江 西	Jiangxi	22200	2773	18311	1116	569.4	410.8	129.5	29.1
山 东	Shandong	79392	10340	67155	1897	1238.9	684.8	367.2	186.9
湖 北	Hubei	34750	4227	28044	2479	830.3	542.9	192.1	95.3
湖 南	Hunan	49062	4462	41610	2990	969.0	643.5	256.6	68.9
广 东	Guangdong	73750	5392	53788	14570	935.2	225.8	325.7	383.6
四 川	Sichuan	50978	5685	43697	1596	614.9	390.8	212.3	11.8
陕 西	Shanxi	30224	3159	27000	65	527.0	415.7	111.1	0.2

注：铁路包括了地方铁路。

Note：Local railway was included in railway.

附录 1－15 社会消费品零售总额(1998)
TOTAL RETALL SALES OF CONSUMER GOODS

单位:亿元 (10^8 yuan)

地区 Region		社会消费品零售总额 Total Ratail Sales of Consumer Goods	市 City	县 County	县以下 County Below	#国有经济 State-Owned Units	#集体经济 Collective-Owned Units	#私营经济 Private-Run Units
全国	Country	29152.5	17825.2	3681.9	7645.4	6021.3	4829.9	164.3
北京	Beijing	1167.2	905.0	111.6	150.6	371.3	290.5	9.6
天津	Tianjin	587.1	466.4	36.9	83.8	115.7	96.0	30.0
辽宁	Liaoning	1568.7	1286.0	87.0	195.7	226.9	156.1	152.6
上海	Shanghai	1471.1	1179.2	71.5	220.4	590.9	417.0	47.5
江苏	Jiangsu	2238.0	1353.4	156.2	728.4	475.9	616.6	137.0
浙江	Zhejiang	1909.2	1036.0	183.6	689.6	228.2	216.3	176.4
安徽	Anhui	924.8	430.2	207.1	287.5	196.3	171.5	16.9
福建	Fujian	1132.5	642.4	145.4	344.7	140.3	181.4	47.4
江西	Jiangxi	605.1	278.4	141.6	185.1	138.4	87.3	20.6
山东	Shandong	2127.2	1304.9	204.9	317.4	403.6	400.9	157.2
湖北	Hubei	1481.4	896.1	156.1	429.2	285.2	213.6	95.1
湖南	Hunan	1125.3	556.8	218.0	350.5	197.1	137.0	38.9
广东	Guangdong	3248.6	2143.8	182.7	922.1	653.9	518.9	206.9
四川	Sichuan	1298.6	620.7	218.2	459.7	207.8	236.3	68.8
陕西	Shanxi	518.8	337.4	89.7	91.7	138.7	93.9	26.8

附录 1－16 外贸进出口总额及外商直接投资额(1998)
TOTAL VALUE OF IMPORT AND EXPORT BY FOREIGN TRADE AND FOREIGN DIRECT INVESTMENT

单位:亿美元 (10^8 USD)

地区 Region		海关进出口总额	Total Value of Import and Export Through Customs		外商直接投资 Direct Foreign Investments		
			进口 Import	出口 Export	项目个数(个) Number of Items	协议投资额 Agreed Value of Investment	实际投资额 Actual Value of Investmet
全国	Country	3239.3	1401.7	1837.6	19799	521.02	454.63
北京	Beijing	157.8	92.8	65.0	651	40.97	21.68
天津	Tianjin	110.8	56.1	54.7	859	30.76	21.14
辽宁	Liaoning	137.6	61.3	76.3	1703	43.80	21.90
上海	Shanghai	311.7	155.3	156.4	1490	58.46	36.01
江苏	Jiangsu	264.3	107.7	156.5	1843	76.86	69.57
浙江	Zhejiang	167.5	51.4	116.1	965	18.34	13.18
安徽	Anhui	24.6	9.5	15.1	206	2.43	2.77
福建	Fujian	181.2	74.0	107.2	2006	50.02	42.12
江西	Jiangxi	14.8	3.5	11.3	334	4.19	4.65
山东	Shandong	191.1	79.0	112.1	1364	22.09	22.03
湖北	Hubei	31.9	15.9	16.0	330	5.25	9.73
湖南	Hunan	20.3	7.0	13.3	416	10.95	8.18
广东	Guangdong	1314.8	551.8	763.0	4348	91.55	120.20
四川	Sichuan	23.9	11.8	12.1	233	7.12	3.72
陕西	Shanxi	21.2	10.2	11.0	196	3.76	3.00

附录 2.

我国经济与主要国家比较

APPENDIX Ⅱ
COMPARISON OF ECONOMY BETWEEN CHINA AND OTHER MAJOR COUNTRIES OF THE WORLD

附录2-1 国土面积和人口(1996)
AREA AND POPULATION

资料来源:《国际统计年鉴—1998》

Source: International Statistical Yearbook (1998)

国家和地区 Country or Territory		国土面积(万平方公里) Area (10000 sq. km)	年中人口数(万人) Mid-year Population (10000 persons)	人口出生率(‰) Birth Rate (‰)	人口死亡率(‰) Death Rate (‰)	人口自然增长率(‰) Natural Growth Rate of Population (‰)
中国	China	960.0	121755	17.0	6.6	10.4
美国	United States	936.4	26545	14.7	8.5	6.3
日本	Japan	37.8	12576	9.6	7.1	2.5
德国	Germany	35.7	8190	9.3	10.8	-1.5
英国	United Kingdom	24.5	5880	12.2	11.0	1.3
法国	France	55.2	5837	12.6	9.2	3.4
意大利	Italy	30.1	5738	9.2	9.5	-0.3
加拿大	Canada	997.1	2996	12.7	7.2	5.5
澳大利亚	Australia	774.1	1831	13.9	7.1	6.8
俄罗斯	Russian Fed	1707.5	14774	8.8	14.3	-5.5
捷克	Czech Rep.	7.9	1032	9.0	11.0	-2.0
波兰	Poland	32.3	3862	11.2	10.0	1.2
匈牙利	Hungary	9.3	1019			
罗马尼亚	Romania	23.8	2261	10.3	12.6	-2.3
印度	India	328.8	93954	25.0	9.0	16.1
印度尼西亚	Indonesia	190.5	19834	22.7	7.7	15.0
菲律宾	Philippines	30.0	7190	28.5	6.6	22.0
泰国	Thailand	51.3	6000	16.5	6.5	10.0
新加坡	Singapore	0.1	361	16.0	5.1	10.9
马来西亚	Malaysia	33	2117	26.8	4.5	22.3
巴基斯坦	Pakistan	79.6	13415	36.6	8.3	28.3
缅甸	Myanmar	67.7	4592	27.3	9.9	17.4
韩国	Korea, Rep.	9.9	4554	15.5	6.3	9.2
巴西	Brazil	851.2	15787	20.8	7.3	13.6

附录2-2 就 业 状 况 (1996)
EMPLOYMENT

资料来源:《中国统计年鉴—1998》
Source: Statistical Yearbook of China (1998)

国家和地区 Country or Territory		就业人数(万人) Employment (10000 persons)	就业人数构成(%) Composition of Employment (%)				
			农林牧渔业 Farming, Forestry, Animal Husbandry and Fishery	矿 业 Mining and Quarrying	制造业 Manufacturing	水、电煤气业 Electricity, Gas and Water	建筑业 Construction
中　　国	China	68850	47.8	1.3	14.2	0.4	4.9
美　　国	United States	12670.8	2.8	0.4	16.2	1.2	6.3
日　　本	Japan	6486.0	5.5	0.1	22.3	0.6	10.3
德　　国	Germany	3598.2	3.0	0.7	23.7	0.9	9.6
英　　国	United Kingdom	2621.9	2.0	0.4	19.2	0.7	6.9
法　　国	France	2229.6①	5.0②	0.3②	19.7②	1.0②	6.8②
意 大 利	Italy	1994.2①	7.5①	0.4①	22.7①	10.2①	8.1①
加 拿 大	Canada	1367.6	4.1	1.2	15.2	1.1	5.3
澳大利亚	Australia	834.4	5.1②	1.1②	14.0②	1.1②	7.2②
俄 罗 斯	Russian Fed	6600.0	15.7①	1.6①	22.2①	1.2①	8.7①
捷　　克	Czech Rep.	497.5	6.2	1.8	28.4	2.0	9.4
波　　兰	Poland	1496.9	22.1	2.8	20.9	1.8	6.2
匈 牙 利	Hungary						
罗马尼亚	Romania	1093.6	37.9	2.2	23.0	2.0	4.3
印　　度	India	2794.1	5.5④	4.1④	24.1④	3.5④	4.7④
印度尼西亚	Indonesia	8570.2	44.0	0.9	12.6	0.2	4.4
菲 律 宾	Philippines	2744.2	41.7	0.4	10.0	0.4	5.7
泰　　国	Thailand	3209.5②	60.3③	0.2③	11.1③	0.4③	3.8③
新 加 坡	Singapore	174.8	0.2	…	23.2	0.4	6.6
马来西亚	Malaysia	840.0	19.4	0.4	22.8	0.5	8.5
巴基斯坦	Pakistan	3333.7①	46.8①	0.1①	10.4①	0.8①	7.2①
缅　　甸	Myanmar	1681.7②	68.7②	0.5②	7.4②	0.1②	1.7②
韩　　国	Korea, Rep.	2076.4	11.6	0.1	22.5	0.4	9.5
巴　　西	Brazil	6962.9①	26.1①	1.2①	12.3①		6.1

注:① 1995年资料;② 1994年资料;③ 1991年资料;④ 1989年资料。
Note: ① Date refer to 1995; ② Refer to 1994; ③ Refer to 1991; ④ Refer to 1989.

附录2-3 人均主要经济指标(1996)
MAJOR PER CAPITA INDICATORS OF ECONOMY

资料来源:《国际统计年鉴—1998》
Source: International Statistical Yearbook (1998)

国家和地区 Country or Territory		人均国民生产总值(美元) Per Capita GDP(USD)	主要农产品产量(公斤) Major Output of Farm Products (kg)			主要工业产品产量(公斤) Major Output of Industrial Products (kg)		
			谷物 Grain	肉类 Meat	水产品 Aquatic Products	煤 Coal	原油 Crude Oil	钢 Steel
中国	China	672	371	39①	21	1141	129	83
美国	United States	28020	1254	127	21	4007	1405	357
日本	Japan	40940	109	25	54	52	6	787
德国	Germany	28870	514	72	4	2835	34	376
英国	United Kingdom	19600	421	61	17	972	2078②	339
法国	France	26270	1073	111	14	138	43②	302
意大利	Italy	19880	365	72	11	7②	94	506
加拿大	Canada	19020	1970	107	30	2531②	3035	969
澳大利亚	Australia	20090	1986	177	12	13387②	1196②	434
俄罗斯	Russian Fed	2410	456	36	30	2182②	2037②	333
捷克	Czech Rep.	4740	649	83	2	5862	13②	630
波兰	Poland	3230	655	75	12	5201②	8②	308
罗马尼亚	Romania	1600	627	56	3	185	292	269
印度	India	380	231	5	5	326	34	14
印度尼西亚	Indonesia	1080	301	10	21	240	379	
菲律宾	Philippines	1160	227	25	32	15	2②	7②
泰国	Thailand	2960	462	26	59	310②	20②	36②
新加坡	Singapore	30550		43	5			
马来西亚	Malaysia	4370	100	46	62	6②	1658②	
巴基斯坦	Pakistan	480	180	14	4	25	21②	
缅甸	Myanmar		401	8	18	2②	11②	
韩国	Korea, Rep.	10610	168	34	60	109	854	
巴西	Brazil	4400	288	67	5	33②	242	157

注:① 为猪、牛、羊肉产量。②为1995年资料。
Note: ① Data refer to the output of pork, beef and mutton. ② 1995's data.

附录2-4 国内生产总值及构成(1996)
COMPOSITION OF GROSS DOMESTIC PRODUCTS

资料来源:《国际统计年鉴—1998》
Source: International Statistical Yearbook—1998

国家和地区 Country or Territory		国内生产总值(亿美元) Gross Domestic Products (10^8 USD)	三次产业构成(%) Composition (%) 第一产业 Primary Industry	第二产业 Secondary Industry	第三产业 Tertiary Industry	1996年比1995年增长(%) Increase in 1996 Over 1995 (%)
中国	China	8179	20.4	49.5	30.1	9.6
美国	United States	73419	1.7①	25.8①	72.5①	2.4
日本	Japan	45997	1.9②	38.0②	60.0②	3.6
德国	Germany	23532	1.3③	38.2③	60.5③	
英国	United Kingdom	11458	2.0④	32.0④	66.0④	2.2
法国	France	15401	2.4②	26.5②	71.1②	1.3
意大利	Italy	12077	3.0④	31.0④	66.0④	0.8
加拿大	Canada	5793				1.5
澳大利亚	Australia	3925	3.5②	28.0②	68.5②	4.0
俄罗斯	Russian Fed	4406	7.3	39.1	53.6	-4.9
捷克	Czech Rep.	549	5.6④	39.3④	55.2④	4.1
波兰	Poland	1345	6.4②	34.4②	59.2②	5.9
匈牙利	Hungary	448				1.3
罗马尼亚	Romania	355	20.9②	40.2②	38.9②	4.1
印度	India	3560	27.8	29.2	43.0	7.5
印度尼西亚	Indonesia	2258	16.3	42.7	41.0	7.6
菲律宾	Philippines	838	21.4	31.7	46.9	5.7
泰国	Thailand	1850	10.7	39.8	49.5	6.4
新加坡	Singapore	941	0.2	35.6	64.3	6.9
马来西亚	Malaysia	992	12.8	46.2	41.0	8.0
巴基斯坦	Pakistan	648	25.8	24.5	49.7	4.6
缅甸	Myanmar		60.3	10.0	29.7	5.9
韩国	Korea, Rep.	4848	6.3	42.8	50.9	7.1
巴西	Brazil	7489	14.0	35.9	50.0	2.9

注:① 为1993年资料;② 为1995年资料;③ 为1991年资料;④ 为1994年资料。
Note: ① Data refer to 1993; ② Data refer to 1995; ③ Data refer to 1991; ④ Data refer to 1994.

附录2－5　中央政府财政收入占国内生产总值比重
CENTRAL GOVERNMENT REVENUE AS PERCENTAGE OF GROSS DOMESTIC PRODUCT

资料来源：《国际统计年鉴—1998》

Source：International Statistical Yearbook（1998）

%

国家和地区 Country or Territory	1980	1985	1989	1990	1991	1992	1993	1994	1995
中　国① China①	25.67	22.36	15.76	15.84	14.57	13.08	12.56	11.19	10.71
美　国 United States	20.85	19.94	20.22	19.86	19.84	19.61	19.72	20.06	19.89
日　本② Japan②	12.05④	12.43	13.87	14.38	22.92	21.42	21.39		
原联邦德国 Germany	28.54	28.89	29.48	28.77	30.53	34.47	35.04	36.23	32.12
英　国 United Kingdom	35.10	35.92	35.45	36.84	36.94	36.04	34.90	35.35	36.34
法　国 France	39.63	40.85	40.51	40.54	40.82	40.60	40.51	37.85	40.61
加拿大 Canada	17.90	19.30	20.12	20.73	20.93	20.79	20.70	20.57	
澳大利亚 Australia	24.85	35.38	34.81	34.76	35.07	36.49	36.71	24.17	24.80
匈牙利 Hungary	53.61②	55.04	54.16	53.18					
捷　克 Czech Rep.			56.83	49.33	50.05	41.71	42.28	41.02	38.85
罗马尼亚 Romania	45.28	42.48	48.29	34.73	37.33	36.78	33.92	29.89	
原南斯拉夫 Former Yugoslavia	8.12	7.66	4.27						
印　度 India	11.85	14.08	14.78	13.51	14.48	14.29	13.56	13.30	13.15
印度尼西亚 Indonesia	21.40	16.23	16.69	19.44	18.01	18.26	16.48	18.30	
泰　国 Thailand	14.99	16.82	17.79	19.20	19.70	18.44	18.45	19.10	18.67
马来西亚③ Malaysia③	26.35	25.73	25.72	27.14	28.73	28.81	28.01	28.83	
新加坡 Singapore	25.31	27.88	28.24	31.09	30.32	31.85	35.14	36.06	34.88
缅　甸 Myanmar	16.00	8.48	9.50	10.56	9.66	8.14	7.78		
韩　国 Korea, Rep.	17.96	17.19	17.40	17.87	17.07	18.22	19.00	20.04	20.52
埃　及 Egypt	47.07②	32.33	29.43	24.39	31.86	35.71	37.79		
墨西哥③ Mexico③	15.78	17.28	18.29	14.05	16.12	16.77	16.35	16.69	
巴　西 Brazil	22.18	20.06	25.57	33.29	27.24	27.99	30.43		
阿根廷 Argentina	21.17	9.26	9.85	10.82	12.09	13.23			

注：① 为国家财政收入占国内生产总值比重；② 1991年以前的数据与此后的数据不可比；③ 1980年数据与以后的数据不可比；④ 1981年数字。

Note：① Refer to government revenue as % of GDP；② The data prior to 1991 were uncomparable with those thereafter；③ Data After 1980 were uncomparable with those thereafter．④ Data refer to 1981．

附录2－6 主要农产品产量（1997）
OUTPUT OF MAJOR FARM PRODUCTS

资料来源：《国际统计年鉴—1998》
Source：International Statistical Yearbook（1998）

国家和地区 Country or Territory		谷物总产量（万吨） Total Output of Grain (10000 tons)	油菜籽产量（万吨） Output of Oil-bearing Crops (10000 tons)	水果产量（万吨） Output of Fruits (10000 tons)	肉类总产量（万吨）（1996年） Total Output of Meat (10000 tons)	水产品产量（万吨）（1995） Total Output of Aquatic Products (10000 tons)
中国	China	44752	958	5089	4595	2517
美国	United States	34146	41	3125	3456	563
日本	Japan	1379		413	313	676
德国	Germany	4541	284	314	584	30
英国	United Kingdom	2361	145	32	339	100
法国	France	6219	349	1019	633	79
意大利	Italy	1991	8	1514	407	61
加拿大	Canada	4832	609	81	317	90
澳大利亚	Australia	2478	75	268	311	22
俄罗斯	Russian Fed	8044	12	359	527	437
捷克	Czech Rep.	693	58	44	93	2
波兰	Poland	2404	54	261	269	45
罗马尼亚	Romania	2050		261	143	7
印度	India	22071	638	3510	430	490
印度尼西亚	Indonesia	5993		967	204	412
菲律宾	Philippines	1583		942	172	227
泰国	Thailand	2523		693	135	350
马来西亚	Malaysia	211		114	95	124
巴基斯坦	Pakistan	2497	25	534	193	54
缅甸	Myanmar	2172		109	34	83
韩国	Korea, Rep.	709		199	155	269
巴西	Brazil	4961		3698	1097	80

附录2－7 我国主要农产品产量居世界位次的变化
CHANGES IN THE ORDER OF PRECEDENCE OF OUTPUT OF MAJOR FARM PRODUCTS

资料来源：《中国统计年鉴—1998》
Source：Statistical Yearbook of China（1998）

项目	Item	1949	1957	1965	1978	1980	1985	1990	1995	1996	1997
谷物	Cereals		3	2	2	1	2	1	1	1	1
肉类①	Meat①	3	2	3	3	3	2	1	1	1	1
棉花	Cotton Lint	4	2	2	3	2	1	1	1	1	1
大豆	Soybeans	2	2	2	3	3	3	3	3	3	3
花生	Groundnuts in Shell	2	2	3	2	2	2	2	1	1	1
油菜籽	Rapeseeds	2	2	2	2	2	1	1	1	1	1
甘蔗	Sugar Cane		3		9	9	4	4	3	3	3
茶叶	Tea	3	3	3	2	2	2	2	2	2	2
水果	Fruit					10	8	4	1	1	1

注：① 1993年以前为猪、牛、羊肉产量的位次。
Note：① Order of precedence of out put of pork, beef and mutton refer to 1993 before.

附录 2－8 主要工业产品产量(1997)
OUTPUT OF MAJOR INDUSTRIAL PRODUCTS

资料来源:《国际统计年鉴—1998》
Source: International Statistical Yearbook (1998)

国家和地区	Country or Territory	钢(万吨) Steel (10000 tons)	发电量(亿千瓦小时) Electricity (10^8 kwh)	水泥(万吨) Cement (10000 tons)	化肥②(万吨) Chemical Fertilizers (10000 tons)	家用电视机②(万部) Household Televison Sets (10000)
中国	China	10894	11356	51174	2548	3496
美国	United States	9500①	33453②	7532②	2559	1388③
日本	Japan	9895①	9900②	9442①	118	902
德国	Germany	4081	5470①	3593	477	323③
英国	United Kingdom	1832	3316②	1129①	147	
法国	France	1760①	4889①	1834①	301	280③
意大利	Italy	2772①	2547①	3416②	95	278
加拿大	Canada	2903①	5490①	1174	1248	
澳大利亚	Australia	809	1728	695	54	3
俄罗斯	Russian Fed	4916①	8675②	2779①	960	101
捷克	Czech Rep.	674	646	502①	26	4
波兰	Poland	1189②	1390②	1396①	190	114
匈牙利	Hungary	182	359	281		
罗马尼亚	Romania	622①	612①	696①	140	37
印度	India	1344①	3937①	7350①	1139	154④
泰国	Thailand		750①	3874①		
马来西亚	Malaysia		587	1235	30	946
巴基斯坦	Pakistan		615①	954	169	10
韩国	Korea, Rep.	3890①	2244	5844①	106	1872
巴西	Brazil	2525①	2754②	3460①	226	642

注:① 为 1996 年数,② 1995 年数,③ 1994 年数,④ 1993 年数。
Note: ① Data refer to 1996. ② Data refer to 1995. ③ Data refer to 1994. ④ Data refer to 1993.

附录 2－9 我国工业主要产品产量居世界位次的变化
CHANGES IN THE ORDER OF PRECEDENCE OF OUTPUT OF MAJOR INDUSTRIAL PRODUCTS

资料来源:《中国统计年鉴—1998》
Source: Statistical Yearbook of China (1998)

产品名称	Item	1949	1957	1965	1978	1980	1985	1990	1992	1994	1995	1996③
钢	Crude Steel	26	9	8	5	5	4	4	3	2	2	1
煤	Coal	9	5	5	3	3	2	1	1	1	1	1
原油	Crude Petroleum	27①	23	12	8	6	6	5	5	5	5	5
发电量	Electricity	25	13	9	7	6	5	4	4	2	2	2
水泥	Cement		8	8	4	4	1	1	1	1	1	1
化肥	Fertilizer		33	8	3	3	3	3	3	2	2	2
化学纤维	Chemical Fibre		26②		7	5	4	2	2	2	2	2
棉布	Woven Cotton Fabrics			3	1	1	1	1	1	1	1	1
糖	Sugar			8	8	10	6	6	3	4	4	4
电视机	Television				8	5	3	1	1	1	1	1

注:① 1950 年数字;② 1960 年数字;③ 估计数。
Note: ① Data refer to 1950; ② Data refer to 1960; ③ Estimates.

附录2－10 工 业 主 要 指 标
MAJOR INDICATORS OF INDUSTRY

资料来源:《国际统计年鉴—1998》
Source: International Statistical Yearbook (1998)

国家和地区 Country or Territory		1996年工业生产指数 (1980＝100) Index of Industrial Products (1996)	制造业主要指标(1995) Major Indicators of Manufacturing (1995)				
			企业数(万家) Number of Enterprises (10000)	雇员数(万人) Employees (10000 persons)	雇员工资(亿本币) Wage of Employees (10^8 Native Currency)	产值(亿本币) Output Value (10^8 Native Currency)	增加值(亿本币) Added Value (10^8 Native Currency)
中国	China						
美国	United States	117	48.83①	1734	5430	35730	17040
日本	Japan	98	38.75②	1050②	449500②	2999290②	1245140②
德国	Germany	96	4.73②	673②	3931②	19222②	8901②
英国	United Kingdom	108	15.69②	423②	643②	3803②	1596②
法国	France	100		384	8478①	39302	14780
意大利	Italy	105	3.90②	283②	1464540②	8122810②	2338240②
加拿大	Canada	114	3.20②	167②	616②	4186②	1538②
澳大利亚	Australia	110	4.46②	91113②	2811②	1839②	680③
印度	India	143	11.82③	783③	2486③	37391③	7444③
印度尼西亚	Indonesia		2.16	416	136290	1946800	670740
菲律宾	Philippines	168	1.11③	90③	603③	7933③	2991③
泰国	Thailand		1.39④	161④	1183④	26814④	16691④
马来西亚	Malaysia	187	0.83②	121②	136②	1969②	495②
韩国	Korea, Rep.	163	9.62	287	378440	3648210	1594480

注: ① 为1992年数;② 为1994年数;③ 为1993年数;④ 为1991年数。
Note: ① Data refer to 1992; ② Data refer to 1994; ③ Data refer to 1993; ④ Data refer to 1991.

附录2－11 一 次 能 源 生 产 量(1995)
OUTPUT OF ENERGY RESOURCES (ONE TIME)

资料来源:《国际统计年鉴—1998》
Source: International Statistical Yearbook (1998)
单位:标准煤万吨 (Standardized coal 10000 tons)

国家和地区 Country or Territory		生产总量 Gross Output	固体 Solid	液体 Liquid	气体 Gas	电能 Electric Energy
中国	China	129034	97163	21420	2452	8000
美国	United States	244422	88633	56035	69173	30581
日本	Japan	13262	520	103	309	12331
德国	Germany	19996	11270	418	2281	6027
英国	United Kingdom	36415	4530	18712	9781	3393
法国	France	16603	785	421	443	14954
意大利	Italy	4293	14	748	2595	936
加拿大	Canada	49601	5652	15515	20941	7493
澳大利亚	Australia	26102	19250	3440	3213	200
俄罗斯	Russian Fed	3898	1362	113	60	2362
罗马尼亚	Romania	4333	1069	996	2063	205
印度	India	31095	22734	4769	2451	1141
印度尼西亚	Indonesia	26674	3610	14375	8338	117
泰国	Thailand	2966	1158	526	1200	83
马来西亚	Malaysia	8915	11	4947	3864	92
韩国	Korea, Rep.	2925	368			

附录 2－12　交通运输、邮电主要指标（1996）
MAJOR INDICATORS OF TRANPORTATION, POSTAL AND TELE－COMMUNICATION SERVICES

资料来源：《国际统计年鉴—1998》

Source: International Statistical Yearbook (1998)

国家和地区 Country or Territory		铁路货物周转量（亿吨公里） Railway Turnover Volume of Freight Traffic (10^8 tons/km)	铁路旅客周转量（亿人公里） Railway Turnover Volume of Passenger (10^8 persons/km)	空运货物周转量（亿吨公里） Air Transport Turnover Volume of Freight Traffic (10^8 tons/km)	空运旅客周转量（亿人公里） Air Transport Turnover Volume of Passenger Traffic (10^8 persons/km)	电话机数①（万部） Telephones (10000)	移动电话数①（万部） Mobil Telephones (10000)
中国	China	12971	3325	25	748	5762	149
美国	United States	19130	81	252	9198	16462	3379
日本	Japan	250	4007	71	1406	6111	1020
德国	Germany	699①	628①	61	633	4040	375
英国	United Kingdom	134	317	40	1232	2941	574
法国	France	506	600	48	575	3240	138
意大利	Italy	225②	471⑤	15①	318①	2485	386
加拿大	Canada	2624③		19	560	1746	259
澳大利亚	Australia			15②	482②	920	230
俄罗斯	Russian Fed	11313	1687	9	527	2502	9
捷克	Czech Rep.	243	81		24	244	5
波兰	Poland	691①	266①	1	39	573	8
匈牙利	Hungary	76	86				
罗马尼亚	Romania	272①	189①		18	297	1
印度	India	2787	3437	6	189①	1198	8
印度尼西亚	Indonesia	39	159		149③	329	22
菲律宾	Philippines			4①	144①	141	49
泰国	Thailand	34	123	14	297	348	109
新加坡	Singapore			42	536	143	31
马来西亚	Malaysia	14	14	12①	234①	333	101
巴基斯坦	Pakistan	55①	186①	5①	104①	213	4
缅甸	Myanmar	7①	43①			16	
韩国	Korea, Rep.	141②	302②	66	521	1860	164
巴西	Brazil	1166④		17	349①	1208	129

注：① 1995 数；② 1994 年数；③ 1991 年数；④ 1992 年数；⑤ 1993 年数。

Note: ① Data refer to 1995; ② Data refer to 1994; ③ Data refer to 1991; ④ Data refer to 1992; ⑤ Data refer to 1993.

附录2-13 进出口贸易额
TOTAL IMPORT AND EXPORT

资料来源:《国际统计年鉴—1998》

Source: International Statistical Yearbook (1998)

单位:亿美元 (100 million US$)

国家和地区	Country or Territory	1985 进口 Import	1985 出口 Export	1995 进口 Import	1995 出口 Export	1997 进口 Import	1997 出口 Export
世界总计	**World**	**20062.3**	**19305.8**	**49986.0**	**49256.7**	**55174.3**	**53377.6**
中国	China	422.5	273.5	1320.8	1487.7	1423.6	1827.0
美国	United States	3616.3	2188.3	7712.7	5847.4	8990.2	6887.0
日本	Japan	1294.8	1756.8	3359.9	4432.7	3386.2	4210.2
德国①	Germany①	1585.5	1840.1	4482.2	5118.7	4418.1	5117.2
英国	United Kingdom	1092.7	1099.9	2653.2	2420.4	3065.6	2810.8
法国	France	1089.1	976.4	2755.5	2868.2	26770.0	2888.7
意大利	Italy	909.9	789.6	2041.0	2312.6	2083.0	2383.6
加拿大	Canada	764.1	847.8	1680.5	1922.0	2008.8	2144.3
澳大利亚	Australia	234.5	228.8	603.2	530.9	680.2	628.9
俄罗斯	Russian Fed.	369.8③	423.8③	466.8	782.9	676.2	873.7
捷克	Czech. Rep.	111.5④	115.1④	252.3	216.8	269.9	225.5
波兰	Poland	108.0	114.9	290.5	228.9	423.1	257.5
匈牙利	Hungary	79.2	82.5	150.5	124.4	158.5②	126.5②
罗马尼亚	Romania	84	101.7	94.2	75.5	114.4②	84.3
保加利亚	Bulgaria	136.6	133.5	50.2	50.9	53.6②	48.1②
印度	India	155.9	87.5	344.0	305.4	403.6	403.6
印度尼西亚	Indonesia	102.6	185.9	409.2	454.2	429.3②	498.1②
菲律宾	Philippines	54.5	46.3	283.4	175.0	341.2②	204.2②
泰国	Thailand	92.4	71.2	707.8	564.6	734.8②	557.2②
马来西亚	Malaysia	126.0	157.2	776.2	737.2	784.2②	783.3②
新加坡	Singapore	262.9	228.1	1245.0	1182.6	1324.5	1250.2
巴基斯坦	Pakistan	58.9	27.2	114.6	79.9	116.0	87.2
缅甸	Myanmar	2.8	3.3	13.4	8.5	22.6	8.7
孟加拉国	Bangladesh	21.7	9.3	65.0	31.7	66.2②	8.6
土耳其	Turkey	113.4	79.3	357.1	216.0	429.3②	230.8②
韩国	Korea, Rep.	311.4	302.8	1351.2	1250.6	1446.4	1366.2
埃及	Egypt	55.0	18.4	117.6	34.5	130.2②	35.4②
尼日利亚	Nigeria	62.1	131.1	93.3	106.4	80.0②	186.1②
墨西哥	Mecxico	137.6	216.6	468.9	484.3	611.6②	593.7②
巴西	Brazil	131.5	256.4	537.8	465.1	650.1	529.9
阿根廷	Argentina	38.1	84.0	201.2	209.7	299.4	246.6

注:① 1991年以前数字仅指原联邦德国;② 1996年数;③ 1993年数;④ 原捷克斯洛伐克数据。

Note: ① Data prior to 1991 refer to the former Federal Rep. of Germany; ② 1996; ③ 1993; ④ Data refer to former Czecholovak.

附录2-14 货 币 汇 率（年末中间价）
EXCHANGE RATES (MID-POINT RATES)

资料来源:《国际统计年鉴—1998》

Source: International Statistical Yearbook (1998)

一美元合该国货币数　　(Unless otherwise stated national currency per U.S. dollar)

国家和地区	货币名称	Country of Area	Currencies	1985	1990	1995	1996	1997
中国	(人民币元)	China	(Renminbi Yuan)	3.20	5.22	8.35	8.30	8.29①
美国	(美元)	United States	(Dollar)	1.00	1.00	1.00	1.00	1.00
日本	(日元)	Japan	(Yen)	200.50	134.40	102.83	116.00	129.95
德国	(德国马克)	Germany	(Deutsche Mark)	2.46	1.49	1.43	1.55	1.79
英国	(英镑)	United Kingdom	(Pound)	0.69	0.52	0.65	0.59	0.60
法国	(法郎)	France	(Franc)	7.56	5.13	4.90	5.34	5.99
意大利	(里拉)	Italy	(Lire)	1678.50	1130.10	1584.70	1530.60	1759.20
加拿大	(加元)	Canada	(Dollar)	1.40	1.16	1.37	1.37	1.43
澳大利亚	(澳元)	Australia	(Dollar)	1.47	1.29	1.34	1.26	1.53
俄罗斯	(卢布)	Russian Fed.	(Rouple)			4640.00	5560.00	5960.00
捷克②	(克朗)	Czech. Rep. ②	(Koruna)	16.00	28.00	26.30	27.33	34.64
波兰	(兹罗提)	Poland	(Zloty)		0.95	2.47	2.88	3.52
匈牙利	(福林)	Hungary	(Forint)	47.35	61.45	139.47	164.93	195.44①
罗马尼亚	(列伊)	Romania	(Lei)	15.73	34.71	2578.00	4035.00	8023.00
保加利亚②	(列弗)	Bulgaria②	(Leva)	1.00	2.80	20.20	487.35	1809.00①
南斯拉夫	(新第纳尔)	Yugoslavia, FR	(New Dinar)	31.28	10.66	5.32	5.54	6.38①
印度	(卢比)	India	(Rupee)	12.17	18.07	35.18	35.93	39.28
印度尼西亚	(卢比)	Indonesia	(Rupiah)	1125.00	1901.00	2308.00	2383.00	4650.00
菲律宾	(比索)	Philippines	(Peso)	19.03	28.00	26.21	26.29	39.98
泰国	(铢)	Thailand	(Baht)	26.65	25.29	25.19	25.61	47.25
马来西亚	(林吉特)	Malaysia	(Ringgit)	2.43	2.70	2.54	2.53	3.89
新加坡	(新加坡元)	Singapore	(Dollar)	2.11	1.74	1.41	1.40	1.68
巴基斯坦③	(卢比)	Pakistan③	(Rupee)	15.98	21.90	34.25	40.12	44.05
缅甸	(缅元)	Myanmar	(Kyat)	7.84	6.08	5.78	5.99	6.36
孟加拉国	(塔卡)	Bangladesh	(Taka)	31.00	35.79	40.75	42.45	45.45
土耳其②	(里拉)	Turkey②	(Lira)	477	2930.10	59650	107775	205605
蒙古②	(图格里克)	Mongolia②	(Tugrik)	3.60	5.60	473.62	693.51	804.86
韩国	(韩圆)	Korea, Rep.	(Won)	890.20	716.40	774.70	844.20	1695.80
埃及③	(埃镑)	Egypt③	(Pound)	0.70	2.00	3.39	3.39	3.39
尼日利亚	(奈拉)	Nigeria	(Naira)	1.00	9.00	21.89	21.89	21.89
墨西哥	(新比索)	Mecxico	(New Peso)	0.37	2.95	7.97	7.85	8.14
巴西	(雷亚尔)	Brazil	(Reai)	3.81	64.39	0.97	1.04	1.12
阿根廷	(比索)	Argentina	(Peso)	0.08	0.56	1.00	1.00	1.00

注：① 8月份数；② 由联合国项目的业务汇率推算的非商业汇率；③ 固定汇率。

Note: ① Data refer to August; ② Data refer to noncommercial rates derived from the operational rates on exchange for United Nations Programs; ③ Fixed rate.

附录3.

主要统计指标解释

APPENDIX Ⅲ
EXPLANATORY NOTES ON MAIN STATISTICAL INDICATORS

主要统计指标解释

总产出 指一定时期内一个国家(或地区)常住单位生产的所有货物和服务的价值,既包括新增价值,也包括转移价值。它反映常住单位生产活动的总规模。

国内生产总值 是按市场价格计算的国内生产总值的简称。它是一个国家(地区)所有常住单位在一定时期内生产活动的最终成果。国内生产总值有三种表现形态,即价值形态、收入形态和产品形态。从价值形态看,它是所有常住单位在一定时期内所生产的全部货物和服务价值超过同期投入的全部非固定资产货物和服务价值的差额,即所有常住单位的增加值之和;从收入形态看,它是所有常住单位在一定时期内所创造并分配给常住单位和非常住单位的初次分配收入之和;从产品形态看,它是最终使用的货物和服务减去进口货物和服务。在实际核算中,国内生产总值的三种表现形态表现为三种计算方法,即生产法、收入法和支出法。三种方法分别从不同的方面反映国内生产总值及其构成。

可比价格 指在不同时期的价值指标对比时,扣除了价格变动的因素,以确切反映物量的变化。按可比价格计算有两种方法:一种是直接用产品产量乘某一年的不变价格计算;另一种是用价格指数换算。

不变价格 指用同类产品的年平均价格作为固定价格,来计算各年产品价值。按不变价格计算的产品价值消除了价格变动因素,不同时期对比可以反映生产的发展速度。新中国成立后,随着工农业产品价格水平的变化,国家统计局先后五次制定了全国统一的工业产品不变价格和农业产品不变价格,从 1949 年到 1957 年使用 1952 年工(农)业产品不变价格,从 1957 年到 1971 年使用 1957 年不变价格,从 1971 年到 1981 年使用 1970 年不变价格,从 1981 年到 1990 年使用 1980 年不变价格,从 1990 年开始使用 1990 年不变价格。

平均每年增长速度 在我国计算平均增长速度有两种方法,一种是习惯上经常使用的"水平法",又称几何平均法,是以间隔期最后一年的水平同基期水平对比来计算平均每年增长(或下降)速度。另一种是"累计法",又称代数平均法或方程法,是以间隔期内各年水平的总和同基期水平对比来计算平均每年增长(或下降)速度。

在一般正常情况下,两种方法计算的平均每年增长速度比较接近,但在经济发展不平衡,出现大起大落时,两种方法计算的结果差别较大。

本《年鉴》内所列的平均每年增长速度,均用"水平法"计算。从某年到某年平均增长速度的年份,均不包括基期年在内。如建国四十六年的平均增长速度是以 1949 年为基期计算的,则写为 1950 - 1995 年平均增长速度。

各个计划时期 表内所用各个"时期"代表的年份如下:恢复时期为 1950 年到 1952 年;第一个五年计划时期(简称一五时期)为 1953 年到 1957 年;第二个五年计划时期(简称二五时期)为 1958 年到 1962 年;第三个五年计划时期(简称三五时期)为 1966 年到 1970 年;第四个五年计划时期(简称四五时期)为 1971 年到 1975 年;第五个五年计划时期(简称五五时期)为 1976 年到 1980 年;第六个五年计划时期(简称六五时期)为 1981 年到 1985 年;第七年五年计划时期(简称七五时期)为 1986 年到 1990 年;第八年五年计划时期(简称八五时期)为 1991 年到 1995 年。

登记注册类型 是指在工商行政管理机关登记注册的各类企业。企业登记注册类型分为以下几种:内资企业包括国有企业、集体企业、股份合作企业、联营企业、有限责任公司、股份有限公司、私营企业、其他企业;港、澳、台商投资企业包括合资经营企业(港或澳、台资)、合作经营企业(港或澳、台资)、港、澳、台商独资经营企业、港、澳、台商投资股份有限公司;外商投资企业包括中外合资经营企业、中外合作经营企业、外资企业、外商投资股份有限公司。

国有企业 是指企业全部资产归国家所有,并按《中华人民共和国企业法人登记管理条例》规定登记注册的非公司制的经济组织。不包括有限责任公司中的国有独资公司。

集体企业 是指企业资产归集体所有,并按《中华人民共和国企业法人登记管理条例》规定登记注册的经济组织。

股份合作企业 是指以合作制为基础,由企业职工共同出资入股,吸收一定比例的社会资产投资组建,实行自主经营,自负盈亏,共同劳动,民主管理,按劳分配与按股分红相结合的一种集体经济组织。

联营企业 是指两个及两个以上相同或不同所有制性质的企业法人或事业单位法人,按自愿、平等、互利的原则,共同投资组成的经济组织。

有限责任公司 是指根据《中华人民共和国登记管理条例》规定登记注册,由两个以上,五十个以下的股东共同出资,每个股东以其所认缴的出资额对公司承担有限责任,公司以其全部资产对其债务承担责任的经济组织。

有限责任公司包括国有独资公司以及其他有限责任公司。

股份有限公司 是指根据《中华人民共和国公司登记管理条例》规定登记注册,其全部注册资本由等额股份构成并通过发行股票筹集资本,股东以其认购的股份对公司承担有限责任,公司以其全部资产对其债务承担责任的经济组织。

私营企业 是指由自然人投资设立或由自然人控股,以雇佣劳动为基础的营利性经济组织。包括按照《公司法》、《合伙企业法》、《私营企业暂行条例》规定登记注册的私营有限责任公司、私营股份有限公司、私营合伙企业和私营独资企业。

合资经营企业(港或澳、台资) 是指港澳台地区投资者与内地的企业依照《中华人民共和国中外合资经营企业法》

及有关法律的规定,按合同规定的比例投资设立、分享利润和分担风险的企业。

合作经营企业(港或澳、台资) 是指港澳台地区投资者与内地企业依照《中华人民共和国中外合作经营企业法》及有关法律的规定,依照合作合同的约定进行投资或提供条件设立、分配利润和分担风险的企业。

港、澳、台商独资经营企业 是指依照《中华人民共和国外资企业法》及有关法律的规定,在内地由港澳台地区投资者全额投资设立的企业。

港、澳、台商投资股份有限公司 是指根据国家有关规定,经外经贸部依法批准设立,其中港、澳、台商的股本占公司注册资本的比例达25%以上的股份有限公司。凡其中港、澳、台商的股本占公司注册资本的比例小于25%的,属于内资企业中的股份有限公司。

中外合资经营企业 是指外国企业或外国人与中国内地企业依照《中华人民共和国中外合资经营企业法》及有关法律的规定,按合同规定的比例投资设立、分享利润和分担风险的企业。

中外合作经营企业 是指外国企业或外国人与中国内地企业依照《中华人民共和国中外合资经营企业法》及有关法律的规定,依照合作合同的约定进行投资或提供条件设立、分配利润和分担风险的企业。

外资企业 是指依照《中华人民共和国外资企业法》及有关法律的规定。在中国内地由外国投资者全额投资设立的企业。

外商投资股份有限公司 是指根据国家有关规定,经外经贸部依法批准设立,其中外资的股本占公司注册资本的比例达25%以上的股份有限公司。凡其中外资股本占公司注册资本的比例小于25%的,属于内资企业中的股份有限公司。

三次产业 根据社会生产活动历史发展的顺序对产业结构的划分,产品直接取自自然界的部门称为第一产业,对初级产品进行再加工的部门称为第二产业。为生产和消费提供各种服务的部门称为第三产业。它是世界上通用的产业结构分类,但各国的划分不尽一致。我国的三次产业划分是:

第一产业:农业(包括种植业、林业、牧业、副业和渔业)。

第二产业:工业(包括采掘工业、制造业、自来水、电力、蒸气、热水、煤气)和建筑业。

第三产业:除第一、第二产业以外的其他各业。由于第三产业包括的行业多、范围广,根据我国的实际情况,第三产业可分为两大部分:一是流通部门,二是服务部门。具体又可分为四个层次:

第一层次:流通部门,包括交通运输业、邮电通讯业、商业、饮食业、物资供销和仓储业。

第二层次:为生产和生活服务的部门,包括金融、保险业,地质普查业,房地产、公用事业,居民服务业,咨询服务业和综合技术服务业,农、林、牧、渔、水利服务业和水利业,公路、内河(湖)航道养护业等。

第三层次:为提高科学文化水平和居民素质服务的部门,包括教育、文化、广播电视,科学研究、卫生、体育和社会福利事业等。

第四层次:为社会公共需要服务的部门,包括国家机关、政党机关、社会团体,以及军队和警察等。

支出法国内生产总值 指一个国家(或地区)所有常住单位在一定时期内用于最终消费、资本形成总额,以及货物和服务的净出口总额,它反映本期生产的国内生产总值的使用构成。

最终消费 指常住单位在一定时期内对于货物和服务的全部最终消费支出,也就是常住单位为满足物质、文化和精神生活的需要,从本国经济领土和国外购买的货物和服务的支出。它不包括非常住单位在本国经济领土内的消费支出。最终消费分为居民消费和政府消费。

(一) 居民消费:指常住住户在一定时期内对于货物和服务的全部最终消费支出。居民关于货物的最终消费支出在货物的所有权发生变化时记录,关于服务的最终消费支出在服务提供的时候记录。居民消费支出按市场价格计算,即按居民支付的购买者价格计算,货物的购买者价格是购买者取得交货所支付的价格,它包括购买者支付的运输和商业费用。居民消费支出除了直接以货币形式购买的货物和服务的消费支出外,还包括以其他方式获得的货物和服务的消费支出,即所谓的虚拟消费支出。居民虚拟消费支出包括如下几种类型:单位以实物报酬及实物转移的形式提供给劳动者的货物和服务;住户生产并由本住户消费了的货物和服务,其中的服务仅指住户的自有住房服务;金融机构提供的金融媒介服务;保险公司提供的保险服务。

(二) 政府消费:指政府部门向社会提供的公共服务支出和对居民提供的消费性货物和服务的转移支出。

资本形成总额 指常住单位在一定时期内获得减去处置的固定资产和存货的净额,包括固定资本形成总额和存货增加两项。

(一) 固定资本形成总额:指常住单位在一定时期内购置、转入和自产自用的固定资产价值,扣除固定资产的销售和转出后的价值。可分为有形固定资产形成总额和无形固定资产形成总额。有形固定资产形成总额包括一定时期内完成的建筑工程、安装工程和设备工器具购置(减处置)价值,以及土地改良、新增役、种、奶、毛、娱乐用牲畜和新增经济林木价值。无形固定资产形成总额包括矿藏的勘探、计算机软件、娱乐和文学艺术品原件等获得减处置。

(二) 存货增加:指常住单位在一定时期内存货实物量变动的市场价值即期末价值减期初价值的差额。存货增加可以是正值,也可以是负值,正值表示存货上升,负值表示存货下降。它包括生产单位购进的原材料、燃料和储备物资等存货,以及生产单位生产的产成品、在制品和半成品等存货。

货物和服务净出口 指货物和服务出口减货物和服务进口的差额。出口包括常住单位向非常住单位出售或无偿转让的各种货物和服务的价值;进口包括常住单位从非常住单位购买或无偿得到的各种货物和服务的价值。由于服务活动的提供与使用同时发生,因此服务的进出口业务并不发生出入境现象,一般把常住单位从国外得到的服务作为进口,非常住单位从本国得到的服务作为出口。货物的出口和进口都按离岸价格计算。

劳动者报酬 劳动者报酬是指劳动者因从事生产活动所获得的全部报酬。它包括劳动者获得的各种形式工资、奖金和津贴,既包括货币形式的,也包括实物形式的,它还包括劳动者所享受的公费医疗和医药卫生费、上下班交通补贴和单位支付的社会保险费等。单位支付的社会保险费,就是单位直接支付给负责社会保险的政府单位(一般指劳动部门)的社会保险金或为本单位职工离退休、发生死亡、伤残、医疗保险等而支付的保险费。对于个体经济来说,其所有者所获得的劳动报酬和经营利润不易区分,这两部分统一作为劳动者报酬处理。

生产税净额 指生产税减生产补贴后的差额。生产税指政府对生产单位生产、销售和从事经营活动以及因从事生产活动使用某些生产要素,如固定资产、土地、劳动力所征收的各种税、附加费和规费。具体包括销售税金及附加、增值税、管理费中开支的各种税、应交纳的养路费、排污费和水电费附加、烟酒专卖上缴政府的专项收入等。生产补贴与生产税相反,是政府对生产单位的单方面收入转移,因此视为负生产税处理,包括政策亏损补贴、粮食系统价格补贴、外贸企业出口退税收入等。

固定资产折旧 指一定时期内为弥补固定资产损耗按照核定的固定资产折旧率提取的固定资产折旧,或按国民经济核算统一规定的折旧率虚拟计算的固定资产折旧。它反映了固定资产在当期生产中的转移价值。各种类型企业和企业化管理的事业单位的固定资产折旧指实际计提并计入成本费用中的折旧费;不计提折旧的单位,如政府机关、非企业化管理的事业单位和居民住房的固定资产折旧则是按照统一规定的折旧率和固定资产原值计算的虚拟折旧。原则上,固定资产折旧应按固定资产的重置价值来计算,但是我国目前尚不具备对全社会固定资产进行重估价的基础,所以暂时只能采用上述方法来计算。

营业盈余 指常住单位创造的增加值扣除劳动者报酬、生产税净额和固定资产折旧后的余额。它相当于企业的营业利润加上生产补贴,但要扣除从利润中开支的工资和福利以及从税后利润中提取的公益金等。

人口 人口数为每年12月31日常住户口人数,不包括户口不在本省的临时户口人数。

出生率(又称粗出生率) 指在一定时期内(通常为一年)平均每千人所出生的人数的比率,一般用千分率表示。计算公式:

$$出生率=\frac{年出生人数}{年平均人数}\times 1000‰$$

出生人数是指活产婴儿,即胎儿脱离母体时(不管怀孕月数),有过呼吸或其他生命现象。

年平均人数是年初、年底人口数的平均数,也可用年中人口数代替。

死亡率(又称粗死亡率) 指在一定时期内(通常为一年)一定地区的死亡人数与同期平均人数(或期中人数)之比,一般用千分率表示。计算公式:

$$死亡率=\frac{年死亡人数}{年平均人数}\times 1000‰$$

人口自然增长率 指在一定时期内(通常为一年)人口自然增加数(出生人数减死亡人数)与该时期内平均人数(或期中人数)之比,一般用千分率表示。计算公式:

$$人口自然增长率=\frac{本年出生人数-本年死亡人数}{年平均人数}\times 1000‰$$

$$人口自然增长率=人口出生率-人口死亡率$$

人口预期寿命 指在一定年龄组死亡率水平下,对某一确定的年龄日后平均还能继续生存的年数(或该年龄组未来的平均寿命)。

从业人员 指从事一定社会劳动并取得劳动报酬或经营收入的全部劳动力。包括:

(1) 全部职工;(2) 城镇私营企业从业人员;(3) 城镇个体劳动者;(4) 农村社会劳动者;(5) 其他社会劳动者。

这一指标反映了一定时期内全部劳动力资源的实际利用情况,是研究我国基本国情国力的重要指标。

各单位的从业人员是指在各级国家机关、政党机关、社会团体及企业、事业单位中工作,取得工资或其他形式的劳动报酬的全部人员。包括在岗职工、再就业的离退休人员、民办教师以及在各单位中工作的外方人员和港、澳、台方人员。

各单位的从业人员反映了各单位实际参加生产或工作的全部劳动力。

在岗职工 指在本单位工作并由单位支付工资的人员，以及有工作岗位，但由于学习、病伤产假等原因暂未工作，仍由单位支付工资的人员。

离开本单位仍保留劳动关系的职工 指由于各种原因，已经离开本人的生产或工作岗位，并已不在本单位从事其他工作，但仍与用人单位保留劳动关系的职工。

离开本单位仍保留劳动关系职工的生活费 指离开本单位仍保留劳动关系职工在离开本单位仍保留劳动关系期间从本单位领取的生活费用。

城镇失业人员 指有非农业户口，在一定的劳动年龄内（16岁以上及男50岁以下、女45岁以下），有劳动能力，无业而要求就业，并在当地就业服务机构进行待业登记的人员。

职工工资总额 指各单位在一定时期内直接支付给本单位全部职工的劳动报酬总额。工资总额包括计时工资、计件工资、奖金、计件超额工资、各种津贴和补贴、加班加点工资、特殊情况下支付的工资（其他工资）等。

工资总额的计算原则应以直接支付给职工的全部劳动报酬为依据。各单位支付给职工的劳动报酬以及其他根据有关规定支付的工资，不论是计入成本的还是不计入成本的，不论是按国家规定列入计征奖金税项目的，还是未列入计征奖金税项目的，不论是以货币形式支付的还是以实物形式支付的，均包括在工资总额内。

职工平均工资 指企业、事业、机关单位的职工在一定时期内平均每人所得的货币工资额。它表明一定时期职工工资收入的高低程度，是反映职工工资水平的主要指标。计算公式为：

$$\text{职工平均工资}=\frac{\text{报告期实际支付的全部职工工资总额}}{\text{报告期全部职工平均人数}}$$

劳保福利费用 指企业、事业、机关根据国家有关劳保福利规定，在工资以外实际支付给职工个人和用于集体的劳动保险和福利设施的费用。具体包括：(1)退职、退休、离休费等；(2)医疗卫生费；(3)职工生活困难补助费；(4)职工及供养直系亲属死亡丧葬费、抚恤费、救济费；(5)农业生产补贴；(6)文艺、体育、宣传费；(7)集体福利事业的补贴；(8)集体福利设施费用；(9)其他福利费用。

劳保福利费用不包括用于职工的劳动保护费用。劳动保护用品的支出是安全生产的需要，不属于福利费用范围。

城镇居民家庭就业人口 指城镇居民从事社会劳动并取得劳动报酬或经营收入的人口。就业人口包括通过国家统筹规划和指导由劳动部门介绍就业，自愿组织起来就业和自谋职业等方式，在国有制、集体所有制、中外合资、中外合作、外资在华独资的企事业单位和私营企业单位工作或从事个体劳动的有固定性职业或临时性职业的人口。被聘用和留用的离退休人员也计入就业人口。本指标可以反映城镇居民的就业情况，是计算就业面、负担系数的重要资料。

现金收入 包括实际收入和借贷收入。

实际收入 指调查户的全部实际的现金收入；不包括借贷收入，如提取银行存款、向亲友借入款、收回借出款以及其他各种暂收款。

借贷收入 指周转性收入。包括提取银行存款、储金会款、借入款、收回借出款、兑售有价证券、赊购、为购房从银行贷款等。

城镇居民家庭可支配收入 指被调查城镇居民家庭在支付个人所得税之后，所余下的实际收入。

消费性支出 指调查户购买商品和用于服务的全部支出，共分八大类：食品；衣着；家庭设备、用品及服务；医疗保健；交通和通讯；娱乐、教育、文化服务；居住；杂项商品和服务。购买商品支出是指从商店、集市、饮食业、工作单位以及直接从工厂和农村购买各种商品的支出，包括自用的和赠送亲友的在内；服务支出是指调查户用于社会提供的各种文化和生活服务方面的支出，包括各种修理费、加工费、洗理美容费、保姆费、劳务费等。

农村住户纯收入 是总收入扣除相应的各项费用性支出后，归农民所有的收入。它是用于生产、非生产投资，改善物质和文化生活，以及用于再分配的支出和结余的收入。这个指标用来观察农民实际收入水平，以及农民扩大再生产和改善生活的能力。

纯收入＝总收入－家庭经营费用支出－生产用固定资产折旧－税收－上交集体承包任务－集体提留和摊派－调查补贴。

农村住户常住人口中整半劳动力 劳动力是农村住户生产的基本要素之一，劳动力的多少和劳动力负担人口的多少，直接影响农村住户收入和生活消费水平的增长变化。整劳动力是指男子18周岁到50周岁，女子18周岁到45周岁；半劳动力是指男子16周岁到17周岁，51周岁到60周岁；女子16到17周岁，46周岁到55周岁，同时具有劳动能力的人。虽然在劳动年龄之内，但已丧失劳动能力的人，不应算为劳动力；在劳动年龄以外，但能经常参加劳动，能顶上一个整劳动力或半劳动力的人，应计在劳动力数内。常住人口中的职工，若这些职工为劳动力，就包括在本户的整半劳动力中。

农村住户生活消费支出 是指农村住户年内用于物质生活和精神生活方面的实际支出,直接反映农民的生活水平、研究农民消费结构变化的基本指标。生活消费支出包括食品、衣着、居住、家庭设备、用品及服务、医疗保健、交通和通讯、文化教育娱乐用品及服务、其他商品和服务等消费支出。

农村住户生活消费现金支出 指农村住户用其货币收入,在市场上购买食品、衣着、家庭用家具器皿、日用杂品、燃料、耐用消费品以及文教卫生用品等生活消费总量。包括向国有商店、集体商店和集市贸易市场以及其他流通渠道购买的全部生活消费品。农村住户生活消费现金支出,是农村住户生活消费支出的一个重要组成部分,是用来反映和分析农村住户生活消费水平的商品化程度,及其由自给性经济向商品经济发展趋势的重要指标,也是研究和预测农村住户对市场消费品需求,制定商品供应计划的重要依据。

城乡储蓄存款余额 城乡储蓄存款,包括城镇居民储蓄存款和农民个人储蓄存款两部分。不包括居民的手存现金和工矿企业、部队、机关团体等集团存款。储蓄存款余额,是指城乡居民存入银行及农村信用社储蓄的时点数(存入数扣除取出数的余额),如月末、季末或年末数额。

全社会固定资产投资 固定资产投资是指建造和购置固定资产的经济活动,它是社会增加固定资产,扩大生产规模发展国民经济的重要手段,也是提高人民物质文化生活水平的条件。

固定资产投资额是以货币表现的建造和购置固定资产活动的工作量,它是反映固定资产投资规模、速度、比例关系和使用方向的综合性指标。全社会固定资产投资包括国有经济单位投资、城乡集体经济单位投资、各种经济类型的单位投资和城乡居民个人投资。按照我国现行计划管理体制划分,固定资产投资总额分为基本建设、更新改造、房地产开发投资、国有其他固定资产投资、城乡集体经济单位投资(包括城镇集体所有制单位投资和农村集体所有制单位投资)、其他各种经济类型的单位投资(包括联营经济、股份制经济、中外合资经营、中外合作经营、外资、与大陆合资经营、与大陆合作经营、港澳台独资及其他经济类型的单位投资)、城乡居民个人投资(包括城市、县城、镇、工矿区所辖范围内的个人建房和农村个人建房及购买生产性固定资产的投资)等九个部分。

从 1997 年起,基本建设、更新改造、其他固定资产投资的起报点由 5 万元提高到 50 万元。

基本建设投资 基本建设是企业、事业、行政单位以扩大生产能力或工程效益为主要目的的新建、扩建工程及有关工作。包括(1)列入中央和各级地方本年基本建设计划的建设项目,以及虽未列入本年基本建设计划,但使用以前年度基建计划内结转投资(包括利用基建设备材料)在本年继续施工的建设项目;(2)本年基本建设计划内投资与更新改造计划内投资结合安排的新建项目和新增生产能力(或工程效益)达到大中型项目标准的扩建项目,以及为改变生产力布局而进行的全厂性迁建项目;(3)国有单位既未列入基建计划,也未列入更新改造计划的总投资在 50 万元以上的新建、扩建、恢复项目和为改变生产力布局而进行的全厂性迁建项目,以及行政、事业单位增建业务用房和行政单位增建生活福利设施的项目。

更新改造投资 更新改造是指企业、事业单位对原有设施进行固定资产更新和技术改造,以及相应配套的工程和有关工作(不包括大修理和维护工程)。包括:(1)列入中央和各级地方本年更新改造计划的项目和虽未列入本年更新改造计划,但使用上年更新改造计划内结转的投资在本年继续施工的项目;(2)本年更新改造计划内投资与基本建设计划内投资结合安排的对企、事业单位原有设施进行技术改造或更新的项目,或增建主要生产车间、分厂等新增生产能力(或工程效益)未达到大中型项目标准的项目;(3)国有企、事业单位既未列入基建计划也未列入更新改造计划,总投资在 50 万元以上的属于改建或更新改造性质的项目,以及由于城市环境保护和安全生产的需要而进行的迁建工程。

房地产开发投资 包括各种经济类型的房地产开发公司、商品房建设公司及其他房地产开发单位统一开发的包括统代建、拆迁还建的住宅、厂房、仓库、饭店、宾馆、度假村、写字楼、办公楼等房屋建筑物和配套的服务设施、土地开发工程,如道路、给水、排水、供电、供热、通讯、平整场地等基础设施工程的投资。包括非房地产企业实际从事房地产开发或经营的活动,不包括单纯的土地交易活动。

其他固定资产投资 全社会固定资产投资中未列入基本建设、更新改造和房地产开发投资的建造和购置固定资产的活动。包括:

(1) 国有单位按规定不纳入基本建设计划和更新改造计划管理,总投资在 50 万元以上的以下工程:①用油田维护费和石油开发基金进行的油田维护和开发工程;②煤炭、铁矿、森工等采掘采伐业用维简费进行的开拓延伸工程;③交通部门用公路养路费对原有公路、桥梁进行改建的工程;④商业部门用简易建筑费建造的仓库工程。

(2) 集体经济单位固定资产投资:包括城镇集体经济单位建造和购置固定资产计划总投资在 50 万元以上的项目。农村集体经济单位建造和购置固定资产计划总投资在 5 万元以上的项目。

(3) 联营经济、股份制经济、外商投资经济、港澳台投资经济及其他经济类型的企、事业单位建造和购置固定资产其计划总投资在 50 万元以上的项目投资。

(4) 城镇、工矿区私人建房投资和农村个人投资。城镇、工矿区私人建房包括:市、县城、镇、工矿区所辖范围内的全部私人建房,不论其房主是否系本地的常住户口均应包括。农村个人投资包括农村个人建房及购置生产性固定资产的投资。农村个人固定资产为农村抽样调查总队根据抽样调查资料推算。

固定资产投资资金来源 是指固定资产投资单位在本年内收到的可用于固定资产建造和购置的各种资金。包括上年末结余资金、本年资金来源小计和各项应付款。其中本年资金来源小计又分为国家预算内资金、国内贷款、债券、利用外资、自筹资金和其他资金来源六种：

(1) 国家预算内资金　分为财政拨款和财政安排的贷款两部分。包括中央财政的基本建设基金(分经营性基金和非经营性基金两部分)、专项支出(如煤代油专项等)、收回再贷(指财政安排的贷款收回再贷)、贴息资金、财政安排的挖潜改造和新产品试制支出、城建支出、商业部门简易建筑支出、不发达地区发展基金等资金中用于固定资产投资的资金；地方财政中由国家统筹安排的资金等。

(2) 国内贷款　指报告期固定资产投资单位向银行及非银行金融机构借入的用于固定资产投资的各种国内借款。国内贷款包括：银行利用自有资金及吸收的存款发放的贷款、上级主管部门拨入的国内贷款、国家专项贷款(包括煤代油贷款、劳改煤矿专项贷款等)、地方财政专项资金安排的贷款、国内储备贷款、周转贷款等。

(3) 债券　是企业(公司)或金融机构通过发行各种债券筹集到的用于固定资产投资的资金，包括由银行代理国家专业投资公司发行的重点企业债券和重点建设债券。

(4) 利用外资　指报告期收到的用于固定资产投资的国外资金(含设备、材料、技术在内)，包括外商直接投资、对外借款、外商其他投资。

(5) 自筹资金　指建设单位报告期收到的，用于固定资产投资的预算外资金，包括中央各部门、各级地方和本单位自有资金。

(6) 其他资金来源　指报告期收到的除以上各种拨款、借款、自筹资金之外，其他用于固定资产投资的资金。

固定资产投资按国民经济行业分　建设项目归哪个行业，按其建成投产后的主要产品或主要用途及社会经济活动性质来确定。基本建设按建设项目划分国民经济行业，更新改造、其他固定资产投资及城乡集体单位投资根据整个企业、事业单位所属的行业来划分。一般情况下，一个建设项目或一个企业、事业单位只能属于一种国民经济行业。

固定资产投资按建设性质分　建设项目的性质一般分为新建、扩建、改建、迁建、恢复。基本建设按建设项目划分建设性质，更新改造、其他固定资产投资及城乡集体单位投资按整个企业、事业单位的建设情况确定建设性质。

(1) 新建　一般是指从无到有、“平地起家”新开始建设的单位。有的单位原有的基础很小，经过建设后其新增加的固定资产价值超过原有固定资产价值(原值)三倍以上的也算新建。

(2) 扩建　一般是指为扩大原有产品的生产能力，在厂内或其他地点增建主要生产车间(或主要工程)、独立的生产线或总厂之下的分厂的企业；事业单位和行政单位在原单位增建业务用房(如学校增建教学用房、医院增建门诊部或病床用房、行政机关增建办公楼等)也作为扩建。

(3) 改建　一般是指现有企业、事业单位为了技术进步，提高产品质量，增加花色品种，促进产品升级换代，降低消耗和成本，加强资源综合利用和三废治理、劳保安全等，采用新技术、新工艺、新设备、新材料等对现有设施、工艺条件进行技术改造或更新(包括相应配套的辅助性生产、生活福利设施)。有的企业为充分发挥现有生产能力，进行填平补齐而增建不增加本单位主要产品生产能力的车间等，也属于改建。

固定资产投资按产业分　固定资产投资分为第一产业、第二产业、第三产业和住宅投资四部分，它是研究不同用途的固定资产投资之间比例关系的重要指标。基本建设投资、更新改造投资、房地产开发投资、其他固定资产投资及城乡集体投资的用途按国民经济行业来确定。

固定资产投资按构成分　固定资产投资活动按其工作内容和实现方式分为建筑安装工程，设备、工具、器具购置，其他费用三个部分。

(1) 建筑安装工程(建安工作量)　指各种房屋、建筑物的建造工程和各种设备、装置的安装工程。包括各种房屋建造工程，各种用途设备基础和各种工业窑炉的砌筑工程；为施工而进行的各种准备工作和临时工程以及完工后的清理工作等；铁路、道路的铺设，矿井的开凿及石油管道的架设等；水利工程；防空地下建筑等特殊工程；以及各种机械设备的安装工程；为测定安装工程质量，对设备进行的试行工作。在安装工程中，不包括安装设备本身的价值。

(2) 设备、工具、器具购置　指购置或自制达到固定资产标准的设备、工具、器具的价值，固定资产的标准按财务部门的规定执行。新建单位、扩建单位的新建车间按照设计和计划要求购置或自制的全部设备、工具、器具，不论是否达到固定资产标准均计入“设备、工具、器具购置”中。

(3) 其他费用　指除建筑安装工程和设备、工具、器具购置以外的投资完成额。

基本建设划分大中小型项目　基本建设划分大中小型项目原则上应按照上级批准的设计任务书或初步设计所确定的总规模或总投资划分，没有正式批准设计任务书或初步设计的，按国家或省、自治区、直辖市年度基本建设投资计划中所列的总规模或总投资划分。上述两条均不具备的，按本年计划施工工程的建设总规模或总投资划分。生产单一产品的工业项目，按产品的设计能力划分；生产多种产品的工业项目，按其主要产品的设计能力划分。品种繁多，难以按生产能力划分的，按全部计划投资额划分。划分标准以国家颁发的《大中小型建设项目划分标准》为依据。国家曾在 1958 年、1962 年、1977 年和 1979 年先后五次修订《大中小型建设项目划分标准》，因此各历史时期的大中型项目数不完全可比。

施工项目　指报告期内曾进行建筑或安装工程施工活动的建设项目。包括报告期内新开工项目、报告期以前开工跨入报告期继续施工的项目以及报告期施工过并在报告期内全部建设投产或停缓建的项目。

全部建成投产项目 工业项目是指设计文件规定形成生产能力的主体工程及其相应配套的辅助设施全部建成，经负荷试运转，证明具备生产设计规定合格产品的条件，并经过验收鉴定合格或达到竣工验收标准，与生产性工程配套的生产福利设施可以满足近期正常生产的需要，正式移交生产的建设项目。非工业项目是指设计文件规定的主体工程和相应的配套工程全部建成，能够发挥设计规定的全部效益，经验收鉴定合格或达到竣工验收标准，正式移交使用的建设项目。

新增生产能力 指通过固定资产投资活动而增加的设计能力或工程效益，它是用实物形态表示的固定资产投资的成果。新增生产能力的计算，是以能独立发挥生产能力或效益的单项工程(或项目)为对象。当单项工程(或项目)建成，经有关部门鉴定合格，正式移交投入生产，即可计算新增生产能力。

新增生产能力或工程效益有以下几种表现形式：

(1) 以建设项目或单项工程建成后的年产能力表示。如煤炭开采、石油开采等。

(2) 以建设项目或单项工程建成后处理原料的能力表示。如选矿工程的年处理矿石能力，洗煤厂年洗原煤能力等。

(3) 以新增的主要设备数量或容量表示。如棉纺锭枚数、发电机组容量等。

(4) 以建筑物容积、容量、面积或长度表示。如水库容量、铁路公路里程等。

新增生产能力的数量一般按设计能力计算。设计能力是指设计文件中规定的在正常情况下能够达到的生产能力，而不论投产后的实际产量如何。以设备数量、建筑物容积、面积、长度等表示的新增生产能力(或效益)，则按建成的实际数量计算。

施工和竣工房屋建筑面积 房屋建筑面积是从房屋外墙线算起的各层平面面积的总和，包括房屋结构(如柱、墙)占用的面积和地下室面积。多层建筑按各自然层面积总和计算，包括房屋内的楼隔层，突出墙面的眺望间、门斗、有柱雨罩的面积。不包括突出墙面结构的构件、艺术装饰等所占的面积，如台阶等。凹阳台、挑阳台按其水平投影面积一半计算建筑面积。

住宅建筑面积 指施工和竣工房屋建设面积中供居住用的施工和竣工房屋建筑面积。

竣工面积 指在报告期内房屋建筑按照设计要求已全部完工，达到住人和使用条件，经验收鉴定合格，正式移交使用单位的建筑面积。

房屋建筑面积竣工率 指一定时期内房屋竣工面积占同期房屋施工面积的比率。它是从房屋建筑施工速度的角度反映投资效果和建筑业经济效益的指标。

新增固定资产 指通过投资活动所形成的新的固定资产价值。包括已经建成投入生产或交付使用的工程价值和达到固定资产标准的设备、工具、器具的价值及有关应摊入的费用。它是以价值形式表示的固定资产投资成果的综合性指标，可以综合反映不同时期、不同部门、不同地区的固定资产投资成果。

建设项目投产率 指一定时期内全部建成投入生产项目个数占同期正式施工项目个数的比率。它是从项目建设速度的角度反映投资效果的指标。

固定资产交付使用率 指一定时期新增固定资产与同期完成投资额的比率。它是反映各个时期固定资产动用速度，衡量建设过程中投资效果的一个综合性指标。

未完工程占用率 指年末未完工程累计完成投资额占全年实际完成投资额的比率。它反映未完工程的相对规模，并可从资金占用的角度反映固定资产投资效果。由于未完工程是指已经开工，但尚未建成交付使用的工程存在有跨年度情况，因此未完工程占用率会出现大于1的情况。

零售价格指数 是反映城乡商品零售价格变动趋势的一种经济指数。零售物价的调整变动直接影响到城乡居民的生活支出和国家的财政收入，影响居民购买力和市场供需平衡，影响消费与积累的比例。因此，计算零售价格指数，可以从一个侧面对上述经济活动进行观察和分析。

居民消费价格指数 是反映一定时期内城乡居民所购买的生活消费品价格和服务项目价格变动趋势和程度的相对数。是综合了城市居民消费价格指数和农民消费价格指数计算取得的。利用居民消费价格指数，可以观察和分析消费品的零售价格和服务价格变动对城乡居民实际生活费支出的影响程度。

城市居民消费价格指数 是反映城市居民家庭所购买的生活消费品和服务项目价格变动趋势及其程度的相对数。编制城市居民消费价格指数，可以观察和分析消费品的零售价格和服务项目价格变动对职工货币工资的影响，作为研究城市居民生活和确定工资政策的依据。

农村居民消费价格指数 是反映农村居民家庭所购买的生活消费品的价格和服务项目变动趋势和程度的相对数。用它可以观察农村消费品的零售价格和服务项目价格变动对农村居民生活消费支出的影响，直接反映农民生活水平的实际变化情况，为分析和研究农村居民生活问题提供依据。

农产品收购价格指数 是反映各种经济类型的商业企业和有关部门收购农产品价格的变动趋势和程度的相对数。农产品收购价格指数可以观察和研究农产品收购价格总水平的变化情况，以及对农民货币收入的影响，作为制订和检查农产品价格政策的依据。

农村工业品零售价格指数 是反映农村市场工业品零售价格水平变动趋势和程度的相对数。通过农村工业品零售价格指数,可以观察工业品零售价格变动对农民货币支出的影响。

工业品出厂价格指数 是反映全部工业产品出厂价格总水平的变动趋势和程度的相对数。其中除包括工业企业售给商业、外贸、物资部门的产品外,还包括售给工业和其他部门的生产资料以及直接售给居民的生活消费品。通过工业生产价格指数能观察出厂价格变动对工业总产值的影响。

固定资产投资价格指数 是反映固定资产投资价格变动趋势和程度的相对数。固定资产投资额是由建筑安装工程投资完成额、设备、工器具购置投资完成额和其他费用投资完成额三部分组成的。编制固定资产投资价格指数应首先分别编制上述三部分投资的价格指数,然后采用加权算术平均法求出固定资产投资价格总指数。

编制固定资产投资价格指数可以准确地反映固定资产投资中涉及的各类商品和取费项目价格变动趋势和变动幅度,消除按现价计算的固定资产投资指标中的价格变动因素,真实地反映固定资产投资的规模、速度、结构和效益,为国家科学地制定、检查固定资产投资计划并提高宏观调控水平,为完善国民经济核算体系提供科学的,可靠的依据。

年底自来水生产能力 指年底城建部门管理的自来水厂和自备水源的社会单位取水、净化、送水、出厂输水干管等环节的实际生产能力。

年底供水管道长度 指从送水泵到用户水表之间所有管道的长度。

全年供水总量 指公用自来水厂和自备水源的社会单位全年的供水总量,包括有效供水量及损失水量。

生活用水量 指居民日常生活与公共福利设施的用水量。包括居民、饮食店、旅馆、医院、理发店、浴池、洗衣店、游泳池、商店、学校、机关、部队等单位的用水量。

城市人口用水普及率 指城市用水的非农业人口数(不包括临时人口和流动人口)与城市非农业人口总数之比。计算公式:

$$用水普及率=(城市用水的非农业人口数\div城市非农业人口数)\times 100\%$$

人工煤气生产能力 指城市煤气厂制气、净化、输送等环节的综合实际生产能力。

输气管道长度 指由压缩机、鼓风机、储气罐的出口到用户立管之间的全部管道长度。

全年供气总量 指全年售给各类用户的全部煤气量。包括工业用量、家庭用量和其他用量。

城市用气普及率 指使用煤气(包括人工煤气、液化石油气、天然气)的城市非农业人口数(不包括临时人口和流动人口)与城市非农业人口总数之比。计算公式:

$$城市煤气普及率=\frac{城市用气的非农业人口数}{城市非农业人口总数}\times 100\%$$

年底实有铺装道路长度 指除土路外,路面经过铺装宽度在3.5米以上的道路,包括高级、次高级道路和普通道路。

城市桥梁 指城市范围内,修建在河道上的桥梁和道路与道路立交、道路跨越铁路的立交桥,以及人行天桥。包括永久性桥和半永久性桥,不包括临时性桥、铁路桥、涵洞。

城市下水道总长度 指所有排水总管、干管、支管及暗渠、检查井、连接井进出水口等长度之和。

城市污水日处理能力 指污水处理厂每昼夜处理污水量的设计能力。

年末实有公共汽(电)车 指年底可参加营运的全部车辆数,包括年底营运车辆数和库存查封未参加营运的车辆,不包括非营运车辆,如架线车、油罐车、工程车、货车及其他专用车辆和借人的客运车辆。

营运线路长度 指设置的固定营运线路长度,包括郊区营运线路长度。不包括临时行驶的线路长度。

城市园林绿地面积 指城市公共绿地、专用绿地、生产绿地、防护绿地、郊区风景名胜区的全部面积。

公共绿地 指供游览休息的各种公园、动物园、植物园、陵园以及花园、游园和供游览休息用的林荫道绿地、广场绿地。不包括一般栽植的行道树及林荫道的面积。

农林牧渔业总产值 是以货币表现的农、林、牧、渔业全部产品的总量,它反映一定时期内农业生产总规模和总成果。

农、林、牧、渔业的统计范围包括国有经济的各种专业农(农、林、牧、渔)场以及国家各级机关团体学校、部队;集体所有制的乡、镇、村各级办农场;工矿企业经营的农、林、牧、渔业,农村各种经济组织和农户经营的农林牧渔业和农民家庭兼营的商品性工业等。

(1) 农业 包括种植业和其他农业。

种植业 包括谷物、豆类、薯类、棉花、油料、糖料、麻类、烟叶、蔬菜、药材、瓜类和其他农作物的种植,以及茶园、桑园、果园的生产经营。

其他农业 包括采集野生植物的果实、纤维、树胶、树脂、油料以及柴草、野生药材、菌类等及农民家庭兼营的商品性工业。

(2) 林业　包括林木的栽培(不包括茶园、桑园和果园的栽培、管理和收获等活动)、林产品的采集和村及村以下合作经济和农户的竹木采伐。

(3) 牧业　包括除渔业养殖以外的一切动物饲养和放牧以及野生动物的捕猎和饲养。

(4) 渔业　包括水生动物和海藻类植物的养殖和捕捞。

农林牧渔业总产值的计算方法通常是按农林牧渔业产品及其副产品的产量分别乘以各自单位产品价格求得,少数生产周期较长,当年没有产品或产品产量不易统计的,则采用间接方法匡算其产值,然后将四业产品产值相加即为农林牧渔业总产值。

1957年以前的农业总产值中包括了厩肥和农民自给性手工业(如农民自制衣服、鞋、袜,自己从事粮食初步加工等)。1958年及以后的农业总产值,林业中增加了村及村以下竹木采伐产值;牧业中取消了厩肥产值;副业中取消了农民自给性手工业产值,增加了村及村以下办的工业产值;渔业中增加了海洋捕捞产品产值。1980年及以后的农业总产值,在副业中增加了农民家庭兼营工业商品部分的产值。从1984年起村及村以下办工业产值划归工业。从1993年起,取消副业,将野生动物的捕猎划入牧业,野生植物采集和农民家庭兼营商品性工业划归农业。

粮食产量　指全社会的产量。包括国有经济经营的、集体统一经营的和农民家庭经营的粮食产量,还包括工矿企业办的农场和其他生产单位的产量。粮食除包括稻谷、小麦、玉米、高粱、谷子及其他杂粮外,还包括薯类和豆类。其产量计算方法,豆类按去豆荚后的干豆计算;薯类(包括甘薯和马铃薯,不包括芋头和木薯)1963年以前按每4公斤鲜薯折1公斤粮食计算,从1964年开始及以后改为按5公斤鲜薯折1公斤粮食计算。城市郊区作为蔬菜的薯类(如:马铃薯等)按鲜品计算,并且不做为粮食统计。其他粮食一律按脱粒后的原粮计算。

油料产量　指全部油料作物的生产量。包括花生、油菜籽、芝麻、向日葵籽、胡麻籽(亚麻籽)和其他油料。不包括大豆,也不包括木本油料和野生油料。花生以带壳干花生计算。

水产品产量　指人工养殖的水产品和天然生长的水产品的捕捞量。包括海水的鱼类、虾蟹类、贝类和藻类以及内陆水域的鱼类、虾蟹类和贝类,不包括淡水生植物。

猪、牛、羊肉产量　指当年出栏并已屠宰后除去头蹄下水后带骨肉(即胴体重)的重量。

耕地面积　指年初可以用来种植农作物、经常进行耕锄的田地,除包括熟地、当年新开荒地、连续撂荒未满三年的耕地和当年的休闲地(轮歇地)外,还包括以种植农作物为主并附带种植桑树、茶树、果树和其他林木的土地,以及沿海、沿湖地区已围垦利用的"海涂"、"湖田"等面积。但不包括属于专业性的桑园、茶园、果园、果木苗圃、林地、芦苇地、天然或人工草地面积。

农作物播种面积　指实际播种或移植有农作物的面积。凡是实际种植有农作物的面积,不论种植在耕地上还是种植在非耕地上,均包括在农作物播种面积中。在播种季节基本结束后,因遭灾而重新改种和补种的农作物面积,也包括在内。

有效灌溉面积　指具有一定的水源,地块比较平整,灌溉工程或设备已经配套,在一般年景下当年能够进行正常灌溉的耕地面积。

农用化肥施用量　指本年内实际用于农业生产的化肥数量。包括氮肥、磷肥、钾肥和复合肥。化肥施用量要求按折纯量计算数量。折纯法化肥施用量是把氮肥、磷肥和钾肥分别按含氮、含五氧化二磷、含氧化钾的百分之一百成份折算后的数量。复合肥按其所含主要成分折算。

农业机械总动力　指主要用于农、林、牧、渔业的各种动力机械的动力总和。包括耕作机械、排灌机械、收获机械、农用运输机械、植物保护机械、牧业机械、林业机械、渔业机械和其他农业机械[内燃机按引擎马力折成瓦(特)计算,电动机按功率折成瓦(特)计算]。不包括专门用于乡、镇、村、组办工业、基本建设、非农业运输、科学试验和教学等非农业生产方面用的动力机械与作业机械。

农林牧渔业劳动力　指直接参加农林牧渔业生产劳动的劳动力。

期初(末)畜禽存栏头(只)数　指本期期初(末)农村各种合作经济组织和国营农场、农民个人、机关、团体、学校、工矿企业、部队等单位以及城镇居民饲养的大牲畜、猪、羊、家食等畜禽的存栏头(只)数。

谷物　指籽实主要供作粮食的作物。这类作物包括稻谷、小麦、玉米、谷子、高粱和其他谷物,不包括豆类和薯类作物。

工业　指从事自然资源的开采,对采掘品和农产品进行加工和再加工的物质生产部门。具体包括:(1)对自然资源的开采,对采矿、晒盐、森林采伐等(但不包括禽兽捕猎和水产捕捞);(2)对农副产品的加工、再加工,如粮油加工、食品加工、轧花、缫丝、纺织、制革等;(3)对采掘品的加工、再加工,如炼铁、炼钢、化工生产、石油加工、机器制造、木材加工等,以及电力、自来水、煤气的生产和供应等;(4)对工业品的修理、翻新,如机器设备的修理、交通运输工具(包括小卧车)的修理等。

1984年以前农村的村及村以下办工业归属农业,1984年以后划归工业。

工业统计调查单位　工业统计调查单位分为两类:独立核算法人工业企业和工业活动单位。

(1) 独立核算法人工业企业　是指从事工业生产经营活动的单位。独立核算法人工业企业应同时具备以下条件:

①依法成立，有自己的名称、组织机构和场所，能够承担民事责任；②独立拥有和使用资产，承担负债，有权与其他单位签订合同；③独立核算盈亏，并能够编制资产负债表。

(2) 工业活动单位　是指在一个场所从事一种或主要从事一种工业生产活动的经济单位。它包括独立核算工业企业按主营业务活动(即工业生产活动)划分的主营业务活动单位和非工业企业所属的工业生产活动单位(即原非独立核算工业生产单位)。工业活动单位，一般应同时具备以下三个条件：①具有一个场所，从事一种或主要从事一种工业活动；②单独组织工业生产、经营或业务活动；③单独核算收入和支出。

限额以上工业统计调查单位　是指全部国有及年产品销售收入 500 万元及以上的非国有工业企业。

轻工业　指主要提供生活消费品和制作手工工具的工业。按其所使用的原料不同，可分为两大类：(1) 以农产品为原料的轻工业，是指直接或间接以农产品为基本原料的轻工业。主要包括食品制造、饮料制造、烟草加工、纺织、缝纫、皮革和毛皮制作、造纸以及印刷等工业；(2) 以非农产品为原料的轻工业，是指以工业品为原料的轻工业。主要包括文教体育用品、化学药品制造、合成纤维制造、日用化学制品、日用玻璃制品、日用金属制品、手工工具制造、医疗器械制造、文化和办公用机械制造等工业。

重工业　是指为国民经济各部门提供物质技术基础的主要生产资料的工业。按其生产性质和产品用途，可以分为下列三类：(1)采掘(伐)工业，是指对自然资源的开采，包括石油开采、煤炭开采、非金属矿开采和木材采伐等工业；(2)原材料工业，指向国民经济各部门提供基本材料、动力和燃料的工业。包括金属冶炼及加工、炼焦及焦炭化学、化工原料、水泥、人造板以及电力、石油和煤炭加工等工业；(3)加工工业，是指对工业原材料进行再加工制造的工业。包括装备国民经济各部门的机械设备制造工业、金属结构、水泥制品等工业，以及为农业提供的生产资料如化肥、农药等工业。

根据上述划分原则，修理业中以重工业产品为修理作业对象的划为重工业，反之划为轻工业。

工业总产值　是以货币表现的工业企业在一定时期内生产的已出售或可供出售工业产品总量，它反映一定时间内工业生产的总规模和总水平。它包括：在本企业内不再进行加工，经检验、包装入库(规定不需包装的产品除外)的成品价值，对外有工费收入，自制半成品、在产品期末期初差额价值。工业总产值采用“工厂法”计算，即以工业企业作为一个整体，按企业工业生产活动的最终成果来计算，企业内部不允许重复计算，不能把企业内部各个车间(分厂)生产的成果相加。但在企业之间、行业之间、地区之间存在着重复计算。

轻重工业总产值的划分也是按“工厂法”计算的，即一个工业企业在正常情况下生产的主要产品的性质属于轻工业，则该企业的全部总产值作为轻工业总产值；一个工业企业生产的主要产品的性质属于重工业，则该企业的全部总产值作为重工业总产值。

工业增加值　是指工业行业在报告期内以货币表现的工业生产活动的最终成果。

固定资产原价　固定资产原价指企业在建造、购置、安装、改建、扩建、技术改造某项固定资产时所支出的全部货币总额。它一般包括买价、包装费、运杂费和安装费等。

固定资产净值　是指固定资产原价减去历年已提折旧额后的净额。

流动资产　流动资产是指可以在一年或者超过一年的一个营业周期内变现或者耗用的资产，包括现金及各种存款、短期投资、应收及预付货款、存货等。

利税总额　指企业利润总额、产品销售税金及附加和应交增值税之和。

资产利税率　指在一定时期内已实现的利润、税金总额与同期的资产(固定资产净值和流动资产)之比。计算公式：

$$资产利税率(\%)=\frac{报告期累计实现利税总额}{固定资产净值平均余额+流动资产平均余额}\times 100\%$$

资金利税率反映每单位(通常是每万元)资金所提供的利润税金额。它是考察和评价部门或企业资金运用的经济效益，分析资金投入效果的主要分析指标。

工业成本费用利润率　指在一定时期内实现的利润与成本费用之比，是反映工业生产成本及费用投入的经济效益指标，同时也是反映降低成本的经济效益的指标。计算公式：

$$工业成本费用利润率(\%)=\frac{利润总额}{成本费用总额}\times 100\%$$

工业增加值率　指在一定时期内工业增加值占同期工业总产值的比重，反映降低中间消耗的经济效益。计算公式：

$$工业增加值率(\%)=\frac{工业增加值(现价)}{工业总产值(现价)+销项税额}\times 100\%$$

流动资产周转次数　指在一定时期内流动资产完成的周转次数，反映流动资产的周转速度。计算公式：

$$流动资产周转次数=\frac{产品销售收入}{全部流动资产平均余额}$$

产品销售率 指一定时期内销售产值与同期全部工业总产值之比，反映工业产品生产已实现销售的程度。计算公式：

$$工业产品销售率(\%)=\frac{报告期现价工业销售产值}{报告期现价工业总产值}\times 100\%$$

产品销售收入 指企业销售产品的销售收入和提供劳务等主要经营业务取得的业务总额。

产品销售成本 指企业销售产品和提供劳务等主要经营业务的实际成本。

产品销售税金及附加 指企业销售产品和提供工业性劳务等主要经营业务应负担的城市维护建设税、消费税、资源税和教育费附加。

产品销售利润 指企业销售产品和提供工业性劳务等主要经营业务收入扣除其成本、费用、税金后的利润。

利润总额 指企业实现的利润。

应交增值税 指企业在报告期内应交纳的增值税额。

产值利税率 指报告期已实现的利润、税金总额（包括利润总额、产品销售税金及附加和应交增值税）占同期全部工业总产值的百分比，计算公式为：

$$产值利税率(\%)=\frac{利税总额}{工业总产值}\times 100\%$$

全员劳动生产率 指根据产品的价值量指标计算的平均每一个职工在单位时间内的产品生产量。是考核企业经济活动的重要指标，是企业生产技术水平、经营管理水平、职工技术熟练程度和劳动积极性的综合表现。目前我国的全员劳动生产率是将工业企业的工业增加值除以同一时期全部职工的平均人数来计算的。计算公式：

$$全员劳动生产率=\frac{工业增加值}{全部职工平均人数}$$

为了使各年度的全员劳动生产率数字可以比较，1990 年以前各年的全员劳动生产率均按指数换算成 1990 年不变价格。

实收资本 指企业实际收到投资者投入企业的可作为长期周转使用的主要经营资本，包括国家资本、法人资本、集体资本、个人资本和外资资本。

总资产 指企业拥有或控制的全部资产。包括流动资产、长期投资、固定资产、无形及递延资产、其他长期资产、递延税项等，即为企业资产负债表的资产总计项。

(1) 流动资产 指企业可以在一年内或者超过一年的一个生产周期内变现或耗用的资产合计。包括现金及各种存款、短期投资、应收及预付款项、存货等。

(2) 固定资产 指企业固定资产净值、固定资产清理、在建工程、待处理固定资产损失所占用的资金合计。

(3) 无形资产 指企业长期使用而没有实物形态的资产。包括专利权、非专利技术、商标权、著作权、土地使用权、商誉等。

总负债 指企业承担并需要偿还的全部债务。包括流动负债和长期负债、递延税项等，即为企业资产负债表的负债合计项。

(1) 流动负债 指企业在一年内或者超过一年的一个营业周期内需要偿还的债务合计，其中包括短期借款、应付及预收款项、应付工资、应交税金和应交利润等。

(2) 长期负债 指企业在一年以上或者超过一年的一个生产周期以上需要偿还的债务合计，其中包括长期借款、应付债务、长期应付款项等。

所有者权益 指企业投资人对企业净资产的所有权。企业净资产等于企业全部资产减去全部负债后的余额，其中包括投资者对企业的最初投入，以及资本公积金、盈余公积金和未分配利润，对股份制企业即为股东权益。

建筑业统计单位 指从事房屋、构筑物建造和设备安装活动的生产单位。根据不同的组织方式，建筑业统计的调查单位可分为法人建筑业企业和附营建筑施工单位。法人建筑业企业是指专门组织的独立核算的法人建筑业企业。它应同时具备的条件是：①依法成立，有自己的名称、组织机构和场所，能够承担民事责任；②独立拥有和使用资产，承担负债,有权与其他单位签订合同;③独立核算盈亏,能够编制资产负债表。附营建筑施工单位是指建筑业以外行业的企业、事业单位为完成本单位固定资产建造任务而自行组织的建筑施工单位。它应同时具备的条件是:①具有一个场所,从事或主要从事建筑安装活动;②单独组织生产经营活动;③在企业内部单独核算收支。

建筑业总产值(即自行完成施工产值) 指建筑业企业或附营建筑施工单位自行完成的按工程进度计算的建筑安装生产总值。建筑业总产值包括:

① 建筑工程产值:指列入建筑工程预算内的各种工程价值。

② 设备安装工程产值:指设备安装工程价值。

③ 房屋、构筑物修理产值:指房屋、构筑物修理所完成的价值,但不包括被修理房屋、构筑物本身的价值和生产设备的修理价值。

④ 非标准设备制造产值:指加工制造没有定型的、非标准的生产设备的加工费和原材料价值,不论是现场还是附属加工厂为本单位承建工程制造的非标准设备的价值,都应计算产值。

建筑业增加值 指建筑业企业在报告期内以货币表现的建筑业生产经营活动的最终成果。目前建筑业增加值采用分配法计算,即从收入的角度出发,根据生产要素在生产过程中应得的收入份额计算。具体计算公式为:

建筑业增加值=本年提取的固定资产折旧+应付工资+应付福利费+管理费用中的劳动待业保险金、税金+工程结算税金及附加+工程结算利润-转作奖金的利润。

房屋建筑施工面积 指在报告期内施工的全部房屋建筑面积。包括本期内新开工的、上期施工跨入本期继续施工、上期停建本期复工的房屋建筑面积;不包括上期开工后又停工,本期未施工的房屋建筑面积。

房屋建筑竣工面积 指在报告期内,按照设计所规定的工程内容全部完成,达到了设计规定的交工条件,经有关部门检查验收鉴定合格的房屋建筑面积。

自有机械设备年末总台数 指归本企业(或单位)所有,属于本企业固定资产的生产性机械设备年末总台数。包括施工机械、生产设备、运输设备以及其他设备。

自有机械设备年末总功率 指本企业(或单位)自有施工机械、生产设备、运输设备以及其他设备等列为在册固定资产的生产性机械设备年末总功率,按设计能力或查定能力计算。包括机械本身的动力和为该机械服务的单独动力设备,如电动机等。计算单位用千瓦,动力换算可按1马力=0.735千瓦折合成千瓦数。电焊机、变压器、锅炉不计算动力。

工程结算收入 指企业(或单位)按工程的分部分项自行完成的建筑产品价值并已与甲方在报告期内办理结算手续的工程价款收入,以及向甲方收取的除工程价款以外的按规定列作营业收入的各种款项,如临时设施费、劳动保险费、施工机械调迁费等以及向甲方收取的各种索赔款。

工程结算利润 指已结算工程实现的利润。如为亏损以"-"号表示。其计算公式为:

$$工程结算利润=工程结算收入-工程算成本-工程结算税金及附加$$

企业总收入 指与企业生产经营直接有关的各项收入,包括工程结算收入和其他业务收入,即:

$$企业总收入=工程结算收入+其他业务收入$$

铁路营业里程 又称营业长度,指办理客货运输业务的铁路正线总长度。凡是全线或部分建成双线及以上的线路,以第一线的实际长度计算;复线、站线、段管线、岔线和特殊用途线以及不计算运费的联络线都不计算营业里程。铁路营业里程是反映铁路运输业基础设施发展水平的重要指标,也是计算客货周转量、运输密度和机车车辆运用效率等指标的基础资料。

铁路正线延展里程 是正线第一线、第二线、第三线和其他正线建筑里程之和,不包括站线、段管线、岔线及特殊用途线的延展里程。它是作为计算铁路线上钢轨、枕木及路基砂石需要量的主要依据。

公路里程 指在一定时期内实际达到《公路工程技术标准 JTJ01—88》规定的等级公路,并经公路主管部门正式验收交付使用的公路里程数。其计算单位为:km。它包括大中城市的郊区公路以及通过小城镇街道部分的公路里程,也包括桥梁、渡口的长度,但不包括大中城市的街道、厂矿、林区生产用道和农业生产用道的里程。两条或多条公路共同经由同一路段,只计算一次,不得重复计算里程长度。公路里程是反映公路建设发展规模的重要指标,也是计算运输网密度等指标的基础资料。

内河航道里程 也称"内河通航里程",是反映内河水运网规模、水平和发展情况的主要指标;是指在一定时期内,能通航运输船舶及排筏的天然河流、湖泊水库、运河及通航渠道的长度。包括全年季节性通航累计三个月以上的航道,但不包括仅供零散流放竹、木排的河道。

民用航空航线里程 指民航运输定期班机飞行的航线长度的总和。航线长度按机场之间的距离计算,通常有两种计算方法:将每条航线长度相加称为重复计算航线里程;如将两线或两条以上航线经过同一区段里程,只计算一次航线长度称为不重复计算航线里程。一般常用的是后者,它能确切反映民航运输网的规模,表明民航事业为国民经济服务和方便人民生活程度的主要指标。

输油(气)管道长度 也称"输油(气)里程",是反映管道运输发展规模和水平的主要指标;是指油品(或天然气)的实际输送距离,一般按输油(气)管道的单线长度计算。若包括复线和备用线长度则称为输油(气)管道延展长度,是指管道铺设的实际长度。我们通常使用的是不包括复线的"输油(气)管道里程"。

货(客)运量 指在一定时期内,各种运输工具实际运送的货物(旅客)数量。是反映运输业为国民经济和人民生活服务的数量指标,也是制定和检查运输生产计划,研究运输发展规模和速度的重要指标。货运按吨计算,客运按人计算。货物不论运输距离长短,货物类别,均按实际重量统计;旅客不论行程远近或票价多少,均按一人一次作为客运量统计。半价票、小孩票也按一人统计。

货物(旅客)周转量 指在一定时期内,由各种运输工具运送的货物(旅客)数量与其相应运输距离的乘积之总和,是反映运输业生产总成果的重要指标,也是编制和检查运输生产计划,计算运输效率、劳动生产率以及核算运输单位成本的主要基础资料。通常以吨公里和人公里为计算单位。计算货物周转量通常按发出站与到达站之间的最短距离,也就是计费距离计算。

沿海主要港口货物吞吐量 指由水运进出沿海主要港区范围,并经过装卸的货物数量,包括邮件及办理托运手续的行李、包裹以及补给运输船舶的燃、物料和淡水。其计量单位为吨。货物吞吐量的货种分类及其主要流向流量,反映了港口在国内外物资交流和对外贸易运输中的地位和作用。吞吐量可以分为进口、出口,又可以分为国内贸易和对外贸易。

邮电业务总量 指以货币表现的邮电部门用于传递信息和提供其他邮电服务的总数量。它综合反映了一定时期邮电工作的总成果,是研究邮电业务量构成和发展趋势的重要指标。根据邮电管理体制不同,分为中央国营业务总量和地方国营业务总量。它用各种邮电分类业务量,如函件件数、电报份数、长话张数、市内电话和农村电话的年均户数、订销报刊累计份数等,分别乘以相应的平均单价(不变价),加总后再加上出租电路和设备的收入、代用户维护电话交换机和线路等设备的收入、其他业务收入求得。

市内电话 指接入县城(包括个别城镇)及县以上城市的市内电话网上,并按市内电话进行经营管理的电话。按计费办法分为包月制和计次制两种。

(1) 住宅电话 指话机装在居民住宅里的电话。它包括私人付费、公费和免费三个部分。

(2) 私人付费电话 指住宅居民自费安装并自己缴纳通话费的电话。

无线寻呼电话用户 指携带小型寻呼机,接收市话用户通过无线寻呼中心,在规定范围内向其发出声音、数字或文字显示信息的用户。目前在邮电部门办理登记手续的无线寻呼电话用户,每一部寻呼机按一户计算。

移动电话用户 指在邮电部门登记,通过移动电话交换机进入移动电话网、占有移动电话号码的电话用户。用户数量以实际办理登记手续进入邮电部门移动电话网的户数进行计算,一部或一台移动电话统计为一户。

社会消费品零售总额 指各种经济类型的批发零售贸易业、餐饮业、制造业和其他行业对城乡居民和社会集团的消费品零售额和农民对非农业居民零售额的总和。这个指标反映通过各种商品流通渠道向居民和社会集团供应生活消费品来满足他们生活需要的情况,是研究人民生活、社会消费品购买力、货币流通等问题的重要指标。包括售给城乡居民用于生活消费的商品(不包括住房)和售给机关、团体、部队、学校、企业、事业单位和城市街道居民委员会、农村村民委员会用公款购买的用作非生产、非经营使用的消费品。

批发零售贸易业商品购、销、存总额 指以各种经济类型的批发、零售贸易业(不包括个体)为总体的商品购进、销售、库存总额。

商品购进总额 指从本企业(单位)以外的单位和个人购进(包括从国外直接进口)作为转卖或加工后转卖的商品。这个指标反映批发零售贸易业从国内、国外市场上购进商品的总量。商品购进总额包括:(1) 从工农业生产者购进的商品;(2) 从出版社、报社的出版发行部门购进的图书、杂志和报纸;(3) 从各种经济类型的批发零售贸易企业(单位)购进的商品;(4) 从其他单位购进的商品,如从机关、团体、企业、单位购进的剩余物资,从餐饮业、服务业购进的商品,从海关、市场管理部门购进的缉私和没收的商品,向居民收购的废旧商品等;(5) 从国(境)外直接进口的商品。不包括企业(单位)为自身经营用,和未通过买卖行为而收入的商品以及销售退回、商品升溢等。

商品销售总额 指对本企业(单位)以外的单位和个人出售(包括对国(境)外直接出口)的商品。这个指标反映批发零售贸易业在国内市场上销售商品以及出口商品的总量。商品销售总额包括:(1) 售给城乡居民和社会集团消费用的商品;(2) 售给工业、农业、建筑业、运输邮电业、批发零售贸易业、餐饮业、服务业等作为生产、经营使用的商品;(3) 售给批发零售贸易业作为转卖或加工后转卖的商品;(4) 对国(境)外直接出口的商品。不包括:出售本企业(单位)自用的废旧包装用品;未通过买卖行为付出的商品;经本单位介绍,由买卖双方直接结算,本单位只收取手续费的业务;购货退出的商品以及商品损耗和损失等。

批发零售贸易业年末库存 指年末各种经济类型的批发零售贸易企业(单位)已取得所有权的商品。它反映批发零售贸易业的商品库存情况及对市场商品供应的保证程度。包括:(1) 存放在批发零售贸易业经营单位(如门市部、批发站、经营处)仓库、货场、货柜和货架中的商品;(2) 挑选、整理、包装中的商品;(3) 已记入购进而尚未运到本单位的商品;(4) 寄放他处的商品,如因购货方拒绝承付而暂时存放在购货方的商品和已办完加工成品收回手续而未提回的商品;(5) 委托其他单位代销(未作销售或调出)尚未售出的商品;(6) 代其他单位购进尚未交付的商品。不包括所有权不属于本单位的商品、拨付除批发零售贸易业以外的其他行业加工厂加工生产尚未收回成品的商品、代国家物资储备部门保管的商品等。期末库存总额计算方法是:农副产品采购单位按购进价计算,批发单位按进货价计算,零售单位按什么价格核算就按什么价格计算。

批发零售贸易业、餐饮业网点 指各种经济类型的批发零售贸易业、餐饮业企业设立的和其他各行业附设的从事批发零售贸易、餐饮业务的自然单位数。

批发零售贸易业、餐饮业人员 指从事批发零售贸易业、餐饮业劳动并取得劳动报酬或经营收入的人员。

进出口总额 海关进出口总额指实际进出我国国境的货物总金额。包括对外贸易实际进出口货物,来料加工装配进出口货物,国家间、联合国及国际组织无偿援助物资和赠送品,华侨、港澳台同胞和外籍华人捐赠品,租赁期满归承租人所有的租赁货物,进料加工进出口货物,边境地方贸易及边境地区小额贸易进出口货物(边民互市贸易除外),中外合资经营企业、中外合作经营企业、外商独资经营企业进出口货物和公用物品,到、离岸价格在规定限额以上的进出口货样和广告品(无商业价值、无使用价值和免费提供出口的除外),从保税仓库提取在中国境内销售的进口货物以及其他进出口货物。进出口总额用以观察一个国家在对外贸易方面的总规模。我国规定出口货物按离岸价格统计,进口货物按到岸价格统计。

商品经营单位所在地进出口额 指所在地海关注册登记的有进出口经营权企业实际进出口额。

商品目的地进口额和商品货源地出口额 目的地进口额是指进口货物的消费、使用或最终抵运地的实际进口额,货源地出口额 是指出口货物的产地或原始发货地的实际出口额。

利用外资 指我国各级政府、部门、企业和其他经济组织通过对外借款、吸收外商直接投资以及用其他方式筹措的境外现汇、设备、技术等。

对外借款 是我国利用外资的主要部分。包括我国通过外国政府贷款,国际金融组织贷款,外国银行商业贷款,出口信贷以及对外发行债券,股票等方式,从境外筹措的资金。

外商直接投资 是指外国企业和经济组织或个人(包括华侨、港澳台胞以及我国在境外注册的企业)按我国有关政策、法规,用现汇、实物、技术等在我国境内开办外商独资企业、与我国境内的企业或经济组织共同举办中外合资经营企业、合作经营企业或作合作开发资源的投资(包括外商投资效率的再投资)以及经政府有关部门批准的项目投资总额内,企业从境外借入的资金。

对外承包工程 包括各对外承包公司以招标议标承包方式承揽的下列业务(1) 承包国外工程建设项目;(2) 承包我国对外经援项目;(3) 承包我国驻外机构的工程建设项目;(4) 承包我国境内利用外资进行建设的工程项目;(5) 与外国承包公司合营或联合承包工程项目时我国公司分包部分;(6) 以服务成果向业主收费的技术服务项目(包括承担地形地貌测绘;地质资源勘探与普查;建设区域规划;提供设计文件、图纸、生产工艺技术资料和工程技术经济咨询;工程项目的可行性考察、研究和评估;进行技术指导和培训人员等);(7) 对外承包兼营的房屋开发业务。对外承包工程的营业额是以货币表现的本期内完成的对外承包工程的工作量,包括以前年度签订的合同和本年度新签订的合同在报告期完成的工作量。

对外劳务合作 指以收取工资的形式向业主或承包商提供技术和劳动服务的活动。我国对外承包公司在境外开办的合营企业,中国公司同时又提供劳务的,其劳务部分也纳入劳务合作统计。劳务合作营业额按报告期内向雇主提交的结算数(包括工资、加班费和奖金等)统计。

旅游人数 指来我国参观、访问、旅行、探亲、访友、休养、考察、参加会议和从事经济、科技、文化、教育、体育、宗教等活动的外国人、华侨、港澳和台湾同胞的人数。不包括外国在我国的常住机构,如使领馆、通讯社、企业办事处的工作人员;来我国常驻的外国专家、留学生以及在岸逗留不过夜人员。

国际旅游(外汇)收入 指入境旅游的外国人、华侨、港澳台同胞在中国大陆旅游过程中发生的一切旅游支出,对于国家来说就是国际旅游(外汇)收入。

财政收入 国家财政参与社会产品分配所取得的收入,是实现国家职能的财力保证。财政收入所包括的内容几经变化,目前主要包括:(1) 各项税收 包括增值税、营业税、消费税、土地增值税、城市维护建设税、资源税、城市土地使用税、印花税、固定资产投资方向调节税、个人所得税、企业所得税、关税、农牧业税和耕地占用税等。

(2) 专项收入 包括征收排污费、征收城市水资源费收入,教育费附加收入等。

(3) 其他收入 包括基本建设贷款归还收入、国家能源交通重点建设基金收入、国家预算调节基金等。

(4) 国有企业计划亏损补贴 这项为负收入,冲减财政收入。

财政支出 国家财政将筹集起来的资金进行分配使用,以满足经济建设和各项事业的需要,主要包括:

(1) 基本建设支出 指按国家有关规定,属于基本建设范围内的基本建设有偿使用、拨款、资本金支出以及经国家批准对专项和政策性基建投资贷款，在部门的基建投资额中统筹支付的贴息支出。

(2) 企业挖潜改造资金　指国家预算内拨给的用于企业挖潜、革新和改造方面的资金。包括各部门企业挖潜改造资金和企业挖潜改造贷款资金，为农业服务的县办“五小”企业技术改造补助，挖潜改造贷款利息支出。

(3) 地质勘探费用　国家预算用于地质勘探单位的勘探工作费用，包括地质勘探管理机构及其事业单位经费、地质勘探经费。

(4) 科技三项费用　国家预算用于科技支出的费用，包括新产品试制费、中间试验费、重要科学研究补助费。

(5) 支援农村生产支出　国家财政支援农村集体(户)各项生产的支出。包括对农村举办的小型农田水利和打井、喷灌等的补助费；对农村水土保持措施的补助费；对农村举办的小水电站的补助费；特大抗旱的补助费；农村开荒补助费；扶持乡镇企业资金；农村农技推广和植保补助费；农村草场和畜禽保护补助费；农村造林和林木保护补助费；农村水产补助费；发展粮食生产专项资金。

(6) 农林水利气象等部门的事业费用　国家财政用于农垦、农场、农业、畜牧、农机、林业、森工、水利、水产、气象、乡镇企业的技术推广、良种推广(示范)、植物(畜禽、森林)保护、水质监测、勘探设计、资源调查、干部训练等项费用，园艺特产场补助费，中等专业学校经费，飞播牧草试验补助费，营林机构、气象机构经费，渔政费以及农业管理事业费等。

(7) 工业交通商业等部门的事业费　国家预算支付给工交商各部门用于事业发展的经费。包括勘探设计费、中等专业学校经费、技术学校经费、干部训练费。

(8) 文教科学卫生事业费　国家预算用于文化、出版、文物、教育、卫生、中医、公费医疗、体育、档案、地震、海洋、通讯、电影电视、计划生育、党政群干部训练、自然科学、社会科学、科协等项事业的经费支出和高技术研究专项经费。主要包括工资、补助工资、福利费、离退休费、助学金、公务费、设备购置费、修缮费、业务费、差额补助费。

(9) 抚恤和社会福利救济费　国家预算用于抚恤和社会福利救济事业的经费，包括由民政部门开支的烈士家属和牺牲病残人员家属的一次性、定期抚恤金，革命伤残人员的抚恤金，各种伤残补助费、烈军属、复员退伍军人生活补助费、退伍军人安置费，优抚事业单位经费，烈士纪念建筑物管理、维修费，自然灾害救济事业费和特大自然灾害灾后重建补助费等。

(10) 国防支出　国家预算用于国防建设和保卫国家安全的支出，包括国防费、国防科研事业费、民兵建设以及专项工程支出等。

(11) 行政管理费　包括行政管理支出，党派团体补助支出，外交支出，公安安全支出，司法支出，法院支出，检察院支出和公检法办案费用补助。

(12) 价格补贴支出　经国家批准，由国家财政拨给的政策性补贴支出，主要包括粮食加价款，粮、棉、油差价补贴，棉花收购价外奖励款，副食品风险基金，市镇居民的肉食价格补贴，平抑市价肉食、蔬菜价差补贴等以及经国家批准的教材课本、报刊新闻纸等价格补贴。

中央财政收入和地方财政收入　按财政体制划分的中央本级收入和地方本级收入。1994 年分税制财政体制以后，属于中央财政的收入包括关税、海关代征消费税和增值税，中央企业所得税，地方银行和外资银行及非银行金融企业所得税，铁道、银行总行、保险总公司等集中缴纳的营业税、所得税、利润和城市维护建设税，增值税的 75% 部分，海洋石油资源税和证券(印花)税 88% 部分。属于地方财政的收入包括营业税，地方企业所得税，个人所得税，城镇土地使用税，固定资产投资方向调节税，城镇维护建设税，房产税，车船使用税，印花税，屠宰税，农牧业税，农业特产税，耕地占用税，契税，增值税 25% 部分，证券交易税(印花税)的 12% 部分和除海洋石油资源税以外的其他资源税。

存款　企业、机关、团体或居民根据可以收回的原则，把货币资金存入银行或其他信用机构保管并取得一定利息的一种信用活动形式。根据存款对象的不同可划分为企业存款、财政存款、机关团体存款、基本建设存款、城镇储蓄存款、农村存款等科目。它是银行信贷资金的主要来源。

贷款　银行或其他信用机构根据必须归还的原则，按一定利率，为企业、个人等提供资金的一种信用活动形式。我国银行贷款分为流动资金贷款、固定资产贷款、城乡个体工商户贷款以及农业贷款等科目。

承保额　又叫保险金额。它是保险人员对被保险人负提损失补偿或约定给付的金额。它是保险合同上的最高责任额，也是计算保费的依据。

保费　又叫保险费。是保险人根据保险合同的有关规定，为被保险人取得因约定危险事故发生所造成的经济损失补偿(或给付)权利，付给保险人的代价。包括财产险和人身险储金收入。

赔款　保险事故发生后，经查证确属保险责任范围以内的保险标的损失，保险人根据保险合同的规定履行赔偿义务，给予被保险人的款项叫做赔款。赔款可分为已决赔款和未决赔款两种。

普通高等学校　指按照国家规定的设置标准和审批程序批准举办，通过国家统一招生考试，招收高中毕业生为主要培养对象，实施高等教育的全日制大学、独立设置的学院和高等专科学校、短期职业大学。

成人高等学校　指按照国家有关规定审批，招收通过全国成人高教统一招生考试的具有高中毕业或同等学历的在职从业人员利用脱产、半脱产、业余或函授等多种形式对其实施高等学历教育，培养高等教育专科或本科毕业水平的专门人才，修业年限、课程设置和总学时数均按高等学历教育要求付诸实施的学校。包括广播电视大学、职工高等学校、农民高等学校、管理干部学院、教育学院、独立设置的函授学院等。

小学学龄儿童入学率 指调查范围内已入小学学习的学龄儿童占校内外学龄儿童总数(包括弱智儿童在内,但不包括盲聋哑儿童)的比重。计算公式:

$$小学学龄儿童入学率=\frac{已入学的小学学龄儿童数}{校内外小学学龄儿童总数}\times 100\%$$

独立研究与开发机构 指有明确的任务和研究方向,有一定学术水平的业务骨干和一定数量的研究人员,具有研究、开发、开展学术工作的基本条件,主要进行科学研究与技术开发活动,并且在行政上有独立的组织形式,财务上独立核算盈亏,有权与其他单位签订合同,在银行有单独户头的单位。包括国务院各部门、中国科学院、中国社会科学院和各省、自治区、直辖市以及地(市)以上[含地(市)]各部门所属的国有独立的科学研究与技术开发机构。

独立研究与开发机构职工 指在科学研究与技术开发机构工作,并由其支付工资的各种人员。包括长期职工和临时职工,不包括编制以外的离休、退休人员和停薪留职人员,但包括招聘人员。

研究与发展经费支出 指报告期内用于研究与实验发展课题活动(基础研究、应用研究、实验发展)的全部实际支出。包括用于研究与发展课题活动的直接支出,还包括间接用于研究与发展活动的一切支出(院、所管理费、维持院、所正常运转的必需费用和与研究发展有关的基本建设支出)。

科学家和工程师 指具有大学本科及以上学历的和不具备上述学历但有高、中级职称的人员。

其他科技人员 指大专、中专毕业和具有初级职称的从事科技活动人员。

专业技术人员 指已取得科学技术职称,或大学、中专的理、工、农、医科系毕业,以及国民经济各部门从工作实践中提拔,从事理、工、农、医等自然科学技术的研究、教学、生产的专业人员和在机关、企业、事业中从事科学技术业务管理工作的专业人员。

工程技术人员 指在国民经济各行业从事工程技术工作的自然科学技术专业人员,包括:高级工程师、工程师、助理工程师、技术员和未评定职称的技术人员。

农业技术人员 指在国民经济各行业从事农业技术工作的自然科学技术专业人员,包括:高级农艺师、农艺师、助理农艺师、技术员和未评定职称的技术人员。

卫生技术人员 指在国民经济各行业从事卫生医务工作的自然科学技术专业人员,包括:正副主任医师、主治医师、医师、医(护)士和未评定职称的技术人员。

科学研究人员 指在国民经济各行业从事科学技术活动的自然科学技术专业人员,包括:正副研究员、助理研究员、研究实习员、技术员和未评定职称的技术人员。

自然科学教学人员 指在国民经济各行业从事自然科学技术方面教学活动的专业人员,包括:正副教授、讲师、助教、教师和在中学人事自然科学技术方面教学活动的人员。

发明 专利法及其实施细则所称的发明,指对有关产品、方法或其改进所提出的新的技术方案。

实用新型 指专利法及其实施细则所称的实用新型,指对产品的形状、构造或者其结合所提出的适于实用的新的技术方案。

文化事业机构 指从事专业文化工作和为专业文化工作服务的独立建制的单独核算的单位。不包括这些单位另外举办独立核算的其他机构和各部门的业余文化组织。

艺术表演团体 指从事戏曲、音乐、舞蹈、杂技等专业艺术表演,有独立帐户,实行单独核算的团体。不包括半工半艺、半农半艺和民间职业剧团。

电影放映单位 指具有放映机器设备、固定或不固定的放映场所与专职与兼职的放映技术人员,经有关部门登记批准,经常为一定的观众对象放映电影的机构。包括批准对外开放进行营业,并与电影发行放映管理机构分帐的专用放映单位和军委系统租片单位。

艺术表演观众人数(人次) 指售票、包场演出或民族地区免费演出的艺术表演观众人次数。不包括彩排审查和内部观摩演出的观看人次数。

医院 指名称为医院,设有固定床位能收容病人住院并能为病人提供医疗、护理服务的医疗机构。包括县及县以上医院、农村乡卫生院、其他医院三部分。按所属性质分为卫生部门、工业及其他部门,集体经济单位三类。其中县及县以上医院按业务性质分为综合医院和专科医院。

卫生技术人员 指卫生事业机构支付工资的全部固定职工和合同制职工中现任职务为卫生技术工作的专业人员。包括中医师、西医师、中西医结合高级医师、护师、中药师、西药师、检验师、其他技师、中医士、西医士、护士、助产士、中药剂士、西药剂士、检验士、其他技士、其他中医、护理员、中药剂员、西药剂员、检验员,其他初级卫生技术人员。

医生 指经卫生部门审查合格,从事医疗工作的专业人员。分为中医医生和西医医生。包括卫生技术人员中的中医师、西医师、中西结合高级医师、中医士、西医士和其他中医。

律师 指受聘参加法律顾问处工作,担任法律顾问、刑(民)事代理人、刑事辩护人,办理非诉讼事件,解答法律询问,代写法律事务文书等主要从事律师业务的专职法律工作者和兼职律师。

公证人员 指在国家公证机关依法办理公证事务的司法人员。包括公证员、助理公证员和在公证处工作的其他人员。

办理公证文书 指公证处在一定时期内办结的公证文书件数。公证文书系按司法部规定或批准的格式制作，包括国内公证和涉外公证两部分。其中国内公证分为经济合同公证和民事法律关系公证两大类。

调解人员 在人民调解委员会担负调解民间一般民事纠纷和轻微违法行为所引起的纠纷的工作人员，包括调解委员会的委员和调解小组的调解员。

调解民间纠纷 指调解委员会依照法律规定，根据自愿原则，用说服教育的方法调解民间发生的有关民事权利和义务的争执，促成当事双方达到协议和谅解，解决纠纷，包括婚姻家庭纠纷、财产权益纠纷等。不包括法院受理调解的民事案件数。

离休、退休、退职人员 指正式办理了离休、退休、退职手续，并享受相应的离休、退休、退职待遇的人员。

保险福利费用 指企业、事业、机关单位在工资以外实际支付给职工和离休、退休、退职人员个人以及用于集体的劳动保险和福利费用。

(1) 职工保险福利费用具体包括：

① 医疗卫生费 指实行公费医疗企业的职工及其供养的直系亲属的医疗费、医务经费、职工因工负伤就医路费以及住院伙食补助费等；卫生部门开支的事业及机关单位职工的公费医疗经费；未参加公费医疗的企业、事业和机关单位职工的医药费。

② 丧葬抚恤救济费 指职工死亡的丧葬费、丧葬补助费和所遗供养直系亲属的抚恤费、救济费、生活补助费以及职工供养直系亲属死亡时的丧葬补助费等。

③ 生活困难补助 指对生活困难的职工实际支付的定期补助和临时性补助。

④ 文体宣传费 指企业、事业和机关单位实际支付的文体宣传费。不包括学习费。

⑤ 集体福利事业补贴费 指对职工浴室、理发室、洗衣房、哺乳室、托儿所等集体福利设施各项支出与收入相抵后的差额补助费。

⑥ 集体福利设施费 指按照国家规定开支的集体福利设施费用。如职工食堂炊事用具的购置费、修理费、职工宿舍的修缮费用。不包括由企业、事业、机关单位自筹经费开支的职工福利设施的基本建设费用。

⑦ 计划生育补贴 指发给职工独生子女的补贴费和保健费。

⑧ 其他 指上述费用以外，单位支付给职工的保险福利费。

(2) 离休、退休、退职人员保险福利费用具体包括：

① 离休金 指发给离休人员的工资和按 1982 年国务院发布的“关于老干部离职休养制度的几项规定”发给符合规定的离休干部相当于 1—2 个月标准工资的生活补贴和国务院[1989]82、83 号文件规定提高离休人员的待遇所增加的费用及粮油价格补贴等。

② 退休金 指按照国家有关规定发给退休人员的退休费和国务院[1989]82、83 号文件规定提高退休人员的待遇所增加的费用及粮油价格补贴等。

③ 退职生活费 指按照 1978 年国务院《关于工人退休、退职的暂行办法》规定定期发给退职人员的生活费用和国务院[1989]82、83 号文件规定提高退职人员的待遇所增加的费用及粮油价格补贴等。

④ 医疗卫生费 指离休、退休、退职人员的医疗费、住院费以及住院伙食补助等费用。

⑤ 护理费 指因工致残、饮食起居需人扶助的离休、退休人员的护理费以及因病不能自理的离休人员的护理费。

⑥ 生活补贴 指按照 1985 年国务院《关于发给离休退休人员生活补贴费的通知》规定，发给离休、退休人员的生活补贴费。

⑦ 交通费补贴 指按月发给离休人员的交通费补贴。

⑧ 丧葬抚恤救济费 指离休、退休、退职人员死亡的丧葬费、丧葬补助费和所遗供养直系亲属的抚恤费、救济费、生活补助费以及供养直系亲属死亡时的丧葬补助费等。

⑨ 其他 包括易地安置的离休、退休、退职人员的安家补助费；离休、退休、退职人员的生活困难补助费、书报费、洗理费、副食品价格补贴、房租价格补贴、水电补贴、少数民族补贴以及老干部活动经费开支的旅游费用等。

工业废水排放量 指经过企业厂区所有排放口排到企业外部的工业废水量。包括生产废水、外排的直接冷却水、超标排放的矿井地下水和与工业废水混排的厂区生活污水，不包括外排的间接冷却水(清污不分流的间接冷却水应计算在内)。

工业废水排放达标量 指各项指标都达到国家或地方排放标准的外排工业废水量，包括未经处理外排达标的和经过处理后外排达标的两部分。国家排放标准见 GB8978—88。

工业废水处理量 指报告期内各种水治理设施实际处理的工业废水量，包括处理后外排的和处理后回用的工业废水量。虽经处理但未达到国家或地方排放标准的废水量也应计算在内。计算时，如遇有车间和厂排放口均有治理设施，并对同一废水分级处理时，不应重复计算工业废水处理量。

工业废气排放量 指企业厂区内燃料燃烧和生产工艺过程中产生的各种排入空气的含有污染物的气体的总量，以标准状态[273K，101325Pa]计。

二氧化硫排放量 指企业在燃料燃烧和生产工艺过程中排入大气的二氧化硫量。

工业烟尘排放量 指企业厂区内的燃料燃烧产生的烟气中夹带的颗粒物的量。

工业粉尘排放量 指企业在生产工艺过程中排放的颗粒物重量。如钢铁企业的耐火材料粉尘、焦化企业的筛焦系统粉尘、烧结机的粉尘、石灰窑的粉尘、建材企业的水泥粉尘等。不包括电厂排入大气的烟尘。

工业固体废物产生量 指企业在生产过程中产生的固体状、半固体状和高浓度液体状废弃物的总量，包括危险废物、冶炼废渣、粉煤灰、炉渣、煤矸石、尾矿、放射性废物和其他废物等；不包括矿山开采的剥离废石和掘进废石（煤矸石和呈酸性或碱性的废石除外）。酸性或碱性废石是指采掘的废石其流经水、雨淋水的pH值小于4或pH值大于10.5者。

工业固体废物处置量 指将固体废物焚烧或者最终置于符合环境保护规定要求的场所并不再回取的工业固体废物量（包括当年处置往年的工业固体废物累计贮存量）。处置方法如：填埋（其中危险废物应安全填埋）、焚烧、专业贮存场（库）封场处理、深层灌注、回填矿井等。

工业固体废物排放量 指将所产生的固体废物排到固体废物污染防治设施、场所以外的量。不包括矿山开采的剥离废石和掘进废石（煤矸石和呈酸性或碱性的废石除外）。

“三废”综合利用产品产值 指利用“三废”（废液、废气、废渣）作为主要原料生产的产品产值（现行价），已经销售或准备销售的，应计算产品产值；但留作生产上自用的，不应计算产品产值。

“三废”综合利用产品利润 指利用“三废”（废液、废气、废渣）生产的产品，销售后所得到的利润。

环境污染与破坏事故 指由于违反环境保护法规的经济、社会活动与行为，以及意外因素的影响或不可抗拒的自然灾害等原因，致使环境受到污染，国家重点保护的野生动植物、自然保护区受到破坏，人体健康受到危害，社会经济和人民财产受到损失，造成不良社会影响的突发性事件。

Explanatory Notes to Major Statistical Indicators

Total Output refer to value of all goods and services by all resident units in a country (or region) during a certain period of time, both including new added value and transfered value, which refers the total scale of production activities by resident units.

Gross Domestic Product refers to gross domestic product calculated at market price, which is all the final products of all resident units of a country (or region) during a certain period of time. Gross Domestic Product is presented in three different forms, i.e. value added, income, and products respectively. The form of value added refers to the total value of all products and services produced by all resident units during a certain period, of time minus total value of inputs of non-fixed assets materials and services or the summation of the value added of all resident units; the form of income includes all the income items produced by all resident units and distributed primarily to all resident and non-resident units; the form of product refers to all final goods and services minus imports of goods and services. In the practice of national accounting, Gross Domestic Product is calculated by three approaches, i.e. product approach, income approach, and expenditure approach respectively to reflect Gross Domestic Product and its composition from different aspects.

Comparable Price is applied when comparing value indicators of different periods to reflect accurately the changes in physical volume. The price is not considered here. Two methods are used for calculating comparable prices: 1. Multiplying the output of products by their constant prices of a certain year; 2. Conversion of the data in current prices by relevant price index.

Constant Prices refer to the average price of a given product in a certain year, which is used to calculate the output value over time. As the output value at constant prices removes the factor of price changes , it reflects the trend of production development over time. Since 1949, with the changes in general price level, the State Statistical Bureau has issued nationally unified constant prices five times: the 1952 constant prices for 1949 – 1957; the 1957 constant prices for 1958 – 1970; the 1970 constant prices for 1971 – 1981; the 1980 constant prices for 1981 – 1990; and the 1990 constant prices have been used since 1991.

Average Annual Growth Rate Two methods for calculating average annual growth rate are applied in China. One is often called "level approach" or the method of calculating geometric average, which is derived by comparing the level of the last year of the interval with that of the base year; the other is called "accumulating approach" or algebraic average or equation method, which is derived by comparing the summation of the actual figure of each year in the interval with the figure in the base year.

Usually the results calculated by the two methods are fairly close, but they differ sharply when uneven economic development occurs with striking fluctuations in growth.

The average annual growth rates listed in this statistical yearbook are calculated by "level approach". The base years are not listed when the years are listed for average annual growth rates. For instance, the average annual growth rate of 43 years since 1949 is listed as average annual growth rate of 1950 – 1995 without listing the base year 1949.

Various Planning Periods The conventional division of time period in this statistical yearbook is as follows: Economic Rehabilitation Period, 1950 – 1952; The First Five – Year Plan period, 1953 – 1957; The Second Five – Year Plan period. 1958 – 1962; The Third Five – Year Plan period, 1966 – 1970; The Fourth Five – Year plan period, 1971 – 1975; The Fifth Five – Year Plan period. 1976 – 1980; The Sixth Five – Year Plan period, 1985; The Seventh Five – Year Plan period, 1986 – 1990; The Eight Five – Year Plan period; 1991 – 1995.

Type of Registeration refer to various kinds of enterprises registered at administrative organization of industry and commerce. The types of registeration are as follows: interior enterprises, including state-owned enterprises, collective-owned enterprises, shareholding cooperative enterprises, joint-owned enterprises, responsibility companies limited, shareholding companies limited, private owned enterprises, other enterprises. Hongkong, Macao and Taiwan invested enterprises, including joint venture enterprises (Hongkong, Macao and Taiwan funds), cooperative corporation enterprises (Hongkong or Macao and Taiwan funds), Hongkong, Macao and Taiwan solely invested enterprises, Hongkong, Macao and Taiwan Shareholding limited companies. Foreign invested enterprises, including sino-foreign joint venture enterprises, sino-foreign cooperative enterprises, foreign investment enterprises, foreign investment shareholding limited companies.

State-owned Enterprises refer to enterprises with the whole properties owned by state, they are registered according to the stipulations of "The Management Regulation of the People's Republic of China Regarding the Registerations of Enterprise Legal Persons" as non-company system economic organizations, but excluding state-owned sole investment company among the responsibility co. Ltd.

Collective-owned Enterprises refer to enterprises with properties owned by collective units, they are registered as the economic organizations, according to the stipulations of "The Management Regulation of the People's Republic of China Regarding the Registerations of Enterprise Legal Persons".

Shareholding Cooperative Enterprises refer to enterprises with the collective system as the base, and established through buying share by staff and workers; absorbing certain proportion of social capital as the investment. It is a sort of collective economy, carrying out the principle of the management of one's own, assuming sole responsibility for its profits and losses, working together, distributing according work and distributing the profits according shares.

Joint-owned Enterprises refer two or more than two enterprise legal persons with same or different ownership, invested together to organize the economic organizations, according to the principle of voluntary, equality and mutual.

Responsibility Co. Ltd. refer to economic organizations registered according to the stipulations of "The Regulations of Registerative Management of the People's Republic of China." They investe together by more than two or less than fifteen of shareholders, each shareholder bears the limited responsibility to company according to his investment value, and the company bears the responsibility to the liabilities with the whole properties. Limited responsibility companies include state-owned sole investment companies and other limited responsibility companies.

Shareholding Co. Ltd. refer to economic organizations registered according to the stipulation of "The Regulation of Registerative Management of the People's Republic of China." Their whole registerated capital raised through issuing share certifications, and structured with equal value of shares. Companies bear the responsibility to liabilities with the thole properties.

Private Owned Enterprises refer to economic organizations based on wage labour to obtain profits, and established according the regulations as "Law of Company", "Law of Partnership", "Temporary Stipulations of Private Enterprises", including private responsibility limited companies, private shareholding limited companies, private partnership enterprises, and private sole investment enterprises.

Joint Venture Enterprises (Hongkong, Macao, and Taiwan Funds) refer to enterprise established by Hongkong, Macao, and Taiwan investers and interior enterprises, according to the regulations of "Law of Sino-foreign Joint Venture of the People's Republic of China" and stipulations of related laws. They share profits and bear risks in accordance with the investment proportion stipulated by contract.

Cooperative Corporation Enterprises refer to enterprises established by the invester of Hongkong, Macao and Taiwan, with interior enterprises, according to the regulation of the "Law of Sino-Foreign Cooperative Corporation of the People's Republic of China" and other relative laws. They invested, provide fovourable factors, share the profits and bear the risks, according to the appointment stipulated by the contract.

Hongkong, Macao and Taiwan Solely Invested Enterprises refer the enterprises established according to the stipulations of the "Law of Foreign Invested Enterprises of the People's Republic of China" and related laws, invested by Hongkong, Macao and Taiwan invester, with whole investment value.

Hongkong, Macao and Taiwan Shareholding Limited Companies refer to companies established according to state related stipulations, and permission of the Ministry of Foreign Economy and Trade, with more than 25 % shares of the registered capital of Hongkong, Macao and Taiwan investers. Whatever the proportion less than 25 %, they belong to the interior limited companies.

Sino-Foreign Joint Venture Enterprises refer to enterprises established by foreign enterprises or foreigners with chinese interior enterprises, according to the stipulations of the "Law of Sino-foreign Joint Venture Enterprises of the People's Repbulic of China" and other related laws. They share the profits and bear the risks in accordance with the investment proportion stipulated by contract.

Sino-Foreign Cooperative Enterprises refer to enterprises established according to the stipulations of the "Law of Sino-Foreign Cooperative Enterprises" and other related laws, by foreign enterprises or foreigners, they invest, provide favourable factors, share the profits and bear the risks, in accordance with the appointment by cooperative contract.

Foreign Investment Enterprises refer to enterprises established according to stipulations of the "Law of Foreign Investment Enterprises of the People's Republic of China" and other related laws, invest in interior land of China with whole investment value.

Foreign Investment Shareholding Limited Companies refer to companies established according to the state stipulations and permission of the Ministry of Economy and Trade, with more than 25 % of the foreign share aomong the registered capital. Whatever the proportion of the foreign share less than 25% among the registered capital, they belong to interior shareholding limited companies.

Economic Units Funded by Overseas Chinese from Hongkong, Macao, and Taiwan refer to enterprises established by enterprises from Hongkong, Macao, and Taiwan in the territory of the mainland China according to related economic laws and regulations of the People's Republic of China in the forms of joint venture, cooperative corporations and ventures with sole investment, including joint ventures, cooperative enterprises, and exclusively invested enterprises.

Three Industries Industry structure has been classified according to the historical sequence of development. Primary industry refers to extraction of natural resources; secondary industry involves processing of primary products; and tertiary industry provides services of various kinds for production and consumption. The above classification is universal although it varies to some extent from country to country. Industry in China comprises:

Primary industry: agriculture (including farming, forestry, animal husbandry, sideline production and fishery).

Secondary industry: industry (including mining and quarrying, manufacture, water supply, electricity gerneration and supply, steam, hot water, gas) and construction.

Tertiary industry: all other industries not included in primary or secondary industries.

Due to the fact that tertiary industry involves a large variety of industries in China, it is divided into two sectors: circulation sector and service sector and further into four levels:

The first level: circulation sector, including transportation, postal and telecommunications, services, commerce, catering trade, material supply and marketing, and storage.

The second level: service sector providing service for production and consumption, including banking, insurance, geological survey, real estates, public utilities, service for residents, consultancy service, and comprehensive technical services, and service for agriculture, forestry, animal husbandry, fishery, water conservancy, and maintenance of roads and inland water ways, etc.

The third level: service sector for upgrading scientific, educational and cultural level of the people, including education, culture, broadcasting, television, science research, public health, sports, and social welfare, etc.

The fourth level: sector providing service for public needs, including government agencies, political and party organizations, social organizations, armies, and policeforce.

GDP Calculated with Expenditure Approach refers to total expenditure on final comsumption, total capital formation and net export of goods and services by resident units of a country in a certain period of time. It reflects the composition of GDP by its use.

Final Consumption refers to the total expenditure of resident units on final consumption of goods and services in a certain period, namely the expenditure of the resident units for purchases of goods and services from domestic economic territory and abroad to meet the requirements of material, cultural and spiritual life. It excludes the expenditure of non-resident units on consumption in the economic territory of the country. The final consumption is classified into resident consumption and government consumption.

(1) Resident consumption refers to the total expenditure of resident households on the final consumption of goods and services in a certain period of time. The expenditure of residents on final consumption of goods is recorded when the change of the ownership of goods happens. The expenditure of residents on the final consumption of services is recorded when the services are provided. The expenditure of the residents on consumption is calculated at market prices, namely the purchasers' prices which the residents pay; the purchasers' prices of goods are the prices the residents pay when they obtain the goods, including the transport and commercial expenses paid by the residents. In addition to the expenditure on consumption of goods and services bought by the residents directly with money, it also includes the expenditure on consumption of goods and services obtained by other means, which is the so-called fictitious expenditure. The fictitious expenditure of the residents on consumption includes the following types: (a) the goods and serviecs provided to the residents by the units in the form of payment in kind and transfer in kind; (b) the goods and services produced and cousumed by the households themselves, in which the services refer only to the services provided by the residential buildings owned by the households; (c) the services of financial intermediary provided by the financial institutions; (d) the insurance services provided by the insurance companies.

(2) Government consumption refers to the transfer expenditure on the public services provided by the government to the whole society and the expenditure on the consumptive goods and services provided to residents.

Total Capital Formation refers to the net amount of the fixed Capital and stock acquired minus those disposed, including the total fixed assets formation and the increase in stock.

(1) Total fixed capital formation refers to the value of fixed assets purchased, transferred in by the resident units and those produced and used by themselves in a certain period, deducting the value of fixed assets sold and transferred out. It can be classified into total tangible assets formation and total intangible assets formation. The total tangible assets formation includes the value of the construction projects, installation projects completed and the equipment, apparatus and instruments purchased as well as the value of land improved, the value of draught animals, breeding stock, milk, wool and recreational animals and the newly increased economic forest in a certain period. The total intangible assets formation includes the prospecting of minerals, the acquisition of computer softwares, the originals of recreational works and works of literature and arts minus the disposal of them.

(2) Increase in stock refers to the market value of the change in stock in a certain period, i. e, the difference of value between the beginning and the end of the period. The increase in stock can be positive or negative. A positive value indicates the

increase in stock while a negative indicates the decrease in stock. The stock includes the raw materials, fuels and reserve materials purchased by the production units as well as the stock of finished products , semi-finished products, work-in-progress, etc.

Net Export of Goods and Services refer to the difference of the exports of goods and services minus the imports of goods and servies. The imports include the value of various goods and services purchased or obtaned gratis by resident units from non-resident units, since the provision and the use of services happen simultaneously, the import and export of services do not appear to have the phenomena of crossing the border of the country. The acquisition of services by the resident units from abroad is usually treated as import while the aquisition of services by non-resident units in its country is usually treated as export. The export and import of goods are calculated at FOB.

Labourers' Remuneration refers to the whole payment earned by the labourers from the productive activities they are engaged in. It includes wages, bonuses and allowances the labourers earn in various forms, including in monetary form and in kind. It also includes the free medical services provided to the labourers and the medicine expenses, traffic subsidies and social insurance fee paid for them by the labourers' working units. The social insurance fee paid by the labourers' working units refers to the social insurance fee paid dircetly by the working units to the government department (usually the department of labour) or the insurance fee paid by the enterprises and institutions for the retirement, death, and medical injury treatment of the staff and workers. As the individual economy is concerned, since the labourers' remuneration is not easily distinguished from the operating profit, both are treated as labourers' remuneration.

Net Taxes on Production refer to the difference of the taxes on production minus the subsidies on production. The taxes on production refer to the various taxes, extra charges and fees levied on the production units on their production, sale and business activities as well as on some factors of production, such as fixed assets, land and labour force, used in the production activities they are engaged in. Specifically speaking, they include sales tax and extra charges, value added tax, various taxes paid in the administrative expenses, road toll payable, sewage charges extra charges on water and electric power consumed, special revenue turned over to the government by the monopolized trade of tobacco and liquor, etc. In contrast to the taxes on production, the subsidies on production is the unilateral transfer of part of the government's revenue to the production units and is therefore treated as the negative taxes on production. They include subsidies on the loss due to implementation of government policies, price subsidies to the grain institutions, foreign trade corporations' receipts from drawback, ect.

Depreciation of Fixed Assets refers to the depreciation of fixed assets drawn in accordance with the stipulated depreciation rate for the purpose of compensating the wear loss of the fixed assets or the depreciation of fixed assets calculated in a fictitious way in accordance with the stipulated unified depreciation rate in the national economic accounting system. It reflects the value of transfer of the fixed assets in the production of the current period. The depreciation of fixed assets in various enterprises and institutions managed as enterprises as well as the houses of residents, the depreciation of fixed assets is the dummy depreciation, which is calculated in accordance with the stipulated unified depreciation rate. In principle, the depreciation of fixed assets should be calculated on the basis of the re-purchased value of the fixed assets. However, there is no actual condition to reevaluate all the fixed assets in China. Therefore, the above-mentioned methods are temporarily adopted at present.

Operating Surplus refers to the balance of the value added created by the resident units deducting the labourers' remuneration, net taxes on production and the depreciation of fixed assets. It is equivalent to the business profit of the enterprises plus subsidies on production, but the wages and welfare expenses paid from the profits and the public welfare fund drawn from the post-tax profits should be deducted.

Population refers to the population with permanent residence registered December 31 every year, excluding migrant population without registered residence in Jiangsu.

Birth Rate (or **Crude Birth Rate**) refers to the birth rate per millenary during a certain period of time (usually a year), which is often presented as ‰. The following formula is used:

$$Birth\ Rate = \frac{Number\ of\ Births}{Average\ Number\ of\ Population} \times 1000‰$$

Number of Births refers to live-born babies, i. e. babies that show breathing or any other vital phenomena regardless of the length of pregnancy.

Average Number of Population is the average of the number of population at the beginning of the year and the end of year and sometimes is substituted with mid-year population.

Death Rate (or **Crude Death Rate**) refers to the ratio of number of deaths to the average population (or mid-year population) during a certain period of time (usually a year), which is often presented as ‰. The following formula is used:

$$Death\ Rate = \frac{Number\ of\ Deaths}{Average\ Number\ of\ Population} \times 1000‰$$

Natural Growth Rate of Population refers to the ratio of natural increase in population (number of births minus number of deaths) in a certain period of time (usually a year) to the average population (or mid-year population) of the period, which is often presented as ‰. The following formulae are applied:

$$Natural\ Growth\ of\ Population = \frac{Number\ of\ Births - Number\ of\ Deaths}{Average\ Number\ of\ Population} \times 1000‰$$

$$Natural\ Growth\ Rate\ of\ Population = Birth\ Rate - Death\ Rate$$

Life Expectancy refer to the average number of years a person of a certain age will live (or the average life-span of an age group if the pattern of mortality for this age group remains as it is).

Persons Employed refers to total number of persons who are engaged in social labor and get labor reward or business earnings, including:

(1) Total staff and workers

(2) Employees in urban private enterprises

(3) Urban individual laborers

(4) Rural laborers

(5) Other social laborers

This indicator reflects the actual utilization of total labor force during a certain period of time and is often used for the research of our national conditions and national strength.

Persons Employed in Various Units refer to total staff working for various levels of government agencies, political and party organizations, social organizations, and enterprises and institutions and receiving wages and other forms of labor reward. It includes employed (on the post) staff, reemployed retirees, non-government paid teachers, foreigners, and Chinese compatriots from Hong Kong, Macao, and Taiwan working in various units. This indicator reflects the total employed (on the post) laborers actually engaged in production or other operations in various units.

Staff and Workers Employed (on the post) refer to those who work in self units which paying wages for them, or they are on the post, but dosn't work due to studying, sickness, injuring, and materity leave, their wages are still paid by the units.

Staff and Workers Who have Left Self-units But Still Remain the labor Relationship with the Units refer to those who have left the production and working posts caused by various reasons and are not taking other positions in the same units, but whose labor relation still remained with units.

Living Exoenses for the Staff and the Workers Who Have Left Self-units But Still Remain Labor Relationship with the Units refer to the those who receiving the living expenses from the units.

Unemployment refers to those non-agricultural population within working age (16-50 for male and 16-45 for female) who are able and willing to work but unemployed and registered in local employment service agencies.

Total Wage Expenditures on Workers and Staff refer to total remuneration payment to permanent workers and staff of various units during a certain period of time. They include time wage, piece wage, bonus, above-quota piecework wage, various allowance and subsidy, overtime premium, wage paid under special circumsfances.

The calculation of total expenditures is in principle based on the total remuneration payment and therefore should include, wages and salaries and other payments to workers and staff regardless of its resources, category, in kind or cash.

Average Wage of Workers and Staff refers to the average wage in money terms per person during a certain period of time for workers and staff of enterprises, institutions, and government agencies, which reflects the general level of wage income during a certain period of time and is calculated as:

$$Average\ Wage\ of\ Workers\ and\ Staff = \frac{Total\ Wage\ Expenditures\ on\ Workers\ and\ Staff\ in\ Reference\ Period}{Average\ Number\ of\ Workers\ and\ Staff\ in\ Reference\ Period}$$

Labor Insurance and Welfare Funds refer to the real cost paid, in line with relative state labor insurance and welfare regulations, to workers and staff outside the wages and used for the collective as labor insurance and welfare facilities funds. It mainly includes: (1)resignation pay, retirement pay and payment for retires with honours; (2)medical and health care fees; (3)subsidies for workers and staff with financial difficulties; (4)funeral expenses for workers and staff and their direct relatives whom they support, pension for the disabled or for the family of the deceased, and relief payment; (5)agricultural production subsidies; (6)funds for cultural, sports and publicity activities; (7)subsidies for collective welfare cause; (8)collective welfare facilities expenses; (9)other welfare cost.

Labor protection cost is not included in the labor insurance and welfare funds. The need of appliances for labor protection is to ensure safety in production and can not be listed in the welfare funds.

Employed Population in Urban Households refers to urban residents engaged in certain work and receiving payment for their labour or income from their business operation, including those who work in state-owned or collective units, joint ventures, foreign-owned units and private units with permanent or temporary jobs. The self-employed individuals and reemployed retirees are also included. This indicator reflects the situation of urban employment and is the basic data for calculating employment rate and dependency ratio.

Cash Income includes real income and credit income.

Real Income refers to the total realized cash income of the sample households, excluding credit income such as withdrawal from bank deposits, borrowed money from relatives and friends, collections of outstanding accounts, suspense receipts of various forms.

Credit Income refers to circulating income which includes withdrawal from bank deposits, reserve fund, borrowed money, collection of outstanding accounts, honoring or selling valuable securities, purchase on credit, bank loan for house purchase. etc.

Disposable Income of Urban Households refers to the income of the actual sample households after the payment of income tax.

Consumptive Expenditure refers to the total expenditure of the sample households on the purchase of goods and services. It is classified into eight categories: food, clothing, home appliances, daily necessities and services, medical and health care, transport and telecommunication, recreational, educational and cultural services, housing, other goods and services. Expenditure on goods refers to the purchase of goods from shops, markets, restaurants, working units or directly from factories or the countryside, including the goods for their own consumption and gifts for other people. Expenditure on services refers to that on various cultural and life services provided in society, including repair charge, processing charge, bathing, hairdressing and cosmetic charges, babysitting charge and other labor charge.

Net Income of Rural Households refers to the income owned by peasants after the deduction of various expenses from toatl income. It is used for Productive and non－productive investment, for improvement of material and cultural life, for expenditure and balance in redistribution. This indicator is employed to observe the actual income level of peasants, and the peasants' capacity of expending reproduction and improving livelihood.

Net income＝total income－expenditure of household operational expenses－depreciation of fixed assets for production－tax－payment for collective units for contracted tasks－collective reserve and apportion－subsidy from survey.

Able-bodied and Semi-ablebodied Laborers of Rural Households refer to permanent residents of rural households who are able to work and actually engaged in social labour, which is one factor of production and sources of rural household income. According to the relevant regulations, male aged 18－50, female aged 18－45 are considered as able-bodied laborers; male aged 16－17 and 51－60, female aged 16－17 and 46－55 are considered as semi-ablebodied laborers. Those who are not in the above age range but able to work and actually engaged in social labour are also considered able-bodied or semi-ablebodied laborers, while those who are within the above age range but unable to work are not counted as able-bodied or semi-ablebodied laborers.

Expenditure of Rural Households for Consumption refers to total expenses of rural households on daily life, including expenses on food, clothing, housing, fuel, articles for daily use, and expenses on cultural life and services. This indicator is used to show the actual consumption level of peasants.

Expenditure of Rural Households on Commodities refers to total expenses of the permanent residents of the rural households on purchases of food, clothing, furniture, household appliances, articles for daily use, fuels, durable goods, and cultural, educational and medicinal articles, including purchases from state-owed shops, collective shops, free markets, etc. Expenditure of peasants for purchase of commodities is an important part of peasants' consumption expenditure, which reflects the extent of commercialization of peasants' consumption and the developing process from self-sufficient economy toward commodity economy. It provides basis for the analysis and research of peasants' market demand and for the formulation of the plan of commodity supply.

Savings Deposits Balance of Urban and Rural Residents savings deposits include the bank savings deposit of urban residents and the bank savings deposit of rural residents. The cash held by residents and the deposits of organizations such as industrial and mining enterprises, army units, institutions, etc. are not included. The outstanding amount of savings deposits refers to the money put into banks and rural credit unions at certain time points (balance between deposit and withdrawal), such as the end of month, quater or year.

Total Investment in Fixed Assets in the Whole Society Total in vestment in fixed assets refers to the economic activity of constructing and purchasing fixed assets. It is an important means for the society to increase fixed assets, expand production scale and develop national economy. It is also a condition for people to improve their cultural and material life.

Amount of investment in fixed assets refers to the volume of activities in construction and purchase of fixed assets in money terms. It is a comprehensive indicator which shows the size, pace, proportional and use orientation of the investment in fixed assets. Total investment in fixed assets in the whole society includes the investment by state-owned units, the investment by the urban and rural collective units, the investment by the units of other types of ownership and the investment by the individuals in the urban and rural areas. According to China's current planning management system, the total investment in fixed assets is classified into the following parts: investment in capital construction, investment in innovation, investment in real estate development, investment in other national fixed assets, investment by the urban and rural collective units (including the investment by the urban collective units and that by the rural collective units), investment by the units of other types of ownership (including the investment by the units of joint-owned economy, share-holding economy, Sino-foreign joint economy, Sino-foreign cooperative economy, economy exclusively with foreign investment, Mainland-Hong Kong or Mainland-Macao or Mainland-Taiwan joint economy, Mainland-Hong Kong or Mainland-Mocao or Mainland-Taiwan cooperative economy, and economy exclusively with investment of Hong Kong or Macao or Taiwan), investment by the individuals in the urban and rural areas (including the investment in personal house building in the areas under the jurisdiction of city, county, town and special industrial and mining areas as well as the investment in personal house building and purchase of productive fixed assets in the rural areas).

Since 1997, the calculating point of projects of capital construction, updating and transformations and other investments of fixed assets was raised to 500,000 yuan above from the originally 50,000 yuan.

Investment in Capital Construction Capital construction refers to the new construction projects or extension projects and the related work of the enterprises, institutions or administrative units mainly for the purpose of expanding production capacity or improving project efficiency. It includes: (1) projects listed in the capital construction plan of the current year of the central government and the local governments at various levels as well as the projects, though not listed in the capital construction plan of the current year, that continued to be constructed in this year, using the investment listed in the plan of capital construction of previous years and carried forward to this year(also using the equipment and materials kept in stock of the capital construction); (2) new construction projects arranged both in the plan of capital construction and the plan of innovation; extension projects with the newly increased production capacity (or project efficiency) up to the standard of a large and medium-sized project; and the projects of moving the whole factory to a new site so as to improve the distribution of productive forces; (3) new construction projects, extension projects or restoration projects with the total investment more than 500 thousand RMB yuan by the state-owned units, though listed neither in the plan of capital construction nor in the plan of innovation; the projects in the state-owned units of moving the whole factory to a new site so as to improve the distribution of productive forces; and the projects of building additional business houses by the administrative units and institutions and building welfare facilities by the administrative units.

Investment in Innovation Innovation refers to the renewal of fixed assets and technological innovation of the original facilities by the enterprises and institutions as well as the corresponding supplementary projects and the related work (excluding major overhaul and maintenance projects). It includes: (1) projects listed in the innovation plan of the current year of the central government and the governments at various levels as well as the projects, though not listed in the innovation plan of the current year, that continued to be constructed in this year, using the investment listed in the plan of innovation of previous years and carried forward to this year; (2) projects of technological innovation or renewal of the original facilities, arranged both in the plan of innovation and in the plan of capital construction; or extension projects (main workshops or a branch of the factory) with the newly increased production capacity (or project efficiency) not up to the standard of a large and medium-sized project; (3) projects of reconstruction or technological innovation whth the total investment more than 500 thousand RMB yuan by the state-owned units, though listed neither in the plan of capital construction nor in the plan of innovation; the projects in the state-owned units of moving the whole factory to a new site so as to meet the requirements of urban environmental protection or safe production.

Investment in Real Estate Development It includes: the investment by the real estate development companies, commerical buildings construction companies and other real estate development units of various types of ownership in the construction of house buildings, such as residential buildings, factory buildings, warehouses, hotels, guesthouses, holiday villages, office buildings, and the complementary service facilities and land development projects, such as roads, water supply, water drainage, power supply, heating, telecommunications, land levelling and other projects of infrastructure. It covers the activities of the non-real estate companies in real estate development or management, but excludes the activities in simple land transactions.

Other Investment in Fixed Assets refers to the construction and purchases of fixed assets not listed in the investment in capital construction, investment in innovation and investment in real estate development. It includes:

Ⅰ. The following projects of the state-owned units with the total investment of more than 500 thousand yuan, which are not included in the plan of capital construction and the plan of innovation: (1) projects of oil fields maintenance and exploitation with the oil fields maintenance funds and petroleum development funds; (2) opening and extending projects with the maintenance funds in coal, ore and other mining enterprises and logging enterprises; (3) project of reconstruction of the original highways and bridges with the highway maintenance funds in the department of communication; (4) projects of construction of warehouses with the funds of simple construction in the commercial department.

Ⅱ. The investment in fixed assets by the collective units: including the projects of construction and purchases of fixed assets by the urban collective units with the planned total investment of more than 500 thousand yuan, and the projects of construction and purchase of fixed assets by the rural collective units with the planned total investment of more than 50,000 yuan.

Ⅲ. The projects of construction and pruchase of fixed assets by the enterprises or institutions of joint-owned economy, share-holding economy, foreign-funded economy, economy funded by the entrepreneurs from Hong Kong, Macao and Taiwan and other economy with the planned total investment of more than 500 thousand yuan.

Ⅳ. The private investment in house construction in the urban areas and industrial and mining areas as well as the individual investment in the rural areas: The private house construction in the urban areas and industrial and mining areas includes all the private house construction under the jurisdiction of cities, counties, towns and industrial and mining areas, no matter whether the owner of the house is registered as the permanent resident in the locality or not. The individual investment in the rural areas includes the investment in house construction and purchase of producitive fixed assets by the individuals in the rural areas. The individual investment in fixed assets in the rural areas is estimated by the Rural Socio-economic Survey Organization, SSB on the basis of the data collected by the sample survey.

Sources of Funds for Investment in Fixed Assets refer to various funds received during the year by fixed assets investments for construction and purchase of fixed assets. They include balance of funds brought forward from the previous year, subtotal of sources of funds in this year, and various payable funds. The subtotal of the sources of funds in this year is further divided into six categories: state budgetary investment, domestic loans, bonds, foreign investment, self-raised funds, and other sources of funds.

(1) State budgetary investment is divided into financial appropriations for arranged financial loans. It includes capital construction fund from central financing (including operational and non-operational fund), special expenditure (loan for replacing petroleum with coal, for example), reloan after recalling (referring to reloan after recalling arranged by financing), fund at discount interest, expenditure arranged by financing on tapping the potential and promoting technical transformation and on developing new products, expenditure on urban construction, expenditure on simple construction in commercial department, fund used as investment in fixed assets from development fund for underveloped areas, fund in local financing of overall atate control, etc.

(2) Domestic loans refer to various domestic loans borrowed by fixed assets investment units from banks and non-bank financial institutions during the reference period for the purpose of investment in fixed assets. Domestic loans include loans issued by banks from their self-owned funds and deposit, loans appropriated by responsible authorities, special loans by government (including loan for replacing petroleum with coal, special loan for reform-through-labour coal mines), loans arranged by local government from special funds, domestic reserve loan, and working loan, etc.

(3) Bonds refer to funds raised by enterprises (companies) or financial institutions through issuing various bonds for the purpose of investment in fixed assets, The bonds include Key Enterprise Bonds and Key Construction Program Bonds issued by the banks on behalf of the state specialized investment companies.

(4) Foreign Investment refers to foreign funds received during the reference period for the purpose of investment in fixed assets, (equipment, material, technology included). Foreign investment includes foreign direct investment, loans from foreign countries, and other foreign investments.

(5) Self-raised funds refer to extra-budgetary funds received by construction enterprises for the prupose of investment in fixed assets during the reference period. They include funds owned by various departments of central and local governments and their own enterprises.

(6) Others refer to funds received during the reference period which are not included in the above-mentioned sources.

Investment in Fixed Assets by Sector The classification of construction projects by sector is determined by the major products or the purpose of the projucts when they are put into production or use, and by the nature of their social economic activities. The invesment in capital construction is classified by construction projects, while investment in innovation, other investment in fixed assets and urban and rural collective units are classified according to the sector which the whole enterprise or institution belongs to. In general, one project of one enterprise or institution can only belong to one sector.

Investment in Fixed Assets by Type of Construction The construction projects in general can be classified by the type of construction into new construction, expansion, reconstruction and moving away. In capital construction, the type of construction is determined by the condition of the project. In investment in innovation, in other investment in fixed assets and investment by urban and rural collective units, the type of construction is determined by the condition of the whole enterprise.

(1) New construction in general refers to newly constructed units. In the case in which value of the original fixed assets is quite small, and the value of newly added fixed assets exceeds the original ones by three times, the expansion construction is considered as new construction.

(2) Expansion refers to construction of new major production workshops or independent production line within a factory or in other locations, or construction branch of a factory so as to increase the production capacity of the original products. Newly constructed business houses in institutions and administrative organizations (such as the newly constructed teaching buildings in schools, clinics or bed building in hospitals, and office building in administrative agencies, etc.) are classified as expansion.

(3) Reconstruction refers to technical innovation and transformation of the existing equipment and technical conditions undertaken by enterprises and institutions for the purposes of technological advancement, improvement in product quality, enlarging variety of products, promoting new generation of products, reducing production consumption and cost, promoting comprehensive utilization of resources, strengthening treatment of waste gas, waste water and solid wastes, and safety in production, etc. through application of new technologies and techniques, use of new equipment and new materials (including accessory facilities for production or for living and welfare purposes). Construction of new workshops for improving existing production capacity rather than increasing production capacity is also considered as reconstruction.

Investment in Fixed Assets by Industry can be classified into four parts, i.e. primary industry, secondary industry, tertiary industry, and residential buildings. It is an important indicator to study proportions among investment of different purposes. The function of the investment in capital construction, investment in innovation, investment in real estate development, and the investment by urban and rural collective units is determined according to national economic industries.

Investment in Fixed Assests by Structure refers to the three major parts of investment activities, i.e. construction and installation, purchase of equipment and instrument, and other expenses.

(1) Construction and installation (work load of construction and installation) refers to construction projects of various houses and buildings and installation of various equipment and instrument, including construction of various houses, equipment foundations and industrial kiln stoves, preparation works for project construction, and clearing up works, post-project construction, pavement of railways and roads, drilling of mines and construction of oil popes, water conservancy, air defence underground constructions and other special projects, installation of various machinery equipment, testing operation for pretesting the quality of installation projects. The value of equipment installed in installation projects is not considered.

(2) Purchase of equipment and intrument refers to the total value of equipments, tools, and vessels purchased or self-produced which come up to standards for fixed assets. Equipment, tools and vessels purchased or self-produced for new workshops by newly established or expanded units are categorized as "purchase of equipment and instrument" no matter whether they come up to the standards for fixed assets or not.

(3) Other expenses refer to investment completed which are not included above.

Capital Construction Projects by Size In principle, the classification of size of capital construction projects should be determined according to the total scale or total investment set in the approved construction plan by higher responsible authorities or in the tentative design, otherwise according to the total scale or total investment set in the current capital construction plan of the state, provinces, autonomous regions, and municipalities directly under central government. Industrial projects which produce unitary products are classified according to its designed capacity of products; projicts which produce multi-products are classified by the design capacity of the major product or by the total planned investment. Standards for the Classification of Construction Projects into large, medium-sized and small ones issued by the government are the base for size division of construction projects, which was revised in 1958, 1962, 1977, and 1979 respectively and therefore, data on projects by size are not entirely comparable from year to year.

Projects Under Construction refer to projects having construction and installation activities undertaken in the reference period, including projects started in the reference period, or continued from the previous period, or completed and put into production or suspended in the reference period.

Projects Completed and Put into Use Industrial projects refer to the major projects and accessory facilities completed which result in forming production capacity and have been checked and accepted while the living and welfare facilities have been completed and can ensure normal production and formally put into production. Non-industrial projects refer to the major projects and accessory facilities completed which possess the designed capacity and have been checked, accepted and formally put into production.

Newly Increased Production Capacity refers to the increase of designed capacity and project efficiency through investment in fixed assets, which relects the accomplishment of investment in fixed assets in kind. The calculation of newly increased production capacity is based on individual projects which operate independently. When an individual project is completed and checked and accepted and put into production, it is counted as newly increased production capacity.

The newly increased production capacity and project efficiency are usually expressed in one of the following forms:

(1) Annual production capacity, such as extraction of coal and petroleum;

(2) Raw material processing capacity, such as ore processing capacity of ore dressing projects, the dressing capacity of a coal washery;

(3) Number or capacity of major equipments increased, such as the number of cotton spindles increased and the capacity of generating sets increased;

(4) Physical measures of construction, such as volume, capacity, area, and length, for instance, the capacity of reservoirs, the length of railways or roads.

Newly increased production capacity in terms of quantity is calculated in designed capacity in general, which refers to the production capacity a project under normal conditions designed in construction documents regardless of the actual output.

Floor Space of Building Under Construction and Completed refers to total floor space in each story of buildings calculated from the outside line of building walls, including the space occupied by construcitions like pillars or walls and basements. The floor space of multi-story building includes the total floor space of each story, including area occupied by separating walls, watching rooms, doorways, and pillars, but excluding protruding wall structures, artistic decoration, etc. (for example, flight of steps). The space of recessed verand and tantilevered balcony is counted by half of the projection area.

Floor Space of Residential Buildings refers to the floor space of the residential buildings under construction and completed among the total space of buildings under construction and completed.

Floor Space of Buildings Completed refers to the floor space of buildings completed in the reference period, which have come up to the designed standards and have been put into use.

Completion Rate of Floor Space of Buildings refers to the ratio of the floor space of buildings completed in certain period of time to the floor space of buildings under construction in the same period, which reflects the investment result and economic efficiency of the construction industry from the angle of the speed of project construction.

Newly Increased Fixed Assets refer to the newly increase value of fixed assets through investment, including the value of projects completed and put into production, the value of equipments, tools, and vessels considered as fixed assets, as well as the relevant expenses as investment in fixed assets. This is a comprehensive indicator of investment in fixed assets, reflecting the achievements of investment in fixed assets in different periods, different sectors, and different regions.

Rate of Construction Projects Completed and Put into Use refers to the ratio of the number of construction projects completed and put into use in certain period of time to the number of projects under construction in the same period. This reflects the investment efficiency from the angle of the speed of projects construction.

Rate of Projects of Fixed Assets Completed and Put into Operation refers to ratio of newly increased fixed assets to total investment made in the same period, This is a comprehensive indicator, reflecting the speed of the employment of fixed assets investment and investment efficiency.

Rate of Investment in Projects Uncompleted refers to the ratio of the accumulated investment in projects uncompleted to the total annual investment in projects. This reflects the relative size of projects uncompleted and the efficiency of investment in fixed assets from the angle of fund utilization. Since projects uncompleted refer to projects started but not completed, they often go beyond one year and therefore, the above ratio could be greater than 1.

Retail Price Index This economic index reflects the general change in retail prices of commodities in urban and rural areas. The change and adjustment in retail prices directly affect living expenditure of urban and rural residents and government revenue, purchasing power of residents and equilibrium of market supply and demand, and the proportion of consumption and accumulation. Therefore, retail price index can predict to certain extent the changes of the above economic activities from a certain perspective.

Consumer Price Index reflects the relative change in prices of consumer goods and services purchased by urban and rural residents, and is derived from urban consumer price index and rural consumer price index. Consumer price index can be used to predict the impact of consumer price change on actual living cost expenditure of urban and rural residents.

Urban Consumer Price Index reflects the relative change in prices of consumer goods and services purchased by urban families and can be used to observe and analyze the impact of price changes in consumer goods and services on money wages of staff and workers, and provide basis for policy making concerning the living cost and wages of urban residents.

Rural Consumer Price Index reflects the relative change in prices of consumer goods and services purchased by rural households and can be used to observe the impact of change in prices of consumer goods and services on living expenditure and actual change in peasants' living cost. It provides basis for analysis and research on peasants' living cost and welfare.

Index of Purchasing Prices of Farm Products reflects the relative change in purchasing prices of farm products purchased by business enterprises of various types of ownership and related departments. It is used to observe and study the impact of change in purchasing prices of farm products on money income of peasants, and it provides basis for making and checking policies concerning prices of farm products.

Retail Price Index of Rural Industrial Products reflects the relative change in prices of industrial products in rural market and can be used to observe the impact of the price change on farmers' money expenditure.

Ex-factory Price Index of Industrial Products reflects the change in general ex-factory prices of all industrial products, including sales of industrial products to commercial enterprises, foreign trade sectors, materials supplying and distributing sectors as well as sales of production means to industry and other sectors and sales of consumer goods to residents. It can be used to analyze the impact of ex-factory prices on gross industrial output value.

Price Index of Investment in Fixed Assets reflects the change in prices of investment in fixed assets. The investment in fixed assests consists of three components, namely the investment in construction and installation, the investment in purchases of equipment and instrument, and the investment in other items. Price index of investment in fixed assets is calculated as the weighted arithmetic mean of the price indices of the three components of investment in fixed assets.

Price index of investment in fixed assets reflects the changes of prices in various goods and services involved in investment in fixed assets and therefore can be used to observe the actual size, speed, structure, and efficiency of investment in fixed assets and provide reliable and scientific data for government planning, management, decision making, and further improving the current national accounting system.

Production Capacity of Tap Water at Year-end refers to the actual production capacity of the waterworks administered by the urban construction department and those owned by enterprises or institutions, taking the capacity of the main links, such as water inflow, purification, conveyance and outflow of the trunk pipelines into account.

Length of Water Supply Pipelines at Year-end refers to the total length of all the pipelines between the water pumps and the users' water meters.

Annual Volume of Water Supply refers to the total volume of water supplied by the public water-works and those owned by individual enterprises and institutions during the whole year, including both the effective water supply and loss during the water supply.

Consumption of Water for Residential Use refers to the water consumption of households for daily life and the water consumption of public welfare facilities, including the consumption of restaurants, hotels, hospitals, barber shops, public bathhouses, laundries, swimming pools, shops, schools, institutions, army units and other units.

Percentage of Urban Population with Access to Tap Water refers to the ratio of the urban non-agricultural population (excluding temporary and mobile population) with access to tap water to the total urban non-agricultural population. The formula is:

$$\frac{\text{Percentage of Population}}{\text{with Access to Tap Water}} \quad \textit{Percentage of Population with Access to Tap Water} = \frac{\textit{Urban Non-agricultural Population with Access to Tap Water}}{\textit{Urban Non-agricultural Population}} \times 100\%$$

Production Capacity of Gaswork Gas refers to the actual comprehensive production capacity of the urban gasworks in gas generation, purification and delivery.

Length of Gas Pipelines refers to the total pipeline length between the outlet of the compressor, blower or gas tank and the shaft pipe of users.

Volume of Gas Supply refers to the total volume of gas sold to user in a year, including the volume for industrial use, residential use and other uses.

Percentage of Urban Population with Access to Gas refers to the ratio of the urban non-agricultural population with access to gas(including gas, liquefied petroleum gas and natural gas) to the urban non-agricultural population (excluding temporary and mobile population). The formula is:

$$\textit{Percentage of Population with Access to Gas} = \frac{\textit{Urban Non-agricultural Population with Access to Gas}}{\textit{Urban Non-agricultural Population}} \times 100\%$$

Length of Paved Roads at Year-end refers to the length of roads with a paved surface, and with a width of more than 3.5 meters, including high-quality, medium-quality and ordinary roads.

Urban Bridges refer to bridges over river courses, great separated junctions and overpasses in urban areas. Permanent bridges and semi-permanent bridegs are included. Temporary bridges, railway bridges and culverts are excluded.

Length of Urban Sewage Pipes refers to the total length of general drainage, trunks, branches and blind drainage, inspection wells, connection wells, inlets and outlets, etc.

Daily Disposal Capacity of Urban Sewage refers to the designed 24-hour capacity of sewage disposal at the sewage treatment works.

Number of Public Vehicles (Buses and Trolley-buses) at Year-end refers to the total number of operational buses available at year-end, including the year-end operational vehicles and vehicles in stock. Non-operational vehicles such as stringing cars, tank cars, machine-shop cars, trucks and other special vehicles and the borrowed passenger vehicles are excluded.

Length of Routes in Operation refers to the length of designated regular routes in operation, including the length of suburban routes in operation. The length of temporary operational lines is not included.

Area of Urban Gardens and Green Areas refers to the total area of urban public green land, special green land, production green land, protection green land and suburban scenic spots.

Public Green Area refers to green areas of various parks, zoos, botanical gardens, cemeteries, amusement parks, tree-flanked boulevards, green-land squares for tourism and relaxation. Areas with trees planted along-side the streets and boulevards are excluded.

Gross Output Value of Farming, Forestry, Animal Husbandry and Fishery refers to the total volume of products of farming, forestry, animal husbandry and fishery in value terms, which reflects the total scale and total result of agricultural production during a given period of time.

The statistical coverage of farming, forestry, animal husbandry and fishery is as follows:

In terms of ownership, China's agriculture includes specialized state farms (farming, forestry, animal husbandry, fishery), farms managed by various government agencies, organizations, schools, research institutions, and army; farms managed by rural collective organizations at levels of township, county, and village; farming, forestry, animal husbandry, fishery run by mining and industrial enterprises; farming, forestry, animal husbandry and fishery and some commodity industries run by various rural collective organizations and individual farmers.

(1) Farming includes cultivation of farm crops and other agricultural activities.

Cultivation includes the cultivation of grain crops, beans, tubers, cotton, oil-bearing crops, sugar crops, fiber crops, tobacco, vegetables, medicinal herbs, melons and gourds, and cultivation and management of tea plantations, mulberry fields and orchards.

Other agricultural activities include gathering fruits, gum and resin of wild plants, oil-bearing plants, grass, wild medicinal herbs, fungus plants, and commodity industries of the rural households.

(2) Forestry refers to planting trees of various kinds (excluding tea plantations, mulbherry fields and orchards), gathering of forest products, and cutting and felling of bamboo and trees by villages and other cooperative organizations under villages.

(3) Animal husbandry refers to raising and grazing of all animals except fishery and aquaculture, and hunting and raising of wild animals.

(4) Fishery refers to cultivation and catching of fish and other aquatic animals and cultivation and collection of seaweed and other aquatic plants.

Gross output value of farming, forestry, annimal husbandry and fishery is obtained by first multiplying the output of each product or by-produdt by its price, resulting in the output value of each single item. For a small number of products, annual output of which is not available or difficult to get due to the long production/growing process involved, the output value is estimated through an indirect approach. The sum of output value of all products of farming, forestry, animal husbandry, and fishery is then equal to their gross output value.

Prior to 1957, China's gross agricultural output value included barnyard manure and handicraft products for self-consumption(clothes, shoes, stocking, and initial grain processing undertaken by peasants). Since 1958, cutting and felling of bamboo and trees by villages and other cooperative organizations under villages have been included in forestry; value of barnyard manure has been excluded from animal husbandry; self-consumed handicrafts have been excluded from sideline occupations, while the output value of industries run by villages and cooperative organizations under village has been included in sideline occupations and the output value of fish catches by motor fishing boats has been added to fishery. Since 1980, the value of handicraft products made for sale by individuals in households has been added to sideline occupations. Since 1984, industries run by villages and cooperative organizations under villages have been included in the sector of industry. Since 1993, the subdivision of sideline occupations has been canceled, and the hunting of wild animals has been classified into animal husbandry, and the gathering of wild plants and commodity industry run by rural household have been included in farming.

Grain Yield refers to the yield in the whole country including grains produced by state farms, collective units, industrial enterprises and mines. Grain includes rice, wheat, corn, sorghum, millet and other miscellaneous grains as well as tubers and beans. Output of beans refers to dry beans without pods. The output of tubers (sweet potatoes and potatoes, not including taros and cassava) was converted into that of grain at the ratio 4:1, i.e. four kilograms of fresh tubers was equivalent to one kilogram of grain up to 1963. Since 1964 the ratio for conversion has been 5:1. Tubers supplied as vegetables (such as potatoes) in cities and suburbs are calculated as fresh vegetables and their output is not included in the output of grain. Output of all other grains refers to husked grain.

Yield of Oil-bearing Crops refers to the total yield of oil-bearing crops of various kinds, including peanuts, (dry, in shell), rapeseeds, sesame, sunflower seeds, flas seeds, and other oil-bearing crops. Soybeans, oil-bearing woody plants, and wild oil-bearing crops are not included.

Output of Aquatic Products refers to catches of both artificially cultured and naturally grown aquatic products, including fish, shrimps, crabs and shellfish in sea and inland water as well as seaweed. Freshwater plants are not included.

Output of Pork, Beef, and Mutton refers to the meat of slaughtered hogs, cattle, sheep and goats with head, feet, and offal taken away.

Cultivated Area (Area under cultivation) refers to farmland which is plowed constantly for growing crops, including cultivated land, newly cultivated land in the current year, farmland left without cultivation for less than three years and fallow land in the current year, rotation land of grass and crops, farmland with some fruit trees, mulberry trees and other trees and cultivated seashore land, lake land, and etc. The land of mulberry fields, tea plantations, orchards, nurseries of young plants, forest land, reed land, natural and man-made grassland and other land are not included in cultivated land.

Sown Area of Crops refers to area of land sown or transplanted with crops regardless of being in cultivated area or non-cultivated area. Area of land resown due to natural disasters is also included.

Irrigated Area refers to areas that are effectively irrigated, i.e. level land which has water source and complete sets of irrigation facilities to lift and move adequate water for irrigation purpose under normal conditions.

Consumption of Chemical Fertilizers in Agriculture refers to the quantity of chemical fertilizers applied in agriculture in the year, including nitrogenous fertilizer, phosphate fertilizer, potash fertilizer, and compound fertilizer. The consumption of chemical fertilizers is required in calculation to convert the gross weight into weight containing 100% effective component (eg. 100% nitrogen content in nitrogenous fertilizer, 100% phosphorous pentoxide content in phosphate fertilizer, 100% potasium oxide content in potash fertilizer). Compound fertilizer is converted with its major component.

Total Power of Farm Machinery refers to total mechanical power of machinery used in farming, forestry, animal husbandry, and fishery, including ploughing, irrigation and drainage, harvesting, transprot, plant protection, stock breeding, forestry and fishery. The power of internal combustion engines is required to convert horsepowers into watts and the power of electric motors is required to be converted into watts. Machinery employed for non-agricultural purposes, such as the machines used in township-run and village-run industry, construction, non-agricultural transport, scientific experiments and teaching, is excluded.

Laborers Engaged in Farming, Forestry, Animal Husbandry and Fishery refers to the total laborers who are directly engaged in production of farming, forestry, animal husbandry and fishery.

Number of Livestock or Poultry on Hand at the Beginning (or End) of the Reference Period refers to the total number of large animals, pigs, sheep, fowls, etc. raised by rural cooperative organizations, state farms, rural individuals, government agencies, schools, industrial and mining enterprises, army and urban residents at the beginning (or end) of the reference period.

Cereals refer to seeds of various kinds of crops which are used mainly for grain. Cereals include paddy, wheat, maize, millet, Chinese sorghum, etc., except beans and tubers.

Industry refers to material production sector which is engaged in extraction of natural resources and processing and reprocessing of minerals and agricultural products, including: (1) extraction of natural recources, such as mining, salt production, logging (but not including hunting and fishing); etc. (2) processing and reprocessing of farm and sideline produces, such as rice husking, flour milling, wine making, oil pressing, cotton ginning, silk reeling, spinning and weaving, and leather making; (3) manufacture of industrial products, such as steel making, iron smelting, chemicals manufacturing, petroleum processing, machine building, timber processing; water and gas production and electricity generation and supply; (4) repairing of industrial products such as the repairing of machinery and means of transport (including cars).

Prior to 1984, the rural industry run by village and cooperative organizations under village was classified as agriculture. Since 1984, it has been grouped into industry.

Units of Industrial Statistics and Inquiry They are classified into two categories (1) corporate industrial enterprises with independent accounting system (2) industrial establishments.

(1) Corporate industrial enterprises with independent accounting system refer to enterprises engaging in industrial production activities, which meet the following requirements: ① They are established legally, having their own names, organizations, location, able to take civil liability; ② They possess and use their assets independently, assume liabilities, and are entitled to sign contracts with other units; ③ They are financially independent and compile their own balance sheets.

(2) Industrial establishments refer to economic units which are located in one single place and engaged entirely or primarily in one kind of industrial activity, including financially independent industrial enterprises and units engaged in industrial activities

under the non-industrial enterprises (or financially dependent). Industrial establishments generally meet the following requirements: ① They have one location and are engaged in one kind of industrial activity each; ② They operate and manage their industrial production activities separately; ③ They have accounts of income and expenditure separately.

Units of Over-norm industrial Statitics and Inquiry refer to the total state-owned industrial enterprises and nonstate-owned industrial enterprises with 5 million yuan above of revenue of product sales.

Light Industry refers to the industry which produces consumer goods and hand tools. It consists of two categories, depending on the materials used:

(1) Industries using farm products as raw materials. These are branches of light industry which directly or indirectly use farm products as basic raw materials, including the manufacture of food and beverages, tobacco processing, textile, clothing, fur and leather manufacturing, paper making, printing, etc.

(2) Industries using non-farm products as raw materials. These are branches of light industry which use manufactured goods as raw materials, including the manufacture of cultural, educational articles and sports goods, chemicals, synthetic fiber, chemical products for daily use, glass products for daily use, metal products for daily use, hand tools, medical apparatus and instruments, and the manufacture of cultural and clerical machinery.

Heavy Industry refers to the industry which produces capital goods, and provides various sectors of the national economy with necessary material and technical basis. It consists of the following three branches according to the purpose of production or the use of products:

(1) Mining, quarrying and logging industry refers to the industry that extracts natural resources, including extraction of petroleum, coal, metal and non-metal ores and logging.

(2) Raw materials industry refers to the industry that provides various sectors of the national economy with raw materials, fuels and power. It includes smelting and processing of metals, coking and coke chemistry, chemical materials and building materials such as cement, plywood, and power, petroleum refining and coal dressing.

(3) Manufacturing industry refers to the industry that processes raw materials. It includes machine-building industry which equips sectors of the national economy, industries of metal structure and cement products, industries producing means of agricultural production, such as chemical fertilizers and pesticides.

According to the above principle of classification, the repairing trades which are engaged primarily in repairing products of heavy industry are classified into heavy industry while these engaged in repairing products of light industry are classified into light industry.

Gross Industrial Output Value is the total volume of industrial products sold or available for sale in value terms which reflects the total achievements and overall scale of industrial production during a given period. It includes the value of the finished products, which are not to be further processed in the enterprises and have been inspected, packed and put in storage, the value of industrial services rendered to other units and the changes in the value of the semi-finished products and products in process between the beginning and closing of the period (only the enterprises with long production cycle are required to calculate the changes). The gross industrial output value is calculated with "factory method". No double calculations are to be made within the same enterprise. However, double counting does occur among different enterprises.

Output value of light and heavy industries is also classified with the "facotry" method. Under normal conditions, if the major products of an industrial enterprise belong to light industry products, the gross output value of that enterprise is classified wholly into light industry; the same principle applies to heavy industry.

Value Added of Industry refers to the final results of industrial production of the industrial trade in money terms during the reference period.

Original Value of Fixed Assets refers to the original value of all fixed assets owned by industrial enterprises, calculated at the cost paid at the time of purchase, installation, reconstruction, expansion, and technical innovation and transformation of the said assets, which includes expenses on purchase, package, transportation, and installation, etc.

Net Value of Fixed Assets is obtained by deducting depreciation over years from the original value of fixed assets.

Working Capital (Circulating Assets) refers to assets which can be cashed or spent or consumed in an operating cycle of one year or over one year, which includes cash, various deposits, short term investment, and receivable payments, and advance payments, stock, etc.

Total Value of Profit and Tax (Pre-tax Profits) refers to the sum of the total profits, products sales tax and surcharges and the value added tax payable of industrial enterprises. It is also called pre-tax profits.

Ratio of Pre-tax Profits to Assets refers to the ratio of pre-tax profits realized in a given period to the total assets in the same period (net fixed assets plus working capital), which reflects the economic efficiency of the assets utilization and is calculated as follows:

$$Ratio\ of\ Pre\text{-}tax\ Profits\ to\ Assets\ (\%) = \frac{Pre\text{-}tax\ Profits\ in\ Reference\ Period}{Average\ Net\ Fixed\ Assets + Average\ Balance\ of\ Working\ Capital} \times 100\%$$

Rario of Pre-tax profits to assets reflects the amount of profit tax provided from per unit capital (usually per 10 thousand yuan). It is a major analytical indicator to observe and assess the economic efficiency of utilizing capital in departments or enterprises, and analyse the input efficiency of capital.

Ratio of Profits to Total Industrial Costs refers to the ratio of profits realized in a given period to the total costs in the same period, which reflects the economic efficiency of input cost and is calculated as follows:

$$Ratio\ of\ Profits\ to\ Total\ Industrial\ Cost\ (\%) = \frac{Total\ Profits}{Total\ Costs} \times 100\%$$

Value Added Rate of Industry refers to the ratio of value added of industry in a given period to the gross output value in the same period, which reflects the economic efficiency of cutting down the intermediate input and is calculated as follows:

$$Value\ Added\ Rate\ of\ Industry\ (\%) = \frac{Value\ Added\ of\ Industry\ (at\ Current\ Prices)}{Gross\ Output\ Value\ (at\ Current\ Prices) + Tax\ Amount\ on\ Sales\ Items} \times 100\%$$

Number of Times of Turnover of Working Capital refers to the number of times of turnover of working capital in a given period of time, which reflects the speed of turnover of working capital and is calculated as follows:

$$Turnover\ of\ Working\ Assets\ (\%) = \frac{Sales\ Revenue\ of\ Products}{Average\ Balance\ of\ Total\ Working\ Capital} \times 100\%$$

Sales Rate of Industrial Products refers to the ratio of total sales in a given period to the gross output value in the same period, which reflects the extent of industrial output sold and is calculated as follows:

$$Sales\ Rate\ of\ Industrial\ Products\ (\%) = \frac{Total\ Sales\ (at\ Current\ Prices)\ in\ Reference\ Period}{Gross\ Output\ Value\ (at\ Current\ Prices)\ in\ Reference\ Period} \times 100\%$$

Sales Revenue of Industrial Products refers to the revenue from the sales of products by industrial enterprises and the revenue from services provided and etc.

Sales Cost of Industrial Products refers to the actual cost of products of industrial enterprises and industrial services provided, etc.

Tax and Extra Charges on Sales of Products refers to the tax on city maintenance and construction, consumption tax, resources tax and extra charges for education, which should be borne by the enterprises in selling products and providing industrial services.

Sales Profit of Products refers to the profit gained by the enterprises by deducting cost, charges and taxes from the business income of the enterprises obtained in selling products and providing industrial services.

Total Profits refers to the profits gained by the enterprises.

Value Added Tax Payable refers to the amount of the value added tax which should be paid by the enterprises in the reference period.

Ratio of Pre-tax Profits to Gross Output Value refers to the radio of the total amount of pre-tax profits gained (including total profits, sales tax and extra charges of products as well as the value added tax payable) in the reporting period to the gross output value in the same period (the ratio is expressed in percentage). The formula is as follows:

$$Ratio\ of\ Pre\text{-}tax\ Profits\ to\ Gross\ Output\ Value\ (\%) = \frac{Total\ Amount\ of\ Pre\text{-}tax\ Profits}{Gross\ Industrial\ Output\ Value} \times 100\%$$

Overall Labour Productivity of Industrial Enterprises refers to the average output per staff and worker in industrial enterprises in value terms. At present, the value added and the average number of staff and workers of an industrial enterprises in a given period are used to calculate the overall labour productivity. The formula used is:

$$Overall\ Labour\ Productivity = \frac{Value\ Added\ of\ Industry}{Average\ Number\ of\ Staff\ and\ Workers}$$

For the purpose of comparison of the overall labour productivity among different years, the data on the overall labour productivity of the years prior to 1990 have been adjusted on the basis of 1990 constant prices.

Actully Received Capital refer the main management capital actually receive by enterprises used for long term circulation, including state capital, legal person capital, collective capital, individual capital and foreign capital.

Total Assets refer to all assets which are owned or controlled by enterprises, including circulating assets, long-term investment, fixed assets, intangible assets and deferred assets, other long-term assets, and deferred taxes, etc. The summation of above items is equal to total assets shown in the balance sheets of the enterprises.

(1) Circulating assets (working capital) refer to assets which can be cashed or spent or consumed in an operating cycle of one year or over one year, including cash, all kinds of deposits, short term investment, receivables, advance payment, stock, etc.

(2) Fixed assets refer to the net value of fixed assets, clearance of fixed assets, project under construction, fixed assets losses in suspense. These are corporations' fund holdings.

(3) Intangible assets refer to the assets without material form used by enterprises over a long time, such as patents, non-patent technologies, trade marks, copyright, land use right, business reputation, etc.

Total Liabilities refer to the debts that enterprises are responsible for repayment, including liquid liabilities, long-term liabilities and deferred taxes, etc. Total liabilities correspond to the summation item of liabilities shown in the balance sheets of the enterprises.

(1) Liquid liabilities (also called quick liabilities or immediate liabilities) refer to an enterprise's total debt payable within an operating cycle of one year or over one year, including short term loans, payables and advance payments, wages payable, taxes payable and profit payable, etc.

(2) Long-term liabilities refer to total debt payable within an operating cycle of one year or over one year, including long-term loans, payable liabilities, long-term payables, etc.

Creditors' Equity refers to investors' ownership of net assets of the enterprise. It is equal to the total assets of the enterprise minus its total liabilities, including the primary input from investors, capital accumulation fund, surplus accumulation fund and undistributed profit. It is the stock holders' equity in stock companies.

Statistical Unit in Construction refers to the establishments engaged in the construction of buildings and structures and in the installation of equipment. They can be divided into two categories: corporate construction enterprises and affiliated construction units, depending upon their way of organization. A corporate construction enterprise is a legal entity with independent accounting system, especially set up to undertake construction activities. It should meet the following 3 requirements: ① being set up in line with relevant legal basis, having its full name, organization and location, and capable of taking civil liabilities; ② independently possessing and using its assets and assuming its liabilities, and entitled to sign contracts with other institutions; and ③ making independent accounts of its profits and losses, and capable of compiling its own balance sheet. On the other hand, the affiliated construction units are subsidiary construction units that are established by enterprises or institutions in other industries to take construction projects to build up their fixed assets. They should also meet 3 requirements: ① engaged exclusively or mainly in construction and installation activities with a fixed site; ② organizing independently their production/management; and ③ with independent accounting capability in the enterprises to which they are attached.

Gross Output Value of Construction (Output Value of Projects Under Construction) refers to the gross output value of construction and installation projects that are undertaken by construction enterprises or affiliated constructing units, calculated in line with the planned schedule. It includes:

(1) Output value of construction projects, that is the value of projects covered by the project budgets;

(2) Output value of installation projects, that is the value of the installation of equipment;

(3) Output value of repair of buildings and structures, that is the value created through the repairs of buildings or structures, but does not include the value of buildings or structures being repaired and the value of the repair of production equipment;

(4) Output value of manufactured non-standard equipment, that is the value of non-standard production equipment (including raw materials and manufacturing cost) made for the contruction project, irrespective of whether the equipment is manufactured on the construction site or by subsidiary workshops.

Value Added of Construction refers to the final result of the activities of production and management of construction in monetary terms in the reference period. At present, the value added of construction is calculated with the method of distribution. In other words, it is the sum of incomes of various production factors in the production process. The formula is as follows:

Value added of construction = *depreciation of fixed assets in the year* + *wages payable* + *welfare expenses payable* +

insurance premium and tax for waiting for employment in the administrative expenses + taxes and surcharges on project settlement + profit gained from project settlement − profit used as bonus.

Floor Space of Buildings Under Construction refers to floor space of building under construction during the reference period, including newly started buildings, buildings started earlier and continued during the referece period, and buildings suspended earlier but restarted during the reference period. Excluded are buildings started and then suspended earlier that have not been restarted during the reference time.

Floor Space of Buildings Completed refers to the floor space of buildings that are completed in the reference period in accordance with the requirements of the design, up to the standard for putting them into use, and have been checked and accepted by concerned departments as qualified ones.

Total Number of Machinery and Equipment Owned by the Construction Enterprises (or Units) by the End of the Year refers to the number of machines and equipment owned by the enterprises (or units, and listed as the fixed assets of the enterprises (or units) by the end of the year, including machinery and equipment for construction, production and transportation.

Total Power of Machinery and Equipment Owned by the Construction (or Units) by the End of the Year refers to the total power of machinery and equipment owned by the enterprises (or units), and listed as the fixed assets of the enterprises (or units) by the end of the year, including machinery and equipment for construction, production and transportation. The power of the machinery is calculate on basis of the designed or verified capacity, covering the power of the machinery/equipment and the separate power equipment serving the machinery/equipment (such as electricmotors), but excluding welders, transformers and boilers. The unit used for the calculation of power is kilowatt, with horsepower converted to kilowatt by 1 horsepower = 0.735 kilowatt.

Income from Settlement of Projects refers to the income received by the construction enterprise/unit from the completed portion of the project through settlement procedures with the contractee during the reference period, and other charges to the contractee as operational costs, such as facility fee, labour insurance premium, moving cost of construction unit, as well as various types of claims to the contractee.

Profit from Settlement of Projects refers to profit realized through settled projects. It is calculated with the following formula:

Profit from Settlement of Projects = Income from Settlement of Projects − Settled Cost − Settled Taxes and Other Cost

Total Revenue of Enterprises refers to the sum of income from production and operation of enterprises, including income from settlement of projects and other operational income, namely:

Total Revenue of Enterprises = Income from Settlement of Projects + Other Operational Income

Length of Railways in Operation refers to the total length of the trunk line under passenger and freight transportation. The calculation is based on the actual length of the first line even if this line has a full or partial double track or more tracks, excluding double tracks, stationsidings, tracks under the charge of stations, branch lines, special purpose lines and the non-payable connecting lines. The length of railways in operation is an important indicator to show the development of the intrastructure for the railway transport, and also the essential data to calculate volume of passenger freight transport, traffic density and utilization efficiency of the locomotives and carriages.

Extention Length of Trunk Lines refers to the sum of the first, the second, the third lines and other constructed length of the trunk railways, excluding the extention length of the station lines, lines under the jurisdiction of depots, sidings and lines for special purpose. It provides important information for the calculation of the needs for rails, sleepers, sand and stone for the construction of railways.

Length of Highways refers to the length of highways which are built in conformity with the grades specified by the highway engineering standard formulated by the Ministry of Communications, and have been formally checked and accepted by the departments of highways and put into use. The length of highways includes that of the suburb highways at large and medium-sized cities, highways passing through streets at small cities and towns, and also the length of bridges and ferries. It does not include the length of streets in big and medium-sized cities and highways built for the production purpose at factories, mines, forest areas and agricultural areas. If two or more highways go the same section of the way, the length of the section is only calculated for once and no duplication is allowed. The length of highways is an important indicator to show the development of the highway construction and to provide essential information to calculate the transport network density.

Length of Navigable Inland Waterways refers to the length of the natural rivers; lakes, reservoirs, canals, and ditches open to navigation during a given period, which enables the tranaport by ships and rafts. It includes the channels open to navigation for over 3 months accumulatively in a year, yet this does not include the river courses which are only used to float odd logs and bamboo rafts.

Length of Civil Aviation Routes refers to the length of all routes for regular civil aviation flights. There are usually two ways to calculate the distance between airports connected by the route length: One is to put the length of all air routes together, called duplicated calculation of the length of the routes; the other is not to allow the duplication in calculation when two or more routes pass the same section. The latter is usually used, as it can precisely show the size of the civil aviation network and indicate the extent of civil aviation serving the national economy and the people.

Length of Oil (Gas) Pipelines refers to the actual transport distance of oil (or gas) products, and is in general calculated in the length of single pipe line. If the length of the double pipelines and alternate pipeline is included, it is called the extention length of the oil (gas) pipelines, which indicates the actual length of the pipelines built. Length of oil (gas) pipelines (excluding double pipelines) is usually used as a chief indicator to show the development, scale and level of the pipeline transportation.

Freight (Passenger) Traffic refers to the volume of freight (passenger) transported with various means. Freight transport is calculated in tons and passenger traffic is calculated in the number of persons. Despite the type of freight and travelling distance, the freight transport is calculated in the actual weight of the goods: and despite the travelling distance and ticket price, the passenger traffic is calculated by the principle that one person can be counted only once in one travel. The passenger who travel with a half-price ticket or a child ticket is also calculated as one person. The freight (passenger) traffic provides a quantitative measure to show how the transport industry serves the national economy and people, and is also an important indicator for planning the transport industry and for studying the development scale and speed of the transport industry.

Freight Ton-kilometers (Passenger-kilometers) refer to the sum of the products of the volume of transported cargo (passengers) multiplied by the transport distance, usually using ton-kilometre and passenger-kilometre as units for measurement. Normally, the shortest distance between the departure station and the destination station (i. e., the payable distance) is the basis to calculate the freight ton-kilometers. This is an important indicator to show the total results of the transport industry, to prepare and examine the transport plan and to measure the efficiency, the labour productivity and the unit cost of transport.

Volume of Freight Handled in Major Coastal Ports refers to the volume of cargo passing in and out the harbor area of the major coastal ports and having been loaded and unloaded. The volume includes that of the postal matters, registered luggages and fuels, materials and fresh water as supplies of the ships. The volume of freight handled may be classified as import, export, or as domestic trade and foreign trade. The volume of freight handled by type of cargo and by main flow direction reflects the position and function of the ports in the inflow of Chinese and foreign commodities and in the transportation for foreign trade.

Business Volume of Post and Telecommunications refers to the total amount of the information delivered and other post and telecommunications services provided by the post and telecommunications departments for the customers. It is derived by first multiplying the business volume of different types, such as number of letters, telegrams, long distance calls, city and rural telephone subscribers and accumulated number of newspapers and journals subscribed and sold, etc. by their respective average unit price (fixed price) and then adding these products together: plus the income from maintenance of telephone exchanges and lines, and the income from other business operations. The business volume of post and telecommunications indicates the total achievements made by the post and telecommunications department during a given period of time in a comprehensive way, and is an important indicator to study the composition and development of the post and telecommunications business.

Local (Urban) Telephone refers to telephones connected to urban telephone network (at and above county level). The telephone charge is at either monthly fixed rate or numerical rate.

(1) Resident telephones refer to telephones installed in resident dwellings, including those with telephone charges paid by individuals, by public units and free of charge.

(2) Personal telephones refer to telephones installed and paid at one's own expense.

Subscribers of Paging Services refers to subscribers who carry small size pagers and receive audio signals, digital signals or literal signals sent out by city telephone through wireless paging center within assigned area. Each pager is counted as a subscriber.

Mobile Telephone Subscribers refers to the persons who own mobile telephone number connected with the mobile telephone communication network and registered by post and telecommunications organization. The unmber of subscribers is calculated only when the subscribers who have gone through all the register formalities and entered into the mobile telephone network. One mobile telephone is treated as a subscriber.

Total Retail Sales of Consumer Goods refers to the sum of retail sales of consumer goods by the establishments in wholesale trade, retail sale trade, catering trade, manufacturing industry and other industries of different types of ownership, to urban and rural residents and social groups. This indicator is used to show the supply of consumer goods through various channels to households and institutions to meet their demands, and is therefore very important for the study of the issues on people's livelihood, on the purchasing power of consumer goods and on the circulation of money. The retail sales of consumer goods include: commodities (excluding houses) sold to urban and rural residents for residential uses, and consumer goods for non-productive and non-operational uses purchased with public money by government agencies, organizations armies, schools, enterprises, institutions, urban neighborhood committees and rural villagers' committees.

Purchase, Sales and Stock of Commodities by Wholesale and Retail Trade refer to the purchase, sales and stock of commodities by wholesale and retail establishments of different ownerships (excluding individual sellers).

Total Purchases of Commodities refer to the purchases of commodities by the establishments from other establisments or individuals (including direct import from abroad) for the purpose of re-selling, either with or without further processing of the commodities purchased. This indicator is used to show the total value of purchases of commodities by wholesale and retail establishments from domestic and overseas markets. The total purchases include: (1) agricultural and industrial products purchased from producers; (2) books, magazines and newspapers purchased from distribution departments of the publishers; (3) commodities purchased from wholesale and retail establishments; (4) commodities purchased from other units, such as surplus materials purchased from government agencies, enterprises or institutions, commodities purchased from catering and service establishments, confiscated goods purchased from customs authorities or market management agencies, second-hand goods and wastes purchased from residents; and (5) commodities directly imported from abroad. Excluded are commodities purchased by establishments (units) for use in their own business operation, commodities obtained without buying or selling procedures, rejected commodities, etc.

Total Sales of Commodities refer to selling of commodities by the establishments to other establishments and individuals (including direct export). This indicator is used to show the total value of sales of commodities at domestic markets and exporting commodities. The total sales include: (1) commodities sold to urban and rural residents and social groups for their consumption; (2) commodities sold to establishments in industry, agriculture, construction, transportation, post and telecommunications, wholesale and retail trades, catering trade and serrice industry for their production and operation; (3) commodities sold to wholesale and retail establishments for re-selling, with or without further processing; and (4) commodities for direct export to other countries. Excluded are selling of waste packaging materials used by the establishments (units) themselves, commodities transferred without buying or selling procedures, commission income from brokerage in transactions whose settlement is directly handled by buyers and sellers, rejected commodities in the purchase, loss in commodities, etc.

Commodity Stock of Wholesale and Retail Enterprises at Year-end refers to total commodities possessed by wholesale and retail enterprises (units) of various types of ownership, which reflects the commodity stock level of various wholesale and retail enterprises and the potential for market supply. It includes: (1) commodities located in storage, garages, counters, and shelves of operating units (such as sale stores, wholesale centers, and operating offices) of wholesale and retail enterprises; (2) commodities in the process of selecting, sorting, and packing; (3) commodities not arrived but recorded as purchase in the account; (4) commodities deposited in other places rather than places mentioned above, for instance: commodities in the hold of purchasers temporarily due to the refusal of payment and commodities not taken back after going through the formalities; (5) commodities entrusted to other units to sell but not sold yet; (6) commodities purchased for other units but not delivered yet. Commodities not included as stock are those not owned by the enterprises (units), those allocated to factories rather than wholesale and retail enterprises for processing but not taken back yet, and finally those put in stock by wholesale and retail enterprises on behalf of the state material reserves units. In the calculation of the value of commodities stock at the end of period, the value is calculated at purchasing prices in agricultural goods purchasing units and wholesale units, and at the accounting prices in retail units.

Outlets of Wholesale and Retail Trade and Catering Trade refer to natural number of units engaged in wholesale and retail trade and catering trade, which are set up by wholesale and retail enterprises and catering enterprises of various types of ownership, and also as captive units by other trades.

Personnel of Wholesale and Retail Trade and Catering Trade refers to those people who are engaged in wholesale and retail trade and catering trade and who get labor reward and operating income.

Total Imports and Exports refer to the value of commodities imported into and exported from the boundary of China. They include the actual imports and exports through foreign trade, imported and exported goods under the processing and assembling trades and materials, supplies and gifts as aid given gratis between governments and by the United Nationals and other international organizations, and contributions donated by overseas Chinese, compatriots in Hongkong and Macao and Chinese with foreign citizenship, leasing commodities owned by tenant at the expiration of leasing period, the imported and exported commodities processed with imported materials, commodities trading, imported and exported small value trading goods in border areas (excluding mutual exchange goods), the imported and exported commodities and articles for public use of the sino-foreign joint ventures, sino-foriegn coopertive enterprises and ventures exclusively with foreign own investment. Also included import or export of samples and advertising goods for whose CIF or FOB value are beyond the permitted ceiling (excluding goods of no trading or use value and free commodities for export), imported goods sold in China from bonded warehouse and other imported or exported goods. The indicator of the total imports and exports at customs can be used to observe the total size of external trade in a country. In accordance with the stipulation of the Chinese government, imports are calculated at CIF, while exports are calculated at FOB.

Import-Export Value by Location of China's Foreign Trade Managing Units refer to actual value of imports and exports carried out by corporations which have been registered by the local customhouse and are vested with right to run impor-export business.

Import Value of Commodities by the Places of their Destination and Expor Value of Commodities by the Places of their Origin in China The former indicator refers to the value of import commodities of the lpaces of their consumption, utilization or the places of the commodities dispatched.

Utilization of Foreign Capital refers to remittance, equipment and technology financed from abroad, by loans, foreign direct investment and other forms undertaken by the Chinese governments at all levels, by various departments, enterprises and other economic units.

Foreign Loans a major part of China's utilization of foreign capital, refer to funds borrowed from abroad, including loans of foreign governments, loans of international financial institutions, commercial loans of foreign banks, export credit, and funds raised by Chinese bonds and shares issued abroad.

Direct Investment by Foreign Enterprises refers to the investments inside China by foreign enterprises and economic organizations or individuals (including overseas Chinese, compatriots from Hong Kong and Macao, and Chinese enterprises registered abroad), following the relevant policies and laws of China, for the establishment of ventures exclusively with foreign sole investment, Sino-foreign joint ventures and cooperative enterprises or for co-operative exploration of resources with enterprises or economic organizations in China, through the utilization of remittance, material objects and technology. It includes the re-investment of the foreign enterprises with the profits gained from the investment and the funds that enterprises borrow from abroad in the total investment of projects which are approved by the relevant department of the government.

Contracted Projects with Foreign Countries refer to projects undertaken by Chinese contractors (project contracting companies) in the form of bidding process. They include: (1) overseas civil engineering construction projects financed by foreign investors; (2) overseas projects financed by the Chinese government through its foreign-aid programs; (3) construction projects of Chinese diplomatic missions, trade offices and other institutions stationed abroad; (4) construction projects in China financed by foreign investment; (5) sub-contracted projects to be taken by Chinese contractors through a joint umbrella project with foreign contractor (s); (6) technical assistance projects in the form of service results and chargeable to the owners (such as topographic surveying, geological prospecting, development zone programming, provision of designing documents, blueprint, materials on production process, technical consultation, project feasibility studies and evaluation, personnel training, etc.); and (7) housing development projects. The business income from international contracted projects is the work volume of contracted projects completed during the reference period, expressed in monetary terms, including completed work on projects signed in previous years.

Service Co-operation with Foreign Countries refers to the activities of providing technology and labour services to employers or contractors in the forms of receiving salaries and wages. Labour services providing by contractual joint ventures of Chinese international contracting corporations should be included in the statistic of service co-operation with foreign countries. The business income of labour service co-operation is the income in the form of wages and salaries, overtime pay, bonuses and other remuneration received from the employers during the reference period.

Number of Tourists refers to the number of foreigners, overseas Chinese, and compatriots from Hong Kong, Macao and Taiwan coming to China for sightseeing, visits, tours, family reunions, vacations, study tours and other activities of an economic, scientific and technological, cultural, physical educational and religious nature. This does not include the number of employees of foreign organizations stationed in China such as embassies, consulates, news agencies, the offices of corporations and enterprises and foreign experts and students residing in China and the persons staying priefly in China but not for passing the night.

Foreign Exchange Earnings from International Tourism refr to the total expenditures of the foreigners, overseas Chinese, compatriots from Hong Kong, Macao and Taiwan in the process of their tourism in the mainland of China. Their expenditures mentioned above are foreign exchange earnings to China.

Government Revenue refers to the revenue of the government finance by means of participating in the distribution of the social products, which is the financial resources for ensuring the government to function. The contents of government revenue have been changed several times. Now it includes the following main items:

(1) Various tax revenues, including value added tax, business tax, consumption tax, land value added tax, tax on city maintenancy and construction, resources tax, tax on use of urban land, stamp tax, tax on adjustment of the orientation of in-

vestment in fixed assets, personal income tax, enterprise income tax, tariff, tax on agriculture and animal husbandry and tax on occupance of cultivated land, etc.

(2) Special revenues, including revenue collected from imposing fee on sewage treatment, revenue collected from imposing fee on urban water resources, and extra-charges for education, etc.

(3) Other revenues, including revenue from the repayment of capital construction loan, the funds for the state key construction projects in energy industry and transportation, and the funds for state budget adjustment, etc.

(4) Planned subsidies for the losses of the state-owned enterprises. This is an item of negative revenue, used to eat up part of the government revenue.

Government Expenditure refers to the distrubution and use of the funds the government finance has raised, so as to meet the needs of economic construction and various causes. It includes the following main items:

(1) Expenditure for capital construction: It refers to the non-gratuitous use and appropriation of funds for capital construction in the range of capital construction, outlay of capital as well as the loans on capital construction approved by the government for special purpose or policy purpose and the expenditure with discount paid in an overall way within the amount of the funds appropriated to the departments for capital construction.

(2) Innovation funds of the enterprises: They refer to the funds appropriated from the government budget for the enterprises to tap the latent power, upgrade the technology and carry out innovation, including the innovation fund of the departments, loan of the enterprises for innovation, subsidies on the innovation of the small fertilizer plant, small cement plant, small coal mines, small machinery plant and small steel plant, the expenditure of interest for the loan for innovation.

(3) Geological prospecting expenses: They refer to the expenses appropriated from the government budget to the geological prospecting units for the expenditure of the prospecting work, including the expenditures of the administrative agencies for geological prospecting and their institutional units as well as the geological prospecting expenditure.

(4) Expenditures for science and technology promotion: They refer to the expenses appropriated from the government budget for the scientific and technological expenditure, including new products development expenditure, expenditure for intermediate trial and subsidies on important scientific researches.

(5) Expenditure for supporting rural production: It refers to the expenditures appropriated from the government budget for supporting the various expenditures of the rural collective units or households for production, including the subsidies to the small water conservancy projects and well drilling, sprinkling irrigation projects run by the villages; subsidies on the rural water and soil conserving measures; subsidies to the small power stations run by the villages; subsidies to the expenditure for fighting against particularly severe draughts; subsidies on the rural waste land exclamation; fund for supporting the township enterprises; subsidies to the expenditure for popularization of the agricultural technologies and plant protection in the rural areas; subsidies to the expenditure for the protection of grasslands and cattle and fowls; subsidies on afforestation and forest protection in rural areas; subsidies on the rural aquatic products industry; special fund for developing grain production.

(6) Operating expenses of the departments of farming, forestry, water conservancy and meteorology etc.: They refer to the expenses appropriated from the government budget for the expenditures of agricultural exclamation, farms, agriculture, animal husbandry, agricultural machinery, forestry, timber industry, water conservancy, aquatic products industry, meteorology, technology popularization in township enterprises, popularization (demonstration) of improved varieties, plant (cattle and fowls, forest) protection, water quality monitoring, prospecting and designing, resources investigation, cadres training, subsidies to horticulture gardens, expenditure of specialized secondary schools, subsidies on the experiments of sowing herbage seeds by flights, expenditures of afforestation agencies and meteorology agencies, expenses for fishery administration and operating expenses for agricultural administration, etc.

(7) Operating expenses of the departments of industry, transport and commerce: They refer to the expenses appropriated from the government budget to the departments of industry, transport and commerce for the expenditure of business development, including expenses for prospecting and designing, expenditures of specialized secondary schools, expenditures of the technical training skills and expenditures for cadres training, etc.

(8) Operating expenses of the departments of culture, education, science and public health: They refer to the expenses appropriated from the government budget for the expenditures of the causes of culture, publication, cultural relics, education, pubilic health, traditional Chinese medical science, free medical services, sports, archives, earthquake, ocean, communications, broadcasting, film and television, family planning; expenditure for training of cadres of government, party and mass organization; expenditures for natural sciences, social sciences, associations for science and technology and the special expenditure for the high-tech researches. They include mainly wages, extra wages, welfare funds, pension for the retirees, stipend, expenses for official business, expenses for equipment purchases, expenses for repairs, business expenses and subsidies to the units which are unable to support their expenditures by their own earnings.

(9) Pension for the disabled or for the families of the bereaved and relief funds for social welfare: They refer to the funds

approriatied from the government budget for the expenditures of pension for the disabled or for the families of the bereaved and relief funds for social welfare, including the lump-sum or regular pension paid by the departments of civil affairs to the members of martyr's families and families of those who died for the public interest, pension to the revolutionary disabled, subsidies for permanent disability of various kinds, subsidies to the military martyr's dependents and the demobilized armymen, expenditure for settling down the demobilized armymen, operating expenses of the consoling institutions, expenses for management and repair of the commemorative buildings for the martyrs, the expenses managed by the departments, of civil affairs for the retirees and those who have quitted their work, expenses for social relief in rural and urban areas, operating expenses for providing relief to the areas of natural calamity and subsidies on the reconstruction after the particularly severe natural calamities, etc.

(10) Expenditures for national defence: They refer to the funds approriated from the government budget for the expenditures for building up national defence and safeguarding national security, including expenses of national defence, expenses of scientific researches on national defence, expenses for building up people's militia and expenditure for special projects, etc.

(11) Administrative expenses: They include expenditure for administration, subsidies to the parties and mass organizations, diplomatic expenditure, expenditure for public security, judicial expenditure, law court expenditure, procuratorial expenditure and subsidies to the expenses to the expenses for treating the cases by the public security departments, procuratroial organs and law courts.

(12) Expenditure for price subsidies: It refers to the expenditure approriated, with the approval of the government, from the government budget for the policy subsidies to price adjustment, including the fund for the increase of grain prices, the subsidies to the difference between the selling prices and purchasing prices of grains, cotton and edible oil, awards in addition to the purchasing prices of cotton, risk fund for non-staple food, subsidies on the prices of meat and meat products, subsidies on the price difference for curbing the high market prices of meat, meat products and vegetables and the subsidies approval by the government on the prices of textbooks and newsprint of newspapers and periodicals.

Revenue of the central government and revenue of the local government In accordance with the classification of the structure of the government finance in 1994 on the basis of the classification of channels for collection of tax revenues, the revenue of the central government and the revenue of the local governments have different coverage. The revenue of the central government includes tariff, consumption tax and value added tax levied by the customs, consumption tax, income tax of the enterprises subordinate to the central government, income taxes of the local banks, foreign-funded banks and non-bank financial institutions, business tax, income tax and profits of railways, head offices of banks, head officed of insurance company, which are handed over to the government in a centralized way, tax on city maintenance and construction, 75% of the value added tax, tax on ocean petroleum resources, 88% of the tax on stock dealing (stamp tax). The revenue of the local governments includes business tax, income tax of the enterprises subordinate to the local government, personal income tax, tax on the sue of urban land, tax on the adjustment of the investment in fixed assets, tax on town maintenance and construction, tax on real estates, tax on the use of vehicles and ships, stamp tax, slaughter tax, tax on agriculture and animal husbandry, tax on special agricultural products, tax on the occupancy of cultivated land, contract tax, 25% of the value added tax, 12% of the tax on stock dealing (stamp tax) and tax on resources other than ocean petroleum resources.

Deposit is a form of credit by which enterprises, institutions, organizations or residents can put money into banks and other credit institutions for safekeeping and interest earning under the principle of free withdrawal. According to different depositors, deposits are divided into enterprise deposits, treasury deposits, deposits of government agencies and organizations, capital construction deposits, urban savings deposits, rural deposits and other deposits. Deposits are major sources of the credit funds of banks.

Loan is a from of credit by which banks and other credit institutions provide funds at certain interest rate to enterprises and individuals in the light of the principle of unconditional repayment. Loans from Chinese banks include circulating capital loans, fixed assets loans, loans to urban and rural individuals engaged in industrial and commercial business and agricultural loans.

Amount Insured refers to the amount of compensation for the loss or agreed sum of money to be paid by the insurer to the insurant. It is the maximum amount of liabilities written in the insurance contract and is also used as a basis to calculate the premium.

Premium is the fee paid by the insurant based on a proportion of the benefit he or she may get from the insurance plus the insurance value. It includes the income from the deposit of property insurance and presonal insurance.

Settled Claim is the compensation paid by the insurer to the insurant in accordance with the insurance contract for the loss which has been checked and found to be in the range of liability of the insurance after an accident has happened to the insured property or to a person who has insured his life. It is further divided into settled and unsettled claim.

Regular Institutions of Higher Learning refer to educational establishments set up according to the government evaluation and approval procedures, which enroll graduates from senior secondary schools and provide higher education courses and training for senior professionals. They include full-time universities, colleges, high professional schools and short-term professional universities.

Institutions of Higher Learning for Adults refer to educational establishments, set up in line with relevant rules approved by the government, which enroll staff and workers with senior secondary school or equivalent education, and provide higher education courses in many forms of full-time, part-time, spare-time, or correspondence for adults. Professionals thus trained receive a qualification equivalent to graduates studying regular courses at regular universities, colleges and professional colleges. Institutions of higher learning for adults include Radio and TV universities, schools of high education for staff and workers and peasants, colleges for management cadres, pedagogical, independent correspondence colleges.

Enrollment Rate of Primary School-age Children refers to the proportion of school-age children enrolled at schools to the total number of school-age children both in and outside schools (including retarded children, but excluding blind, deaf and mute children). The formula is:

$$\textit{Enrollment Rate of Primary School}-\textit{age Children}=\frac{\textit{Total Primary School}-\textit{age Children at Schools}}{\textit{Total Primary School}-\textit{age Children Both at and Outside Schools}}\times 100\%$$

Independent Research and Development Institutions refer to the state-owned insitutions which have direct mission and research purpose, a certain number of core members with higher research level and a certain number of research personnel, favorable conditions for R & D and engaging in scientific research and technological development. The institutions also have their own independent organization and finance, authority to sign contracts with other units, their bank accounts. Independent research and development institutions include the institutions attached to central government agencies, Chinese Academy of Sciences, Chinese Academy of Social Sciences and the institutions attached to local governments.

Personnel of Independent Research and Development Institutions refer to the persons who work and receive payment in research and development institutions. It includes regular full-time and temporary staff and workers, but excludes retirees and persons who leave their work temporarily without payment but still retain their posts.

Total Expenditure on Research and Development refer to all actual expenditure made for R & D (basic research, applied research and experimental development) in reference period. It includes direct expenditure on R & D and indirect expenditure on R & D (including management expenses, administrative expense and investment in capital construction relating to R & D.

Scientists and Engineers refer to persons who have completed university or higher education or obtained titles of senior and middle-level professional positions.

Other Technical Personnel refers to persons involved in science and technology with secondary specialized education or three-year college college education and persons with junior professinal titles.

Natural Scientific and Technical Personnel refers to those professionals holding scientific and technical titles or taking such positions, or being graduated from departments of science, engineering, agriculture and medicine, and/or having been promoted in practice in different sectors of the national economy and working on research, teaching and production technique in the scientific and technological fields such as science, engineering, agriculture and medicine, etc. and the professionals doing administrative work related to science and technology in government agencies, enterprises and institutions.

Engineering Professionals refer to the persons who are engaged in engineering science and technology in different sectors of the national economy, including senior engineers, engineers, assistant engineers, technicians and technical personnel without professional titles.

Agricultural Professionals refer to the persons who are working on the science of agriculture in different sectors of the national economy, including senior agronomists, agronomists, assistant argonomists, technicians and technical personnel without professional titles.

Public Health Professionals refer to the persons who are engaged in medical and health work in different sectors of the national economy, including director doctors and their deputies, doctors in charge, doctors, paramedics, nurses and technical personnel without professional titles.

Scientific Research Personnel refers to those personnel engaged in scientific and technical activities in different sectors of the national economy, including research fellows and their deputies, assistant research fellows, research trainees, technicians and technical personnel without professional titles.

Teaching Personnel of Natural Sciences refers to those professionals engaged in the teaching of natural sciences and technology in different sectors of the national economy, including professors, associate professors, lecturers, teaching assistants, teachers and teaching personnel in science and technology in middle schools.

Inventions refer to the inventions as specified by the patent law and its detailed rules and regulations for implementation. They refer to the new technical proposals to the products or methods or their modifications.

Utility Models refer to the utility models as specified by the patent law and its detailed rules and regulations for implementation. They refer to the practical and new technical proposals on the shape and structure of the product or the combination of both.

Cultural Institutions refer to units which have their own organizational system and independent accounting system and specialize in or serve cultural development. They exclude other establishments run by these cultural institutions and amateur cultural groups established by various departments.

Art Troupe refers to the troupe which is engaged in drama, opera, music, dance, acrobatics or other art performance, opens independent accounts with banks and has self-supporting accounting system; excluding the troupes which are engaged partly in industrial or agricultural activities, partly in art performance and the professional troupes organized by the people.

Film Projection Units refer to units with film projection equipment, full or part-time projectionists, permanent or non-permanent places, approved by related administrative departments to show films regularly for certain groups of audience, including those film projection units which have been approved to give commercial shows and run business with independent accounting system as well as those film-renting units of the military system.

Number of Spectators at Art Performance refers to the number of attendants at commercial shows, completely booked shows or free shows given in minority national areas, and does not include the number of spectators at rehearsals for examination and internal shows for study.

Hospitals refer to medical institutions named as "hospital" with permanent hospital beds, which are able to take in patients and provide them with medical and nursing services. They include three kinds: hospitals at or above the county level, hospitals of rural townships, and other hospitals. According to their ownership, hospitals can be classified into three categories: hospitals under the public health departments, hospitals under industrial and other departments and collective-owned hospitals. Hospitals at or above county level are divied into comprehensive and specialized hospitals.

Medical Technical Personnel refers to all permanent medical staff and workers employed by medical institutions, including doctors of Chinese and Westerm medicine, senior doctors who integrate traditional Chinese therapeutics with Western therapeutics in practice, senior nurses, pharmacists of Chinese and Western medicine, laboratory specialists, other specialists, paramedics of Chinese and Western medicine, laboratory technicians, other technicians, other practitioners of Chinese medicine, nursing attendants, pharmacological workers of Chinese and Western medicine, laboratory workers, and other primary medical personnel.

Doctors refer to qualified professional medical workers approved to practice by public health departments. They are classified into doctors of Chinese medicine, doctors of Western medicine, senior doctors who integrate traditional Chinese therapeutics with Western therapeutics in practice, paramedics of Chinese medicine and Western medicine, and other specialists of Chinese medicine.

Lawyer refer to the personnels invited to attend the work in consultative department of the law; hold the post of law adviser, criminal (civil) deputy, and criminal defender, handle non-law suits events, answer whoinquiring about law, write law affairs documents on sb's behalf ect. as a law worker mainly engaged in law affairs with fulltime or part-time.

Notary refer to judicial personnels who handle the notarial affairs in the state notarial organs according to law, including notary, assistant notary and other personnels worked in notarial department.

Handle notarial documents refer to notarial departments which handle the notarial documents by number of pieces in a certain stage; notarial documents refer to make the documents according to the regulations or permission of the Ministry of Justice, including two parts: domestic notarial documents and concerning foreign notarial documents, among which, the domestic notarial documents were divided into two kinds: economic contract notarization and law relationship of civil notarization.

Mediator refer to personnels who hold the post of mediating the disputs, caused by general civil disputs among the people and slight illegal activities in people's mediative committee, including committee members of mediative committee and mediator of mediative groups.

Mediating the disputs among the people refer to mediative committee which mediate the disputs of civi rights and duties among the people by the method of persuasion and education according to the principle of voluntary, so as to reach agreement and understanding on both sides of liligants. Disputs to be solved are including marriage disputs and family disputs, property and right disputs, but excluding the civil cases accepted and mediated by the court.

Retired or Resigned Personnel refers to the persons who have formally gone through the formalities for their retirement or quitting work and enjoy the corresponding treatments.

Insurance and Welfare Funds refer to labour insurance and welfare fund paid by enterprises, organizations and institutions to their staff and workers as well as retired and resigned persons in addition to their wages and salaries.

(1) **Insurance and Welfare Funds for Staff and Workers** include:

① Medical Care Allowance: It refers to the cost of medical care of staff and workers and their dependent family members who are covered by the medicare system of enterprises, travelling expenses of injured employees to hospital and their per diem subsidies during hospitalization, cost of medical care of employees who are covered by the medicare system of institutions and organizations, as well as cost of medicine of employees of enterprises and institutions who are not covered by the medicare system.

② Funeral Expenses and Pensions for Family of the Deceased: They refer to funeral expenses of staff and workers, and pensions and allowance for their dependent family members, as well as subsidies to funeral expenses of staff and workers' dependent family members.

③ Subsidies for Living Expenses: They refer to regular or ad hoc subsidies to staff and workers who have difficulties in making ends meet.

④ Expenses for Recreational, Sports and Publicity Activities: They refer to actual payment made by enterprises and institutions in recreational, sports and publicity activities, excluding training cost.

⑤ Subsidies to Collective Welfare Undertakings: They refer to subsidies to the operation of welfare undertaking that can not fully cover their cost, such as public bathrooms, barber shops, laundries, nurseries and kindergartens.

⑥ Expenses for Collective Welfare Facilities: They refer to expenses for collective welfare facilities that are spent in line with state regulations, such as the purchase and repair of cooking utensils for canteens, and repair of living quarters of staff and workers, but excluding the expenses for welfare projects that are constructed with self-raised funds.

⑦ Family Planning Subsidy: It refers to subsidy and health allowance paid to the one-child family of staff and workers.

⑧ Others: They refer to other insurance and welfare funds paid to staff and workers.

(2) **Insurance and Welfare Funds for Retired and Resigned Staff and Workers**

① Pensions for retired veteran cadres: They refer to pensions and other subsidies paid to the retired in line with relevant government documents.

② Pensions for Retirement: They refer to living allowance and other subsidies paid to retired staff and workers in line with the relevant government documents.

③ Resignation Allowances for Living Expenses: They refer to living allownce and subsidies paid to resigned staff and workers in line with relevant government instructions.

④ Expenses for Medical Care: They refer to the costs for medical treatment, hospitalization and food subsidies in hospitals for retired and resigned staff and workers.

⑤ Nursing Cost: It refers to cost for nursing retired or resigned staff and workers who are unable to take care of themselves and need the help from nurses.

⑥ Living Subsidy: It refers to living subsidy paid to retired employees in line with the instructions in a 1985 State Council document.

⑦ Traffic Subsidy: It refers to the monthly traffic subsidy paid to senior retired staff.

⑧ Funeral Expenses and Pensions for Family of the Deceased: They refer to the funeral expenses of retired staff and workers, and pensions and allowance for their dependent family members, as well as subsidies to funeral expenses of retired staff and workers' dependent family members.

⑨ Others: They refer to other expenses, including moving and settlement allowance, allowance for difficult families, book and newspaper allowance, subsidy for non-staple foods, housing subsidy, water and electricity subsidy, special allowance for staff and workers of national minorities, travelling cost for senior retired staff, etc.

Volume of Industrial Waste Water Discharged refers to the volume of industrial waste water discharged, through all outlets, to the outside of industrial enterprises, including waste water produced, direct-cooling water, underground water from mines that does not meet the standard of discharge, and the domestic sewage mixed up with industrial waste water when discharged, but excluding discharged indirect-cooling water.

Volume of Waste Water up to the Standard for Discharge refers to the volume of discharged industrial waste water that, with or without treatment, has come up to the national or local standards for discharge.

Volume of Treated Industrial Waste Water refers to the volume of industrial waste water after being treated and purified through various water treatment facilities in the reference period, including the volume discharged or recovered after being treated. The volume of waste water that fails to meet the national or local standards after treatment is also included. If there are treatment facilities both at the outlets of workshops and at the outlets of the factory, and the same volume of waste water has been treated twice, duplication should be avoided in the calculation of the volume of treated industrial waste water.

Volume of Waste Gas Emission refers to waste gas emitted from burning of fuels and from production process in the area of the factory, and is measured by 10000 standard cubic metres each year under normal condition.

Volume of Sulphur Dioxide Discharged refers to the volume of sulphur dioxide discharged to the air in the process of fuel burning or in the production process.

Volume of Industrial Soot Discharged refers to the volume of solid soot in the smoke discharged in the process of fuel burning in the area of the factory.

Industrial Dust Discharged refers to the total weight of solid dust discharged by industrial enterprises in the production process, such as dust of refractory materials from iron plants, dust from coke-screening system or from sintering machines of coking plants, dust from lime kilns, cement dust from building material enterprises, etc., but excluding smoke and dust discharged by power plants.

Volume of Industrial Solid Wastes Produced refers to the total volume of solid, semi-solid or highconcentration liquid residue produced by industrial enterprises in their production process, including dangerous wastes, residues from melting, slag, powdered coal ash, gangue, chemical residues, tailings, radioactive residues and other residues, but excluding stripped or dug stones in mining (except gangue and acid or alkali stones which are stones washed or soaked by water with a pH value smaller than 4 or larger than 10.5).

Volume of Industrial Solid Wastes Treated refers to solid wastes disposed of in a non-recoverable place that meet the requirement of environmental protection, such as burying (The dangerous wastes should be buried safely), burning, piling in designated sites, pouring water into the deep strata, filling of old mines, etc. (including treatment of solid wastes piled up in the previous years).

Volume of Industrial Solid Wastes Discharged refers to the volume of industrial solid wastes produced and discharged at the places outside the special facilities or special sites for preventing against pollution, excluding stripped or dug stones in mining (except gangue and acid or alkali waste stones).

Output Value of Products Made from Utilization of Waste Gas, Waste Water and Industrial Solid Wastes refers to the value of products (calculated at current prices) made by industrial enterprises using recovered waste water, waste gas or solid wastes as main raw materials. Only the value of the products which have been sold or are ready to be sold should be included. The value of the products which will be used in the production of the enterprises should not be included.

Profit Obtained from Utilization of Waste Gas, Waste Water and Industrial Solid Wastes refers to profit obtained from selling or self-consumption of products made by industrial enterprises using recovered waste water, waste gas or solid wastes as main raw materials.

Accidents of Environment Pollution and Destruction refer to sudden accidents, due to economic and social behavior or activities in contrast with environment protection legislation, unexpected factors or irresistible natural disasters, that cause the pollution of environment, the destruction of natural protection zones, wild plants and animals, the danger to the health of people, and the loss in the property of the society and people.

企事业单位选介

BUSINESS ENTERPRISES SELECTED
INTRODUCTION OF THE UNITS

1998年江苏省建立现代企业制度企业进展情况

1998年,全省建立现代企业制度工作从试点转向在面上展开。从全省调查统计的245家原省级试点和国家重点联系企业的情况看,建立现代企业制度工作继续深化,并朝着力争在本世纪末大多数国有大中型骨干企业初步建立现代企业制度的目标迈出了新的步伐。但社会保障制度不完善、历史债务包袱沉重和市场体系不健全成为推进企业建立现代企业制度的主要障碍。

被调查的245家企业拥有注册资本527.32亿元,其中国家资本266.92亿元,占总数50.62%;集体资本17.84亿元,占3.38%;法人资本168.52亿元,占31.96%;个人资本20.87亿元,占3.96%;外商资本53.17亿元,占10.08%。从控股情况看,国有绝对控股企业为201家,占82.04%;国有相对控股15家,占6.12%;集体绝对控股11家,占4.49%;其他占7.35%。从企业登记注册类型看,国有企业89家,国有独资公司45家,其他有限公司54家,股份有限公司47家,其他类型企业10家,分别占总数的36.33%、18.37%、22.04%、19.18%和4.08%。调查企业中有大型以上企业180家,有上市公司22家。

1998年被调查企业生产经营情况的主要特点是:(1)对外投资进一步增加,投资收益明显提高。至1998年末累计对外投资136.07亿元,同比增长20.15%,其中对境外投资增长15.52%;投资收益增度较大,比去年同期增长67.7%,达18.8亿元。(2)经济效益下滑,利润降幅较大。被调查企业的主营业务收入、应交增值税、实现利润均呈负增长,其中企业主营业务收入为1615.51亿元,较去年同期下降4.35%,1998年实现利润46.79亿元,同比下降15.4%,应缴增值税55.52亿元,下降0.2%;出口额也比去年同期下降3.29%。(3)科研开发费用增加较多。1998年被调查企业投入研究开发的费用达14.31亿元,同比增长14.5%。表明企业对新产品开发和技术改造较以往更为重视。

企业改制工作取得新的进展。被调查企业中,有195家企业已进行改制后的注册登记,改制面达79.59%。通过改制,企业的内部的法人治理结构进一步完善。被调查企业中有45.31%的企业成立了股东代表大会,有76.73%的企业成立了董事会,有43.09%的董事会有专家董事,有70.2%的企业成立了监事会,有19家企业已派驻稽察员。在总经理的产生方式中,有26.94%企业总经理由企业主管部门任命,21.63%的企业由由董事会任命,26.53%的企业由政府部门提名,董事会任命,有21.63%的企业由上级组织部门任命;企业中层管理人员的产生方式中,有27.76%的企业由总经理自主决定,有37.96%的企业由总经理提名,董事会任命,这说明企业经营的自主权进一步扩大。

富余职工分流和企业办社会职能分离工作力度加大。1998年末,被调查企业从业人员为81.35万人,同比减少6%,在岗职工减少7%,其他从业人员增加8%,离开本单位仍保留劳动关系的人数大幅度上升,1998年末达8.8万人,较去年增长120%,人均报酬有所提高,98年末较去年同期提高5%。在分离的91754名富余职工中,12.78%安排到其他单位,企业内部消化22.96%,下岗及待业占40.94%,提前退休占23.32%,主要分离去向为工业、批发零售贸易餐饮业和其他行业。98年共分离机构44个,分离8977人。

江苏省建立现代企业制度企业调查名单

中国石化集团金陵石油化工公司
熊猫电子集团公司
南京卷烟厂
江苏省海外企业集团有限公司
江苏省汽车工业销售总公司
金城集团有限公司
南京容光达电子(集团)有限责任公司
南京晨光集团有限责任公司
南京精密机械集团公(第二机床厂)
南京友谊华联(集团)有限公司
江苏舜天国际集团公司
南京交电家电总公司
南京玻璃厂
江苏省物资集团总公司
跃进汽车集团公司
南京机轮酿造集团有限公司
江苏宏图电子信息集团有限公司
江苏省石油集团有限公司
江苏省燃料总公司
南京金陵饭店
南京华宏(集团)有限公司
南京汽轮电机(集团)有限责任公司
南京天环食品(集团)有限公司
南京钢铁集团有限公司
中国石化集团扬子石油化工有限公司
南京化学工业集团有限公司
南京雷电集团有限公司
化工部南京化工厂
江苏双龙集团有限公司
南京电子网板有限公司
南京塑料包装材料总厂
南京木器厂
南京高速齿轮箱厂

江苏时花电器集团
无锡市太极实业股份有限公司
无锡庆丰集团有限公司
无锡中润集团有限公司
无锡商业大厦集团有限公司
无锡威孚集团有限公司
无锡橡胶集团有限公司
无锡锅炉厂
江苏锡钢集团公司
无锡压缩机股份有限公司
无锡市小天鹅股份有限公司
无锡市丝绸印染厂
无锡山禾集团有限公司
江苏海星电机集团有限公司
无锡协新集团有限公司
无锡开源机床集团有限公司
无锡化工集团股份有限公司
无锡宏源集团有限责任公司
江苏新苏机械制造有限公司
中国华晶电子集团公司
法尔胜集团公司
江苏省宜兴陶瓷公司
无锡华源行星动力有限公司
锡山华源行星机械有限公司
红豆集团公司
江苏北方氯碱集团有限公司
江苏六朝松集团有限公司
徐州轮胎集团公司
徐州钢铁总厂
江苏铝厂
江苏天宝电子集团有限公司
徐州压力机械股份有限公司
徐州海鸥集团有限公司
徐州市百货大楼股份有限公司
徐州蓝天商业大楼
江苏巨龙集团有限公司
徐州工程机械集团有限公司
江苏力大建材机械有限公司
江苏银宇集团有限公司
徐州飞虹网架集团有限公司
徐州矿务集团有限公司
徐州帘子布厂徐州电子仪器总厂江
苏凤鸣集团股份有限公司
大屯煤电(集团)有限责任公司
徐州华纺化纤有限责任公司
大地食品股份有限公司
维桑集团
江苏霸王集团公司

维维集团
徐州市第五制药厂
江苏省新沂热电有限公司
江苏省邳州水泥厂
常州药业股份有限公司
常州化工厂
常州机电集团有限责任公司
大成纺织集团有限公司
黑牡丹＜集团＞股份有限公司
天马集团公司
常州连环集团公司
常州糖烟酒股份有限公司
常州金狮自行车集团公司
常州长江客车集团有限公司
丽宝第集团公司
常州无线电总厂
常柴股份有限公司
上海华源化纤股份常州化纤公司
常林股份有限公司
东风农机集团公司
常州变压器厂
江苏正昌集团公司
江苏五菱柴油机股份有限公司
苏州机械腔股集团有限公司
江苏化工农药集团有限公司
苏州商业大厦有限公司
苏州精细化工集团有限公司
江苏光明丝绸集团有限公司
苏州市孔雀电器集团有限责任公司
苏州振亚集团有限责任公司
江苏苏州物贸中心(集团)有限公司
苏州化学纤维厂
苏州亚细亚商厦
江苏春花电器集团股份有限公司
江苏苏净集团有限公司
苏州钢铁股份有限公司
银河电子集团公司
江苏华昌(集团)有限公司
江苏沙钢集团有限公司
昆山昆化集团(实业)公司
江苏吴江丝绸集团有限公司
国营吴江绸缎炼染二厂
苏州宏达集团有限公司
苏州制氧机有限公司(苏州制氧机厂)
南通五交化股份有限公司
江苏冠达集团股份有限公司
南通江山农药化工股份有限公司
江苏宝灵化工股份有限公司

南通医药股份有限公司
南通玻璃有限公司
南通机床股份有限公司(集团)
南通电容器厂
南通钢绳(集团)有限公司
江苏南通二棉集团有限公司
南通华容电子集团有限责任公司
南通天生港发电有限公司
江苏大生集团有限公司
江苏苏中建材装备集团股份有限公司
江苏黄海汽配股份有限公司
江苏双猫纺织装饰集团有限公司
启东盖天力制药股份有限公司
江苏南天集团股份有限公司
江苏南浦机电集团股份有限公司
江苏通丝联股份有限公司
连云港华泰塑料有限公司
连云港市百货大楼有限责任公司
江苏东堡集团股份有限公司
连云港纺织机械厂
江苏华龙石油化工机械集团有限公司
连云港华威电子集团有限公司
东北输变电设备集团连云港变压器
有限公司
连云港涤纶厂
连云港机械厂
连云港连众玻璃钢集团有限公司
江苏恒瑞医药股份有限公司
连云港华东铝塑包装有限公司
连云港康源制药有限公司
江苏德邦化学工业集团有限公司
江苏双菱化工集团有限公司
新海发电厂
江苏省清印集团有限公司
江苏省清棉集团有限公司
江苏省淮阴市清江商场有限公司
淮阴清江石油化工有限公司
江苏淮钢集团
淮阴市电化厂
江苏双穗鞋业有限公司
江苏省清江轴承集团有限公司
一拖清江拖拉机有限公司
淮阴清江化肥厂
江苏省清江电机股份有限公司
江苏省韩泰轮胎有限公司
江苏淮河化工总厂
国营淮安棉纺织厂
新光集团有限公司

江苏悦达集团有限公司	江苏亚星客车集团有限公司	江苏丹棉集团有限公司
江苏江动集团有限公司	扬州江扬船舶集团公司	江苏丹化集团公司
江苏众想集团有限公司	扬州制药厂	江苏通华集团有限公司
盐城化纤集团有限公司	扬州水箱厂	泰州绝缘材料厂
江苏阳春集团有限公司	扬州玻璃厂	国营靖江葡萄糖厂
江苏八菱集团公司	扬州布厂(华源有限公司)	泰州吉泰毛纺织染厂
江苏燕舞电器集团有限公司	扬州冶金机械有限公司	苏北电机厂
江苏天虹集团公司	江苏扬农化工集团有限公司	江苏陵光集团
江苏大圣集团有限公司	江苏宝胜集团有限公司	扬子江药业集团
盐城市物资控股集团有限公司	仪征化纤股份有限公司	春兰集团公司
江苏盐阜人民商场集团有限公司	镇江金威集团有限责任公司	泰州梅兰电化集团
江苏盐阜公路运输集团有限公司	镇江焦化煤气集团公司	江苏天伦染织实业有限公司
江苏飞驰股份有限公司	江苏惠通集团有限责任公司	江苏靖江工程机械集团有限公司
江苏阜宁肉联厂	江苏华通机械集团公司	泰兴市金属材料公司
江苏东方化工集团	镇江钛白股份有限公司	扬动股份有限公司
江苏新洋集团有限公司	华东铝加工厂	江苏玻璃集团有限公司
盐城市磷肥厂	江苏索普(集团)有限公司	江苏省宿迁市禾友化肥有限公司
江苏森威集团飞达股份有限公司	江苏镇纺集团有限责任公司	江苏泗绢集团有限公司
江苏珍丰集团股份有限公司	江苏三维服装集团有限公司	江苏洋河集团有限公司
江苏亲亲集团股份有限公司	江苏恒顺集团有限公司	泗洪油嘴油泵厂
江苏扬州机械集团	江苏船山集团有限责任公司	江苏泗洪酒厂
扬州柴油机厂	镇江华讯集团有限公司	江苏双沟酒业集团有限公司
扬州晶体管厂(晶来半导体有限公司)	江苏金猴机械集团公司	

1998年江苏省重点企业集团发展情况

1998年,全省重点企业集团努力克服亚洲金融危机和洪涝灾害的影响,在宏观经济和市场环境比较困难的条件下,积极探索,知难而进,保持了较好的发展势头。在实施规模经济,促进全省经济结构调整中继续发挥了龙头和骨干作用,推进了我省经济集中度的提高。

据对包括省政府批准成立的27家省重点企业集团和列入全省经济结构规划的50多家市重点企业集团在内的全省116家企业集团的调查统计,1998年企业集团的运行主要有以下几个特点:一是资产规模扩大,对外投资增加。1998年末,资产总计达2362.52亿元,较97年末增长10.76%,其中,固定资产净值799.85亿元,增长12.91%。累计对外投资147.50亿元,同比增长10.99%,其中,对境外投资1.15亿元,增长23.94%。二是主营业务收入增加,实现利润减少。1998年,实现主营业务收入1734.5亿元,较上年增长3.3%,其中出口额达166.91亿元,增长2.55%。但全年实现利润60.79亿元,同比下降15.3%。三是企业集团内部管理更趋规范。全省重点企业集团在致力于生产经营,实现资本不断扩张的同时,也着力推进和深化集团内部的各项改革,不断完善集团内部的管理制度和生产经营机制。到1998年末,被调查的企业集团中有100家已经建立了母子公司体制,占调查企业集团的86.2%;有44家企业集团成立了股东会,有103家企业集团成立了董事会,有77家企业集团成立了监事会,分别占被调查企业集团的37.9%、88.8%和66.4%。

重点企业集团在我省经济发展中已发挥着举足轻重的作用,但处于组建和发展过程中的企业集团,目前仍存在着一些有待进一步提高和完善的问题。一是集团组建速度快,但规范化运作程度低。迄今为止,我省有各类省级企业集团2500多家,但集团的规范化运作程度却不尽如意。表现在集团的母子公司制度及集团内部的组织机构及管理体制不健全。一些企业集团仍然沿用计划经济管理直属厂的办法管理子公司,没有赋予子公司相应的经营自主权。有些集团的母子公司是行政捏合而成,不存在资产及控股关系,使集团名存实亡。二是企业集团的规模偏小,总体效益不高。全省统计的116家重点企业集团平均资产规模为20.37亿元,而总资产超过100亿元的仅有春兰集团一家。销售收入在50亿元以上的仅有金陵石化、春兰集团、扬子石化、仪化集团、跃进集团等少数几家。

1998年企业集团的主营业务收入虽较上年增长3.3%，但利润却比去年同期下降15.3%。三是企业集团的母公司的带动作用不够明显。总体上看，目前我省重点集团母公司在投融资、科研开发、对外资本扩张及结构调整等方面的带动作用还不够显著，影响了集团的整体发展和实力的壮大。

1998年江苏省重点企业集团前一百家

（按销售收入排序）

中国石化金陵石油化工公司
中国石化集团金陵石油化工公司
江苏春兰集团
中国石化集团扬子石油化工有限公司
仪征化纤集团
跃进汽车集团
常柴集团有限公司
江苏沙钢集团有限公司
熊猫电子集团
南京钢铁集团
江苏小天鹅集团有限公司
华东电子集团
江苏阳光集团公司
维维集团
江苏国泰国际集团有限公司
江苏舜天国际集团公司
南京化学工业集团有限公司
徐州工程机械集团有限公司
江苏华西集团公司
江苏捷达摩托集团公司
江苏汇鸿国际集团有限公司
金城集团有限公司
南京金蛙集团
常州塑料集团
徐州矿务集团有限公司
江苏江动集团
江苏新科电子有限集团公司
红豆集团公司
江苏省海外企业集团有限公司
南京同创信息产业集团有限公司
江苏输变电设备集团
江苏宏图电子信息集团有限公司
江苏亚星客车集团
江苏法尔胜集团公司
江苏吴江丝绸集团有限公司
苏州丝绸集团有限责任公司
江苏淮钢集团
江苏悦达实业集团
江苏森达集团
江苏华容集团有限公司
三毛集团公司
江苏牡丹汽车集团有限公司
江苏锡钢集团公司
江苏富士通通信技术有限公司
无锡山禾集团有限公司
江苏三房巷实业集团总公司
扬州江扬船舶集团
无锡庆丰集团有限公司
江苏林海动力机械集团
鹰翔集团公司
江苏双良集团公司
江苏综艺股份有限公司
江苏五菱集团
永鼎集团公司
江苏化工农药集团有限公司
江苏苏钢集团有限公司
中大工业集团
苏州医药集团有限公司
江苏新伍集团公司
南京金陵制药(集团)有限公司
江苏宝胜集团
常州长江客车集团公司
无锡威孚集团有限公司
无锡开源机床集团有限公司
扬动股份有限公司
大地集团
连云港恒瑞集团有限公司
江苏扬子江药业集团
江苏陵光集团
徐州钢铁总厂
江苏长江电器集团公司
江苏艺龙集团公司
江苏索普集团
申达集团公司
苏州精细化工集团有限公司
南京金陵饭店集团
中国华晶电子集团公司
江苏高能集团
无锡太平洋集团有限公司
江苏洋河集团有限公司
江苏大亚集团公司
江苏中洋集团
江苏沿山实业集团总公司
江苏华润集团公司
无锡化工集团股份有限公司
江苏扬农化工集团
正茂集团有限责任公司
江苏双沟酒业集团有限公司
江苏苏州物资中心(集团)有限公司
江苏众想集团
江苏正昌集团公司
江苏马北集团公司
江苏北方氯碱集团有限公司
无锡橡胶集团有限责任公司
江苏天宝电子集团有限公司
江苏振阳集团
华东铝业集团
无锡宏源集团
常林股份有限公司
大成纺织集团有限公司
江苏巨龙水泥集团

1998 年江苏省工业企业前一百家

（按销售收入排列）

中国石化金陵石油化工公司
中国石化扬子石油化工有限责任公司
希捷国际科技（无锡）有限公司
跃进汽车集团公司
仪征化纤股份有限公司
江苏沙钢集团有限公司
苏州飞利浦消费电子有限公司
江苏维维集团
南京钢铁集团有限公司
徐州工程机械集团有限公司
华飞彩色显示系统有限公司
江苏阳光集团公司
金城集团有限公司
常柴股份有限公司
江苏华西集团公司
江苏永钢集团
徐州矿务集团有限公司
东海粮油（张家港）工业有限公司
丹徒县龙山鳗业联合公司
无锡市摩托车厂
无锡小天鹅股份有限公司
夏普办公设备（常熟）有限公司
徐州卷烟厂
江苏新科电子集团公司
江苏春兰制冷设备股份有限公司
熊猫电子集团公司
吴江丝绸集团公司
法尔胜集团公司
苏州罗技电子有限公司
苏州明基电脑有限公司
南京金蛙集团有限公司
江苏森达集团公司
一汽无锡柴油机厂

泰州春兰空调器厂
江苏石油勘探局
江苏三房巷实业集团总公司
江苏牡丹汽车集团
江苏锡钢集团公司
江苏富士通通信技术有限公司
南京爱立信通信有限公司
南京化学工业集团有限公司
无锡威孚集团有限公司
南京同创信息产业集团有限公司
大屯煤电（集团）有限责任公司
无锡山禾集团有限公司
南京大金山实业有限公司
扬州江扬船舶集团公司
仁宝电脑工业（中国）有限公司
江阴市兴澄钢铁有限公司
中国鹰翔集团公司
江苏亚星客车集团有限公司
江苏双良一特灵溴化锂制冷机有限公司
江苏雪浪钢铁集团公司
南京金城精密机械有限公司
江苏长虹电视机有限公司
江苏澄星磷化工集团公司
江苏三毛集团公司
江苏江动集团有限公司
南通顺达集装箱有限公司
江苏江阴模塑集团总公司
武进柴油机厂
淮阴卷烟厂
江阴振华港口机械有限公司
南京卷烟厂
吴县防爆电机厂
戚墅堰机车车辆厂
江苏化工农药集团有限公司

江苏三笑集团有限公司
徐州华润电力有限公司
南通醋酸纤维有限公司
江苏苏钢集团有限公司
南京金陵制药（集团）有限公司
江苏新伍集团
无锡开源机床集团有限公司
徐州胜阳木业有限公司
无锡电缆厂
江苏华纺集团公司
扬动股份有限公司
大地集团公司
江苏亚邦集团公司
南京夏普电子有限公司
江苏通润机电集团有限公司
南京南瑞集团公司
牧田（中国）有限公司
南京华新电线电缆有限公司
吴江光电通信线缆总厂
华芳实业总公司
南京浦镇车辆厂
江苏扬子江药业集团公司
淮阴利淮钢铁有限公司
金桐石油化工有限公司
化学工业部南京化工厂
江苏林海动力机械集团公司
无锡市第一棉纺织厂
江苏陵光集团
无锡夏普电子元器件有限公司
昆山统一企业食品有限公司
中讯电子（昆山）有限公司
南京化学工业集团有限公司连云港碱厂
无锡锅炉厂

1998年江苏贸易零售企业前一百家

（按销售额排列）

南京市新街口百货商店股份有限公司
无锡市商业大厦集团有限公司
南京中央商场股份有限公司
南京商厦股份有限公司
中国旅游品工艺品镇江展销馆
苏州五金交电集团公司
无锡市第一百货(集团)有限公司
南通文峰大世界
常州百货大楼股份有限公司
无锡市八佰伴商贸中心有限公司
苏州商业大厦有限公司泰华商城
江苏苏南股份有限公司
苏州人民商场股份有限公司
江苏华地企业股份有限公司
仪征怡华商贸发展有限公司
淮阴供销大厦股份有限公司
徐州市百货大楼股份有限公司
南京市山西路百货大楼
苏州亚细亚商厦
南京友谊华联(集团)有限责任公司
常州市百货公司
宜兴市丁蜀商业总公司
南京太平商场
镇江百盛商城有限公司
常熟华联商厦
昆山商厦股份有限公司
徐州供销大厦
江阴医药股份有限公司
盐城商业大厦股份有限公司
苏州市石路国际商城
江苏省徐州医药采购供应站
常州家电城
海门市供销大厦
无锡天惠超市股份有限公司
徐州市华联商厦
武进市洛阳供销合作社
南通市百货大楼股份有限公司
常州商业大厦
南京桂花鸭(集团)公司
江苏省宜兴市医药总公司
苏州市第一百货商店
南通市华联商厦股份有限公司
无锡市锡佛装潢家具商业总公司
南京市新华书店
宜兴市物资经营总公司
江苏省石油总公司淮阴公司
扬中商城
下关商厦
江阴市粮油集团总公司
江都商城股份有限公司
吴江市盛泽供销社
扬州商场
扬中市通达商业总公司
江苏盐阜人民商场集团有限公司
苏州长发商厦有限责任公司
高邮市人民商城
吴江市莘塔供销社
泰州市第一百货商店股份有限公司
江苏省太仓市百货总公司
张家港市商业大厦
南通王府井百货有限责任公司
中外合资扬州百盛商业大厦有限公司
无锡永安集团有限公司
徐州蓝天商业集团总公司
南京金陵饭店购物中心有限公司
苏州市百汇连锁店总公司
常州国际商城有限公司
徐州市白云大厦股份有限公司
江阴国际购物中心
徐州市友谊商场
南京湖南路商场
清江商场
南京南浦商贸(集团)有限责任公司
常州商厦家电广场
南京中山大厦商场
武进市湖塘供销合作社
华润超级市场(苏州)有限公司
昆山华厦实业总公司
连云港市百货大楼有限责任公司
南通七彩商厦
江苏省泰兴市金凤商城股份有限公司
泰州市商业有限公司
丹阳商业广场
太仓市五金交电化工总公司
泰兴市农业机械总公司
金天都实业总公司
江苏华诚百姓自选商场有限公司
南京市粮食局第二分局
徐州古彭商业大厦
埝头供销社
连云港华联商厦
江苏省姜堰市五交化总公司
南京金贸(集团)公司
扬州丰祥商业有限公司万家福商城
吴县市陆慕供销社
江苏商厦有限公司
镇江商业大厦
溧阳市医药总公司
江苏省姜堰市百货大楼
徐州人民商场有限公司

1998年江苏省建筑企业前五十家

（按总产值排列）

江苏省建筑安装工程股份有限公司
江苏省南通市第三建筑安装工程公司
南通市第二建筑安装工程公司
江苏省南通市第七建筑安装工程公司
金坛市建筑安装工程公司
通州市建筑安装工程总公司
江苏苏中建设股份公司
南京大地建设(集团)股份有限公司
中国核工业华兴建设公司
海门市建筑安装工程公司
南京市第六建筑安装工程公司
金坛市第三建筑安装工程公司
盐城市天虹建筑总公司
邗江县建安总承包公司
南通市第四建筑安装工程公司
中国建筑第八工程局第三建筑公司
江都市建筑安装工程公司
江苏海门常乐建工集团有限公司
江苏邮电建设工程局
高邮市第二建筑工程公司
江苏省交通工程总公司
启东市建筑安装工程公司
江苏省泰兴市第一建筑安装工程公司
江苏正太建设股份有限公司
海门市设备安装工程公司
南通市第六建筑安装工程总公司
常熟土木建筑有限公司
兴化市建筑安装工程总公司
南京三建(集团)公司
兴化市边城建筑工程公司
海门市第一建筑安装工程公司
江苏铜山建筑工程公司
江苏省建筑工程总公司
江苏省送变电公司
南京市第一建筑工程公司
中国石化第二建设公司
南通市宏大建安公司
江都市建设工程总公司
常州通达工程总公司
南通市建筑安装工程总公司
中煤第五建设公司
江苏苏州第二建筑工程集团公司
南通五建集团有限公司
江苏摩天建工集团
建湖县建筑工程总公司
江都市第二建筑安装工程公司
江都市第三建筑安装工程公司
泰兴市焦荡建筑安装工程公司
张家港市兴港建筑安装工程总公司
铁道部大桥二处

1998年江苏房地产企业前五十家

（按销售面积排列）

徐州市经济实用住房发展中心
无锡市适用住宅发展中心
苏州市郊区住宅建设有限公司
南京市栖霞建设(集团)公司
苏州新创建设发展有限公司
武进市房地产开发总公司
南通苏通房地产开发实业公司
徐州同昌集团有限公司
南京市下关城镇建设综合开发公司
淮阴市房屋开发实业公司
苏州新港建设发展有限公司
苏州工业园区房地产发展有限公司
连云港市房屋建设开发总公司
武进市新城房产开发有限公司
东台市东亭房地产开发有限公司
苏房房地产开发实业公司扬州分公司
阜宁县富建房地产开发有限公司
连云港市经济房开发中心
兴化市城市建设综合开发总公司
扬中市房地产开发总公司
无锡市房地产开发公司
连云区房地产综合开发公司
徐州市金城房地产开发有限公司
溧阳市昆仑房地产开发公司
南京富城房地产开发有限公司
南京市秦淮区城镇建设综合开发公司
徐州市园林房地产开发公司
南京经济实用住房发展中心
南京亚东国际实业有限公司
阜宁县四建房地产开发有限公司
苏州市沧浪区房地产发展公司
金山桥开发区房地产开发公司
苏州房地产经营总公司
江苏省房地产开发总公司泰州公司
南京振东房地产开发有限公司
南京宁威房地产开发有限公司
常州市常信房地产开发有限公司
苏州房地产有限公司
南京市建设发展总公司
盐城市房地产公司
南通市房屋建设开发公司
苏州城市建设开发总公司
无锡市小天鹅房地产建设开发有限公司
金坛市华罗庚科技城房产开发总公司
扬州市鸿大房地产开发公司
淮阴市清浦区房地产开发公司
扬州市经济技术开发区房地产公司
东台市地产开发总公司
中房集团无锡房地产开发公司
苏州市地产开发经营公司

1998年江苏外商投资企业前一百家

（按实际投资规模排列）

江苏金东纸业有限公司
中新苏州工业园区开发有限公司
华飞彩色显示系统有限公司
京阳水泥有限公司
金华盛纸业(苏州工业园区)有限公司
东丽合成纤维(南通)有限公司
金红叶纸业(苏州工业园区)有限公司
苏州工业园区亚太纸品有限公司
正新橡胶(中国)有限公司
江南－小野田水泥有限公司
狮王啤酒饮料(苏州)有限公司
南通远洋船务工程有限公司
苏州工业园区亚太纸板有限公司
徐州华润电力有限公司
无锡星洲工业园投资有限公司
苏州杜邦聚脂有限公司
南京依维柯汽车有限公司
张家港保税区东海粮油工业有限公司
张家港浦项不锈钢有限公司
昆山华成织染有限公司
常熟兴华长江发展有限公司
苏州三星电子有限公司
常州华源雷迪斯聚合物有限公司
三星电子(苏州)半导体有限公司
苏州紫兴纸业有限公司
东丽酒伊织布(南通)有限公司
长江浮法玻璃有限公司(新)
中国贝卡尔特钢帘线有限公司
江苏迪斯耐食品有限公司
俐马(苏州)织染有限公司
新苏工业厂房(苏州)有限公司
南京锦湖轮胎有限公司
扬子巴斯夫苯乙烯系列有限公司
申华化学工业有限公司
江阴苏龙发电有限公司
华渊电机(江苏)有限公司
江苏韩泰轮胎有限公司
苏州罗技电子有限公司
南亚塑胶工业(南通)有限公司
苏州明基电脑有限公司
南通天生港发电有限公司
牧田(中国)有限公司
南通帝人(第二)有限公司
南京金城机械有限公司
江阴兴澄钢铁有限公司
南京富城房地产开发有限公司
昆山统一企业食品有限公司
昆山六丰机械工业有限公司
江阴永丰余造纸有限公司
夏普办公设备(常熟)有限公司
武进亚能热电有限公司
东丽酒伊印染(南通)有限公司
苏州爱普生有限公司
沪士电子(昆山)有限公司
卡特彼勒徐州有限公司
水山造船(通州)有限公司
苏州飞利浦消费电子有限公司
无锡松下冷机有限公司
张家港永旺钢铁有限公司
江阴兴澄特种钢铁有限公司
昆山大上海企业发展有限公司
张家港扬子纺纱有限公司
苏州罗马瓷砖有限公司
永丰余纸业(昆山)有限公司
华能国际电力股份有限公司
  南通分公司
小松常林工程机械有限公司
张家港东华优尼科能源有限公司
镇江奇美化工有限公司
旭日(苏州)科技有限公司
东丽印染(南通)有限公司
东海粮油工业(张家港)有限公司
希捷国际科技(无锡)有限公司
江苏福迈特纤维板有限公司
常熟埃尔夫阿托化学三爱富氟化工
  有限公司
张家港浦扬钢板有限公司
昆山恩斯克虹山有限公司
张家港保税区南港发展有限公司
张家港保税区利辉国际有限公司
张家港雁江房地产开发有限公司
昆山世界名人城房产开发有限公司
苏州工业园区亚太纸品加工有限公司
马佳利机械(无锡)有限公司
锡山市锡金供水有限公司
维德木业(苏州)有限公司
捷安特自行车(中国)有限公司
常州光星精机有限公司
无锡龙达荣成纸业有限公司
吴江远通公路建设发展有限公司
美浮(太仓)石油化工贮运有限公司
江苏东海圣戈班玻璃有限公司
南通醋酸纤维有限公司
苏州福太智慧科技娱乐有限公司
张家港越洋实业有限公司
张家港保税区长发仓储有限公司
常州超级食品有限公司
长江浮法玻璃有限公司
张家港保税区金麒麟国际贸易
  有限公司
张家港保税区培根商品展示
  交易中心有限公司
苏州华苏塑料有限公司
苏州阳澄湖兴丽娱乐度假有限公司

1998年江苏外贸公司出口超亿美元二十家

江苏舜天国际集团有限公司
江苏国泰国际集团有限公司
中设江苏机械设备进出口集团公司
江苏汇鸿国际集团有限公司
江苏省丝绸进出口集团股份有限公司
江苏省轻工业品进出口集团股份有限公司
江苏省纺织品进出口集团股份有限公司
苏州市进出口(集团)有限公司
江苏省海外企业集团有限公司
南京市纺织品进出口股份有限公司
中国江苏国际经济技术合作公司
常熟市外贸公司
常州市对外贸易公司
南通市对外贸易有限公司
江苏省工艺品进出口集团股份有限公司
扬州市对外贸易公司
连云港市对外贸易公司
南通市经济技术开发总公司
中化江苏进出口公司
江苏省技术进出口公司

1998年江苏生产企业出口超千万美元三十五家

苏州精达电子电器公司
江苏通润机电集团
江苏晨风集团股份有限公司
无锡市第一棉纺织厂
常州柴油机厂
江阴钢绳厂
春兰集团公司
无锡市第一色织厂
常州市第四针织厂
张家港市医疗器械厂
常州黑牡丹集团
苏州化工农药集团公司
江苏江淮动力机集团公司
苏州助剂厂
苏州阀门厂
南京金城机械厂
江苏亚邦集团公司
常熟市标准件厂
徐州铁合金厂
镇江焦化煤气集团公司
太仓香塘集团有限公司
常熟市不锈钢制品厂
扬子江船厂
徐州工程机械集团进出口公司
正茂集团有限责任公司
靖江市天伦染织实业公司
江苏高淳陶瓷股份有限公司
无锡市震球服装厂
南通冠达股份有限公司
江苏通盟色织(集团)股份有限公司
张家港市沙洲纺织印染公司
江苏澄星磷化工集团公司
扬州制药厂
江阴市红星染织厂
无锡市光明内衣厂

1998年江苏外商投资企业出口超五千万美元十四家

希捷国际科技(无锡)有限公司
夏普办公设备(常熟)有限公司
苏州罗技电子有限公司
苏州明基电脑有限公司
仁宝电脑工业(中国)有限公司
南通顺达集装箱有限公司
三星电子(苏州)半导体有限公司
苏州飞利浦消费电子有限公司
中讯电子(昆山)有限公司
牧田(中国)有限公司
无锡夏普电子元器件有限公司
苏州爱普生显示元器件有限公司
昆山富士康电脑接插件有限公司
张家港扬子纺纱有限公司

1998 年江苏旅行社前五十家

（按营收净额排列）

中国康辉无锡旅行社
苏州市中国青年国际旅行社
苏州永安旅游公司
南京中北国际旅行社
苏州海外旅游公司
苏州中国国际旅行社
无锡中国旅行社
南京招商国际旅行社
南京市中国旅行社
南京友好国际旅行社
南京国际旅行社
苏州太湖国际旅行社
苏州风光旅行社
江苏省中国旅行社
金鸡湖假日旅行社
苏州国际体育旅行社
无锡海外旅游公司
苏州东吴中国旅行社
苏州市文化国际旅行社
苏州市和平国际旅行社
常熟中国国际旅行社
江阴市友好旅行社
江苏省青年旅行社
苏州职工国际旅行社
苏州民族国内旅行社
江南旅行社（无锡）
吴江天马旅行社
江阴市华西旅行社
昆山春秋国内旅行社
无锡天天游旅行社
苏州国旅（集团）观光旅行社
南京原野旅行社
江阴市旅游公司
南京航空有限公司旅行社
南京青年旅行社
南京海外旅游公司
南京万通旅行社
镇江青年旅行社
南京长江大桥旅游公司
江苏金陵商务旅行社
常熟中国旅行社
吴江吴都旅行社
苏州铁路旅行社
南京希望旅行社
南京春秋旅行社
南京市东方旅行社
南京铁路分局旅行社
南京园林旅游实业有限公司
扬州金阳光旅行社
南京长江旅游公司

1998 年江苏旅游涉外饭店前五十家

（按营业收入排列）

金陵饭店（南京）
中山大厦（南京）
中心大酒店（南京）
玄武饭店（南京）
丁山宾馆（南京）
状元楼酒店（南京）
常州大酒店
竹辉饭店（苏州）
古南都饭店（南京）
无锡大饭店
南京希尔顿国际大酒店
南京饭店
南通文峰饭店
新城花园（苏州）
雅都大酒店（苏州）
江阴市国际大酒店
南通大饭店
湖滨（水秀）饭店（无锡）
凯莱大酒店（苏州）
宜兴国际饭店
虹桥饭店（南京）
江苏省钟山宾馆（南京）
南京怡华假日酒店
国际饭店（无锡）
东方大酒店（连云港）
南京国际会议大酒店
金谷大厦（南京）
扬州市西园饭店
江苏省山水大酒店（南京）
吴江宾馆（苏州）
金利酒店（晶丽酒店）（南京）
江苏中日友好会馆（南京）
常州江南春宾馆
江阴市暨阳山庄
明都大饭店（常州）
梁溪饭店（无锡）
南通市华能宾馆
海悦大酒店（盐城）
苏州饭店
江苏新世纪大酒店（南京）
南郊宾馆（徐州）
胥城大厦（苏州）
昆山宾馆（苏州）
馨苑度假村（苏州）
常州宾馆
南通国际大酒店
白鹭宾馆（南京）
华美达酒店（无锡）
江阴市法尔胜大酒店
美丽都大酒店（无锡）

奋进中的江苏外汽

江苏省外事旅游汽车公司(简称江苏外汽)是全省外事旅游的骨干企业,解放初期组建,至今已有近50年的历史。几十年来,公司对完成中央首长和外国元首及宾客来江苏的视察访问以及各类外事任务起到了重要的作用。

党的十一届三中全会以后,随着改革开放的不断深入和旅游事业在我国的蓬勃发展,公司的工作重点也由过去单一的外事接待转变为以旅游接待为主,兼顾外事任务的以经济和政治任务同时并举的专业汽车公司,承担着南京市境外旅游客人的用车和本省、市人代会等大型会议的用车任务,并多次被国家旅游局评为全国旅游系统先进集体。面对不断深入的市场经济,针对挑战与机遇并存的时机,公司领导和全体员工抓住机遇、解放思想,转变观念,走出计划经济框框,从内部改革着手,向市场要效益,特别是经过近几年的努力,取得了令人瞩目的成绩。公司坚持走"一业为主,多种经营"的道路,已初步形成了集交通、修理、配件、饮食、娱乐及商、贸为一体的综合性公司。企业规模不断扩大,固定资产由创业时的几万元增加到3亿多元,下设十六个经营单位,公司90%以上员工分别实行了责任指标承包,干部职工的收入与自己的实绩挂构,多劳多得,鼓励员工依法致富,并摸索出了"一家公司,多种体制"的经营模式,公司还利用自身的力量和良好的政策更新车辆,有效地遏制了汽车经营萎缩的局面,得到了上级领导和同行的肯定和赞同。经营机制的转换,调动了员工的积极性,公司的服务质量和信誉也得到了提高,连续多年被评为省市旅游客运行业文明单位,同时,在市场疲软,客源下降、竞争激烈的情况下,公司从1993年起,利润、税收、固定资产每年均以20%以上的幅度递增,员工的收入也得到了大幅度提高。

改革春风吹拂了江苏外汽,使效益之花争奇斗艳,公司面貌日新月异,近五十年来,江苏外汽干部员工辛勤耕耘,不断求索,为公司的发展作出了不懈的努力,在新世纪到来之际,外汽人将继续努力,负重前进,力争为江苏旅游事业的发展,为公司的腾飞拼搏,拼搏,再拼搏。

总经理:张传尧

电话总机:(025)8822811　　　　传真:(025)8823089

公司总部地址:南京市江东北路88号　邮编:210011

南京凯米亚明胶有限公司

南京凯米亚明胶有限公司,由中意双方共同投资,注册资金为168万美元,采用意大利伊凯玛公司先进的设备和工艺,是生产工业、食用及医药明胶的专业厂。

凯米亚公司位于南京东郊尧化门,在南京新港经济技术开发区内,距新生圩港6公里,紧邻沪宁铁路、沪宁高速公路,毗邻312国道和环城公路,交通十分便捷。

公司成立于1997年9月,拥有标准厂房4000平方米,年生产各类明胶及明胶制品1500余吨,部分产品已进入欧洲市场。

该产品主要用于感光材料、药品制剂、食品添加剂和工业粘合剂,产品用途广泛,其产品的特性有着广阔的深加工前景。

公司本着"优质的产品,优惠的价格,优质的服务"的原则,服务于全国各地之用户,同时竭诚欢迎国内外同行携手为发展中国的明胶事业做出贡献。

公司经理:周　敏

联 系 人:邹宝贵

垂询电话:(025)5562007

江苏省环保利用世界银行贷款办公室
江苏省环境经济技术国际合作中心

江苏省环保利用世界银行贷款办公室/江苏省环境经济技术国际合作中心系经江苏省政府批准成立,直属江苏省环境保护局领导的外事机构,其宗旨为:

引进国际金融组织、国外政府贷款等多种渠道的资金用于环境保护,并为国外政府机构、世界金融组织、提供省内代理服务。

引进国际组织、国外政府的技术援助用于环境保护战略研究、项目准备、新技术设备开发等。

江苏省环保利用世界银行贷款办公室/江苏省环境经济技术国际合作中心受省政府委托管理世界银行苏南环保项目,贷款额达2.5亿美元。以下是项目执行一览表。

(单位:百万元,总投资以人民币计,世行贷款以美元计)

项目名称	世行贷款	项目完成时总投资	项目名称	世行贷款	项目完成时总投资
无锡锡凯包装材料厂	0.40	17.02	建材253厂	2.00	42.00
锡山市化工助剂厂	1.27	34.84	溧阳化工厂	2.75	64.20
江阴向阳实业公司	1.28	33.02	无锡炼油厂	2.50	43.25
宜兴江洲生物制药厂	1.20	24.56	无锡新苑化工集团	2.19	40.28
无锡前洲印染厂	1.87	43.72	无锡化工集团	8.76	171.91
锡山泉山化工厂	1.00	25.40	无锡热交换器厂	3.99	108.12
无锡酿酒总厂	0.50	12.80	江阴沿山工业集团	4.00	303.00
锡山开宝磁性材料厂	0.30	17.79	无锡橡胶厂	3.00	77.49
锡山毛纺厂	0.30	8.69	无锡钢铁厂(a)	5.60	117.18
无锡第三钢铁厂	0.50	23.75	无锡第四橡胶厂	2.19	82.59
锡山变压器厂	0.50	18.70	江阴造纸厂	3.95	230.60
张家港丝绒一厂	0.40	9.05	江阴新伍集团	3.35	57.22
张家港礼帽厂	0.51	7.59	宜兴鼎球实业	3.50	66.45
苏州新风丝织厂	0.44	5.99	无锡橡胶集团公司	2.50	70.55
吴江工艺织造厂印染分厂	0.75	22.96	无锡染料厂	2.50	72.35
吴江平望染料化工厂	1.00	13.46	宜兴菲达化工厂	1.00	29.50
太仓针织印染厂	0.80	15.78	无锡第二橡胶厂	1.21	30.98
苏州牛奶公司	1.00	18.00	无锡石化总厂	1.00	141.10
平江起重机械厂	0.50	7.39	无锡利达焊管厂	3.88	105.40
苏州电瓷厂	0.50	11.73	无锡钢铁厂(b)	3.30	151.54
苏州长青轧钢厂	0.44	29.34	苏州第五制药厂	2.80	64.50
苏州姑城造粒厂	0.50	11.29	张家港化工厂	1.67	21.24
太仓酿酒总厂	0.91	20.60	江苏化工农药集团	6.43	107.00
甪直污水处理厂	0.58	13.00	苏州合成化工厂	2.57	46.82
镇江市第二化工厂	1.81	29.80	张家港化工助剂厂	4.75	77.40
丹阳化工厂	7.46	132.00	苏州安利化工厂	3.64	74.34
金河纸业集团	4.50	90.88	苏州精细化工集团	3.99	49.45
镇江水泥厂	1.52		苏州中港化纺集团	1.98	23.00
丹阳磷肥厂	1.76	31.13	苏州炭黑厂	5.52	139.09
丹徒水泥厂	6.35	143.89	苏州枫桥水泥厂	2.80	90.00
镇江冶炼总厂	1.97	45.00	江苏苏钢集团	12.93	514.00
丹阳钢铁厂	1.76	91.88	常熟化工厂	6.83	130.00
常州化工厂	13.35	241.60	乡镇企业周转金	17.44	446.47
常州酿酒总厂	9.90	242.45			

1998年重大涉外合作项目:

项目名称	国外合作机构	国外赠款	项目执行期限
江苏环境技术支持	英国海外开发署	140万英镑	1996—1999
江苏中小企业应用管理与环保	加拿大国际开发署	500万加元	1999—2004
德国巴府州-江苏环保合作	德国巴府州政府	50万美元	1997—1999
世行城市水管理咨询项目	美国CDM公司	40万美元	1994—1999

地址:南京市北京西路71号　　电话:025-3727278　　传真:025-3312450

南 京 理 工 大 学

南京理工大学，是首批全国重点大学之一，座落在六朝古都南京中山陵风景区。校园占地173公顷，50多万平方米的校舍掩映在一片绿荫之中，曲塘潋滟，佳木葱茏，是江苏省首批“花园式校园”。学校成立于1953年，经过四十多年的建设，现已发展成为以工为主，理、工、文、经、管等多学科综合配套、协调发展的理工科大学。

学校下设机械学院、化工学院、电子工程与光电技术学院、制造工程学院、信息学院、经济管理学院、动力工程学院、理学院、人文学院、成人教育学院、高等职业技术学院、紫金学院等12个学院和材料科学与工程系、外语系2个直属系以及研究生部。学校共有8个一级学科博士后流动站，博士点覆盖了11个一级学科中的17个学科点，硕士点覆盖了22个一级学科中的37个学科点，此外还有MBA和工程硕士学位授予权，44个本科专业。学校现有教职工3580人，其中有高级职称近900人，中国工程院院士1人。各类在籍生19300余人，其中博士生、硕士生1514人，本专科生1万余人。几十年来，学校共为国家培养了4万多名各类高级专业技术人才，深受社会各行业的欢迎和赞誉。

学校的主要学科集中在机械、电子、光学、化工、计算机、自动控制、动力、材料、财经、管理和外贸领域，现有2个国家级重点学科、27个部、省级重点学科，有2个国家级重点实验室、3个国家级工程技术研究中心。

学校设有科学研究院，下辖18个研究所(室)。改革开放以来，学校共完成研究与发展项目1500余项，获得部省级以上奖励589项，其中国家级奖65项；拥有国家专利206项，其中50余项获国际国内发明展览会奖牌。学校科技经费逐年上升，1998年突破亿元大关。学校的科技贸易活动已覆盖全国26个省市区，并享有科技产品进出口贸易权。

改革开放以来，学校已与美、英、法、德、日、意、俄等十几个国家50多所大学和科研院(所)建立了良好的合作关系，并多次举办国际性学术会议，邀请来校讲学、工作、交流的国外专家学者千余人，是“全国引进国外智力工作先进单位”。学校先后派出700余名教师出国访问、考察或留学等，学校具有外国留学生招收权。

1995年4月，学校通过了国家“211工程”部门预审，1998年6月，国家发展计划委员会正式批准立项，目前学校正抓紧实施“211工程”国家立项建设工作，基本目标是：经过十多年的建设，使南京理工大学成为学科水平特色突出，在国际上有一定影响，以工为主，理、工、文、经、管协调发展的多科性国内一流理工科大学。

1998年9月，江泽民同志亲笔为学校题写了“南京理工大学”校名。

南 京 造 币 厂

南京造币厂隶属于中国人民银行印钞造币总公司，系国家大型企业、中国100家最大金属制品企业。主要从事印钞造币专用机械、金属流通硬币以及增值税专用发票的制造、生产。同时还兼营生产、销售、设计制造各种纪念章(卡)、金属工艺品、有价证券、钙塑包装用品等。

工厂以“抓住机遇，深化改革，强化管理，依靠科技，提高素质，振兴南币”为宗旨，坚持以生产为中心，狠抓“两个文明”建设，励精图治，从严治厂，艰苦奋斗，团结拼搏，为提高我国印制机械制造能力和工艺装备水平，为新型印钞、造币设备的研制和批量生产作出了贡献。历年来被命名为“国家安全级企业”、“机械工业安全生产先进单位”、南京市“明星企业”、“管理先进企业”、“安全先进企业”、“环境保护先进企业”、“文明工厂”等，并荣获中国印钞造币总公司“现场管理先进企业”称号。

厂　长：王儒明
地　址：南京市江宁105信箱
电　话：(025)2282820(总机)、2282704
传　真：(025)2281511
电　报：0448
邮　编：211100

江苏教育学院

江苏教育学院座落在人文荟萃，素有“六朝古都”之誉的南京城西清凉山麓石头城下，始建于1952年10月，是一所具有师范性质的成人本科高等学校。江苏省中学教师培训中心、江苏教育行政干部培训中心都设在这里。学院承担着全省重点中学、完全中学、中等师范学校、县(市、区)教师进修学校和县(市、区)教育局等教育行政干部和教师培训任务，又是江苏省中小学、幼儿园教师高等教育自学考试的主考学校。

校园占地面积170亩，校舍建筑面积91000m^2。现有教职工480人，专任教师237人，其中正副教授99人。图书馆现有藏书近40万册，中外文期刊、装帧期刊5万册。全院拥有实验室18个，各专业均备有现代化教学仪器设备。学院出版的《江苏教育学院学报》以及《学校管理》杂志在全国公开发行。目前在册学生共有5023人。

学院现设有教育管理、汉语言文学、数学教育、英语教育、政治教育、历史教育、地理教育、物理教育、化学教育、生物教育、音乐教育、美术教育、经济管理、微机及其应用、实用美术、生化技术等二十一个专业。还设有体育教研室、现代教育技术中心、教育科学研究所、学报编辑部等直属机构。

学院定期聘请美国、加拿大、英国、澳大利亚等国家的专家、学者来院授课或讲学。在教学过程中，学院重视发挥自己的优势，强化基础理论教育，加强实践性环节，注重能力培养。目前，全院师生员工正在积极推进和深化学校内部改革，决心为发展江苏的教育事业作出更大的贡献。

南京外国语学校

南京外国语学校创建于1963年，是在周恩来总理直接关怀下，全国首批创建的外国语学校之一。该校是具有专业性教育的省重点中学。其主要任务是为高等院校输送外语水平较高、一般文化知识较好的学生，为培养高级外语人才和精通外语的其他专门人才打下坚实基础。

学校座落在鸡鸣古寺附近，校园占地73亩。设有语言实验室、听音室、录放相室、电影放映室等较完备的外语教学设施。理化生实验室、外文打字室、计算机教室、多媒体演示室等设备齐全，中外文图书馆藏书10万册，有声资料千余盘(盒)。

学校开设英、德、法、日四个语种，生源在全市范围择优录取，在校学生1462人。现有教职工195人，其中高级教师58人，外籍教师6人，青年教师中硕士研究生结业27人，师资力量雄厚。

学校倡导“求实、奋进、博学、谦逊”的校风，并将办学宗旨具体化为“爱祖国、有教养、通外语、知识广、图进取、能力强”的十八字素质要求，全面提高学生素质，扎扎实实地实施素质教育。学校重视学生思想品德教育和行为规范的养成；严格教学计划，不搞加班加点和题海战术，充分保证学生的休息时间和自己支配的时间；改革课程结构，增设选修课，完善劳技课，强化社会实践课；开展丰富多彩的校园活动，发挥学生个性特长，提高他们的能力。

经过长期的教育教学实践，学校逐步形成了自己的特色。在德育工作中，学校十分重视学生的社会能力培养，以使他们将来能适应社会主义市场经济的需要。学校的外语教学独树一帜，授课形式已形成听说领先，读写跟上，阶段侧重，容量大、节奏快、方法多、气氛活跃的特色。很多学生进入大学后，直接上二年级或编入高起点班。

学校从1984年起开始强化理科教学，开设理科班。经过长期不懈努力，理科教学逐渐与文科教学平衡发展，并形成相对优势。教学硕果累累：中考、高考升学率与考试成绩在全省领先，学科竞赛大面积丰收。

作为具有外语专业教育的重点中学，学校每年接待市内外、省内外数十所学校的领导和教师来校听课交流；每年向全市中、小学外语教师开公开课、示范课；向全国10多所外语学校及其他学校提供外语教材和音像资料……，以发挥外语教学的示范作用。

学校十分重视国际友好交流，自80年代以来，学校先后聘请了来自12个国家的近百名外籍专家和外籍教师来校任教，并与日本、澳大利亚、法国、英国、德国、美国、香港等19所学校正式建立友好交流关系，并开展了实质性交流，学校已先后派出百余名师生出国学习、进修、工作和讲学。像这样大规模、全方位、多层次的对外交流在全国中等学校中是罕见的。

建校36年来，我校为国家培养了3700余名毕业生。他们正在各条战线上为社会主义建设事业贡献力量。

江苏省靖江高级中学

江苏省靖江高级中学1941年由中国共产党和抗日民主政府创办，是一所办学有一定特色、在省内外有一定知名度的省属重点中学。学校现有面积54253平方米，建筑面积30980平方米。教职工170人，其中特级教师1人，中学高级教师34人，中学一级教师58人。高中班级24个，学生1296人。校园环境优美，教学设施齐备。近年来学校积极启动教育现代化工程，校内教育教学管理实现微机联网，并接入"江苏省公用信息网"；新建了演播中心，开通了闭路电视；建有软件制作中心和电子阅览室；拥有两个微机房，一个多媒体教室，一个语音教室；图书馆、食堂使用IC卡，实行电脑管理。

江苏省靖江高级中学坚持从严治校，倡导"既重教书，尤重育人"，逐步形成了"爱国、团结、严谨、求实"的校风，"严、精、新、爱"的教风，"勤、实、博、活"的学风。学校坚持对学生进行思想品德的系列教育，结合社区教育和社会实践教育，充分利用本校德育资源"烈士纪念馆"、"校史陈列馆"、"校庆纪念册"和其它德育基地，逐步建立起德育教育工程，逐步形成科学有序的德育教育体系。学校参与了"九五"国家教委重点课题《中小学班主任与学生素质发展》、《当代中小学优等生与后进生的状况成因及适应性教育方法》的研究，并取得阶段性成果。

学校全面贯彻教育方针，面向全体学生，坚持教育改革，模范执行教育法律、法规，努力实施素质教育，在教学、科研、师资队伍建设、教学改革等方面取得丰硕成果。智育方面，注重发展智力、培养能力，注重学生整体素质的提高。多年来，高考升学率均居全省前列。1995年高考本科上线率为92%；1996年高考本科上线率为94%；1997年上线率为95%。近几年来，学生中约有300人次在国家、省、市学科竞赛中获奖，其中在全国竞赛中获奖的有40多人次。重视艺术教育，强化素质教育，坚持开设各种门类的选修课。学校多次获省、市青少年科技先进单位称号。1994年和1996年分别获省青少年科技活动无线电测向竞赛团体冠军和个人前四名，学生科技制作获全国二等奖、江苏省小发明一等奖。学校是江苏省OEH多媒体教育网络实验学校，已取得一批省级成果，电化教育发展较快，一批自编电教教材已获多项省级奖。

江苏省靖江高级中学是省级田径传统项目学校，群体活动蓬勃开展，竞技体育成绩在省、市位于前列。1983年以来向体育院校、省级体工队共输送体育人材60余名，培养一、二、三级运动员100余名。学校是中国体育科学学会立项的《21世纪中国学校体育发展实验性研究》实验学校，现正积极从事多项研究。

江苏省靖江高级中学劳技教育经过十多年探索研究，逐步走向规范化、系列化，并向高层次发展。学校参加了国家教委"七·五"、"八·五"期间教育科研项目《中小学劳动教育研究》课题的研究，成果显著。

多年来，在全校师生的努力下，江苏省靖江高级中学办学成绩引人注目。1981年获国家"两部两委"颁发的"体育卫生先进单位"光荣称号；1982年获省政府嘉奖；1987年以来，连续被命名为"江苏省文明单位"；1988年被命名为"江苏省德育工作先进学校"和"江苏省劳技教育先进集体"；1991年被命名为"全国体育先进传统项目学校"。1993年获"江苏省体育项目先进学校"称号；1995年获江苏省贯彻《两个条例》"体育卫生先进单位"称号；1996年学校被省政府授予"江苏省先进集体"称号。1992年以来，学校团委、学生会被省教委、团省委连续授予"江苏省先进集体"称号；1996年获省爱国主义教育活动优秀组织奖；1997年学校被南京军区评为"招飞工作先进集体"并再次被省教委评为"江苏省德育工作先进学校"。学校现为北师大教育实验基地。为创办一所现代化、高质量、有特色的省内一流重点中学和国家级示范性高中，江苏省靖江高级中学全体教职工正在不懈努力！

江苏省文化学校

江苏省文化学校是江苏省文化厅直属的一所中等艺术专业学校。她主要是为本省群众文化艺术、图书、博物、电影发行等文化艺术门类培养中等业务和管理人才,同时还承担着全省文化系统干部的轮训工作。

学校创建于1953年5月,原名为江苏省文化干部学校,其主要是以长期、短期培训的形式,培养和轮训全省文化干部。学校先后开办了文化局长、文化行政干部训练班;文化馆、站长培训班;城市群艺馆、工人文化宫工作讲习班;业余文艺骨干训练班;图书馆长、业务干部培训;剧团编导训练班;剧场经理训练班;图书发行训练班;电影管理干部、放映检片维修人员、电影放映培训师资训练班等。从1953年至今,学校开设长、短期培训班56期,培训行政和业务干部5133名,经过培训,大部分学员成为全省文化系统中的骨干力量,有的成为文化艺术专业的专家,不少学员被充实到各级领导岗位,为江苏省文化事业的发展和繁荣发挥了重要作用。学校还为安徽、西藏等兄弟省和自治区代培了100余名电影技术人员和师资。

1984年6月,江苏省人民政府批准学校改名为江苏省文化学校,学校肩负中专学历教育和干部培训两大任务。学校设有电影技术管理、舞美音响、群众文化音乐、美术四大专业。1998年起与有关院校联办文化事业管理大专、本科班,初步形成了多层次、多形式的办学体制。

学校占地面积25亩,建筑面积7600平方米。学校有电影技术专业所需的放映机械、检测仪器及电化教学设备;音乐专业有琴房一幢、钢琴26台,舞蹈排练厅二个;美术专业有展览厅、画室、摄影暗房,还建有现代化的电脑设计教学中心,中心拥有成套专业级的"苹果"电脑设计系统和40台"PC"电脑,可供教师进行图型设计研究和开发及学生电脑绘画和"三维"动画制作。图书馆艺术类藏书3万余册。

学校现有教职工50人,其中专任教师28人,高中级职称占专任教师总数的61%,学校还有一支由驻宁艺术院校、艺术院团专家组成的长期、稳定的外聘教师队伍,共计32人。学校现有在校生447人,培养中专毕业686人。

校　长:董正淮
地　址:南京市中山门外马群百水桥　　邮编:210049
电　话:4431931(校长室)　　4431716(办公室)

锡山市前洲中学

前洲中学(前洲职业高级中学)座落于锡山市前洲镇,南邻312国道和古运河,北依沪宁高速公路。学校占地88亩,建筑面积20018平方米。开设了机电,计算机维修和应用、农机工程、电子技术与贸易、多种经营与管理等五个专业,在校学生近2000人,教职工200余人,其中有研究生3人,高级职称15人,中级职称65人。近年来,出版著作6部,在市级以上报刊发表论文50余篇,获奖教学设计60余篇。

一所朝气蓬勃的学校:1998年是前洲中学发展较快的一年。一年中,明确了以高职预备教育为主体的发展方向,通过了教育现代化工程和无锡市爱国卫生先进单位验收,建成了锡山市高等职业预备教育基地,锡山市人民防空教育基地和常州技术师范学院教育实习基地。1999年又成为常州技术师范学院电化教育实验学校和常州技师成教学院锡山分校。是锡山市1998年报考人数最多的职业学校之一。

一个真正读书的地方:自1939年建校以来,前洲中学坚持走内涵发展之路。学校环境优美悦目,教育设施配套齐全,有专业实验室12个,实习工厂4个,校外实习基地11个。学校坚持"面向全体学生,全面提高素质"的办学方针,夯实文化基础,强化专业技能,学生文化课统考、技能达级竞赛均居于同类学校领先水平。被评为市法制教育、执行中学生行为规范、人民防空教育、体育达标、校园文化建设先进学校、锡山市文明单位、无锡市文明卫生单位,毕业生受到了用人单位的广泛欢迎。

一条充满希望的道路:1998年,前洲中学在教委支持下,成为锡山市高职预备教育基地,为职教学生开辟了进大学升造之路。高职预备班学生在通过规定的技能考核后均能参加全国对口高校考试,进入高校深造,还能通过成人高考直升本校常州技术师范学院"机电一体化"、"计算机应用"等专业联办班,边工作边参加大专函授,获得全国通用的大专文凭。这对于那些企盼圆大学梦的学生,无疑是一个振奋人心的佳音。此外,学校还与中国船舶总公司无锡蓝海舾装设备有限公司等10多家企业实行联合办学,为学生就业提供了保障。

地　　址:锡山市前洲镇中兴路　邮政编码:214181
联系电话:(0510)3391783-9(校长室)
　　　　　(0510)3391783-8007(招办)

仪征市马集乡

马集乡位于古城真州(今仪征市区)北郊,东傍古龙河,南临宁扬一级公路,西北紧靠景色宜人的铜山、捺山自然风景区。省际公路仪(征)天(长)线穿境而过,是省对外开放卫星镇之一。现辖15个行政村,1个街道居委会,224个村民小组,全乡总面积64平方公里,总人口2.8万人。

该乡自然资源丰富,境内蕴藏大量黄砂、青石和优质矿泉水。近10条3至6公里不等的冲坝,田块方整、道路林网、小桥流水,星罗棋布的水塘,水库点缀其间,展示着丘陵山区的独特风貌。令踏青、垂钓、息暑的城里人流连往返。

党的十一届三中全会以来,特别是近年来,该乡党委政府按照"稳步发展农业,积极发展副业,突击主攻工业,努力拓展三产、外贸业"的思路,带领全乡人民奋力进取,真抓实干,经济建设和各项社会事业得到蓬勃发展,取得了令人瞩目的成就。1998年,全乡三业总产值突破3亿元,实现国内生产总值9550万能元,人均纯收入达2550元,连续多年被省市评为"依法治乡先进乡"、"安全乡(镇)"和"双文明建设先进乡镇"。

在加快步伐奔小康的道路上,该乡时刻不放松农业这个基础产业,农业综合开发取得了实效。以小流域治理、中低产田改造、蓄水工程建设为重点的农田水利建设取得了突破性进展,每年完成水利土方60多万方,改造中低产田1500亩,扩浚当家塘近20口。先进农业适用技术推广较快,全面实行了水稻肥床旱育稀植,机收、机播面积大幅度增加,各类农用机械近2000台套,总动力16395千瓦,全乡基本达到旱涝保收。农业产业化经营迈出新的步伐,着力实施了"4321"工程,"九五"期末,将如期形成4个基地,即:4000亩意杨林基地、3000亩蔬菜基地、2000亩水产基地、1000亩茶果基地。八里雪菜种植初具规模,并成为南京、扬州市场的抢手货。多种经营项目由过去的10多个发展到近40个,涌现了一批传统、特种养殖专业大户。

工业经济平稳发展。该乡注重投入,依靠科技,在发展中调整,在调整中发展,经过10多年的努力走出了资源工业的粗放型圈子,形成了一个以环(活塞环)、缸(气缸体、缸套)、簧(活塞环螺旋撑簧),座(气门座)为主导产品,集车辆玻璃、钢板弹簧、车用蓄电池等为一体的内燃机配件基地。1998年实现工业总产值2.30亿元,利税1000万元。全乡有乡村企业近50家,一大批优势产品跻身国内外市场,骨干企业威龙活塞环有限公司和金派内燃机配件有限公司,不断叫响自己的品牌,活塞环产销量处于全国同行前列,螺旋撑簧占据国内市场80%以上。被《新华日报》誉为贫困山区升起的一颗新星的金营村,不安于过去的穷样板,艰苦创业,开拓创新,成为该乡的排头兵,作为江苏省农村现代化示范村,该村有全国唯一的活塞环衬簧研究中心,苏北第一家村办变电所,金营人免费就医、就学。

基础设施建设力度不断加大,第三产业发展迅速。乡党委政府十分重视基础设施建设,仅1998年就投入900多万元,用于兴办社会事业。如今全乡村村通砂石路,组组通程控,并拥有两个较大的农贸市场,两座35千伏变电所,一所完中……。中心集镇实施绿化、亮化、美化工程。近年来,每年都有几十户家民进镇经商办实体,商贸运输十分兴旺。1998年全乡实现三产增加值3000万元。

独特的地理位置,便利的交通、通迅,雄实的基础设施,丰富的土地、劳力资源、再加上马集人思想的不断解放,构成了良好的投资环境,同时,不断的改革,使得马集的经济建设及社会事业始终保持强劲的发展势头。重点企业全部实现了股权流动。一批来自城里的下岗职工和工程技术人员还来此安营扎寨,事业红火。私营经济在全乡经济总量中占有较大比重。路漫漫,万里征途新起点。勤劳智慧的马集人民在党的路线、方针、政策的指引下,在社会各界的关心支持下,以自己的心血和汗水创造了美好的今天,为了马集明天更加繁荣,马集乡党委和政府将提供更加优惠的政策,更加优良的服务,热忱欢迎各方宾客来马集施展才华,共创大业。

书　记:吴春和
乡　长:张长金
电　话:0514－3660023
邮　编:211414

·中国统计出版社最新资料书简目·

中国统计年鉴—1999(汉英)
中国统计摘要—1999
国际统计年鉴—1999
中国农村统计年鉴—1999
中国城市统计年鉴—1998
中国劳动统计年鉴—1999（汉英）
中国人口统计年鉴—1999
中国建筑业统计年鉴—1999
中国对外经济统计年鉴—1999
中国固定资产投资统计年鉴—1998
中国物价及城镇居民家庭收支调查统计年鉴—1999
北京统计年鉴—1999（汉英）
天津统计年鉴—1999
河北经济年鉴—1999
山西统计年鉴—1999
内蒙古统计年鉴—1999
辽宁统计年鉴—1999
吉林统计年鉴—1999（汉英）
黑龙江统计年鉴—1999
上海统计年鉴—1999（汉英）
江苏统计年鉴—1999（汉英）
浙江统计年鉴—1999（汉英）
安徽统计年鉴—1999
福建统计年鉴—1999
江西统计年鉴—1999
山东统计年鉴—1999
河南统计年鉴—1999
湖北统计年鉴—1999
湖南统计年鉴—1999
广东统计年鉴—1999（汉英）
广西统计年鉴—1999
海南统计年鉴—1999
重庆统计年鉴—1999（汉英）
新疆生产建设兵团统计年鉴—1999
柳州地区社会经济统计年鉴—1999
南宁地区统计年鉴—1999
开封统计年鉴—1999

四川统计年鉴—1999
贵州统计年鉴—1999
云南统计年鉴—1999
西藏统计年鉴—1999
陕西统计年鉴—1999
青海统计年鉴—1999
宁夏年鉴—1999
新疆统计年鉴—1999
石家庄统计年鉴—1999
唐山统计年鉴—1999
邯郸统计年鉴—1999
衡水统计年鉴—1999
廊坊经济统计年鉴—1999
呼和浩特经济统计年鉴—1999
四平统计年鉴—1999
延吉统计年鉴—1999
哈尔滨统计年鉴—1999
双鸭山社会经济统计年鉴—1999
延边统计年鉴—1999
徐州统计年鉴—1999
杭州统计年鉴—1999
苏州统计年鉴—1999
无锡统计年鉴—1999
常州统计年鉴—1999
宁波统计年鉴—1999
绍兴统计年鉴—1999
嘉兴统计年鉴—1999
金华统计年鉴—1999
舟山统计年鉴—1999
温州统计年鉴—1999
台州统计年鉴—1999
济南统计年鉴—1999
青岛统计年鉴—1999
泰安统计年鉴—1999
潍坊统计年鉴—1999
德州统计年鉴—1999
南昌统计年鉴—1999
齐齐哈尔经济社会统计年鉴—1999
三门峡统计年鉴—1999

平顶山统计年鉴—1999
洛阳统计年鉴—1999
武汉统计年鉴—1999
十堰统计年鉴—1999
宜昌统计年鉴—1999
海口统计年鉴—1999
广州统计年鉴—1999
惠州统计年鉴—1999
珠海统计年鉴—1999
东莞统计年鉴—1999
南宁统计年鉴—1999
宜春统计年鉴—1999
西安统计年鉴—1999
成都统计年鉴—1999
西宁统计年鉴—1999
乌鲁木齐统计年鉴—1999
巴音郭楞统计年鉴—1999
吐鲁番统计年鉴—1999
广安统计年鉴—1999
九江经济统计年鉴—1999
深圳统计信息年鉴—1999
桂林经济社会统计年鉴—1999
临汾统计年鉴—1999
上海浦东新区统计年鉴—1999（汉英）
大理统计年鉴—1999
甘肃年鉴—1999
沈阳年鉴—1999
福州年鉴—1999
宝山年鉴—1999
兰州年鉴—1999
厦门经济特区年鉴—1999
福州经济技术开发区马尾区年鉴—1999
黑龙江垦区统计年鉴—1999
广东农村统计年鉴—1999
湖北农村统计年鉴—1999
福建农村统计年鉴—1999
柳州经济统计年鉴—1999